*D*ictionary *of Native American Literature*

Garland Reference Library of the Humanities
(Vol. 1815)

Dictionary of Native American Literature

Andrew Wiget, EDITOR

Garland Publishing, Inc.

New York and London

1994

Library of Congress Cataloging-in-Publication Data

Dictionary of Native American literature / edited by Andrew Wiget.
    p.   cm. — (Garland reference library of the humanities ; vol.
1815)
  Includes bibliographical references (p.   ) and index.
  ISBN 0–8153–1560–0 (alk. paper)
  1. Indian literature—United States—Encyclopedias. 2. American
literature—Indian authors—Encyclopedias.   I. Wiget, Andrew.
II. Series.
PM155.D53   1994
897—dc20   94–3811
                                                CIP

Printed on acid-free, 250-year-life paper
Manufactured in the United States of America

*C*ontents

Contents

The Historical Emergence of Native American Writing

C*ontents*

A Native American Renaissance: 1967 to the Present

Contents

Contents

List of Figures

Introduction

Following the award of the 1969 Pulitzer Prize for Fiction to N. Scott Momaday's *House Made of Dawn* (1968), readers in all quarters began to give serious attention to "Native American Literature." Precisely what that term denominated was heatedly argued by those who produced, taught, and read it. Many sought to embrace within the bounds of this term the vast corpus of Native American folklore generated by American anthropology. Some of them argued pragmatically that Momaday and writers of his stature could not be effectively understood without reference to the oral traditions which served as their artistic resource. Others, influenced by the redefinition of ethnography and folklore that was overtaking the ways in which those disciplines had been practiced in America, argued for a more expansive definition that would comprehend "oral literature." Strangely, literature departments founded on the study of Homer and Chaucer foundered on the notion of "oral literature" when applied to Native American materials. Complicating this situation further was the fact that much of the most vigorous publishing activity was happening at small presses.

Some years later, these debates do not seem so strange. Today we understand how and accept that questions of evaluation are linked to models of interpretation. In ways that were not at the time so obvious in the case of African-American literature or even Chicano or Asian literature, Native American literature opened the difficult questions of tradition and influence, of the relationship between speech and writing, precisely at that moment in the evolution of literary criticism in the West when those topics were coming under the closest scrutiny. The argument over what was worth reading was clearly a transformation of the argument over how to read. While it was clear that contemporary Native American writers wanted to repudiate any kind of cultural determinism in the formation of their work, they were often driven, both by the needs of mass-market merchandising and by the presence of readers from their own communities of origin, to unambiguously address in their own persons that which had always been ambiguous: their own conflicted identities and the multiplicity of voices these generated. In this way, determinations of what counted as Native American literature often devolved into arguments over what and who were authentically Native American. Arguments over *who* speaks, and *how*, were endlessly debated in professional conferences, donut shops, classrooms, and, in not a few cases, on Indian reservations.

This volume emerged out of a sense that some basic frame of reference was needed for these always frustrating but often fruitful arguments. It was originally begun around 1980 by Jeffrey Huntsman at Indiana University. In 1987, it was passed on to the present editor, who formed an advisory board of individuals who had come to be regarded among the most respected scholars in different areas within the emerging field: for Native American oral literatures, Larry Evers (University of Arizona); for historical writing by Indians, A. LaVonne Brown Ruoff (University of Illinois–Chicago) and Daniel F. Littlefield, Jr. (University of Arkansas–Little Rock); and for contemporary Indian writing, Joseph Bruchac (*Greenfield Review*). The task of researching and writing this volume was brought before the Association for the Study of American Indian Literatures, composed of the principal scholars and university teachers in the field, who embraced it, not without trepidation, as an urgent need. This is ultimately their work; fifty-two of them, including five non-American scholars, are represented in the more than seventy essays here. The present editor has permitted them to assume their own writing styles and to advance their own critical judgments. In such a new field, it is too early to canonize any critical interpretation, if that is ever advisable at all.

The advisory board and the Association scholars contributed significantly to the definition of the volume. The decision not to use a simple alphabetical listing of articles, for instance, but to organize the contents roughly by subject and period evolved from a shared concern to give some explicit shape to the field. These scholars also helped in identifying topics to be included (even up to these last few months) or excluded. So it was that after consultations, the decision was made not to include articles on film or journalism or children's literature, which, however interesting in themselves, were also judged to be of enormous scope and would have taken the volume far afield. The fundamental question of whom to include also emerged from this group, though, given the length of the project from conception to publication, it is inevitable that, even with one major updating of the manuscript in 1991–92, the significance of some individuals has been underrepresented.

In terms of topical articles, the real issue was how to keep the volume focused on literature, oral and written. The decision to include some topical articles, on Indian policy, for instance, was based on the desire to provide teachers and the general reader with a concise in-text guide to background material essential for framing any reading of historical or contemporary Native writing. The same goal motivated the inclusion of the few maps and charts supplied. Serious secondary reading on history and ethnography should begin with the new *Handbook of North American Indians* (ed. Sturtevant et al.).

On the other hand, some topics that would have been especially interesting in conjunction with the study of Native oral literatures were not included. While it would seem logical to have a general article on "Songs," for instance, it was clear from the beginning that Native American songs from over 350 different tribes did not have as a subject the same kind of formal coherence that oral narrative did, and that such an article, while an interesting and valuable exercise, would be not only spotty in its coverage but also fragmented into a multiplicity of subtopics, each of which would be important but impossible to explicate fully. The same may be said for an article on what has come to be popularly called "Ritual Drama," a term that in some circles has almost become synonymous with "ceremony" or "ritual." Unfortunately, the term itself is loaded with Western notions of representation and function that cannot be assumed to apply to Native peoples. And, like song, the topic quickly devolves into a discussion of multiple components (masking, dance, oratory, songs, prayers, processions, shrines, altars, etc.), the interrelationship of which is too complicated to be discussed briefly and too serious to be treated glibly. To have included articles on song or ritual drama would have been to invite their authors to create the most speculative kind of typology with which to frame a brief and spotty discussion of an enormous topic. For discussions detailed enough to provide serious consideration of such complex topics, the reader is referred to the many specialized articles cited in the *Ethnographic Bibliography of North America* (Murdock and O'Leary), which is organized by tribe, and, for literary topics, to Ruoff's *American Indian Literatures*.

There are many ways to use a handbook such as this. People familiar with the field and seeking specific information might go immediately to the relevant article and follow the references supplied in the index. Relative newcomers to the field might be best advised to first read in sequence the overview articles by Wiget, Ruoff, and Bruchac that introduce each section and are designed to provide an orientation to the more specific articles that follow. Like all editors, the present one is conscious that in attempting to produce something definitive, something much more limited has resulted. Nevertheless, we believe that most readers will find this volume useful both as a source of information and as a means to opening critical discussion. If those modest aims are achieved, the volume will have served the fundamental purposes for which it was published.

I would like to thank the many patient scholars whose contributions give this volume its essential value; they have waited a long time for its publication. I wish to thank the advisory board, especially A. LaVonne Brown Ruoff, who, with James Ruppert, were not only attentive to lapses in the volume's scope but willing to contribute their time and scholarship to mend them. And I would also like to thank the many students who helped with the many word-processing and correspondence tasks associated with this work: Patricia Ruiz, Monty Mince, Barbara Robins, Barbara Tresko, Irene Hammond, Lorena Reyes, and Tammie Camp.

Andrew Wiget
New Mexico State University

BIBLIOGRAPHY

Ethnographic Bibliography of North America. Eds. George Murdock and Timothy O'Leary. 5 vols. New Haven: Human Relations Area Files, 1985.

Handbook of North American Indians. Gen. Ed. William Sturtevant. 20 vols. Washington, DC: Smithsonian Institution Press, 1978– .

Ruoff, A. LaVonne Brown. *American Indian Literatures*. New York: Modern Language Association, 1990.

*A*dvisory Board and Contributors

Advisory Board

Joseph Bruchac
  The Greenfield Review

Larry Evers
  University of Arizona

Daniel F. Littlefield, Jr.
  University of Arkansas—Little Rock

A. LaVonne Brown Ruoff
  University of Illinois—Chicago

Contributors

Gogisgi Carroll Arnett
  Mecosta, MI

Barbara Babcock
  University of Arizona

Donald Bahr
  Arizona State University

Franchot Ballinger
  University of Cincinnati

Gretchen M. Bataille
  Arizona State University

William Bright
  University of Colorado

Alanna K. Brown
  Montana State University

Joseph Bruchac
  The Greenfield Review

David Brumble
  University of Pittsburgh

Laura Coltelli
  University of Pisa

Jay Cox
  University of Arizona

Gordon M. Day
  Canadian Ethnology Service
  Canadian Museum of Civilization

Roger Dunsmore
  University of Montana

Thomas A. Erhard
  New Mexico State University

Michael K. Foster
  Canadian Ethnology Service
  Canadian Museum of Civilization

Hanay L. Geiogamah
University of California—Los Angeles

Robert F. Gish
California State Polytechnic University—San Luis Obispo

Birgit Hans
University of North Dakota

Elaine A. Jahner
Dartmouth College

Ronald A. Janke
Valparaiso University

Sue M. Johnson
University of South Dakota

Thomas King
University of Minnesota

M. Dale Kinkade
University of British Columbia

Arnold Krupat
Sarah Lawrence College

George E. Lankford
Arkansas College

Andrea Lerner
California State University—Chico

Daniel F. Littlefield, Jr.
University of Arkansas—Little Rock

John Lowe
Louisiana State University

Kenneth M. Morrison
Arizona State University

Phyllis Morrow
University of Alaska—Fairbanks

Robert M. Nelson
University of Richmond

James W. Parins
University of Arkansas—Little Rock

Bernd C. Peyer
Johann Wolfgang Goethe University

John Lloyd Purdy
Central Oregon Community College

Jarold Ramsey
University of Rochester

Julian Rice
Florida Atlantic University

Barbara K. Robins
New Mexico State University

Kenneth M. Roemer
University of Texas—Arlington

Gretchen Ronnow
Wayne State College

A. LaVonne Brown Ruoff
University of Illinois—Chicago

James Ruppert
University of Alaska—Fairbanks

Scott Rushforth
New Mexico State University

Kathleen M. Sands
Arizona State University

Robert F. Sayre
University of Iowa

Susan Scarberry-Garcia
Fort Lewis College

Mary A. Stout
Tucson Public Library

Kathryn S. Vangen
University of Washington

Alexander Vaschenko
*A. M. Gorky Institute of World Literature
Moscow, Russia*

Alan R. Velie
University of Oklahoma

Andrew Wiget
New Mexico State University

Norma C. Wilson
University of South Dakota

Terry P. Wilson
University of California—Berkeley

*N*ative American Oral Literatures

Native American Oral Literatures: A Critical Orientation

The title of this essay begs an etymological question: How can that which is unwritten, that is, without letters, be called literature? To this, Krupat has responded effectively: "Literature, from the Latin *littera*, as is well-known, served broadly to indicate anything that had been written down and—*to achieve a measure of social circulation*—copied over. (For oral societies without alphabetic 'letters,' literature is whatever language is deemed worthy of sufficient repetition to assure it will be remembered and passed along.)" (1989:39, my emphasis.) Moreover, for the longest time, the kinds of materials we today call literature were not called literature at all, but "poetry," to set them apart from other kinds of written language. While the ethnographic and ethnohistorical literature of Native Americans is voluminous (see Jennings and Swaggerty; Prucha 1977, 1982; Murdock and O'Leary), and there are several useful collections of critical essays on the subject of oral literature (Hymes 1981; Tedlock 1983; Kroeber 1981; Swann 1983; Wiget 1985; Swann and Krupat 1987), there are few volumes of extended critical discourse on oral literature as literature (but see Finnegan, Krupat 1992). Critical discussion of Native American oral literature evolves along two lines, evaluative and descriptive.

Value and Evaluation

The argument on value, however finely or crudely expressed ("But is it any good?"), consistently turns on one question: Do these forms, or particular examples of them, when translated and represented textually, evoke from competent Euroamerican readers the same kinds of judgments of satisfaction as the masterworks with which the Euroamerican reader is familiar? This, I believe, is an accurate formulation of the crux of the problem as perceived by both advocates and antagonists, but there are, nevertheless, several difficulties with this way of understanding evaluation.

First, judgments of satisfaction are intimately linked to the reader's prior literary experiences. Knowledge of the conventions of plot, form, and style for a range of genres is acquired slowly during the course of an individual's enculturation. This much is true in any cultural setting. Nor is the Euroamerican pattern of providing formal instruction in how to recognize, understand, and employ such conventions unique. What does appear distinctive is the role of certain Euroamerican aesthetic values in this process. Some of these values, such as the manipulation of form, the concern for eliciting certain kinds of affective responses, and the exaltation of the individual artist, while taking on a certain urgency in the last two hundred years, nevertheless remain rooted in the ancients, such as Aristotle, Horace, and Longinus, and inform most formal, and many informal, literary experiences. That these values are not standard in every culture is clear almost immediately upon encountering verbal art outside the Euroamerican traditions, and then one's own experience prompts one to judge works to be literature to the degree that they not only resemble more familiar works, but also to the degree that the aesthetic values they project resonate with one's own.

Second, judgments of satisfaction about literary experiences are rooted in the reader's experiences of life as lived. "Experience" is both a subjective and social formulation. While Euroamericans in the post-Romantic age are quick to identify the subjective dimensions of experience, they have been slow to recognize that the mental construction of an individual's "world" involves the complex interplay of many social forces. Classical anthropology exacerbated this confusion. The "patterns of culture" studies obliterated individuality in mass identity, while the "culture and personality" studies, in attempting to account for personality, often left the impression that individuation was a form of cultural deviance. While it is not arguable that some elements of that social formulation are roughly isomorphic within a society, and properly called "cultural," many are formulated by small, shared experience groups in which any individual participates. Knowledge of the "world" thus fractures along many lines of stress, usefully complicating both "intra"-cultural communication as well as "cross"-cultural communication. Appeals to universalism and the broad project of "translation" cannot undo this problem. Identifying a story as a "typical Oedipal plot" or "a classic example of the Magical Helper motif" or "a fine expression of mankind's deepest longing to experience some kind of transcendent reality" really says nothing about what the tradition bearer and his audience value in the tale and serves only to valorize the categories of significance of those for whom such appeals are made.

Third, recognizing a fundamental gap between our actual and literary experiences and those of Native Americans and their literature, we confront our own ethnocentrism as the basis of evaluation. Alan Merriam, a highly regarded ethnomusicologist, criticized one tribe, and through it Indians generally, because they did not have a lexicon of aesthetic and critical terms, nor did their values seem to conform to our own, such as manipulation of aesthetic form for its own sake. Merriam's position is understandable in historical terms as a product of neoscholastic, New Critical thinking, for which the Beautiful was a transcendent category and the task of criticism was to describe the formal structures by which the revelation of beauty was more or less successfully achieved. Culture and history might condition the means of expression, but the category of the Beautiful remained transcendent, universal. Such an assumption still undergirds the unreflective commentary of some critics who seek to articulate the value of Native American literatures as local instances of universal forms, themes, and values. Why people should be so obtuse as to maintain performance traditions with evident delight for centuries when these traditions supposedly lack any evident aesthetic value is a question Merriam never asks. Like other universalists, he never asks the question because he has already dismissed the only answer that counts: "aesthetics," Merriam writes, "is not considered to be the same as the values implied in making choices" (Merriam 1967:45). While the consequences for aesthetics of holding such a principle are still resonating through our cultural institutions, such a statement is no longer possible in serious critical discourse since the deconstruction of aesthetic programs into their ideological antecedents has been well established. Having conceded that aesthetic values are transformations of other, antecedent cultural and historical values, the critic-reader's task is to describe how such transformations occur (see Murray).

While some might assume that ethnocentrism precludes a just understanding, dialogic anthropology argues that it is the basis for all parties' achieving some kind of necessarily inadequate, but nevertheless fundamentally equitable understanding. If it is true that some Euroamerican readers find Native American stories repetitious and boring, Native Americans might respond that Euroamerican stories are cluttered with insignificant detail. In short, evaluation is a two-way street.

In the remainder of the essay, I want to promote a dialogic consideration of the nature of Native American oral literature and the nature of Euroamerican literature as phenomena. A number of heuristic strategies could be effectively employed. Arnold Krupat has used some key terms in Western critical language (author, literature, mode of production, canonicity) in this manner, and such a list could be expanded. I have chosen the familiar diagram (see figure 1) as a place to start. In either case, the reader needs to be continually reminded that these are heuristic devices for provoking dialogue about the functions adumbrated by the terms, which remain problematic even in Western critical discourse. This is not really comparison for the sake of evaluation, in which a critic might dismiss an instance of Native American oral literature because, unlike a modern Western novel, it does not have an author whose life can be explored in order to establish a number of genetic relationships to her novel. Such a critic takes for granted precisely what needs to be established, because "author" is a term denominating a set of functions, the relevance of each of which is itself debatable, whether or not it can be demonstrated that a particular historical person accomplished any of them. In short, we are not doing sums in cross-cultural account books, but questioning the very usefulness of the way in which we as Euroamericans conceptualize and talk about the stuff we customarily, and too casually, call literature. Though my examples of oral literature will be drawn from Native American cultures, much of what I write is applicable to "oral literature" in cultures beyond North America.

Oral Literature as Phenomenon

A familiar diagram of the forces and interests involved in literary experience locates the work at the intersection of two axes. The axis of communication locates the work as a transaction between a writer, responsible for the work's creation (the Genetic pole), and a reader, responsible for the work's apprehension and realization (the Affective pole). The axis of representation locates the work, as a unique configuration of signs, between a particular socially sanctioned, culturally constituted view of the world (the Mimetic pole) on the one hand and a set of prior linguistic configurations (the Intertextual pole) on the other. Despite its limitations, this model is particularly useful as a heuristic device because it highlights the single but nonetheless critical difference between written and oral communication. In writing, the axis of communication is unidirectional, whereas oral communication is genuinely bilateral and interpersonal. Let us take up in turn each of these poles, along their respective axes.

The Mimetic Pole

The mimetic pole calls attention to the way in which the work shapes forth a particular understanding of the world. Do the issues of representation familiar to us from Western literary tradition arise in Native American oral literatures? In the broadest sense, yes. That is, insofar as all verbal arts, whether oral or written, are fictions, they are selective, ideologically charged, linguistic structures, and so the question remains for all of them: How does the world signified by the linguistic structure conform to our sense of the world as experienced extraliterarily? Whether the representation is true to the world as it in fact exists cannot be tested, for the latter is not accessible in itself. Verity, in short, is never the issue. In every culture, and

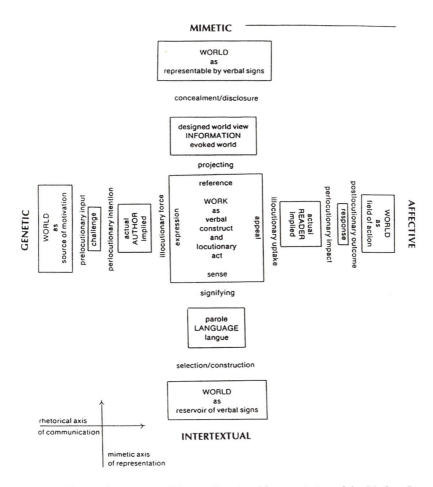

Figure 1. The Work as Focus of Forces. (Reprinted by permission of the Modern Language Association of America from Joseph Gibaldi, *Introduction to Modern Languages and Literatures*, Modern Language Association, 1981.)

independent of the mode of communication (whether orality or inscription), claims for verisimilitude will vary depending upon the relationships of the "author" to the world he is claiming to represent, to the audience and the occasion, and to previous attempts at representation.

An audience's assent to the claim occurs on two levels, engrossment and reflection. The first is the tacit assent, sometimes called the "willing suspension of disbelief," that measures the verisimilitude of a representation by its capacity to imaginatively involve the audience in the performance. The second is the distanced, critical judgment about the likelihood of such an event's ever happening in view of culturally shared assumptions about the structure of reality and human behavior, the "truthfulness," if you will. Verbal representations that are unpersuasive in their claims to verisimilitude preclude or rupture the audience's engrossment by driving them to judgments about credibility. In performative terms, then, the representational aim of verbal art is to create a sense of verisimilitude appropriate to the nature of the communication which engrosses the audience sufficiently to preclude serious questions of credibility that threaten to destroy the frame of the communication.

A number of formal and stylistic features are useful in establishing and managing audience expectations for credibility. Because meaning is fundamentally a matter of co-occurrence, the perpetual association of certain subject matters with certain places, seasons, or verbal formulas creates experiential frames which characterize different claims of verisimilitude (Goffman 1975). Tedlock (1983:164) has noted that the Zunis, like many other Native American communities, use verbal and temporal frames which make claims about the credibility of narrative forms while establishing audience expectations for appropriate kinds of verisimilitude. Origin stories, which can be told at any time during the year, lack a verbal frame, an absence which they share with explicitly historical narratives about events of the recent past. Zuni *telapna:we*, however, always begin with a verbal formula ("*Sonahchi. Sonti ino:te*") and end with a verbal formula ("*Le: Sem:konikya*"), which establishes a frame around the narrative that instructs the audience (who acknowledge by answering "*E:so*") to understand that this story, while believable, is not certifiably true.

Storytellers can also express varying degrees of confidence in the credibility of what they are narrating. Authorizing particles are a common means, though their frequency and lack of organic relation to "story" often led early translators to delete them from translations as boring and repetitive. Reportatives (often translated as "they said" or "it is said") recur throughout narrations to assert credibility on the basis of reliable tradition rather than personal testimony. There may also be a class of particles I would call speculatives, which establish degrees of probability. In my fieldwork with stories at Zuni, the particle *imat* (often glossed by Zunis as "I guess") was used throughout *telapna:we* where it was clear that the storyteller was not guessing, in the strict sense of choosing between existing alternatives, but inventing, speculating. Such a use is common in English as well, but at Zuni the speculative particle was used frequently enough in this manner to suggest an overall qualification of the credibility of some stretches of narrative.

Expectations of credibility established by frames, authorizing particles, and other conventions provide the standard against which verisimilitude is measured. Verisimilitude can be created performatively by embodying the characters in the narration by means of gestures, manipulation of voice qualities such as timbre, volume and pitch, and direct quotation (Tedlock 1983; Wiget 1987; Burns 1983). At Zuni, performative styles, touching upon matters like gestures and voice manipulation, vary considerably, but invariably Zuni *telapna:we* predominantly feature direct quotation. Verisimilitude can be created superficially, by a kind of thick description that lards the performance with details about social life, ritual, material culture, and so on. The Boasian tradition of studying oral literature as a repository of custom has produced many excellent examples of the Native American propensity to domesticate even the most widely disseminated kinds of oral narratives in this manner.

Finally, the most organic kind of verisimilitude arises from the values and beliefs upon which the motivations and behaviors of characters are grounded (see, for example, Kluckhohn and Leighton 1946; Fenton 1962). Oral literature dramatizes the cognitive models of the universe and appropriate behaviors and relationships within it (Geertz 1973). This educative value is one of four principal functions Bascom (1954) attributes to folklore, the others being institutional validation, cultural commentary, and norm maintenance. Structuralism attempts to understand how a particular text reflects the values of the "audience" as most broadly conceived. Structuralist discourse presumes that the circulation of a work of a particular kind is sustained because the work reflects the interests of the audience which sanctions the circulation. The task then becomes one of identifying aspects of the work which instantiate those interests. A nonexclusive listing of probable audience interests would include aesthetic values (it gives pleasure to recognize relationships between innovation and traditional forms), social values (the story tells how one group came to dispossess another), political values (the story demonstrates the justice of that dispossession), or cultural values (the protagonist participates in, reenacts, or even establishes important cultural practices). The classic study is Lévi-Strauss's 1963 analysis of the Zuni Emergence myth. The usefulness of structuralist criticism is that it locates the value of oral literature in relationship to other, recognized values and so identifies literature as a central, rather than a marginal component of cultural life. This strength is also its limitation, for it effectively addresses only the normative, the central, the traditional, the communal, the thematic, and thus is reductive. For the most part, this limitation is induced by the nature of that which is studied when dealing with received texts, as opposed to a careful documentation of the interaction between performer and audience. Only the latter would enable one to specify with some degree of confidence the immediate performance conditions that might account for innovation, idiosyncrasy, in short, the difference between one performance and another. Moreover, while material culture elements may be glossed in notes and performative features indicated in scriptlike annotations, the compelling vision that informs the world as experienced by the storyteller cannot be translated in any compelling matter. A system of beliefs can be understood as a system, but the sense of its own rightness or correctness that is brought to bear in every experience cannot be mediated through notes. Here, at the most crucial moment, the foreign, alien reader, however willing, is nevertheless least able to "translate" and to assent.

Native Americans, for example, had no notion of sin. Now, one might respond that today Sin—with its biblical overtones, its rootedness in will, its covenanted sense of responsibility to God and neighbor—increasingly is being rejected by Euroamericans as an acceptable description for certain kinds of human behavior, and no longer occupies the imagination or compels the intellectual assent that it did in ninth-century France. In our liberal attempt to reduce sin to weakness, we have only confused the two, with the result that people are accumulating guilt for what was formerly denominated as weakness and refusing guilt for what was formerly denominated as sin. Nevertheless, questions of a predisposition to evil, mythologized in the story of the Fall, provide a fundamental assumption about human nature with which Euroamerican authors must still come to grips in creating credible motives for their characters, so that, despite the generalized loss of belief, it remains difficult for most Western readers to account for certain kinds of behaviors in ways which are not informed by a residuum of the concept of sin. Because Native Americans were not so encumbered, they imagined characters in a fundamentally different way. Our attempts to understand the causes and consequences of negatively valued behavior, or even to recognize it as negative, in Native American narrative often limp along on weak analogies to our own Euroamerican experience.

Other equally metaphysical questions include the notion of human freedom; value and processes of individuation; concepts of destiny, time, and history; the nature of heroism, tragedy, humor, and romance; and a variety of personal relationships. While these concepts are often recognizably culture-bound, it is often more difficult to recognize as culture-bound the assumptions upon which the concepts are based. It is clear that any serious appreciation of Native American literature requires real effort to discover the cultural limitations of our own belief and recognize and value difference (see, for example, the valuable works on Navajo metaphysics by

McNeley and by Farella). Yet, however more valuable our reading when it is informed by a knowledge of relevant tribal customs and values, the force of the reading is nevertheless diminished because that knowledge is analytic rather than experiential.

The Intertextual Pole

Because "intertextual" explicitly refers to written literature, this is perhaps better denominated the Traditional Pole, for what is at stake in this corner is the collective cultural memory of expressive forms, understood most broadly as the range of possibilities within the language (stylistics) and the literature (genres and works), precisely the kind of "tradition" which, T. S. Eliot wrote, both shapes and is shaped by each new instance.

At first glance, oral and written literatures would seem to be fundamentally different here. A writer establishes a relationship between his work and other texts, a singer or storyteller between his work and other performances. The entitivity of a text, its persistent historical identity, may seem to constrain a writer more rigorously than an ephemeral performance would constrain subsequent performers. Yet a writer, as Harold Bloom has pointed out, is more apt to transgress than imitate, because of his desire to establish difference in spite of evident continuity. Indeed, it is precisely the obviousness of continuity—whether in language, plot, occasion, reference, image, theme, characterization, and so on—that motivates the inscription of difference. Performers, on the other hand, never truly replicate, even when that is their aim, as in those genres most constrained for social or religious reasons. In short, this sense of the presence of the past is felt keenly by both the writer and the performer, who struggle to find acceptable ways to locate their work in a meaningful relationship to tradition. The motives for this struggle are many, and more properly discussed later under *The Author*, for this negotiation between tradition and innovation is really one dimension of the authoring function.

Every literature, oral or written, is characterized by a concept of genre, which clusters culturally sanctioned conditions of appropriateness. Consequently, discussions which treat examples of Native American oral literature analogously as instances of some Western genre have a very limited usefulness, for the real aesthetic value of genre is culturally specific. This is true even of the most discriminating analysis, such as Bascom's cross-cultural typology of narrative forms (1965). Some of the most heated arguments in ethnopoetics, for instance, have concerned the usefulness of denominating some kinds of oral literature as poetry or prose, and whether those Euroamerican categories correspond to various Native American terms for distinguishing speech and song. This argument over "analytic categories" (Ben-Amos 1975) doesn't really touch the Native performer, who is much more concerned with her "ethnic genres." Such systems can be quite complex, as Basso (1984) demonstrated for the Western Apache (see figures in "Oral Literature of the Southwest") and Gossen (1974:51–52) for the Chamula Maya. Because these conditions are either prescriptive or normative, they are experienced as constraints by the singer or narrator, who must choose at every moment whether and by what means she will accept or transgress those restraints.

Several widespread, though probably not universal examples of constraining conventional structures for narrative are well known, and can be manipulated for self-consciously artistic purposes.

1. *Verbal Framing.* The presence/absence as well as the degree of complexity/depth of opening and closing formulas.
2. *Songs.* The presence of singing, the number and location within the story of repetitions.
3. *Initial Particles.* The recurrent use of selected particles, corresponding roughly to the adverb of traditional English grammar, to mark units of narrative into lines, groups, episodes. May be repeated in different numbers, embedded, or stacked.
4. *Vocalization.* Modification of voice (especially timbre and pitch) or the use of specialized vocabulary to distinguish between characters.
5. *Special Vocabulary.* Specialized vocabulary to distinguish between characters or mark genres.
6. *Repetition.* The use of culturally significant numbers to structure narrative at all levels.
7. *Formulaic Expressions.* Recurrent syntactical units ranging from a phrase through a line to a group of several lines.

Similar lists could be constructed for songs and would include: repetition, refrains (especially vocables), parallelism, melody, accompaniment, and vocal arrangement. By manipulating content as well as these formal resources, the performer establishes the unique relationship of performance to the genre tradition. So the Navajo storyteller Yellowman was able to identify for Toelken (1969) the marks of different genres in which Coyote would appear. Radical transformations of material from one genre form to another, known as metaphrasis, have also been identified in Native American oral literatures (Hymes 1981:87).

Stylistic innovations are more intimately related to two linguistic and performative conventions. It used to be widely assumed in the nineteenth century that American Indian languages were so bound up with the experience of the natural world that they were nearly incapable of being used for abstract reasoning. The Imagist poets of the twenties were quick to embrace what they viewed as the poetically compressed and fundamentally metaphorical nature of American Indian oral literature. Even today, a common mistake of translators is to assume that a linguistic unit that looks to us like a metaphor carries that metaphorical force to original speakers. To translate the Choctaw word for "horse" into "big deer" or the word for "sugar" into "sweet salt" would simply be precious. Each language carries with it certain capacities, not all of which are authorized or actualized by every segment of the speech community in any one era. Stylistic artistry emerges from the surprisingly (because previously unrecognized or unauthorized or simply infrequent) appropriate expression. Performatively, the kinesic and paralinguistic resources of the speech community provide a range of resources, which have not been fully explored (but see Wiget 1987). Too frequently, performative style has been overlooked or confused with genre form. We do not yet have a range of performances by different individuals, adequately evaluated by community members, from any tribe, even after Tedlock's work with the Zuni, that could tell us whether there is a normative performance style for any particular genre and what is the range of acceptable variation.

The Author

It is more appropriate, as Foucault suggests, at this level of description to speak of an authoring function, rather than an author, but our historical inclinations in the West have been biographical, at least since the emergence of states. It appears that when states emerged in the Americas, keeping biographical records, at least of some distinguished individuals, also came into being. Certainly, some naming customs, such as the accumulation of names associated with deeds or experiences within a lifetime or the custom of naming a child after a relative of two or three generations earlier, suggest a biographical habit of mind, regarding the social value of preserving personal identity and the association of identity with achievement.

It is nevertheless true that authoring in an oral, as opposed to a written, literature did not usually imply the kind of proprietary interest that today accrues to the creator of something unique. Moreover, to continue the analogy to contemporary copyright practices, one needs to distinguish between ownership and use. With regard to ownership or proprietary identification, most genres of literature, spoken or sung, were the common property of a group, even if the group were a segment of the whole community, such as a medicine society or priesthood. The most obvious exception to this are certain classes of songs, articulating personal sources of spirit power acquired in dreams, some kinds of which could be sold as personal property. Among the Inuit, some songs came in dreams as the words of deceased people, so the song, even when sung for the first time, was spoken of as having belonged to someone else. Only among the Aztecs is there evidence of a tradition of identifying people specifically as creators of original poetry and preserving the corpus of poetry in their names. Whether the uniqueness of the Aztec phenomenon results from inadequate attention to the question of authorship in the history of ethnography, the early and thorough recording of Aztec poetry before centuries of contact and assimilation, or from a biological impulse emerging in conjunction with the Aztec state will never be known.

That most oral literature was common cultural property does not exclude consideration of performance from the condition of art. Consider the condition of European literature through the Renaissance, when not just the broad knowledge of past was the shared basis for literature—the matter of Greece, the matter of Rome, the matter of Britain—but whole, complex plots were appropriated from earlier writers. And readers, knowing full well the story, took pleasure not in the novelty of the whole but in the innovative details of setting, twists of plot, or turns of phrase. The audience for a storyteller often had the same expectations, while in some Native American song traditions, for instance, pleasure derived from fitting innovative lyrics to "traditional" melodies. This is precisely why a critic errs when he assumes that a performer is disclaiming responsibility for performance when he says, "I'm just telling you what I heard" (Vizenor 1989:199).

Because most oral literature was common cultural property does not mean, however, that all genres of oral literature could be performed appropriately or competently by everyone. Clearly, every society sanctions the production and dissemination of expressive forms of culture in a variety of ways (Becker 1982). Traditional forms of deference behavior—sometimes expressed through silence or disclaimers of ability—often manifested themselves when the invitation to perform was issued in a group where more than one individual was competent to do so. In addition to aesthetic correlates of competence (discussed below under *Audience*), indices of competence were often associated with role or status, so that the prerogative to perform correlated with characteristics such as age, gender, membership in the appropriate clan or organization, and so on. There is also a sense in which authoring is to claim a peculiar kind of personal interest in what is being performed. In some senses, then, works can be spoken of as autobiographical. Perhaps because of her detailed knowledge of the distinctive personalities of well-known Navajo medicine men, Gladys Reichard worked mightily to undo the notion that oral traditional performers were "transparent," mere windows into or vehicles for the voice of the past. In her article "Individualism and Mythological Style," Reichard demonstrated how Hastiin Klah introduced innovations into the Emergence story consonant with his own experiences and individual temperament. While the anthropologists responsible for transcribing the materials which have come to be appreciated under the rubric of oral literature were concerned less with individuals and with variation than they were with establishing broad patterns of culture—an attitude that built the myth of the anonymous author—Reichard and others can legitimately point to the value of genetic biographical criticism.

Audience

Literary theorists have revived a consideration of audience with their concern for reception studies and reader-response analysis. But the interpersonal relationship between audience and performer characterizes folk literacy as a mode of expression. Indeed, the most widely accepted definition of performance highlights the role of audience:

> Fundamentally, performance as a mode of spoken verbal communication consists in the assumption of responsibility to an audience for a display of communicative competence. This competence rests on the knowledge and ability to speak in socially appropriate ways. Performance involves on the part of the performer an assumption of accountability to an audience for the way in which a communication is carried out, above and beyond its referential content. From the point of view of the audience, the act of expression on the part of the performer is thus marked as subject to evaluation for the way in which it is done, for the relative skill and effectiveness of the performer's display of competence. (Bauman 1977:11)

While one can rightly argue that the audience function in both modes is principally one of evaluation, how evaluation occurs in each situation is considerably different. An admittedly simple model of writing, but useful for the moment, sees the writer as alternating roles between that of the author and that of the audience during the production of the work, as he anticipates the values, beliefs, and experiences of the audience to whom he appeals. His second audience, over which he has even less control, is the readers and editors responsible for publishing and circulating his work. His third audience, larger and even more complex, consists of the work's readers, who appropriate it according to their various interests. Only the first two—the writer-as-audience and the editor-as-audience—are in a position to affect the final shape of the work. The responses of critics and other readers may, in fact probably will, help shape subsequent works, but the one at hand is fixed. All of these various audiences are also present to the performer of oral literature. Like the writer, the performer tries to anticipate his audience's responses, but unlike the writer, who can dismiss a hostile or incredulous audience after the fact as philistines because the work is already complete and in circulation, the performer, confronted with the audience in his face, must incorporate his responses to their evaluations into the work as it is developing. Like editors and first readers, audiences in performance have a kind of co-creative function.

The active participation of the audience in evaluating the performance as it occurs is what distinguishes performance as an *emergent form* from

15

textuality as *fixed form* (though if we accept, as some reader-response critics do, that each reader actualizes texts differently, then the text-as-read is certainly also an emergent phenomenon). Very few useful observations of performances have been done, but two are worth remarking on here. In her record of a Cree storytelling performance, Regna Darnell describes several ways in which the storyteller she was documenting adapted his performance to his audience. In the first place, he refrained from including subject matter which he thought the young woman who was present as a translator would judge to be obscene. Second, he augmented the ending of his story by creating a narrative bridge which prophesied the return of men with beards, because white men with beards were present at the storytelling. In short, both the form and the content of the storytelling event were substantially altered by the presence of the audience. In addition to shaping the emergent form, audience response can also identify values peculiar to different audience fractions representing what I earlier called "shared experience groups." Since I know of no Native American example to illustrate this point, I will mention that offered by Bruce Grindal, who was working among the Sisala tribe. Grindal observed that different age groups in the audience laughed at different moments during the performance of Trickster stories. Older people laughed at the story's conclusion, when Trickster got his comeuppance, while younger people laughed during the middle part of the story, as Trickster successfully evaded punishment.

In the evolution of performance analysis, the role of the audience deserves much more careful study. Too frequently, contemporary studies of Native American oral literature focus on familiar issues of form, theme, and style and less on context, function, and audience. To a degree, such studies remain encumbered by a textual rather than a performative paradigm, ignoring characteristics that set oral tradition apart from writing.

In this brief essay, I have tried to sketch out a framework for understanding Native American oral literature. The points of contact between writing and orality are numerous; the difference between them is crucial. Some have argued that orality as a mode of expression limits the capacity of the imagination and the intellect in a variety of ways, but there is no way of testing such a hypothesis that does not founder on its own ethnocentrism. In the fifteenth century, Native Americans, like many tribal peoples throughout the world, could offer examples of sophisticated mathematics, affecting poetry, a vision of history, and a complex social organization all equal to the capacities of literate European societies. Indeed, understanding the nature and dimensions of the oral tradition enables us to understand why today it not only survives, but in many cases flourishes, alongside writing and electronic media.

Andrew Wiget
New Mexico State University

BIBLIOGRAPHY

Bascom, William. "The Four Functions of Folklore." *Journal of American Folklore* 67 (1954): 333–49.

———. "The Forms of Folklore: Prose Narrative." *Journal of American Folklore* 75 (1965): 3–20.

Basso, Keith. "'Stalking with Stories': Names, Places and Moral Narratives Among the Western Apache." *Text, Play and Story: The Construction and Reconstruction of Self and Society.* Washington, DC: American Ethnological Society, 1984. 19–55.

Bauman, Richard. *Verbal Art as Performance.* Rowley, MA: Newberry House, 1977.

Becker, Howard. *Art Worlds.* Berkeley: U of California P, 1982.

Ben-Amos, Dan. "Analytical Categories and Ethnic Genres." *Folklore Genres.* Ed. Dan Ben-Amos. Austin: U of Texas P, 1975. 215–42.

Burns, Allan. *An Epoch of Miracles: Oral Literature of the Yucatec Maya.* Austin: U of Texas P, 1983.

Darnell, Regna. "Correlates of Cree Narrative Performance." *Explorations in the Ethnography of Speaking.* Eds. Richard Bauman and Joel Sherzer. Cambridge: Oxford UP, 1974. 315–36.

Farella, John. *The Main Stalk: A Synthesis of Navajo Philosophy.* Tucson: U of Arizona P, 1984.

Fenton, William. "'This Island, the World on Turtle's Back.'" *Journal of American Folklore* 75 (1962): 283–300.

Finnegan, Ruth. *Oral Poetry.* Oxford: Cambridge UP, 1977.

Geertz, Clifford. "Religion as a Cultural System." *Interpretations of Culture.* New York: Basic Books, 1973.

Goffman, Irving. *Frame Analysis.* Cambridge, MA: Harvard UP, 1975.

Gossen, Gary. *Chamulas in the World of the Sun: Time and Space in Maya Oral Tradition.* Cambridge: Oxford UP, 1974.

Grindal, Bruce. "The Sisala Trickster Tale." *Journal of American Folklore* 86 (1973): 173–75.

Hernadi, Paul. "Literary Theory." *Introduction to Scholarship in Modern Languages and Literatures.* New York: Modern Language Association, 1981. 98–115.

Hymes, Dell. *"In Vain I Tried to Tell You": Essays in Native American Ethnopoetics.* Philadelphia: U of Pennsylvania P, 1981.

Jennings, Francis, and William Swaggerty. *The Newberry Center for the History of the American Indian Bibliographical Series.* Bloomington: Indiana UP.

Kluckhohn, Clyde, and Dorothea Leighton. *The Navajo.* Cambridge, MA: Harvard UP, 1946.

Kroeber, Karl, ed. *Traditional American Indian Literatures: Texts and Interpretations.* Lincoln: U of Nebraska P, 1981.

Krupat, Arnold. "An Approach to Native American Texts." *Critical Inquiry* 9 (1982): 323–38.

———. *The Voice in the Margin: Native American Literature and the Canon.* Berkeley: U of California P, 1989.

———. *Ethnocriticism: Ethnography, History, Literature.* Berkeley: U of California P, 1992.

Lévi-Strauss, Claude. "The Structural Study of Myth." *Structural Anthropology.* New York: Basic Books, 1963. 209–31.

McNeley, James. *Holy Wind in Navajo Philosophy.* Tucson: U of Arizona P, 1981.

Merriam, Alan. *Ethnomusicology of the Flathead.* Chicago: Aldine, 1967.

Murdock, G. P., and T. L. O'Leary. *Ethnographic Bibliography of North America.* Fourth Edition. New Haven: Human Relations Area Files, 1989.

Murray, David. *Forked Tongues: Speech, Writing and Representation in North American Indian Texts.* Bloomington: Indiana UP, 1991.

Prucha, Francis Paul. *A Bibliography-Guide to Indian-White Relations in the United States*. Chicago: U of Chicago P, 1977.

———. *Indian-White Relations in the United States: A Bibliography of Works Published, 1975–1980*. Lincoln: U of Nebraska P, 1982.

Ramsey, Jarold. *Reading the Fire: Essays in the Traditional Indian Literatures of the Far West*. Lincoln: U of Nebraska P, 1983.

Reichard, Gladys. "Individualism and Mythological Style." *Journal of American Folklore* 57 (1944): 16–25.

Swann, Brian, ed. *Smoothing the Ground: Essays on Native American Oral Literature*. Berkeley: U of California P, 1983.

Swann, Brian and Arnold Krupat, eds. *Recovering the Word: Essays on Native American Literature*. Berkeley: U of California P, 1987.

Tedlock, Dennis. "Pueblo Literature: Style and Verisimilitude." *New Perspectives on the Pueblos*. Ed. Alfonso Ortiz. A School of American Research Book. Albuquerque: U of New Mexico P, 1972.

———. *The Spoken Word and the Work of Interpretation*. Philadelphia: U of Pennsylvania P, 1983.

Toelken, Barre. "The 'Pretty Languages' of Yellowman: Genre, Mode and Texture in Navajo Coyote Stories." *Genre* 2 (1969): 211–35.

Vizenor, Gerald, ed. *Narrative Chance: Postmodern Discourse on Native American Literatures*. Albuquerque: U of New Mexico P, 1989.

Wiget, Andrew. *Native American Literature*. Boston: Twayne, 1985.

———, ed. *Critical Essays on Native American Literature*. Boston: G. K. Hall, 1985.

———. "Telling the Tale: A Performance Analysis of a Hopi Coyote Story." In Swann and Krupat, 1987. 297–338.

Witherspoon, Gary. *Language and Art in the Navajo Universe*. Ann Arbor: U of Michigan P, 1977.

Oral Literature of the Alaskan Arctic

In many respects, the oral literatures of Alaskan Yupik and Inupiaq peoples are thematically and structurally varied, yet the range of variation is consistent. Alaskan traditions are clearly related to the verbal art of Inuit peoples in Canada, Greenland, and Siberia, and many elements are also shared with other Native North American groups.[1] Rather than considering the distribution of specific forms and motifs, however, the following concentrates on features of genre, performance, transmission, function, and content specific to Alaskan Inuit oral literature.

Native Genre Distinctions

A basic, although not rigid, distinction is made between two categories of narratives. The first of these consists of narratives considered to be of great antiquity and importance. Traditional tales which are not ultimately attributable to any known storyteller, and which include stock characters, rather than named persons who are known to have existed, are among those included in this genre. Etiological stories, detailing origins of celestial and geographic features, human customs and ceremonies, and animal characteristics; accounts of the legendary exploits of culture heroes; and ancient tales of animals in their human forms and of human/animal transformations are usually in this class. In most areas, the terms for this genre are cognate: Central Siberian Yupik *unigpaghaq*; Alaskan Inupiaq *unipkaaq/unipchaaq/ulipkaaq*; Naukanski Siberian Yupik *unikparaq*; Norton Sound *univkaraq*; Alutiiq *unigkuaq* (Fortescue and Kaplan 1989). Although *univkaraq* is used by some Central Alaskan Yupik speakers, the divergent form *quliraq* is more common. Here, the designation *unipkaaq/quliraq* will be used.

The second genre includes narratives which are considered to be more recent. These may describe events in the lives of known (extant or deceased) individuals, and are thought to be attributable to a particular person, a source who may or may not be known to the storyteller (Woodbury 1984). One Inupiaq storyteller, for example, distinguished between a "legend" (*unipkaaq*) such as Raven's theft of daylight, and his own "stories of people with names" (*quliaqtuaq*) (Okakok 1981). These narrative accounts range from memorates, including encounters with ghosts and other supernatural beings, to ethnohistories of such events as interregional warfare or early contacts with Europeans. *Qanemciq* is the Central Yupik designation; *quliaqtuaq* the Inupiaq one.[2] A comparison of Central Yupik *quliraq* with Naukanski *quliramsuk*, and Central Siberian Yupik *ungipaghaq* and *ungipausuk*, suggests that the essential distinction is expressed by the postbase -*msuk*, "something newer" or "less important."

These distinctions, however, are relative, and stories are sometimes classified ambiguously. For example, in one story Raven spears a tussock to pull a named local hill out of the vast ocean flood, thereby creating the contemporary landscape and causing the waters to recede. The narrator explains that it "is not really a story (*unipkaaq*), but rather an account (*quliaqtuaq*) of our origin" (Ingstad 1987). Yupik stories about Raven are also "told as accounts" although they are considered to be *qulirat* (pl.). Similarly, a narrative of a war which occurred in a specific locality but "a fairly long time ago, maybe three hundred years ago," was said to be an "account" (*quliaqtuaq*) that was like a "legend" (*unipkaaq*) (Ingstad 1987).

Other Narrative Genres

In addition to these two categories, more specialized forms exist, notably short stories in which characters compete through ritualized insult songs (Inupiaq *atuutilgautrat*), illustrated tales, string figure stories, and formulaic rhymes and finger plays for children. These are categories defined primarily by form and mode of performance. Central Yupik storyknife tales, for example, are distinctive because they are told only by females (most commonly, girls) and consist of simultaneous narration and illustration with stylized symbols etched in mud or snow. They may be imaginary stories, or accounts of personal experience. Illustrations of house plans are prominently featured. North Slope Inupiaq women apparently had a related tradition, unreported in the literature, which involved drawing house plans and illustrating stories in beach sand. Similarly, string stories accompany and explain single (static or moving) or sequential cat's cradle-type string figures. Like that of Coyote stories in the American Southwest, the telling of string figure stories is variously restricted. The Inupiaq tell them only in the winter months; the consequences for violating this injunction, themselves elaborated in the oral tradition, involve the appearance of the spirit of string figures who may extinguish all the lamps, causing paralysis and death, or challenge the transgressor to a deadly competition, using its own intestines or an invisible string to make figures (Jenness 1923).

Other genres, such as the Central Yupik *inqutaq*, are specific to young children. *Inqutaq* are set to a recognizable metrical scheme and spoken with a high-pitched "cooing" intonation pattern, but consist of words and syllables personalized to a particular child. Finger ditties, clapping games, and songs are also used to distract or amuse children, or to encourage obedience. Children learn to perform these, in turn, for the amusement of adults.

Also reported historically in many areas are bawdy chants, such as women's juggling chants (Koranda 1964) and boys' chants to accompany games with the hunting bola.

Ownership and Performance Rights

With a few exceptions, Inuit narratives may be told by anyone who has been "lucky enough to catch (i.e., hear and remember) them." Customarily, however, storytellers defer formally and politely to each other's expertise, and actively request additions or corrections to their tellings. An observer in the late 1800s reported that in some Yupik areas, "important tales" were told by two men, one of whom narrated, while the other marked significant junctures in the narrative by placing small sticks on the floor between them, and corrected his partner's errors (Nelson 1983). Storytellers may also verify the source from whom they "acquired" a particular variant, calling it, for example, "Nageak's story." This serves to provide a reference point for the introduction of other people's versions.

Certain formalized verbal expressions used in ritual contexts, and hunting charms, might be explicitly owned. During the Yupik Messenger Feast, for example, men called out formulaic references to unusual events experienced by an ancestor. These introduced certain gift request songs, and the performance of dances with inherited motions (Mather 1985).

Narrative Setting and Focus

The setting and focus of narrative performances might vary depending upon the age and gender of the narrators and audience, the season, and the narrative genre. During the winter months, when subsistence pursuits were reduced, Inuit men in both North and Southwest Alaska spent much of their time in the ceremonial house (Inupiaq *qargi*; Central Yupik *qasgi*). Here elders told stories, both for entertainment and to teach their juniors the rules of proper behavior when traveling, hunting, courting, and pursuing other activities. These rules were codified in aphorisms, prescriptions, and injunctions, which were repeated frequently so that youth would ab-

21

sorb and be able to recall them when the appropriate situation arose. In the Central Yupik area boys were barred from exiting while such instruction occurred.

In addition to these explicit forms of instruction, many Inuit stories serve as implicit parables for behavior. An abbreviated Northwest Alaskan tale of a mouse's delusions of grandeur (he sings that he is so big his back touches the sky and his belly the earth, when in fact he is merely lying underneath a piece of sealskin), for example, suggests that boasting is an empty pursuit apt to make one look foolish (*Unipchaallu*).

Learning and Listening

Short tales like these are learned from repeated tellings, but young men learning more complicated tales traditionally repeated them "verbatim, even with the accompanying inflections of the voice and gestures." In a Kuskokwim River village in 1879, an observer reported being kept awake for several nights by young men repeating stories that they were attempting to memorize, while the others slept (Nelson 1983:451). Today, it is not unusual for men to end stories by saying that they do not know any more because as young boys they fell asleep and never heard the recitations completed.

In the *qargi*, too, were told lengthy episodic accounts of wars, tales of revenge, and cycles of the adventures of Raven and of legendary heroes. It is said that some narratives took a month to complete, but rarely have full accounts survived, since the *qargi* was discontinued with Christianization. Men continue to tell stories when they work together making or repairing gear, at hunting and fishing camps, and, in the Yupik area, in the family steambaths which have replaced the sweatbaths of the *qasgi*.

Especially in the Central Yupik area, where women traditionally entered the *qasgi* only to serve food or for ceremonial occasions, women have passed on their oral traditions primarily in the home. Girls may continue to learn norms through traditional prescriptions and proscriptions. Older female relatives tell them animal tales, memorates, ghost stories, and origin stories; isolated story motifs may reappear, along with dreams, movie and television plots, and personal experiences, in the girls' storyknife tales. Hunting and war stories, however, are still generally told by men.

New Contexts for Narrative

In contemporary Alaskan Inuit societies, the oral tradition is also transmitted more sporadically during formal elders' conferences. There, audience and storytellers include both males and females. Agencies and community groups also sponsor efforts to record and preserve oral literature; often, these reflect a concern with documenting placenames and other evidence of land use for regulatory purposes. Although in the restricted setting of the classroom, elders may be uncomfortably isolated from the confirming presence of other tradition-bearers, the schools are also increasingly a setting for narrative performance. Finally, with language shift some narrative traditions are being reshaped in English versions, while others are disappearing.

Form and Content Distinctions

In addition to these characteristics of setting, narrator, and audience, there are content and form distinctions associated with different oral genres. Consistent with the relatively egalitarian nature of Inuit societies and the lack of story ownership, narratives do not include lengthy genealogies of either characters or narrators, although the storyteller often briefly credits his/her source and that person's relationship to him/her. Narratives in the *quliaqtuaq/qanemciq* category often specify the story's location immediately, by placename and in relation to identifiable geographical features; they also quickly identify named characters. In contrast, *unipkaaq/quliraq* narratives often begin with generalized locations ("there was a village by a river") and characters. Especially in stories accounting for animal characteristics or natural features, it is common for the narrator to corroborate the story with his/her own observations. An Upper Kobuk narrator, for example, tells of two fish, Pike and Mudsucker, who flung arrows at each other, one from his body and the other from his tail. Because pike have bony bodies and mudfish bony tails, the narrator concludes, "they both are as the story says, which is why [it] is so believable" (*Unipchaanich* 1980:8).

A common story type centers around a grandmother and orphaned grandchild. Lacking an adult male provider, the two live in poverty. The child is often teased and mistreated by, variously, a beautiful girl, a shaman, and/or the other villagers. If a boy, the orphan may be supported by the village's great hunter, and may find a supernatural or animal helper. He eventually shames or defeats those who have rejected him, often by gaining shamanic powers, and rewards his benefactor. In female-centered variants (such as storyknife tales), the granddaughter often disobeys her grandmother; consequently, the child is exposed to supernatural danger. Here, it may be the grandmother who turns out to have magical powers (Oswalt 1964; Ager 1971).

In other stories, the main characters may be a couple living far from other people. Their lonely desolation creates a dramatic tension that leads up to an encounter with a "person" who turns out to be a supernatural being or an animal in human form. In one Yupik story, the lonely man sees another person in the ice, but cannot get him to respond; angered, he stabs the unfriendly stranger. Later, the being comes to threaten the man and his wife; when he kills it, we realize that it is his own reflected image, as the man himself dies (Morrow, *Yupik Language Center Collection* 1981).

While stories like this explore powerful metaphysical themes of life, death, loneliness, and human striving, others are more playful. A light-hearted Inupiaq variant on the mistaken reflection theme concerns a young hunter in his kayak who repeatedly dives into the water in pursuit of a beautiful young woman—unaware that he is chasing his own image (*Unipchaallu*).

Songs are often integral to the *unipkaaq/quliraq*. When sung by animals (or animal-people), they may be imitative of that animal's calls set to words. Songs are often actualized in magical events: one may sing animals into the *qasgi*, landslides down onto a village, or game into the hunter's hands. A narrator may gesture the dance motions that accompany songs in the story; some are merely portions of longer dance songs, which themselves may tell a story. Because of the structure of Eskimo languages, which incorporate tense, case, and person in postbases and endings such that words commonly end in the same sequence of syllables, rhyme is not important to song or story structure, although rhythm is.

As in other Native American traditions, the numbers four and five are significant ones in Inuit cultures. Stories are often structured accordingly, with parallel events occurring four/five times, the last of these being emphasized. Close analysis reveals other complex rhetorical features. In his study of the modular structure of one Yupik narrative, for example, Woodbury (1987) identifies "three distinct types of recurrent hierarchic organization . . . : nondiscrete hierarchy (in pause phrasing), discrete hierarchy (in prosodic phrasing and syntactic constituency), and numerically constrained hierarchy (in form-content parallelism in the narrative, and in a variety of components in the song)." Woodbury suggests a complex interaction among components and notes the storyteller's use of dramatic techniques (intonation shifts, nonverbal signs, and register and code-switching to characterize different voices and to heighten affect).

Quliaqtuaq/qanemciq narratives, other than brief memorates, can also be highly structured. A well-known Yupik legend, for example, describes a war which began when one boy accidentally blinded another during a dart game. Violence escalated as people took sides in the resulting conflict, and the story is constructed around a variable number of incidents following the warriors' trail.

Such war and revenge stories often describe the agony of a tortured family member and the justice wrought by his/her relatives, the destruction of villages that leaves only one survivor, or the shrewd and/or magical means by which people manage to escape death. The effect is of a series of intimate and personal vignettes—violence and revenge as experienced by members of a scattered band society. There is no epic glorification of conquest.

It should be clear, even from this superficial survey, that Alaskan Inuit oral arts are more complex and varied than they appear to be in the popular English literature, which has tended to include highly edited versions of relatively short tales. While readers can never experience the full richness of these oral art forms, more careful transcriptions and translations and more respectful analyses have begun to give us a better appreciation of these subtle traditions.

Phyllis Morrow
University of Alaska—Fairbanks

Notes

1. While "Eskimo" is often used among Alaska Natives, Inuit has become the accepted circumpolar designate.
2. Appropriately, *qanemciq* also refers to television/radio news broadcasts.

Thanks are due to Chase Hensel, Steven Jacobson, Elsie P. Mather, James Nageak, Leona Okakok, and Mary C. Pete for their critical comments and suggestions.

Bibliography

Primary Sources

Ingstad, Helge. *Nunamiut Unipkaanich: Nunamiut Stories Told in Inupiaq Eskimo by Elijah Kakinya and Simon Paneak of Anaktuvuk Pass, Alaska*. Trans. and ed. Knut Bergsland. Barrow, AK: North Slope Borough Commission on History and Culture, 1987.

Kaplan, Lawrence D. *Ugiuvangmiut Quliapyuit King Island Tales: Eskimo Tales and Legends from Bering Strait*. Fairbanks, King Island Native Community and the Alaska Native Language Center: U of Alaska, 1988.

Mather, Elsie Pavil. *Cauyarnariuq*. Bethel, AK: Lower Kuskokwim School District, 1985.

Morrow, Phyllis. Unpublished transcripts and translations. Yupik Language Center Collection of Oral Narratives. Bethel, AK: Kuskokwim Community College, 1979–81.

Okakok, Leona. *Puiguitkaat: The 1978 Elder's Conference*. Barrow, AK: North Slope Borough Commission on History and Culture, 1981.

Unipchaallu Uqaaqtuallu: Legends and Stories. Vols. 1 and 2. Anchorage: National Bilingual Materials Development Center, 1979–80.

Unipchaanich Imagluktugmiut: Stories of the Black River People. Anchorage: National Bilingual Materials Development Center, 1979-80.

Woodbury, Anthony C. *Cev'armiut Qanemciit Quliraot-llu: Eskimo Narratives and Tales from Chevak, Alaska*. Fairbanks: Alaska Native Language Center, U of Alaska, 1984.

Secondary Sources

Ager, Lynn Price. *The Eskimo Storyknife Complex of Southwestern Alaska*. Thesis. U of Alaska, 1971.

Fortescue, Michael, and Lawrence Kaplan. *Comparative Eskimo Dictionary*. Fairbanks: Alaska Native Language Center and Institute of Eskimology, 1989.

Jenness, Diamond. "Eskimo String Figures." *Journal of American Folklore* 36 (1923): 281–94.

Koranda, Lorraine D. "Some Traditional Songs of the Alaskan Eskimos." *Anthropological Papers of the University of Alaska* 12.1 (1964): 17–32.

Morrow, Phyllis. "It Is Time for Drumming: A Summary of Recent Research on Yup'ik Ceremonialism." *Études/Inuit/Studies* 8 (1984): 113–40.

Nelson, Edward W. *The Eskimo About Bering Strait*. 1899. Washington, DC: Smithsonian Institution Press, 1983.

Oswalt, Wendell. "Traditional Storyknife Tales of Yuk Girls." *Proceedings of the American Philosophical Society* 108 (1964): 310–36.

Woodbury, Anthony C. "Rhetorical Structure in a Central Alaskan Yupik Eskimo Traditional Narrative." *Native American Discourse: Poetics and Rhetoric*. Ed. Joel Sherzer and Anthony Woodbury. Cambridge: Cambridge UP, 1987.

Yuut Qanemciit/Yupik Lore: Oral Traditions of an Eskimo People. Bethel, AK: Lower Kuskokwim School District, 1981.

Oral Literature of the Subarctic Athapaskans

Approximately twenty-three Northern Athapaskan languages are spoken by different tribal groups in the western subarctic (Alaska, the Yukon Territories, northern British Columbia, the Northwest Territories, and northern Alberta). These languages are related to others of the Athapaskan family which are spoken on the American Pacific Coast and in the American Southwest. They are more distantly related to Eyak and Tlingit. Taken together, Athapaskan, Eyak, and Tlingit constitute the NaDene linguistic phylum.

Anthropologists sometimes organize discussions of subarctic Athapaskans by differentiating (1) the Mackenzie River Drainage—including Bearlake, Slavey, Dogrib, and other *Dene*, (2) the subarctic Cordillera—embracing, among others, Kutchin (*Gwich'in*) and Tutchone, and (3) subarctic Alaska—including, for example, Koyukon (*Ten'a*) and Tanaina (*Dena'ina*). All of these peoples subsisted by fishing and hunting. In the west, an abundance of resources like salmon allowed for a more sedentary existence than was possible in the east, where peoples relied on more variable and less productive seasonal resources. In the west, matrilineal descent and phratries or moieties were important to social organization and structure. In the east, bilaterality and very flexible kin-based band organization were more characteristic. Throughout the Athapaskan subarctic, shamanistic religious institutions predominated. Fundamental beliefs focused on spiritual power acquired by dreaming about and through the aid of various "animal helpers." Religious rituals were somewhat less formalized (more individualistic) in the east than in the west, where such public ceremonial occasions as funerary potlatches were more frequent. Concerning intergroup communication, peoples in the east had relatively few contacts with speakers of languages other than their own or a closely related Athapaskan dialect. In the west, opportunities to interact with speakers of other languages occurred more regularly—especially among groups bordering and trading with Northwest Coast peoples.

The ensuing discussion of subarctic Athapaskan oral literature is organized into three sections: a history of study; typical genres, performances, and functions; and "Distant Time" stories (mythology).

History of Study

The earliest collectors of subarctic Athapaskan oral literature were late nineteenth- and early twentieth-century Christian missionaries. Among the most prominent of these were the Catholic priests Émile Petitot (Mackenzie Drainage *Dene* [1886]), Adrien Morice (Chilcotin and Carrier), and Julius Jetté (Koyukon [1908, 1913]) and the Episcopal missionary, John W. Chapman (Ingalik [1914]).

Anthropologists have also collected and studied subarctic Athapaskan folklore and mythology, frequently with the intention of describing the world view of these peoples. Prominent anthropologists contributing to our knowledge of Mackenzie Drainage oral literature include Kaj Birket-Smith (Chipewyan), John Honigmann (Slavey), and June Helm (Slave and Dogrib [Helm and Thomas 1966, Helm and Gillespie 1981, MacNeish 1955]). Anthropologists who have documented subarctic Cordillera oral literature include James Teit (Kaska and Tahltan [1917, 1919–21]), Diamond Jenness (Carrier [1934]), Douglas Leechman (Kutchin [1950]), Robert A. McKennen (Kutchin and Taniana [1959]), Catherine McClellan (Tagish and Tutchone [1970]), Richard Slobodin (Kutchin [1975]), Robin Riddington (Beaver [1978]), and Julie Cruikshank (Tutchone [1983]). Ethnographers writing about subarctic Alaskan Athapaskan oral literature include Cornelius Osgood (Tanaina and Ingalik), Annette McFayden Clark (Upper Koyukon), Joan Townsend (Tanaina), and Richard Nelson (Koyukon [1983]).

Prominent linguists who have contributed to the study of subarctic Athapaskan oral literature include Pliny Goddard (Beaver and Chipewyan [1917a, 1917b]), Fang-Kuei Li (Chipewyan), Ronald and Suzanne Scollon (Chipewyan), and a number of scholars working at the Native Language Center at the University of Alaska, Fairbanks: Michael Krauss (Eyak, which is related to Athapaskan languages [1982]), James Kari (Ahtna and Tanaina [1986, Kalifornsky 1977]), and Eliza Jones (Koyukon [1979; Jones and Henry 1976]).

Additional references to the work of the above scholars may be found in the *Handbook of North American Indians*, Vol. 6, *Subarctic*, ed. June Helm.

Typical Genres, Performances, and Functions

There are three principal genres of traditional Northern Athapaskan oral literature: (1) mythical accounts of "Distant Time" (Nelson), (2) historical narratives focusing on such remarkable events as feuding or raiding between groups, the arrival of "whitemen," and the discovery of gold or oil (Helm and Gillespie), and (3) personal narratives (Cruikshank). Other traditional genres include riddles (Jetté), songs, prayers, and stories of "bushmen" or "bogeymen," powerful human-like creatures occupying the forests and behaving in asocial ways (Basso 1978).

All genres of subarctic Athapaskan oral literature, including epic accounts of Distant Time, were performed in both informal and formal situations. Distant Time stories, riddles, songs, and prayers were intrinsic parts of shamanistic practices, feasts, dances, and gambling. Among subarctic Alaskan and Cordilleran Athapaskans, slightly greater restrictions were placed on the recitation of Distant Time stories than among the Mackenzie Drainage *Dene*. Among the former peoples, myths were most appropriately recited by knowledgeable "old timers" during the evenings of late fall or winter days, during "Winter Ceremonies," or during funerary potlatches. Such groups as the Ahtna, Tahltan, and Kaska engaged in competitive storytelling.

Northern Athapaskan oral literature was used to entertain and educate. Distant Time stories accounted for the origins of everything in the subarctic universe. They explained the significant characteristics of plants, animals, and the natural landscape and they specified and justified appropriate human behavior—establishing for Northern Athapaskans a code of ethical conduct (Nelson). Historical and personal narratives, as well as "bushman" stories, frequently displayed the appropriate behavior or misguided actions of characters, along with the advantages of the former and the negative consequences of the latter.

Distant Time Stories

The mythologies or Distant Time stories (e.g., *Sukdu* in Tanaina, *Kk'adonts'idnee* in Koyukon, and *Yaníít'ó godi* in Bearlake) of Northern Athapaskan peoples share many common features. These are stories about the first three of five eras distinguished more or less explicitly by subarctic Athapaskans. The chronology, although implicit and even ambiguous for some peoples (as represented in published accounts), is: (1) distant time, (2) an era dominated by a great flood, (3) an ambiguous period of re-creation and great transformation by culture heroes, (4) a period of distant history or legend, and (5) an era of recent history and personal narrative (Nelson). During the first three of these periods, the mythical universe was dominated by anthropomorphic animals existing much like humans of the

29

modern world—animals possessed of all the psychological traits of human agents, as well as language, culture, and a kin-based social organization. The boundary between animals and humans is often blurred in the mythical universe, and spiritual power, transformation, and transfiguration were common events. The ambiguity between animals and humans is representative of the frequent conceptual inversions of the modern world which occur in the mythical universe.

Various more specific elements are also common to much of subarctic Athapaskan mythology. "Raven" is generally creator, transformer, and trickster of the Distant Time universe. After the great flood, Raven organized the animals who survived and re-created the earth (common characters in accounts of the flood and other myths are Beaver, Wolf, Bear, Mouse, and various birds). The flood itself marked the end of the first world and the beginning of a second world. Human linguistic and cultural diversity began to develop at that time. Following the flood, a great traveler, hunter, and transformer emerged as culture hero (for example, *Yamodéya* in Bearlake, *Yamontashe* or *Tsa-o-sha* in Tanana, *Etsuya* in Tutchone, *Tsuguyain* in Kaska, and *k't talqani* in Koyukon). This man hunted giant animals, married various women (who might be transfigured animals), became entangled in various kin relationships, fought giants or cannibalistic animals, and transformed many Distant Time places and animals into their modern forms. In some accounts, this hero is the elder of two brothers who journeyed throughout the world (e.g., Bearlake, Slavey, Kaska, Chipewyan, and Kutchin). In other accounts, he is identified with "Beaver Man" (e.g., Kaska, Beaver, Tanana, and Tutchone). Most Northern Athapaskans also tell stories relating to this era about an unfortunate woman who married a capable hunter. In reality, however, her husband was a dog capable of transforming itself into human form. She discovered the truth about her husband and then killed him, but not before becoming pregnant. She eventually gave birth to dog-children which, through a series of events, were finally transformed into stones forever sitting in a river. During this same period, two sisters became so infatuated with the stars that they were transported to the sky and married two star-beings. Eventually, however, they became homesick, escaped to the earth, and, with the help of animals, returned home.

Distant Time stories share with other genres certain types of themes and events. Some of these features are almost as likely to be associated with historical or even personal narratives as with accounts of the mythological world. For example, principles of kinship and marriage are fundamentally important to the organization of social life in all of the worlds described in traditional subarctic Athapaskan oral literature. In Distant Time, anthropomorphic animals might suffer the consequences of their misguided behavior toward kin. In a personal narrative, some individual known to the storyteller might be shown to have benefited greatly from his or her past generosity toward relatives. Social relationships are also stressed in narratives about "stolen women" (Cruikshank). Throughout time, women have been lost or stolen from their families and husbands. Accounts of such events from Distant Time and recent history become epics about the failures and successes surrounding the responsibilities of kinship and marriage and about the causes and consequences of warfare. Many of these stories also illustrate four other elements common to various subarctic Athapaskan genres: the existence of multiple worlds, journeys to and from those worlds, the ever-present threat of starvation, and the imperatives of both self-reliance and mutual support for survival. The presence of multiple worlds is reflected through distinctions between the natural world and either the Distant Time world or a contemporaneous supernatural world, often located underground and at some distance. The current supernatural world is much like the Distant Time world, and many stories do not make explicit distinctions between the two. The supernatural worlds are frequently visited by self-reliant, capable, and powerful men or women who subsequently return with special knowledge or skills which allow them to overcome starvation and other problems faced by peoples in the real world.

In conclusion, Northern Athapaskan oral literature focuses at many points on social and cultural features directly or indirectly tied to life in the subarctic environment. Whether in Distant Time or the modern world, industriousness, self-reliance, mutual aid, special knowledge, and kinship relations are of fundamental importance.

Scott Rushforth
New Mexico State University

BIBLIOGRAPHY

Basso, Ellen B. "The Enemy of Every Tribe: Bushman Images in Northern Athapaskan Narratives." *American Ethnologist* 5.4 (1978): 690–710.

Chapman, John W. *Ten'a Texts and Tales from Anvik, Alaska*. Publications of the American Ethnological Society VI (1914).

Cruikshank, Julie. *The Stolen Women: Female Journeys in Tagish and Tutchone*. National Museum of Man Mercury Series. Canadian Ethnology Service Paper 87. Ottawa: National Museum of Man, 1983.

Deacon, Belle. *Eng'thidong Xugixudhoy: Their Stories of Long Ago Told in Deg Hit'an Athabaskan by Belle Deacon*. Recorders: James Kari and Karen McPhergon. Ed. and trans. James Kari. Fairbanks: Alaska Native Language Center, U of Alaska, 1987.

Goddard, Pliny Earle. *Beaver Texts*. Anthropological Papers of the American Museum of Natural History 10.5. New York: American Museum of Natural History, 1917. 295–397.

———. *Chipewyan Texts*. Anthropological Papers of the American Museum of Natural History 10.1. New York: American Museum of Natural History, 1917, 1–65.

Helm, June, and Beryl C. Gillespie. "Dogrib Oral Tradition as History: War and Peace in the 1820s." *Journal of Anthropological Research* 37.1 (1981): 8–27.

Helm, June, and Vital Thomas. "Tales from the Dogrib." *The Beaver* 297 (1966): 16–20, 52–54.

Helm, June, ed. *Handbook of North American Indians.* Vol 6. *Subarctic.* Washington: Smithsonian Institution, 1981.

Jenness, Diamond. "Myths of the Carrier Indians of British Columbia." *Journal of American Folklore* 47 (1934): 97–257.

Jetté, Julius. "On Ten'a Folk-Lore." *Journal of the Royal Anthropological Institute of Great Britain and Ireland* 38 (1908): 298–367.

———. "Riddles of the Ten'a Indians." *Anthropologica* 8 (1913): 181–201, 630–51.

Jones, Eliza. *Chief Henry Yuqh Noholnigee: The Stories Chief Henry Told.* Fairbanks: Alaska Native Language Center, U of Alaska, 1979.

Jones, Eliza, and Chief Henry. *Kooltsaah Ts'in (Koyukon Riddles).* Fairbanks: Alaska Native Language Center, U of Alaska, 1976.

Kalifornsky, Peter. *Kahtnuht'ana Oenaqa: The Kenai People's Language.* Ed. James Kari. Fairbanks: Alaska Native Language Center, U of Alaska, 1977.

Kari, James. *Tatl'ahwt'aenn nenn'—The Headwaters People's Country.* Fairbanks: Alaska Native Language Center, U of Alaska, 1986.

Krauss, Michael E., ed. *In Honor of Eyak: The Art of Anna Nelson Harry.* Fairbanks: Alaska Native Language Center, U of Alaska, 1982.

Leechman, Douglas. *Folk-lore of the Vanta-Kutchin.* National Museum of Canada Bulletin, Anthropological Series 126. Ottawa: National Museum of Canada, 1950.

MacNeish, June Helm. "Folktales of the Slave Indians." *Anthropologica* 1 (1955): 37–44.

McClellan, Catherine. *The Girl Who Married the Bear: A Masterpiece of Indian Oral Tradition.* National Museum of Man Mercury Series. Canadian Ethnology Service Paper 57. Ottawa: National Museum of Man, 1970.

McKennen, Robert A. *The Upper Tanana Indians.* Yale U Publication in Anthropology 55. New Haven: Yale UP, 1959.

Nelson, Richard K. *Make Prayers to the Raven: A Koyukon View of the Northern Forest.* Chicago: U of Chicago P, 1983.

Petitot, Émile Fortune. *Traditions Indiennes du Canada Nord-Ouest.* Paris: Maisonneuve frères et C. Leclerc, 1886.

Riddington, Robin. *Swan People: A Study of the Dunneza Prophet Dance.* National Museum of Man Mercury Series. Canadian Ethnology Service Paper 38. Ottawa: National Museum of Man, 1978.

Slobodin, Richard. "Without Fire: A Kuhtchin Tale of Warfare, Survival, and Vengeance." *Proceedings: Northern Athapaskan Conference.* 2 vols. Ed. A. McFayden Clark. National Museum of Man Mercury Series. Ethnology Service Paper 27. Ottawa: National Museum of Man, 1975. 259–301.

Teit, James A. "Kaska Tales." *Journal of American Folklore* 30 (1917): 427–73.

———. "Tahltan Tales." *Journal of American Folklore* 32 (1919): 198–250; 34 (1921): 223–53, 335–56.

Tenenbaum, Joan M. *Dena'ina Sukdu'a, I–IV: Tanaina Stories, I–IV.* Fairbanks: Alaska Native Language Center, U of Alaska, 1976.

Williamson, Robert G. "Slave Indian Legends." *Anthropologica* 1 (1955): 119–43; 2 (1955): 61–92.

Native Oral Literature of the Northwest Coast and the Plateau

The northern Northwest Coast is noted for its spectacular art and architecture as well as its complex and highly structured social organization. The southern half of the Northwest Coast and the adjacent Plateau appear less elaborate in these respects, and correspondingly receive less attention. Just over a dozen, often powerful, language groups occupied the northern half of the coast, with a roughly equal number on the Plateau, but over thirty along the southern coast. This diversity along the coast was possible because of a temperate climate and abundant resources, the latter allowing the accumulation of great wealth in some areas. The Plateau, by contrast, is less hospitable, with a much greater range of temperatures, large semi-desert regions, and less abundant food supplies. Throughout both regions, salmon was a major food source, and large quantities were dried or smoked for winter use, along with other fish, game, roots, and berries. Villages on the coast were semi-permanent and often large, while those on the Plateau were probably smaller; residents of both made seasonal migrations to take advantage of available resources. The more open country of the southern Plateau allowed the development of a culture dependent on the horse for transportation, whereas the canoe played this role elsewhere, especially on the coast, where the many waterways made extensive use of horses impractical. The literatures of these regions show as much diversity.

The sections which follow will survey in turn (1) the history of the collection and study of Native literature of the Northwest, (2) typical genres to be found there, (3) what the nature of the myth world was and who populated it, (4) when and why stories were told, and (5) the form this literature takes and what stylistic features characterize it.

History of Study

Much of the Native folklore of the Indians of the Northwest Coast and the Plateau has been written down since the first arrival of Euroamericans in the area. It is safe to assume that only a fraction of the mythology and folktales that were told before white contact has been so recorded, however, and nothing like a complete collection exists for even a single original language or social group. Yet it has been claimed that "in regards to what has been done about oral literature, it is the best known area of all the non-Western world" (Jacobs 1967:18). Publication often lagged far behind collection, and some materials still remain unpublished.

The collection and analysis of the Native literature of the Northwest falls into three periods, divided by decade-long periods of little activity at the times of World Wars I and II. The first period, from 1890 to 1915, was dominated by one man, the great anthropologist Franz Boas. Prior to Boas's arrival in the Northwest in 1886, the only Native folklore collection of any significance in the area had been the one by Albert Gatschet and Jeremiah Curtin in Oregon (both working for the Bureau of American Ethnology) and the missionary Myron Eells in western Washington. Boas himself actively collected materials for over forty years, and was responsible for the publication of several major collections of Northwest folktales—thirteen volumes in English and the original language (as well as individual tales or small collections) from *Chinook Texts* (1894) to *Kwakiutl Tales* (1935–43), and including myths and tales of the Chinook (1894), Kathlamet (1901), Kutenai (1918), Kwakiutl (1910; 1935–43), Bella Bella (1928; 1932), Bella Coola (1898), and Tsimshian (1902; 1912; 1916). In addition, he persuaded his Columbia University colleague Livingston Farrand to join the Jesup North Pacific Expedition (1897–1901) to collect ethnographic and folkloristic material (Farrand 1900; Farrand and Kahnweiler). He encouraged and trained James Teit to take advantage of his friendship with the Indians of south-central British Columbia and collect data on (especially) the Thompson, Lillooet, and Shuswap Indians (Teit 1898). He trained two British Columbia Indians to write their Native languages and collect folklore; this collaboration resulted in two volumes on Kwakiutl with George Hunt (1902–5, 1906), and a volume (1916) based on Tsimshian materials provided to Boas by Henry W. Tate. Boas also trained numerous students who went on to collect huge quantities of folkloristic materials from Northwest Indians; most notable beginning in this earliest period were John R. Swanton on Haida (1905, 1908) and Tlingit (1909); Edward Sapir on Takelma (1909), Wishram (1909), and, with Morris Swadesh, Nootka (1939); and Leo J. Frachtenberg on Coos (1913), Siuslaw (1914), and Alsea (1920).

There were few others who had no direct connection to Boas who were actively collecting Northwest Indian folklore during this early period; worth noting are Charles Hill-Tout in southwestern British Columbia (his writings are collected in Maud 1978); Edward S. Curtis, the Seattle-based photographer-ethnographer, who published numerous tales (in English) in his monumental series *The North American Indian* (1907–30); and Marius Barbeau, who worked out of the Canadian National Museum (at first under Sapir; Barbeau 1953), and who published myths collected by himself and William Beynon (1961), a Tsimshian who assisted Barbeau from 1915 to 1957 (others were published posthumously as Barbeau and Beynon's *Narratives* I and II).

The second period extends from 1920 to 1940, and again is dominated by Boas through his students, although the Canadian National Museum sent T. F. McIlwraith to the Bella Coola and Diamond Jenness to the Carrier and Halkomelem. Both published limited numbers of texts, and in English only. Of Boas's students, several published major collections of texts, often incorporating materials collected by earlier investigators Melville Jacobs on Sahaptin (1929, 1934–37), Chinook Jargon (1936), Coos (1939, 1940), Kalapuya (1945), and Clackamas Chinook (1958, 1959); Manuel Andrade on Quileute (1931); Thelma Adamson on several Salishan groups of southwestern Washington (1934; in English only); Archie Phinney on Nez Perce (1934); Edward Sapir and his student Morris Swadesh on Nootka (1939); and Gladys Reichard on Coeur d'Alene (1947; in English only, although Coeur d'Alene versions were collected). Jacobs is clearly the dominant figure here, and often worked with the last speakers of languages. Other, usually shorter, collections of myths and tales were also gathered by various scholars during this period, such as Elmendorf on Twana and other Coast Salish (1961) and Elizabeth Jacobs on Tillamook (1959), but all are in English only, except for the Kalispel texts published by the Norwegian linguist Hans Vogt (1940).

Several collections of tales were also published by nonacademic collectors at this time. The most significant of these was Ballard's (1929); recognition should also be given to publications by Indians themselves. Archie Phinney, noted above, was Nez Perce, and his published texts are in Nez Perce and English. Small collections, in English only, are by the Colville speaker Mourning Dove (Christine Quintasket; 1933), the Northern Lushootseed speaker Martin J. Sampson (1938), and the Lushootseed-Wenatchee William Shelton (1932).

New projects were not begun during the 1940s, although established scholars continued publishing materials already collected. A new period began in the 1950s; this time there was no central figure, and researchers had more diverse backgrounds than before. It also became more difficult to publish texts in the Native languages, and the publishers too became more diversified. Major collections since 1950 are on Southern Puget Sound Salish (Snyder 1968), Klamalh (Barker 1963), Nez Perce (Aoki 1979), Eyak (Krauss 1982), Squamish (Kuipers 1967, 1969), Shuswap (Kuipers 1974; Bouchard and Kennedy 1979, in English), Lillooet

(Bouchard and Kennedy 1977; in English), Bella Coola (Davis and Saunders 1980), Oowekeeno (Hilton and Rath 1982), and Tlingit (Dauenhauer and Dauenhauer 1987). Mattina (1985) provides a long tale in Colville; it is an unusual document in that it is a tale of European origin thoroughly transformed into Native style.

Native collectors were again active in this period. Harris (1974) collected Gitksan legends (in English). Hilbert (1980; 1985) carefully prepared collections of Lushootseed tales in English. Others were not just collected by Natives, but even produced by Native communities; Slickpoo (1972) collected Nez Perce legends, Beavert (1974) collected Sahaptin legends, and a group of Gitksan people assembled *We-Gyet Wanders On: Legends of the Northwest* (1977). This last does not give versions of stories from individuals (which might be considered private property), but offers amalgams of individual versions.

A few scholars have used Northwest Coast and Plateau myths as the basis for syntheses and analyses of content, structure, and style. Easily the most important of these are Jacobs (*Content and Style*, 1959; *The People*, 1960), both based on Clackamas Chinook texts. More popular in style are Clark ("Indian Story-telling," 1953; "The Mythology," 1953) which provide an overview of the context and content of myth in the area. Ramsey (*Reading*, 1983) collected articles on western oral literature, while *Coyote Was Going There* (1977) is an annotated compilation of Coyote stories and similar tales from Oregon. Early comparative studies are Boas (1895) and Boas (*Tsimshian*, 1916:872–81).

Some collection of myths and tales continues in the Northwest; however, knowledge of Native languages has diminished greatly in the area, and along with this has occurred loss of knowledge of the traditional literature. In many cases today, only reanalysis of material collected earlier is possible.

A general and useful discussion of mythology on the Northwest Coast is Hymes 1989, and for British Columbia specifically see Maud (1982). More extensive references to work that has been done in the area can be found in Thompson (1973), and a thorough inventory of Native folklore in Washington State is included in Walls (1987).

Genres

Several distinct genres of Native literature exist, although the boundaries between some varieties are blurred in the Northwest. The Native languages of the area rarely distinguish more than two varieties, having a specific name for a myth or traditional story, and lumping everything else together, whether traditional, anecdotal, or of European origin (this dichotomy was recognized early in Boas [1916:565]). This is the situation in all twenty-three Salishan languages, where stories of the myth age have a specific designation and all other types are called by a word based on forms meaning "tell, narrate." A variant of the named variety occurs at least among the Gitksan, Kwakiutl, and Nootka (and probably the other northern groups as well) where the specific name refers to those legends that explain, and hence validate, the history (often legendary) of a family along with its crests and rights.

This labelled category may be termed "myth." Within the non-myth category, however, one can recognize several distinct types of narrative. There are tales of a traditional nature, often with anthropomorphic animal actors, that take place somewhere between the myth age and historic times. Biblical stories and European folktales and fables are easily adapted to this type of story, as in a Columbian tale when a Reynard the Fox tale is turned into a Coyote Story (such tales were spread through the region by missionaries and teachers). There are also contemporary stories which may be based on actual incidents; these may or may not be rendered using the formal apparatus of myths and tales.

Along with these more traditional categories, one can identify various genres which can be considered literature in a broad sense. Songs of various types were known everywhere; some occurred as parts of myths, and spirit power songs, love songs, and gambling songs were popular (see Densmore and Herzog for classic studies of Northwest Coast music). Speeches and prayers can also be seen as distinct categories, although few have been accurately recorded, and hence have received little scholarly attention. Efforts to reconstruct such famous Indian speeches as those by Chief Joseph renouncing warfare or Chief Seattle extolling nature have resulted in more fiction than fact. Aphorisms and adages were common, but have not been systematically collected. Another distinctive type of story that is well known by Indians throughout the area is the Sasquatch story. Most literature on this subject is concerned with whether or not such creatures really exist, and actual stories or anecdotes about them appear only sporadically. Indian lore throughout the Northwest is replete with stories about such creatures—Sasquatch (also known as stick-Indian, seatco, or bigfoot), little-earths, tree-strikers (and other dwarfs), two-headed snakes, water monsters, unicorns, and thunderbirds; recorded versions of these stories in the Native languages are virtually nonexistent, apart from their appearance in myths (for a study of Native characterizations of the Sasquatch, see Suttles 1972).

Cosmogony and Myth Roles

Northwest mythologies do not always include creation stories, and the preexistence of a world is often assumed. It is an imperfect world, however, and is full of animals and physical objects with human characteristics and ogres of many varieties. Where there are actual humans present, they are ill-formed and deficient in essential knowledge. This situation has to be fixed, the people have to be taught to behave correctly, ogres have to be killed, various foods provided, the sun and moon established, day and season lengths set, and numerous other matters arranged before it is time for the transition to the present world. All this has to be done because (as in the title of Jacobs's 1960 study) "the people are coming soon"—everything has to be gotten ready for modern man.

On the north coast it is often Raven who does much of the changing and is a combined trickster-transformer, and on the Plateau and in the Willamette Valley it is Coyote. On the Plateau and in western Washington it is difficult to assign roles like "transformer" and "trickster" since characters may be both (Jacobs 1959:196). A sort of culture hero is present—*wíget* among the Gitksan, *q'waeti* among the Quileute and Southern Wakashans, xwən or *xwənáexwənae* among the Chehalis and Cowlitz, məsp among the Quinault, and *dukwibal* among the Lushootseed and Twana. He is a man, although human attributes are not specifically assigned to him; at least he is certainly not an animal. Although he does make many changes and kills many ogres, he is not in all cases the principal transformer (he is among the Quileute and Wakashans)—among the Lushootseed, Upper Chehalis, and Cowlitz, that role belongs to Moon. The culture hero is certainly not a deity either. Nor is he merely a trickster; much of what he does is benevolent, and the trickster role is shared with a number of other creatures, such as Bluejay in all of southwestern Washington.

Supreme beings are not typical of the Northwest, and Raven, although he performs many god-like functions, is no god. He may provide light for the people, but he does so by stealing it from someone else who would not share it. One reported exception to the absence of a supreme being is among the Colville, where this role has been attributed to Sweathouse; he is never, however, equated with the Christian god.

Even death is not firmly established at the beginning of the myth age. People die, but not permanently until some central figure makes a crucial mistake making it impossible for someone (often his daughter or son) to return to life, and permanent death thereby becomes established. Even then there are different kinds of death and different worlds of the dead. Some kinds of death, as by accident or fire, are immediately permanent; others, as by illness, can be overcome if a shaman can recover the soul in time. In Upper Chehalis lore, the latter kind of soul is located in a land of the dead across a river, and the former lives in a house beyond that. Shamans are thus important in soul-recovery, as well as for curing in general. Even more important to the individual is his spirit-power, and myth figures regularly call upon their powers for advice and assistance. A comic figure may be given an outlandish spirit power to make him seem even more ridiculous, as when Coyote's power is his sisters, who in reality are his own feces; whenever they give him the advice he has sought of them, he claims that he knew it already so as not to give them any credit.

Other characters in myths come in a wide variety of shapes and sizes; all act like people, albeit people with special characteristics. Among inanimate objects or phenomena appearing as characters in Northwest myths are Spear, Southwest Wind, the Snow brothers, and Fire and his daughters in Upper Chehalis; Moon and Urine Boy in Cowlitz; Pitch Woman and a Yellow Cedar Bark ogre in Nootka; Flint Boy in Santiam Kalapuya; and Awl in Clackamas Chinook. More usual, however, are animal characters. They may have special myth names, as in Kalispel, where mythic Coyote is called by a name borrowed from Sahaptin, or the myth name may be a variant of the usual word for that animal, as in Nez Perce, where a real fox is called *tilípe ?* and mythic fox is *tilípcxi ?*. The myth animal character often takes on some of the character of the real animal: Grizzly Woman (Chinook) is fierce and murderous, Great Horned Owl (Columbian, Colville) is an ogress who preys on children, Coyote (Plateau) is crafty, Cougar (Upper Chehalis) is a great hunter, Great Blue Heron (Columbian) has long legs that can be used as a bridge. Conversely, the character may be given attributes opposite to those of the real animal: Wren (Columbian) has a huge bow and is the best shot, Wood Tick (Columbian) controls the deer, Waterbug (Clackamas Chinook) overcomes Grizzly Woman. These animal characters also intermarry like ordinary people, and animals are often related as might be expected (Bobcat is the younger brother of Cougar, Coyote and Fox are brothers); unexpected linkings also occur (on the Plateau, Coyote's wife is Mole, one of his sons—all Coyotes—marries a duck, Chipmunk's grandmother is Snowshoe Hare in Columbian, Wren's grandmother is Bluebird in Upper Chehalis, Spring Salmon marries Mourning Dove in Columbian).

Setting and Function

Non-myth literature could be performed at any time or as occasion demanded, although myth performance was traditionally restricted to the winter. Even today, many of those who still remember myths believe that telling them out of season will bring bad luck. It is also widely believed that it would be unlucky to tell only part of a story, and individuals will not attempt to tell one if they are not sure they know the whole thing.

On the northern part of the coast, where myths validated family crests and histories, they were told primarily as part of winter ceremonials and at potlatches. Farther south and on the Plateau, an elder might tell myths to a group of children at night, rather like bedtime stories, although other adults enjoyed listening too. Audiences were expected to respond with a traditional word from time to time to indicate continued attention. Restrictions might be placed on the listeners (Upper Chehalis audiences were not allowed to ask for food during a recitation), and a story would be broken off if the taboo was violated. Some Plateau groups report traveling storytellers who would make their rounds during the winter, spending a week or so with family after family and narrating stories in the evening; it was more usual, however, for an elder within the family unit to tell the stories. Most of these traditions are no longer observed, although there are still individuals who tell the old myths to their grandchildren at bedtime, and at least one Columbian elder begins telling Coyote stories at two or three o'clock in the morning during wakes to help keep other mourners awake.

Stories were told for several reasons. Portrayal of family histories has been mentioned, but other myths were related for their educational value, since lessons on social norms and expectations were interjected into stories, and good or bad behavior by myth characters served as a model for children. Various bits of explanation, true or fanciful, occur frequently in stories, educating audiences on the origin of some animal characteristic, geographical formation, or the like. Not to be slighted was the sheer entertainment value of these traditional stories; they were filled with both suspense and rollicking, often ribald humor. They are still valued as entertainment, and audiences can still judge if a story is well presented or not, or if necessary components are omitted.

Form and Style

The telling of myths and tales has been likened to a dramatic performance; this is emphasized and demonstrated in particular in Jacobs's *Clackamas Chinook Texts Part II* (1959). Jacobs's "Areal Spread of Indian Oral Genre Features in the Northwest States" (1972) includes this "play structure" in a list of twenty-one style features that recur in Northwest folklore. Some of the other features that he thought characteristic of the area are specific myth and tale introductions; closings; pattern numbers; terse indications of distance, location, and time; virtual lack of reference to environment, feelings, or personal traits; audience behavior and response words; humor; laconic style; and the use of titles of myths and tales.

Dell Hymes carried this notion even further by showing that a good myth performance has systematic structure at many levels, and proposed that a free verse structure is an appropriate way to present myths and tales on paper (particularly accessible demonstrations can be found in Hymes [1981], and in papers by Virginia Hymes [1987] and Kinkade [1987]). The ultimate unit of this verse structure is the line, and the performance as a whole can be broken down into successively smaller components, from myth to act to scene to stanza to verse to line. Internal patterning, in both dramatic content and linguistic form, indicates these units. For example, listening to a recording of an Upper Chehalis myth leaves little doubt about line structure; pauses and falling intonation patterns consistently correlate with clause endings. Groups of lines can be combined to form verses, which can be seen as a single unit of activity. The beginnings of units at various levels are often regularly marked by a word that seems to have little other meaning; thus, in one Columbian narrative virtually every stanza begins with i, a particle that occurs almost nowhere else. Upper Chehalis uses *huy* "and then" this way, but a bit more freely, Upper Chinook (Kiksht) uses *aGa* "now," Sahaptin *au* "now then," or *ku* "and, but, so"—all at the beginning of sentences; Quileute uses *da kil* "then, well" as the second word in a line.

Even the number of verses, stanzas, scenes, or acts within a larger unit is not random or arbitrary, but usually accords with whatever pattern number is dominant in a society. Just as European folklore has groups of three as its pattern, so in the Northwest four and five are dominant (the latter among the southernmost Salishan groups, Sahaptin, Chinookan, and some groups in Oregon). The importance of pattern numbers carries over into expressive content as well. Thus, in Upper Chehalis units of five are common and overtly expressed: there are five Cougar brothers, five daughters of fire, five baskets of water are given to Bluejay to put out the fires on the five prairies he must cross. The pattern number may be expressed more subtly, and may not be specifically stated as it is in Upper Chehalis; we can tell that the pattern number in Columbian is five because Coyote has five (named) sons, whereas in nearby Kalispel he has only four—and there the pattern number is four.

Narratives organized on the printed page along the lines mentioned here take a very different form from the traditional printing of texts on the page in block paragraphs. They not only look different, they will be read differently, and their literary qualities become more apparent. This is an outsider's view, of course, since evaluations by natives are generally unavailable. It is not necessarily the case that all myths and tales have such formal organization, nor is every storyteller equally good at organizing his presentation; yet some structure is usually present, if only to help the narrator keep track of where he is and what still needs to be told.

Also to be found in the Northwest are some long cycles of tales. These have not received much attention in the literature as cycles; the component stories are often printed as discrete units, although rhetorical devices were used in the telling to indicate that the cycle was to be continued. It is known, however, that Coyote stories on the Plateau were often told as cycles over several successive evenings, and in 1927 Boas wrote down over two hundred pages of Upper Chehalis *xwənáexwənae* stories. It remains to be seen how the structural features found in individual stories are interwoven into these cycles.

M. Dale Kinkade
University of British Columbia

BIBLIOGRAPHY

Primary Sources

Adamson, Thelma. *Folk-Tales of the Coast Salish*. American Folklore Society Memoir 27. New York: The American Folklore Society, 1934.

Andrade, Manuel J. *Quileute Texts*. Columbia University Contributions to Anthropology 12. New York: Columbia UP, 1931.

Aoki, Haruo. *Nez Perce Texts*. University of California Publications in Linguistics 90. Berkeley: U of California P, 1979.

Ballard, Arthur C. *Mythology of Southern Puget Sound*. University of Washington Publications in Anthropology 3.2 (1929): 31–150.

Barbeau, Marius. *Haida Myths Illustrated in Argillite Carvings*. National Museum of Canada Bulletin 127, Anthropological series 32. Ottawa: National Museum of Canada, 1953.

———. *Tsimsyan Myths*. National Museum of Canada Bulletin 174, Anthropological series 51. Ottawa: National Museum of Canada, 1961.

Barbeau, Marius, and William Beynon. *Tsimshian Narratives I; Trickster Shamans and Heroes*. Eds. John J. Cove and George F. MacDonald. Canadian Museum of Civilization Mercury Series. Directorate Paper No. 3. Ottawa: National Museum of Canada, 1987.

———. *Tsimshian Narratives II: Trade and Warfare*. Eds. John J. Cove and George F. MacDonald. Canadian Museum of Civilization Mercury Series. Directorate Paper No. 3. Ottawa: Canadian Museum of Civilization, 1987.

Barker, M. A. R. *Klamath Texts*. University of California Publications in Linguistics 30. Berkeley: U of California P, 1963.

Beavert, Virginia, Project Dir. *The Way It Was: (Anaku Iwacha) (Yakima Legends)*. Toppenish, WA: The Consortium of Johnson O'Malley Committees of Region IV, State of Washington and the Yakima Tribe, 1974.

Boas, Franz. *Chinook Texts*. Bureau of American Ethnology Bulletin 20. Washington, DC: GPO, 1894.

———. *The Mythology of the Bella Coola Indians*. American Museum of Natural History Memoir 1. New York, 1898. 25–127.

———. *Kathlamet Texts*. Bureau of American Ethnology Bulletin 26. Washington, DC: GPO, 1901.

———. *Tsimshian Texts*. Bureau of American Ethnology Bulletin 27. Washington, DC: GPO, 1902.

———. *Kwakiutl Tales*. Columbia University Contributions to Anthropology 2. New York: Columbia UP, 1910.

———. *Tsimshian Texts* (new series). American Ethnological Society Publication 3 (1912): 65–285.

———. *Tsimshian Mythology*. Based on texts recorded by Henry W. Tate. Bureau of American Ethnology Annual Report 31. Washington, DC: GPO, 1916. 27–1037.

———. *Kutenai Tales*. Bureau of American Ethnology Bulletin 59. Washington, DC: GPO, 1918.

———. *Bella Bella Texts*. Columbia University Contributions to Anthropology 5. New York: Columbia UP, 1928.

———. *Bella Bella Tales*. American Folklore Society Memoir 25. New York: Columbia UP, 1932.

———. *Kwakiutl Tales* (new series). Columbia University Contributions to Anthropology 26. New York: Columbia UP, 1935–43.

Boas, Franz, and George Hunt. *Kwakiutl Texts*. American Museum of Natural History Memoir 5. New York, 1902–5.

———. *Kwakiutl Texts*. 2nd series. American Museum of Natural History Memoir 14. New York, 1906. 1–269.

Bouchard, Randy, and Dorothy I. D. Kennedy, eds. *Lillooet Stories*. Sound Heritage 6.1 Victoria, British Columbia, n. p. 1977.

———. *Shuswap Stories*. Vancouver: CommCept., 1979.

Curtis, Edward S. *The North American Indian: Being a Series of Volumes Picturing and Describing the Indians of the United States and Alaska*. Ed. Frederick Webb Hodge. Norwood, MA: Plimpton Press, 1907–30. Reprint. New York: Johnson Reprint, 1970.

Dauenhauer, Nora Marks, and Richard Dauenhauer. *Haa shuka, Our Ancestors: Tlingit Oral Narratives*. Seattle: U of Washington P, 1987.

Davis, Philip W., and Ross Saunders. *Bella Coola Texts*. British Columbia Provincial Museum, Heritage Record No. 10. Victoria: British Columbia Provincial Museum, 1980.

Elmendorf, William W. "Skokomish and Other Coast Salish Tales." *Washington State University Research Studies* 29.1 (1961): 1–37; 29.2 (1961): 84–117; 29.3 (1961): 119–50.

Farrand, Livingston. *Traditions of the Chilcotin Indians*. American Museum of Natural History Memoir 4. New York, 1900. 1–54.

———, and W. S. Kahnweiler. *Traditions of the Quinault Indians*. American Museum of Natural History Memoir 4. New York, 1902. 77–132.

Frachtenberg, Leo J. *Coos Texts*. Columbia University Contributions to Anthropology 1. New York: Columbia UP, 1913.

———. *Lower Umpqua Texts and Notes on the Kusan Dialects*. Columbia University Contributions to Anthropology 4. New York: Columbia UP, 1914.

———. *Alsea Texts and Myths*. Bureau of American Ethnology Bulletin 67. Washington, DC: GPO, 1920.

Harris, Kenneth B. *Visitors Who Never Left: The Origin of the People of Damelahamid*. Vancouver: U of British Columbia P, 1974.

Hilbert, Vi. *Huboo. Lushootseed Literature in English*. Seattle: U of Washington P, 1980.

———. *Haboo: Native American Stories from Puget Sound*. Seattle: U of Washington P, 1985.

Hilton, Susanne, and John C. Rath, eds. *Oowekeeno Oral Traditions as Told by the Late Chief Simon Walkus Sr*. National Museum of Man Mercury Series, Canadian Ethnology Service Paper 84. Ottawa: National Museum of Man, 1982.

Jacobs, Elizabeth Derr. *Nehalem Tillamook Tales*. University of Oregon Monographs, Studies in Anthropology 5. Eugene: U of Oregon Books, 1959.

Jacobs, Melville. *Northwest Sahaptin Texts 1*. University of Washington Publications in Anthropology 2.6 (1929): 175–244.

———. *Northwest Sahaptin Texts*. Columbia University Contributions to Anthropology 19. New York: Columbia UP, 1934–37.

———. *Texts Chinook Jargon*. University of Washington Publications in Anthropology 7.1 (1936).

———. *Coos Narrative and Ethnologic Texts*. University of Washington Publications in Anthropology 8.1 (1939): 1–126.

———. *Coos Myth Texts*. University of Washington Publications in Anthropology 8.2 (1940): 127–60.

———. *Kalapuya Texts*. University of Washington Publications in Anthropology 11 (1945).

———. *Clackamas Chinook Texts Part 1*. Indiana University Research Center in Anthropology, Folklore, and Linguistics Publication 8. *International Journal of American Linguistics* 24 (1958).

———. *Clackamas Chinook Texts Part II*. Indiana University Research Center in Anthropology, Folklore, and Linguistics Publication 11. *International Journal of American Linguistics* 25 (1959).

Krauss, Michael E., ed. *In Honor of Eyak: The Art of Anna Nelson Harry*. Fairbanks: Alaska Native Language Center, U of Alaska, 1982.

Kuipers, Aert H. *The Squamish Language: Grammar, Texts, Dictionary*. Janua Linguarum, series practica 73. The Hague: Mouton & Co., 1967.

———. *The Squamish Language: Grammar, Texts, Dictionary*. Janua Linguarum, series practica 73.2. The Hague: Mouton, 1969.

———. *The Shuswap Language: Grammar, Texts, Dictionary*. Janua Linguarum, series practica 225. The Hague: Mouton, 1974.

Mattina, Anthony, ed. *The Golden Woman: The Colville Narrative of Peter J. Seymour*. Tucson: U of Arizona P, 1985.

Maud, Ralph, ed. *The Salish People. The Local Contribution of Charles Hill-Tout*. 4 vols. Vancouver: Talonbooks, 1978.

Mourning Dove (Humishuma) (Christine Quintasket). *Coyote Stories*. Caldwell, ID: The Caxton Printers, Ltd., 1933.

Phinney, Archie. *Nez Perce Texts*. Columbia University Contributions to Anthropology 25. New York: Columbia UP, 1934.

Reichard, Gladys A. *An Analysis of Coeur d'Alene Indian Myths*. American Folklore Society Memoir 41. New York: Columbia UP, 1947.

Sampson, Martin J. *The Swinomish Totem Pole. Tribal Legends*. (Told to Rosalie Whitney.) Bellingham, WA: Union Printing Co., 1938.

Sapir, Edward. *Takelma Texts*. University of Pennsylvania, The Museum, Anthropological Publication 2.1 (1909): 1–267.

———. *Wishram Texts*. American Ethnological Society Publication 2. Leiden: E. J. Brill, 1909.

———, and Morris Swadesh. *Nootka Texts: Tales and Ethnological Narratives with Grammatical Notes and Lexical Materials*. Philadelphia: Linguistic Society of America, 1939.

Shelton, William. *The Story of the [Everett] Story Pole*. Everett, WA: Kane and Harcus, 1932.

Slickpoo, Allen, Sr., et al. *Nu-Mee-Poom Tit-Wah-Tit: Nez Perce Legends*. Lapwai, ID: Nez Perce Tribe of Idaho, 1972.

Snyder, Warren A. *Southern Puget Sound Salish: Texts Place Names and Dictionary*. Sacramento Anthropological Society Paper 9 (1968).

Swanton, John R. *Haida Texts and Myths*. Bureau of American Ethnology Bulletin 29. Washington, DC: GPO, 1905.

———. *Haida Texts—Masset Dialect*. Publications of the Jesup North Pacific Expedition 5.2. New York, 1908.

———. *Tlingit Myths and Texts*. Bureau of American Ethnology Bulletin 39. Washington, DC: GPO, 1909.

Teit, James. *Traditions of the Thompson River Indians of British Columbia*. American Folklore Society Memoir 6. New York: Houghton, Mifflin, 1898.

———. *Mythology of the Thompson Indians*. Publications of the Jesup North Pacific Expedition 8. New York, 1912.

Vogt, Hans. *The Kalispel Language: An Outline of the Grammar with Texts, Translations, and Dictionary*. Oslo: Det Norske Videnskaps Akademi, 1940.

We-Gyet Wanders On: Legends of the Northwest. Saanichton, British Columbia: Hancock House Publishers Ltd., 1977.

Secondary Sources

Boas, Franz. "Die Entwickelung der Mythologien der Indianer der nordpacifischen Kuste America's." *Verrhandlungen der Berliner Gesellschaft für Anthropologie, Ethnologie und Urgeschichte* (1895): 487–523. Rpt. in *Indianische Sagen von der Nord-pacifischen Kuste Amerikas.* Berlin: A. Asher, 1895.

Clark, Ella. "Indian Story-telling of Old in the Pacific Northwest." *Oregon Historical Quarterly* 54.2 (1953): 91–101.

———. "The Mythology of the Indians in the Pacific Northwest." *Oregon Historical Quarterly* 54.3 (1953): 163–69.

Densmore, Frances. *Nootka and Quileute Music.* Bureau of American Ethnology Bulletin 124. Washington, DC: GPO, 1939.

Herzog, George. "Salish Music." *Indians of the Urban Northwest.* Ed. Marian W. Smith. New York: Columbia UP, 1949. 93–109.

Hymes, Dell H. *"In Vain I Tried to Tell You": Essays in Native American Ethnopoetics.* Philadelphia: U of Pennsylvania P, 1981.

———. "Mythology." *Handbook of North American Indians* 7: *Northwest Coast.* Ed. Wayne Suttles. Washington, DC: Smithsonian Institution, 1989.

Hymes, Virginia. "Warm Springs Sahaptin Narrative Analysis." *Native American Discourse: Poetics and Rhetoric.* Eds. Joel Sherzer and Anthony C. Woodbury. Cambridge Studies in Oral and Literate Culture 13. Cambridge: Cambridge UP, 1987.

Jacobs, Melville. *The Content and Style of an Oral Literature: Clackamas Chinook Myths and Tales.* Seattle: U of Washington P, 1959.

———. *The People Are Coming Soon: Analysis of Clackamas Chinook Myths and Tales.* Seattle: U of Washington P, 1960.

———. "Our Knowledge of Pacific Northwest Indian Folklores." *Northwest Folklore* 11.2 (1967): 14–21.

———. "Areal Spread of Indian Oral Genre Features in the Northwest States." *Journal of the Folklore Institute* 9.1 (1972): 10–17.

Kinkade, M. Dale. "Bluejay and His Sister." *Recovering the Word: Essays on Native American Literature.* Eds. Brian Swann and Arnold Krupat. Berkeley: U of California P, 1987.

Maud, Ralph. *A Guide to B.C. Indian Myth and Legend: A Short History of Myth-Collecting and a Survey of Published Texts.* Vancouver: Talonbooks, 1982.

Ramsey, Jarold. *Coyote Was Going There: Indian Literature of the Oregon Country.* Seattle: U of Washington P, 1977.

———. *Reading the Fire: Essays in the Traditional Indian Literatures of the Far West.* Lincoln: U of Nebraska P, 1983.

Suttles, Wayne. "On the Cultural Track of the Sasquatch." *Northwest Anthropological Research Notes* 6.1 (1972): 65–90.

Thompson, Laurence C. "The Northwest." *Current Trends in Linguistics 10: Linguistics in North America.* Ed. Thomas A. Sebeok. The Hague: Mouton, 1973.

Walls, Robert E., comp. and ed. *Bibliography of Washington State Folklore and Folklifes: Selected and Partially Annotated.* Seattle: U of Washington P, 1987.

Oral Literature of California and the Intermountain Region

Among the peoples of Native North America, the tribes of California occupy a position geographically and culturally intermediate between those of the Northwest Coast—famous for their sea-hunting, their wood carving, and their potlatches—and those of the Southwest Pueblos, noted for their dry-land agriculture, their rich ceremonialism, and their ceramic art. Life in Native California was less complex; a largely sedentary lifestyle was supported by hunting, fishing, and the gathering of acorns as a staple food. A temperate climate and abundant natural resources permitted a higher population density than in any other part of North America, with a correspondingly high diversity of tribal groups and languages. The most developed art was basketry. The tribes to the east, in the Great Basin region between the Sierra Nevada and the Rocky Mountains, had cultural and linguistic links with those of California; the more arid environment was correlated with reliance on pinyon nuts as a dietary staple, and with greater seasonal movements in search of food.

The following account will survey (1) the history of the study of the Native literature in the region; (2) the genres of this literature; (3) its function with respect to cosmography and religion; (4) typical roles and plots in Native narratives; and (5) relationships to non-Native literatures. Unfortunately, it will by no means be possible to do justice here to the great diversity found in the oral literatures of the region.

History of Study

In California and the Great Basin, as elsewhere in Native North America, a great part of the study of oral literature has been carried out by anthropologists. From 1900 onward, extensive ethnographic fieldwork, on the model originated by Franz Boas at Columbia University, was done by A. L. Kroeber with his students and colleagues at the University of California, Berkeley; these scholars put on record a considerable body of Native narrative, some of it in the original languages as well as in English translation. Outstanding examples include Sapir, *Yana Texts* (1910); Lowie, "Shoshonean Tales" (1924); Voegelin, *Tubatulabal Texts* (1935), and, from a separate research project in the Great Basin, Sapir's "Texts of the Kaibab Paiutes and Uintah Utes" (1930). A second wave of research, starting around 1955, again emanated from Berkeley and was done by anthropological linguists, who seized the opportunity to work with the last generation of storytellers who spoke the Native languages fluently. The result has been a series of bilingual volumes of texts, in which close attention is given to the linguistic accuracy of both transcription and translation (e.g., Bright, *The Karok Language* [1957]; Hill & Nolasquez, *Mulu'wetam* [1973]; Miller, *Newe Natekwinappeh* [1972]).

Most of the fieldworkers who have recorded these literatures have been interested in their material primarily insofar as it functioned as myth, or reflected Native ethnography, or documented linguistic patterns. A relatively rare example of a comparative study is Gayton's "Areal Affiliations of California Folktales" (1935). Studies of Native narratives from the viewpoint of literary aesthetics are almost nonexistent; but see T. Kroeber, *The Inland Whale* (1959).

A pioneering linguistic study of the ways in which grammatical patterns are adapted to oral narrative is Newman's "Linguistic Aspects of Yokuts Style" (1940). More recently, some anthropological linguists have attempted "ethnopoetic" analyses of traditional narratives, following the lead of Tedlock (*Finding the Center* [1972]) and Hymes ("*In Vain I Tried to Tell You*" [1981]). For some tribes of northern and central California, it can be shown that myths are organized in terms of characteristic units which may be called "verses" and "lines"—understanding these concepts not in terms of traditional European rhyme or meter, but in terms of the occurrence of initial particles ("And so . . . , And then . . .") and of recurrent patterns of grammatical and lexical structure (cf. Bright, "A Karok Myth in Measured Verse" [1979]; McLendon, "Meaning, Rhetorical Structure, and Discourse Organization in Myth" [1982]). Useful surveys, with bibliographies, are provided for California by Heizer, "Mythology" (1978) and Wallace, "Comparative Literature" (1978), and for the Great Basin by Hultkrantz, "Mythology and Religious Concepts" (1986) and Liljeblad, "Oral Tradition" (1986). Some important recent collections are Blackburn, *December's Child* (1975); A. L. Kroeber, *Yurok Myths* (1976); Golla and Silver, *Northern California Texts* (1977); A. L. Kroeber and E. W. Gifford, *Karok Myths* (1980); and Laird, *Mirror and Pattern* (1984).

Genres

Poetry existed only in the form of words to songs; it was not rhymed. Such songs were sometimes interpolated in myths, as sung by the characters at crucial points (cf. Sapir, "Song Recitative in Paiute Mythology" [1910]). Other songs formed part of rituals. Most were short; however, song cycles were used in ceremonies of the Southern Californian tribes, and they were rich in figurative language (Joughlin and Valenzuela, "Cupeño Genesis" [1953]).

The principal type of oral literature everywhere was narrative; two major types can frequently be distinguished as "myth" and "tale." These terms have counterparts in some of the Native vocabularies, and some languages distinguish them by special linguistic features; for example, Karok myths begin with *'uknîí* (comparable to "Once upon a time . . ."), and use a special "ancient tense" suffix with verbs. The action of myths occurs before the human species existed; the characters are members of a prehuman race which may be called the "First People." Most of them have names like Coyote and Bear; they have at least some human characteristics, but are thought of as the prototypes of the corresponding present-day animal species. (Thus the prehuman era is occasionally referred to as "When the animals were people.") Among certain tribes, the plots of many myths move toward the point when the First People ordain some great change: for example, salmon are released into the river, or death is instituted. Thereupon, the First People are transformed into animals, and human beings come spontaneously into existence.

In tales, by contrast, the main actors are human beings who lived long ago. Such tales may, nevertheless, involve magical or supernatural beings and happenings. This genre seems to have been somewhat less popular, at least in California.

Public speeches and prayers by chiefs are considered highly valued forms of verbal art in the Great Basin (Shimkin 1947).

It is often said that Native American people did not have riddles, proverbs, or traditional sayings. However, the Karok, who were obsessed with possessing wealth, are reported to have had a saying that "No matter how poor a man may be, he still has his penis." In the Great Basin, Liljeblad reports that aphoristic expressions are common (1986:643).

Cosmogony and Religion

Northwestern California is notable for lacking myths of the origin of the world, and in ascribing the human species to spontaneous generation. Elsewhere, the world and the First People are said to have come into existence through the will of a creator—but this personage does not always stay around to supervise the results. Human beings were then created by the First People, with Coyote often playing a leading role. In all areas, myths describe how the necessary elements of human life, such as fire and acorns, were provided by the First People. Some tribes say that death was invented by Coyote to prevent overpopulation; when his own child was the first to die, he tried to repeal the ordinance, but it was too late. According to the Karok, the Klamath River used to run upstream on one side, and downstream on the other. "That's no good," said Coyote, "the young married men will get lazy. Let the river flow only *down*stream, so the men will have to row *up*stream."

Myths form an essential part of religious and magical practice among many tribes. Especially in northwest California, before a ceremonial dance can be performed, the myth of its origin must be recited by a person who possesses the esoteric knowledge.

Typical Roles and Plots

It is not possible to discuss Native literature without mention of Coyote, the most salient of the First People. As indicated above, he is typically a major figure in ordaining the conditions of human life—not as a deity who created the world, or indeed as a "culture hero," but rather as the *bricoleur* responsible for The Way Things Are. As elsewhere in western North America, he is the prototypical trickster, magically powerful, but gluttonous, lecherous, dishonest, and clownish—often the victim of his own mischief, yet ultimately indestructible. (For details and bibliography, see Bright, "The Natural History of Old Man Coyote" [1987].)

Many mythologies also include a noble or heroic character who kills monsters and makes the world fit to live in; among Great Basin tribes like the Chemehuevi (Laird, *Mirror and Pattern* [1984]), this role is played by Wolf, in explicit contrast with his brother Coyote. In Southern California, a religious cult was focused on an all-powerful divinity who is magically poisoned by his daughter, dies, and is transformed into the moon; in later ages he is succeeded by a semi-divine figure, Chinigchinich, who instructs human beings in morality and ceremonialism (Boscana, *Chinigchinich* [1978]). It has been suggested that the myth may owe something to Christian teaching (Kroeber, "Problems on Boscana" [1959]).

Tribes of the Great Basin and adjacent parts of California tell many tales about the Water Baby, a type of malicious sprite said to live in streams and lakes; this small but powerful being is said to be responsible for child disappearances and drownings (Liljeblad, 1986:653). Apart from all the plots relating to origins, the Native literatures clearly have entertainment value as well. Typically told by grandparents to children around a winter fire, they offered amusement as well as instruction. Coyote stories in particular are rich in surprises, narrow escapes, outrageous violations of morals, and good knockdown humor.

Relationships to Non-Native Literatures

In spite of possible Christian mixture in the Chinigchinich myth, as mentioned above, very few examples of European tale-types have been recorded from California. If the Native languages and cultures had survived longer, we might know more examples like the one recorded by Hinton on the Mexican border ("Coyote Baptizes the Chickens" [1978]). In the Great Basin, considerable European influence is reported (Liljeblad, 1986:658).

Rather more conspicuous is the impact which Native traditions, and Coyote stories in particular, have had on Anglo-American writers, particularly those related to the Beat poetry movement of San Francisco in the 1950s. The most influential figure in introducing Old Man Coyote to English-language literature has been Gary Snyder, drawing on his experience with Indians of Oregon, but writing in California ("A Berry Feast" [1957]; "The Incredible Survival of Coyote" [1977]). Some especially effective "new" Coyote stories, in English verse, have been written by Peter Blue Cloud, an Iroquois transplanted to California (*Elderberry Flute Song* [1982]). As the mechanized and urbanized society of the white man advances—and the Native cultures approach extinction—it is clear that, for some writers and readers, Coyote is a valuable mediator between original nature and impinging culture; his impulsive creativity and his humor are, perhaps, more needed now than ever.

William Bright
University of Colorado

BIBLIOGRAPHY

Primary Sources

Blackburn, Thomas. *December's Child: A Book of Chumash Oral Narratives*. Berkeley: U of California P, 1975.

Blue Cloud, Peter. *Elderberry Flute Song: Contemporary Coyote Tales*. Trumansburg, NY: Crossing Press, 1982.

Boscana, Geronimo. *Chinigchinich*. A revised and annotated version of Alfred Robinson's translation; annotations by John P. Harrington. Banning, CA: Malki Museum Press, 1978.

Bright, William. *The Karok Language*. University of California Publications in Linguistics 13. Berkeley: U of California, 1957.

Golla, Victor, and Shirley Silver, eds. *Northern California Texts*. International Journal of American Linguistics, Native American Texts Series 22. Chicago: U of Chicago P, 1977.

Hill, Jane H., and Rosinda Nolasquez. *Mulu'wetam, the First People: Cupeño Oral History and Language*. Banning, CA: Malki Museum Press, 1973.

Hinton, Leanne. "Coyote Baptizes the Chickens." *Coyote Stories*. Ed. W. Bright. International Journal of American Linguistics, Native American Texts Series, Monograph 1. Chicago: U of Chicago P, 1978. 117–20.

Joughlin, Roberta, and Salvadora G. Valenzuela. "Cupeño Genesis." *El Museo* n.s. 1.4 (1953): 16–23.

Kroeber, A. L. *Yurok Myths*. Berkeley: U of California P, 1976.

——, and E. W. Gifford. *Karok Myths*. Berkeley: U of California Press, 1980.

Laird, Carobeth. *Mirror and Pattern: George Laird's World of Chemehuevi Mythology*. Banning, CA: Malki Museum Press, 1984.

Lowie, Robert H. "Shoshonean Tales." *Journal of American Folklore* 37 (1924): 1–242.

McLendon, Sally. "Meaning, Rhetorical Structure, and Discourse Organization in Myth." *Analysing Discourse Text and Talk*. Ed. Deborah Tannen. Washington, DC: Georgetown UP, 1982. 284–305.

Miller, Wick R. *Newe Natekwinappeh: Shoshoni Stories and Dictionary*. Anthropological Papers 94. Salt Lake City: U of Utah, 1972.

Sapir, Edward. *Yana Texts*. University of California Publications in American Archaeology and Ethnology 9.1. Berkeley: U of California, 1910. 1–235.

——. "Texts of the Kaibab Paiutes and Uintah Utes." *Proceedings* of the American Academy of Arts and Sciences. Boston, 1930. 652.

Snyder, Gary. "A Berry Feast." *Evergreen Review* 2 (1957): 110–14.

Tedlock, Dennis. *Finding the Center: Narrative Poetry of the Zuni Indians*. New York: Dial Press, 1972.

Voegelin, C. F. *Tubatulabal Texts*. University of California Publications in American Archaeology and Ethnology 34.3. Berkeley: U of California, 1935. 191–246.

Secondary Sources

Bright, William. "A Karok Myth in Measured Verse: The Translation of a Performance." *Journal of California and Great Basin Anthropology* 1 (1979): 117–23.

——. "The Natural History of Old Man Coyote." *Recovering the Word*. Ed. Brian Swann and Arnold Krupat. Berkeley: U of California P, 1987. 339–87.

Gayton, Anna H. "Areal Affiliations of California Folktales." *American Anthropologist* 37 (1935): 582–99.

Heizer, Robert F. "Mythology." *Handbook of North American Indians 8: California*. Ed. R. F. Heizer. Washington, DC: Smithsonian Institution, 1978. 654–58.

Hultkrantz, Ake. "Mythology and Religious Concepts." *Handbook of North American Indians 11: Great Basin*. Ed. Warren L. D'Azevedo. Washington, DC: Smithsonian Institution, 1986. 630–40.

Hymes, Dell. *"In Vain I Tried to Tell You": Essays in Native American Ethnopoetics*. Philadelphia: U of Pennsylvania P, 1981.

Kroeber, A. L. *Problems on Boscana*. U of California Publications in American Archaeology and Ethnology 47.3. Berkeley: U of California, 1959. 282–93.

Kroeber, Theodora. *The Inland Whale*. Bloomington: Indiana UP, 1959.

Liljeblad, Sven. "Oral Tradition Content and Style of Verbal Arts." *Handbook of North American Indians 11: Great Basin*. Ed. Warren L. D'Azevedo. Washington, DC: Smithsonian Institution, 1986. 641–59.

Newman, Stanley S. "Linguistic Aspects of Yokuts Style." *Yokuts and Western Mono Myths*. Eds. A. H. Gayton and S. S. Newman. Anthropological Records 51. Berkeley: U of California P, 1940. 48.

Sapir, Edward. "Song Recitative in Paiute Mythology." *Journal of American Folklore* 23 (1910): 455–72.

Shimkin, Demitri B. "Wind River Shoshone Literary Forms: An Introduction." *Journal of the Washington (DC) Academy of Sciences* 37 (1947): 329–76.

Snyder, Gary. "The Incredible Survival of Coyote." *The Old Ways*. Ed. William J. Wallace. San Francisco: City Lights, 1977. 67–93.

Wallace, William. "Comparative Literature." *Handbook of North American Indians 8: California*. Ed. R. F. Heizer. Washington, DC: Smithsonian Institution, 1978. 658–62.

Oral Literature of the Southwest

History of the Native American Southwest

While difficult to circumscribe precisely, the Native American Southwest has traditionally been centered on what are now the states of Arizona and New Mexico, with fringes extending into the surrounding United States as well as into the states of Chihuahua and Sonora, Mexico. This is the homeland of the well-known archaeological cultures: the Anasazi on the Colorado Plateau of the northern tier of the region; the Mogollon below the Mogollon Rim in the south central and southeastern parts of the region; the Hohokam to their westward in what is now southern Arizona; and farthest west, the Patayan culture of the Lower Colorado River. These cultures began to emerge between 300 B.C. and A.D. 100 on the archaeological horizon when peoples native to the Southwest, each in their own way, began to incorporate agriculture, technologies, resources, and patterns of belief brought north from Mexico, perhaps by traders, perhaps by immigrant colonists. The relationship of these archaeological cultures to historic Indian tribes of the area is not always clear. The Patayan and Hohokam cultures are clearly formative to Yuman-speaking tribes and to the Pima and Papago (Tohona O'odham) respectively, but the Anasazi culture had several different phases each of which, either singly, in combination, or in combination with elements of other archaeological cultures such as the Hohokam and Mogollon, contributed to the formation of the various Puebloan peoples. The most recent arrivals are the Athapaskan speakers, the Navajos, and various Apachean peoples, whose languages differ enough from those of the nearest-related speakers in Canada to suggest they came to the Southwest between 700 and 1,000 years ago.

The first contacts with Euroamericans came with the Coronado expedition of 1540. The period of frequent European contact and permanent colonization began with the 1598 expedition of Don Juan de Oñate, which led to the founding of the New Mexico colony, headquartered initially at San Juan Pueblo. By the 1620s Spain's colonial effort had established civil, military, and religious presence in the area as far west as the Hopi villages. The single most important event in the Spanish period was the Pueblo Revolt of 1680, a nativistic movement led by a Tewa priest, Popé, to expel the Spanish and restore the kachina religion and the authority of the Native religious figures. The Revolt and the decades which followed were responsible for several developments that had long-term consequences for the evolution of Native cultures in the region: (1) refugee pueblos established connections with the Navajo, then in northwest New Mexico; (2) there was considerable population movement, such as the migration of some Rio Grande Tewas to the Hopi area; (3) the reconquest in 1692 seriously undermined the kachina religion in the northern Rio Grande but failed to have the same effect in the West at Zuni and Hopi; and (4) the policy of settling Indians around missions, centralizing trade, and tolerating Indian slave trading provided long-term acculturative pressures. These effects were visible when Mexico claimed the region after its independence in 1821, and persisted when Mexico ceded the area to the United States in 1848. Despite its age, Spicer (1962) remains the best ethnohistoric record of the Native American Southwest.

History of Study

Spanish records have produced information of ethnographic value for the area, as have the journals of early English-speaking traders and travelers. The earliest intensive ethnography was originally done by civilians attached to military posts, like Washington Matthews, the Army doctor and ethnographer of the Navajo, or Matilde Coxe Stevenson, whose husband was a doctor at Zuni. In 1879, the Bureau of American Ethnology was founded and soon sent Frank Hamilton Cushing to Zuni. The work of the BAE's ethnographers, though often bound to theories of cultural evolution that were current in the late nineteenth century, nevertheless set new standards for detailed recordation, especially when informed by the demands and methods of Franz Boas, who sent several generations of scholars to the Southwest (Basso in Ortiz, 1979). Especially to the point of this volume, Boas urged the collection of Native-language texts of all genres because they provided important linguistic, cultural, and historical information. A number of different language families, several as large and complex as Indo-European, are represented in the area (Hoijer 1946). Athapaskan languages include Navajo, San Carlos Apache, Chiricahua Apache and Mescalero Apache, Jicarilla Apache, Lipan Apache, and Kiowa

Apache. Keresan languages are spoken at a number of the northern Rio Grande pueblos and at Acoma and Laguna west of the Rio Grande. Other Rio Grande Pueblos speak one of three Tanoan languages: Tewa, Tiwa, or Towa. Yuman languages are spoken by a number of tribes, such as the Mohave and Maricopa, in the Lower Colorado and Lower Gila River area. Uto-Aztecan languages are spoken by the Hopi, the Pima, and the Tohona O'odham (Papago). Zuni is a linguistic isolate, whose affiliation with any other language family in the area has not been convincingly demonstrated.

The Boasian model of linguistic transcription was the standard in the study of Southwestern Native languages and literatures until it was challenged, though not supplanted, by the example of Tedlock's Zuni materials. The form of Tedlock's work demonstrated the virtues of considering oral literature on the model of performed speech rather than literary text, though there are few examples of extended performance analyses (Basso, *Whiteman*, 1979; Wiget 1987). The impact of sociolinguistics and speech act theory has provided new and more precise ways of identifying significant elements of context, form, and style in oral literature. In order to capture nonlinguistic dimensions of performance, efforts have been made to document oral literary performances on videotape. Evers (1979) has produced a series of VHS-format video recordings of Hopi and Western Apache folktales, Navajo and Laguna songs, and portions of the Yaqui Deer Dance. Evers and Molina (1987) fused dialogic anthropology and performance analysis to provide a keen study of the social, functional, religious, and performative dimensions of Yaqui Deer Songs, and one can easily assess how far the treatment of oral literature has come in just the last few decades by comparing their work to the earlier standard (Wilder 1963).

Genres and Styles

Of all genres, narrative forms are the best represented in the ethnographic record. Today, ethnographers recognize the value of distinguishing Native genres in their own terms (cf. Ben-Amos 1975). For example, the environmental frame which restricts the telling of Hopi *tuwuutsi* or Zuni *telapna:we* to the period between the first frost and the first thunder in spring, and ideally only in December or January, suggests that an essential component of the Hopi and Zuni understandings of these genres has to do with the way in which stories interact with nature, a concept which is not part of the European notion of "folktale."

Ethnic genre systems can be quite complex. Basso has outlined Western Apache narrative genres in figure 2.

In addition, of course, there are not only significant subdivisions of the other two categories ("prayer" and "ordinary talk"), but undoubtedly a second set of distinctions, equivalent to those of speaking, which would

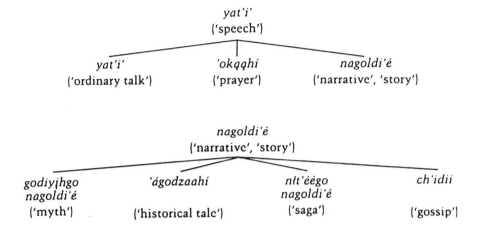

NARRATIVE CATEGORY	TEMPORAL LOCUS OF EVENTS	PURPOSES
godiyįhgo nagoldi'é ('myth')	*godiyąqná'* ('in the beginning')	to enlighten, to instruct
'agodzaahí ('historical tale')	*doo'ánííná* ('long ago')	to criticize, to warn, to 'shoot'
nłt'éégo nagoldi'é ('saga')	*dííjįįgo* ('modern times')	to entertain, to engross
ch'idii ('gossip')	*k'ad* ('now')	to inform to malign

Figure 2. Western Apache Narrative Genres. (From Keith H. Basso, "Stalking with Stories," *Western Apache Language and Culture: Essays in Linguistic Anthropology.* University of Arizona Press, 1990. Reprinted by permission of the University of Arizona Press, 1990.)

typologize ethnic genres of "singing." Dancing, too, is distinguished by form, though little work has been done to determine whether more complex events, such as ceremonials, are conceptualized as unified wholes or as combinations of discretely identified speaking, singing, dancing, and musical components. Despite the complexity and nuances of ethnic genre systems, analytical categories remain useful for cross-cultural comparisons, and if the Apache and Zuni cases are taken as representative, native ethnic narrative genre terms do roughly correspond to the Western terms myth and folktale, while showing the most semantic slippage in the area of history/legend (Bascom 1965).

Myth

Throughout the Southwest the origin story everywhere is the myth of emergence, which describes how the ancestors of the present population emerged onto the earth's surface from within the earth. This story has been summarized succinctly by Wheeler-Voegelin and Moore (1957):

> Following ascent by natural or artificial means, the people and/or supernaturals (all living things) issue from a hole in the ground after preparation of the earth for their habitation (or a scout's discovery of it as habitable).
>
> The hole is thought to be pre-existing or to be a cave or to have been bored by an animal, a series of animals, or by the culture hero(es).
>
> The means of ascent is either a vine, a stretching plant, a tree or a mountain, a ladder, or a combination of two or more of these.
>
> The emergence is actuated either by the coming or subsidence of a flood (the termination of some other catastrophe)—in which case the emerging peoples are refugees—or by the desire for a place lighter, larger, and better provided for with subsistence forms than the underground habitation. (73)

Wheeler-Voegelin and Moore emphasize the connection between the emergence myth and agricultural traditions, which is enforced in several versions by identifying the Earth Mother with the Corn Mother. They also point out the role of the myth in authorizing fetishes and medicine bundles brought up from worlds beneath the earth. The primeval flood and the existence of protoworlds and creations antecedent to the present era also suggest that the emergence myth was rather easily mapped over the Earthdiver cosmology when agriculture was acquired. This suspicion is reinforced by the fact that in many emergence myths, the Sky Father dispatches guides or rescuers along an *axis mundi* to the underworld whence they lead the people out to the earth's surface, thus recapitulating the fall from the sky, the animals' dives to the underworld, and the bringing to the surface the mud of which the world is made. Among a number of important variable motifs which Wheeler-Voegelin and Moore do not mention in their article are the variation in the number of underground worlds: the Tewa have only one, the Navajo variously three or four. Zolbrod (1984) compiles several versions of the Navajo story, which differ in a number of significant ways from the Puebloan tradition; differences include the motive for the emergence (their expulsion for misconduct by the inhabitants of the lower worlds), the creation of the world twice, a special creation as opposed to evolution of human beings, a period when the sexes separated, and the discovery by the emerging Navajo that Puebloan peoples are already living on the earth's surface.

Bahr (1977) notes significant differences in complexity and well-formedness between versions of the emergence myth that are recited and those that are chanted. Interestingly, while chanted versions are better formed—revealing a story-grammar that structures each myth around a journey, and with each episode of that journey is divided into four scenes:

departure, travel, arrival, and actions—they are not as complex, that is, rich in detail. Moreover, Bahr hypothesizes that complexity is not always a principal value, since the skeletalization of the chanted versions represents an attempt to secure the core of the tradition as a sequence of journey-stages as outlined by the story-grammar.

As Wheeler-Voegelin and Moore also observe, emergence myths are usually coupled with a migration sequel, in which the emergent population travels over the earth surface until they discover the most suitable locale for their habitation, which is, of course, their present location. As a group, the migration sequels do not appear to have the integrity of the emergence story tradition, but two components are frequently found. First, during the course of the migration, events happen which account for the origins of many elements of social organization or economy or religion. Second, the adventures of culture heroes are often narrated as part of this migration or, if narrated separately, are said nevertheless to have occurred during this time period. The culture heroes are usually referred to as brothers; the older is characteristically ambitious, aggressive, and strong, while the younger is gifted with wisdom, foreknowledge, or clairvoyance and sometimes protects his brother magically while remaining at home during the other's adventures. The southern Athapaskan cycle of the Navajo and Apache, while not responsible for Pueblo culture hero stories, has greatly influenced the Puebloan traditions, especially in the West, and regularly features the slaying of first the giant, then the horned monster, and third the giant eagles or thunderbirds. These incidents are usually narrated in a particular order.

Finally, stories about the origins of different cults within the kachina religion (Zuni: Kyaklo, Poseyemu) might also be subsumed under the analytical category of myth, but that must remain conjecture since no field-elicited taxonomies for these kinds of stories have been produced. Well-known stories, such as that of the Gambler who bet for human lives as a price for rain, may also be classified as myth, provided the same caution is exercised.

Folktale

This analytical category describes several different kinds of stories, and my own fieldwork at Zuni indicates that they are all encompassed by the Zuni ethnic genre term *telapna:we*, commonly glossed as "fiction story." This gloss may have to do not with the truth value of the story's content, but rather with the fact that these stories are told as "hearsay," a status communicated by the recurrent use of a reportative particle, which early translators often omitted because they tired of repeating phrases like "it seems" or "they say."

One group of folktales are stories of man-animal marriages, transformations, and cohabitations, the most common of which in the Southwest involve a boy who lives with the deer and (in New Mexico) a boy who lives with the buffalo. These stories account for hunting rituals still practiced today by describing the close relations that formerly existed between human persons and animal persons, who understood each other's thoughts and language and who altered their physical forms by putting skins on and off as easily as changing a shirt.

A second set of stories involves human beings with ogres and other creatures. These appear to be stories which have been spun out of reflection upon the social order and the institutions within society. By putting individuals in unusual situations—abandoned children, girls as hunters, and the like—these stories offer the opportunity to reflect upon the efficacy of the present social structure.

Yet a third set of stories are animal tales, including those featuring the Trickster figure. The Trickster is a creature dominated by appetites which frequently bring about his downfall; this is Trickster the Overreacher. Many of the most widely disseminated Trickster stories are found throughout the Southwest, including the Reflected Fruit and the Eye Juggler. Trickster can be imagined as either male or female, though only the former seems to be featured in stories involving sexual appetites.

Poetry

This heading is not meant to reopen the tendentious discussion about whether spoken narratives are better understood as examples of what is called "poetry" in the West. Rather, we want to distinguish in this category all of those items that are encompassed by the terms "chant" and "song" to distinguish them from "speech." Clearly, we are concerned with more than content and form criteria here, for as Bahr (1977) has pointed out, myth narratives can be both chanted and recited. But insofar as these represent distinct kinds of speech events, apart from their content, it is worth inquiring into how well these have been addressed.

Historically, songs have been the object of study for some time. An important early article by Matthews (1894) examined the function of repetition and the place of song in complex Navajo ceremonials. Most of the recordings of Frances Densmore were done when Indians visited Washington, and while they are of value, her theoretical orientation and lack of extended fieldwork in the Southwest limited her ability to address issues of function and significance in anything more than a purely formal way. Like Cronyn (1918), Austin (1923) and Barnes (1925), Walton and Waterman (1925) recognized early on that the texts of such songs corresponded closely to Anglo-American poetic conventions, and Walton took after Matthews in addressing questions of structure in Navajo songs (1930). In the 1930s, three important works epitomized the recovery and appropriation by Anglo-Americans of American Indian poetry. The song texts-as-poetry tradition generated Spinden's *Songs of the Tewa* (1933), an exquisitely beautiful but not widely circulated volume. Boasian anthropology's contribution was Ruth Bunzel's "Zuni Ritual Poetry," a masterful combination of textmaking, linguistics, and sensitive anthropological contextualization. The most successful and popular attempt to bridge the belletristic and anthropological approaches was Ruth Underhill's *Singing for Power: The Song Magic of the Papago Indians* (1938), which provided the first major assessment of the nature and function of song in a southwestern Indian tribe. Underhill's book influenced the development of many anthologies (Astrov 1946; Day 1951) which attempted to bring American Indian poetry to a popular audience.

In the modern era, songs continue to be the object of important studies. While some, like Bierhorst (1971, 1974), continue to take an almost purely textual approach to songs, the issue of how texts can best represent oral poetry has been problematized (Rothenberg 1968; Hymes 1965; Bevis 1975; Bahr 1987). Moreover, purely formalist studies modeled on an analogy to New Critical approaches to Anglo-American poetry no longer seem possible. Wiget (1980) discusses the structure of a Zuni ritual poem in relationship to the Zuni ceremonial calendar. Hinton (1980) offers functional hypotheses about the occasions for vocables in Havasupai songs. Barbara Tedlock (1980) discusses the composition, rehearsal, and performance of Zuni kachina songs. These studies share with many studies of what Wyman and Kluckhohn (1938) call Navajo "song ceremonials" a common difficulty in integrating an analysis of songs with the other components of complex ceremonials in a comprehensive study of ritual drama as emergent form. Perhaps the best attempt at this to date, and a model of cooperative inquiry, is Evers and Molina's *Yaqui Deer Songs/Maso Bwikam: A Native American Poetry* (1987).

Other Forms

A number of events meet the essential requirements of *drama*, i.e., formalized scene setting and role transformation. Some of these are enormously complex ceremonial behaviors properly called *ritual drama* (Frisbie 1980). The Zuni Shalako, for example, involves many players and a variety of speaking, chanting, and singing parts, in several venues over several days, and might properly be thought of as drama. On the other hand, as scholars become more attentive to varieties of speech play and minor genres, they discover smaller, more ephemeral dramatic forms, such as the "whiteman joking" of the Western Apache (Basso, *Whiteman*, 1979). Several important *oral historical narratives* have been studied with special attention paid not only to the historicity of the narrative, but also to typologizing unique events (Eggan 1967; Wiget 1982). And in the Southwest, as elsewhere, *oratory* (Underhill et al. 1979; Voegelin and Euler 1957) has not been the object of much study. Obviously, much work needs to be done. The continuing vitality of the oral tradition in the Southwest is evidenced by the adaptation of traditional forms to written expression in Native languages, as Zepeda's collection of Tohona O'odham language poems (1982) from a number of different Native language writers attests.

Andrew Wiget
New Mexico State University

BIBLIOGRAPHY

Astrov, Margot. *The Winged Serpent: American Indian Prose and Poetry.* New York, 1946.

Austin, Mary. *The American Rhythm.* New York, 1923.

Bahr, Donald. "On the Complexity of Some Southwest Emergence Myths." *Journal of Anthropological Research* 33 (1977): 317–49.

———. "Pima Heaven Songs." In Swann and Krupat (1987): 198–246.

Barnes, Nellie. *American Indian Love Lyrics and Other Verse.* New York, 1925.

Bascom, William. "The Forms of Folklore: Prose Narrative." *Journal of American Folklore* 78 (1965): 3–20.

Basso, Keith. "History of Ethnological Research." In Ortiz (1979): 14–21.

———. *Portraits of the Whiteman: Linguistic Play and Cultural Symbols Among the Western Apaches.* Cambridge: Oxford UP, 1979.

———. "'Stalking with Stories': Names, Places, and Moral Narratives Among the Western Apache." *Text, Play and Story: The Construction and Reconstruction of Self and Society.* Washington, DC: American Ethnological Society, 1984. 19–55.

Ben-Amos, Dan. "Analytic Categories and Ethnic Genres." *Folklore Genres.* Ed. Dan Ben-Amos. Austin: U of Texas P, 1975. 215–42.

Bevis, William. "American Indian Verse Translations." In *Literature of the American Indians: Views and Interpretations.* Ed. Abraham Chapman. New York: New American Library, 1975. 308–23.

Bierhorst, John. *In the Trail of the Wind: American Indian Poems and Ritual Orations.* New York: Farrar, Straus & Giroux, 1971.

———. *Four Masterworks of American Indian Literature.* New York: Farrar, Straus & Giroux, 1974.

Cronyn, George. *The Path on the Rainbow.* 1918; Rpt. New York: Liveright, 1934.

Day, A. Grove. *The Sky Clears: Poetry of the American Indians.* Lincoln: U of Nebraska P, 1951.

Dobyns, Henry F., and Robert C. Euler. *Indians of the Southwest: A Critical Bibliography.* Bloomington: Indiana UP, 1980.

Eggan, Fred. "From History to Myth: A Hopi Example." *Studies in Southwestern Ethnolinguistics.* Ed. Dell Hymes and William Bittle. The Hague: Mouton, 1967. 33–53.

Evers, Larry. *Words and Place: Native American Literature of the Southwest.* New York: Clearwater Publishing Co., 1979.

———, ed. *The South Corner of Time: Hopi, Navajo, Papago, Yaqui Tribal Literature.* A Sun Tracks Volume. Tucson: U of Arizona P, 1980.

Evers, Larry, and Felipe Molina. *Yaqui Deer Songs/Maso Bwikam: A Native American Poetry.* Tucson: U of Arizona P, 1987.

Frisbie, Charlotte J., ed. *Southwestern Indian Ritual Drama.* A School of American Research Book. Albuquerque: U of New Mexico P, 1980.

Hinton, Leanne. "Vocables in Havasupai Song." In Frisbie (1980): 275–305.

Hoijer, Harry. *Linguistic Structures of Native America*. Viking Fund Publications in Anthropology 6. New York: Viking Fund, 1946.

Hymes, Dell. "Six North Pacific Coast Poems: A Problem in Anthropological Philology." *American Anthropologist* 67 (1965): 316–37.

Lévi-Strauss, Claude. "The Structural Study of Myth." *Structural Anthropology*. New York: Basic Books, 1963. 209–31.

Matthews, Washington. "Songs of Sequence of the Navajos." *Journal of American Folklore* 7 (1894): 185–94.

Murdock, G. P., and T. L. O'Leary. *Ethnographic Bibliography of North America*. Fourth ed. New Haven: Human Relations Area Files, 1989.

Ortiz, Alfonso, ed. *The Tewa World: Space, Time, Being and Becoming in a Pueblo Society*. Chicago: U of Chicago P, 1969.

———. Handbook of North American Indians 9: *The Southwest*. Washington, DC: Smithsonian Institution, 1979.

Parsons, Elsie Clews. "Pueblo Indian Folk-Tales, Probably of Spanish Provenience." *Journal of American Folklore* 31 (1918): 216–55.

———. "Spanish Elements in the Kachina Cult of the Pueblos." *Proceedings* of the Twenty-First International Congress of Americanists 1 (1928): 582–603.

———. *Pueblo Indian Religion*. 2 vols. Chicago: U of Chicago P, 1939.

Parsons, Elsie Clews, and Franz Boas. "Spanish Tales from Laguna and Zuni." *Journal of American Folklore* 33 (1920): 47–72.

Rothenberg, Jerome. *Technicians of the Sacred*. Garden City, NY: Doubleday, 1968.

Spicer, Edward. *Cycles of Conquest: The Impact of Spain, Mexico and the United States on the Indians of the Southwest, 1533–1960*. Tucson: U of Arizona P, 1962.

Spinden, Herbert. *Songs of the Tewa*. New York, 1933.

Swann, Brian, and Arnold Krupat. *Recovering the Word: Essays on Native American Literature*. Berkeley: U of California P, 1987.

Tedlock, Barbara. "Songs of the Zuni Kachina Society: Composition, Rehearsal and Performance." In Frisbie (1980): 7–35.

Tedlock, Dennis. *Finding the Center: Narrative Poetry of the Zuni Indians*. New York: Dial Press, 1972.

———. *The Spoken Word and the Work of Interpretation*. Philadelphia: U of Pennsylvania P, 1983.

Underhill, Ruth. *Singing for Power: The Song Magic of the Papago Indians*. Berkeley: U of California P, 1938.

———, et al. *Rainhouse and Ocean: Speeches for the Papago Year*. Flagstaff: Museum of Northern Arizona Press, 1979.

Voegelin, C. F., and Robert C. Euler. "An Introduction to Hopi Chants." *Journal of American Folklore* 70 (1957): 115–36.

Walton, Eda Lou. "Navajo Song Patterning." *Journal of American Folklore* 43 (1930): 105–18.

Walton, Eda Lou, and T. T. Waterman. "American Indian Poetry." *American Anthropologist*, n. s. 27 (1925): 25–52.

Wheeler-Voegelin, Erminie, and R. W. Moore. "The Emergence Myth in Native America." *Indiana University Publications in Folklore* 9 (1957): 66–91.

Wiget, Andrew. "Sayatasha's Night Chant: A Literary Textual Analysis of a Zuni Ritual Poem." *American Indian Culture and Research Journal* 4.1 & 2 (1980): 99–140.

———. "Truth and the Hopi: An Historiographic Study of Documented Oral Tradition Concerning the Coming of the Spanish." *Ethnohistory* 29 (1982): 181–99.

———. "Telling the Tale: A Performance Analysis of a Hopi Coyote Story." In Swann and Krupat (1987): 297–338.

Wilder, Carleton S. "The Yaqui Deer Dance: A Study in Cultural Change." Anthropological Paper No. 66, in *Bulletin 186 of the Bureau of American Ethnology*. Washington, DC: Smithsonian Institution, 1963.

Wyman, Leland C., and Clyde Kluckhohn. "Navajo Classification of Their Song Ceremonials." *Memoirs of the American Anthropological Association* 50 (1938): 1–38.

Zepeda, Ofelia. *When It Rains: Papago and Pima Poetry*. A Sun Tracks Volume. Tucson: U of Arizona P, 1982.

Zolbrod, Paul. *Diné Bahané: The Navajo Creation Story*. Albuquerque: U of New Mexico P, 1984.

Oral Literature of the Plains Indians

Among the peoples most consistently classified as Plains rather than Prairie or Plateau Indians, the Arapaho, Blackfeet, Cheyenne, Crow, and Sioux held many narrative traditions in common, even though some tribes were enemies, like the Blackfeet and Crow, or spoke mutually unintelligible languages, like the Sioux and Cheyenne.

With the individuality characteristic of Plains culture, narrators provide much variation even within a single tribe. In a typical hero story, the beginnings are similar, though never exactly the same, while subsequent adventures are drawn from a stock of episodes freely assigned to any hero. "Blood Clot Boy" initially presents a condition abhorrent to hunting societies, who survived by generously distributing food, especially to those who could not obtain it themselves. An old man has been forced by his son-in-law to kill buffalo and to relinquish all claim to the meat and hides. Starving, the old man hides a blood clot in his clothes and brings it home (Grinnell 1962:29). In a Sioux version (Deloria 1932:113), the old man is a rabbit and the tyrant is a bear with no kinship tie. The rabbit places the clot in a sweat lodge where it becomes a boy who will grow up to defend and feed his relatives. The ceremonial creation of the power to continue tribal life is the answer to internecine abuse. Though the bear and the rabbit are unrelated by blood, they are neighbors, thereby assuring that they will act as relatives (see Walker 1982:5–6).

Through the purification lodge, the Sioux narrator releases a dynamic force to scourge divisiveness in a community. A Blackfeet narrator does not solve the problem ritually but simply has the blood clot turn into a child, who begins to cry when the kettle where it lies begins to boil (Grinnell 1962:298). In a Cheyenne version also told to Grinnell, the starving old man takes a stick, carves it to look as though it held a bow and arrows, then puts the stick to bed from which it arises in the morning as an armed young man (Grinnell 1971:206–11). An Arapaho blood clot turns into a child spontaneously in the old man's robe as he brings it home (Dorsey and Kroeber 1903:298–304). In every version (see Lowie 1960:285–357; Wissler and Duvall 1975:53–58), the young man grows with miraculous rapidity and unforgivingly ends the life of the son-in-law, and sometimes of the disloyal daughters (or of the bear and his children). An additional common element has him sparing the life of the youngest daughter (or cub) because she had risked her own life to save morsels of food for the old ones to keep them alive.

The Arapaho Blood Clot Boy overcomes enemies with transformative abilities that allow him to fight or escape in such shapes as a tree stump, a feather, or a bird. His last conquest, though formulaic and intertribal, requires a different kind of imagination. A girl in a band he has saved scorns his attentions, but the effect of herbs rubbed into his flute causes her to be humbled by an irresistible attraction, when he plays it outside her tipi. They do not live happily ever after since he soon returns to his parents and then to his supernatural "father," but he has taught her and the listeners something about the unreliability of romantic attraction and the need to value others on the basis of their contributions to collective well-being.

This last lesson is important for Deloria's Sioux Blood Clot Boy (1932:113–20), who is a more fallible and dynamic character than other Plains heroes with his name (see Jahner 1982:42–49). Before the adventures section begins, the rabbit advises his son not to travel west, the direction of difficulty, because "something very deceptive" awaits him there, but travel to the west is necessary for spiritual development, as the younger man intuitively knows, and he proceeds to take his chances. Iktomi, the trickster, meets him, plays upon the young man's training in kinship by calling him "younger brother," and persuades him to kill a bird and retrieve it from the top of a tree. The hero sheds his clothes and weapons to comply and Ikto promptly steals them, leaving the boy stuck to the tree, unable to answer guile with the physical courage that had enabled him to kill the bear. Ikto dons the clothes, enters a camp circle, marries the daughter of a chief, and receives undeserved praise. But like many who manage to achieve social prominence, he cannot feed the people spiritually or physically, failing abysmally when he tries to bring buffalo by ritual summons.

In the meantime, Blood Clot Boy is freed from the tree by a young girl who has been abused by her elder sister, Ikto's jealous wife. Feeling compassion for him, presumably because of her own suffering, she chops down the tree and frees Blood Clot Boy from the potential pursuit of adventure and fame. Such adolescent egotism is properly returned to the trickster, who is exposed and forced to leave the camp. Having passed his own trickster phase, Blood Clot Boy calls a large herd of buffalo, and having learned compassion from the girl, he can quell tricksters and prepare others for their own encounters. In the end, he and the girl return to the rabbit and the small bear, sharing a kinship of benevolent regard rather than blood, since the rabbit had adopted him and the bear was the child of his enemy (see Rice 1989:974).

But while this Sioux story is more sophisticated than intertribal variants, no tribe's stories are consistently more complex by any literary criterion. The trickster in the Sioux Blood Clot Boy story typifies the antagonistic figure of most of the extant Sioux oral narratives. Iktomi can be brutally destructive and he educates other characters only by narration, inadvertently warning them of their vulnerabilities. This narrative trickster figure is represented in all Plains collections by ancient stories, some told primarily in the region, and others known throughout North America (see Thompson 1966:294–300). These stories relate how the trickster induces ducks (pheasants, prairie chickens, prairie dogs, etc.) to dance with their eyes closed, while he kills them with a club; how he promises some women a valuable treasure, which they leave him to pursue while he cooks and eats their babies; or how he finds a way to marry his own daughter without being detected until, as usual, he gets careless and is run out of camp, and so proceeds to further adventures, promised by his survival at each story's end.

The trickster is more familiar in these outrageous acts than in his other identity as the Creator of the earth and all its life or, if not quite so exalted, the one who confers language and other attributes of culture on human beings in the early days of the world (see Bright 1987:348–49, 374–75; Powers 1986:154–55). The most developed of these trickster-transformers is Old Man in the Blackfeet version given to Wissler and Duvall (1975:19–21). In Plains Creation stories, the Creator is not God, the ultimate Great Mystery, in that he himself is subordinate to a remote disincarnate power, collectively the celestial bodies for the Blackfeet. Creation reflects the human process of tentative suggestion and accomplishment learned by failure. In the familiar Algonquian beginning, the first three animals Old Man sends to dive for earth are drowned. The last diver, the duck, is also drowned, but he brings a tiny ball of dirt, from which Old Man ritually forms the earth.

Then, in another tale of the earth's early days, Old Man is accompanied by Old Woman, whose origin is not given. Not only is Old Man far from omnipotent in his initial creation, he is often overruled by Old Woman, who, in general, advocates the necessity of difficulty and frailty. She gains the "second say" in all things, making hides very hard to tan so that good workers may be known; giving people only half the ten fingers on each hand proposed by Old Man, lest too many get in the way; correcting Old Man on the proper placement of the human genitals because if they were at the navel, childbirth would be too easy. Perhaps the most profound of Old Woman's revisions, and the most oft-quoted, is the decision that man

67

must die forever rather than for only four days. This issue of human mortality elicits Old Man's resistance. He proposes to decide it by throwing a buffalo chip in the water. If it floats, the people will not die forever. It does float, but Old Woman simply refuses to accept the whole test, much less the conclusion. She throws a rock into the water and, when it sinks, she makes one of the most memorable comments in world literature: "If the people did not die forever, they would not feel sorry for each other and sympathy would not exist in the world." Old Man concedes without an argument. But the continuing inseparability of deity and trickster is then remarkably expressed in the reversal at the story's end. When Old Woman's daughter dies, she tries to undo their agreement on death. This time Old Man incorporates the virtues of courage and acceptance; his firm refusal speaks of a transcendent wisdom coexisting in the world, and in an individual person, with trickster impulses to manipulate the process. In most later tales, however, Old Man uses his mind only for triumph and pleasure (Grinnell 1962:153–73; Wissler and Duvall 1975:24–39).

Commonly in Plains literature, diverse human qualities are either combined in a single figure or divided into separate characters who together form the story's single protagonist, mankind. In Walker's synthesized version of Sioux Creation stories, wisdom and folly exist in one figure, subsequently split into two more distinct selves than those of Old Man (see 1983:214–15, 286–87). Iktomi was originally Ksa, the god of wisdom, whose powers were used to invent the means and practice of creative expression including stories and "science." But his odd shape makes him vulnerable to mockery by most of the gods, and he is convinced by the demonic Crazy Buffalo to use his intelligence to humiliate and dominate others in revenge for their disrespect. When he has wasted his powers long enough, he is condemned by Skan, the Great Spirit, to an eternal game of strategy in which many losses are assured and victory never matters.

The Crow world is begun by a trickster-transformer, Old Man Coyote. After forming the earth and the males and females of various species, he is suddenly joined by a younger coyote named Cirape. As with the Blackfeet Old Man and Old Woman, their dialogue reflects the creative process in a single mind. Cirape makes suggestions which Old Man Coyote usually respects, though only he has the power to execute them. One of Cirape's suggestions has the same reverse impact as Old Woman's connection of death and compassion. Human beings should dislike each other and speak different languages, he argues, so that they can live a greater range of experience with more intensity. If they cannot feel rage, he says, they cannot feel happiness. If good and bad are not mixed together, he concludes, the people will have nothing to do. And as these paradoxical portraits of Trickster imply, there would be fewer kinds of stories to reimagine and tell (Lowie 1960:204–21; see also Bright 1987:367).

The stories most seriously and carefully told, however, in each tribe convey the culture heroes specific to those tribes. Intertribal heroes often begin as tribal outcasts, demonstrate bravery on perilous journeys, and return to comfort their families with the assurance of continuing life without submission to enemies or invasion by tricksters. The most revered culture heroes bring gifts even more crucial to each tribe's survival as a people. These culture heroes either emerge as spirit-beings to begin with, or they are born into human bodies and manifest their supernatural identities gradually as they grow up. Unlike the definitively perfect savior of Christianity, the Plains culture hero reflects a process of human development. As a young man, the Cheyenne Sweet Medicine demonstrates power over the physical body by arranging his own decapitation and then restoring himself. Later he lives in isolation from the tribe, having killed a chief in a hunting dispute over ownership of a kill. This period suggests the competitiveness and individualism of adolescence, but unlike a trickster, Sweet Medicine returns to bring buffalo when the people are starving (see Harrod 1987:101). After this physical contribution, he departs again, this time in the manner of various questers, and eventually brings the tribe one of their two vitalizing symbols, the four medicine arrows. As Sweet Medicine teaches the use of ordinary arrows to bring down game, so he introduces a symbol to feed the mind and heart (Grinnell 1971:263–68; Powell 1969:xviii, xxiii, 443).

The other Cheyenne culture hero is Erect Horns, the original wearer of the buffalo horn cap, reverenced as greatly as the arrows. Erect Horns teaches the sun dance, to celebrate, among many blessings, the spiritual meaning of human sexuality. He refuses to attend to his new wife until they have both learned the body's symbolic function as a medium of the larger creation. The private act of sexual intercourse in the Cheyenne sun dance lodge between the "sacred woman" and the chief priest consummates the mythical marriage between Erect Horns and his wife, the spiritual and physical worlds (Grinnell 1971:257–68; Powell 1969:447–50).

The Blackfeet story of Scarface (Grinnell 1971:92–103; Wissler and Duvall 1975:61–66; Harrod 1987:124–27) does not include physical sexuality as a metaphor of spiritual union, but the hero mediates contraries that cause self-hatred and brutality. The culture hero begins as a young man literally scarred with human imperfection. He wishes to marry the most beautiful woman in his tribe and is not deterred when the other young men mock him because of the ugly scar on his face. The girl tells him that she belongs to the Sun, but if Scarface travels to the sky and requests the girl in marriage, she may yet be his. She will know if he has gained consent when he returns to her without the scar. Scarface travels, saves the Sun's child, Morning Star, from an attack of giant birds, and in reward, the Sun teaches him the lessons most needed by the people. The raven is the wisest animal and should be heeded; the buffalo is the most sacred animal and should be used for food and shelter; the tongue of the buffalo should be left for the Sun; the sweat lodge and the sun dance lodge would be used to cure sickness and should be built in a special way. He then returns to earth without his scar to marry the girl so that the people may follow his example of courageous sacrifice for the sake of unity and generation.

The choosing of the difficult way has a sexual dimension in the story of the Lakota culture giver, the White Buffalo Calf Pipe Woman. The spontaneous reactions of the two scouts who first see her represent the antithetical sides of human nature, sterile and creative, here in two separate bodies. One scout expresses the usual pleasure from the sight of the beautiful woman. The other young man cautions him to behold what appears with interest and care. Lust represents any kind of narrow possessiveness here, and the woman turns the bad scout into an image of the rudimentary being he already was, a skeleton covered with snakes. But the good young man is rewarded by becoming her messenger. After he informs the chiefs how to ceremonially receive it, the pipe, center of all expressions of prayer, healing, and kinship, is presented and explained by the woman. Like the woman herself, the pipe is not to be appropriated for individual gain but is to be used only as a means of creating and sustaining life (Densmore 1972:63–66; Walker 1980:109–12; Black Elk 1984:283–85).

Explicit sexuality as a source of metaphor or humor is largely absent from these collections, all of which were edited early in the twentieth century. In some instances, passages considered obscene are translated into Latin rather than English. The Arapaho Creator teaches the first man and woman the proper use of their sexual parts by direct application after the usual trial-and-error sequence. Finally, when the two are properly joined, he asks the man what he thinks: "Bene est," he responds (Dorsey and Kroeber 1903:6). The humor of the passage is only partly supplied in any translation, although in an ironic sense, the Latin translation adds humor.

Plains oral literature is extensive. Ella Deloria's complex orthography and extensive notation are unique features of her texts. Lakota myths rewritten by Walker, on the other hand, are among the earliest examples of written Native American mythology. George Sword, original author of much of the Walker myth cycle, wrote the stories in the Lakota language, after which an interpreter wrote a translation which was then rewritten by Walker (see 1983:13–16). Beckwith, Wissler, Grinnell, Dorsey and Kroeber, all present long, complex stories, translated straightforwardly without the Victorian refinement that occasionally mars Walker's prose. Lowie's translations are interesting for their lack of such improvement and for their physical explicitness, though they are stiffly literal and do not translate the tone of the original.

One teller of traditional stories is exceptional in that he has long had an international reputation. In 1944, Black Elk told John Neihardt narratives in every Plains genre, and although they were never published in an edited form, the stenographic record of their translated versions has recently been published in *The Sixth Grandfather* (1984). These stories include culture hero myths, myth-histories of the early days of the world, and historical accounts, especially of peace treaties concluded between the tribes before the white man came. Through the stories, Black Elk sends a clear message about the future to his varied English-speaking readers (see Rice 1989:25–26). In a story of the prophet Wooden Cup, Black Elk tells of a holy man who predicted the ascendancy of the white man long before it occurred, and the survival of Lakota culture throughout the period of conquest. No matter what happens, he tells them, they will live if they hold onto the pipe and the way of prayer it defines (1984:337–41; the holy man is renamed Drinks Water in *Black Elk Speaks* [1972:8]). Similar tales of prophecy by the Cheyenne Sweet Medicine (Grinnell 1971:277; Stands in Timber and Liberty 1972:40), and the naming of the Cheyenne and Arapaho tricksters with their respective tribal words for "white man," *veho* and *nihancan* (Wissler and Duvall 1975:11), reminded the Plains peoples that radical changes in their way of life were encompassed by a spiritual tradition with no beginning and no end. The stories trace this larger circle to center each listener in a world of tricksters and spirit-guides, avoided or invoked more readily for each story responsibly told.

Julian Rice
Florida Atlantic University

BIBLIOGRAPHY

Primary Sources

Beckwith, Martha Warren. "Mythology of the Oglala Dakota." *Journal of American Folklore* 43 (1930): 339–439.

Black Elk. *Black Elk Speaks*. Told through John G. Neihardt. New York: Pocket Books, 1972.

———. *The Sixth Grandfather*. Ed. Raymond J. DeMallie. Lincoln: U of Nebraska P, 1984.

Buechel, Eugene, S.J. *Lakota Tales and Texts*. Pine Ridge, SD: Red Cloud Lakota Language and Cultural Center, 1978.

Bullchild, Percy. *The Sun Came Down*. San Francisco: Harper & Row, 1985.

Deloria, Ella. *Dakota Texts*. 1932. Reprint. New York: AMS, 1974.

———. *Teton Myths* [The George Bushotter Collection]. Ca. 1937. MS 30 (x8c3). Boas Collection, American Philosophical Society, Philadelphia.

Densmore, Frances. *Teton Sioux Music*. 1918. Reprint. New York: Da Capo, 1972.

Dorsey, George A., and Alfred L. Kroeber. *Traditions of the Arapaho*. Chicago: Field Columbian Museum, 1903.

Grinnell, George Bird. *Blackfoot Lodge Tales*. Lincoln: U of Nebraska P, 1962.

———. *By Cheyenne Campfires*. Lincoln: U of Nebraska P, 1971.

Lowie, Robert H. *Crow Texts*. Berkeley: U of California P, 1960.

Stands in Timber, John, and Margot Liberty. *Cheyenne Memories*. Lincoln: U of Nebraska P, 1972.

Theisz, R. D., ed. *Buckskin Tokens*. Aberdeen, SD: North Plains Press, 1975.

Walker, James R. *The Sun Dance and Other Ceremonies of the Oglala Division of the Teton Dakota*. 1917. Reprint. New York: AMS, 1979.

————. *Lakota Belief and Ritual*. Eds. Raymond J. DeMallie and Elaine A. Jahner. Lincoln: U of Nebraska P, 1980.

————. *Lakota Society*. Ed. Raymond J. DeMallie. Lincoln: U of Nebraska P, 1982.

————. *Lakota Myth*. Ed. Elaine A. Jahner. Lincoln: U of Nebraska P, 1983.

Wissler, Clark. "Some Dakota Myths." *Journal of American Folklore* 20 (1907): 121–31, 195–206.

————, and D. C. Duvall. *Mythology of the Blackfoot Indians*. 1909. Reprint. New York: AMS, 1975.

Secondary Sources

Bright, William. "The Natural History of Old Man Coyote." *Recovering the Word*. Ed. Brian Swann and Arnold Krupat. Berkeley: U of California P, 1987. 339–87.

Harrod, Howard E. *Renewing the World: Plains Indian Religion and Morality*. Tucson: U of Arizona P, 1987.

Jahner, Elaine A. "Cognitive Style in Oral Literature." *Language and Style* 14 (1982): 32–51.

Powell, Peter J. *Sweet Medicine: The Continuing Role of the Sacred Arrows, the Sun Dance, and the Sacred Buffalo Hat in Northern Cheyenne History*. 2 vols. Norman: U of Oklahoma P, 1969.

Powers, William K. *Sacred Language*. Norman: U of Oklahoma P, 1986.

Rice, Julian. *Lakota Storytelling: Black Elk, Ella Deloria, and Frank Fools Crow*. New York: Peter Lang, 1989.

Thompson, Stith. *Tales of the North American Indians*. Bloomington: Indiana UP, 1966.

Oral Literature of the Northeastern Algonquians and the Northern Iroquoians

The term Northeastern Algonquian refers to Algonquian-speaking peoples in the Atlantic provinces of Canada and the New England states. Oral literatures in this area differ somewhat from those of other Algonquian groups to the north and west such as the Cree and Ojibwa. Within the Northeastern area itself, there is only fragmentary information on the oral literatures of the southern New England tribes (the Mahican, Pawtucket, Massachusetts, Narragansett, Niantic, Pequot, and Mohegan). Abundant information exists on the Micmac, Malecite, Passamaquoddy, Penobscot, and St. Francis Abenaki, known collectively as the Wabanaki. The Northern Iroquoians consist of a dozen or more tribes inhabiting an area to the west of the Northeastern Algonquians around the lower Great Lakes. The oral literature of the League Iroquois—particularly the Seneca and Onondaga—and their ancient political rivals to the north, the Hurons, is voluminous. Nothing is known of the oral traditions of the St. Lawrence Iroquoians, the Erie, the Neutral, or the Petun, except as the last group contributed to the "Huron-Wyandot" identity of immigrant groups whose oral traditions were studied early in the present century by Marius Barbeau. With the exception of a few folktales, there is little similarity between the oral literature of the Cherokee, the sole Southern Iroquoian group, and that of the Northern Iroquoians.

Contacts between the League Iroquois and the Northeastern Algonquians were generally hostile, and the two language families are unrelated. Not surprisingly, their oral traditions are quite different, although there are instances of diffusion between the two areas, like, for example, the borrowing of Trickster tales by the Huron and Seneca from their Algonquian neighbors, and the borrowing of the rival twins theme from Iroquois into Micmac cosmology. Some of the elements in the mythologies of one or both groups have a wider distribution in North America or even beyond: the themes of the earth diver, the rival twins, the overworld thunderer vs. the underworld serpent, and the magic flight.

As elsewhere in North America, neither group had a true system of alphabetic or hieroglyphic writing before contact, though both used mnemonic devices of various kinds for keeping track of longer recitations. Such recitations must be regarded as extraordinary feats of memory, but study of different versions of myths, tales, and other speeches shows that they were, in general, not recited verbatim, and performers developed their own characteristic styles and enjoyed varying reputations for effectiveness in their communities. For both groups, recitation of myths and tales was a nighttime activity restricted to the winter months; only the Micmac appear to have lacked such a taboo. Performances of the longer cycles could last days or even weeks. The Iroquois, but not the Northeastern Algonquians, discouraged children from attending these sessions. They provided food and gifts of tobacco to the narrator. Historical traditions were well developed among the Wabanaki tribes, less so among the Northern Iroquoians. The latter, on the other hand, developed legendary oratorical skills and styles in their calendrical ceremonies and political activities. Although neither group had a formal taxonomy of speech types, several genres can be identified for both on the basis of the occasion, sitting, participants, speaking style and event duration.

The Northeastern Algonquians

For the Northeastern Algonquians, we can distinguish myths, seen as true accounts of events occurring in the earliest times when the earth and the animals received their forms, from shorter tales recited for amusement or to teach a moral lesson. The latter were generally conceived as fiction. Both of these types are distinguished from traditional histories which recount relatively recent events.

Algonquian mythologies are dominated by Transformers, who converted the primal earth and its creatures into their historical forms, and Tricksters, who were involved in numerous escapades, either with or without a moral purpose. The Northern Algonquians, such as the Cree and Ojibwa, combine these antithetical personalities in one figure. The Wabanaki groups, on the other hand, resolve the psychological contradiction of an all-powerful culture hero and a blundering buffoon by separating them into a culture hero Transformer and a host of animal Tricksters, commonly Wolverine, Hare, and Raccoon. Wabanaki mythologies distinguish a series of earlier Transformers from a later series. The earliest group were grotesque, had awesome power, and confined their activities largely to converting a featureless world into one with mountains, rivers, and bodies of water. The Abenaki Ojihozo is the archetype. The later group took over and adapted the world to mankind's use. The wise and good hero Gluskap, with his special concern for Indians, is the best known of the later Transformers, and there are others of the same type.

The Wabanaki have a store of shorter narratives which revolve around the exploits of Tricksters and the adventures of animals. These "wigwam tales," as they have been called, are frequently humorous, are usually regarded as fiction, and may have an immediate moral purpose or serve to explain how an animal came by its appearance or characteristic habits. In Micmac and Passamaquoddy tales, Wolverine brings disaster on himself by playing mean tricks on those he meets. Hare often begins as a bungler but develops extraordinary powers by which he outwits Lynx. In Penobscot and Abenaki tales, Raccoon plays tricks of all sorts, often out of sheer exuberance, though sometimes with all the meanness of Wolverine. The style and setting of these tales was informal, and there was considerable performance variation among narrators. Some performances were directed at children. The most important collections of Wabanaki myths and tales were made by Rand, and Wallis and Wallis for the Micmac; Mechling, and Szabo for the Malecite; Leland, and Leland and Prince for the Passamaquoddy; Speck, and Nicolar for the Penobscot.

Wabanaki tribes had well-developed traditional histories. Micmac narratives tell of their early experiences with the Red Indians (Beothuk), their wars with the Eskimo and the Montagnais, the Malecite, and the Penobscot, the coming of the white man, and their participation in the Seven Nations of Canada, whose capital was the Mohawk village of Caughnawaga. Malecite, Passamaquoddy, and Penobscot traditions treat similar events. Some traditions were the property of individual families for whom the event had special significance. The destruction of the first Abenaki village on the St. Francis River was known to the whole tribe, but the longest and best version was passed down in one family whose earliest-remembered ancestor was made a chief at an impromptu council after the battle. Traditional histories have been much neglected by historians, although they often contain accurate information about real events which may be missing from the documentary record penned by white men (Day 1972). In earlier times, both myths and historical narratives were recited in a metrical chant, a device which aided the memory. The unit of delivery was the line, which was divided into phrase groups and had a characteristic terminal pitch contour. A long historical narrative in chanted form was collected as late as 1961 (Day, Abenaki field notes), but the style has since disappeared.

Ceremonial performance did not develop among the Northeastern Algonquians to anything like the degree it did among other Algonquian groups such as the Ojibwa, Sac, Fox, and Menominee, who had medicine societies, or among the Northern Iroquoians, who had complex calendrical ceremonialism and well-developed traditions of political oratory. Chief-making and other Wabanaki ceremonies were largely a matter of song and dance. It is known that the Abenaki appointed an individual, called a *mikwobaid*, "the rememberer," to keep track of tribal councils. Regrettably, little effort was made to record the traditions of the *mikwobaid* before the last person so designated died. Wabanaki treaty ceremonialism developed largely in response to contact with the Iroquois, notably with the Caughnawaga Mohawk after 1750.

The Northern Iroquoians

For the Northern Iroquoians, as for the Northeastern Algonquians, the category of narrative (*kaka:a?* [Seneca], *oká:ra?* [Mohawk] "story, tale") can be distinguished from ceremonial speaking on grounds of setting, participants, occasion, and style. The great founding myths of the Iroquois are no longer recited, and we lack sound recordings of them, but they have been well documented in dictated form, often in the original languages with interlinear translations. The tradition of story narration, on the other hand, survives on all Iroquois reservations where the languages are still spoken, although the content of the tales has shifted to some extent away from traditional to more contemporary themes over the hundred-year period they have been intensively collected. There are extensive, if still incomplete, collections of both dictated and taped speeches associated with Northern Iroquoian calendrical ceremonialism and political institutions.

The myth or story narrator is usually an older male (*hakeota?* [Seneca] "he raises up a story"), though the record shows there were also gifted female narrators. The traditional setting for story and myth narration was the longhouse during winter nights. The narrator began by smoking a pipe or burning tobacco at the hearth fire, ritual acts of cleansing the self, and preparing a communicative path to the overworld. He announced a story by uttering a stock opening formula, to which the audience responded with a term of assent which was also uttered periodically during the performance to indicate continued concurrence and involvement in the event. He might use wooden counters or other devices as aids to memory or as the basis for his choice of a story. If he could not finish a narrative on a given occasion, he "tied it" for a future occasion (Barbeau 1915; Parker 1923).

Myths were regarded by the Northern Iroquoians as being true explanations of the origins of natural phenomena and social institutions. They began with an opening formula such as "This happened long ago" (Barbeau 1915:15). The best known and longest of these is the "cosmogonic" myth of the Earth Grasper or Sky Woman, of which some two dozen versions are on record. The same essential features are found in Huron versions collected in the early seventeenth century as in League Iroquois versions collected in the late nineteenth century; Sky Woman is expelled from the world on the other side of the Sky when her mysterious pregnancy arouses the jealousy of her husband, the Keeper of the Tree of Light; with the help of waterfowl she descends gently to the back of the Great Turtle swimming in a limitless sea; Muskrat dives to the sea bottom and brings up a clod of earth; from this the world is formed; Sky Woman gives birth to a daughter, who matures and bears twins, the Good Minded and the Evil Minded; the twins compete for control of the earth and the Good Minded finally wins out (Barbeau 1915, 1960; Hewitt 1903, 1928; Fenton 1962). The physical universe of the Iroquoians is thus accounted for, as are the central features of Iroquoian society. In some versions, the origin of the clans and their division into moieties are also recounted.

Shorter myths account for the origin of the extraterrestrial "man-beings" the Pleiades, Orion's Belt, Thunderer, Sun, Moon, Wind, and Morning Star; or detail the exploits of the supernaturals Flying Head, Horned Serpent, Dew Eagle, and Blue Panther (Converse 1908; Curtin and Hewitt 1918; Parker 1923). A good part of Huron mythology is concerned with powerful *oki*, either benevolent spirits contained in some animals, plants, and people, or malevolent spirits contained in witches and monsters (Barbeau 1915).

The Northern Iroquoians distinguish a second set of narratives which they regard as pure fiction. These usually involve human foibles and begin with an opening formula such as "It is as if a man walked" (Barbeau 1915:18). Some are Trickster stories borrowed from neighboring Algonquians, and involve a witch being fooled by the Trickster when she covets something he has. For the Cayuga, the Trickster figure represents unrestrained male sexuality (Randle 1953:626). Similar to these are the animal stories in which Raccoon outwits Fox or some other animal. Another set of stories involves human adventures, and often features a youth who triumphs over evil relatives after a series of initial hardships (Barbeau 1960:12–14). In still other tales, the Northern Iroquoians borrowed elements of plot and theme from European folklore (Barbeau 1960:26–27; Randle 1953:627–29).

The category of narrative history is not as well developed among the Northern Iroquoians as it is among the Northeastern Algonquians. Text collections nevertheless contain some historical or quasi-historical accounts, such as stories of the coming of the white man, the seventeenth-century Iroquois-Huron wars or wars with other groups, and, for the Huron-Wyandot, their removal to Ohio and Oklahoma. A typical opening formula for narrative histories is "They started for the winter hunt" (Barbeau 1960:15).

As indicated, there are extensive published narrative collections for Huron, Seneca, and Onondaga in the work of Barbeau, Converse, Curtain, Hewitt, and Parker. Only recently have narrative materials been added for the remaining Six Nations languages by Williams for Mohawk, by

Lounsbury and by Michelson for Oneida, and by Rudes and Crouse for Tuscarora. One collection consists of closely analyzed texts in all the Five Nations languages (Mithun and Woodbury, *Northern Iroquoian Texts*, 1980). An extensive unpublished collection of mainly Cayuga narratives was recorded only in English (see Randle, "The Waugh Collection," 1953).

Ceremonial speaking was highly developed among the Northern Iroquoians. It includes political oratory, the speeches associated with the first-fruits and agricultural ceremonies and the curing ceremonies, and the Code of Handsome Lake. Lengthy published and unpublished original-language texts exist to complement a vast store of translated Indian speeches and the record of observations about these events made by missionaries, government workers, and anthropologists.

It is a commonplace to cite the Iroquois as brilliant orators and diplomats in the forest councils held with white colonial officials and the spokesmen of other Indian tribes during the seventeenth and eighteenth centuries. The literary merit of Indian council oratory and the Indian treaty was recognized by eighteenth-century literati like Benjamin Franklin (Van Doren 1938; see also Drummond and Moody 1953; Wroth 1928). The primary and secondary source literature on the forest councils is enormous (see Fenton 1957), but there is a need to interpret it afresh in the light of traditions of council speaking which still survive among the Iroquois in the original languages, and which more faithfully preserve the Indian point of view than the earlier translations (Foster 1984). From these accounts we learn crucial details regarding the purpose and meaning of the councils to the Iroquois, and new light is shed on the use of wampum as a mnemonic device (Foster 1985). The Iroquois ingeniously adapted to the needs of forest diplomacy the Condolence Ceremony for mourning dead chiefs and installing successors; the Condolence rituals provided a carefully paced protocol for greeting visiting delegations, dividing into "sides of the fire," and arriving at decisions. The Condolence Ceremony itself belongs to a larger cycle of literature which includes an account of Deganawida's founding of the Iroquois League and a recitation of the Great Law; the latter contains the rules governing the comportment of chiefs and the operations of the League. The best-known versions of the Great Law are the two translations which appear in Parker (*The Constitution of the Five Nations*, 1916). The most complete version of the entire cycle, dictated by John Arthur Gibson to Alexander Goldenweiser in 1912 in Onondaga, is under preparation as a fully analyzed and translated text by Hanni Woodbury. Excerpts in Mohawk and Onondaga of the Condolence Ceremony were prepared and interpreted by Beauchamp (*Civil, Religious and Mourning Councils*, 1907) and Hale (*The Iroquois Book of Rites*, 1883 [1963]), and the ceremony has been the subject of intensive study by many Iroquoianists, from Lewis Henry Morgan to William N. Fenton.

At the time of contact, the Northern Iroquoians had practiced agriculture for nearly a millennium, but they had retained some elements of an earlier hunter-gatherer economy as well. Longhouse calendrical ceremonialism today reflects both these lifeways, as well as remnants of other complexes such as dream guessing and the medicinal-therapeutic rituals. Each phase of the year is marked by a major ceremony conducted in the Longhouse: the general plan of these ceremonies is an extended dialogue conducted between appointed speakers (*hahtha:ha?* [Cayuga]) for the two moieties (groupings of clans), punctuated by ritual singing and dancing. There is no formal training for Longhouse speakers; younger men of promise are encouraged to perform and perfect their skills. Study of a range of speeches by different ritualists based on the hierarchy of spirit forces that comprise the Iroquoian universe shows that speakers do not recite speeches verbatim, but compose them to a certain extent anew on each occasion. The basic unit of composition in Longhouse speeches is the line, which is best defined on grounds of pitch, stress, and rhythm, rather than on syntactic grounds. The speaker draws from a stock of set formulas, combining these into lines, and the lines into sections, according to compositional rules. Performances are similar enough to be counted as the same by the participants, but different enough for speakers to be continually evaluated and to earn reputations as masters of particular genres (Foster 1974). The style of Longhouse speaking has been characterized on intonational grounds by Chafe (1961:147–48), and certain parallels between formal spoken Seneca and non-Iroquoian written prose have also been suggested (Chafe 1981). Fenton's exhaustive study, *The False Faces of the Iroquois* (1987), has a wealth of detail on one type of medicine rite, and contains transcribed and translated Seneca and Onondaga texts.

The Longhouse also serves as a religious center for "preaching" the Code of Handsome Lake (*káiwi:yo:h* [Seneca], known in English as "The Good Message"). At the very end of the eighteenth century, following the devastating effects of the American Revolution, the Seneca prophet *Skanyotaiyo?* ([Seneca] "beautiful lake," a chief's title) began to have a series of visions which lasted intermittently until 1815. In them, the Creator spoke to him through supernatural intermediaries about providing the Indians with a new social order. Following a pattern typical of the Iroquois, Handsome Lake's teachings were gradually codified as they were handed down from speaker to speaker over time, until they have become today a set piece of oratory. The Good Message is preached at fall "conventions" in Iroquois Longhouses. It consists of some 130 sections which are spread over the mornings of three days. The preacher (*haihwaHsáweHa?* [Cayuga]) must earn recognition from the Tonawanda council before he is allowed to preach at conventions. He grasps strings of wampum collected from each of the longhouses on that year's circuit in one hand and intones the Good Message in a measured, high-pitched chant. The preaching style is entirely distinct from the normal Longhouse speaking style (Chafe 1961:148). The Good Message is given primarily in Seneca and Cayuga, although it is occasionally heard in Mohawk. Parts of a Seneca performance have been recorded and transcribed, and a manuscript copy exists of Edward Cornplanter's original Seneca version, which served as the basis for the best-known English translation (Parker, *The Code of Handsome Lake*, 1913).

Gordon M. Day
Michael K. Foster
Canadian Ethnology Service
Canadian Museum of Civilization

BIBLIOGRAPHY

Primary Sources

Barbeau, C. Marius. *Huron and Wyandot Mythology*. Canada, Department of Mines, Geological Survey, Memoir 80, Anthropological Series 11. Ottawa: Government Printing Bureau, 1915.

―――. *Huron-Wyandot Traditional Narratives in Translations and Native Texts*. National Museum of Canada Bulletin 165, Anthropological Series 47. Ottawa: Department of Northern Affairs and National Resources, 1960.

Beauchamp, William M. *Civil, Religious and Mourning Councils and Ceremonies of Adoption of the New York Indians*. New York State Museum Bulletin 113. Albany: New York State Museum, 1907. 341–451.

Chafe, Wallace L. "Seneca Thanksgiving Rituals." Bureau of American Ethnology Bulletin 183. Washington, DC, 1961.

Converse, Harriet Maxwell. *Myths and Legends of the New York State Iroquois*. Ed. Arthur C. Parker. New York State Museum Bulletin 125. Albany: New York State Museum, 1908.

Curtin, Jeremiah, and J. N. B. Hewitt. *Seneca Fiction, Legends, and Myths*. 32nd Annual Report of the Bureau of American Ethnology for the Years 1910–1911. Washington, DC: GPO, 1918.

Day, Gordon M. Unpublished field notes on Abenaki. ca. 1957–79.

Foster, Michael K. *From the Earth to Beyond the Sky: An Ethnographic Approach to Four Longhouse Iroquois Speech Events*. Canadian Ethnology Service, Mercury Series 20. Ottawa: National Museums of Canada, 1974.

Hewitt, J. N. B. *Iroquoian Cosmology, First Part*. 21st Annual Report of the Bureau of American Ethnology for the Years 1899–1900. Washington, DC: GPO, 1903. 127–339.

―――. *Iroquoian Cosmology, Second Part*. 43rd Annual Report of the Bureau of American Ethnology for the Years 1925–1926. Washington, DC: GPO, 1928. 449–819.

Leland, Charles G. *The Algonquin Legends of New England, or Myths and Folk-Lore of the Micmac, Passamaquoddy, and Penobscot Tribes*. Boston: Houghton Mifflin, 1884.

―――, and John D. Prince, trans. *Kuloskapto Master, and Other Algonkin Poems*. New York: Funk and Wagnalls, 1902.

Lounsbury, Floyd G. *Oneida Verb Morphology*. Yale University Publications in Anthropology 48. New Haven: Yale UP, 1953.

Mechling, William H. *Malecite Tales*. Canada, Department of Mines, Geological Survey, Memoir 49, Anthropological Series 4. Ottawa: Government Printing Bureau, 1914.

Michelson, Karin, ed. *Three Stories in Oneida*. Canadian Ethnology Service, Mercury Series Paper 73. Ottawa: National Museums of Canada, 1981.

Mithun, Marianne, and Hanni Woodbury, eds. *Northern Iroquoian Texts*. Native American Text Series 4. Chicago: U of Chicago P, 1980.

Nicolar, Joseph. *The Life and Traditions of the Red Man*. Bangor, ME: n.p., 1893.

Parker, Arthur C. *The Code of Handsome Lake, the Seneca Prophet*. New York State Museum Bulletin 163. Albany: New York State Museum, 1913.

———. *The Constitution of the Five Nations*. New York State Museum Bulletin 184. Albany: New York State Museum, 1916. 7–158.

———. *Seneca Myths and Folk Tales*. Buffalo Historical Society Publications 27. Buffalo: Buffalo Historical Society, 1923.

Rand, Silas T. *Legends of the Micmacs*. Wellesley Philological Publications. New York: Longmans, 1894.

Rudes, Blair A., and Dorothy Crouse. *The Tuscarora Legacy of J. N. B. Hewitt*. Canadian Ethnology Service, Mercury Series Paper 108. Ottawa: National Museums of Canada, 1987.

Speck, Frank G. "Penobscot Transformer Tales." *International Journal of American Linguistics* 1 (1918): 187–244.

———. *Wawenock Myth Texts from Maine*. 43rd Annual Report of the Bureau of American Ethnology for the Years 1925–1926. Washington, DC: GPO, 1928. 165–97.

———. "Penobscot Tales and Religious Beliefs." *Journal of American Folklore* (1935): 1–107.

Szabo, Laszlo. "Malecite Tales." Ms. in the Archives of the Canadian Ethnology Service, Canadian Museum of Civilization, Ottawa.

Wallis, Wilson D., and Ruth S. Wallis. *The Micmac Indians of Eastern Canada*. Minneapolis: U of Minnesota P, 1955.

Williams, Marianne, ed. *Kanien?kéha? okara?shón:?a*. New York State Museum Bulletin 427. Albany: New York State Museum, 1976.

Secondary Sources

Chafe, Wallace L. "Differences Between Colloquial and Ritual Seneca, or How Oral Literature Is Literacy." *Report from the Survey of Californian and Other Indian Languages* 1. Eds. Alice Schlichter, Wallace L. Chafe, and Leanne Hinton. N.p., 1981. 131–45.

Day, Gordon M. "Oral Tradition as Complement." *Ethnohistory* 19 (1972): 99–108.

Drummond, A. M., and Richard Moody. "Indian Treaties: The First American Dramas." *Quarterly Journal of Speech* 39 (1953): 15–24.

Fenton, William N. *American Indian and White Relations to 1830: Needs and Opportunities for Study*. Chapel Hill: U of North Carolina P, 1957.

———. "This Island, the World on the Turtle's Back." *Journal of American Folklore* 75 (1962): 283–300.

———. *The False Faces of the Iroquois*. Norman: U of Oklahoma P, 1987.

Fisher, Margaret W. "Mythology of the Northern and Northeastern Algonkians in Reference to Algonkian Mythology as a Whole." *Man in Northeastern America*. Ed. Frederick Johnson. Papers of the Robert S. Peabody Foundation for Archaeology 3 (1946): 226–62.

Foster, Michael K. "On Who Spoke First at Iroquois-White Councils: An Exercise in the Method of Upstreaming." *Extending the Rafters: Interdisciplinary Approaches to*

Iroquoian Studies. Eds. Michael K. Foster, Jack Campisi, and Marianne Mithun. Albany: State U of New York P, 1984. 183–207.

———. "Another Look at the Function of Wampum in Iroquois-White Councils." *The History and Culture of Iroquois Diplomacy.* Eds. Francis Jennings, William N. Fenton, and Mary A. Duke. Syracuse: Syracuse UP, 1985. 99–114.

Hale, Horatio, ed. *The Iroquois Book of Rites.* 1883. 2nd ed. Toronto: U of Toronto P, 1963.

Randle, Martha Champion. "The Waugh Collection of Iroquois Folktales." *Proceedings of the American Philosophical Society* 97 (1953): 611–33.

Van Doren, Carl. Introduction. *Indian Treaties Printed by Benjamin Franklin 1736–1762.* Ed. Julian P. Boyd. Philadelphia: The Historical Society of Pennsylvania, 1938.

Wroth, Lawrence C. "The Indian Treaty as Literature." *Yale Review* 17 (1928): 749–66.

Oral Literature of the Southeast

In assessing the oral literature of Native Americans of North America, it is always tempting to treat the collections from a given tribe or nation as a synchronic corpus to be accepted as "their lore," if only because it is so difficult to deal with the diachronic reality that the materials change over time. Nowhere is that temptation greater than in the Southeast, because the last four centuries have been a period of extraordinary upheaval for the Native Americans of that area. The historic dimension of the collections is intimidatingly hard to deal with, but the importance of it make any simple synchronic picture suspect from the outset.

History of Study

From prehistoric times, the Southeast has been a melting pot of diverse peoples, particularly as disease and warfare reduced the numbers of small ethnic groups to the point of absorption into larger groups for survival. In other cases, however, the metaphor of the stew pot might be more appropriate in view of the stubborn persistence of ethnic identity, even through centuries of intimacy with other peoples. The Alabama and Coushatta, for example, lived adjacent to each other in Alabama for a century before moving together to Texas, where they have been since the late eighteenth century. Even today, after complex intermarrying, members of the group can discuss the extent to which they are Alabama or Coushatta. At the same time, however, no one can remember a time when they spoke significantly different dialects of Muskhogean, but in the late eighteenth century it was pointed out that seven different languages were spoken in the vicinity of Fort Toulouse (now Montgomery, Alabama). The nature of the basic political structure of the Southeast, the "town," made confederacies of alien peoples both a possibility and a reality. Complicating even more the international quality of southeastern life and lore was the tradition of Africans at an early period. It has long been a truism that Native Americans picked up few oral literary materials from the Europeans, but the same is not true in regard to African lore. Whether from affinities of content and structure between Native American and African folklore or from the quality of the relationships between the two groups, albeit master and slave, the southeastern peoples added significant numbers of African tales, particularly those about animals, to their repertoire (Dundes 1965).

Daunting to any attempt to understand the collections of southeastern material is the reality of the Removals of the 1830s and 40s. It is clear from the examination of other collections that many legends are linked directly to the land, both as etiology and as the locale for important events. Thus this story happened on that butte, while that tale explains the origin of that river. Those legends which could not stand the transplantation to Oklahoma died. This reality becomes even more daunting when the lateness of the collecting of the materials is considered. Most of the ethnographers and folklorists visited Oklahoma and other locations in the Southeast in the decades from 1880 to 1920, with most of the visits occurring in the later years, when many of the bearers from the old homeland had already died. That means that the collections of Swanton, in particular, have to be seen as bodies of filtered material which survived both the geographic transplant and transmission to an Oklahoma-born generation.

Then, too, there are the historical influences which must be assessed by students of any region of North America—the syncretism which may be present due to changes in the Native religious system. Christianity is the most obvious influence which must be considered, and the power of this force is well known. Christian ethical dualism, for example, can easily be identified in the change of the Iroquoian twins from culture hero and trickster to Jesus and the Devil. Christianity is only one of the syncretistic influences, however, for the wave of Ghost Dance revitalization in the nineteenth century indicated the ease of major alteration of beliefs, and the success of peyote religion in this century points to growing pluralism in Native American thought. Moreover, the growth of the Pan-Indian movement is a warning to students of the history of narratives—if a people will borrow and adapt dances (for example) of other peoples in a short period of time, have they not done the same with their myths and legends?

Further complicating the picture are the remnant groups. The Cherokee and Choctaw, in particular, have attempted to maintain close contact with the bands which remained in the old country of North Carolina and Mississippi, but differences were bound to be accentuated through time, if only by environmental and political pressures. Moreover, the very adaptability which led to the appellation the "Five Civilized Tribes" has also led some of the remnant groups to develop their own version of modern

Euro-American culture, with a resulting loss of the traditional oral literature. Collecting and comparing the old-country literature with that from
Oklahoma, in fact, remains one of the interesting projects yet to be done
by students of the Southeast.

Major published collections mostly stem from the turn of the century,
which means that today's standards for collecting, including extensive note-
taking on the context and informant, and verbatim recording of the telling
in the original language, were seldom observed. One of the questions
which hangs over the collections in print, in fact, is whether the English
version is a translation, a paraphrase, or a complete rewriting. The list of
published collections and studies is not long, for many literatures were not
recorded at all, and others were collected only one time. The two major
collections are Mooney's from the Eastern Cherokee (1900) and Swanton's
volume from the Muskhogean peoples (Creek, Hitchiti, Alabama, Koasati,
Natchez), issued separately (1929) from his ethnographies. The other major collections are: Cherokee (Mooney 1900; Kilpatrick and Kilpatrick
1964, 1966); Choctaw (Bushnell 1909; Swanton 1931); Creek (Brinton
1870; Gatschet 1884; Tuggle 1973; Speck 1907; Swanton 1911, 1922,
1928, 1929); Alabama (Swanton 1929; Martin 1977); Seminole (Greenlee
1945); Yuchi (Speck 1909; Wagner 1931); Catawba (Speck 1934), Caddo
(Dorsey 1905; Swanton 1942), Tunica (Haas 1950). Other texts are scattered through the ethnographic volumes and various journals. The only
attempt to bring all of these sources into a single representative volume is
Lankford's recent study (1987), which has an extensive bibliography.

Genres

Determining the genres of the oral literature of the Southeast is difficult.
Speck observed, on the basis of his work among the Yuchi (1909), that
there were two major genres, a sacred one and a "commonplace" class. In
the latter he included the Trickster stories and animal stories, but that is
not a clear distinction, since in the Southeast the animals are very frequently mythic characters connected with the primal time, and the Trickster appears in narratives which are clearly sacred myths. It is intriguing to
speculate that this late separation of genres may reflect the southeastern
awareness that many of the animal and Trickster stories had been derived
from Africans. If that is true, then the genre separation would actually
signify Native versus imported. Most of the narratives that were collected
fall in the mythic category, since they deal with events of the primal time
or have overtones of culture heroes, power people, and so on. The other
type of narrative which was collected in many other regions—the historical legend of great events in recent times—was rarely collected in the
Southeast. The few which made the transition from field notes to published texts make it clear that the Southeast was not deficient in the telling

of contemporary legends of tribal life. Perhaps it is safer to follow Hultkrantz's suggestions (1981) that all Native American narrative historical legends be termed "myths," since it is difficult to separate religious texts from entertainments. That is certainly true in the Southeast, where animal roles range from the cosmic to the trivial, and the Trickster sometimes resembles the Algonquian culture hero Rabbit, and at others seems the pure African Hare. Verbal forms other than narratives have seldom been collected in the Southeast, even though they certainly existed in varieties of forms.

Beliefs and Plots

As myths, the narratives normally enshrine beliefs about the structure of the cosmos, the nature of its inhabitants, and the customs and traditions of the particular people whose story they are. The general cosmological picture seems to have been the same across the Southeast. The ancient "earth diver" motif is the creation theme, with the resulting image of the earth as an island floating on the sea and covered over with a solid dome supporting the sky world, a world which can be reached by leaping to the other side of the dome at its edge, then climbing into the celestial plane. Birds, as representatives of religious powers (sun, thunderstorms, wind, planets) and as inhabitants of the upper world, are important actors in the basic myths. The Southeast has the distinction of having produced or participated in a visual iconography well known from various prehistoric sites. This "Southeastern Ceremonial Complex" has been a subject of great debate, since its archaeological source leaves the images uninterpreted. One image which does seem to be linked directly to the oral traditions is a hawk or eagle which represents the thunderstorm and thus is part of the general eastern thunderbird concept.

That mythic bird is matched by the alternate figures of the water serpent or the underwater panther, the "piasa" so widely known throughout the Eastern Woodlands. The structural dualism of the celestial sphere over against the underwater world is thus neatly expressed in the opposing figures of the bird and the serpent/panther, and their footprints are present in the oral traditions. The widespread solar worship of the Southeast finds expression in the legends, for both the sun and fire, its earthly representative, are featured in many texts. Curiously, there are examples of a female sun, anomalies which suggest the presence of some alternate cosmological traditions, but they are too ambiguous for clarification. In a similar way, the Choctaw and Alabama retained elements of an emergence myth, but they did not elaborate on levels of terrestrial reality as is found among the southwestern and Meso-American peoples. The emergence is represented as simple fact, with the focus of the mythic tradition on the subsequent migration legend, which seems to be shared by all the speakers of the Muskhogean language family.

The economic base of the peoples of the Southeast is well celebrated in the oral traditions. A wide array of animals appears in both etiological narratives and in stories which deal with the relationships of humans with "people" from other tribes—deer, alligators, serpents, and so on. The shamanistic vision quest pattern is frequently the structure of legends, for the human frequently visits the home of the animal people, where he receives special powers for healing and hunting. Others undergo a transformation into animals, another shamanistic theme.

At the same time that there is a great emphasis on relationship to the animal peoples, the agricultural rooting of the southeasterners is equally well manifested in the literature. Most of the important food and medicine plants are mentioned in the myths, with many of them given a firm origin in etiological or culture-hero legends. Maize, as the chief staple, is featured in many stories, and the variety of origin myths for corn indicates the complex history of the arrival and ethnic relations of the types of maize.

Accompanying the subsistence lore is the usual body of cultural information, from the details of rites to the architecture of the towns—lodges, square grounds, ball play grounds and pole. As is true of any oral literature, the details of daily life are part of the very weave of the stories and can be extracted by the scholar as easily as the young can absorb them for survival knowledge.

Culture heroes abound in the collections, and it is an interesting fact that the Southeast does not possess a single overarching myth of the Manabozho type. Basic themes (theft of fire, origin of tobacco, and so on) are widespread, of course, but the identity of the culture hero changes from text to text, even among the same people. No single character stands out, but it seems impossible to know whether that is a loss from the lore or stems from the original belief system. There are signs of earlier stronger mythic figures, such as the Cherokee Twins and the Creek "Orphan," both of which are probably related to counterparts in other regions, but which have in the Southeast become understated persons in the narratives as collected.

Belief in the "Little People" was widespread, and it is reflected in many narratives, some of which reveal a careful categorization of them by powers and functions. As can be seen in the many hero legends, various kinds of ogres inhabited the southeastern world, from Sharp-buttocks to the Iroquoian Stonecoat of the Cherokee. In later centuries the Europeans found their place in the oral accounts of the kinds of creatures in the world, but they are presented not so much as ogres as fortunate people well favored by the powers. The lack of Southeastern mythic tools to deal with the whites is reflected in the borrowing of African stories which attempt to explain the origin of the different races and their technological differences.

Perhaps the most fascinating single topic in the study of southeastern materials is the problem of the Trickster. As already noted, Africans, whether slave or free, contributed a significant number of animal stories and plot elements, and many of those stories are trickster incidents. The southeastern collection has many such which are clearly Native American, as seen in their distribution across North America, but the African trickster stories fit right in with their variety of trickster figures. So strong is the relationship between the two trickster bodies of lore that nineteenth-century scholars debated at length and with some rancor the question of African influence. The development of type indexes for Africa has ended the question, for the preponderance of certain types in Africa and the West Indies makes clear the direction of transmission. In the light of that reality, however, the mystery of a single Trickster for the Southeast seems insoluble. The Rabbit is a major figure in the Creek collection, but that person is virtually nonexistent for the Cherokee. Moreover, the Rabbit, which is an important culture-hero/divinity in the Great Lakes region, may be present in the Creek corpus, since so many other northern and Plains connections are apparent. Even so, there is the equally important Hare figure from Africa, and there is always the unknown syncretistic process by which either figure (or both) could have been transformed so as to become a part of the southeastern narrative world. It seems unlikely that the mystery will ever be unraveled, and the student of the Southeast can only long for the relative clarity of a Coyote in attempting to understand the complexity of the ethnic mix and blending of traditions that is the hallmark of the Southeast.

George E. Lankford
Arkansas College

BIBLIOGRAPHY

BAEB = Bureau of American Ethnology Bulletin
BAEAR = Bureau of American Ethnology Annual Report

Brinton, D. G. *National Legend of the Chahta-Muskokee Tribes*. Morrisiana, New York, 1870.
Bushnell, David I. *The Choctaw of Bayou Lacomb, St. Tammany Parish, Louisiana*. BAEB 48, Washington, DC: GPO, 1909.
Dorsey, George A. *Traditions of the Caddo*. Carnegie Institution 41, 1905.
Dundes, Alan. "African Tales Among the North American Indians." *Southern Folklore Quarterly* 29 (1965): 207–19.
Gatschet, Albert S. *A Migration Legend of the Creek Indians*. Philadelphia, 1884.
Greenlee, R. F. "Folktales of the Florida Seminole." *Journal of American Folklore* 58 (1945): 138–44.
Haas, Mary R. *Tunica Texts*. Berkeley: U of California P, 1950.

Hultkrantz, Ake. "Myths in Native American Religions." *Belief and Worship in Native North America.* New York: Syracuse UP, 1981.

Kilpatrick, J. F., and Anna Gritts Kilpatrick. *Friends of Thunder Folktales of the Oklahoma Cherokees.* Dallas: SMU Press, 1964.

———. "The Wahnenauhi Manuscript." BAEB 196, Washington, DC: GPO, 1966.

———. "Eastern Cherokee Folktales: Reconstructed from the Field Notes of Frans M. Olbrechts." BAEB 196, Washington, DC: GPO, 1966.

Lankford, George E. *Native American Legends.* Little Rock: August House, 1987.

Martin, Howard N. *Myths and Folktales of the Alabama-Coushatta Indians.* Austin, Texas: Encino Press, 1977.

Mooney, James. *Myths of the Cherokees.* Washington, DC: BAEAR, 1900.

Speck, Frank G. *The Creek Indians of Taskigi Town.* American Anthropological Society Memoirs 2. Menasha, WI: 1907.

———. *Ethnology of the Yuchi Indians.* University of Pennsylvania: Museum of Anthropology Publications I. Philadelphia, 1909.

———. *Catawba Texts.* New York: Columbia UP, 1934.

Swanton, John R. "Mythology of the Indians of Louisiana and the Texas Coast." *Journal of American Folklore* 20 (1907): 285–89.

———. *Indian Tribes of the Lower Mississippi Valley and the Adjacent Coast of the Gulf of Mexico.* BAEB 43, Washington, DC: GPO, 1911.

———. *Early History of the Creek Indians and Their Neighbors.* BAEB 73, Washington, DC: GPO, 1922.

———. "Social Organization and Social Usages of the Indians of the Creek Confederacy." BAEAR 44, Washington, DC: GPO, 1928: 169–273.

———. *Myths and Tales of the Southeastern Indians.* BAEB 88, Washington, DC: GPO, 1929.

———. *Source Material for the Social and Ceremonial Life of the Choctaw Indians.* BAEB 103, Washington, DC: GPO, 1931.

———. *Source Material on the History and Ethnology of the Caddo Indians.* BAEB 132, Washington, DC: GPO 1942.

Tuggle, W. O. *Shem, Ham, and Japeth: The Papers of W. O. Tuggle.* Athens: U of Georgia P, 1973.

Wagner, Gunter. *Yuchi Tales.* Publications of the American Ethnological Society 13. New York: G. E. Stechert, 1931.

Oral Historical Epic Narratives

Several North American Indian tribes produced narratives of epic proportions dealing with the mythic and historical past. These vary significantly in complexity of form and mode of presentation, ranging from sets of laconic oral formulae to historical epics of advanced prose or poetic form. Two types of subject matter, the chronicle (an annalistic sequence of discrete events) and the fabulistic (emplotted) narrative, are present. Oral presentation is frequently accompanied by a mnemonic aid, such as wampum or pictographs.

It is difficult to generalize about when these forms first appeared in the Native oral literatures as a distinct genre; each case must be considered separately. Subject matter often deals with the origins of the tribe and its migration to and settlement in a given area as a series of events which are presumed to have taken place long before the arrival of the Europeans. More rarely, a single event is regarded as central to the narrative. The traditions themselves, however, must have developed through a long process involving several stages. Because the epic-forming tendency often appears to be the result of intertribal experiences, the final and more advanced shape of the narrative probably occurred as part of the process of tribal confederation, or even later. The arrival of Europeans seems to have intensified the process of composition in some cases and stifled it in others. Where strong disintegrating tendencies were at work, only mere rudiments of the narrative survived.

Evidence of these epic oral historical narratives exists from colonial times. Tribal "genealogies" are sometimes mentioned by such authors as John Lawson or the Moravians Ziesberger and Loskiel among the Delawares. Cushman mentions the succession of "Suns" as governors of the Natchez. Charles Beatty speaks of the wampum records of the Algonkians.

Adair writes of historical records of the Creeks, and Haywood of the Cherokees. Almost every traveler through the New York State region mentions sundry details of the Great League epic, although it was understood at the time to be entirely fictitious and the basis for rhetoric. The mode of perpetuating this historical knowledge was often mentioned, and focused especially on the narratives' recitation during acts of succession of leadership. Such narratives were reproduced in full at general councils of the Iroquois Confederacy or at certain points during principal tribal or intertribal ceremonies, such as the Green Corn ceremony of the Creeks or Cherokees. Since vital details and ideas in these narratives were regarded as sacred by Indians and kept from the eyes of strangers, the nature of these narratives and their epic character were often recognized only at a much later date.

The Wallamolum and Chronicles of the Northeastern Algonkians

The Walam Olum (more correctly, Wallamolum) or Red Score, an old chronicle of proto-Algonkian migrations, survived within the Delaware or Leni Lenape tribe. It was brought to public light in 1820 by Rafinesque, who received it as a gift from a Dr. Ward in Indiana, who in turn got it from the White River community of Delawares. The Wallamolum tradition is preserved in two media, consisting of 183 pictographs, originally painted in red on wooden sticks (hence the name Red Score), each accompanied by a verse in the Delaware language which textualized the traditional interpretation of the pictograph.

In Rafinesque's papers, the content of these verses is organized into five sections. The first tells of the creation of the world and the people and of the primordial harmony that prevailed in the beginning (twenty-four pictographs). The second describes the deluge myth, a disaster brought upon the people by the Great Serpent from which they are rescued by Nanapush, together with the Turtle and a "daughter of the manito" (sixteen pictographs). The third section, in Western terms, shifts from mythology to the mythologization of history, telling of the beginning of the Delaware migration from the fabulous Turtle Land to the Snake Land or island via a strait covered with ice (twenty pictographs). The fourth section begins with a description of life in the "land of the Pines" and continues the record of the migration by enumerating chiefs and marking the significant events of the term of leadership of each. Having crossed the Nemassippi (Mississippi) River, the Lenape defeat the mysterious Talligewi people and occupy their lands (sixty-four pictographs). The fifth and final section tells of coming to "Sassafras Land" (Pennsylvania?) and to the seacoast, and of local wars and the separation of tribes. It ends with the arrival of whites, and the question: "Friendly people with great possessions: who are they?" (fifty-nine pictographs). In all, the Wallamolum mentions the names of ninety-eight chiefs and twenty tribes, some of which have been tentatively identified as the Cherokees, Hurons, Shawnees, Nanticokes, and others.

The Lenape text appeared to Brinton to be distinctly metrical; it is unified by assonance and repetition, which often produce the effect of rhyme. The principal structural dynamic is the opposition between "Turtle Land" as the place of mythological harmony and "Snake Land" as the sphere of all unknown and hostile elements. Semimythological places mentioned along the route of migration contribute to the atmosphere of a heroic age in which the epic tribe, the "men among men," move from chaos toward cultural stability.

"Wallamolum" appears to be the term for a genre of similar chronicles which were known among the Lenape and perhaps some of the related tribes who entered the confederacy with them. The structure of the chronicle is many-layered, reflecting a long process of development. Thus the content of sections 4 and 5 seems more traditional, whole sections 1 and 2 and parts of 3 may have been added later from myths in response to a need for tribal self-valorization during the turmoil of the colonial period. As an epic, the Wallamolum is unique, the only more-or-less-complete narrative to reflect the culture and history of tribes north of Mexico which retains its pictographic form.

The authenticity of the chronicle has been questioned, especially in the second half of this century, despite the fact that the text was apparently recorded by a non-Indian from an Indian recitation. Most scholars of the chronicle, however, from Squier to Brinton, Weslager, Speck, and Voegelin never doubted the genuinely aboriginal origin of the Wallamolum. There are three English translations, by Rafinesque (1836, slightly altered by Squier in 1849), Brinton (1833), and E. Voegelin (1954).

The many mythological parallels between elements of the Wallamolum and the general oral historical tradition of eastern Algonkians (including the crossing-the-ice motif, the creation story, the deluge, and migration from the west) support claims for the authenticity of the text. An interesting "Fragment on the history of the Linapis since about 1600 when the Wallamolum closes," given in English, also comes from Rafinesque. It resembles the chronicle in form, adding twenty verses of lamentations dealing with the history of Delaware-white relations during colonial times. Although "Lekhibit" (a corruption of the "Lekhitin" in the fifth section of the Wallamolum) is mentioned as the author of the chronicle, he apparently was only one of many recordkeepers.

Other historical narratives among the Algonkians are underdeveloped. One fragment of a similar chronicle with the crossing-the-ice motif has been recorded from the Algonkian-influenced Tuscarora (Wallace and Reyborn 1951). Different communities of Ojibwa/Chippewa possess pictographic birchbark scrolls containing sacred Midewiwin maps with schematic rendering of the creation and migration route. Only the succession of place names with scanty commentary remains.

National Legends of the Creeks and Cherokees

The so-called national (sometimes "origin") legends of the southeastern tribes have come mainly from the Choctaws and Chickasaws, but they are also known among the Cherokees, who are Iroquoians culturally influenced by the Creeks.

We possess only abbreviated or fragmented versions, which were often handed down in the form of mythic narratives. Earlier versions, though, show traces of formulaic and even rhythmical organization. The best preserved is the Chekilli version or the Kashita migration legend, which was presented to Europeans by Chekilli, chief of the Creeks, in 1733. It tells of the Kashita's coming from the west, the acquisition of magical talismans, and medicines (four herbs and the sacred fire). Functionally important is the magic red-and-white-striped pole, which directed the way during the course of the Kashita's migration. Having crossed the Mississippi River, the Kashita come to the Southeast, where they settle and establish a confederacy after a dispute with rival tribes, the question of sovereignty being solved either by a ball-stick game or a scalp acquisition contest. In other versions, two legendary brothers, Chahta and Chikasha, lead the migration and in the end separate. A recurring motif, the carrying of the bones of their deceased ancestors, is resolved with the burial of the bones inside a sacred mound named Nanih Waiya. "Living mounds," which make noise and contain bones from which assistance may be secured if needed, abound in southeastern Indian folklore. The Taskay Mico version is shorter, but complements the Chekilli version.

Thus it appears that the earlier versions are closer to the traditional form, which deteriorated significantly from the rapid acculturation of the southeastern tribes, the effects of the removal policy, and so on. The genre has been studied by Brinton, Gatschet, and Swanton. The only known Native-language text (Gatschet 1884) is actually a back translation from English.

There are evidences that similar narratives were common among the Cherokees, who called them "eloh" (Meredith and Milam 1975). However, these vanished very early in the historical period. There are two or three retellings and one attempt to restore the narrative. In content, "eloh" resemble the national legend of the Creeks, differing in some motifs. In the early ethnographic literature, there are scattered mentions of mnemonic aids; Adair tells of bead annals, and Chekilli's version originally appeared on a hide.

Narrative Histories of the Plains Tribes

Epic oral historical narratives did not develop as a prominent genre among Plains tribes. Still, one characteristic genre which did develop to become a part of the whole Plains cultural complex in the historical period seems related to this discussion. This is the winter count. The winter counts of the Dakotas are not epics, but pictographic calendar histories covering a number of years, each picture marking one event for a single year. Practically no formulas are present to save the "name" of the year. Most calendars come from the Dakota bands and present band histories. At least nine are known; others are in archives or mentioned in the literature (Brown Hat or Battiste Good, years 1700–1879, Brule; Lone Dog, years 1800–71, Yanktonai; Red Horse Owner, years 1786–1968, Oglala). The only one in Dakota is Ben Kindle's, years 1759–1925. The Kiowa winter counts are more recent, having been adopted from the Dakota; six are known. There is one Blackfeet winter count (Bad Head, years 1810–83). Winter counts were usually kept by the appointed historians. The events to be recorded were discussed by the elders before being painted onto the buffalo hide.

So far, the only known epic historical narrative from the Plains area emerged among the members of the Dhegiha Confederacy, the Osages in particular. The genre of *wi-gi-e*, or mythological epic poems (from 300 to 1,500 lines in length) was studied by Francis LaFlesche, himself an Osage. The narratives tell the Osage story of their creation, their mythological journey from the sky, and their quest for sacred life-symbols. The epic quality is apparent in the well-developed system of parallelisms, repetitions, and formulae, and even fixed line endings. The historic plain is vague, only hinted at through the content; the hero is the epic tribe (the "children") and the ancestors accomplish glorious deeds.

The Great League Narratives of the Iroquois

These cluster around the central event of Iroquois history, the forming of the Great League (Great Peace, Great Law) Confederacy. Although parts of these narratives have been known from colonial times, their publication and serious study began only at the end of the last century. Then it became clear that there are three bodies of material within the cycle. One is the Condoling Council or Condolence Ritual, which is rooted in a precolonial-period Feast for the Dead. The other two emerged with the development of the League. "The Constitution of the Six Nations" (the Ever-Binding Law) and the Deganawideh legend tell the story of the actual founding of the League. With the formation of the confederacy, the three were brought together. Many existing versions show that under natural conditions, the general plot comprises vital elements of all three narratives, the nucleus being the Deganiwideh or Peacemaker legend. The Huron demigod

Deganawideh and the Onondaga chief, Hiawatha (Ayonhawatha, Hayowentha), cooperate for the purpose of uniting the tribes and establishing lasting peace. The first is exiled from his tribe, while the second is dispossessed by a gorgon-like cannibal monster, Atotarho (Thadodaho). Nevertheless, in five years' time they succeed in uniting the five tribes of the Iroquois to form the League. This could be done only after the Condolence Ritual had been performed over Hiawatha and, in its pacification aspect, over Thadodaho.

The Condolence Ritual in full consists of several parts, the most important being the address "At the wood's edge" with its three "rare words" of Requickening; the glorification elegy, "Roll Call of the Founders," wherein all fifty chiefs are named; and the remaining fifteen "words" of the Requickening address. Six songs are sung, and then the appeal to the new candidate to replace the deceased chief is sounded. The incorporation of the Condolence material into the epic has enlarged the scope of its meaning. The Peacemaker legend events are followed by the Constitution, the wampums of the Ever-Binding Law, which in its longest known form comprises 117 articles and is full of metaphorical formulae.

The impact of Native historical narratives upon the growth of Native American literature has been considerable, from the development of ideological and cultural imagery, such as Turtle Island, to D. Q. University, the appearance of Iroquoian philosophy in journalism, and the treatment of League ideas in the poetry of Maurice Kenny, especially his *Blackrobe*. The principles of the winter count have been incorporated into the fiction of Momaday, Dallas Chief Eagle, James Welch, and others, while the *wi-gi-e* tradition figures in the work of John Joseph Mathews.

Alexander Vaschenko
A. M. Gorky Institute of World Literature
Moscow, Russia

BIBLIOGRAPHY

Primary Sources

Beauchamp, W. M. "Civil, Religious and Mourning Councils and Ceremonies of Adoption of the New York Indians." *New York State Museum Bulletin 113*. Albany: State Museum, 1907. 341–51.

Brinton, D. G. *The National Legend of the Chahta-Muskokee Tribe*. New York: Morrisania, 1870.

———. *The Lenape and Their Legends*. Philadelphia: D. G. Brinton, 1885.

Fenton, William, ed. *Parker on the Iroquois*. Syracuse: U of Syracuse P, 1968.

Gatschet, A. S. *A Migration Legend of the Creek Indians*. Philadelphia: D. G. Brinton, 1884.

Hale, Horatio. *The Iroquois Book of Rites*. 1883. Rpt. Toronto: U of Toronto, 1965.

LaFlesche, Francis. *War Ceremony and Peace Ceremony of the Osage Indians*. Bureau of American Ethnology Bulletin 101. Washington, DC: GPO, 1939.

Lawson, John. *The History of Carolina*. Raleigh: 1860.

Loskiel, G. H. *History of the Mission of the United Brethren Among the Indians of North America*. London, 1794.

Mallery, Garrick. *Picture Writing of the North American Indians*. Tenth Annual Report of the Bureau of American Ethnology. Washington, DC: GPO, 1893.

Starr, Emmet. *Early History of the Cherokees, Embracing Aboriginal Customs, Religion, Laws, Folk Lore and Civilization*. Claremore, OK: Emmet Starr, 1817.

Swanton, John R. *Source Material for the Social and Ceremonial Life of the Choctaw Indians*. Bureau of American Ethnology Bulletin 103. Washington, DC: GPO, 1931.

Vaschenko, Alexander. *Historical-Epic Folklore of the North American Indians: Typology and Poetics*. (In Russian.) Moscow: Academy of Science Press, 1989.

The Walam Olum or Red Score: The Migration Legend of the Lenni-Lenape or Delaware Indians. Eds. C. and E. Voegelin. Indianapolis: Indiana Historical Society, 1954.

Zeisberger, David. "Some Remarks and Annotations Concerning the Traditions, Customs, Languages, &c. of the Indians of North America." *Olden Time* I (1846): 271–81.

Secondary Sources

Meredith, H. L., and V. E. Milam. "A Cherokee Vision of Eloh." *The Indian Historian* 8.4 (1975): 19–23.

Wallace, Anthony F. C., and W. D. Reyborn. "Crossing the Ice: A Migration Legend of the Tuscarora Indians." *International Journal of American Linguistics* 12 (1951): 42–47.

The Native American Trickster

This article reviews the most popular, problematic, and powerful figure in Native American literature, follows the ubiquitous trickster through various incarnations in oral and written literature, and examines significant scholarly interpretations of the meanings and uses of this promiscuous figure. Trickster is popular, problematic, and powerful for the same reason—he/she knows no bounds, lives in a world before/beyond classification, and is always in motion. Timeless, universal, and indestructible, this "ragged four-legged verb" eludes and disrupts all orders of things, including the analytic categories of academics (Smith 1983:192). Paradoxically, trickster is "multiform and ambiguous" by definition (Turner 1968:580). The "irreducible polymorphism" attests, Serres would argue, to the primacy, the necessity of disorder (Serres 1982:xxvii). Mythic and primordial, this champion of possibility and enemy of spatial, temporal, and cultural boundaries has been variously conceived in Jungian terms as "an archetypal structure of extreme antiquity," from the Freudian perspective as the personification of the id or life principle, and in the Navajo world view as "a symbol of that chaotic everything" (Jung 1956:200; Roheim 1952:193; Toelken 1969:231).

In the Native American imagination, trickster assumes a variety of masks and personae. For some he/she is raven, for others rabbit, for many coyote; and it is as coyote that trickster has crossed over into the Anglo imagination. For convenience, in the remainder of this article, we will use the terms coyote and trickster interchangeably. For over a century, coyote stories have been collected, transcribed, and translated by anthropologists, linguists, and folklorists, who have struggled to make sense of this confusing and amusing character as he/she appears in a variety of cultural forms and genres from jokes to sacred myths to contemporary painting. Not surprisingly, trickster transgresses both genres and periods of tribal literature (Wiget 1990:7). In mythic time and narrative, coyote appears as one of the first beings, responsible for "the world-as-it-is," in historic legend he takes on the white man, and in the contemporary paintings of Fonseca and writings of Vizenor, he is the crazy, creative Indian negotiating urban America. Polysemic as well as multifunctional, coyote and his stories just keep "going along," somewhere beyond interpretation, epitomizing resistance and survival. (See Bright for a discussion of parallels between the biological coyote and his literary cousins in this respect.) As such, he/she has inspired ancient storytellers as well as both Indian and Anglo writers in recent decades.

Whatever animal mask trickster wears, he is always understood as human—a human, however, who can shift his shape at will and for whom the human/animal boundary does not exist. Wadkjunkaga, the Winnebago "Foolish One," transforms himself into a deer (Radin 1956); coyote rides a bus to Second Mesa (Silko 1981:260); raven shoots arrows and carves canoes (Stone 1971). Sexual ambiguity is also characteristic of trickster, despite his repeated appearance as an ambient phallus. Tricksters frequently transform themselves into women and are sometimes represented as hermaphrodites. Moreover, female coyotes are not unknown in either traditional or contemporary Native American literatures (see Kendall 1980; Haile 1984; Silko 1981). That trickster is generically male and characterized by exaggerated phallicism may be the result of male bias in the collection and interpretation of trickster compounded by the Anglo bias of identifying Indian women with stability (Wiget 1990).

While trickster's animal/human transformations and gender ambiguity have not vexed interpreters, the coincidence of the sacred and the scatological, of culture hero and fool, in a single figure certainly has. Coyote steals, lies, and lusts and in the process shapes and endows the world as we know it. Countless scholars have tried to explain or explain away this characterological ambiguity. Nineteenth-century commentators, notably Daniel Brinton, espoused a devolutionary approach and saw trickster as a fallen god. Boas and his followers reversed this, reading trickster as embodying and evolving from an earlier stage of consciousness, as do Jung and Radin as well. These and other explanations of the combination of disparate elements into one mythical personality are summarized by Ricketts.

In recent decades, the most compelling interpretations of coyote's ambiguous and contradictory nature have derived from a structuralist perspective. Arguing that "mythical thought always progresses from the awareness of oppositions toward their resolution," Lévi-Strauss (1967:221) describes trickster as a "mediator," occupying, as do raven and coyote, a position between two polar terms—herbivores and carnivores—and being of ambiguous and equivocal character, i.e., scavengers and omnivores. Concerned with the dialectic of structure and anti-structure, Turner also places trickster betwixt and between categories in a position that he describes as "liminal" (1968:576). This mythic "coincidence of opposite processes and notions in a single representation" (Turner 1967:98) may also be described, following Bakhtin and Julia Kristeva, as "dialogic" or, following Robertson Smith, as "the ambiguity of the sacred." The function of such sacred ambiguity, of such anomalous, "dirty" characters as trickster, is not, as Mary Douglas argues, simply mediation between binary oppositions, but reflexive, provoking a recognition of cultural categories for "the fictive, man-made, arbitrary creations that they are" (Douglas 1970:200; see also Babcock-Abrahams, "Frogs" 1975). Babcock-Abrahams summarizes and applies these various theories of order and disorder to the phenomenon of trickster in general, and to the Winnebago trickster in particular, and suggests six social functions played by his antisocial narratives (Babcock-Abrahams, "Trickster" 1975). Regrettably, however, too few collectors of coyote's stories have solicited an explanation of trickster's inexplicable behavior from the storytellers themselves. When Barre Toelken did ask about coyote's contradictory deeds, the Navajo Yellowman told him, "If he did not do all those things, then those things would not be possible in the world," for "through the stories everything is made possible" (Toelken 1969 [see also Toelken 1987 and Wiget 1990 for further discussion of the differential meanings of a particular tale]).

As a "negation offering possibility" (Babcock-Abrahams, "Trickster" 1975:182), the adventures of coyote constitute metasocial commentary, for by breaking rules, he/she throws into sharp relief the relationships, categories, and patterns of his culture. His tales are at the same time a form of metanarration, for telling stories is, after all, coyote's *modus vivendi*. Not surprisingly, therefore, the contemporary Native American storyteller frequently presents him/herself in the ratty fur of coyote.

Coyote creeps into contemporary writing with great frequency and ease. "Cultural contact"—that is, the conquering of native lands and the colonizing of native people—has created within tribal imaginations a sense of discomfort (at the very least), perhaps best exemplified by the now traditional intrusion into storytelling sessions of the non-Native ethnographer with microphone. This discomfort is the perfect proscenium for the persona of trickster and all his/her revolutionary subversion, inversion, and reflexivity. The liminal space where cultures clash is simply the best place to command power, to confuse the "enemy," and to spin out a good story.

Since several excellent surveys of contemporary Native American poetry and fiction exist, we will examine only a few of trickster's appearances in recent Native American literature. (See Lincoln 1983; Smith 1987; Wiget 1985.) The first of these reincarnations occurs in N. Scott Momaday's (Kiowa) *House Made of Dawn* (1968). The protagonist, Abel, must find a cure for the sickness that stems from his mixed heritage and the spiritual rupture that manifests itself in inarticulateness. (See Evers 1977 for further discussion.) The words are eventually given to him by the Right Reverend John Big Bluff Tosamah, who delivers them in his great dog voice with all the ambiguity and clowning for which trickster is well known. Not accidentally, Tosamah's sermon, *The Way to Rainy Mountain*, shares its title with Momaday's own very popular book (1969). By incorporating these same words into Abel's healing process, through the mouth of Tosamah, Momaday comments extratextually on the role of the novelist, specifically the Native American novelist. Perhaps more important, the invocation of the oral traditions and tribal history in *The Way to Rainy Mountain* emphasizes trickster's ability to teach and heal through contraries, parables, and the collective tribal imagination. So, in this first novel of the Native American renaissance, trickster emerges as central to Abel's reconciliation with his tribal past and is identified with the novelist himself, and the craft of fiction in general.

In the work of Leslie Marmon Silko (Laguna), coyote undergoes a number of transformations; while still resembling the traditional figures from Boas's Keresan collections, Silko's coyotes usually wear the sheep's clothing of the iconoclast. In "Coyote Holds a Full House in His Hands," the final piece in *Storyteller* (1981), trickster wears a fringed vinyl jacket and "heals" women by massaging their thighs with juniper ash. This aspect of trickster invites comparison with southern white tricksters and confidence men, such as the Rainmaker and the faith healer, who satisfy their appetites and still effect beneficial change for their marks. In *Ceremony* (1977), trickster becomes healer. Betonie, like Momaday's Tosamah, uses medicine—sand paintings, magazines, stars, and stories—from both cultures to heal Tayo of his need to vomit up what the war and white culture have forced down his throat. In Betonie, Silko demonstrates one of trickster's best attributes—his ability as accomplished scavenger and *bricoleur* to use beneficially what appears to be the waste of human cultural existence.

Simon Ortiz (Acoma) and Gerald Vizenor (Ashininabe) are two writers whose names and work are nearly synonymous with trickster (on Ortiz, see Smith 1983, Lincoln 1984, Wiget 1986; on Vizenor, see Scholer 1984). Their use of and reliance on trickster demonstrates the symbiosis between trickster/storyteller in dramatically different ways. Ortiz claims trickster's power to conglomerate storytelling, poetry, and politics in order to fuel the revolution that will tear down barriers and build "common walls" (see Ortiz 1984). *A Good Journey* (1977) follows coyote truckin' along from Canada to Laguna to Los Angeles to Acoma to Florida, stressing the importance of chili, survival, children, and stories. Ortiz fully comprehends and emphasizes the need to participate—to listen, tell, and act—in the stories, because they engender knowledge (Ortiz 1984:59) and tribal knowledge is tribal power that ensures a continuance of tribal identity (see also Wiget 1986).

In both Gerald Vizenor's fiction and scholarship, the ability of trickster to deconstruct order and live a sort of Keatsian negative capability—dwelling in mysteries, fears, and doubts—demonstrates the slipperiness of language itself. In his enigmatic, incomprehensible, ambiguous, ambivalent language, Vizenor encodes and decodes tribal meaning, and opens up the potential of language without for a moment feeling compelled to suggest or fix meaning. For Vizenor, the battleground is academe and trickster a word warrior. Vizenor's recurring tricksters, among them Griever de Hocus and Luster Browne, appear in a number of academic shrines and do what Vizenor calls a cultural striptease, à la Roland Barthes, that tantalizes to expose yet reveals nothing, maybe because there is nothing to reveal. Vizenor's veiled and twisted images call the academic study of urban Native American literature itself into question. In fact, in *Narrative Chance*, Vizenor posits that trickster *is* his/her narration, a language game in him/herself (Vizenor 1989:187).

In contemporary writing, the inversion of gender might just be trickster's best disguise. Silko's "Yellow Woman" (*Storyteller*) and other Kochininako stories are based on the traditional Keresan figure whose power to leave the center of her people and return with gifts—twins, corn, summer—is very similar to the machinations of trickster, who operates boldly on the margin and (sometimes discretely) within the community (see Boas 1928; Haile 1984; and especially Malotki 1987, "Coyote and the Witches"). In many of Silko's stories, the river acts as the liminal space where cultural boundaries are breachable and breached and contrarily fruitful. Other female tricksters might be at work, changing, recombining, revolutionizing: in the fiction of Louise Erdrich (Turtle Mountain Chippewa)—Fleur in *Tracks* (1988) and *The Beet Queen* (1986), in the poetry of Joy Harjo (Creek) or nila northSun (Shoshoni-Chippewa), or in the artistry of Nora Naranjo-Morse (Santa Clara Pueblo) whose figure Pearlene is a playful, clowning alter ego both in clay and in verse.

Doings which are undoings, reorderings through disorderings, epitomize trickster and are the essence of cultural critique. The poetry and fiction of contemporary Native American storytellers such as Silko, Erdrich, Vizenor, northSun, Momaday, and Ortiz attest that trickster is indeed going right along, merrily reinventing, embellishing, and subverting the language, theme, and structure of Native and Euro-American literary traditions. More often than not, trickster today holds a pen, or sits at a typewriter or computer, "processing" words which heal, fool, incite, inspire, anger, and empower all who read in/between the lines. Recent films and videotapes created and/or produced by Native Americans also feature coyote at work either in front of the camera or as the motivating spirit behind it. So it should not surprise us that this "animate principle of disruption" is now read as the deconstructionist of Native American literature (Kroeber 1979) or that he/she is lauded as a role model for radical feminists (Haraway 1988). There is indeed wisdom in this folly, for coyote knows that to know is to eschew fixity for the uncertainty of the journey and he/she just keeps going along, across the desert, the barroom, and the page.

Barbara Babcock
Jay Cox
University of Arizona

BIBLIOGRAPHY

Primary Sources

Boas, Franz. *Keresan Texts.* 2 vols. Publications of the American Ethnological Society 8. 1928.

Bright, William. *A Coyote Reader.* Berkeley: U of California P, 1992.

Erdrich, Louise. *The Beet Queen.* New York: Holt, 1986.

———. *Tracks.* New York: Holt, 1988.

Haile, Father Berard. *Navajo Coyote Tales: The Curly to Aheedliinii Version.* American Tribal Religions Series, No. 8. Gen. ed. Karl Luckert. Lincoln: U of Nebraska P, 1984.

Harjo, Joy. *She Had Some Horses.* New York: Thunder's Mouth Press, 1983.

Kendall, Martha. *Coyote Stories.* International Journal of American Linguistics, Native American Texts Series. Chicago: U of Chicago P, 1980.

Malotki, Ekkehart, ed. *Hopi Coyote Tales.* American Tribal Religions Series, No. 9. Gen. ed. Karl Luckert. Lincoln: U of Nebraska P, 1987.

Momaday, N. Scott. *House Made of Dawn.* New York: Harper & Row, 1968.

———. *The Way to Rainy Mountain.* Albuquerque: U of New Mexico P, 1969. New York: Ballantine, 1972.

Naranjo-Morse, Nora. *Earth Hands and Life.* Heard Museum Exhibit and Ceramic Figures Symposium. Phoenix, Arizona. January 20–21, 1989.

northSun, nila. *Diet Pepsi and Nacho Cheese.* Fallon, NV: Duck Down Press, 1977.

Ortiz, Simon. *A Good Journey.* Tucson: Sun Tracks and U of Arizona P, 1977.

———. Introduction. *Earth Power Coming: Short Fiction in Native American Literature.* Ed. Ortiz. Tsaile, AZ: Navajo Community College Press, 1983. vii–ix.

———. "Always the Stories: A Brief History and Thoughts on My Writing." In Schöler (1984), 57–69.

Radin, Paul. *The Trickster.* New York: Philosophical Library, 1956.

Silko, Leslie Marmon. *Ceremony.* New York: Viking, 1977.

———. *Storyteller.* New York: Seaver Books, 1981.

Vizenor, Gerald. "Luminous Thighs: Mythic Tropisms." *Genre* 18 (1985): 131–49.

———. *The Trickster of Liberty: Tribal Heirs to Wild Baronage.* Minneapolis: U of Minnesota P, 1988.

———, ed. *Narrative Chance.* Albuquerque: U of New Mexico P, 1989.

Secondary Sources

Babcock-Abrahams, Barbara. "'A Tolerated Margin of Mess': The Trickster and His Tales Reconsidered." *Journal of the Folklore Institute* 11 (1975): 147–86. Rpt. in *Critical Essays on Native American Literature.* Ed. Andrew Wiget. Boston: G. K. Hall, 1985. 153–85.

———. "Why Frogs Are Good to Think and Dirt Is Good to Reflect On." *Soundings* 58 (1975): 167–81.

Bright, William. "The Natural History of Old Man Coyote." *Recovering the Word: Essays on Native American Literature.* Eds. Brian Swann and Arnold Krupat. Berkeley: U of California P, 1987. 339–87.

Douglas, Mary. *Purity and Danger: An Analysis of Concepts of Pollution and Taboo.* London: Pelican, 1970.

Evers, Larry. "Words and Place: A Reading of *House Made of Dawn.*" *Western American Literature* 11 (1977): 297–320. Rpt. in *Critical Essays on Native American Literature.* Ed. Andrew Wiget. Boston: G. K. Hall, 1985. 211–30.

Haraway, Donna. "Situated Knowledges: The Science Question in Feminism and the Privilege of Partial Perspective." *Feminist Studies* 14 (1988): 575–99.

Jung, Carl. "On the Psychology of the Trickster Figure." In Radin (1956): 195–211.

Kroeber, Karl. "Deconstructionist Criticism and American Indian Literature." *Boundary* 2.7 (1979): 73–89.

Lévi-Strauss, Claude. *Structural Anthropology.* Trans. Claire Jacobson and Brooke Grundfest Schoepf. New York: Doubleday, 1967.

Lincoln, Kenneth. *Native American Renaissance.* Berkeley: U of California P, 1983.

———. "Common Walls: The Poetry of Simon Ortiz." In Scholer (1984), 79–94.

Ricketts, Mac Linscott. "The North American Indian Trickster." *History of Religions* 5 (1966): 327–50.

Roheim, Geza. "Culture Hero and Trickster in North American Mythology." *Papers of 29th International Congress of Americanists* (1952): 190–94.

Schöler, Bo, ed. "Trickster and Storyteller: The Sacred Memories and True Tales of Gerald Vizenor." *Coyote Was Here: Essays on Contemporary Native American Literary and Political Mobilization.* Århus, Denmark: U of Århus, 1984. 134–44.

Serres, Michel. *Hermes: Literature, Science, Philosophy.* Baltimore: Johns Hopkins UP, 1982.

Smith, Patricia Clark. "Coyote Ortiz: Canis Latranslatrans." *Studies in American Indian Literature.* Ed. Paula Gunn Allen. New York: MLA, 1983. 192–210.

———. "Coyote's Sons, Spider's Daughters: Western American Indian Poetry 1968–1983." *Literary History of the American West.* Fort Worth: Texas Christian UP, 1987. 1067–78.

Stone, Peter. "Reciprocity: The Gift of a Trickster." Paper delivered to "The Social Use of Metaphor" Symposium. 69th Annual Meeting of American Anthropological Association. San Diego, California, 1970. Rev. draft, 1971.

Toelken, Barre. "The 'Pretty Language' of Yellowman: Genre, Mode and Texture in Navajo Coyote Narratives." *Genre* 2 (1969): 1–25. Rpt. in *Folklore Genres.* Ed. Dan Ben-Amos. Austin: U of Texas P, 1979. 145–70.

———. "Life and Death in the Navajo Coyote Tales." *Recovering the Word: Essays on Native American Literature.* Eds. Brian Swann and Arnold Krupat. Berkeley: U of California P, 1987. 388–401.

Turner, Victor W. "Betwixt and Between: The Liminal Period in *Rites de Passage.*" *The Forest of Symbols: Aspects of Ndembu Ritual.* Ed. Victor W. Turner. Ithaca, NY: Cornell UP, 1967.

———. "Myth and Symbol." *International Encyclopedia of Social Sciences.* 1968. 576–82.

Wiget, Andrew. *Native American Literature.* Boston: Twayne, 1985.

———. *Simon Ortiz.* Boise State University Western Writers Series. Boise, ID: Boise State U, 1986.

———. "His Life in His Tail: The Native American Trickster and the Literature of Possibility." *The New American Literary History.* New York: MLA, 1990.

Oratory

Some form of speechmaking has been called by a form of the Latin word *oratoria*, or a derivative, such as the English "oratory," since the time of the Roman republic. Oratory's fortunes as human-to-human speech (the word was also applied to prayers) waned under feudalism but waxed under classicism and republicanism in the seventeenth, eighteenth, and nineteenth centuries in the debate, or myriad of subdebates, over the creation of the modern world. In those centuries, Europeans brought oratory to Indians and, somewhat to their surprise, received oratory back from them. Thus were Indians' speeches from Metacomet's (1660) to Chief Joseph's (1877) entered into anthologies, mostly American, of classic elocution.

This is one meaning of Native American oratory: speeches addressed to Euroamericans in defense of Indian life, property, and liberty. One naturally supposes that Indians used oratory or something like it on other occasions; and one wishes to know how such speeches compared with those given to Europeans. Was there a single Native oratory or were there many, which varied according to language, culture, and setting? I think that there were many, of which only a few are known, and I will try to show how those few differed from the oratory that was addressed to Europeans. Thus, the present article has three parts: a trial definition of oratory, a discussion of the Indian oratory that responded to the European expansion, and a sampling into studies of other more or less Native oratorical traditions.

An oration is a speech by a mortal person to mortal people. The speech argues a position on what is good for the community. The key words in this definition are "argues" and "community." By the first, I mean that the speech must give reasons for the position that it takes. It must be an engine of persuasion with equivalents for such English expressions as "therefore,"

"I think," "it is false that," etc. Thus, if there is an argumentative function for language (and it would fall between Roman Jakobson's referential and cognitive functions), then oratory, although perhaps not alone, serves that function. Second, the speech, the speaker, and the speaker's community must allow for and anticipate disagreement. This disagreement might be informal and delayed, or formal and immediate, but it must be allowed, that is, institutionalized. Thus, I tie the notion of oratory to the practice of contentious (although not necessarily rowdy or unreasonable) communal argument: politics.

There is no doubt that to the European colonists, oratory was attached to politics, specifically to parliamentary politics. As the colonists came, their home states were in debate and revolution over the constitution of parliamentary systems, e.g., how parliaments should represent the citizenry, how parliamentary seats should be filled, and the relation between parliament (senate, chamber of deputies, etc.) and monarchy. When those issues were debated, it was by oratory.

We immediately see what was peculiar about Indians engaging in oratory with or against Europeans: Indians were not or did not think that they were citizens or subjects of the states to whose representatives they were orating. I believe that in the early stages of colonization the colonizing states did think so, but, paradoxically, this may be why little oratory was recorded from that time. Thus, the monarchies and empires of Spain, England, Holland, and France extended subject status to Indians, with (Spain) or without (England, Holland, France) physically conquering them. It appears that as subjects, these Indians did little orating against their monarchical sovereigns.

They did something similar, however. In New Spain, for example, they routinely petitioned the colonial courts for redress in documents written in Indian languages, called *Titles* (Titulos). Munroe Edmonson characterizes this literature as "a litigious and industrious attempt on the part of the doomed noble lineages to stave off their destruction by wearing Spanish courts with petitions and appeals . . . with all the charm of a collection of legal briefs" (1985:119). (The Spanish conquest subordinated but did not liquidate the stratified, ranked Native social system.)

The most famous Indian oratory was occasioned by the westward advance of the U.S. republic, under whose laws Indians were not subjects but on the contrary were sovereign and, therefore (not fully or abjectly subject), foreigners.

The oratory occurred in diplomacy, not in parliament. This may have been a novelty both for the classical European oratorical tradition and for European diplomacy. Conventional diplomacy, I believe, was conducted in quiet meetings of ambassadors. Oratory was absent in moments of diplomatic contact because, by convention, the place for oratory was in parliament. Diplomacy was supposed to be undemonstrative, canny, and poker-faced. Oratory was highly demonstrative. Sometimes it was florid, but, more to the point, it always explored the implications of an opponent's concept of what was good for the community. Thus we have the classical (so-called in the nineteenth century) oration's seven-part scheme: the entrance or *exordium*, to catch the audience's attention; the narration, to set forth facts; the exposition or definition, to define terms and open issues; the proposition, to clarify the points at issue and state exactly what is to be proved; the confirmation, to set forth arguments for and against; the confutation or refutation, to refute the opponent's arguments; and the conclusion or *epilogue*, to sum up the arguments and stir the audience (Holman 1981:311). Such a speech is designed for debate. It is adversarial and it supposes that adversarial to be negative. The classical oration deals with both sides. It encapsulates the opposing position and tries to show that its own position is better.

The following bit of text exemplifies that concept of oratory. It is from a petition sent by the Cherokees to Congress in 1829. The text is in English and was transmitted only in that language. I do not know if there was a written Cherokee original or translation, but there is circumstantial evidence that it was a specialized foreign affairs product. The names attached to the document include a mixture of English-style (for Cherokees, however) and "Indian" names, the former signed and the latter marked with an "X." The man designated as Speaker of the Council has an Indian name with an "X." He was at least somewhat dissociated from the English petition, which reads:

> From time immemorial, our common Father, who is in heaven, has given our ancestors the land we occupy. . . . Permit us to ask you humbly what better right a nation can have to a country than the right of inheritance and immemorial possession? . . . At what time have we lost it? . . . Are we being reproached for having fought under the flag of . . . Great Britain in the War of Independence? If this is the crime . . . why, in the first treaty following this war, did you not declare that we had lost the ownership of our lands? Why did you not insert an article . . . "The United States wishes to grant peace to the Cherokees but to punish them . . . it is declared that they shall . . . be subjected to departing when their neighboring states demand that they shall do so?" That was the moment to speak thus. . . . (de Tocqueville 1969:38)

Official America, too, had a style for talking to Indians that was different from the style used in Congress. It was a patronizing and unctuous style, as the following excerpt shows:

> Brethren,
> Our business with you, besides rekindling the ancient councilfire, and renewing the covenant . . . is . . . to inform you of the advice that was given . . . by your wise forefathers . . . when Cannassateego spoke to us, the white people. . . . Our forefathers rejoiced to hear . . . these words. . . . They said to one another, "The six nations are a wise people. Let us hearken to them, and take their counsel, and teach our children to follow it. Our old men have done so. They have frequently taken a

single arrow, and said, Children, see how easy it is broken . . . divided a single man may destroy you; united, you are a match for the whole world." We thank the Great God that we are all united . . . at Philadelphia, and have sent sixty-five counsellors to speak and act in the name of the whole, and consult for the common good of all people, and of you. . . . (Tooker 1988:309–10)

If the reader thinks that is a polite speech, I agree, but add that it is probably untrue that the whites actually spoke to each other as the Commissioner said.

The following text was created for a delegation of Chippewas who came to Washington in 1864, and is less than classically oratorical because it does not lay bare an opponent's concept of what is good for the community (the Cherokee text does this wickedly, asking in effect, "Why didn't you say forty years ago that as punishment for fighting you, you might wish to remove us?"). This text is near to Edmonson's characterization of the *Titles*, a wearying (but real) list of U.S. failures to live up to past treaties:

1.1. This statement made by the Indians according to the best of their knowledge in regard to the promises made to them while living in peace among themselves.

1.2. At a certain time there came to us a word of our "Great Father" calling us to a Council to be held at Prairies Du Chien. Summer of 1825.

1.3. Then the word of our "Great Father" was made known to us, the result of which [was] proved to be, to know what was the division that the Indians regarded permanently.

1.4. This much the Indian knew was the reason that he was called upon to attend at the Council by his Great Father.

1.5. Again another word from our "Great Father" was reported to us. Your Great Father takes from you your "Tomahawks" and buries them in the earth as deep as his arm can reach so that you will not be able to take it again. . . .

2.4. The next time that the word was spoken to the Indian, was a promise, that there would be a farm opened for him and every one of their villages.

2.5. Then again spoke one of the Commissioners to the Indians; "I shall return to your Great Father, and report to him your condition. I shall tell him how poor his Chippewa Children are. He will send you a price of Two Thousand Dollars. $2000." This we fail to see fulfilled, this promise that our Father made to us. (Nichols 1988:12–13)

Because the text is in paragraph-for-paragraph bilingual alignment, one can see how its particular message is stated in Chippewa. John Nichols has given the Chippewa a new phonemic transcription, given a new running interlinear morphemic classification, and new word glosses, but he hasn't analyzed the text as discourse or literature. Nor will I, except to note sociolinguistically that the old men who ordered it sent to Washington in both languages (we know their names and that they engaged a mixed-blood government interpreter as their scribe) imposed their own talk on America in a way that the Cherokee Speaker of the Council did not.

Interestingly, Washington did not keep or copy the physical document. The Indian Commissioner "booked" the delegation's arrival and a Wisconsin senator wrote some notes on the gist of the statement, but the delegation, whatever their intentions, left with the document they had so carefully made. It was eventually deposited at the Wisconsin Historical Society (Nichols 1988:2). I speculate that this disappointed them, and that their blunt request, unpolished English, and insistence on writing Chippewa were all to blame.

The above were petitions, not debates. What was the linguistic exchange at face-to-face meetings? The main source of information on this is descriptions written shortly after a meeting by white participants. Less abundant are Indian recollections gathered by oral historians some years after the event. From what one can tell, the meetings, while face-to-face, had a certain remoteness due to the need, or preference, for the parties to speak in their own languages.

We lack, I think, Indian-language versions of any of the famous eighteenth- and nineteenth-century orations. From Metacomet to Chief Joseph (I use the sequence given in Sanders and Peek), we know this oratory only in English. Rudolf Kaiser demonstrated the cost of this in a good study of the famous speech of Seattle, a chief of the Suquamish and Duwamish Indians of Puget Sound. The speech was made in 1853 and was first published in a newspaper article dated 1887. The published text was based on notes taken in 1853 by a white man, Dr. Henry Smith. Kaiser, who encountered a version in Germany, has retraced the history of the speech. He points out that the 1887 text accepts the then current U.S. doctrine of Manifest Destiny, while the 1970s version warns of impending white-caused ecological doom. Since there are details in the 1887 version of things that Seattle probably did not know in 1853 (references to slaughtered buffalo on the plains and to transcontinental railroads), it is not known how much to credit Seattle or Smith for this version. And since the 1970s ecology oration was based on the 1887 Manifest Destiny oration, the ecology emphasis is secondary elaboration: not a forgery, but an editing.

If we cannot know Seattle's speech as it was actually given, we can appreciate its derivative use in later oratorical projects. Such is its use in Sanders and Peek's anthology of oratory, a collection of twenty-four speeches that begins on the East Coast, proceeds west to the Pacific (Seattle, but the Smith version), then doubles back to end on the northern plains with Chief Joseph's famous "I will fight no more forever." The titles alone have the power of a single, superoration:

We Find the Christians Depraved, Conestoga Chief
You Have Now Got the Most of Our Lands, Cornplanter
Do Not Ask Us to Give Up the Buffalo for the Sheep, Ten Bears

We Preferred Our Own Way, Crazy Horse
The Surrender Speech of Chief Joseph

Europe did invade North America and did draw Indians into its oratory, as Sanders and Peek indicated, but what separate and diverse oratorical traditions did Indians bring to this conflict, and how did (and do) they use those traditions among themselves? The remainder of this article tries to answer those questions.

Perhaps the most beautiful work of modern scholarship on Native American literature is John Bierhorst's *Four Masterworks of American Indian Literature* (1974). Two of the masterworks in question are ceremonies which Bierhorst presents as scripts for ritual dramas: the Iroquois Condolence Ceremony and the Navajo Night Chant. The other two, entitled "Quetzalcoatl" and "Cuceb," from the Aztecs and Yucatec Mayas respectively, are purely spoken (not enacted) pieces. All four are assumed to have been formed largely free of European influence. Bierhorst's work on each was to "reconstitute" it (define parts, combine and possibly repair fragments), then retranslate (especially the Aztec, in which he is trained) and comment on the whole. He depended on ample published scholarship for each work.

He classified each work as to "style" (in the following order): oratorical, incantatory, bardic, and prophetic. I will start to answer the above questions by applying my definition of oratory to the work he so designated. The Condolence ceremony is occasioned by the death of one of the fifty "sachems" (high councillors or his chiefs) of the Iroquois (Five Nation) Confederacy. Representatives of the confederacy assemble and give speeches about what is good for the community in this crisis. In Bierhorst's analysis, the council of fifty represented the whole of Iroquois nationhood, which was also symbolized as a house on one hand and a woman on the other. "In the vivid imagery of the Condolence texts, 'she' becomes a grieving widow whose eyes fill up with tears, whose throat and ears are clogged with ashes as she grovels in the dead coals in her darkened house" (109). The Condolence ceremony is to cure this woman, who is society, the Iroquois confederacy, and a house. The cure coaxes and gently manipulates her return to normal, civil life. Should the cure fail, "she" (that is, the confederacy) might fly apart in violent dark grief.

The following excerpts offer a taste:

> It is ever true that the organs within the breast and the flesh-body are disordered and violently wrenched without ceasing, and so also is the mind. Now, verily, therefore, there always develop yellow spots within the body. Verily, now, the life forces of the sufferer always become weakened thereby. This ever takes place when the Great Destroyer puts forth excessive ferocity against one in causing such great affliction. (144)
>
> It is this, that where a direful thing befalls a person, that person is invariably covered with darkness, that person becomes blinded with thick darkness itself. It is

always so that the person knows not any more what the daylight is like on the earth, and his mind and life are weakened and depressed. (149)

Now, oh, my offspring, do thou know it, that now the Three Brothers have made their preparations, and now, therefore, let them say, "Now therefore, we make it daylight again for thee. Now, most pleasantly will the daylight continue to be beautiful when again thou wilt look about thee whereon is outspread the handiwork of the Finisher of Our Faculties on the face of the earth." (149–50)

The English diction is almost unchanged from that of Horatio Hale, the first (1883) of a series of translators of still earlier Iroquois-written Native-language scripts of the ceremony. While it now appears dated, a more up-to-date diction would not necessarily be more true to the Iroquois. If English sentence structure is basically different from Iroquois, then the replacement of one variety of English diction with another is tempting (neither can be perfect) but idle unless the retranslator knows the Native language better than the earlier translator. It is an editing toward currency just as was practiced on Seattle's speech, albeit on the level of diction rather than theme.

The ceremony basically consists of speeches by a "clearheaded" and comforting party to a darkened and bereaved party. This two-sided drama is somewhat like the structure of a debate. A language of "clear" versus "dark" thinking is common to both. In both, the resort to this language is temporary, that is, the parties to the verbal exchange cease using this language and go back to normal when the event (ceremony or debate) is finished. But purposes and procedures differ between debate and ceremony: to argue policy (debate) versus to stimulate a mourning party to appoint a new sachem (ceremony); and by mutual accusation (debate) versus mutual acceptance (ceremony) to demonstrate that, for this occasion, one side is clear and the other is darkened. Thus the resemblance is thematic rather than functional, but there is a final similarity to note. Both pertain to sacralized, formalized representative government, and at present there is controversy over how much the U.S. form of that government actually owes to the Iroquois. According to Elizabeth Tooker, Iroquois governmental debate (apart from Condolence rituals) took place at the meeting of the Great Council of the League of the Iroquois, and also at council of the League. The Great Council meetings concerned League diplomacy and the tribal meetings concerned internal affairs. Three points emerged in these meetings: that unanimity was required in all final decisions; that the councils were preoccupied with keeping peace in their sphere (the League, the nation/tribe) and that they appointed war-to-war chiefs who acted in a private, extracouncillor capacity; and that besides the above-mentioned sachem chiefs and war chiefs, there were local, ordinary chiefs with influence and oratorical skills. Red Jacket was one. Such persons were considered potentially disruptive to the Great Council and were not appointed to it (Tooker 1988:313–20). On balance, the Iroquois seemed to know combative oratory and to keep their councils free of it. No written accounts of council proceedings are known to me. The councils in question were those of the League of the eighteenth century as reconstructed by Lewis Henry Morgan in the 1840s. Iroquois politics have continued until today, but their internal workings are probably more closed to outsiders now than they were in Morgan's time.

I give a third example from the Iroquois because another of their more or less oratorical genres is the subject of the best linguistic study to date of a form of Native American public speaking. The study is by Michael Foster (1974). Its inspiration is the Yugoslav and Homeric epic verse studies of Milman Parry and Albert Lord, and its materials are "Longhouse speeches." These are used in an annual round of religious ceremonies (not the same as the Condolence ceremony) concerning "spirit forces," of which there are seventeen, in ascending order, from low on the earth to high beyond the sky. Foster translates the Iroquois names of the whole ceremonies, or ceremonial components (he calls them "speech events"), as Thanksgiving Address, Great Feather Dance, Skin Dance, and Tobacco Invocation. A form of public speaking, which he calls an address, occurs either in or in connection with all four events. These addresses are the objects of his oral formulaic analysis.

He first establishes that each address must proceed through the full span of spirit powers, from low to high, either to thank or to supplicate to the Creator for the things (grasses, fruits, the moon, the Creator Himself) that pertain to that level. Then Foster explains how speakers are able to give short, medium, and long versions of the selfsame speech, depending on the circumstances, by their skilled use of "formulas" similar to those posited by Parry and Lord.

He states that the Iroquois have oratory, but he does not use that word in reference to these addresses. Nor do the addresses fit this article's definition of oratory. They are said by mortals to mortals about what is good for the community, but their language does not invite, nor do they receive, debate. They could be called sermons. They are more sermonlike than the speaking at the Condolence ceremony. The latter's multiple speaking roles, pomp, apparently fixed texts, and stormy emotions are ritual drama rather than a sermon.

We end with three additional studies of contemporary Native public speaking. Each was called oratory, but none is quite political oratory. They are from the Tlingit, the Pima-Papago, and Colville-Okanagan. I review them because they are based on, and cleave to, Native-language texts.

The Tlingit studies are by Nora and Richard Dauenhauer (1986; 1990) and Sergei Kan (1983). They are for funerals and death memorials, that is, for occasions similar to the Iroquois Condolence ceremonies. Like the latter, the Tlingit speeches are by mortals to mortals. They seek to give comfort and heal grief. They typically start with references to the speaker's relation to the deceased. The society is divided into moiety "halves" for social and religious purposes. Those halves regulate who speaks to whom at funerals, which again is like the Iroquois, at least in general terms. After the introductory part of the speech, there commonly comes a shift into a parabolic story on the having and the lessening of grief, roughly the same issue as in Condolence speeches. It seems that where the Iroquois speeches concentrate on grief as blind, dark, and raging, the Tlingits express it as drifting, that is, as a species of floating. The following text illustrates this. First a river and then an uprooted and floating tree personify grief:

> We [speakers] are in need of our [deceased] mother's brothers. [As for example] The river would swell. When it had swollen it would flow. The earth would crumble away. That's when it [subject switches to tree] would think of breaking it would drift down the river. On this great ocean it would drift. It would drift ashore. . . . In the morning the sun would begin to shine on it. It would begin to dry out. From this my hope is that you become like it [and stop grieving] my brothers-in-law. . . . (Dauenhauer 1986:110–11)

Next, my own study of Pima-Papago "ritual oratory" shows primarily how these speeches are built on the theme of a single hero's journeying. An apparatus for defining lines (there being no concept of "line" in the folk literary theory) and multiline "parts" (corresponding to verses or stanzas) was founded on the pervasive language of motion in these texts, which are used, analogous to Longhouse speeches, in an annual round of ceremonies. The speeches narrate shamanic adventures and express the same fascination with traveling that Margot Astrov noted for Navajo literature in 1950. Thus conceived, they are not at all tools for debate. In contrast to the Longhouse speeches, they are memorized word for word, or nearly so, and thus do not expand or contract to suit the occasion. It is fair to say that they are too sacred for that. They are chants or spells rather than sermons.

The above two oratories or near-oratories (and the Longhouse speeches) still exist in their home communities, but they are dying as the public life becomes dominated by miniature parliamentary systems: tribal governments modeled on modern nation-states. Each tribe reveres the memory of a distinct ancestral culture, but the material and governmental lives of all are increasingly similar. The principal vocation is social services, especially health and education, in the Anglo-American mold (it is different in Mexico, where peasant and pauper economies exist). The parliamentary tribal governments devote much of their energy to sustaining those social services.

I know of no studies of the formal and informal speech practices of these governments. Despite their being designed for debate, it is likely that something approximating the Iroquois principle of unanimity prevails in them. In fact, these small-scale parliaments have little to debate about, being dependencies of the United States, Canada, or Mexico. Their ultimate official acts are resolutions and contracts which are written in English, French, or Spanish. The official minutes of their deliberations are almost always written in white men's languages (I know of no exception), but at the other extreme, every self-governing Indian community must have someone who thinks about government in an Indian language. Somewhere between private thinking and public resolving, Indian languages give way to white.

The following speech comments on this situation:

1. Thank you my relatives, you are gathered here.
2. This is a big day.
3. A long time ago before the White people got here to us, the Indians were truly happy on this earth.
4. They survived, the Indians ate from this land, . . . [and] from the water.
5. Time went by, and the White people got here to us.
6. They fenced in the Indians on undesirable land.
7. They told them, "You will stay there, and you will die there."
8. They told the Indians.
9. From the fenced-in land the Indians went to school.
10. They went to school, and they wrote, they learned the language of the Whites.
11. It was then that the two heads were born, the Indians' heads, one White, the other Indian. . . .
38. Not only our native language has died, this whole world is lonesome.
39. It never hears the Indian language spoken.
40. The world is lonesome.
41. When a person speaks Indian this whole world stops, and listens to the speaker. . . .
72. When Indian is spoken the land is glad, the Indian is glad, and now my fellow elders and I talk about fixing the reservation.
73. We fix it so it will grow spawning salmon, and squaw fish, spring salmon, and everything.
74. My fellow elders say to me, "What are you making?
75. Are they making a spawning facility?"
76. "I guess so."
77. And so they're changing the earth.
78. The White people thought of it.
79. The knowledgeable children went along.
80. They all agreed.
81. Now I quit talking.
82. In a little while I'll translate into English.
83. I'll translate what I said, I'm sorry when I speak English I get lost for words, because English is not my language, no, Indian is my language.
84. It's recently that I have learned the English language.
85. That's how it was made, one of my heads in English, and one of my heads Indian. (Mattina 1988:8–10)

The speech was made by William Charlie at a common type of reservation occasion, the groundbreaking for a new tribal facility, in this case a fish hatchery on the Colville reservation. White people thought of it, the knowledgeable children on the council went along with it (no doubt in lines 78,

79). The speech was not offered in debate. It was an ably made (and impeccably recorded, transcribed, and translated) tart remark.

Donald Bahr
Arizona State University

BIBLIOGRAPHY

Astrov, Margot. "The Concept of Motion as the Psychological Leitmotif of Navaho Life and Literature." *Journal of American Folklore* 63 (1950): 45–56.

Bahr, Donald. *Pima and Papago Ritual Oratory: A Study of Three Texts.* San Francisco: Indian Historian Press, 1971.

Bierhorst, John. *Four Masterworks of American Indian Literature.* New York: Farrar, Straus & Giroux, 1974.

Dauenhauer, Nora, and Richard Dauenhauer. "Tlingit Oratory." *Alaska Quarterly Review* 4.3 (1986): 103–31.

———. *Haa Tuwunáaga Yís, for Healing Our Spirit: Tlingit Oratory.* Seattle: U of Washington P, 1990.

Edmonson, Munro. "Quiché Literature." Ed. M. Edmonson. *Literatures, Supplements to The Handbook of Middle American Indians.* Vol. 3. Austin: U of Texas P, 1985.

Foster, Michael. *From the Earth to Beyond the Sky: An Ethnographic Approach to Four Iroquois Speech Events.* National Museum of Man Mercury Series. Canadian Ethnology Service Paper 20. Ottawa: National Museum of Man, 1974.

Holman, Hugh. *A Handbook to Literature.* Indianapolis: Bobbs-Merrill, 1981.

Kaiser, Rudolf. "Chief Seattle's Speech(es): American Origins and European Reception." *Recovering the Word.* Eds. B. Swann and A. Krupat. Berkeley: U of California P, 1987.

Kan, Sergei. "Words That Heal the Soul: Analysis of the Tlingit Potlatch Oratory." *Arctic Anthropology* 20.2 (1983): 47–59.

Mattina, Anthony. "William Charlie's 'Two Headed Person.'" Preliminary Notes on Colville-Okanagan Oratory. 23rd International Conference on Salishian Linguistics, Eugene, Oregon, 1988.

Nichols, John. "Statement Made by the Indians: A Bilingual Petition of the Chippewas of Lake Superior, 1864." Text Series, Languages and Cultures. Centre for Research and Teaching of Canadian Native Languages, U of Western Ontario. London, Ontario, 1988.

Sanders, Thomas, and Walter Peek. *Literature of the American Indian.* Beverly Hills: Glenco, 1973.

Tocqueville, Alexis de. *Democracy in America.* Reprint. Garden City, NY: Doubleday, 1969.

Tooker, Elizabeth. "The United States Constitution and the Iroquois League." *Ethnohistory* 35 (1988): 305–36.

Underhill, Ruth, Donald Bahr, D. Lopez, and J. Pancho. *Rainhouse and Ocean, Speeches for the Papago Year.* Lincoln: U of Nebraska P, 1979.

Dreams, Song and Narrative

"Dream song" refers to a song that enters someone's consciousness during a dream. The term pertains to the history of a song, not to the song's musical or narrative qualities except if the dreamer tells the content of the dream, and if such telling is institutionalized as dream stories or dream literature; in this case, the song is a part, possibly even a privileged part, of a dream story/literature. Such was and is the case among the "dream cultures" of Southern California and Southern Arizona. Among these peoples, dream song is not only an ontogenic category (how a person got a song) but also a narrative one (how a song tells, even is, a dream).

Before considering this special development I will make two points on ontogenic dream songs. First, this notion asserts that a person came to know a song while dreaming. The song might logically have existed before that person encountered it, and hence we are actually discussing the origin of a song-in-someone's-consciousness, not a song-in-the-universe. This is important throughout Native North America where dreams, or relatedly "visions," were and are understood as means for humans to acquire songs as gifts from supernaturals. Presumably the supernaturals had the songs before, during, and after transmitting them to humans. Second, that a song was once dreamt does not mean that it is always dreamt, and specifically this does not preclude that songs could be transmitted between humans wakefully. Dreaming would be a one-way gate for songs from supernaturals to humans, who might keep the songs indefinitely.

Such ontogenic, one-way-gated songs were ubiquitous in North America, but not all songs were/are of that nature. Some peoples, especially the Pueblos (as described by George List, for example) made a point of the wakeful creation of some songs, e.g., Kachina songs. Furthermore, nearly all peoples had a notion of "scriptural" songs, that is, of songs that

119

were supposedly sung in mythic times and were retained in the tribal memory without having been dreamt by anyone. Thus, dream song, humanly composed song, and scriptural song are alternative song histories or ontogenies. A given people might have all three types, although possibly with different emphases, which differences could entail different attitudes toward time, spirit, and creativity. The remainder of this article explores differences associated with low and high emphases on dreaming, and particularly on dreaming for literary purposes.

Although the notion of dream song was ubiquitous, one does not often find the phrase "dream song" in accounts of North American singing. To my knowledge, it is used by scholars only in the "dream culture" area, and even there it is a Euroamerican imposed, not a Native, term. Why would this be? Very simply, songs tended to be named for their supernatural sources (e.g., Deer, Peyote), subject matter, purpose (e.g., curing, war), associated dance step, or other matters in preference to their ontogeny. For example, Ghost dance songs (Mooney, Vander) were and are very nearly dream songs—they came during trances—but they are named for the dance that is associated with them. Similarly, Peyote songs also come or came during trances or dreams, but they are named for the cactus that is eaten in connection with singing them (McAllester). A further fact about those two types of songs is that they were used in spreading, proselytizing religions. Thus, a favorite song traveled far beyond its original dreamer. It became a hymn whose broad or long use became more important than the fact of its dreamt origin.

We come now to the exceptional dream cultures. Here it is not only a question of songs being continually, freshly dreamt, but also, at the heart of the matter, of obtaining songs for no purpose other than as textual souvenirs of another, highly interesting reality. The classic case is the Mojave Indians of California and Arizona, and the classic description is by Alfred Kroeber. Let us consider what he said in a masterpiece of literary criticism:

> The Mojave adhere to a belief in dreams as the basis of everything in life. . . . Not only all shamanistic power, but most myths and songs, bravery and fortune in war, success with women or gaming, every special ability, are dreamed. . . . [Mojaves] learn, indeed, as much as other people; but since learning seems an almost valueless nothing [unless it is vouched in a dream], they dream over, or believe they have first dreamed, the things which they . . . know. (1925:754)

What impressed Kroeber was not the sheer frequency of Mojave dreaming, for he knew little about that, but what they did with their dreaming. They not only dreamt for songs to aid them as omens or clues for pragmatic action, as did most North American peoples, but they also dreamt for songs as the librettos of myths, and they considered these song myths to be ends in themselves. This second, purely literary and aesthetic use struck Kroeber as rare, and was the reason why he conferred the title "dream culture" on the Mojave and a few of their neighbors.

The Mojave song myth is a narrative consisting of segments of plain speech (prose) interspersed with short series of songs. The songs are ontogenic dream songs; they had been heard in a dream. The prose segments were not heard in a dream, but are waking tellings of what the dreamer saw (saw, but not did—apparently the dreamer of a song myth is always an onlooker and never an actor). The songs are the supernaturals' very words. The prose is stage directions, witness testimony, or transition.

Why is the prose necessary? One can get a sense of the problem by comparing the Mojave and other Riverine Yuman (Yuma, Cocopa, Maricopa) song myths with the proseless dreamt song sets of the neighboring Pima-Papago. Both peoples' songs describe moments: something, but not much, moves, but not for long. The successive, cross-song moments of a Pima-Papago set have enough internal and juxtapositional drama to suggest a story, but the successive Riverine Yuman moments do not. In Riverine Yuman song myth, the prose supplies the drama (scene shifts, abrupt speech, the placement of actors in conflict—see Appendix in this article). On the other hand, the Riverine Yuman (prose-and-)song myths are far longer than the neighboring pure song sets. The former run to hundreds of songs and comprise a total of a few score to a few hundred sung words.

Kroeber summarized the Mojave Yuman song myth stories as follows:

> The myths are enormously long, and almost invariably relate to the journey of a single person. . . . Each locality reached . . . is named, and its features are frequently described. All that happens, however, at most of these stops is that the hero thinks of something that he left behind, . . . marvels at the appearance of a rock, . . . or suddenly . . . plots the death of his brother. . . . As a story the whole is meaningless. (1925:756–57)
>
> The idea is that the dreamer followed, or was taken on, this long journey. We are thus face to face with a style . . . which is as frankly decorative as a patterned textile. . . . It is its intricacy . . . that [has] meaning, not the action told by its figures. (757)

These myths were in addition to the Mojave creation myth, which, according to Kroeber, was songless. They were a special development as distinct from a Yuma, Cocopa, or Maricopa development. Unfortunately, the Yuma version quoted in [his] Appendix I is the closest we can come to them because Kroeber published only the prose, not the songs, of the Mojave song myths that he encountered.

Do such dream songs still exist? Barely. Outside interest in them lapsed between 1940 and 1970. Recently, academics have found dream song survivals among the Yaqui (Evers and Molina), Shoshone (Vander), and Pima-Papago (Bahr), but few signs of freshly dreamt songs. (There are no recent studies of Riverine Yuman singing, but it continues among them.)

A new wave of Indian literature is being written in English, but writing and English should not be obstacles to dream songs. Rather, the obstacle is the status of the language quoted from dreams. Formerly, such language was credited to spirits, but now it is credited to the dreamer. Fresh Indian writing denies the spirits to the degree that it extols the scribe. A respect for those spirits along with a love for scribeship has fossilized dream songs.

Appendix 1. Dream Songs with and without Prose.

A. Three Pima-Papago Songs from the beginning, middle, and end of a proseless song set.

> Make a new sun.
> Toss it East.
> It will climb,
> Will light the ground,
> Will pass over me,*
> Will descend into West.
>
> Sun dies.
> Sun dies,
> Earth everywhere black,
> Then every bird stops cooing.
> World doesn't echo.
>
> Mocking bird sounds pitiful
> In distant, isolated talk.
> We stop singing and scatter.
> Wind springs from our singing place,
> Runs back and forth,
> Erases the marks of people,
> Nothing left at the end

(Sung by an oriole to a Pima, learned and resung by Vincent Joseph, translated by D. Bahr)

*First-person language refers to a supernatural, in this case an oriole.

B. Selection from near the beginning of a Yuma (Prose-and-)Song Myth.

> Having descended, he says, "I will go throughout the length of this earth describing things." He said that it was song. "I will name it, and people will call it 'lightning.'" He is going along with the intention of heading only in one direction.

He** stands and looks from afar
He looks from afar and sees
He sees from afar and describes
The land belongs to him, he says, "Fog Bearer [San Jacinto Peak]," and he went off describing it. He arrived there and saw it; it stood there as a high white mass; he is on its summit dancing and so he describes it.
He stands and looks from afar at San Jacinto Peak
He goes along looking from afar at San Jacinto Peak
He arrives at San Jacinto Peak and stands
He sees that San Jacinto Peak is white
He stays on the summit of San Jacinto Peak and is dancing

(Presumably sung by a supernatural who made lightning to Charles Wilson, a Yuma. Resung by William Wilson to A. Halpern, edited by L. Hinton and L. Watahomigie, 1984)

**I am surprised that this is a "he" instead of an "I." Presumably the song was sung by the person who made lightning.

Donald Bahr
Arizona State University

BIBLIOGRAPHY

Bahr, Donald. *Pima and Papago Ritual Oratory: A Study of Three Texts*. San Francisco: Indian Historian Press, 1971.

Evers, Larry and Felipe Molina. *Yaqui Deer Songs*. Tucson: U of Arizona P, 1987.

Kroeber, Alfred. *Handbook of the Indians of California*. Bureau of American Ethnology of the Smithsonian Institution 78. Washington, DC: GPO, 1925.

List, George. "The Hopi as Composer and Poet." *Proceedings of the Centennial Workshop on Ethnomusicology*. Ed. P. Crossley-Holland. Vancouver: Government of the Province of British Columbia, 1968.

McAllester, David. *Peyote Music*. Viking Fund Publications in Anthropology, No. 13. New York, 1949.

Mooney, James. *The Ghost Dance Religion and the Sioux Outbreak of 1890*. Bureau of American Ethnology of the Smithsonian Institution, 1892–1893. 14th Annual Rpt. Part 2. Washington, DC: GPO, 1896.

Vander, John. *Ghost Dance Songs and Religion of a Wind River Shoshone Woman*. Monograph Series in Ethnomusicology 4. Los Angeles: U of California at Los Angeles, Dept. of Music, 1986.

Wilson, William. Excerpts from the "Lightning Song." *Spirit Mountain: An Anthology of Yuman Song and Story*. Eds. L. Hinton and L. Watahomigie. Tucson: Sun Tracks and U of Arizona P, 1984.

Revitalization Movements and Oral Literature

Although much ignored in the historical literature, oral tradition—including mythology, folklore, and ritual performance—provides the necessary key to understanding Native American revitalization movements. In the first place, creation mythology encodes basic understandings of world order, including the people's relationships with transcendent beings, and with the plant and animal persons of nature, their relationships with each other, and their own responsibility for social and cosmic order. At a second level, folklore remembers the way in which the events of creation structure historical struggle. Folklore reminds people not only of folly, viciousness, and pain, but also of the transformative opportunities of human life.

Thomas Blackburn (1975) has used creation mythology to reveal the existential principles which sustain tribal solidarity—the power of sharing, for example—and to isolate the way in which folklore encapsulates the normative postulates by which people make sense of changing circumstance. As Gary Witherspoon has shown (1977), story shapes past and present and so engenders the future. Drawing on a broad interdisciplinary consensus, Sam D. Gill (1982) similarly demonstrates that stories have performative significance. Informing song, dance, and gesture, stories shape religious action and concretize the flux and flow of creation in the here and now. Revitalization movements thus attempt to conjoin understanding and action. They are, in short, efforts to utter effective stories.

Critical reflection about oral tradition offers the possibility of rethinking revitalization history in humanistic and cross-cultural terms. The primary issue that must be confronted is the tension between impersonal, literate history and the kind of intimate social orientation that oral tradition conveys. Two assumptions stand out for challenge. First, there is the idea that myth somehow fails to be historical. Second, scholars too often

125

assume that only literacy makes critical self-scrutiny possible. In actuality, Natives and Euroamericans have distinctive, though complementary, modes of historical consciousness, as Alfonso Ortiz has argued (1977). Ortiz observes that Native Americans ground their stories primarily in spatial terms, in the here and now, rather than in the there, then, and when. Literate Euroamericans focus instead on past and future. In these senses, myth and history seem to value radically different realities.

Myth and history are modes of consciousness that have the same purpose and function, although they appreciate human experience in radically different ways. Psychologically, all individuals reach for a story-line that says "I am because ——." Socially, the textual task consists of being able to declare "We are because ——." Both oral and literate people are historical, then, because both seek a meaningful story to account for the troubled present. The telling difference is that myth highlights the present and so spotlights human responsibility.

In cultures that stress the need for positive relations between human beings and cosmic persons, impersonal causes—the economic, political, religious, and ideological forces of literate history—do not show up, until, of course, literacy displaces orality. Literate history distorts myth's vital concerns. Written history thinks at the world; myth provides a way of experiencing. History explains; myth motivates, as a few exemplary revitalization movements demonstrate.

Long before European contact, the Iroquois peoples of upper New York State used story in diagnostic and value-shifting ways. At issue was an ineffective story. A law of clan revenge required males to avenge wrongs done to their kinsmen. The result was pervasive violence because the revenge story institutionalized retaliation. But the Iroquois also had a transformative story: they say that a prophet always appears to counter crisis. And so it happened. Hiawatha, in visionary communication with Dekanawideh, learned not only how to diagnose the Iroquois' responsibility for the devastation, but also how to rectify the situation. The result, reconstructed by Anthony F. C. Wallace (1958), was a story that worked. The prophet convinced his people to abolish the law of clan revenge and, more positively, revealed a ritual to console grieving relatives. Ultimately, the prophet created a political institution, the famous League of the Iroquois, that achieved interclan solidarity and extended kinship internationally.

After the American Revolution, the League of the Six Nations entered another period of crisis and again a prophet arose to revitalize and adapt tradition (Wallace 1970). With the military defeat of the League, the old solidarity, based on men's hunting, war, and diplomacy, evaporated. As seriously, the Iroquois had little choice but to adopt an American-style nuclear-family farm that made their matrilineal clans dysfunctional. The prophet, Handsome Lake, proclaimed a story of promise and on the basis of visionary experience produced a new cultural text. Like Hiawatha before him, Handsome Lake gave the Iroquois a story of cooperation that not only revitalized the traditional ideal of kin solidarity, but also recognized the antisocial threats of the impinging American capitalist economy: there was an antisocial, antitribal tale. The Handsome Lake story ritually enacted in the Longhouse has empowered Iroquois ethnic survival ever since.

Recognizing the storied character of revitalization must lead to a new appreciation of the classic movements. For example, historians commonly devalue the Ghost Dance of the late nineteenth century as a failure. The materialistic conventions of literate history hold that ritual activity is irrelevant. To ask why demoralized people dance, however, invites a fresh understanding of literary phenomena in religious terms. Dance becomes meaningful text. The Ghost Dance did not spread as rapidly as it did because it was simply an expression of despair. Rather, the Ghost Dance sprang from an ancient tale of world rejuvenation, a narrative that stipulated human responsibility.

The real story of the dance rests in the prophet Wovoka's call that only enlivened social values could ensure Native Americans' health and well-being. Wovoka even urged Indians to tolerate their white neighbors. The dead at Wounded Knee were not hostiles. They only sought, as Black Elk put it, to do their religious duty (see DeMaillie). Everywhere the dance produced results. People spoke with dead relatives, renewed solidarity, and exchanged promises of mutual support. The Pawnee used contact with dead shamans, according to Alexander Lesser (1978), to create a textual revolution in which lost knowledge—including myths, prayers, and ceremonies—was recovered. Finally, the Ghost Dance became an Indian, rather than a tribal, story. As such, the dance gave birth to the pan-Indian consciousness of the present century.

Apart from the prophetic stories which directly countered large-scale crisis, revitalization occurred in countless microshifts in myth. Peter Powell (1969, 1981) has detailed the ways in which the Cheyenne exemplify the narrative reorientation of the tribal peoples who moved out onto the Great Plains. Before their migration, the Cheyenne's life had centered on the creation story, in which Maheo, the All-Father, gave the people the great Person-Bundle, Mahuts, the Four Sacred Arrows. Once on the plains, Mahuts played a much greater role in Cheyenne life, and the people remember his power, which made men successful warriors and hunters. Life on the plains brought the Cheyenne another great Person-Bundle Story. She was Is'siwun, the Buffalo Hat, who ensured the fertility of buffalo and Cheyenne women. As manifestations of cosmic caring, Mahuts and Is'siwun stabilized the migratory tribal life of the plains. More, Cheyenne tradition asserts that the people's failure to reciprocate the gifts of Mahuts and Is'siwun led directly to military defeat and the demise of the buffalo.

Numerous small shifts in story likewise accommodated the realities of impinging Euroamerican culture. These stories share two characteristics. First, they revalue tradition with nativistic self-confidence. Second, the tales embrace cautiously selected aspects of Euroamerican life. Old stories were retold by conservatives bent on constructive change. Northeastern Algonquians, for example, came to understand that their culture hero, Gluskap, served as Christ's co-creator. They also realized that Adam was both the father of European people and of evil in the world (Morrison 1981). Charles Hill-Tout (1978) records a similar story, in which the culture hero, Benign-face, gave plows, wagons, and gunpowder not only to the Salish but to Europeans as well. The Apache and the Navajo went so far as to comprehensively recast creation mythology to account for the marvelous discovery of horses (Clark 1966). Everywhere, Native Americans called on Mother Earth to explain to materialistic Euroamericans their special relationship to the land (Gill 1987).

Many other stories record Native Americans' worried assessment of Euroamerican character and so empowered the survival of ethnic distinctiveness. Percy Bullchild reports the Blackfeet sense that God did not exist until Europeans brought him into the world in order to excuse their misdoings. An Ojibwa recounts a disturbing, after-death encounter with St. Peter. The gatekeeper of heaven told the Christian Indian that there was no room for him (Berkhofer 1965). Yaqui pascola clowns parody the English "You're welcome" with the phrase "you work them" (Painter 1986). The Navajo declare that Euroamericans behave as if they have no kin (Witherspoon 1975). And more than once, Native Americans have equated the newcomers with the monsters of myth (Morrison 1979; Roscoe 1988).

These stories, and many more, declare the enduring power of myth in shaping Native American cultures and driving their creative revitalization before and since Euroamerican contact. The stories demand a new examination of the resiliency of Native American values. They declare that, far from being victims, Native Americans told stories to empower survival.

Kenneth M. Morrison
Arizona State University

BIBLIOGRAPHY

Berkhofer, Robert. *Salvation and the Savage: An Analysis of Protestant Missions and American Indian Response, 1787–1862*. Lexington: U of Kentucky P, 1965.

Blackburn, Thomas. *December's Child: A Book of Chumash Oral Narratives*. Berkeley: U of California P, 1975.

Bullchild, Percy. *The Sun Came Down: The History of the World as My Blackfeet Elders Told It*. San Francisco: Harper & Row, 1985.

Clark, Laverne Harrell. *They Sang for Horses: The Impact of the Horse on Navajo and Apache Folklore*. Tucson: U of Arizona P, 1966.

DeMaillie, Raymond J., ed. *The Sixth Grandfather: Black Elk's Teachings Given to John G. Neihardt*. Lincoln: U of Nebraska P, 1985.

Gill, Sam D. *Native American Religions: An Introduction*. Belmont, CA: Wadsworth Publishing Co., 1982.

———. *Mother Earth: An American Story*. Chicago: U of Chicago P, 1987.

Hill-Tout, Charles. *The Salish People: The Local Contribution of Charles Hill-Tout*. Ed. Ralph Maud. Vancouver: Talon Books, 1978.

Lesser, Alexander. *The Pawnee Ghost Dance Hand Game: Ghost Dance Revival and Ethnic Identity*. Madison: U of Wisconsin P, 1978.

Morrison, Kenneth M. "Towards a History of Intimate Encounters: Algonkian Folklore, Jesuit Missionaries, and Kiwakwe, the Cannibal Giant." *American Indian Culture and Research Journal* 3 (1979): 51–80.

———. "The Mythological Sources of Abenaki Catholicism: A Case Study of the Social History of Power." *Religion* 11 (1981): 235–36.

Ortiz, Alfonso. "Some Concerns Central to the Writing of 'Indian' History." *The Indian Historian* 10 (1977): 17–22.

Painter, Muriel Thayer. *With Good Heart: Yaqui Beliefs and Ceremonies in Pascua Village*. Tucson: U of Arizona P, 1986.

Powell, Peter. *Sweet Medicine*. Norman: U of Oklahoma P, 1969.

———. *The People of the Sacred Mountain*. San Francisco: Harper & Row, 1981.

Roscoe, Will, ed. *Living the Spirit: A Gay American Indian Anthology*. New York: St. Martin's, 1988.

Wallace, Anthony F. C. "The Dekanawideh Myth Analysed as the Record of a Revitalization Movement." *Ethnohistory* 5 (1958): 118–30.

———. *The Death and Rebirth of the Seneca*. New York: Alfred A. Knopf, 1970.

Witherspoon, Gary. *Navajo Kinship and Marriage*. Chicago: U of Chicago P, 1975.

———. *Language and Art in the Navajo Universe*. Ann Arbor: U of Michigan P, 1977.

Myth and Religion of Native America

Although scholars commonly distinguish between shamans, medicine men, and priests, the terms obscure Indian religious knowledge and practice. Even the term religious specialist distorts the actuality. No dividing line separates shamans from priests, or from medical diagnosticians, masked dancers, ritual clowns, prophets, singers, musicians, seers, and even witches. All religious practitioners translate gifts of power into cultural texts. They all understand the existential rules given in myth and, in meeting the changing needs of their communities, variously combine the functions of the dramatist, historian, philosopher, economist, psychologist, politician, and minister.

People at different life stages and with varying degrees of power read the world and interpret the shifting text of life for others less skillful. In religious systems where life-text is always personal, reading becomes dialogical interaction, a mutually empowering conversation between some human beings, and between them and transcendent persons, about how things are and ought to be. Native American religions are experientially intimate, rather than dogmatic, and they are performance driven rather than rationalistic (Gill 1982). These religions focus on two crucial questions: Who is at cause? How are we responsible? Human beings, plants, animals, "natural forces," and great mythological others interact in complex systems of cooperative and competitive otherness (Hallowell 1960).

These are religions created by and for everyone. In religious theory and performance, the ecstatic character of shamanism, the diagnostic and curing activity of doctors, and the cosmological mediation of priests merge on a continuum of power. Throughout North America, extraordinary religious insight comes in everyday dreams, in much sought visions, and in the taxing labor of ritual practice. Native American religions focus on personal knowledge and responsibility, and are thus scripted dramas acted out in daily life. Native American cosmologies center religious reality in the here and now, and so stress the need for religious action. Every human shares with other sentient beings the pivotal power to create, and in particular to speak persuasively. Since a creative imperative lies behind all expression, human and otherwise, religious equality characterizes some humans and the great transcendent others. In vision, Black Elk realized that he himself had become the Sixth Grandfather with the grave responsibility of directing ritual dramas to lead the people.

For religious practitioners, the world is not only compellingly personal; the great persons of myth and nature also demand attention. Gathering herbs, shaping a pot, or framing a canoe, as well as the life-sustaining activities of alleviating individual and social crisis, predicting the future, conducting war, curing, hunting, and farming all require the aid of great transcendent others. Such activities derive from the power-charged, paradigmatic texts, and transformative gestures that mythic others made in the beginning. Myth persons still affect the world. The Abenaki peoples of the Northeast declare that Gluskap, their Culture Hero, literally lives in the telling of his story (Morrison 1981).

Reverenced as generative, healing forces in their own right, mythic narratives constitute the vehicles through which religious practitioners focus their use of power (Witherspoon 1974). In Navajo creation myth, First Man (who does not have human form) models the power of future Earth people, and declares the way in which the world is continually created and sustained through thought and speech. Symbolically integrating mind and all the senses in a totalistic apprehension of reality, serious stories bring myth persons into being, and connect human communities with cosmological others. In narratives uttered in words, gesture, and music, and as often embodied in dance, mythic persons share their abilities with religiously powerful humans. Like human mediators, the persons of myth transform the ordinary. In this way, everyday life has cosmological significance because offended powers retaliate with hunger, sickness, and death. Mollified, the very same powerful others lend assistance.

If human religious actors share the same personal nature as cosmic others, then power, constituted both in knowledge and in the ability to apply power in novel situations, differentiates persons (Adams and Fogelson 1977). Applied to religious practitioners, as well as to transcendent others, the terms for power—manitou, wakan, orenda, etc.—demark unusual ability and responsibility. In all Native American societies, some individuals stand out for their demonstrated success in responding to disease, disaster, and psychosocial disorder. Since Indian religions are pragmatically grounded, rather than systems of belief, the community itself actively arbitrates religious status. Religious leadership, whether expressed in sustenance activities, war, politics, or in medicine, is always an achieved status,

132

even in those situations where individuals inherit or purchase power. Success matters and confers respect. Power, personal competence, and religious activity intersect. Ability exists not as an abstract, impersonal force, but rather as a matter of transformative action taken in the present.

Just as is true for the persons of myth, human power wielders are always empowered by others. Gift-giving is both the great cosmological source of interpersonal solidarity, and the central means of human religious practice (Mauss 1954). Native American religions ritually embody the cosmological imperative to share. The great others not only give human beings power (plants and animals literally give life), they also expect reciprocity in return. Navajo myth declares, for example, that Sun requires human lives in return for his light. Continent-wide hero stories declare the positive benefits derived from giving, and exemplify the ideal of religious practice. These myths model the struggle and dignity of religious practitioners. At first helpless and powerless, great others take pity on the hero-to-be. After trials, devastation, and sometimes complete destruction, the great others empower the hero to return to his people with transformative ritual performances (Spencer 1957). In this way, Native American religious practitioners channel power to benefit not only human beings, but transcendent persons as well. Power circulates cosmologically in compassionate acts of giving, offering, and sacrifice. Kwakiutl religious personnel, the named chiefs as well as medicine people, mediate the cosmological dictum that life has to do with eating and being eaten (Goldman 1975). Native American religious personnel play a crucial role because power itself is neutral. Power can be, and is, used for ill as well as good. If, on the one hand, religious practitioners receive high status for their essential services, they also, on the other hand, focus fearful ambivalence. The fact is that powerful humans do abuse power in acting against their fellows. In both myth and in ritual, religious mediators confront monstrous impersonality, and so make a constructive difference. But powerful humans, like powerful transcendent others, experience selfish impulses. Acting out of self-interest and refusing to share creates cosmic entropy. In the end, then, Native American religious practitioners meet an inescapable challenge. The power of sharing requires that religious persons transform pride and surrender to others' well-being.

Kenneth M. Morrison
Arizona State University

BIBLIOGRAPHY

Adams, Richard N., and Raymond D. Fogelson, eds. *The Anthropology of Power.* New York: Academic Press, 1977.

Gill, Sam D. *Native American Religions: An Introduction.* Belmont, CA: Wadsworth Publishing Co., 1982.

Goldman, Irving. *The Mouth of Heaven: An Introduction to Kwakiutl Religious Thought.* New York: John Wiley & Sons, 1975.

Hallowell, A. Irving. "Ojibwa Ontology, Behavior and World View." *Culture in History: Essays in Honor of Paul Radin*. Ed. Stanley Diamond. New York: Columbia UP, 1960. 19–52.

Mauss, Marcel. *The Gift*. 1925. Trans. Ian Cunnison. London: Cohen and West, 1954.

Morrison, Kenneth M. "The Mythological Sources of Abenaki Catholicism: A Case Study of the Social History of Power." *Religion* 11 (1981): 235–36.

Spencer, Katherine. *Mythology and Values: An Analysis of Navaho Chantway Myths*. Memoirs of the American Folklore Society 48. Philadelphia: American Folklore Society, 1957.

Witherspoon, Gary. *Language and Art in the Navajo Universe*. Ann Arbor: U of Michigan P, 1974.

The Bible and Traditional Indian Literature

We will never know the full extent of the assimilation of Bible stories by Native Americans into their oral repertories in the nineteenth century because most linguistic and ethnographic fieldworkers simply ignored such assimilations in their campaign to collect "classical" Native narratives. While understandable under the circumstances, this neglect of Native Bible stories is regrettable, in that such texts as we do have shed valuable light on (1) the practical circumstances of evangelical work among the Indians, (2) the theological dispositions of various tribes before and during the Contact Era, (3) Native imaginative and philosophical responses to the acculturative traumas of Anglo contact and conquest, and (4) the governing "rules" and conventions of the traditional Indian mythologies, as revealed in the ways these myth-systems absorbed the missionaries' Bible stories. (The same claims and complaints might be made, of course, on behalf of largely unrecorded Bible-adaptations in all colonialized cultures, as far back as sixth-century England. Augustine's letters back to Rome neglect to record, alas, what imaginative and literary sense his "converts" were making of the stories of the Old Testament and the Gospels.)

In the American and Canadian West, Indians were hearing and absorbing biblical stories (as well as French folktales) from French-Canadian trappers and *voyageurs* before 1800, but the Bible's main literary impact in the West came in the 1830s and 1840s with the arrival of Protestant and Catholic missionaries such as Jason Lee, Henry Spalding, Cushing Eells, Father Peter De Smet, and Father F. N. Blanchet. "Preaching"—often across two or even three translations, and often ending in Chinook jargon—most often took the form of telling simplified stories from Scripture, notably the Creation and Fall, the Tower of Babel and Confusion of

Tongues, Noah and the Flood, Jonah, Daniel, and the Life of Christ, sometimes supplemented with illustrations and diagrams depicting biblical history according to the Protestant or Catholic viewpoint.

The forms of scriptural assimilations into Native oral repertories can be broken into three broad categories: (1) *incorporation*, in which a Bible story was accepted with few changes in general because it corresponded to a Native story; (2) *adaptation*, in which a Bible story was altered in the process of assimilation more or less drastically, often so as to conform to a Native cycle or mythic scheme; (3) *mythopoetic refiguration*, in which, as a consequence of what appears to have been a genuinely free play of imagination over both scriptural and Native traditions, a new, synthetic narrative owing something to both traditions but fully governed by neither, was created.

Examples of simple incorporation include numerous versions of the Flood and the rise and fall of the Tower of Babel, in which Native alterations are limited to details of setting (most Indian myth-repertories had "Flood" and "Babel" stories, to begin with). In the case of adaptation, the Indians' alterations of biblical narratives often seem to be deliberately ironic, and sometimes anti-white, as in a Northern Paiute twisting of Genesis, in which the serpent in the garden is identified as a white man ("White people have eyes just like a rattlesnake") who prevents the Indians from eating the apples on the Edenic tree. Another kind of adaptation is the remarkable "adjustment" of Christ to fit Native understandings in a number of Northwest repertories: recognizing that Christ's mediative position between God and mankind was analogous to the position of Coyote the Trickster-Transformer, Indians grafted Him onto their Transformation Era cycles, with God's Son cast in the role of an unsuccessful precursor of Coyote! In the words of a Thompson River narrative recorded by James Teit, "the Chief [God] looked over the world, and saw that things had not changed much for the better. Jesus had only set right a very few things. He had done more talking than anything else" (1917:80).

Examples of truly "mythopoetic" responses to Bible narratives are rare, perhaps because of the indifference of most transcribers, even those who were receptive to incorporative and adaptive biblical stories. One fieldworker who *did* take a special interest in such material was James Teit, collecting in British Columbia for Franz Boas at the turn of the century. In one of Teit's Thompson River transcriptions, there is a virtually seamless intermixing of elements of the Elijah story and of Native journeys to the afterworld, and of Christian references to Hell, Satan, etc., and Thompson's traditional ideas about morality. The overall imaginative quality of this narrative (and others of its kind) is that of a romance. It is a reasonable speculation that the same unstable imaginative interplay of traditional Native forms and new Christian material that produced stories of biblical assimilation also led to the rise of new adaptive forms of Indian worship—as in the Native "Shaker" and "Feather" cults of the Pacific Northwest.

Jarold Ramsey
University of Rochester

BIBLIOGRAPHY

Landerholm, Carl, ed. *Notices and Voyages of the Famed Quebec Mission to the Pacific Northwest.* Portland, OR: Champoeg Press, 1956.

Miller, Christopher. *Prophetic Worlds.* New Brunswick, NJ: Rutgers UP, 1985.

Ramsey, Jarold. "The Bible in Western Indian Mythology." *Journal of American Folklore* 90 (1977): 442–52. Rpt. in Jarold Ramsey, *Reading the Fire: Essays in the Traditional Indian Literatures of the Far West.* Lincoln: U of Nebraska P, 1984.

Teit, James. *Folk-tales of Salish Tribes. Memoirs of the American Folklore Society* 11 (1917).

Thompson, Stith. "Sunday School Stories Among Savages." *Texas Review* (1917): 109–16.

———, ed. *Tales of the North American Indians.* Bloomington: Indiana UP, 1968.

Todorov, Tzvetan. *The Conquest of America.* Trans. Richard Howard. New York: Harper & Row, 1984.

Utley, Francis Lee. "The Bible of the Folk." *California Folklore Quarterly* 4 (1945): 1–17.

The White Man in Native Oral Tradition

The depiction of Anglos in Native American oral tradition dates back to the earliest Indian/Anglo contacts in the sixteenth and seventeenth centuries, and ranges in tonality from awe and wonder at these mysterious, impatient, potent newcomers, to perplexity over their strange ways, to anger and outrage, to sly or open contempt. What Indians have seen in the Anglos over the centuries has been imaginatively *refracted* in their traditional narratives, according to what they wanted or expected to see and according to the Native literary "rules" and conventions governing the way such alien material was assimilated. Hence the imaging of whites in traditional stories is almost never matter-of-fact or neutral; it is, on the contrary, full of a sense of Anglo otherness.

If the pictographic *Walum Olum* of the Delawares is authentic as a record of their pre-Contact history (some scholars doubt its authenticity), then there is special poignancy in the chronicle's final entry:

> Watcher was chief; he looked toward the sea.
> At this time, from north and south, the whites came.
> They are peaceful; they have great things.
> Who are they? (Brinton 1969:217)

The oral traditions of some Native groups record the arrival of the whites as an auspicious fulfillment of ancient prophecy. Thus the Aztecs at first welcomed Hernando Cortez as their long-promised white-skinned messiah and deliverer; and when Anglo miners and adventurers first came into Northern Paiute country in Nevada in the 1840s, they were initially hailed by Truckee and other headmen as long-lost brothers, according to a Paiute myth of dispersal in which the light-skinned children of the first family were separated from their dark-skinned siblings for quarreling.

So the light girl and boy disappeared, and their parents saw them no more. . . . And by and by, the dark children grew into a large nation, and we believe it is the one we belong to, and that the nation that sprang from the white children will some time send someone to meet us and heal all the old trouble. (Winnemucca 1883:6–7)

(Such mythic identifications of "the other" were by no means limited to the Indians, of course: through much of the nineteenth century, Anglo missionaries and even some early ethnologists went looking for evidence to support the notion that the Indians were really descendants of the Lost Tribes of Israel!)

In 1808, when Simon Fraser came down the river in British Columbia that now bears his name, the Salish tribes through which he and his canoe-flotilla passed were as startled by the intrusion as we might be by a visitation from outer space. One such group, the Thompson River band, managed to make traditional sense of the event by interpreting it as the historical sequel to a Myth Age story about how a band of Thompson mythic heroes, including Sun, Moon, Morning-Star, Coyote, and others, once traveled *up* the river, transforming the world as they went. Fraser, who apparently wore some kind of shiny badge, was identified by the Thompsons as "Sun"—and the astonishing power of myth-systems to transmogrify raw and shocking "news" into natively intelligible mythic patterns is illustrated by this story, recorded in summary-form by James Teit around 1900, based on an actual canoe-capsizing suffered by Fraser's party: "The canoe was of birch-bark and disappeared under the water with all hands. The first to appear very early in the morning was Morning Star, who rose to the surface and came ashore. At noon, Sun rose and came ashore; and in the evening, Moon rose holding the canoe, and came ashore. During the night, the canoe and all disappeared" (Teit 1912:416).

Thus myth accounts for and legitimates historical event, even when the event brings the sudden appearance of a new and formidable race of people—but such first sightings of the white man, although translatable into traditional mythic terms as here, were often subsequently understood (perhaps with hindsight) as portending change and trouble to come.

When the Contact Era ensued, the depiction of whites in Indian storytelling became, not surprisingly, a form of imaginative coping with a new reality indeed full of drastic change and trouble. A narrative like the Cathlamet Chinook's, "The Sun's Myth" in fact contains no direct images of or references to Anglos, but as Dell Hymes has pointed out, this tragic story, told by Charles Cultee to Franz Boas in 1900, seems to dramatize the irresistible and often ruinous appeal of Anglo goods and ways to Indians during the initial Contact Era. Cultee's protagonist, a chief, travels to the household of the Sun, and although she befriends him and offers him any traditional Indian treasure he sees in her well-appointed house, he insists on claiming a mysterious "shining thing" that hangs on the wall.

Sun warns him of its powers; and when he returns home with it, it comes alive in his arms and destroys all the villages of his people. At length Sun comes down and reclaims the lethal thing, and denounces the chief for bringing disaster to the land. She tells him, "It is you who chose": a stern affirmation of the Indians' option, at least early in the Contact Era, to avoid cultural death by choosing to reject the fatal novelties and "shining things" of white culture (Hymes 1975:367).

More commonly, Indian anxieties about and resentment of Anglos and their ways expressed themselves directly in stories featuring whites as villains and fools. Native resistance to Protestant and Catholic evangelism appears, for example, in stories pointing at white missionaries. A Northern Paiute twisting of Genesis declares that Eden was made for the Indians, but a white man in the form of a rattlesnake got into the apple tree and has kept Indians out of Paradise ever since. And in a latter-day Kiowa tale, Saynday the Trickster meets "Smallpox," in the form of a tall, skinny, pock-marked Anglo preacher who asks for directions to the Kiowas. (Saynday recovers some of his lost status among the Kiowas by misdirecting Smallpox away from them and, instead, on to the Pawnees!)

A broader impulse of cultural resistance animates the popular modern-day Coyote stories of many western and southwestern Indian communities, in which Coyote, shifty and resourceful as always, scores symbolic victories over Anglo laws and technology both on and off the Rez. In one North Coast tale, for example, it is Coyote, not the Apollo astronauts, who first lands on the moon; the astronauts find that he has left it barren. Sexual tensions between the races seem to color stories like the Clackamas Chinook "She Deceived Herself with Milt," in which a widow's wishes transform a quantity of salmon milt (male sexual fluid) into a handsome white-skinned but vacuous man, who is promptly stolen away by another woman, and is then magically reduced to milt again by the vengeful widow. The racial and sexual animus of such tales is amusingly recorded in a comment by Mrs. Victoria Howard, the great Clackamas storyteller: "When some white person would pass by [our house], my mother-in-law would look at that white person, and she would laugh. She would say [in Clackamas] 'Dear oh dear, it is a light one! Possibly it is milt!' And then she would sing. This is what she would say in the words of the song, 'She deceived herself with milt.'"

This same vein of satirical and defensive humor at the expense of Anglos runs deep in much modern Indian writing—in the work of Simon Ortiz and Gerald Vizenor, for example—and it is yet another line of literary continuity between oral/traditional Indian literature and its modern written renaissance.

Jarold Ramsey
University of Rochester

141

BIBLIOGRAPHY

Basso, Keith. *Portraits of "the Whiteman": Linguistic Play and Cultural Symbols Among the Western Apache*. Cambridge: Cambridge UP, 1979.

Brinton, Daniel. *The Lenape and Their Legends*. New York: AMS Press, 1969.

Hymes, Dell. "Folklore's Nature and the Sun's Myth." *Journal of American Folklore* 88 (1975): 345–69.

———. *"In Vain I Tried to Tell You": Essays in Native American Ethnopoetics*. Philadelphia: U of Pennsylvania P, 1981.

Jacobs, Melville. *Clackamas Chinook Texts*, Part Two. Research Center in Anthropology, Folklore, and Linguistics, Publication 11. *International Journal of American Linguistics* 25.2.

Ramsey, Jarold. *Reading the Fire: Essays in the Traditional Indian Literatures of the Far West*. Lincoln: U of Nebraska P, 1984.

———, ed. *Coyote Was Going There*. Seattle: U of Washington P, 1977.

Teit, James. *Mythology of the Thompson Indians*. Memoirs of the American Museum of Natural History, Vol. 12, Pt. 1. New York: American Museum of Natural History, 1912.

———. *Folk-tales of Salish Tribes*. Memoirs of the American Folklore Society 11. Menasha, WI, 1917.

Todorov, Tzvetan. *The Conquest of America*. Trans. Richard Howard. New York: Harper & Row, 1984.

Winnemucca, Sarah. *Life Among the Piutes*. Ed. Mrs. Horace Mann. Boston and New York: G. P. Putnam and Sons, 1883.

The Historical Emergence of Native American Writing

Native American Writing: Beginnings to 1967

Beginnings to 1899

Prior to contact, some North American tribes made pictographic accounts of rituals and important events, and the Maya of Mesoamerica preserved their sacred literature in books. Most Native American literature, however, was transmitted orally. The emergence of Native American authors parallels whites' conquest of Indian lands and the subsequent education of Native children in white-run schools. Some of the earliest of these were seventeenth-century texts written in Latin and Greek by students at Harvard's Indian College: Caleb Cheeshateaumauk, "Honoratissimi Benefactores" (1663), and Eleazar (no last name given), "In obitum Viri veré Reverendi D. Thomae Thackeri" (1679) (Hochbruck and Dundensing-Reichel 1992). Probably the first published work by an Indian author is Samson Occom's *A Sermon Preached at the Execution of Moses Paul, an Indian* (1772). Here Occom, a Mohegan, demonstrates his rhetorical skill in appealing to Indian and white audiences through the popular genre of the execution sermon. Sounding a warning echoed by later Native American writers, Occom vividly describes how Indian families had been devastated by alcoholism.

Most nineteenth-century Indian authors wrote nonfiction prose. They published protest literature, autobiographies, and ethnohistories in response to the curtailment of Native Americans' rights and attempts to remove Indians from their traditional homelands. Prior to the Civil War, one of the greatest threats to Indians was the implementation of the Indian Removal Act of 1830, under which tribes east of the Mississippi River were removed either to Indian Territory (now Oklahoma) or to other lands deemed appropriate. Indian tribes also faced local threats to abrogate their rights.

An eloquent example of Indian protest writing is Elias Boudinot's *An Address to the Whites* (1826), in which he declares that speculations and conjectures about the practicability of "civilizing the Indians must forever cease." The achievements of the Cherokees, Boudinot argues, demonstrate how Indians can improve. The most effective Indian protest writer of the 1830s was William Apes (Pequot). His "An Indian's Looking Glass for the White Man," appended to the 1833 edition of his *Experiences of Five Christian Indians of the Pequot Tribe*, forcefully attacks white prejudice against Indians exemplified in the new miscegenation laws of Massachusetts. His *Indian Nullification of the Unconstitutional Laws of Massachusetts, Relative to the Marshpee Tribe* (1835) recounts his role in the Mashpee's successful struggle for self-determination, the only such victory in the 1830s. His most eloquent protest writing is *Eulogy on King Philip* (1836), in which Apes contrasts the Puritans' inhumane treatment of the New England tribes with Native people's generosity to the new arrivals. Another powerful protest writer is George Copway (Ojibwa), who lectured in the East and addressed the thirty-first Congress on his proposal, *Organization of a New Indian Territory, East of the Missouri River* (1850).

Nineteenth-century American Indians also wrote autobiographies to inform their readers about Indian life and history. These autobiographies often included forceful commentaries on what whites had done to Indian people. Perhaps the first full-length autobiography to be written and published by an Indian author is Apes's *A Son of the Forest* (1829), which combines the literary tradition of the spiritual confession with sharp criticism of white treatment of Indians. It was published at the height of the debate over the Indian Removal Bill. Copway's *The Life, History, and Travels of Kah-ge-ga-gah-bowh* (1847) was undoubtedly written in response to attempts to move the Minnesota Ojibwas from territories ceded to them in 1842. It blends the Western European traditions of the confession and the missionary reminiscence with Ojibwa myth, tribal ethnohistory, and personal experience, a combination that characterizes most later Indian autobiographies.

In the second half of the nineteenth century, Native Americans faced new threats, reflected in works by Indian authors. After the discovery of gold in 1849, rapidly increasing numbers of immigrants encroached on Indian land as they traveled to the California gold fields, Idaho ore deposits, or Oregon timber. Slowed during the Civil War, westward migration increased when the end of the war brought new demands for land. By the end of the 1880s, the government had forced the last of the tribes onto reservations by destroying their food supplies—the buffalo and stored winter caches. As part of its policy of assimilation, the government passed the General Allotment Act of 1887, supported by both land grabbers and by assimilationist Indians and non-Indians. Popularly called the Dawes Act after its sponsor, Henry L. Dawes, it allotted in severalty land previously owned by tribes. The Allotment Act was disastrous for Indians, who lost approximately 60 percent of the land they owned in 1887 (Washburn 1975:242–43). One final attempt at Indian resistance was the Ghost Dance, a messianic religious movement that gained many converts from Plains tribes in the late 1880s and 1890. It was led by Wovoka, or Jack Wilson (Paiute), who predicted that the Plains would again support millions of buffalo and that whites would disappear. By 1890, it had aroused the Plains tribes and terrified whites. The tragic end to the movement and to the Indian wars came in 1890, when Big Foot's band of Sioux Ghost Dancers was massacred at Wounded Knee, South Dakota, after a dispute over turning in their weapons.

One of the most powerful books to chronicle the impact of westward migration on tribal life and the abuses by government agents is *Life Among the Piutes* (1883) by Sarah Winnemucca [Hopkins] (Paiute). She may have been the only Indian woman writer in the nineteenth century to publish a personal and tribal history. Her account is more personal and detailed than most such books in the period. Especially interesting are Winnemucca's discussion of the status of Indian women in Paiute society and her accounts of her harrowing experiences as she rode between the white and Indian lines during the Bannock War of 1876. Winnemucca also castigates federal Indian policy and the agents who abused her people or ignored their needs.

As traditional tribal life changed when Indians were put on reservations or moved from ancestral lands, numerous Indian authors published accounts of their tribe's myths, history, and customs. Among the first was *Sketches of Ancient History of the Six Nations* by David Cusick (Tuscarora). It may have been published as early as 1825, the date of the preface, but was probably published in 1827. The first history of the Ojibwas by a tribal member was Copway's *The Traditional History and Characteristic Sketches of the Ojibway Nation* (1850), later published under the title *Indian Life and Indian History* (1858). Two other Ojibwas also wrote histories: Peter Jones [Kakewaquonaby], *History of the Ojebway Indians* (published posthumously in 1861), and William Whipple Warren, *History of the Ojibway, Based upon Traditions and Oral Statements* (completed in 1852 but not published until 1885). Among those who also authored ethnohistories of their tribes are Peter Dooyenate Clark (Wyandot), *Origin and Traditional History of the Wyandotts, and Sketches of Other Indian Tribes of North America* (1870); Chief Elias Johnson (Tuscarora), *Legends, Traditions and Laws, of the Iroquois* (1881); and Chief Andrew J. Blackbird [Mackawdegbenessy] (Ottawa), *History of the Ottawa and Chippewa Indians of Michigan* (1887). In March, April, and May 1862, John Rollin Ridge published in the California newspaper *Hesperion* three essays on "North American Indians," which examined their history, customs, and beliefs.

Journals kept by Native Americans recounting their experiences among Indian tribes also were printed. One of the earliest is *A Short Narration of My Last Journey to the Western Country* by Hendrick Aupaumut, a Mahican sachem (d. 1830). Recorded in 1794 and published in 1827, it describes his journey and negotiations with various tribes during his service in the early 1790s as government liaison to the Indians of the Northwest Territory. The journals of Peter Jones, who served as a missionary to the Ojibwa and helped them adjust to the encroachment of white culture, were published posthumously in *Life and Journals of Kah-ke-wa-quo-na-by* (1860).

Native Americans also published travel literature in the nineteenth century. An early example is *An Account of the Chippewa Indians, Who Have Been Travelling Among the Whites* ... (1848) by George Henry or Maungwudaus (Ojibwa), a lapsed Methodist missionary whose formation of a "wild Indian" troupe considerably embarrassed his half brother, the devout missionary Peter Jones. The pamphlet, which appeared in various forms in 1847 and 1848, describes Maungwudaus's impressions as the group toured the United States, Great Britain, France and Belgium in 1844 and 1845. Especially titillating is Maungwudaus's description of how English women insisted that the Indians kiss not only their cheeks but also their mouths. The first full-length travel book is Copway's *Running Sketches of Men and Places* ... (1851), which contains some interesting character portraits of members of London society.

By the mid-nineteenth century, Native American writers began writing fiction. The first novel by an Indian author is the romance *The Life and Adventures of Joaquim Murieta* (1854) by John Rollin Ridge. Though not specifically about Indians, the novel portrays how whites' unjust treatment of a Metizo protagonist causes him to seek revenge against the race that oppresses him. Murieta, the hero, possesses the nobility, intelligence, and gentlemanliness expected of a Byronic "noble outlaw." Apparently the only novel published by an Indian woman in the nineteenth century is *Wynema: A Child of the Forest* (1891) by S. Alice Callahan (Creek), which reflects the influence of the domestic romance common in women's literature of the period. Callahan incorporates explanations of Creek customs and an impassioned fictional account of the events that led to the murder of Sitting Bull and the massacred at Wounded Knee. Callahan also embeds in her novel strong pleas for women's rights and suffrage. In 1899, *O-gî-mäw-kwe Mit-i-gwä-kî* [Queen of the Woods] was published posthumously under the name of Simon Pokagon (Potawatomi), whose authorship has been questioned. The novel is a romance that laments the Potawatomi's loss of their Edenic past and warns about how alcohol can destroy Indians and whites.

The few American Indians who wrote poetry in the nineteenth century were strongly influenced by romanticism. One of the first to publish was Jane Johnston Schoolcraft (Ojibwa), wife of Henry Rowe Schoolcraft. Some of her poems appeared in *The Literary Voyager or Muzzeniegun*, a literary magazine founded by her husband in 1826. Ridge's *Poems* (1868), published posthumously, may be the first book-length collection of poetry by a Native American. Although few of the poems have Indian themes, several reveal Ridge's ability to create realistic characterization and to use dialect. E. Pauline Johnson (Mohawk) gained critical acclaim in Canada and Great Britain with her *The White Wampum* (1895), praised for its lyricism and its dramatic, sometimes melodramatic, poems on Indian subjects. *Flint and Feather* (1912) includes this volume and her less successful *Canadian Born* (1903).

As tribes established newspapers, Native Americans became journalists. Elias Boudinot exercised his considerable rhetorical skills in his editorials for the *Cherokee Phoenix*, which in 1826 became the first Native American newspaper in the United States. After Removal, many Indian newspapers were started in Indian Territory. They included considerable news about Indian affairs as well as accounts of national and international news. The Cherokees were especially active journalists. William P. Ross was the first editor of the *Cherokee Advocate*, which was later edited by Boudinot's brother, William Penn Boudinot, and his grandson, Elias Cornelius Boudinot, Jr. John Lynch Adair edited the *Cherokee Advocate*, *Indian Chieftain*, and the *World*, the latter published at Vinita, Indian Territory, while Robert Latham Owen owned and edited the *Indian Chieftain*. Like Ross, Owen also edited the *Osage Herald*. Tribes in other parts of the country established newspapers as well. In 1886, the *Progress* was established on the White Earth Ojibwa reservation, with Theodore H. Beaulieu as editor and Augustus H. Beaulieu as publisher. The first tribal newspaper to be seized by federal agents, it was succeeded two years later by the *Tomahawk*.

Three Cherokees owned or edited newspapers outside Indian Territory. Both Edward W. Bushyhead and Ridge went to California during the gold rush of 1850 and became journalists. From 1868 to 1873, Bushyhead was half-owner of the *San Diego Union*, one of only two daily papers in Southern California. Ridge wrote for and edited such newspapers as the *Sacramento Bee*, *California Express* at Marysville, *Marysville National Democrat*, *Trinity National*, *San Francisco Herald*, and *Grass Valley Daily National*. Elias Cornelius Boudinot, son of Elias, became editor of the Little Rock *True Democrat* and the Fayetteville weekly *Arkansian*.

1900 to 1967

During the late nineteenth and early twentieth centuries, Native Americans from western tribes struggled to adjust to life on reservations. Many of their children were shipped off to boarding schools in such places as Carlisle, Pennsylvania, and Riverside, California, where they were separated from their families for years, given new Anglo-European names, and forbidden to speak their Native languages or practice their tribal customs and religions. Not until 1924 did Congress grant Native Americans citizenship. Ten years later it passed the Wheeler-Howard Indian Reorganization Act, which ended allotment in severalty, confirmed cultural pluralism, and reestablished tribal government. By 1953, however, politicians sought to end the "Indian problem" by passing House Concurrent Resolution 108, which began the campaign to terminate the federal government's role in Indian affairs. Under this policy, tribes like the Klamath and Menominee lost their reservation status and the government actively encouraged Indians to move to cities. The Menominees finally won in 1973 their battle to reverse termination and to regain their status as wards of the government.

Most of the autobiographers publishing early in the century focused on the ethnohistory of their tribes and their own adjustments to life on reservations. Because most of them were the first generation from their tribes to be educated in white-run schools, they also described their traumatic initiations to life in white-run schools. A widely read autobiographer during this period is Charles Eastman [Ohiyesa] (Sioux), who collaborated with his wife, Elaine Goodale Eastman, on two life histories. *Indian Boyhood* (1902) describes his boyhood before the reservation period, and *From the Deep Woods to Civilization* (1916) chronicles his adjustments to reservation and white schools and his experiences as a doctor. Others whose stories describe similar reservation life or adjustment to schools include Francis La Flesche (Omaha), Standing Bear (Sioux), and Zitkala Sa [Gertrude Bonnin] (Sioux). A forceful personal history and ethnohistory written from a woman's perspective is *Mourning Dove: A Salishan Autobiography*. Edited by Jay Miller from drafts written by Mourning Dove primarily in the 1930s, it was published posthumously in 1990. The most literary autobiography of this period is *Talking to the Moon* (1945) by John Joseph Mathews (Osage). This stylistically sophisticated book is strongly influenced by the philosophical autobiographies of Henry David Thoreau and John Muir as well as by Osage traditions.

Two Native American satirists gained prominence early in the century. Alexander Posey (Creek) became very popular in Indian Territory for his Fus Fixico letter, written in Creek-style English. While Posey focuses on the politics of the Indian Territory and the Creek nation, Will Rogers (Cherokee) satirized national and international politics both in his newspaper columns and books.

The numbers of American Indians writing versions of tribal stories as well as studies of American Indian anthropology, ethnohistory, contemporary issues, and philosophy greatly increased in this period. Among those publishing anthropological studies or collections of oral literature are Ella C. Deloria (Sioux), William Jones (Fox), and Archie Phinney (Nez Perce), all of whom were trained by Franz Boas, the founder of American anthropology. Others who published such studies include John N. B. Hewitt

(Tuscarora), Francis La Flesche (Omaha), William Morgan (Navajo), and Arthur C. Parker (Seneca). Many Indians also published popularizations of tribal stories: Jesse Cornplanter (Seneca), Charles Eastman (Sioux) (in collaboration with Elaine Eastman), E. Pauline Johnson (Mohawk), Mourning Dove (Colville), Edmund Nequatewa (Hopi), Standing Bear (Sioux), and Zitkala Sa [Gertrude Bonnin] (Sioux).

Charles Eastman published several books on Indians that gained wide readership. In *The Soul of the Indian* (1911), he explains Native American beliefs, using a Sioux model. In *The Indian Today* (1915), he examines the problems his people faced and describes their achievements. In *Speaking of Indians* (1944), Deloria describes Sioux beliefs and customs and examines how her people adapted these after they moved onto reservations. Ruth Muskrat Bronson (Cherokee) provides a general introduction to Indian life and culture in her *Indians Are People Too* (1944).

The most important Indian ethnohistorian to begin publishing during this period is D'Arcy McNickle (Cree/Flathead). His *They Came Here First* (1949) and *The Indian Tribes of the United States* (1962) added a long-missing Indian perspective to Native American history. Equally important are his books *Indians and Other Americans* (1959), written with Harold E. Fey, and *Native American Tribalism* (1962). Using oral tradition, John Joseph Mathews creates a fascinating history of his people in *The Osages* (1961). Thomas Wildcat Alford narrated the history of the Shawnee to Florence Drake, published as *Civilization* (1962). Lois Marie Hunter (Shinnecock) gives a general history of her tribe in *The Shinnecock Indians* (1950). As a youth, John Oskison (Cherokee) won a prize for his essay "Remaining Causes of Indian Discontent" (1907), reprinted in Peyer (1989:152–58).

Native Americans also began to write biographies. Eastman offers short biographical sketches of tribal leaders in *Indian Heroes and Great Chieftains* (1918). Perhaps the only full biography of an Indian written by a Native American in this period is Oskison's *Tecumseh and His Times* (1938). Two other Native Americans wrote biographies about non-Indians: McNickle, *Indian Man: A Biography of Oliver La Farge* (1971), and Mathews, *Life and Death of an Oilman: The Career of E. W. Marland* (1951).

Fiction began to supplant nonfiction prose as the genre to which Indian authors increasingly turned. Many Native American novels dealt with mixed-bloods' quests to find their places in the Indian and white worlds and with the survival of tribalism. Mourning Dove [Christine Quintasket] (Colville), Mathews, and D'Arcy McNickle incorporate these themes in their novels. In *Cogewea, the Half Blood* (1927), written in collaboration with Lucullus V. McWhorter, Mourning Dove combines the portrayal of a strong-willed heroine who temporarily rejects her tribal heritage with plot elements from westerns. Mathews's *Sundown* (1934) focuses on the problems faced by the Osage after allotment and during the oil boom of the

1920s. The protagonist is a mixed-blood Osage whose abandonment of his ancestral past and inability to adjust to the white-dominated present end in alcoholism. The most polished novel by an Indian writer in the 1930s is McNickle's *The Surrounded* (1936). Set on the Flathead reservation after allotment had deprived many Indians of their lands and Catholicism had replaced their tribal religion, *The Surrounded* powerfully depicts the dilemma of a mixed-blood inadvertently caught up in unpremeditated murders that his mother and girlfriend commit. His strongly traditional mother and a tribal elder lead the protagonist back to the Flathead culture he had rejected.

The importance of place is the theme of John Oskison's (Cherokee) *Brothers Three* (1935), a vivid account of a family's struggle during the Depression to hold on to an Oklahoma farm established by their father and their quarter-Cherokee mother. Oskison's *Wild Harvest* (1925) and *Black Jack Davy* (1926) are "southwesterns" set in Indian Territory before statehood and deal with the surge of white settlers onto Cherokee land.

Two novels describe tribal life. The adjustments of the Osage to the reservation and the acculturation of their agent, Major Laban J. Miles, to tribal world views and customs are the focus of Mathews's *Wah'Kon-Tah* (1932), whose last chapter introduces the prototype of the hero of *Sundown*. Completed in draft form by 1944 but not published until 1988, Deloria's (Sioux) *Waterlily* recreates, from a woman's perspective, nineteenth-century Sioux life before the reservation period.

The most prolific novelist is Todd Downing (Choctaw, 1902–1974), who published nine detective novels in the 1930s and 1940s. Primarily set in Mexico, these detective stories often contain allusions to Indian beliefs or minor characters with some Indian ancestry. Among these are *The Cat Screams* (1934), *Night over Mexico* (1937), and *The Lazy Lawrence Murders* (1941).

Many Indian writers wrote short fiction in the first half of the century. One of the earliest collections is E. Pauline Johnson's *The Moccasin Maker* (1913), which primarily consists of sentimental but often powerful stories about Indian and Canadian women. Her *The Shagganappi* (1913) contains stories for young boys. The Eastmans' stories about life before the reservation period are collected in *Old Indian Days* (1907). Some stories by Zitkala Sa [Gertrude Bonnin] are published in *American Indian Stories* (1921), which also includes her autobiographical articles and nonfiction. Short stories by Susette La Flesche (Omaha), Francis La Flesche (Omaha), Angel Decora (Winnebago), Johnson, William Jones (Ojibwa), Eastman, Oskison, Mathews, and McNickle have been collected in *The Singing Spirit* (1989), edited by Bernd Peyer. Francis La Flesche wrote many short stories, which are now being edited by Daniel F. Littlefield, Jr., and James M. Parins.

The only major Native American dramatist of the period was (Rolla) Lynn Riggs (Cherokee), who had several plays produced on Broadway. He is best known for his *Borned in Texas*, produced as *Roadside* (1930), and *Green Grow the Lilacs* (1931), the basis for *Oklahoma!* (1943). His only play with an Indian theme is *The Cherokee Night* (1936), which focuses on the sense of loss felt in the period by Cherokee mixed-bloods alienated from their Cherokee heritage.

Few Indian poets published in the first half of the century. *The Poems of Alexander Lawrence Posey* (1910), primarily consisting of work written in the author's youth, was published posthumously. The book reflects Posey's fondness for the English pre-Romantic and Romantic poets. Far more sophisticated is Riggs's *The Iron Dish* (1930), which contains some beautifully phrased descriptions of nature and some realistic observations. One poet whose career began in the 1950s was Maurice Kenny (Mohawk), who wrote two chapbooks in this period: *Dead Letters Sent* (1958) and *With Love to Lesbia* (1959). This prolific writer published most of his work after the 1970s.

Indian newspapers continued to be published and founded in the twentieth century. Alexander Posey made the *Indian Journal*, the only Indian daily, a popularly read newspaper in Indian Territory. After 1900, Charles Gibson, a friend of Posey's, wrote extensively for the *Journal* and other Indian newspapers. C. H. Beaulieu (Ojibwa), son of Clement H., assumed the editorship of the White Earth *Tomahawk* in 1917 after his brother Gustave died. Later in the century, many other newspapers emerged, such as *Indian Speaking Leaf* (1937, New Jersey), *Standing Rock Eyapaha* (1943, Fort Yates, North Dakota), and *Adhhoniigii: Navajo Language Monthly* (1943, Windowrock, Arizona).

Several pan-Indian journals developed as well. In 1916, Carlos Montezuma (Yavapai) established and edited *Wassaja*, a magazine on Indian affairs. Montezuma used the journal to rail against the Bureau of Indian Affairs, which he felt should be abolished. The Society of American Indians published two magazines. Arthur C. Parker (Seneca) edited the *Quarterly Journal* (1912–16) while Zitkala Sa served in a similar capacity for its successor, *American Indian Magazine* (1917) of the National Congress of American Indians, offered Native Americans national forums to express their views on Indian issues.

In the period 1772 to 1967, Native Americans established themselves as important authors, scholars, and journalists. Unfortunately, much of their work soon went out of print, so that few contemporary authors were able to read the writing of their predecessors. As scholars have gradually recognized the significance of their work, many of these works have been reprinted.

A. LaVonne Brown Ruoff
University of Illinois—Chicago

BIBLIOGRAPHY

Hochbruck, Wolfgang, and Beatrix Dudensing-Reichel. "'Honoratissimi Benefactores': Native American Students and Two Seventeenth-Century Texts in the University Tradition." *Studies in American Indian Literatures*. 2nd Ser. 4 (1992): 35–47.

Kenny, Maurice. *Love to Lesbia*. New York: Aardvark Press, 1959.

Littlefield, Daniel F., and James W. Parins, comps. *A Biobibliography of Native American Writers 1772–1924*. Native American Bibliography 2. Metuchen, NJ: Scarecrow, 1981.

———, comps. *American Indian and Alaska Native Newspapers and Periodicals, 1826–1924*. Westport, CT: Greenwood, 1984.

———, comps. *A Biobibliography of Native American Writers, 1772–1924: A Supplement*. Native American Bibliography 54. Metuchen, NJ: Scarecrow, 1985.

Murphy, James E., and Sharon M. Murphy. *Let My People Know: American Indian Journalism, 1828–1978*. Foreword by Jeannette Henry. Norman: U of Oklahoma P, 1981.

Peyer, Bernd, ed. *The Singing Spirit: Early Short Stories by North American Indians*. Tucson: U of Arizona P, 1989.

Ruoff, A. LaVonne Brown. *American Indian Literatures: An Introduction, Bibliographic Review, and Selected Bibliography*. New York: MLA, 1990.

Vizenor, Gerald. *The People Named the Chippewa: Narrative Histories*. Minneapolis: U of Minnesota P, 1984.

Washburn, Wilcomb E. *The Indian in America*. New York: Harper & Row, 1975.

Wiget, Andrew. *Native American Literature*. Twayne's United States Authors 467. Boston: Twayne, 1985.

Population, Reservations, and Federal Indian Policy

Early Indian-European Policy

The initial course of action pursued by the United States Government toward the American Indian had its roots in the actions of the European colonies in America. The important national groups with whom the Indians came in contact in the mid-1600s were the Spaniards in Florida and the Rio Grande valley, the French in the St. Lawrence valley, and the English on the Atlantic coast. The direction of Indian modification varied, of course, according to the culture and the policies of these European nations.

Spanish policy was basically one attempting to "civilize" the Indian according to Spanish ideas and then to bring him under Spanish political control. This policy was accomplished primarily by integrating the Indian into either Spanish-type communities or into the mission system. Both of these systems were dynamic centers of cultural change for the incorporated Indians of California and the Southwest (Robinson 1979; Spicer 1962). Because all of Spain's efforts were directed toward the establishment of these systems, little attention was paid to Indian tribes more distant from areas of colonization, who, being nomadic for the most part, could not be incorporated into the Spanish way of life. However, these tribes were indirectly influenced by Spain with the introduction of the horse. This indirect influence spread by means of intertribal trade north through the plains and then east into the prairies and west into the steppes. Many Indian tribes were influenced by the horse and drifted into the plains, and many tribes who had not previously met were now thrown into close cultural contact.

The French policy was similar to the Spanish policy in that France also wanted to "civilize" the Indian according to French ideas. However, it was accomplished not by forcing the Indians to resettle into compact units, but simply by living with the Indians. Parkman clearly states this policy: "mingled with French traders and French settlers, softened by French manners, guided by French priests, ruled by French officers, their now divided bands would become the constituents of a vast wilderness empire" (1867:131). Far more important than these social and religious attempts to "civilize" the Indian was the economic process that developed under the French fur trade. Unlike the Spanish contacts through intertribal trade, the French fur trade with its influx of European goods exerted influence on Indian tribes far beyond its settled areas. This economic influence was a powerful factor, producing changes not only in the location of tribes, but also in their attitudes and values and affecting the Native cultures of numerous tribes throughout the Great Lakes and the Plains.

Unlike the French and Spanish policies, which tried to "civilize" the Indians, British policy treated the Indians as a distinct and inferior people not worthy of civilization. The British tried to separate the Indian from the colonial settlements by recognizing the Indian tribe as an independent nation and limiting his territory through treaties (Jacobs 1972). As a result of this policy, fewer direct social and religious contacts existed than among the French or Spanish settled areas. However, as in the French fur trade, the British fur trade exerted a great economic influence far beyond its settlement boundaries.

Treaties for Indians

After the American Revolution and the formation of a new government under the Articles of Confederation, the United States inherited the title asserted by Great Britain to all lands occupied by the Indians. The U.S. Indian policy generally passed through a number of different stages. Originally, the first stage of U.S. policy was similar to the British colonial policy, although this policy was by no means homogeneous, as instanced by the religious differences among the English colonies. However, most British colonials, like U.S. citizens, rejected the idea that the Indian could be "civilized" and later absorbed into white society. Thus, as in British policy, the Indian was separated from the white settlers. In pursuing this policy, the United States in effect recognized the tribes as quasi-sovereign nations, thereby setting precedents that were to persist for over a century, and because the Indians asserted claims to vast territories, there ensued a long history of treaty-making and land cession with a number of consequences that persist to the present day.

The United States' first Indian treaty was made with the Delawares on September 2, 1778 (Royce 1930:591–93). Subsequent treaties were made with most of the remaining Indian tribes east of the Appalachians before the turn of the century. After 1790, the government adopted the practice of setting aside certain areas to be reserved exclusively for Indian use. The various tribes of the Iroquois in western New York were the first to be confined to these "reservations."

Removal and Concentration Westward for Indians

Following the War of 1812, the character of Indian-American relations changed. When the threat of British intervention faded, the United States felt less need to conciliate the Indian nations and began negotiating new treaties by which the tribes relinquished their holdings in the East and consented to removal farther west. By the end of the 1830s only the Seminoles and a remnant of the Cherokees had resisted removal. The Chickasaws, Choctaws, and Creeks all had surrendered their homes in Georgia, Alabama, and Mississippi, and were transported over the "trail of tears" to their new homes beyond the Mississippi (Foreman 1953; Viola 1974). The tribes of the Iroquois, whose reservations were in western New York, also were relocated west of the Mississippi and other tribes had ceded their claims in Ohio, Indiana, and Illinois. Except for the Seminole reservation in Florida, the Cherokee reservation in western North Carolina, and a few small reservations in northern Wisconsin and Michigan, most of the Indian reservations were created west of the Mississippi.

Reservations for Indians

The confinement of the Indian tribes to reservations increased steadily during the nineteenth century, with periods of quiescence occurring only when the white man temporarily halted his westward movement. The greatest number of reservations were established between 1851 and 1860 (Royce 1930:590–1190; Foreman 1933:35–78). By 1880, 297 separate areas of land were reserved for Indian use (Danziger 1974).

These reservations ranged in size from tiny settlements of only a few acres in California to a 13-million-acre Navajo reservation in Arizona. These reservations were located almost exclusively west of the Mississippi, with marked concentrations in the deserts of the Southwest and the yet-to-be-settled northern and central Great Plains. Six present-day states contained 80 percent of the total land on Indian reservations. (See Table 1.)

Table 1

Distribution of Indian Lands—1880

Area/State	Percent of Total Indian Lands
Southwest	
Arizona	28
New Mexico	10
Northern Great Plains	
Montana	10
South Dakota	9
North Dakota	8
Central Great Plains	
Oklahoma	15
Total	80

"Civilization" for Indians

The initial governmental policy of isolating the Indian on reservations began to change in the 1870s and 1880s. In 1872, recognizing the anomalous situation of dealing with Indians as independent nations, the United States Congress prohibited the further making of treaties with any Indian tribes. This was a move in the direction of an explicit recognition of a problem involved in the political, economic, and social incorporation of the Indian into the American nation. The program of isolating the Indian had proven to be shortsighted. No spot in the United States could any longer be thought of as a permanently isolated area. Isolation being patently impossible, there was nothing to do but consider ways and means of integration. During the 1880s, citizens and officials steadily evolved a program of "civilization" which crystallized in the passing of the General Allotment Act in 1887 (Prucha 1978).

The central idea of this act was the assimilation of Indian cultures into the white culture by means of individualization. "The Reservation system belongs to the past; Indians must be absorbed into our national life, not as Indians, but as American citizens; the Indian must be 'individualized' and treated as an individual by the Government" (U.S. Department of the Interior 1962:583). The primary method of individualizing the Indian was the allotting of land in individual assignments to Indian families. It was thought that the basis of civilization consisted in knowing how to handle individual property. From this experience would come responsibility and awareness of the obligation of citizenship. Hence, if tribal lands were now reassigned on an individual basis, there would appear stimulus for economic improvement. The tribal ties, which were believed to be conducive to lack of industry and lack of individual responsibility, would melt away and the Indians would become industrious participants in the American nation. Thus, the Allotment Act was an attempt to assimilate the individual Indian into the American yeoman farmer myth (Fritz 1963; Keller 1983).

The major result of the General Allotment Act of 1887 was the loss of 86 million acres of Indian land in the next forty-seven years (*U.S. Bureau of Indian Affairs 1934*:1–16). There were several means whereby this land was transferred from Indian to white ownership: the sale of surplus lands, alienation to whites through fee patents, and the sale of original and heirship allotments. After the individual allotments had been made, the remaining lands were sold to the government for its disposal (apparently the assumption was that Indians were not to have any children). At least 61 million acres of Indian land were lost in this way. The second means of loss, alienation through fee patents, involved the granting of fee patents to Indian landowners at the end of the trust period which removed sale restrictions allowing individual Indians to sell their land to whites. Since much of the land was sought eagerly by whites, this method accounted for the loss of about 23 million acres. Augmenting the effects of the General Allotment Act was a new act of Congress passed on March 1, 1907 (Kinney 1937:42–87). This act gave the Interior Secretary the power to dispose of the original allottees' land if the Indian could be proven an "incompetent" user of this land. Since any simple argument could be made for its application to individual cases, this act became an effective instrument in the dissipation of the individually owned Indian land. Under this act, a total of 3,370,265 acres of the best land was alienated from Indian ownership.

A compilation by the Bureau of Indian Affairs in 1934 revealed the following general classification of Indian-owned lands:

Table 2

Distribution of Indian-Owned Land

Type of Land	Acres	Percent of Total
Tribal land	34,287,336	65.5
Allotted land	17,622,700	34.0
Reserves set aside for schools	232,899	0.5
Total	52,142,935	100.0

At first glance, it appears that the larger share of Indian land is tribally owned. However, it is important to note the location of this tribally owned land. Over 75 percent of the tribally owned land is located in the hot deserts of the Southwest (Arizona and New Mexico) and the colder deserts of the Basin and Range region (eastern California, Nevada, western Utah, and southwestern Idaho). (See Table 3.)

Table 3

Concentration of Tribally Owned Land

State	Acres
Arizona	18,400,000
New Mexico	4,800,000
Utah	1,470,000
Nevada	600,000
California	300,000
Idaho	150,000
Total	25,720,000

The concentration of allotted Indian lands is in the grazing areas of the Great Plains and the forested mountains of the Pacific Northwest and the forests of northern Wisconsin and Minnesota. Ninety percent of the allotted land is concentrated in these areas. (See Table 4.)

Table 4

Concentration of Allotted Owned Land

State	Acres
Montana	5,000,000
South Dakota	4,600,000
Oklahoma	2,900,000
North Dakota	1,000,000
Washington	950,000
Oregon	500,000
Minnesota	130,000
Wisconsin	120,000
Total	15,200,000

The location of the allotted and tribally owned lands reflects their suitability for agriculture. According to the General Allotment Act, land not suitable for agriculture or grazing was not allotted; therefore, the tribally owned reservations are located in the poorest land. Most reservations are located in arid or semi-arid areas with 80 percent of all the reservation land receiving less than 20 inches of rain in a year. Tribal reservations are concentrated in the arid Southwest; Arizona, New Mexico, Nevada, and Southern California are the leading areas. A few tribal reservations outside the Southwest are among the allotted reservations, but these are poorly suited for agriculture.

Indian allotted land is located in the most suitable economic areas. However, if the Indian could or wanted to adapt his culture to conform to the white methods of exploiting the natural resources, he would encounter a number of obstacles in using land inside the allotted reservations. Not only is a large percentage of the best land inside the reservation white-owned, but the allotted land is also intermingled and fragmented. Both Indian and non-Indian lands are located in close proximity, creating a checkerboard land pattern. This makes it difficult or impossible for Indian owners to use their land for grazing or lumbering. It is important to note that most allotted reservations are located either in the Great Plains or northern Great Lakes area, where the primary economic activity is not farming. Practical utilization of these grazing and timber regions by whites requires large tracts for efficient operation. The allotment of timberlands discouraged the practice of scientific forestry and a sustained-yield cutting, while the allotment of grazing lands encouraged the idle, non-use of huge acreages because a herd of cattle could not be sustained on such small land plots (Carlson 1981).

Of all the problems resulting from the allotment system—the lost Indian lands, the fragmenting of grazing and timberland into small plots, and the fragmentations of land through inheritance—none had a more profound effect in destroying the purpose of the allotment system than the leasing act. Four years after the passage of the General Allotment Act, Congress passed the Leasing Act which stated in part: "That whenever it shall be made to appear to the Secretary of the Interior that, by reason of age or other disability, any allottee under the provisions of said act, or any other act or treaty, cannot personally and with benefit to himself occupy or improve his allotment or any part thereof, the same may be leased upon such terms, regulations, and conditions as shall be prescribed by such Secretary, for a term not exceeding five years for farming or grazing, or ten years for mining purposes" (*U.S. Leasing Act* XXVI: 412).

The term "disability," as used in the act, was applied to a person who for any reason was unable to cultivate all or any part of his land. Thirty years after the act was passed, some 14 million acres of grazing land and 3 million acres of farmland were leased. In sustaining the statute, proponents of leasing argued that the Indians would be stimulated by the successful farm operations of their white neighbors, to whom they had turned over a portion of their allotment. It was also argued that the income from rentals would provide the Indians with funds to make improvements upon the land they were working (Harger 1943:181–83). Instead, the Leasing Act encouraged idleness and forced the Indian to exist on small pittances of unearned income.

This section has concentrated on the land problems which were created by the Allotment Act. The basic philosophy of this act was to change the Indian by breaking up tribal unity. In order to further individualize the Indian, a section of the Allotment Act required all Indian children to attend off-reservation boarding schools. Civilization was to be achieved by both agriculture and education. Another feature of this change through education was the giving of government funds to various church groups so that religious schools could be established on reservations to promote white beliefs and moral codes. The application of these educational programs extended throughout all reservations, allotted and unallotted, so that probably one-fourth or more of the Indian children from the 1890s to the 1930s experienced some boarding school life (U.S. Congress. House 1934:428). The majority of these children, under the complex forces of change, came back to the reservations and continued to participate to some degree in the Indian cultures. The missionary school program resulted in some change of Native religion, but the major effect was not complete replacement, but rather the creation of a diversity of cult practices and beliefs.

Tribal Reorganization for Indians

The federal government was not unaware of the problems created by the General Allotment Act. In 1922, the Secretary of the Interior commissioned hundreds of prominent citizens to investigate the Bureau of Indian Affairs and to make recommendations (Mardock 1971). The study was released in 1928 as *The Problems of Indian Administration*, but it is popularly known as the Meriam Report (Meriam, Lewis et al.). The report stirred up considerable controversy, and its careful identification of problems made it very difficult to ignore. It was now evident that Indians were not members of a dying race, that the federal Indian program had created a complex mess, and that specific Indian problems would not just go away. In 1932, John Collier introduced legislation which would shift power from the Secretary of the Interior to newly approved tribal councils (Kelly 1983). With the election of Franklin Delano Roosevelt as President, the Indian "New Deal" was about to begin. The Great Depression had weakened many of the beliefs about individualism inside American society and made Indian communal beliefs somewhat more acceptable. John Collier was appointed Commissioner of Indian Affairs in 1934 by President Roosevelt and that same year he was able to pursue his reform ideas with the passage of the Indian Reorganization Act (I.R.A.). This act not only completely stopped the land allotments as injurious to the Indian and shifted emphasis

Figure 3. Western Indian Reservations, 1890. (From Arrell Gibson, *The American Indian*, University of Oklahoma Press.)

from off-reservation boarding schools to on-reservation day schools, it also proposed that influences from Anglo culture could be best assimilated through the medium of the tribe. The I.R.A. was based on the principle that "communal enterprise was the most efficient and expedient means for economic betterment" (Kelly 1954:32).

The effectiveness of the Reorganization Act in solving the basic land problems resulting from the Allotment Act was limited. The first problem, that of lost Indian lands, appeared to have been solved, since the I.R.A. stopped the sale of Indian lands and even set aside $2 million annually for the repurchase of lost lands. The general increase in tribal lands after the year 1934 appears to bear this out. The total amount of tribal lands increased from 29 million acres in 1934 to 33 million acres in 1945. However, the total amount of Indian lands remained about the same throughout this period. Most of the increase in tribal lands can be accounted for by the loss of allotted lands during this same period: a drop from 18 million acres to 14 million acres. Thus, all the Reorganization Act accomplished was to buy Indian-allotted land and return it to the reservation for tribal use. The basic problem of having too little land for Indian use was never resolved because the total Indian land acreage did not increase.

Likewise, the problem of having white and Indian landowners intermixed on small plots of land was not solved by the Reorganization Act. Furthermore, most of the land located inside allotted reservations remained white-owned. The Indian Reorganization Act also provided for the education of the Indian in the principles of sustained-yield forestry and livestock raising. However, these principles could be applied only on tribally owned reservations where no complicated land ownership pattern existed. Therefore, only tribally owned reservations benefited from this educational provision in the Indian Reorganization Act. The heirship and leasing problems still remained, and in recent years have become magnified. Under the Reorganization Act, the estate could not be sold to non-Indians; thus, heirs were left with only two choices in disposing of their inherited property, both of which were used and both of which created severe obstacles to effective land use. The first system resulted in land fragmentation, with each plot of land being subdivided upon the death of its owner, thereby creating smaller landholdings with each successive generation. In some extreme cases, plots were fragmented into pieces so small that no effective economic use of them was possible. The alternative was to keep the original plot intact by operating it as a single unit, with all heirs receiving a share. In order to obtain income from the unit, it was usually leased to non-Indian operators such as lumbermen or ranchers; the rent they paid to the estate was divided among the owners. With the passing of a new leasing law in the 1940s, the period of time for which Indian land could be leased was extended. Leases could now be obtained for periods of up to twenty-five years, with the exception of those for grazing purposes, which were limited to ten years or less. In 1945, some 15 million acres of grazing land and 4 million acres of farm land were being leased to whites.

Therefore, the I.R.A. failed to solve the Indian land problems that were created by the General Allotment Act. As early as 1944, an investigation by the O'Connor-Hundt House Committee on Indian Affairs reported that "although the I.R.A. had in some instances aided the Indians, progress toward assimilation had lagged because of inadequate land, education, and the government's failure to settle claims and to consolidate scattered holdings owned by several heirs" (U.S. Congress. Senate 1944:17). In sum, the Indian Reorganization Act was destined by its design to limited success. The I.R.A. was largely an administrative reorganization following a century of mismanagement and mistaken policies. Tribes were encouraged to form chartered corporations and operate essentially as local governments. One important condition of the original law was that it would apply only to those tribes that by majority vote decided to come under its provisions. Initially, only 181 tribes accepted the I.R.A. and 77 rejected it. Many Indians felt that the I.R.A. was another method to get more land away from them (Scudder 1948:213). Furthermore, many of the Indians who accepted the I.R.A. did not adopt constitutions and few were organized economically under tribal corporate charters. None of the reservations were able to reestablish their old land base. Another problem with the I.R.A. was the refusal of Congress to support the program. House members cut appropriations for the purchase of additional lands and refused to allow the concept of tribal self-government to have any chance for sustained growth by refusing to force allotments into communal ownership.

After 1937, John Collier ran into increasing opposition. World War II turned the nation away from internal concerns, and in 1945 John Collier resigned. Forces opposed to the Indian New Deal stressed assimilation of Indians into the mainstream of American society, and the policy of termination was about to begin.

Termination for Indians

After World War II, in a new spirit of nationalism, senators and congressmen began to preach for equality and freedom for the Indians. They demanded that the government stop treating Indians differently from other citizens and demanded that the Indians be allowed to survive on their own. After Collier resigned in 1945, the executive branch of the government shifted from a policy of assistance for Indians to a goal of getting out of the Indian business. Between 1945 and 1950, federal policy was in a period of transition from the old policy of Indian self-determination to the new policy of termination. This involved both a new policy of federal withdrawal from Indian affairs by freezing Indians out from government control and dependency, as well as the old policy of Indian assimilation. Emphasis again was on individual responsibility with the idea of removing all federal protection and services from various Indian tribes and making the Indian subject to the same laws and the same privileges and responsibilities as other citizens of the United States. The design of Congress was to get out of the "Indian business" and to "terminate" their federal trust relationship.

In 1953, Congress formally endorsed the policy of termination with the passage of House Concurrent Resolution 108. This act created a permanent procedure whereby states could extend civil and criminal jurisdiction over Indian tribes, thus undermining the powers of tribal governments to govern themselves and restricting their ability to utilize tribal resources as they wished. Between 1953 and 1962, 109 reservations were terminated, affecting some 1,369,000 acres of Indian land and affecting some 12,000 Indians (Fixico 1986:183). Perhaps the best-known examples of termination were those of the large Menominee reservation in Wisconsin and the equally large Klamath reservation in Oregon. The termination of federal responsibilities produced unforeseen complexities in the across-the-board transfer of functions from the federal to the state governments. Serious economic problems developed on many of these terminated reservations due to reduced federal aid and the taxing of Indian lands and property by the states. With land no longer protected by the government, there was also a strong desire on the part of Indians to sell their land, especially because of increasing land values. Some terminated reservations which had never before been allotted began to develop land problems similar to those of allotted Indian reservations during the allotment period (U.S. Congress. Senate 1935:318–29). The termination legislation produced tribal factions on many reservations—those that favored and those that opposed termination. The opposition to the policy of rapid termination was so strong on some reservations that it affected the willingness of many tribes to embark on new programs which might make them more self-sufficient. Tribes were afraid that a successful new program would lead to termination (Taylor 1959).

Relocation for Indians

The end of World War II also served as a stimulus for the first large-scale Indian population movements from reservations to urban areas. After the war, about 100,000 Indians who had served in the armed forces returned to the reservations (Higgins 1982:110). In response to this overcrowding and widespread unemployment on these reservations, the Bureau of Indian Affairs began a full-scale relocation program for Indians who desired permanent employment away from the reservation. Relocation was similar to termination because it was another way to disperse Indians among the general population in order to enhance assimilation. With assimilation, the federal government could again withdraw from the business of Indian affairs.

Relocation efforts intensified during the 1950s, emphasizing labor recruitment and financial assistance to aid in the resettling of Indians. In 1962, the voluntary program was renamed the Employment Assistance Program and its scope widened to include job placement in certain large metropolitan areas. To discourage Indians from returning to their reservations, large cities distant from reservations were selected for these programs. Employment assistance centers were established in Chicago, Cleveland, Dallas, Denver, Los Angeles, Oakland, San Jose, Tulsa, Oklahoma City, and Seattle. Over 160,000 Indians, approximately one-third of the estimated urban Indian population, were relocated to urban areas through these various government programs (Rhodes 1987:261). Many other Indians moved to smaller regional centers which were nearby their reservations such as Tulsa, Oklahoma City, Tucson, Minneapolis, and Albuquerque. Urbanization was difficult for most Indians, many of whom simply were not prepared socially, psychologically, or economically for the sudden removal of all federal trust status. The trauma of adjusting to the urban environment of unemployment, slum living, and alcoholism has been described in much of the current American Indian literature. It was not surprising that approximately 30 percent to 75 percent of the American Indians who participated in the Bureau of Indian Affairs relocation programs returned to their reservations (Lazewski 1982:121).

Self-Determination for Indians

In the 1960s, a government task force reviewed the Indian program and concluded that the emphasis on termination and relocation had impaired Indian morale and produced a "hostile or apathetic response" to federal Indian programs. The task force did not list termination or relocation as one of the Bureau's main objectives, as it had done during the 1950s, but emphasized the social, economic, and political development of the Indian community (U.S. Department of the Interior 1961). This shift in Indian policy became more explicit during the Kennedy and Johnson administrations. In presidential messages by both Kennedy and Johnson, the idea of termination was rejected. Control and responsibility were to be transferred from the federal government not to the states, but rather to the Indian community. During their terms in office, they initiated programs based on the belief that changes could best be brought about by establishing conditions for stimulating Indian communities to choose and develop their own patterns of adjustment. The Kennedy administration established the Area Redevelopment Program, and fifty-six reservations were designated reservation development areas. Emphasis was placed on Indian lead-

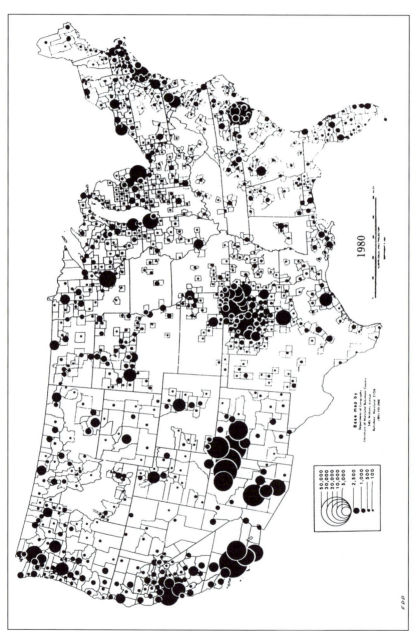

1980

Figure 4. Indian Population by Counties and SMSAs, 1980. (Reprinted from *Atlas of American Indian Affairs*, by Francis Paul Prucha, by permission of the University of Nebraska Press. Copyright © 1990 by the University of Nebraska Press.)

ership and Indian initiative in solving Indian problems, and funds were provided for specific programs in economic improvement, Indian education, and health. These programs were continued under the Johnson administration and Indians were intended to be part of President Johnson's "Great Society."

During the Nixon administration, Indian policy was broadened to encourage more Indian participation in programs. Federal policy became firmly committed to Indian self-determination, and past policies were rejected. In December 1973, Congress voted to reverse the termination of the Menominee Indian Reservation (Peroff 1982:189). From 1973 to 1980, six terminated tribes were restored to federally recognized status by the federal government (Fixico 1986). The emphasis on relocating Indians in cities was replaced with a greater emphasis on increased funding and on creation of reservation employment possibilities and education in job skills. In recent years, the case for Indian self-determination has been strengthened by court decisions concerning Indian jurisdiction over reservation populations as well as land, resources, and water rights. Over 80 percent of the Bureau of Indian Affairs work force and 90 percent of the agency superintendents are now Indians (Ross 1987:317). The administrations of Gerald Ford and Ronald Reagan demonstrated that the federal government will continue to assist Indians in self-determination, but with limited funding and reduced services. Reaganomics severely affected federal funding of Indian services. The Reagan administration cut back one-half of the health care services, one-half of funding for Indian higher education, and the Bureau of Indian Affairs budget was cut back by $80 million (Barsh 1981:24). In 1988, some Americans glowed with pride as they watched Ronald Reagan on television, delivering to the Russian people a compact history of this nation's treatment of its Native people. Clearly, his statement that we should not have humored Native Americans and should have forced them to join us indicated that his cutbacks were driven by thinking that closely followed the termination policy of the 1950s. Could it be that recent government policy is based on a belief that if American Indians were able to totally supervise their own affairs, there would be no need for special federal services and funding?

Urbanization of Indians also contributes to the plans to eventually dissolve federal services. Today, one-half of the total Indian population, an estimated 1.5 million people, reside in urban areas (U.S. Census). States such as Texas and California, which contain few Indian reservations, now have large numbers of American Indians residing in their cities. (See figure 4.) The highest concentrations of urban Indians are in the megalopolises of the Northeast and Midwest, where there are few reservations. Today, Indians are found in all fifty states, though well over 75 percent are living in fourteen states and almost one-half live in only four states. (See Appendix in this chapter.) The very location of urban Indians, like the location of reservation Indians, clearly reflects past federal Indian policies.

American policy may be characterized generally as having moved from indifference about Indian internal affairs to intensive concern with them. It has moved from the absence of programs for changing Indian culture to a program of replacement: replacement of tribal landholdings with individual landholdings, replacement of Native religions with various forms of Christian religion, replacement of informal home education with formal education, and replacement or improvement of Indian economics. The land problems which were initiated by the General Allotment Act still exist today, despite the community aid programs of the Indian Reorganization Act, the rapid assimilation programs of the early 1950s, the relocation programs of the 1960s, and the self-determination programs of the 1970s. Today, much remains to be done by the federal government to assist the Indians in restoring their land, regenerating their communities, and developing their economies.

Ronald A. Janke
Valparaiso University

APPENDIX

American Indian Population Living On and Off Reservations by State—1980 (in descending order of total population)

State	Population	On Reservation	Off Reservation
California	198,275	9,342	188,933
Oklahoma	169,292	4,749	164,543
Arizona	152,498	114,228	38,270
New Mexico	107,338	83,432	23,906
North Carolina	64,536	4,844	59,692
Washington	58,186	16,750	41,436
South Dakota	44,408	33,125	11,283
Texas	39,740	859	38,881
Michigan	39,734	1,790	37,944
New York	38,967	6,734	32,233
Montana	37,598	24,044	13,554
Minnesota	34,831	10,119	24,712
Wisconsin	29,320	9,440	19,880
Oregon	26,591	3,084	23,507
Alaska	21,869	942	20,927
North Dakota	20,120	13,040	7,080
Utah	19,158	6,885	12,273
Florida	19,134	1,303	17,831
Colorado	17,734	1,966	15,768
Illinois	15,846		15,846
Kansas	15,256	715	14,541
Nevada	13,306	4,739	8,567

State	Population	On Reservation	Off Reservation
Missouri	12,129		12,129
Ohio	11,985		11,985
Louisiana	11,969	395	11,574
Idaho	10,418	4,774	5,644
Arkansas	9,364		9,364
Virginia	9,211		9,093
Pennsylvania	9,179		9,179
Nebraska	9,145	2,846	6,299
New Jersey	8,176		8,176
Maryland	7,823		7,823
Indiana	7,682		7,682
Alabama	7,502		7,502
Massachusetts	7,484	1	7,483
Georgia	7,442	30	7,412
Wyoming	7,057	4,159	2,898
Mississippi	6,131	3,166	2,065
South Carolina	5,665	728	4,937
Iowa	5,369	492	4,887
Tennessee	5,013		5,013
Connecticut	4,431	27	4,404
Maine	4,057	1,235	2,822
Kentucky	3,518		3,518
Rhode Island	2,872		2,872
Hawaii	2,655		2,655
West Virginia	1,555		1,555
Delaware	1,307		1,307
New Hampshire	1,297		1,297
Washington, DC	996		996
Vermont	968		968

Source: Adapted from *American Indian Areas and Alaska Native Villages: 1980.* 1980 Census of Population, Supplementary Report PC80S113. August 1984. U.S. Department of Commerce, Bureau of the Census, page 14.

BIBLIOGRAPHY

Primary Sources

Cadwalader, Sandra L., and Vine Deloria, Jr. *The Aggression of Civilization: Federal Indian Policy Since the 1880's.* Philadelphia: Temple UP, 1984.

Deloria, Vine, Jr. *American Indian Policy in the Twentieth Century.* Norman: U of Oklahoma P, 1985.

Dippie, Brian W. *The Vanishing American: White Attitudes and United States Indian Policy.* Middletown, CT: Wesleyan UP, 1982.

Foreman, Grant. *Advancing the Frontier: 1830–1860.* Norman: U of Oklahoma P, 1933.

———. *Indian Removal: The Emigration of the Five Civilized Tribes.* Norman: U of Oklahoma P, 1953.

Kelly, W. H. *Indian Affairs and the I.R.A.* Tucson: U of Arizona P, 1954.

Kinney, J. P. *Indian Land Tenure in America.* Baltimore: Johns Hopkins UP, 1937.

Meriam, Lewis, et al. *The Problems of Indian Administration.* Baltimore: Johns Hopkins UP, 1928.

Prucha, Francis Paul. *Americanizing the American Indians*. Cambridge: Harvard UP, 1978.

———. *The Great Father: United States Government and the American Indians*. Lincoln: U of Nebraska P, 1984.

Royce, Charles C. "Indian Land Cessions in the United States." 18th Annual Report of the Bureau of American Ethnology. Washington, DC: GPO, 1930.

Smith, Jane F., and Robert M. Kuasnicka. *Indian-White Relations: A Persistent Paradox*. Washington, DC: Howard UP, 1976.

Spicer, Edward H. *Cycles of Conquest*. Tucson: U of Arizona P, 1962.

Taylor, Theodore W. "The Regional Organization of the Bureau of Indian Affairs." Diss. Harvard U, 1959.

———. *American Indian Policy*. Mt. Airy, OK: Lomond Public Press, 1983.

Tyler, Lyman S. *A History of Indian Policy*. Washington, DC: GPO, 1973.

United States. Bureau of Indian Affairs. *Annual Statistical Reports for 1934*. Washington, DC: GPO, 1934.

———. Congress. Senate. *Aspects of Indian Policy*. 79th Cong., 1st Sess. Washington, DC: GPO, 1944.

———. Congress. House. "House Concurrent Resolution 108." *United States Statutes at Large*. 67588–90. Washington, DC: GPO, 1953.

———. Congress. House. "Leasing Act Statutes at Large." XXVI. Washington, DC: GPO, 1991.

———. Dept. of Interior. Office of Indian Affairs. *The United States Indian Service*. Washington, DC: GPO, 1962.

Washburn, Wilcomb E. *The American Indian and the United States: A Documentary History*. New York: Random House, 1973.

———. *The Assault on Indian Tribalism: The General Allotment Law (Dawes Act) of 1887*. Philadelphia: J. B. Lippincott, 1975.

———. Dept. of Commerce. Bureau of Census. *American Indian Areas and Alaska Native Villages 1980*. Washington, DC: GPO, 1980.

Secondary Sources

Barsh, Russel. "The Reagan Budget." *Nations: The Native American Magazine* 11 (1981): 21–25.

Burt, Larry W. *Tribalism in Crisis: Federal Indian Policy, 1953–1961*. Albuquerque: U of New Mexico P, 1982.

Carlson, Leonard A. *Indians, Bureaucrats, and Land: The Dawes Act and the Decline of Indian Farming*. Westport, CT: Greenwood, 1981.

Danziger, Edmund Jefferson, Jr. *Indians and Bureaucrats Administering the Reservation Policy During the Civil War*. Urbana: U of Illinois P, 1974.

Fixico, Donald Lee. *Termination and Relocation: Federal Indian Policy 1945–1960*. Albuquerque: U of New Mexico P, 1986.

Fritz, Henry E. *The Movement for Indian Assimilation 1860–1890*. Philadelphia: U of Pennsylvania P, 1963.

Harger, Allan. "Indian Land Problems in the United States." *The North American Indian Today*. Toronto: Toronto Press, 1943. 181–83.

Higgins, Bryan. "Urban Indians: Patterns and Transformations." *Journal of Cultural Geography* 2.2 (1982): 110–19.

Jacobs, Wilbur R. *Dispossessing the American Indian: Indians and Whites on the Colonial Frontier*. New York: Charles Scribner's, 1972.

Janke, Ronald A. "The Loss of Indian Lands in Wisconsin, Montana, and Arizona." *A Cultural Geography of North American Indians*. Ed. Thomas E. Ross and Tyrel G. Moore. Boulder, CO: Westview, 1987. 127–49.

Keller, Robert H., Jr. *American Protestantism and United States Indian Policy 1869–1882*. Lincoln: U of Nebraska P, 1983.

Kelly, Lawrence C. *The Assault on Assimilation: John Collier and the Origins of Indian Reform Policy*. Albuquerque: U of New Mexico P, 1983.

Lazewski, Tony. "American Indian, Puerto Rican and Black Urbanization." *Journal of Cultural Geography* 2.2 (1982): 119–34.

Mardock, Robert. *The Movement for Indian Reform*. Columbia: U of Missouri P, 1971.

Neils, Elaine. *Reservation to City: Indian Migration and Federal Relocation*. Research Paper 131. Chicago: U of Chicago P, 1971.

Nichols, Roger L., ed. *The American Indian: Past and Present*. Tucson: U of Arizona P, 1981. 1–283.

Parkman, Francis. *The Jesuits in North America in the Seventeenth Century*. Boston: Little, Brown, 1867.

Peroff, Nicholas C. *Menominee Drums: Tribal Termination and Restoration, 1954–1974*. Norman: U of Oklahoma P, 1982.

Philp, Kenneth R., ed. *Indian Self-Rule: First Hand Accounts of Indian-White Relations from Roosevelt to Reagan*. Salt Lake City: Howe Brothers, 1986. 1–343.

Rhodes, Terrel. "The Urban American Indian." *A Cultural Geography of North American Indians*. Ed. Thomas E. Ross and Tyrel G. Moore. Boulder, CO: Westview, 1987. 259–97.

Robinson, W. Stitt. *The Southern Colonial Frontier, 1607–1763*. Albuquerque: U of New Mexico P, 1979.

Ross, Thomas E. "American Indian Problems and Prospects." *A Cultural Geography of North American Indians*. Ed. Thomas E. Ross and Tyrel G. Moore. Boulder, CO: Westview, 1987. 313–19.

Scudder, McKeel. "An Appraisal of the Indian Reorganization Act." *American Anthropology* 46 (1948): 213.

Stern, Theodore. *The Klamath Tribe: A People and Their Reservation*. Seattle: U of Washington P, 1965.

United States. Congress. House. *History of the Allotment Policy by D. S. Otis*. 73rd Cong., 2nd sess. H. Doc. 7902: 428. Washington, DC: GPO, 1934.

———. Congress. Senate. *The Status of Termination of the Menominee Indian Tribe*. 89th Cong., 1st Sess. 5. Doc. 1935: 318–29. Washington, DC: GPO, 1958.

———. Dept. of Interior. Office of Indian Affairs. *Task Force on Indian Affairs Report for July 10, 1961*. Washington, DC: GPO, 1961.

Viola, Herman J. *Thomas L. McKenney, Architect of America's Early Indian Policy 1816–1830*. Chicago: Swallow, 1974.

Waddell, Jack, and Michael Watson, eds. *The American Indian in Urban Society*. Boston: Little, Brown, 1971.

Autobiography

Autobiography, as it is generally understood in the West, did not traditionally exist as a genre of discourse among the indigenous peoples of the present-day United States. Necessary for the production of autobiography in the Western sense are, minimally, a culturally sanctioned concentration on the individual self or person and the technology of alphabetic writing. Neither of these was present in the Native cultures of America, which tended, in the first instance, to construct conceptions of the person in more nearly collective (family, clan, moiety, tribe) than individualistic terms, and, in the second, to employ oral rather than written means to communicate, store, and transmit information. Although as Lynne O'Brien has shown, there most certainly are aboriginal records of personal activity, achievement, and inspiration in coup stories, pictographs, and the recitation of visions and visitations, the typical Western autobiographical concern to record the whole of an individual's life, usually from an evolutionary or developmental perspective (e.g., I started *here* and arrived, in time, *there*) took hold among Indian people (so far as it does so at all) only as a consequence of the pressures upon them of Euroamerican people.

Arnold Krupat (1985) has distinguished between what he calls autobiographies-by-Indians and Indian autobiographies. Autobiographies-by-Indians are self-written texts produced by Native people who had accepted Western "civilization" at least to the extent of learning how to write (usually they had accepted "christianization" as well). Indian autobiographies are compositely produced texts, the result of a collaboration between a Euroamerican editor who fixes the text in writing and a traditional Indian person who is the subject of the text. Typically one or more mixed-blood persons have been involved as translator, as well.

Collaborative Indian Autobiographies (by Arnold Krupat)

A number of commentators have referred to these collaborative autobiographies as "as told to" autobiographies. Such an appellation is anachronistic, ethnocentric, patronizing, inaccurate, and simplistic. Anachronistic because the category of "as told to" autobiographies is entirely a twentieth-century one and thus is often misleading in its connotations when projected backwards onto nineteenth-century texts. Ethnocentric because the category derives largely from a Euroamerican context ("largely" rather than exclusively because a number of "as told to"–form autobiographies are of African-American subjects). What is sure is that there are no versions of the "as told to" in indigenous cultural production. Patronizing because "as told to" autobiographies are most commonly of celebrities, usually luminaries of popular culture, sports, entertainment, etc., specifically *not* celebrated for their literary or narrative abilities. They tell their stories to others because they cannot tell them themselves: this is not at all the case with Native American subjects of composite autobiography. Inaccurate because some of the presumptively "as told to" autobiographies originate not with Indian speech but with Indian writing (or drawing, in the case of Joseph White Bull), as in "Crashing Thunder's" autobiography, originally composed in a stenographic notebook in the Winnebago syllabary. Simplistic because the term reductively obscures the often-complex conditions of production of these composite texts, the varying roles of subjects, translators, editors, and so on.

The first Indian autobiographies produced by collaboration appeared in the nineteenth century under the sign of history, as Euroamericans sought out Native American people who had been prominent in the battles and encounters of various types that made up the "history" of Indian-white relations. J. B. Patterson's edition of *The Life of Ma-ka-tai-me-she-kia-kiak, or Black Hawk*, published in Cincinnati in 1833, just after the conclusion of the Black Hawk "War," was the first of these texts. Among others are the belatedly gathered accounts of such as Wooden Leg, "a warrior who fought Custer" (1931), of Joseph White Bull, the "warrior who killed Custer" (1931), and of Yellow Wolf, participant, with Chief Joseph, in the 1879 "flight" of the Nez Perces (1940).

If the first Indian autobiographies came out of a certain concern on the part of Indians and Euroamericans to set the historical record straight, the next group of these texts came from a concern to set the cultural record straight. Produced under the sign of science, from the first part of this century even to the present, a considerable number of Indian autobiographies were collected, not by amateur historians but by professional anthropologists who set out to record the "life histories" not of world-historical chiefs who had played a prominent part in the publicly recorded events of history, but of private individuals who might be taken as representatives of their cultures. Truman Michelson's early work with Fox and Cheyenne women is noteworthy here, although major attention to autobiography as a key to cultural understanding may be said to begin with the work of Paul Radin among the Winnebago (1913, 1920, 1926). Anthropologically inspired Indian autobiographies are too many to enumerate here (for a listing, see Brumble 1981 and 1982), although it may be worthwhile to name some of the better-known examples such as Walter Dyk's *Son of Old Man Hat* (1938), Leo Simmons's *Sun Chief* (1942), Ruth Underhill's *Papago Woman* (1936), and Nancy O. Lurie's *Mountain Wolf Woman* (1961).

But some of the best-known autobiographies of relatively unacculturated Indians were based not on transcriptions of interviews, but on narratives written by the Indians themselves. In some cases, the Indian's own sense of autobiographical form survives the work of editing. This is the case, for example, with *The Autobiography of a Winnebago Indian* (ca. 1917), a book written by Sam Blowsnake (Winnebago) in a Winnebago syllabary, then translated and edited by the anthropologist Paul Radin.[1] Here the form is Blowsnake's own adaptation of the oral confessional form he knew as a participant in the Peyote Cult rituals as they were practiced by the Wisconsin Winnebago (Brumble 1988:147–64).

In other cases, however, even when the Indian wrote most of the material upon which the autobiography is based, the form may be largely of the editor's devising. Don Talayesva wrote some 9,000 pages, for example, for the sociologist Leo Simmons, but the form of *Sun Chief* (1974) is nearly entirely owing to Simmons. The same may be said of the deeply moving autobiography of Rosalio Moises (Yaqui; 1954–58).

Some later editors are more tolerant of non-standard English, and more willing to allow the autobiographers' sense of form and order to stand. Nuligak (Eskimo; ca. 1960) had relatively little editorial assistance so he speaks to us in a voice quite his own about his life, projected upon a screen large enough for legend. Kathleen Sands strikes a fine balance between readability and fidelity in her edition of the autobiography of Refugio Savala (Yaqui; 1964–69). Anthony Apakark Thrasher (Eskimo; 1970–75) began writing down disjointed personal anecdotes while he was in jail awaiting trial. Later, in prison, he began to work with two journalists. One suspects that their editorial hand was heavy early on, and lighter as Thrasher began to educate himself in the prison school. The book is powerful, combining all the everyday brutalities of prison life with the psychological consequences of acculturation which have been common in Native American autobiographies from the start.

While these collaborative books were appearing, other Indians were writing quite without the aid of editors, Indians whose art and outlook were quite different from Eastman's or Griffis's or Standing Bear's. Maria Campbell (Metis; 1973) writes of her life, her people, and her life-long struggle with the problems of racial injustice (Bataille and Sands 1984:113–26). John Joseph Mathews (Osage; 1945), for example, was educated at the

University of Oklahoma and Oxford. In *Talking to the Moon* he seems quite self-consciously to have written a kind of Osage *Walden*. Like Thoreau, Mathews felt it necessary to retreat "from the roaring river of civilization" (p. 3). Thoreau had his pond; Mathews, the Oklahoma hills of his Osage people. Both built cabins, and both describe in detail the technology of their self-consciously primitive ways of life. And both fill their books with close observations of animals, people, and plants. Mathews weaves into his narrative a good deal of Osage history, myth, and nature lore, but the viewpoint is clearly that of a thoroughly educated, Western man. Probably this is why this good book is seldom read.

John Neihardt's collaboration with the Lakota holy man, Black Elk, *Black Elk Speaks* (1932) has been the subject of much recent study. Although Black Elk's life is extremely interesting from a historical point of view (he was present at the Custer fight and at the massacre of Wounded Knee), and from an ethnographic point of view (he was a traditional holy man who had been vouchsafed an elaborate vision deemed most powerful by his people), Neihardt's interest in it is neither historical nor scientific, so much as it is—if the terms be taken broadly—poetic and religious. Because the transcripts of Black Elk's work with Neihardt have been preserved, it is possible to answer questions concerning, for example, the specific contributions and purposes of each of the participants in the autobiographical encounter, questions of a sort that have not been answerable for other, less-well-documented texts.[2]

Collaborations between traditional Native people and non-Native editors continue to the present. We may cite, for example, the interesting autobiographies of Frank Fools Crow prepared by Thomas E. Mails (1979), and that of Lame Deer, by Richard Erdoes (1972), among others. Increasingly, however, texts of this sort have been somewhat eclipsed by the appearance of the highly sophisticated, individually composed autobiographical texts of such Native American artists as N. Scott Momaday, Leslie Marmon Silko, and the contributors to *I Tell You Now: Autobiographical Essays by Native American Writers* (1987), edited by Brian Swann and Arnold Krupat.

Autobiographies by Indians (by David Brumble)

It is not surprising that the earliest Indian autobiographical narratives should have been written by christianized Indians. In the first place, in the eighteenth century the missionaries were about the only people interested in teaching reading and writing to Indians. In the second place, there are strong traditions of Christian autobiographical narrative, confessional narratives, and stories of individual salvation and other faith-promoting experiences. Samson Occom's "A Short Narrative of My Life" (Mohegan; 1762)[3] may be understood largely in this context, as can the autobiographical passages in letters written by his fellow students: Samuel Ashpo (Mohegan; 1763–66), Hezekiah Calvin (Delaware; 1766–68), Joseph Johnson (Mohegan; 1767–74), and Tobias Shattock (Narraganset; 1765–67). All these Indians left—or were snatched out of—their tribes to learn hygiene, Greek, Latin, English, Calvinism, and guilt from Eleazar Wheelock at Dartmouth College. The letters of Ashpo, Johnson, Calvin, and Shattock (see McCallum 1932) describe struggles with drunkenness and the frontier Indians whom they were trying to convert. Taken together, there are few less fortunate examples of acculturation than these letters present.

The first extended christianizing autobiography was written by William Apes (1829). Apes also published a collection of such autobiographical conversion stories (1833), including a brief version of his own autobiography, wherein his insistence on the ill effects of white prejudice and interference stands out even more starkly than in his original. For three other early pietistic autobiographies, see George Copway (Ojibwa; 1846), Peter Jacobs (Ojibwa; 1852–57), and Peter Jones (Ojibwa; 1825–56).

Not all of the earliest Indian autobiographies are pietistic. In 1792, Hendrick Aupaumut convinced the government to commission him to travel to what were then the western tribes, the Onondagas, the Ottawas, the Shawnees, and the Wyandots among others, in order to convey to them the intentions—and the armed might—of the United States. He kept a journal of his eleven months' travel (Mahican; 1792 [the 1791 date in the published version is wrong]). This is one of the most remarkable of the Indian narratives that might be called autobiographical. Aupaumut felt his mission to be urgent. He also writes a good deal about the customs of the tribes he visits, about their speech making, their gift giving—and their usually disappointing responses to his message. Aupaumut shows us eighteenth-century Indians, Indians who knew *very* little of the white man, Indians still secure in their sense of permanence. We see them from the point of view of an acculturated Indian, but one with an acute sense of the fragility of all that he is describing.

Aupaumut's journal, then, is quite unusual for its point of view, but like the pietistic autobiographies it is not unusual in its form. All these were written fairly well in accord with Western traditions. But many Indians have written autobiographies which draw upon the Indians' own pre-literate, oral autobiographical traditions. At least six such pre-literate traditions have been identified (Brumble 1988): (1) the coup tales, (2) the less formal and usually more detailed stories of war and the hunt, (3) the self-examinations, (4) the self-vindications, (5) the educational narratives, and (6) the tales of the acquisition of powers.

As one might expect, the closer the Indian autobiographer is to his or her tribal traditions, the more the writer tends to rely upon pre-literate autobiographical traditions. *The Personal Narrative of Chief Joseph White Bull* (Teton Sioux; 1931) is a fine example of this. White Bull did not learn to write until after his surrender in 1876; and then he learned to write only in a Sioux syllabary. In 1931, a Fargo, North Dakota, businessman paid White Bull to write an account of his remarkable life. What White Bull produced was as close to traditional coup tales as writing would allow, and his written account of each coup was accompanied by a thoroughly traditional pictograph.

White Bull's traditional form mirrors his traditional intent. He is not at all concerned to explain the forces that shaped him, nor how he came to be just such a person as he was; he does not even mention his childhood. When the Fargo businessman paid him to write down the story of his life, he wrote down his adult deeds, all the glorious deeds that define him. He is the sum total of his deeds.

And White Bull does not provide connections between individual accounts of individual deeds. Indeed, in general the more unified the autobiography, the more we see connections between episodes, the more we are seeing the influence of European-American autobiographical traditions.

Sarah Winnemucca Hopkins's autobiography (Paiute; 1883) provides another example of the uses of pre-literate autobiographical traditions. Winnemucca was born in a Paiute brush hut, but she grew up to know a good deal more of white ways than White Bull did. Orally, she was quite fluent in English; in fact, she lectured on many occasions before white audiences on Indian subjects. But her education was not extensive; she seems not to have been at all widely read (Fowler 1978). While her autobiography is not as close to pre-literate forms as White Bull's, it still owes more to pre-literate autobiographical traditions than it does to Western autobiographical models.

Winnemucca's book has nearly as little to do with the development of the self as White Bull's. Winnemucca's narrative is more continuous than White Bull's collection of individual coup tales, but her book does concentrate on deeds; Winnemucca is more concerned with the cumulative effect of her deeds upon the reader than she is with the connections between events. Like many pre-literate autobiographers before her, she was concerned to tell the deeds that define her. She was also concerned to vindicate herself and her people—and this, too, was one of the traditional uses of first-person storytelling (Brumble 1988). Modern autobiographies are very much concerned with "turning points" and formative events. But Winnemucca is relying on a traditional sense of what it means to tell the story—or rather the stories—of a life. And so she does not talk about turning points or formative events.

Such autobiographers as Charles Alexander Eastman (Santee Sioux; 1902, 1916), Luther Standing Bear (Oglala Sioux; 1928, 1931), and Joseph Griffis (Osage; 1915) were thoroughly educated. Eastman, for example, earned a degree from the Boston University Medical School. It is not surprising that their autobiographies are quite close to the modern, Western sense of autobiography. There are clear turning points in these autobiographies. Both Eastman and Standing Bear were taken out of tribal life just at the point where they were entering upon manhood. Standing Bear was sent off to boarding school just after he killed his first buffalo. He was a student in the first class at Carlisle. Eastman, too, was taken away to enter into the white man's world just as he was entering upon the life of a warrior hunter. And there are other turning points along the way. In *Indian Boyhood*, Eastman describes the moment at which he first felt the instinct to hunt which is, he believed, native to the Indians:

> I was scarcely three years old when I stood one morning with my little bow and arrow in my hand. . . . Suddenly the instinct to chase and kill seized me powerfully. Just then a bird flew over my head and . . . Everything else was forgotten and in that moment I had taken my first step as a hunter. (87)

One simply does not find such passages in White Bull or Winnemucca. But such passages are basic to the autobiographies of Eastman, Griffis, and Standing Bear—for not only are they educated and aware of Western autobiographical traditions, they testify to the influence of Social Darwinist ideas. White Bull and Winnemucca do not think of the stories of their lives as descriptions of the evolution of a *self*; Eastman, Griffis, and Standing Bear see themselves as quintessential examples of the ways in which whole races of people evolve. Eastman, for example, begins *Indian Boyhood* with the assertion that the "North American Indian was the highest type of pagan and uncivilized man." The old ways may be recalled as glorious—as wonderful in the way that the remembered summers of childhood may be wonderful—but his autobiography shows him maturing, evolving from the highest type of pagan to the highest level of human. As he writes, he is competing at an equal level with white, American Christians in Herbert Spencer's laissez-faire world. The "Introduction" to Griffis's book makes such assumptions explicit. Griffis, we read,

> is a man who has passed through a series of transitions that have led him up from savagery, through the experiences of an Indian warrior . . . to the state of broad culture that fits him for his association and friendship with scientists, statesmen and leaders of world-thought. (7)

These autobiographers, then, hew as closely to European-American autobiographical models as they can. This is one of the ways in which they can demonstrate that they *have* evolved, that they are worthy of association with "leaders of world-thought." These autobiographers see themselves as having evolved even as their people must evolve. Their autobiographical mode expresses their belief that they have been assimilated into modern American society.

Americans and Europeans had long been interested in what Indians *do*; Eastman, Griffis, and Standing Bear spoke quite directly to those interests.

They described customs, hunting, warfare, and Indian history, along with their own experiences. But as interest in psychology waxed in America, readers became ever more interested in the ways Indians *thought*, especially the unacculturated Indians. It was always tempting to regard them as the "real Indians." Many social scientists and other Indian enthusiasts worked with Indians to produce Indian autobiographies.

With his Ph.D. from Stanford, N. Scott Momaday (Kiowa; 1966–69, 1976) is also thoroughly educated. But Momaday chose to write autobiography in ways that recalled oral Indian storytelling. In general, Momaday begins *The Names*,

> my narrative is an autobiographical account. Specifically, it is an act of the imagination. . . . When Pohd-lohk told a story he began by being quiet. Then he said *Ah-keah-de*, "They were camping," and he said it every time. I have tried to write in the same way, in the same spirit. Imagine: They were camping. (n.p.)

Momaday has written elsewhere ("The Man Made of Words") about his interest in the "evolution" of oral traditions into literature. In *The Way to Rainy Mountain* and *The Names*, Momaday is, as it were, trying to give us a sense in writing of what it would be like to experience stories in an oral culture. And so he eschews long narrative passages; brief stories, descriptive passages, and images tumble out one after another with *very* few explicit connections or transitions. The effect is very like White Bull's *Personal Narrative*, and even the purpose would seem to be very much the same. Both Momaday and White Bull expect us to formulate a sense of *who they are* by hearing the stories that constitute them. Both Momaday and the tellers of the coup tales tell their tales in order to build up in the minds of their audiences a sense of who they are essentially.[4]

Momaday's autobiographical work has done a good deal to establish the form of the present generation of Indian autobiographers. Leslie Silko's *Storyteller* (1981) follows Momaday very closely. She is a storyteller, concerned like Momaday to render the experience of oral storytelling in print. Her verse in particular is designed to convey a sense of oral performance. But most strikingly, her autobiography, like Momaday's, is discontinuous; it is one story, image, poem, after another, with very little explicit as to how the one relates to another (see Lincoln 1983:222–50).

Momaday's influence is similarly pervasive in many of the autobiographical essays collected by Swann and Krupat. This book provides the latest words from Indian autobiographers: Paula Gunn Allen, Jim Barnes, Joseph Bruchac, Barney Bush, Elizabeth Cook-Lynn, Jimmie Durham, Jack Forbes, Diane Glancy, Joy Harjo, Linda Hogan, Maurice Kenny, Duane Niatum, Simon Ortiz, Carter Revard, Wendy Rose, Ralph Salisbury, Mary Tallmountain, and Gerald Vizenor.

Conclusion

Critical attention to Indian autobiography, like the genre itself, has not a long history although developments of late have been most exciting. The indispensable starting point for study is H. David Brumble's *Annotated Bibliography of American Indian and Eskimo Autobiographies* (1981), and its "Supplement . . ." (1982). Brumble's *American Indian Autobiography* (1988) provides a fine sense of the history of the genre and readings of a number of selected texts, both autobiographies by Indians and Indian autobiographies. Arnold Krupat's *For Those Who Come After: A Study of Native American Autobiography* (1985) is more theoretical, bringing to bear on this subject aspects of continental criticism. For the life stories specifically of Native American women, there is *American Indian Women: Telling Their Lives* (1984) by Gretchen Bataille and Kathleen M. Sands, which contains a useful annotated bibliography. New work in this field is ongoing and most interesting.

David Brumble
University of Pittsburgh
Arnold Krupat
Sarah Lawrence College

Notes

1. Radin later reworked this material, keeping the order of the *Autobiography* and virtually all of its material, but adding to it substantially from material he had collected on other occasions. This was *Crashing Thunder*. See Krupat (1985:75–106) for the best account of the genesis of this book.
2. These questions are just those referred to in the note above as to who said what, who did what, etc. The works of Raymond DeMallie (1984), Clyde Holler (1984), and Julian Rice (1988) are particularly important for an understanding of *Black Elk Speaks*. Krupat's Appendix to the Nebraska edition of Paul Radin's *Crashing Thunder* goes some ways toward indicating the relative contributions of "Crashing Thunder" and of Radin; Brumble's "Sam Blowsnake: Adapting Oral Forms to Written Autobiography" is also an important contribution in these regards.
3. In what follows, the date of the autobiography is given in parentheses. Sometimes this is simply the date of publication; but where there is a lapse of years between writing and publication—as there often is for Indian autobiographers—I give the date of writing. The date of publication, of course, is always given in the bibliography.
4. Momaday's writing was, of course, profoundly affected by other than Indian oral traditions. The best introduction to Momaday's intellectual background is Schubnell (1985). For Momaday and the history of Indian autobiography, see Brumble (1988); for Momaday and oral tradition, see Evers (1977), Brumble (1983), and Lincoln (1983:82–121).

BIBLIOGRAPHY

Primary Sources

Apes, William. *A Son of the Forest: The Experience of William Apes, a Native of the Forest. Comprising a Notice of the Pequot Tribe of Indians. Written by Himself.* New York: By the author, 1829.

Apess, William (variant spelling of William Apes). *Experiences of Five Christian Indians of the Pequot Tribe.* Boston: By the author, 1833.

Aupaumut, Hendrick. *A Narrative of an Embassy to the Western Indians from the Original Manuscript of Hendrick Aupaumut.* Ed. B. H. Coates. *Pennsylvania Historical Society Memoirs* 2 (1827): 61–131.

Black Elk. *Black Elk Speaks.* 1932. Ed. John G. Neihardt. Rpt. Lincoln: U of Nebraska P, 1979.

Black Hawk. *The Life of Ma-ka-tai-me-she-kia-kiak or Black Hawk.* 1833. Ed. J. B. Patterson. Rpt. Urbana: U of Illinois P, 1955.

Blowsnake, Sam (pseudonym: Crashing Thunder). *The Autobiography of a Winnebago Indian.* Ed. Paul Radin. 1920. Rpt. New York: Dover, 1963.

Campbell, Maria. *Halfbreed.* Toronto: McClelland and Stewart, 1973.

Copway, George (Kah-ge-ga-gah-bowh). *Life, History, and Travels of Kah-ge-ga-gah-bowh.* Albany: Weed and Parsons, 1847.

Eastman, Charles Alexander. *Indian Boyhood.* 1902. Rpt. Boston: Little, Brown and Co., 1922.

———. *From the Deep Woods to Civilization: Chapters in the Autobiography of an Indian.* 1916. Rpt. Lincoln: U of Nebraska P, 1977.

Fools Crow, Frank. *Fools Crow.* Ed. Thomas E. Mails. Garden City, NY: Doubleday, 1979.

Griffis, Joseph K. *Tahan: Out of Savagery into Civilization.* New York: George H. Doran Co., 1915.

Hopkins, Sarah Winnemucca. *Life Among the Piutes: Their Wrongs and Claims.* Ed. Mrs. Horace Mann. 1883. Rpt. Bishop, CA: Sierra Media, Inc., 1969.

Jacobs, Peter. *Journal of the Reverend Peter Jacobs.* New York: By the author, 1857.

Jones, Peter. *Life and Journals of Kah-ke-wa-quo-na-by: Rev. Peter Jones, Wesleyan Missionary.* Ed. Wesleyan Missionary Committee. Toronto: Anton Green, 1860.

Lame Deer, John (Fire). *Lame Deer: Seeker of Visions.* Ed. Richard Erdoes. New York: Simon and Schuster, 1972.

Lurie, Nancy O., ed. *Mountain Wolf Woman, Sister of Crashing Thunder: The Autobiography of a Winnebago Woman.* Ann Arbor: U of Michigan P, 1961.

Mathews, John Joseph. *Talking to the Moon.* Chicago: Chicago UP, 1945.

Moises, Rosalio. *A Yaqui Life: The Personal Chronicle of a Yaqui Indian.* Ed. Jane Holden Kelly and William Curry Holden. Lincoln: U of Nebraska P, 1977.

Momaday, N. Scott. *The Way to Rainy Mountain.* 1969. New York: Ballantine, 1973.

———. "The Man Made of Words." *Literature of the American Indians.* Ed. Abraham Chapman. New York: NAL, 1975. 96–110.

———. *The Names.* New York: Harper & Row, 1976.

Nuligak. *I, Nuligak.* Ed. Maurice Metayer. Toronto: Peter Martin Associates Ltd., 1966.

Occom, Samson. "A Short Narrative of My Life." *The Elders Wrote: An Anthology of Early Prose by North American Indians, 1768–1931.* Ed. Bernd Peyer. Berlin: Dietrich Reimer Verlag, 1982. 12–18.

Radin, Paul, ed. "Personal Reminiscences of a Winnebago Indian." *Journal of American Folklore* 26 (1913): 293–318.

———. *The Autobiography of a Winnebago Indian.* 1920. New York: Dover, 1963.

————. *Crashing Thunder: The Autobiography of an American Indian.* 1926. Lincoln: U of Nebraska P, 1983.

Savala, Refugio. *The Autobiography of a Yaqui Poet.* Ed. Kathleen Sands. Tucson: U of Arizona Press, 1980.

Schubnell, Matthias. *N. Scott Momaday: The Cultural and Literary Background.* Norman: U of Oklahoma P, 1985.

Silko, Leslie Marmon. *Storyteller.* New York: Seaver Books, 1981.

Simmons, Leo W. *Sun Chief: The Autobiography of a Hopi Indian.* New Haven: Yale UP, 1974.

Standing Bear, Luther. *My People the Sioux.* 1928. Rpt. Lincoln: U of Nebraska P, 1975.

————. *My Indian Boyhood.* New York: Houghton Mifflin, 1931.

Swann, Brian, and Arnold Krupat, eds. *I Tell You Now: Autobiographical Essays by Native American Writers.* Lincoln: U of Nebraska P, 1987.

Thrasher, Anthony Apakark. *Thrasher . . . Skid Row Eskimo.* Eds. G. Deagle and A. Mettrick. Toronto: Griffin House, 1976.

Underhill, Ruth, ed. *Papago Woman.* 1936. Rpt. New York: Holt, Rinehart and Winston, 1979.

White Bull, Chief Joseph. *The Warrior Who Killed Custer.* Ed. James H. Howard. Rpt. Lincoln: U of Nebraska P, 1968.

Wooden Leg. *Wooden Leg: A Warrior Who Fought Custer.* 1931. Ed. Thomas B. Marquis. Rpt. Lincoln: U of Nebraska P, 1962.

Yellow Wolf. *Yellow Wolf: His Own Story.* 1940. Ed. Lucullus V. McWhorter. Rpt. Caldwell, ID: The Caxton Prints, 1987.

Secondary Sources

Bataille, Gretchen, and Kathleen M. Sands. *American Indian Women: Telling Their Lives.* Lincoln: U of Nebraska P, 1984.

Brumble, H. David. *An Annotated Bibliography of American Indian and Eskimo Autobiographies.* Lincoln: U of Nebraska P, 1981.

————. "A Supplement to *An Annotated Bibliography of American Indian and Eskimo Autobiographies.*" *Western American Literature* 17 (1982): 242–60.

————. "Indian Sacred Materials: Kroeber, Kroeber, Waters, and Momaday." *Smoothing the Ground: Essays on Native American Oral Literature.* Ed. Brian Swann. Berkeley: U of California P, 1983. 283–300.

————. *American Indian Autobiography.* Berkeley: U of California P, 1988.

DeMallie, Raymond. *The Sixth Grandfather: Black Elk's Teachings Given to John G. Neihardt.* Lincoln: U of Nebraska P, 1984.

Fowler, Catherine. "Sarah Winnemucca, Northern Paiute, ca. 1844–1891." *American Indian Intellectuals.* Ed. Margot Liberty. St. Paul: West Publishing Co., 1978. 33–44.

Holler, Clyde. "Lakota Religion and Tragedy: The Theology of *Black Elk Speaks.*" *Journal of the Academy of Religion* 52 (1984): 19–45.

Krupat, Arnold. Foreword and Appendix. *Crashing Thunder: The Autobiography of an American Indian.* 1926. Ed. Paul Radin. Lincoln: U of Nebraska P, 1983.

————. *For Those Who Come After: A Study of Native American Autobiography.* Berkeley: U of California P, 1985.

Lincoln, Kenneth. *Native American Renaissance.* Berkeley: U of California P, 1983.

McCallum, James Dow. *The Letters of Eleazar Wheelock's Indians.* Hanover, NH: Dartmouth College Publications, 1932.

O'Brien, Lynne Woods. *Plains Indian Autobiographies.* Boise: Boise State College Press, 1973.

Rice, Julian. *Lakota Storytelling.* Houston: The Hague, 1988.

Women's Autobiography

The image of Indian women in American culture has been largely a product of misinformation, stereotyping, and political convenience, yet Indian women have, over the past century and a half, been frequent and eloquent spokespersons for their tribes and activists for Indian causes. Many tribal women have also chosen to tell or write their life stories for a nontribal readership, giving voice to a wide range of personal intentions and experiences. However, despite the substantial canon of American Indian women's autobiographical texts, little attention has been given until recently to these works even by scholars in the fields of autobiography and American Indian literatures. In many cases, this is because the works are hard to find, often obscured by misclassification in libraries, not kept in print by publishers, or not marketed widely. And, of course, like all women's literature, they suffer from marginalization, but to a much higher degree, particularly when they challenge the princess/squaw image of Indian women held by American culture. As critic Sidonie Smith points out:

> if the autobiographer is a woman of color or a working class woman, she faces even more complex imbroglios of male-female figures: Here ideologies of race and class, sometimes even of nationality, intersect and confound those of gender. As a result, she is doubly or triply the subject of other people's representation, turned again and again in stories that reflect and promote certain forms of selfhood identified with class, race, and nationality as well as sex. In every case, moreover, she remains marginalized in that she finds herself resident on the margins of discourse, always removed from the center of power within the culture she inhabits. (1987:51)

Indian women autobiographers participate in two cultures, tribal and Euroamerican, and the marginality of Indian women's autobiographies is complicated by factors unique to their tribal source. Autobiography is not an indigenous form of literature for American Indian peoples. The traditional literature of tribal peoples is oral in nature and communal, consisting of myths, tales, songs, and chants performed in ceremonial context or told for the purpose of instructing and entertaining the community. Only since the nineteenth century have Indian peoples used written forms to record their histories and produce literary works, and until this century, only a minority of Indians wrote in English. Furthermore, individualism is not a highly regarded value in tribal societies, so to relate one's life story is to put oneself forward in a way that may elicit criticism from one's own community.

Representing Indian experience is further complicated by the fact that Indian culture is not homogeneous but is made up of several hundred separate cultures with separate languages and literatures. And, as in mainstream and other American minority cultures, the female autobiographical tradition is separate from the male tradition. Autobiographies of Indian men tend to focus on public lives; their subjects are figures of historical importance—chiefs, warriors, medicine men—while the autobiographies of Indian women tend to focus on private lives—the examination of personal relationships and individual growth, concentrating on everyday events and activities (see Jelinek 1980, 1986).

Finally, the process of Indian personal narrative is often collaborative—a tribal person narrating to a nontribal collector/editor. The intervention of a mediator between the narrator and the reader complicates the issues of voice and reliability inherent in autobiography because the published narrative is actually a bicultural composition.

Many of the autobiographies of American Indian women were collected and edited by anthropologists seeking case histories to support their ethnographic studies of American Indian tribes. Early ethnographers such as Truman Michelson and Gilbert Wilson sought out Indian women to serve as informants for longer studies on tribal traditions or agricultural practices. That events in their lives became a part of the narrative was often incidental. In some cases, this ethnographic intent leads to short, episodic narrative; in others, a full life history is presented but with little attention to aesthetic techniques or style. Thus the term autobiography, which is always difficult to define, is particularly problematical in reference to Indian personal narrative, since autobiography generally presumes literary intention and form. "Personal narrative" or "life story" are generally more accurate terms, although there are some Indian women's narratives that, despite their origins in ethnography, have recognized literary merit and fit commonly held conventions of autobiography, and others have been written consciously as literary works. Whether literary or ethnographic, the cross-cultural discourse required to represent the life and cultural context of a tribal woman to a nontribal reader is complex and adds to the already problematical nature of the autobiographical process.

To further complicate the study of Indian women's personal narrative, there are three separate traditions: composite, written, and multigenre. The bicultural composite (Krupat 1981:24) is most easily discussed using the terms "as-told-to" or "life history" since it is characterized by oral narration by the subject and recording, structuring, and editing by a nontribal person to form an extensive record of the subject's life. This form should not, however, be seen as an early stage in the development of Indian autobiography because it is still being produced today and has co-existed with written autobiographies by Indian women over the past century and a half. The written tradition is often affected by extensive editing by a nontribal person, so it too may share, in varying degrees, the bicultural method of composition. The multigenre form is a recent innovation by contemporary Indian women—creative writers, such as Leslie Marmon Silko, who mix oral tradition, personal narrative, fiction, and poetry into works that might best be called cultural memoirs.

Although the three processes referred to are not gender specific, gender must be considered in examining autobiographical works by American Indians, because it not only establishes the public/private contrast in these texts but has impact on the issues of reader reception and critical assessment. Because warriors and medicine men like Geronimo or Black Elk have historical recognition apart from their narratives, the reception of and critical attention to their autobiographical texts is far greater than to those written by Indian women who have no public reputations. Hence, female narratives are, as in mainstream literature, marginalized on the basis that their content is deemed not significant. Indian women, until recently, have not generally been active in the public arena; thus, it is assumed that their narratives must be essentially repetitious of one another, focusing on childhood, puberty, marriage and childbearing, and old age. Little variety or significance is expected. Even for the purpose of ethnography, women's lives are frequently seen as interesting only in terms of their generative and male-supporting roles, so in some cases little beyond data supporting representative social roles has been gathered and published. Because it has traditionally been a negative characteristic for tribal people to put themselves forward, the woman who narrates her individual experiences, particularly if she presents herself as other than representative of tribal norms, calls particularly negative attention to herself. She places herself in double jeopardy, criticized within her tribe and unlikely to find validation for her experiences or narration in the world of the nontribal audience either, because it generally upholds male-dominated criteria for autobiographical writing and clings tenaciously to the princess/squaw image. The American Indian woman who, either through a nontribal collector/editor, or by her own pen, ventures to call attention to her life, whether as representative or, more dangerously yet, as unique, risks censure at home, tepid reception in the dominant culture, and indifference from scholars.

It is a wonder, given this personal and literary peril, that any Indian women have chosen to share their life stories. Some have, in fact, remained anonymous informants for anthropologists, but most of the over 130 autobiographies by Indian women carry the narrator's names, and many are powerful and eloquent statements of personal and cultural survival.

One of the earliest written autobiographies by an American Indian is Sarah Winnemucca Hopkins's *Life Among the Piutes: Their Wrongs and Claims*, published in 1883. As the title suggests, this autobiography is not only a personal narrative but also a cultural history of the Northern Paiute tribe from early contact with whites to the 1880s, and a plea for an end to unjust treatment of her people.

Sarah Winnemucca, daughter of a shaman and chief, was born into a time of rapid and bewildering change for her people. In her youth she overcame a severe fear of whites and eventually became a battle leader and spokeswoman for her tribe, lecturing throughout the country and writing her life story to finance her advocacy of tribal causes. Winnemucca is a public person, and her autobiography is very much in the tradition of nineteenth-century male autobiography, focusing on her public roles and deeds. It is also, however, in the female tradition in her attention to domestic detail, her concern with the role of women within her tribe, and her role as teacher to the children of her tribe. Winnemucca's narrative is not typical of the more private nature of most Indian women's autobiographies; in fact, it is a defense against the criticism that her unusual and public life has attracted. It demonstrates the peril Indian women face when they enter the public arena and violate the squaw stereotype.

Almost exactly a century later, another autobiography, *During My Time*, narrated by Florence Edenshaw Davidson, a Haida woman, demonstrates the continuing viability of the collaborative method of Indian autobiography. Collected and edited by anthropologist Margaret B. Blackman, Davidson's life history presents a far more conventional portrait of Indian womanhood. Born in 1896, five years after Winnemucca's death, Davidson focuses on the domestic activities and family relationships that are commonly the concern of women's autobiography. As one of the last Haida women to go through traditional puberty rituals and an arranged marriage, she represents the old ways of her tribe. As a Christian woman active in her community on the seaward side of Queen Charlotte Island off the coast of western Canada, she also represents the changing experience of tribal women. As with many women's autobiographies, she expresses a nostalgia for the past, but she is not bitter about the changes in her life. Nor is her narration a conversion narrative. Rather, like many other Indian women's autobiographies, her narrative is one of cultural change and adaptation which focuses on her roles in the home and family as a stabilizing factor in a time of radical change in male roles. As editor Blackman points out, "Despite the social position she has enjoyed as the daughter of high-ranking parents and the esteem she has earned, Florence Davidson views her life as 'ordinary,' in the sense of being uneventful" (7). In this, and in her representative character, she is similar to many women who have related their life stories.

Production of autobiographical literature by fiction writers and poets has a long tradition in Euroamerican letters, but when American Indian women poet/novelists produce multigenre works, the conventional notions of Indian women's autobiography become expanded and redefined. Laguna Pueblo Indian writer Leslie Marmon Silko is an example of a contemporary writer of fiction and poetry who has ventured into areas of women's writing that are radically unlike the forms of autobiography discussed above but which are bicultural in nature and form of expression. Silko's collection of traditional stories, short fiction, poetry, and photographs, *Storyteller*, is a new kind of autobiographical text which uses fragments of personal narrative to bind together traditional stories, contemporary fiction, and poetic versions of stories central to the identity of the Laguna people. Personal reminiscences link the past and present in her book, cementing the individual to the tribal experience and memory and elucidating "the way remembrance works" in autobiography (Bataille and Sands 1984:139). Silko, in a distinctly tribal and innovative way, demonstrates the remarkable flexibility of autobiographical writing: it adapts to new needs, accommodates non-Western ways of knowing and expressing one's life, generates new concepts of text, and expands the definition of what is literary.

As new developments in the process of Indian women's autobiography influence the shape and understanding of personal narrative, new developments in literary and feminist theory may also open up new areas of discourse for interpreting these texts. Woman-centered mythology and ceremonial roles may receive more attention, and gossip, a powerful narrative tradition among Indian women, may gain legitimacy as a genre. Both written and orally narrated life stories will probably continue to be told, but with less involvement by nontribal collector/editors as Indian women take greater control of presenting their lives to the American public.

Whatever the future forms Indian women's autobiography may take, personal narrative by American Indian women will continue to be one of the few means open to nontribal people in America to learn the realities of life in tribal cultures; their autobiographies present detailed and intimate ways of knowing Indian women that demand that stereotypes be set aside. The voices of the past and the present verify and vivify the range and variety of experiences and roles in American Indian women's lives. Although it is unrealistic to expect the voices of the next generation of Indian women narrators to radically change popular attitudes about Indian women, with new forms and narrative strategies opening to them and with support from feminist theory and scholarship, Indian women have the potential to counter the superficial, flat stereotypes that clutter the American imagination.

Gretchen M. Bataille
Kathleen M. Sands
Arizona State University

BIBLIOGRAPHY

Primary Sources

Blackman, Margaret B., ed. *During My Time: Florence Edenshaw Davidson, a Haida Woman.* Seattle: U of Washington P, 1982.

Hopkins, Sarah Winnemucca. *Life Among the Piutes: Their Wrongs and Claims.* Boston: Printed for the Author, 1883. Facsimile rpt. Bishop, CA: Chalfant Press, 1969.

Silko, Leslie Marmon. *Storyteller.* New York: Seaver Books, 1981.

Secondary Sources

Bataille, Gretchen. *Native American Women: A Biographical Dictionary.* New York: Garland Publishing, Inc., 1991.

————, and Kathleen M. Sands. *American Indian Women: Telling Their Lives.* Lincoln: U of Nebraska P, 1984.

————. *American Indian Women: A Guide to Research.* New York: Garland Publishing, Inc., 1991.

Jelinek, Estelle C. *Women's Autobiography: Essays in Criticism.* Bloomington: Indiana UP, 1980.

————. *The Tradition of Women's Autobiography: From Antiquity to the Present.* Boston: Twayne Publishers, 1986.

Krupat, Arnold. "The Indian Autobiography: Origins, Type and Functions." *American Literature* 53.1 (1981): 22–42.

Smith, Sidonie. *A Poetics of Women's Autobiography: Marginality and the Fictions of Self-Representation.* Bloomington: Indiana UP, 1987.

Coyote's Jokebook: Humor in Native American Literature and Culture

For much of our history, that stern, unyielding profile of the Indian that used to grace our nickels has dominated the popular imagination. Indians, it was believed, never laughed, despite early testimony to the contrary by Washington Irving. Writing about his 1832 trip to the prairies, Irving declared Indians to be by "no means the stoics that they are represented. . . . When the Indians are among themselves . . . there cannot be greater gossips. . . . They are great mimics and buffoons, also, and entertain themselves excessively at the expense of the whites . . . reserving all comments until they are alone. Then it is that they give full scope to criticism, satire, mimicry, and mirth" (in Basso 1979:x). Freud pointed out that humor as a social process requires a social ground, so when we factor in the highly structured tribal communities, it would be surprising if Indians were *not* comically gifted. Yet even today, as Vine Deloria notes, whites have yet to understand how humor permeates virtually every area of Indian life; indeed, he asserts that nothing in Indian national affairs is possible without it, and that people are frequently educated and made militant by biting, activist humor (1969:147).

The Oral Comic Tradition, Yesterday and Today

The origins of many oral comic narratives may be found in religious ceremonies involving sacred clowns and shamans. Ritual clowns were an integral part of most early Western Indian cultures, forming a comic counterpoint to sacral events. The clowns were privileged to ridicule, burlesque, and defile even the most sacred religious festivals. Dressed outrageously, frequently in rags and masks, they would mimic the serious kachina dancers, stumbling, falling, throwing or even eating filth or excrement, setting up rival fake-Gods and "worshipping" them in an exaggerated fash-

193

ion, only to beat them a few seconds later. Much of their humor was sexual, and some of them were permitted to grab spectators' genitals. Although Europe had a parallel tradition carried on by monks until the sixteenth century called the Feast of Fools, Indian traditions probably actually derive from Mayan customs of "ceremonial madness." Moreover, as Steward noted in 1930, echoing Irving, the clowns were intermediaries, for "Humor of everyday occurrence, to be sure, was much in evidence in native life, but this is not available for our purpose because observers have paid little attention to it and made less record of it" (Steward 1930:187). Indeed, even today, some tribes prohibit religious ceremonies from beginning until all the people have laughed (Tedlock 1975:106). Black Elk once said that the people are caused "to feel jolly and happy at first [at ceremonies] so that it may be easier for the power to come to them" (Neihardt 1961:192).

As for the shaman, the magical qualities of his performances often elicited laughter as well as wonder, especially when he employed puppets. Sometimes the healing aspects of shamans were granted to clowns as well, as in Zuni, Ojibwa, and Canadian Dakota cultures, where clowning (especially caricature) was deemed therapeutic (Kirby 1974:10–14). Artists and shamans both draw what is feared into the open, enabling people to cope with it, a point to bear in mind with such brutally graphic but comic contemporary works as the plays of Hanay Geiogamah or the novels of Gerald Vizenor, James Welch, and others.

The key player in Indian humor, from the early narratives up to today, is the Trickster figure, who is sometimes wrongly confused with the shaman. As a comedian, he operates in a similar way, for all comic artists enable people to deal with feared subjects easily. Trickster is a figure known in virtually all Native American cultural traditions; his character is personified, but usually he can exchange animal and human forms. Transformation and trickery are his hallmark, yet he bears aspects of the divine. Most frequently he appears as Coyote, but in the Northwest he is Raven; in the East he becomes Hare. Other forms include Spider, Jay, or Wolverine. His scandalous behavior frequently has salutary results for mankind, for Trickster also figures in creation stories, especially the Earth diver tales and those of the flood and the re-creation of the world. Humor thus has a role in the beginning of things; in the Klamath creation story, sports and amusements are created before game animals, and the progenitor Kamukamts and Gopher pause in their creative activities to listen: "[They] heard the sound of people talking, and of children laughing. . . . " (Ramsey 1983:7). The Joshua Indians of Oregon report that "The Giver" (their creator) allows his human creation to smoke a pipe, which creates a horse, out of which appears a beautiful woman. The creator wryly remarks, "Now we shall have no more trouble in creating people" (Ramsey 1983:19). Stories such as these explain the mysteries—cosmic riddles—and Archer

Taylor's 1944 study was the first of several that outlined the popularity of riddles among tribes.

The biggest comic mystery is Trickster himself, breaker of all boundaries and thus source of delight, laughter, and narrative. Gerald Vizenor sees him as "a comic discourse and language game," one that establishes a "comic and communal discourse" (Vizenor 1978:x). Trickster is frequently depicted, too, as the giver of song (prototype of narrative), as in the myths of the Maidu of California.

Until recently, there were few literary studies of Trickster; perhaps one of the reasons critics hesitated is precisely that he is so very difficult to pin down. Unlike the picaro, whom he resembles in some ways, he isn't just a type of man; he lives in a timeless world and is apparently immortal, although he does die (only to be resurrected) in some tales told in the various cycles. Trickster is between God and man, and as such is both a link to God and a comic butt who mirrors man's own failings and glories. His appearance in written form in the current century has stimulated much critical interest.

Functions of Oral Comic Narrative

Trickster's comic characteristics lent themselves well to the crucial performance aspect of the telling of tales in winter, when the people gathered together in the lodges after the growing season was over. Across many Indian cultures, oral narration, sometimes even of ostensibly serious stories, would be calculated both to create humor and to draw it from the audience in their responses and questions. Trickster tales frequently center on bodily functions, and man's inability to control them; indeed, Trickster is generally blamed for all things that go wrong, which loss of body function symbolizes. In fact, the most popular tales have always been the ones that depict him as a buffoon, especially where he is known as Coyote, whose bawdy excesses are notorious. He uses his incredibly long, rope-like penis in endless affairs (including some with his own daughters); eats a laxative bulb, then breaks wind and defecates with hurricane-like force; charges his rectum to stand guard and then beats it for disobeying; and transforms himself into a woman and marries the chief's son in order to eat well. Such tales actually support the norms they rupture, while providing comic "release" from societal pressure. The tales, moreover, no matter how scabrous or obscene, were told in the presence of children, for they were meant to be instructive as well as entertaining. To expurgate the tales would also strip them of spontaneity and verisimilitude, as the tales reflect actual modes of discourse; Hopi verbal humor, for instance, relies heavily on puns, many of them sexual (Malotki 1983:205). And indeed, Indian humor is associated with more than the comic: Yellowman, a Navaho teller of Coyote stories, told Barre Toelken that Coyote tales "are not funny stories . . . [the people] are laughing at the way Ma'i does things, and at the way the story is told. Many things about the story are funny, but the story is not funny. . . . If my children hear the stories, they will grow up to be good people; if they don't hear them, they will turn out to be bad. . . . Through stories everything is made possible" (Toelken and Scott 1981:80). Furthermore, the tales were modified to fit instruction needed for the colonial period; one tale has Trickster "preaching" a sermon to furred animals and giving them "communion" that is poisoned, thereby permitting him to pay his debts with their skins, a devastating attack on the role of Catholic priests and the French fur trade (Wiget 1985:18).

As Karl Kroeber notes, Trickster stories permit fantasy indulgence in taboo behavior, release psychic tension, and simultaneously present a cautionary tale; but more important is the storytelling itself, which the audience participates in. "Stories teach skill in living. . . . A story teaches skill in a specific way of life, a culture . . . [which] cannot be divorced from long-term engagement in its performances" (Kroeber 82). Humor, moreover, is connected with memory, which pervades all Indian literature; the songs and tales until the last two centuries were oral and their survival depended on listeners remembering them and creatively repeating them; as Alfred Lord has noted of Western oral narratives, tradition can truly be preserved only if it is constantly re-created, via the singer of tales (Lord 1960:26). On a related note, a great deal of Native American literature centers on irony and paradox, possibly because, as Duane Niatum puts it, "complete survival is at stake, survival of the traditions and survival of what [the Indian] represents as a people . . ." (Bruchac 1987:196), and because a partly tragic history demands detachment to be comprehended.

Native American Literary Humor

Paradoxically, even though we now know much more about Native oral traditions, many still assume that being a member of a "tragic race" of "vanishing Americans" precludes the existence of a comic literature. But Indians, like Jews, blacks, and other oppressed peoples, have proved capable of taking what appears to be a tragic history, winnowing out and cherishing what contradicts it, and inverting the rest; thus the communal verbal tradition of joking lives, with a vengeance, providing a cornucopia of jokes and comic motifs for writers. Indians say, for instance, that Custer was well dressed for the Little Big Horn. When the Sioux found his body, he had on an Arrow shirt. He had boasted that he himself could ride through the entire Sioux nation with his Seventh Cavalry—he was half-right, Indians tell you—he got half-way through. Meanwhile, one of his soldiers, seeing that defeat was imminent, stripped, covered himself with mud, painted his face like an Indian, and crawled over to Indian lines, whispering "Don't shoot—I'm joining you." When asked why, he replied,

"Well, better red than dead." When an Indian gets old, people say he is "too old to muss the Custer anymore." Other, sadder events, such as the days when the Sioux had to eat dogs to keep alive after the buffalo were slaughtered, are turned into occasions for jokes by other tribes, who announce that their chef has prepared a special treat for the Sioux guests at the annual banquet through the special cooperation of the local dog pound (Deloria 1969:149, 164). This good-natured kidding has a long history, for in a sense, ethnic humor in North America began with gibes by one tribe about another, a much-documented practice that still goes on today; Robert Jarvenpa has shown that Chipewyans and Crees in Saskatchewan still tell stories about each other even though the causes of their ancient animosity (competition during the French fur-trading era) are long gone, and they live a somewhat symbiotic and neighborly life. In a more sinister vein, Simon Ortiz's poem "Indian Guys at a Bar" documents intragroup slurs; Chippewas and Pueblos get slammed by the speaker and his tribesmen, ironically followed by the speaker's recollection of a prison guard calling, "Get your red ass in gear, you're going home," followed by the reply, "I know. Here, have another drink of culture" (Bruchac 1983:190). Humor thus still functions within the tribal community as a corrective for mistaken behavior; Indians commonly refer to certain Indian brothers and sisters as "apples"; red on the outside, white on the inside. "Apples" thereby join a long parade of other ethnic in-joke victims, such as oreos (blacks), bananas (Asians), and coconuts (Hispanics). Similarly, artists who create stereotyped Indian art for lucrative tourist shops are sarcastically termed members of the "bambi" school—for creating a "proliferation of deer prancing over purple mountains" (Katz 1980:75), or members of the "beads-and-feathers" school of art. By contrast, the Mission/Luiseno Indian painter Fritz Scholder creates subtly ironic studies of contemporary Indians that tend toward caricature, feeling that distorted figures are expressive of paradoxical lives. "I reject the visual cliché of the noble savage bending over a fire sharpening his arrows. My buffalo dancer may wear traditional garb, but he'll hold an ice-cream cone or a beer can. I have depicted the Bureau of Indian Affairs as a Rhinoceros" (Katz 1980:77).

The Bureau, notorious for its mismanagement and insensitivity throughout a long history, has historically been the butt of Indian jokes. An example: Injun Joe went to the Public Health Service with a headache. The white doctor decided to cut Joe's brain out to take a look at it. When a messenger ran in with news that Joe's house was on fire, Joe headed for the door. "Wait, Joe," cried the doctor—"you forgot your brain!" "That's OK, Doc," said Joe. "After I put the fire out, I'm going to work for the BIA" (Deloria 1969:161).

Jokes like these enable a sometimes taciturn people to deal with infuriating and dangerous issues, especially relations with whites, which the Custer jokes also epitomize. Keith Basso has written an entire book that documents Apaches' fondness for mocking white speech with high-pitched English exclamations such as "I don't like it, my friend, you don't look good to me. Maybe you sick, need to eat aspirins! You come to clinic every day, my friend. Sure I help you over there. Sure got lots of aspirins. Maybe you drink too much, that why you sick . . . you got to sleep, my friend. . . . " In such verbal play, the code-switching, stock phrases, specific lexical items, recurrent sentence types, and patterned modifications in pitch, volume, tempo, and voice quality signal to those familiar with it that a particular form of joking has begun (and many of these devices may be found in contemporary Indian literature). This verbal dueling also signals the speaker's confidence in his special joking relationship with a friend; the participants test and affirm their relationship through mock-insult. Although Basso doesn't pursue the matter, here the Apaches are working in the framework of what humor theorists have termed an irony of irony: an extreme insult (under specific conditions) is more likely taken as a "left-handed" insult or compliment in disguise than is a mild insult. The illusion is created that the recipient is amused by a joke that attacks him, when in fact he laughs after cognitively restructuring the exchange nonliterally, as a compliment (LaFave et al. 1977:285). The existence of structures like these creates another criticism of superiority humor—the insultee is not threatened, and in fact feels a sense of mastery because he understands the incongruity and also appreciates being selected as someone savvy enough to know the convention. Basso's study finds the Apache jibes at whites useful, for in the joking relationship, tentative or "stiff" friendships get stretched and strengthened, like a worked-upon deerhide. The "Portraits" also quite obviously suggest the superiority of Apache manners and reticence over Anglo-Americans.

Critics of Indian literatures have quite properly warned themselves and others to avoid the assumption that any one description or literature represents all American Indians; we may, however, find somewhat of a common ground in many aspects of the humor employed, especially in the contemporary era. Joy Harjo, Diane Burns, Simon Ortiz, Hanay Geiogamah, Louise Erdrich, Leslie Silko, and many others frequently create comic treatments for underlying tragic themes such as drunkenness, alienation, aimless lives, poverty, and clashes among cultures, within families, and between men and women. We see these basic stances in poetry, drama, and fiction alike, and also in the acerbic and penetrating essays of Vine Deloria and the multigenre texts of Gerald Vizenor, the two of them in many ways the Diderot and Voltaire of the Native American Renaissance.

The tendency toward pan-tribal comic themes began virtually simultaneously with written humor at the turn of the century, with the newspaper satire of Alexander Posey (1873–1908), who used a fictional ethnic "reporter," Fus Fixico, to comment on the wrongs done to the Creek people by the U.S. government. His paradigm for this genre was surely Finley Peter Dunne's talkative Irish-American bartender, Mr. Dooley, who doled out drinks and wisdom in equal measure to his rather dense sidekick, Mr. Hennessy, in the pages of the nation's newspapers. Originally intended at least in part to counter anti-Irish sentiment which Dunne had felt himself, Mr. Dooley accepted the stereotype imposed on him and inverted it, commenting astutely on American events in Irish brogue. Posey, like other ethnic writers across the nation, knew Mr. Dooley's column, as well as popular cartoons and songs of the period which cruelly caricatured Indians alongside other ethnic groups in a kind of negative comic gallery favored by many ordinary patrons of popular culture. *Judge's* and *Puck* were two of the most popular magazines of this type, and Posey subscribed to both. He no doubt recognized that widely held stereotypical attitudes would seem to be variations on the "form," that is, on the general image (frequently negative) that the ethnic group is assigned by the dominant culture, and that Dunne had inverted and exploded them. Like Dunne, Posey hoped to shepherd his people through a difficult period of transition, the "end" of the Creek nation and the "transformation" of the people into Oklahomans. He used the character of Fus Fixico (the words mean "Fearless Bird") as a reporter on the conversations he has heard and participated in within the local Creek community. Fus at first is the dominant voice, but soon other characters take over, especially the volatile and salty Hotgun, who serves as a less refined version of Fus.

Like Dunne, Posey began to alter his style, his humor, and his characters once the columns began to gather momentum, consequently using humor as a come-on and a mask, for under the pose was a preacher, and under the jokes was a jeremiad. Indians were being bilked and duped by both lawyers and federal agents; Posey tried to expose these outrages, using a rich cast of Indians and corrupt politicians that rivals Mark Twain's uproarious crew in *The Gilded Age*. The "book" constituted by the letters actually more resembles Sut Lovingood stories, where "It is good to be shifty in a new country." Instead of *Orpheus Seeker*, we have real figures like Senator Owen dubbed "Col. Robert L. Owes-em." Significantly, Posey sometimes used the pen name Chinnubbie Harjo, who in Muskogee mythology was a trickster who could change character. Fixico's comic wisdom is rendered from a realistic rural perspective; Fus speaks nonstandard English, mixing tenses and negatives freely, as in "I didn't had not time to write," and crop reports, observations on the all-important weather, and so forth frequently precede his vignettes of life on the reservation and Indian–U.S. government relations. This type of writing, still practiced today by Indian writers, illustrates Mary Douglas's formulation of a joke as a play upon form, bringing disparate elements into configuration, in that "one accepted pattern is challenged by the appearance of another which in some way was hidden in the first . . . a successful subversion of one form by another completes or ends the joke for it changes the balance of power" (Douglas 1968:365).

In the early twentieth century, pressures of acculturation and competition from white writers "going Indian" created a decline in the volume of Indian publications, which was reversed by the appearance of Indian autobiographies and "serious" novels by John Joseph Mathews, D'Arcy McNickle, and John Milton Oskison in the 1930s. The "mainstream" black humor of the 1960s, however, had its parallel in the paradoxical, ironic humor of the early Native Renaissance writers. Alan Velie has shown that Trickster figures prominently in contemporary "serious" novels such as Momaday's *House Made of Dawn* and Welch's *Winter in the Blood*, going so far as to say that the latter novel is "a masterpiece of comic fiction" (Velie 1989:92); the humor in this dark book, however, is frequently surreal and indebted more to modernist "black" humor than to traditional Indian styles. Humor plays a role in another quite serious work, Leslie Silko's *Ceremony* (1977), in scenes such as the one where she depicts one antagonist's army adventures; using a doubly comic mode, he creates an obscene poem to relate how he comes on to two white women in a bar, a commentary on casual cross-ethnic humor and a parody of Native American prosody: "I used Mattuci's name that night—this Wop / in our unit." The next day his friend learns he scored with both women: "Shit, Chief, / that's some reputation / you're makin for Mattuci!" / "Goddam," I said / "Maybe next time / I'll send him a bill!" (60–61).

Even the titles of texts promise hip, angry humor, as in Charles Trimble's *Shove It, Buster, We'd Rather Have Our Land*, or anthropologist/poet Wendy Rose's chapbook, *Academic Squaw: Reports to the World from the Ivory Tower*.

Other Indian writers target for satirical treatment, the Bureau of Indian Affairs, white do-gooders, missionaries, and tourists but various factions within the community draw their ire as well, as in *Love Medicine*, when Louise Erdrich satirizes Nector Kashpaw's involvement with the tribal council's plan to take the land of his mistress. There's also the comic love story of the gargantuans Dot Adare and Gerry Nanapush; he's eternally on the lam, largely because of his status as Houdini-like escape artist, on a treadmill of incarceration, escape, and capture because he can't abide enclosed spaces. He clearly resembles Trickster, and indeed, the Chippewa name for Trickster/Hare is "nanabush." Erdrich, like many other contemporary Indian novelists, writes of anguished lives, poverty, and multicultural angst, employing naturalism and tragedy, yet humor plays a leading role in all her narratives; the sharp edges largely depend on a judicious use of Indian humor.

Gerald Vizenor's novels, including *The Trickster of Liberty* and *Griever*, but especially *Darkness in Saint Louis Bearheart*, fit the categories of both the Trickster narrative and the comic postmodern novel (Alan Velie and Louis Owens have done detailed "postmodern" readings of the book—see

Vizenor 1978). Andrew Wiget sees a parallel with Trickster's classic encounter with the Evil Gambler in *Bearheart*'s Sir Cecil Staples episode; the mythic original depicts the Gambler's defeat as the avenue to restored life and rain (Wiget 1985:96). Vizenor undeniably employs traditional Native American myths and comic devices, especially with Trickster characters, and is the best example of how Native American traditions are merging with the cutting edge of contemporary writing.

It should be noted that white writers, knowing a good thing when they see it, have appropriated Indian subjects and characters in humorous novels and stories, such as those by the Canadian writers W. P. Kinsella (*The Moccasin Telegraph* and *Shoeless Joe*), W. H. Drummond, author of the "Leetle Bateeste" poems; and Dan Cushman, whose *Stay Away, Joe* is quite popular on reservations.

Coyote appears repeatedly in the poetry and prose of contemporary writers; Peter Blue Cloud uses him because he enables coverage of any kind of material, and you can make fun of current events; "People are still doing the same stupid and good things that they were doing hundreds of years ago, so why not tell the same stories and just bring them up to today?" (Bruchac 1987:31). Freely transcribed and updated *Tales of Nanabozho* (ed. Dorothy M. Reid) get taken much further by the contemporary and hip *Coyote's Journal* (ed. James Koller et al.), an anthology of Coyote's appearance in short poems, stories, and essays by contemporary Native American writers; the collection amply documents the fact that Coyote is alive and well and living just about everywhere, trendy or traditional. Also a joy is Joseph Bruchac's collection of contemporary American Indian poetry, *Songs from This Earth on Turtle's Back* (1983). Most of the brightest new stars of the Native American Renaissance have contributed to these two volumes, both in prose and poetry. Leslie Silko's great comic poem "Toe'osh: A Laguna Coyote Story—for Simon Ortiz" (Bruchac 1983:228) typically updates Coyote, encompassing traditional tales and contemporary tribal events, even negotiations with pipeline executives.

Diane Burns's "Sure You Can Ask Me a Personal Question" epitomizes the wry humor used to skewer white attitudes toward Indians; the poem gives an Indian woman's side of a conversation with an ignorant white woman, who asks the speaker if she's Chinese or Spanish, if Indians are extinct, and so on, before announcing that her own grandmother was a "Cherokee Princess," and admitting that she's had an Indian friend, an Indian lover, and an Indian servant. After apologizing for historical wrongs, she asks where she can buy peyote, is Cher really Indian, and so on (Bruchac 1983:40). There is bitter humor, too, as in Gogisgi's "Song of the Breed," where the title figure is forced by the world to stand in the middle of the "god-damned road" between "fullbloods" and "whites" to get hit (Bruchac 1983:14). Humor's serious use and its continuing link to the spiritual is hinted at in Robert J. Conley's "Untitled": "My poem might be a prayer /

an offering or a joke / and it is sacred / only insofar as it is honest / no more—no less" (Bruchac 1983:52). Maurice Kenny, in "Corn Planter," takes deadly comic aim at the loss of traditional skills and occupations, first limning the various catastrophes of a would-be corn planter, whose solution after eight seasons of failure is: "The ninth spring I make chicken-feather headdresses, / plastic tom-toms and beaded belts. / I grow rich, / buy an old Ford, / drive to Chicago, / and get drunk / on Welfare checks" (Bruchac 1983:132). Peter Coyote (and who should know better) reminds us that "Coyote is never (except in Native traditions) pictured as house-holder and community man. The rush to overlook this is a Coyote tricking that bears watching . . . Coyote is the miss in your engine / He steals your concentration in / the Zendo Mates for life. A good / family man who helps raise the kids" (Koller 1982:45) And Peter Coyote is right—for Paul Radin, in his classic *The Trickster*, noting Wakdjunkaga's youthful vora-ciousness and notorious early adventures, points nevertheless to final facts: "He has relatives. He has attachments. His task is to grow up and to see that human beings grow up with him. Most of the incidents in the cycle illustrate how this is accomplished . . . what happens to him happens to us" (1972:166–69). Coyote does indeed seem more and more to fit in with our image of ourselves—hedonistic, existential, but evolving, changing, maybe ready to put down roots—certainly interested in community; and the real coyotes are moving into the suburbs. Coyote may or may not be a charac-ter in a modern play, story, or poem, but his tradition—of using humor to present a universal truth or value—goes on, for he has become a symbol for the chaos of modern life. As Paula Gunn Allen notes, he survives because of his creative prowess, and therefore has special meaning for the ongoing Native American literary renaissance, providing life-saving hu-mor as a resource against horror (Allen 1986:158).

Finally, in addition to inspiring action, uniting the people, providing sheer play and laughter, humor frequently works to heal and unite; the older women in Paula Gunn Allen's story "Tough Love" take care of each other, "using joking and jibing to convey love and concern. It worked" (1983:200). As Rayna Green states, "This Indian world fills the empty spaces with laughter, with humor. Laughing is one way Indians, like all people, get around the tragedy, the trouble, the one-way street they stumble into" (1984:11). Her remarks suggest the obvious, that the oral tradition did not die with the introduction of the printed word; indeed, it flourishes today, in both traditional and innovative forms, such as the contemporary songs sung at '49s, ritualized nocturnal gatherings of young Native Ameri-cans where song, dancing, drinking, and sexual excitement provide a con-temporary equivalent to more ancient gatherings, and a youthful version of adult powwows. This in turn has led to a provocative and hilarious play, Hanay Geiogamah's *49*, which juxtaposes an 1885 ceremony with a '49 occurring in the same place today. Traditional Indian music and chants punctuate the exuberant celebration of ethnicity, presided over by the ancestral spirit of Night Walker, whose sacral language intertwines with the comic, hip exclamations of the young people. The comic exchanges of a car full of kids coming to the event are broken off, however, by a fatal wreck, and the play ends with the young defying the efforts of white police to disperse them; the humor is used to underline deeply serious matters of tradition and cultural assertion. Similarly, Geiogamah's *Body Indian* follows a drunken binge in a filthy apartment through five comic scenes, taking an Indian cast through Rabelaisian physical comedy that culminates in the theft of the central figure's artificial leg, to be sold to buy booze. Geiogamah courageously accepts and then explodes one tired stereotype about Indians after another. The unsparing humor is self-directed, but ultimately forces the audience to face, via laughter and tears, both the degradation and endurance of a proud people.

Not surprisingly, Geiogamah and other writers willing to examine poverty, drunkenness, and other problems in the community have been attacked for washing dirty linen in public. Geiogamah looks without, however, as well as within; *Foghorn* offers a surreal collage of hilarious caricatures of red-white relationships over the years, all occurring against the backdrop of the dramatic seizure of Alcatraz Island by Indians in 1978, painting a damning portrait of contemporary federal policies. In a different vein, *Coon Cons Coyote*, based on a Nez Perce coyote story, encourages the audience to identify the lusty, earthy humor of the foolish animals with human behavior, and thereby to laugh at themselves in a comic shock of recognition.

In these plays, Geiogamah arguably displays the most impressive comic gifts of all the Native American Renaissance writers, possibly because his art, like its ancient heritage, is so tied to performance.

Humor, always present in the oral narratives, has taken on even more important dimensions in the ongoing Native American literary renaissance; in a postmodern age, it helps man analyze the absurdities, contradictions, and injustices in what sometimes seems to be a nightmare world, an image that has plagued Native Americans since the white man landed on this continent. As current Indian writers demonstrate, Native American humor now seems to speak for all citizens of this land. It is not too much to say that Trickster and the Indian humor he creates keep tribal culture and all that it contributes to America from stagnating; the very engine of dynamism, humor forces us to reinvent the world anew.

John Lowe
Louisiana State University

BIBLIOGRAPHY

Allen, Paula Gunn. "Tough Love." *Earth Power Coming: Short Fiction in Native American Literature.* Ed. Simon Ortiz. Tsaile, AZ: Navajo Community College Press,

1983. 196–215.

———. *The Sacred Hoop: Recovering the Feminine in American Indian Traditions*. Boston: Beacon Press, 1986.

Basso, Keith H. *Portraits of "the Whiteman": Linguistic Play and Cultural Symbols Among the Western Apache*. Cambridge: Cambridge UP, 1979.

Blue Cloud, Peter. "Coyote Meets Raven." *Earth Power Coming: Short Fiction in Native American Literature*. Ed. Simon Ortiz. Tsaile, AZ: Navajo Community College Press, 1983. 120–22.

Bruchac, Joseph, ed. *Songs from This Earth on Turtle's Back: Contemporary American Indian Poetry*. Greenfield Center, NY: The Greenfield Review Press, 1983.

———, ed. *Survival This Way: Interviews with American Indian Poets*. Tucson: Sun Tracks and the U of Arizona P, 1987.

Deloria, Vine, Jr. "Indian Humor." *Custer Died for Your Sins*. New York: Macmillan, 1969. 146–67.

Douglas, Mary. "The Social Control of Cognition: Some Factors in Joke Perception." *Man* 3 (1968): 361–76.

Green, Rayna. *That's What She Said: Contemporary Poetry and Fiction by Native American Women*. Bloomington: Indiana UP, 1984.

Jarvenpa, Robert. "Intergroup Behavior and Imagery: The Case of Chipewyan and Cree." *Ethnology* 21 (1982): 283–99.

Katz, Jane B., ed. *This Song Remembers: Self-Portraits of Native Americans in the Arts*. Boston: Houghton Mifflin, 1980.

Kirby, E. T. "The Shamanistic Origins of Popular Entertainments." *Drama Review* 18 (1974): 5–15.

Koller, James. "Gogisgi." *Coyote's Journal*. Eds. Carroll Arnett, James Koller, Steve Nemirow, and Peter Blue Cloud. Berkeley: Wingbow Press, 1982.

Kroeber, Karl. "Deconstructionist Criticism and American Indian Literatures." *Boundary* 2, 7, 3 (1979): 73–89.

LaFave, L., R. Mannell, and A. M. Guilmette. "An Irony of Irony: The Left-Handed Insult in Intragroup Humour." *It's a Funny Thing, Humour*. Eds. Anthony J. Chapman and Hugh C. Foot. New York: Pergamon, 1977. 283–89.

Lincoln, Kenneth. *Native American Renaissance*. Berkeley: U of California P, 1983.

Lord, Albert B. *The Singer of Tales*. Cambridge: Harvard UP, 1960.

Malotki, Ekkenhart. "The Story of the 'Tismonmanmant' or Jimson Weed Girls." *Smoothing the Ground: Essays on Native American Oral Literature*. Ed. Brian Swann. Berkeley: U of California P, 1983. 204–20.

Neihardt, John G. *Black Elk Speaks*. Lincoln: U of Nebraska P, 1961.

Radin, Paul. *The Trickster: A Study in American Indian Mythology*. New York: Schocken Books, 1972.

Ramsey, Jarold. *Reading the Fire: Essays in the Traditional Indian Literatures of the Far West*. Lincoln: U of Nebraska P, 1983.

Silko, Leslie. *Ceremony*. New York: Viking, 1977.

Steward, Julian. "The Ceremonial Buffoon of the American Indian." *Papers of the Michigan Academy of Science, Arts, and Letters* 21 (1930): 187–207.

Taylor, Archer. "American Indian Riddles." *Journal of American Folklore* 57 (1944): 1–15.

Tedlock, Barbara. "The Clown's Way." *Teachings from the American Earth: Indian Religion and Philosophy*. Ed. Dennis Tedlock and Barbara Tedlock. New York: Liveright, 1975. 105–18.

Toelken, Barre, and Tacheeni Scott. "Poetic Retranslation and the 'Pretty Languages.'" *Traditional American Indian Literatures: Texts and Interpretations*. Ed. Karl Kroeber. Lincoln: U of Nebraska P, 1981.

Velie, Alan. "The Trickster Novel." *Narrative Chance: Postmodern Discourse on Native American Indian Literatures.* Ed. Gerald Vizenor. Albuquerque: U of New Mexico P, 1989. 121–40.

Vizenor, Gerald. *Wordarrows: Indians and Whites in the New Fur Trade.* Minneapolis: U of Minnesota P, 1978.

Wiget, Andrew. *Native American Literature.* Boston: Twayne, 1985.

William Apes *(January 31, 1798–1839)*

William Apes is one of the most intriguing personalities who emerged in the early stages of Native American literature. His four monographs stand out in their times for their critical interpretation of New England's association with Native Americans. In addition to his literary achievements, Apes is also remembered today for his important role in the Mashpee struggle for autonomy during the Jacksonian era.

The limited data currently available on Apes is derived solely from his own autobiographical accounts. According to these, he was born near Colrain, Massachusetts, in 1798. His father was a half-blood Pequot who had chosen to live with the tribe and eventually married a full-blood, reputed to be a relative of King Philip. Apes's parents separated shortly after his birth and left him and his siblings in the care of maternal grandparents in Colchester, Connecticut. In 1803, he was so severely beaten by his alcoholic grandmother that the town selectmen removed him from her care. Lacking any financial means, he was bound out to three different families between 1804 and 1813. At age fifteen he ran away and enlisted in the army, participating in the furtive campaign against Canada during the War of 1812. Following his release in 1814, he led a wandering life until 1818, when he was baptized by Methodists and turned to preaching as a vocation. He was ordained by the Methodist Society in 1829. In 1833, he visited the Mashpee in Cape Cod and became actively involved in their long-standing dispute with the state of Massachusetts over their political sovereignty. Under Apes's leadership—he was officially adopted into the tribe—the Mashpee managed to attain a certain degree of autonomy by March 1834. His efforts on their behalf, which included legal as well as

---

*Apes also gave January 30 as the day of his birth.

disruptive tactics, were much publicized by New England newspapers like William Lloyd Garrison's *Liberator*. Apes thus became a popular figure among contemporary eastern abolitionists, while incurring the ill feelings of local agents and speculators (Campisi 1979; McQuaid 1977). According to a recent study on the Mashpee (Brodeur 1985), Apes continues to be honored by them as a folk hero.

William Apes began to publish fairly extensively after his ordination in 1829. His first work, *A Son of the Forest* (1829), is a detailed account of his difficult childhood, adventurous wanderings, and ultimate conversion to Christianity. Content and style reflect the influence of two types of auto-biographical writings popular at the turn of the nineteenth century: spiritual autobiographies, which are concerned primarily with the author's path to salvation (or conversion testimony); and slave narratives, in which the author's trials as a member of a discriminated-against ethnic minority are depicted with the intention of stimulating public consciousness. It was reprinted in a revised edition in 1831, supplemented by a long essay on Native American "moral character." The latter is a compilation of annotated quotations from a wide range of books then available on Native Americans, focusing upon the popular notion of the "Ten Lost Tribes of Israel" as expounded by the philanthropist Elias C. Boudinot. Apes's autobiography is the first to be written by a Native American (in English), predating Black Hawk's famous "as-told-to" autobiography by four years.

In 1833, Apes published *The Experiences of Five Christian Indians of the Pequot Tribe*. This monograph is composed of five brief autobiographies: a summarized version of *A Son of the Forest*, followed by the conversion testimonies of his Anglo-Spanish wife (Mary Apes) and three Pequot women. These are supplemented by an essay entitled "An Indian's Looking Glass for the White Man," in which Apes bitterly denounces racism and lists alcohol, unemployment, legal dependency, unclear land titles, improper education, and corrupt agents as the essence of the "Indian problem" being publicly discussed in the course of removal policies. The use of humor to convey social criticism is similar to the use of humor in the blossoming period of Native American literature that began some 130 years later.

In 1835, Apes completed his most ambitious piece, *Indian Nullification of the Unconstitutional Laws of Massachusetts, Relative to the Marshpee Tribe: Or, the Pretended Riot Explained*. This monograph of about 200 pages outlines the Mashpee conflict and Apes's role therein, underscored by numerous reprinted letters and newspaper articles. The author concludes from his experiences that "Indian policy" is merely calculated to divest Native Americans of their lands, that it is "one continued system of robbery." Apparently the manuscript was edited for publication by William J. Snelling, but the extent of his participation remains unclear.

The last monograph Apes wrote is *Eulogy on King Philip* (Boston: By the author, 1837). This forty-eight-page tract was originally read at the Odeon in Boston on January 8, 1836. Here Apes carries on the example set by Washington Irving's "Traits of Indian Character" in his *Sketch Book* (1819), which Apes had cited extensively in *A Son of the Forest*, and depicts the famous Native American leader as a heroic patriot who fought a just war against Puritan aggressors, a point of view that was undoubtedly of a more volatile nature when publicly proclaimed by an Indian. The tragic fate of King Philip and his family, however, is merely the background against which Apes mounts a remarkable attack on Puritan treatment of Native Americans in general, which does not spare from criticism venerable figures like Increase Mather. Well ahead of his times, Apes declares December 22 (the date of the pilgrims' landing) a day of mourning for all Native Americans. Together with "An Indian's Looking Glass for the White Man," the *Eulogy* represents the best of Apes's writing.

Apes was also the author of a number of tracts, at least one of which has survived: "The Increase in the Kingdom of Christ: A Sermon" (1831). His appeal for Methodism was due in part to the relatively egalitarian views expounded by this society and the more spontaneous, emotionally charged oratorical style of its preachers. Apes himself shared the notion of nonsectarian religion, and the concept of a "religion for the common man," as expressed in the tract mentioned above, reflects Methodist principles during the "Second Great Awakening" in the first half of the nineteenth century.

Perhaps it was Apes's marginal position—in his own words, as a "cast-off member of the tribe" (Apes, *A Son of the Forest*, 22)—that sharpened his sensitivity to social injustice and made him so critical of dominant society. Unfortunately, he disappears from the pages of history shortly after leaving the Mashpee in 1835. A ticket for one of his public addresses, contained in the Newberry Library's Ayer Collection along with a portrait, bears the following handwritten message: "Pequot Indian Chief . . . died, 1839." His whereabouts then and cause of death remain a mystery.

Bernd C. Peyer
Johann Wolfgang Goethe University

BIBLIOGRAPHY

Primary Sources

Apes, William. *A Son of the Forest*. 1829. New York: By the author, 1831.
———. "The Increase in the Kingdom of Christ: A Sermon." New York: By the author, 1831.
———. *The Experiences of Five Christian Indians of the Pequot Tribe*. Boston: By the author, 1833.

———. *Indian Nullification of the Unconstitutional Laws of Massachusetts, Relative to the Marshpee Tribe: Or, the Pretended Riot Explained.* Boston: Press of J. Howe, 1835. Stanfordville, NY: Earl M. Coleman, 1979.

———. *Eulogy on King Philip.* 1836. Boston: By the author, 1837.

Secondary Sources

Brodeur, Paul. *Restitution, the Land Claims of the Mashpee, Passamaquoddy, and Penobscot Indians of New England.* Boston: Northeastern UP, 1985.

Campisi, Jack. Foreword to William Apes, *Indian Nullification of the Unconstitutional Laws of Massachusetts, Relative to the Marshpee Tribe: Or, the Pretended Riot Explained.* Stanfordville, NY: Earl M. Coleman, 1979. v–x.

McQuaid, Kim. "William Apes, Pequot: An Indian Reformer in the Jackson Era." *The New England Quarterly* 50 (1977): 605–25.

B*lack Elk* (1863–1950)

Black Elk, the Oglala Lakota (Sioux) holy man, became widely known when his "Life Story," originally told to John G. Neihardt in 1931 and first published in 1932, was reissued in 1961 by the University of Nebraska Press and eventually translated into more than half a dozen languages. In Neihardt's poetic prose, *Black Elk Speaks* became a virtual manifesto of Native American revival and a source of inspiration for 1960s counterculture causes. The book's eventual popularity with those seeking to restore Native culture and value was based on the general assumption that it was Black Elk's authentic testimony and that Neihardt was only a translator and reporter. But Neihardt had come to Black Elk as a self-professed epic poet in the Christian tradition of Milton, seeking information for his typological *Song of the Messiah* from Lakota elders who had participated in the Ghost Dance (Black Elk, *The Sixth Grandfather* 1984:26–27). But Neihardt found Black Elk himself so interesting that he decided to write his "autobiography" before resuming work on the *Song*. Neihardt's poem, eventually published in 1935, shows the Lakota advancing through the Ghost Dance to Christian illumination.

Black Elk spoke of his birth in 1863, and the historical and social vicissitudes of the last years of life in the hoop before Wounded Knee, where the story ends. The story's most remarkable chapter and its beginning is Black Elk's description of his "Great Vision," experienced during an illness when he was nine years old. The vision synthesizes the major symbols and conceptions of Lakota culture and indicates that the spirits usually granted visionary experience to enable the dreamer to heal, to restore, and to perpetuate the inner consciousness of the people. A *hanbloglaka* or vision talk was itself a ritual of restoring and transmitting the powers within it, but it is unlikely that Neihardt understood Black

211

Elk's ritual purpose. Instead, Neihardt's attitude, more explicitly present in his other works, reflects a perception of Black Elk lamenting the inevitable disappearance of his religion and his people (see *The Sixth Grandfather* 37, 62, and 66; see also Holler, "Lakota Religion," 27–28, 34, and 38).

Ironically, the Jesuits at Holy Rosary Mission in Pine Ridge were angry at Neihardt for inducing Black Elk and possibly others to regress to pagan beliefs, thus undoing missionary efforts (*The Sixth Grandfather* 58–63). Actually, Neihardt's philosophy was conventionally Christian in its assumption that Black Elk's sorrow was pitiful but providential, like the blindness of the hero in Milton's *Samson Agonistes*. For Neihardt, Black Elk was a "natural Christian," a righteous pagan who would be saved without benefit of the true faith. To emphasize Black Elk's direct but unconscious inspiration from the Christian God, Neihardt made the visionary passages read like the King James Bible. The personal and historical sections about Black Elk's boyhood, on the other hand, often sound like *Huckleberry Finn* (see *Black Elk Speaks* 1979:138–39 on the death of Crazy Horse, a passage entirely invented by Neihardt). The beginning and ending of the story proper are admittedly Neihardt's, and his consciousness rather than Black Elk's is responsible for the despairing tone of the epilogue (see Rice, "*Akicita*," 20; Holler, "Lakota Religion," 38–39).

Undeniably, much of what Black Elk spoke in Lakota, which was then rendered into English by his son, Ben Black Elk, was conscientiously preserved: "Neihardt would repeat Ben's translation, rephrasing it for clarity in more standard English. When necessary, the sentence was repeated to Black Elk in Lakota for further clarification. As each sentence came forth in revised form from Neihardt's repetition, Enid wrote it down in shorthand" (*The Sixth Grandfather* 32). Nevertheless, the book's appeal is based on the pity Neihardt artfully evokes in his readers, predicated on the convention that the suffering of the tragic hero, like that of Christ on the cross, should realize love, compassion, and conversion in the world. The image of Black Elk as pitiful in his ordeal of transition has been changed considerably since the publication of the original transcript, typed by Neihardt's daughter, Enid, from her shorthand notes. Neihardt's changes in wording from the transcript have been pinpointed by Raymond J. DeMallie in his introduction to the transcript (*The Sixth Grandfather* 77, 94–99). DeMallie explains that the Great Vision was a Thunder being vision, emphasizing a dynamic power to purify (destroy) and to renew (*The Sixth Grandfather* 94–99). The Western powers expressed themselves through animal messengers or *akicita* of their direction, and these particular animals are most prominent in Black Elk's visionary experience—horses, dogs, butterflies, dragonflies, and swallows (*The Sixth Grandfather* 99; Rice, "*Akicita*," 7–15). Black Elk's dog vision and *heyoka* or sacred clown ceremony also come from the Western powers. While this power of destruction and renewal is Black Elk's dominant power, as it was that of Crazy

Horse and great warrior leaders, Black Elk includes all of the major Lakota sacred symbols associated with each direction in the Great Vision and in his description of other ceremonies. Neihardt took advantage of the abundance of symbolic material to minimize the dynamic lightning qualities in Black Elk because he apparently read the metaphors of destruction too literally, as if they were useful only in physical battle (see Rice, *"Akicita,"* 1–8, 15–18). Instead, Neihardt balanced all the powers to make Black Elk a man of pre-Christian revelation on the road to salvation.

In the old Lakota culture, powers were necessarily balanced in a man, but one particular power was typically predominant, so that each person could contribute a particular strength to the nation. In the horse dance, Black Elk leads because he is a Thunder dreamer, but in the bear and buffalo ceremonies Black Elk only assists because he has not dreamed of the bear and because he has not had a strong enough buffalo dream to lead. War and lightning metaphors predominate in Black Elk's narrative to effectuate its ceremonial purpose. When Neihardt and his family arrived in 1931, a ritual ground for invoking the thunder power had been prepared: a tipi "with the flaming rainbow of Black Elk's vision painted above the doorway and the vision power symbols painted on the sides" (*The Sixth Grandfather* 30). Since almost all Lakota ceremonies involved healing, Black Elk's narrative was apparently spoken to accomplish his lifelong purpose of restoring the nation's hoop (see Holler, "Lakota Religion," 38–39). Neihardt's purpose was universal and ecumenical. He considered the cultural survival of the Lakota to be an impossibility (see *The Sixth Grandfather* 55); by 1946, Neihardt favored termination of the reservation system (DeMallie 1984:130–31). And so his editing, as outlined by DeMallie, consistently has Black Elk reaching out to the world more often than he actually did, and shows him less intently concerned with perpetuating Lakota consciousness than he actually was.

The Sixth Grandfather also contains a large number of stories—historical, mythical, and fictional—as well as extensive descriptions of the old Lakota society including kinship relations, the care of children, and games. All show the intelligence and humanity of the old Lakota. This material was given to Neihardt in 1944, but most of it was not used by him, remaining unpublished until *The Sixth Grandfather* (1984). Several stories express the theme of cultural restoration, especially that of Sharp Nose, the Arapaho, who spiritually moved some Crow leaders to restore the Arapaho horses by presenting them with a pipe and a sacred bundle (*The Sixth Grandfather* 371–76), much as Black Elk himself offered his culture to the whites to restore his own people rather than to save the world. Surely Black Elk knew about narrative persuasion in white society, since he had been a Catholic catechist for almost thirty years before speaking to Neihardt.

This fact, having become widely known through *The Sixth Grandfather* (14), has disillusioned many of Black Elk's adherents, who knew him only through Neihardt. When Neihardt asked Black Elk why he had changed his religion, he merely said, "my children had to live in this world" (*The Sixth Grandfather* 47). He never said Christianity was a better religion. His adaptation to reservation life was practical and protective, consistent with the primary purpose of the warrior he was raised to be—to defend the helpless, to continue the nation's life. Given the first opportunity to perpetuate the inner life of the Lakota, he used Neihardt as readily as in his youth as he would have used a good Crow horse. Young people were speaking less Lakota, and he himself did not speak English well. Neihardt was a professional writer. After Neihardt supplied English in a first major effort, Black Elk continued to sing and dance traditionally for tourists in the Black Hills (*The Sixth Grandfather* 63–66).

In 1947, three years before he died, he took the initiative in employing another visitor, who did not originally intend to write a book, in the task of setting down descriptions of Lakota ceremonies. *The Sacred Pipe*, edited by Joseph Epes Brown (first published in 1953), gives a much fuller account than *Black Elk Speaks* of the sweat lodge, vision quest, and sun dance as well as ceremonies not described at all for Neihardt: the ghost keeping, making of relatives, buffalo woman, and throwing of the ball. This time, Black Elk ensured a written record of ceremonies which were not openly performed in 1947, but he, or perhaps Brown, adjusted many symbols to fit Christian religious conventions. For example, the black race paint worn by returning warriors after a victorious raid was explained by Black Elk as "we know that we have done something bad and we wish to hide our faces from *Wakan Tanka*" (92); the black road of difficulty or hardship becomes the black road of "error and destruction" (7). Black Elk's inside practice of missionary rhetoric may have affected his thinking at the age of eighty-three, or he may have attempted to make Lakota spirituality more acceptable to Christians so that they in turn would help his people, much as Sharp Nose, the Arapaho, moved the Crow chiefs. Brown's effect on the book's text is hard to determine, but his copious footnotes betray Hindu and Buddhist emphases in such interpretations as "the Spotted Eagle corresponds exactly, in the Hindu tradition, to the *Buddhi* . . . a ray directly emanating from the *Atma*, the spiritual sun" (6); or emergence from the sweat lodge represents "liberation from the universe . . . or microcosmically the liberation from the ego" (42).

At present, the original transcript of *The Sixth Grandfather* appears to be the most authentic expression of the Black Elk who fought, hunted, had visions, and performed healing ceremonies in the hoop before the reservation period. His way of being was formed in the old culture and he did not necessarily stop living within its perceptions after the age of thirty-seven. Since he was virtually coerced to become a Catholic, when his healing ceremony was desecrated by the zealous Father Lindebner in 1904 (*The*

Sixth Grandfather 14), Black Elk may not have inwardly conformed to the socially feasible image which protected his family.

In *The Sixth Grandfather*, Black Elk's mood after Wounded Knee, verbally repeated in its recollection for Neihardt, shows a resolute will to endure. Neihardt's fictive termination includes some of Black Elk's most widely believed emotions: "you see me now a pitiful old man who has done nothing, for the nation's hoop is broken and scattered . . . and the sacred tree is dead" (*Black Elk Speaks* 270). But his actual last words recall his youthful desire for revenge before returning to tribal protection: "the next day we were supposed to make peace. We made a law that anyone who should make trouble in the fort (agency) should be arrested and tried and if found guilty he would be punished. Two years later I was married" (*The Sixth Grandfather* 282).

When *Black Elk Speaks* through the agency of Neihardt, it appears to a Jesuit writer to be a past-tense tale of "weeping old men" (Starkloff 1984:171) rather than a ceremonial infusion. *The Sixth Grandfather*, in both Black Elk's ongoing life story (1931) and the supplementary stories (1944), affirms Lakota continuity. In one story the prophet Wooden Cup foretells the white man's coming and magically wears white man's clothing long before historical contact. He explains how the Lakota people can survive in the strange world to come: "But people . . . Remember your peace pipe . . . even when you come to the time I am telling about . . . The hat I am wearing was given to me by my grandfather the Thunder-beings. The power lies in this hat; the Thunder-beings have given me the power" (*The Sixth Grandfather* 340). Although he became a Catholic in 1904, by 1944, at the age of eighty, Black Elk's *persona*, Wooden Cup, was still healing through the pipe and the thunder rather than the cross. *Black Elk Speaks* may now have less credibility than it once had, but Black Elk's own voice can reach us more clearly than before. Neihardt edited out Black Elk's comment that the voice of the Western spirit in the black stallion was so powerful it went "all over the universe like a radio and everyone heard it" (*The Sixth Grandfather* 133). Black Elk's authentic voice conveys the pan-tribal theme advanced by such moderns as Momaday, Silko, and Welch, whose spiritual adaptabilities he prefigures and shares.

Julian Rice
Florida Atlantic University

BIBLIOGRAPHY

Primary Sources

Black Elk. *Black Elk Speaks*. Told through John G. Neihardt. New York:William Morrow, 1932. Rpt. Lincoln: U of Nebraska P, 1979.

———. *The Sacred Pipe*. Ed. Joseph Epes Brown. 1953. Rpt. New York: Penguin, 1971.

———. *The Sixth Grandfather.* Ed. Raymond J. DeMallie. Lincoln: U of Nebraska P, 1984.

Secondary Sources

Aly, Lucile F. *John G. Neihardt: A Critical Bibliography.* Amsterdam: Rodopi, 1977.

Bataille, Gretchen M. "Black Elk—New World Prophet." *A Sender of Words: Essays in Memory of John G. Neihardt.* Ed. Vine Deloria, Jr. Salt Lake City: Howe Brothers, 1984. 135–42.

Brown, Joseph Epes. *The Spiritual Legacy of the American Indian.* New York: Crossroad, 1982.

Brumble, H. David, III. *An Annotated Bibliography of American Indian and Eskimo Autobiographies.* Lincoln: U of Nebraska P, 1981.

Castro, Michael. *Interpreting the Indian: Twentieth Century Poets and the Native American.* Albuquerque: U of New Mexico P, 1983.

DeMallie, Raymond J. "John G. Neihardt's Lakota Legacy." *A Sender of Words: Essays in Memory of John G. Neihardt.* Ed. Vine Deloria, Jr. Salt Lake City: Howe Brothers, 1984. 110–34.

Dunsmore, Roger. "Nicolaus Black Elk: Holy Man in History." *A Sender of Words: Essays in Memory of John G. Neihardt.* Ed. Vine Deloria, Jr. Salt Lake City: Howe Brothers, 1984. 143–58.

Holler, Clyde. "Black Elk's Relationship to Christianity." *American Indian Quarterly* 8 (1984): 37–49.

———. "Lakota Religion and Tragedy: The Theology of *Black Elk Speaks.*" *Journal of the American Academy of Religion* (January 1984): 19–43.

Krupat, Arnold. *For Those Who Come After.* Berkeley: U of California P, 1985.

Lincoln, Kenneth. "Native American Literatures." *Smoothing the Ground: Essays on Native American Oral Literature.* Ed. Brian Swann. Berkeley: U of California P, 1983. 3–38.

———. *Native American Renaissance.* Berkeley: U of California P, 1983.

McCluskey, Sally. "Black Elk Speaks and So Does John Neihardt." *Western American Literature* 6 (1972): 231–42.

Momaday, N. Scott. "To Save a Great Vision." *A Sender of Words: Essays in Memory of John G. Neihardt.* Ed. Vine Deloria, Jr. Salt Lake City: Howe Brothers, 1984. 30–38.

Nichols, William. "Black Elk's Truth." *Smoothing the Ground: Essays on Native American Oral Literature.* Ed. Brian Swann. Berkeley: U of California P, 1983. 334–43.

Olson, Paul A. "*Black Elk Speaks* as Epic and Ritual Attempt to Reverse History." *Vision and Refuge: Essays on the Literature of the Great-Plains.* Lincoln: U of Nebraska P, 1982. 3–27.

Rice, Julian. "*Akicita* of the Thunder: Horses in Black Elk's Vision." *MELUS* 12 (1985): 5–23.

———. *Lakota Storytelling: Black Elk, Ella Deloria, and Frank Fools Crow.* New York: Peter Lang, 1989.

Sayre, Robert F. "Vision and Experience in *Black Elk Speaks.*" *College English* 32 (1971): 509–35.

Starkloff, Carl J., S. J. "Renewing the Sacred Hoop." *A Sender of Words: Essays in Memory of John G. Neihardt.* Ed. Vine Deloria, Jr. Salt Lake City: Howe Brothers, 1984. 159–72.

Waters, Frank. "Neihardt and the Vision of Black Elk." *A Sender of Words: Essays in Memory of John G. Neihardt.* Ed. Vine Deloria, Jr. Salt Lake City: Howe Brothers, 1984. 12–24.

Elias Boudinot *[Buck Watie, or Gallegina] (ca. 1802–June 22, 1839)*

Elias Boudinot was an early spokesman for the Cherokees from the mid-1820s to 1835 when he signed the removal treaty at New Echota. After that he was one of the leaders of the Treaty Party of Cherokees. His most famous work is *An Address to the Whites*, published in 1826. A religious tract with the title *Poor Sarah* is also attributed to him, but it is likely that it was written by someone else and that Boudinot translated the piece into Cherokee. Perhaps best known as the first editor of the *Cherokee Phoenix*, the first American Indian newspaper, Boudinot contributed a number of original pieces to its pages. In addition, he contributed to periodicals issued on the Eastern Seaboard. He is recognized today as one of the first American Indians to write and publish in English.

Buck Watie or Gallegina was born in the eastern Cherokee Nation around 1802, the son of Oo-watie, a prominent man in the tribe. He studied there in missionary schools before being chosen to attend the American Board of Commissioners for Foreign Missions school at Cornwall, Connecticut. While there, he distinguished himself through his studies and took the name of a benefactor who had sponsored him at the school. Before returning home, he married Harriet Gold, whose family lived in Cornwall. Back in the Cherokee Nation, Boudinot was involved in organizing the *Cherokee Phoenix* and establishing a Cherokee academy. To this end, he visited many major cities to raise funds for these endeavors. His *Address to the Whites* was delivered on this tour. He became the first editor of the *Phoenix* and, as such, defended his tribe's right to their homeland. Soon, however, he became discouraged in the cause and signed the removal treaty. For this act, he was assassinated on June 22, 1839.

An Address to the Whites. Delivered in the First Presbyterian Church on the 26th of May, 1826 is an eloquent argument presented in polished prose.

217

Boudinot's purpose was to convince his audience that the original inhabitants of the continent were intelligent human beings capable of achieving the same level of civilization as their European counterparts. He argues that Indians are made of the "same materials" as whites by the same Creator. Inhabitants of Britain eighteen centuries ago, he writes, were in the same uncivilized condition as the Indians today. He offers himself as an example that Native Americans are capable of achieving an education and can conduct themselves as well as whites. Boudinot suggests that the arguments against the "practicability" of civilizing the Indians must end, citing the condition of his own people as irrefutable evidence. He recounts how the Cherokees, in a few short years, have made significant progress toward civilization, emulating their white neighbors in agricultural, commercial, governmental, and educational practices. Taking note of the success of Sequoyah's Cherokee syllabary and the widespread use of English in the Nation, he shows how the Cherokees are eager to learn more and advance themselves still further. The address closes with a plea for assistance, asserting that the choice for the American Indian is clear: civilization and happiness, or extinction. Boudinot's *Address* itself proves many of his points. It is written in the best tradition of eighteenth- and nineteenth-century oratory and shows more than a passing knowledge of contemporary social and philosophic thought.

As editor of the *Cherokee Phoenix*, Boudinot wrote a number of pieces. The *Phoenix* was established to publish the laws and documents of the Cherokee Nation, note the progress being made by the people, report the news, and furnish articles to promote civilization. Boudinot wrote articles on a number of topics, but ultimately all argued against removal. He pointed out errors in statements regarding the Cherokees in Congress, documented progress being made in the Nation by citing statistics, and exposed the actions of intruders and maneuverings of the State of Georgia. By 1832, however, he was convinced that the Cherokees could not win. His writings from that time argued that they must remove or become extinct and later argued the validity of the Treaty of New Echota.

James W. Parins
University of Arkansas—Little Rock

BIBLIOGRAPHY

Primary Sources

Boudinot, Elias. *Poor Sarah; or Religion Exemplified in the Life and Death of an Indian Woman.* Mount Pleasant, OH: Elisha Bates, 1823. Rpt. 1833.

———. *An Address to the Whites. Delivered in the First Presbyterian Church on the 26th of May, 1826.* Philadelphia: William F. Geddes, 1826.

———. *Letters and Other Papers Relating to Cherokee Affairs; Being a Reply to Sundry Publications Authorized by John Ross. By E. Boudinot, Formerly Editor of the Cherokee Phoenix.* Athens, GA: Southern Banner, 1837.

————. *Documents in Relation to the Validity of the Cherokee Treaty of 1835 . . . Letters and Other Papers Relating to Cherokee Affairs; Being a Reply to Sundry Publications Authorized by John Ross*. Washington, DC: Blair and Rives, 1838.

Secondary Sources

Gabriel, Ralph Henry. *Elias Boudinot, Cherokee, and His America*. Norman: U of Oklahoma P, 1941.

Perdue, Theda, ed. *Cherokee Editor: The Writings of Elias Boudinot*. Knoxville: U of Tennessee P, 1983.

S. *Alice Callahan*
(January 1, 1868–January 7, 1894)

S. Alice Callahan's *Wynema: A Child of the Forest* is one of the earliest novels by a Native American woman. Born near Sulphur Springs, Texas, Callahan was the daughter of Samuel Benton Callahan and Sara Elizabeth Thornberg Callahan. One-eighth Creek, Samuel was the captain of a company of the First Creek Regiment of the Confederate Army and later was elected to represent the Creeks and Seminoles at the Confederate Congress at Richmond, Virginia. After the Civil War, he held many important positions within the tribe, often serving as a delegate to Washington. He also edited the *Indian Journal* and was superintendent of the Wealaka Boarding School for Creek children. Samuel made and lost several fortunes as a merchant, rancher, and farmer.

Little is known about Callahan's life. She probably spent her early years in Sulphur Springs. Although her father returned to the Creek Nation in approximately 1865 to establish a ranch near Okmulgee, accounts differ as to whether he brought his family with him or moved them there in 1885. For ten months his daughter attended the Wesleyan Female Institute in Staunton, Virginia, from which she returned in June 1888. When *Wynema*, her only book, was published in 1891, she was teaching at Muskogee's Harrell International Institute, a Methodist high school. In 1892–93, she taught at the Wealaka School, a Creek school. In late 1893, she moved back to Harrell. Callahan planned to return to the Female Institute in 1894 to complete her studies so that she could open her own school. Before she could fulfill her plans, she died of pleurisy at age twenty-six.

That Callahan's purpose in writing *Wynema* was to arouse her readers' anger about the outrages perpetuated against Indians is clear from her dedication of the book to the Indian tribes of North America "who have felt the wrongs and oppression of their pale-faced brothers." The plot focuses on the acculturation and romances of two heroines, Genevieve Weir, a non-Indian Methodist teacher from a genteel southern family, and Wynema Harjo, a full-blood Creek child who becomes Genevieve's best student and dear friend. The first part chronicles Genevieve's adjustments to life as a Methodist teacher in the Creek Nation. Wynema and Gerald Keithly, a Methodist missionary, help her understand Creek culture. A reverse acculturation theme is introduced in part 2, when Genevieve takes Wynema on a visit to the Weir home. There the heroines must adjust (or readjust) to southern lifestyles. Genevieve, who has turned down Gerald's proposal because she has an understanding with Maurice Mauran, a child-hood friend, breaks off the relationship when she realizes how prejudiced this southern gentleman is against Indians and women. She then accepts Gerald's proposal. In the meantime, Wynema and Robin Weir, Genevieve's sensitive and politically correct brother, fall in love. Both women return to the Creek Nation, where they marry their beloveds. The first two parts of the novel are clearly influenced by the domestic romance plots popular in America from 1820 to 1870. At a time when few women left home before marriage, Callahan makes Genevieve an unusually independent heroine. By providing Genevieve with a husband who is her equal in intelligence and sensitivity, Callahan keeps her heroine within the boundaries that, as Larzer Ziff points out in *The American 1890s* (1966), were characteristic of that decade. Callahan also undercuts the stereotypical plot of the plucky white heroine who risks life and limb to bring education and religion to the "savage Heathens" by beginning the novel with a description of the Creeks' Edenic life in a virgin landscape and by her characterization of the warm family relationship between Wynema and her doting father, Choe Harjo.

The final section of the book is such a departure from the earlier romance plot that it may well have been added to an almost completed novel. Callahan drops the domestic romance plot and sends Robin and his friend Carl Peterson, formerly a missionary to the Sioux, off to the North-west. There Carl acts as an intermediary between Sioux chiefs and the army. Callahan incorporates allusions to the murder of Sitting Bull and the massacre at Wounded Knee, both of which occurred in late 1890.

Callahan uses multiple voices and perspectives, Indian and non-Indian, female and male, to educate her readers. Gerald Keithly is the author's spokesperson to explain the significance of Creek customs and to argue for their retention. Callahan also includes discourses on such Indian issues as allotment and the causes of the Sioux hostilities in late 1890. Although Callahan devotes most of the novel to Indian issues, she also includes some strong statements about the equality of women—a movement that gained strength in the 1890s. Not only Wynema and Genevieve express the author's commitment to this cause; Robin does so as well. Like many works by

African-American and popular women writers of the nineteenth and twentieth centuries, Callahan's novel lacks the complex plots, multidimensional characters, and elevated style of belles lettres. Nevertheless, her novel makes important statements about issues important to Indians and women.

A. LaVonne Brown Ruoff
University of Illinois—Chicago

BIBLIOGRAPHY

Primary Sources

Callahan, S[ophia] Alice. *Wynema: A Child of the Forest.* 1891. Edited with an introduction by A. LaVonne Brown Ruoff. Lincoln: U of Nebraska P, 1990.

Secondary Sources

Foreman, Carolyn Thomas. "S. Alice Callahan." *Chronicles of Oklahoma* 33 (1955): 306–15, 549.

Ruoff, A. LaVonne Brown. "Justice for Indians and Women: The Protest Fiction of Alice Callahan and Pauline Johnson." *World Literature Today. From This World: Contemporary American Indian Literature* 66.2 (1992): 249–55.

"Samuel Benton Callahan." Appendix to *Chronicles of Oklahoma* 33 (1955): 314–15.

Ziff, Larzer. *The American 1890s.* New York: Viking, 1966.

George Copway [Kahgegagahbowh] (1818–1869)

George Copway was one of the first American Indians to publish a written autobiography. Although this is his most important work, he also wrote both a history of the Ojibwa and a travel book, and edited a short-lived Indian newspaper.

Born in 1818, Copway or Kahgegagahbowh ("Standing Firm") was a member of the Mississauga band of the Ojibwa, located near Rice Lake, Ontario. He was raised as a traditional Ojibwa until 1827, when his parents converted to Christianity. In 1830, Copway himself became a Christian convert and later occasionally attended the Methodist Mission School at Rice Lake. After helping Methodist missionaries spread the gospel among the Lake Superior Ojibwa in 1834–36, he entered Ebenezer Manual Labor School at Jacksonville, Illinois, in 1838. For the next nineteen months he received his only real formal education. Following his graduation in late 1839, Copway traveled in the East before returning to Upper Canada. There he met and married Elizabeth Howell, a white woman.

Until 1842, the Copways served as missionaries to the Indian tribes of present-day Wisconsin and Minnesota. Accepted as a preacher by the Wesleyan Methodist Canadian Conference, Copway also served briefly as a missionary in Upper Canada. The high point of his career in Canadian Indian affairs was his election in 1845 as vice president of the Grand Council of Methodist Ojibwas of Upper Canada. Later that year, both the Saugeen and Rice Lake bands accused him of embezzlement. Briefly imprisoned in the summer of 1846, Copway was expelled from the Canadian Conference of the Wesleyan Methodist Church and left Canada for the United States.

With the help of American Methodists, Copway launched a new career as a lecturer and writer on Indian affairs. Although he called himself a

225

"chief" in his lectures and books, he never held this position in his band. His first book was his autobiography, *The Life, History, and Travels of Kah-ge-ga-gah-bowh (George Copway)* (1847). After its publication, Copway lectured in the East, South, and Midwest on his plan for a separate Indian state, advocated in his pamphlet *Organization of a New Indian Territory, East of the Missouri River* (1850). Copway's lectures in the East enabled him to meet the well-known scholars Henry Rowe Schoolcraft and Francis Parkman, as well as such famous writers as Henry Wadsworth Longfellow, Washington Irving, and James Fenimore Cooper, who provided moral and financial encouragement for his later publishing projects. Copway's second book was *The Traditional History and Characteristic Sketches of the Ojibway Nation* (London, 1850; Boston, 1851). The publication of all three of these works was undoubtedly influenced by the government's efforts from 1847 through 1850 to remove the Ojibwas from ceded territory to central Minnesota, an effort the Indians strongly resisted (Knobel 1984:180).

Copway achieved his greatest recognition in 1850–51, when he was selected to represent the Christian Indians at the Peace Congress held in Germany. Before attending the meeting, Copway visited Great Britain and the Continent. At the Peace Congress, he created a great stir by delivering a lengthy antiwar speech while garbed in full Ojibwa dress. Returning from Europe in December 1850, Copway hastily wrote *Running Sketches of Men and Places, in England, France, Germany, Belgium, and Scotland* (1851). Between July and October 1851, he published a newspaper, *Copway's American Indian*. The year 1851 marked the end of his successful career as a writer and of his close relations with eastern intellectuals, now impatient with his too frequent appeals for money. Copway and his wife also suffered family tragedies: between August 1849 and January 1850, three of their four children died.

From 1849, he courted the support of the nativists whose anti-immigration, anti–Roman Catholic beliefs were widespread and who later formed the political party called the Know-Nothings. In 1852, he was elected to membership in the New York chapter of the Nativist Order of United Americans. During most of the 1850s, Copway, no longer a popular lecturer and almost bankrupt, spent much of his time attempting to secure funds or jobs. Little is known about the last decade of his life. In 1864, he recruited Canadian Indians to serve in the American Civil War and surfaced again in 1867, when he advertised himself as a healer in the *Detroit Free Press*. The following year, Copway arrived alone at Lac-des-deux Montagnes, a large Algonquian-Iroquois mission about thirty miles northwest of Montreal. Describing himself as a pagan, Copway announced his intention to convert to Catholicism. On January 17, 1869, he was baptized "Joseph-Antoine." Several days later he died, on the evening of his first communion as a Catholic.

Copway's best work is his autobiography, originally published as *Life, History, and Travels of Kah-ge-ga-gah-bowh (George Copway)* in 1847. Enthusiasm for this autobiography was so great that it was reprinted in six editions in one year. A slightly revised edition, to which Copway added speeches and published letters, appeared in 1850 under two different titles: *The Life, Letters and Speeches of Kah-ge-ga-gah-bowh, or G. Copway* (New York) and *Recollections of a Forest Life or, The Life and Travels of Kah-ge-ga-gah-bowh, or George Copway* (London).

Copway's autobiography incorporates elements from the spiritual confessions and missionary reminiscences that were popular in the period as well as traditions from American Indian oral narratives. In its emphasis on documentation, it reflects the influence of the slave narratives as well. Copway divides the autobiography into an ethnographic account of Ojibwa culture; descriptions of the conversions of his band, family, and himself; his role as mediator between Indians and whites; and the history of Ojibwa-white relations in the recent past. He blends myth, history, and personal experience. Later American Indian autobiographers used a similar blend in their personal narratives. This mixed form of life history, which differs from the more linear personal confession or life history found in non-Indian autobiographies, was congenial to Indian narrators and writers accustomed to viewing their lives within the history of their tribes, clans, and families.

Like other Christian Indian writers, Copway undertook the dual task of demonstrating to their audiences both the virtues of traditional tribal life and the capacity of their races to adapt to white civilization after conversion to Christianity and education in Western European traditions. In the ethnographic sections on Ojibwa life, Copway presents Indians as children of nature and uses himself as an example of Indian adaptability to white civilization. He stresses the Ojibwa moral code, which embodies universal human values and links Indian and white culture. Throughout, he emphasizes that the differences between the two races consist of language and custom rather than humanity. Copway uses his own experiences to personalize his generalizations about Ojibwa world views and customs. Particularly moving are the sketches of his relationship with his parents. Copway's descriptions of Ojibwa conversion exemplifies the power of Christianity to uplift all Indians from what he calls the "darkness" of tribal religions and the degradation inflicted by whites, who lure Indians into alcoholism. His account of his spiritual awakening follows the literary conventions of spiritual confessions. The sections that deal with his experiences as a missionary replace the conventional fall from grace and subsequent recapture of faith found in confessional narratives. Copway also discusses Indian-white relations in the autobiography, strongly criticizing whites for their introduction of alcohol to the Ojibwa and for their failure to send missionaries to the Indians. In his autobiography, Copway uses a plain, journalistic style in the narrative portions, an oratorical one in his discussions of government policy, and a rhapsodic one in the philosophical sections.

Although Copway clearly contributed the information in the autobiography, his wife, Elizabeth, may have smoothed the style. In the preface, Copway acknowledges the assistance of a friend, probably his wife, who corrected serious grammatical errors. Donald B. Smith indicates in "The Life of George Copway" that Elizabeth's style in her letters is easy and graceful, whereas George's is awkward. By the end of her life, she gained some reputation for her talent as a writer. The well-read Elizabeth probably also contributed the literary quotations (Smith 1988:13–14, 18).

In the glow of the popularity of his autobiography and lectures, Copway proposed a separate Indian state in his pamphlet *Organization of a New Indian Territory, East of the Missouri River* (1850), which he presented in addresses from South Carolina to Massachusetts. Copway's proposal resembled two other plans with which he was undoubtedly familiar: four converted chiefs had proposed in 1836 the establishment of an Indian territory in the Saugeen area of Upper Canada, and James Duane Doty, governor of the Wisconsin Territory, had proposed in 1841 that such a territory be located in what is now the Dakotas. Copway's plan, which especially resembles Doty's, attracted considerable support from eastern intellectuals. To help Copway raise money to implement his plan, Julius Taylor Clark, a former Indian Agent, gave Copway a copy of his poem, *The Ojibway Conquest*. With the author's permission, Copway published it under his own name in 1851, adding an altered introduction, a poem to his wife, and revised endnotes.

Copway's second book was *The Traditional History and Characteristic Sketches of the Ojibway Nation*, published in London in 1850 and in Boston in 1851. The first history of that tribe to be published by an Indian, it later appeared under the title *Indian Life and Indian History* (1858). In addition to describing the topography of traditional Ojibwa territory, Copway traces his people's migrations as contained in their legends and discusses their wars with such perpetual enemies as the Iroquois, Huron, and Sioux. He also describes the tribe's religious beliefs, forms of government, language and pictograph writings, modes of hunting, and games. The volume is notable for its emphasis on the importance of oral tradition as the basis for Indian history and for Copway's incorporation of ancient myths, stories from the historical period, and accounts of personal experience. Copway includes the story of his boyhood bear hunt both in the autobiography and the history.

Like other contemporary writers, Copway incorporates verbatim excerpts from other published sources. Donald B. Smith states that nearly 100 of the book's 298 pages consist of reprinted passages, including excerpts from works by General Lewis Cass, the Rev. Edward Neil, and William Warren (Ojibwa), whose fine *History of the Ojibways* was completed in 1852 but published posthumously in 1885. Copway was undoubtedly familiar as well with *History of the Ojebway Indians* by his fellow Methodist and Ojibwa friend, the Rev. Peter Jones, published posthumously in 1861. Copway's history lacks the unity and substantial content of those by Warren and Jones.

Copway's final book was *Running Sketches of Men and Places, in England, France, Germany, Belgium and Scotland* (1851), the first full-length travel book by an Indian. Copway begins with an account of his ocean voyage, described in Byronic terms. His accounts in subsequent chapters of the people and places he visited are buttressed by copies of his letters to his father and friends, lengthy newspaper accounts of Copway's public appearances, versions of his lectures, an enraptured description of a Jenny Lind concert that he published in a New York newspaper, an extended quotation from Byron's *Childe Harold's Pilgrimage*, a day-by-day account of the Peace Congress, and extensive extracts from guidebooks. Elizabeth, who accompanied her husband on the trip to Britain, undoubtedly helped to select the material from the travel guides. Although the book suffers from this padding, it does contain Copway's reactions to Europe and to such famous people as Benjamin Disraeli, Lord John Russell, Baron de Rothschild, and Jenny Lind.

After his return from Europe, Copway published a weekly newspaper called *Copway's American Indian* from July to October 1851. Dale T. Knobel points out in "Know-Nothings and Indians" that although the newspaper claimed to be "neutral in politics and creeds," its political positions were essentially those of the New York Whigs, aligned behind Vice President and later President Millard Fillmore. According to Knobel, the newspaper took its political stance from James Watson Webb's *New York Courier and Enquirer*, which in this period expressed nativistic Whig positions. Knobel also stresses that there was a sustained, anti-abolitionist element in Copway's plea for an Indian territory. In August 1851 Copway questioned why most American and British philanthropists were so totally indifferent to the Indian cause and so zealous in that of the African American (Knobel 1984:185). Aside from these political allegiances, there was little in the newspaper to sustain long-term readership because it primarily reprinted or restated Copway's earlier lectures and comments.

Much of Copway's life and career remains enigmatic. While the reliability of his history of his people suffers by comparison with such Ojibwa writers as the Reverend Peter Jones and William Warren, he remains important as one of the first Indian authors to write about his life and his people.

A. LaVonne Brown Ruoff
University of Illinois—Chicago

BIBLIOGRAPHY

Primary Sources

Copway, George. *The Life, History, and Travels of Kah-ge-ga-gah-bowh (George Copway).* Albany, NY: Weed and Parsons, 1847. Rev. as *The Life, Letters and Speeches of Kah-ge-ga-gah-bowh, or G. Copway.* New York: Benedict, 1850. Rev. as *Recollections of a Forest Life or, The Life and Travels of Kah-ge-ga-gah-bowh, or George Copway.* London: Gilpin, 1850.

———. *Organization of a New Indian Territory, East of the Missouri River.* New York: Benedict, 1850.

———. *The Traditional History and Characteristic Sketches of the Ojibway Nation.* London: Gilpin, 1850; Boston: Mussey, 1851. Rpt. as *Indian Life and Indian History, by an Indian Author.* Boston: Colby, 1858.

———. *Running Sketches of Men and Places, in England, France, Germany, Belgium and Scotland.* New York: Riker, 1851.

Secondary Sources

Knobel, Dale T. "Know-Nothings and Indians: Strange Bedfellows?" *The Western Historical Quarterly* 15 (1984): 175–98.

Ruoff, A. LaVonne Brown. "George Copway: Nineteenth-Century American Indian Autobiographer." *Auto/Biography* 3.2 (Summer 1987): 6–17.

———, and Jerry W. Ward, Jr., eds. "Nineteenth-Century American Indian Autobiographers: William Apes, George Copway, and Sarah Winnemucca." *Redefining American Literary History.* New York: MLA, 1989.

Smith, Donald B. "The Life of George Copway or Kah-ge-ga-gah-bowh (1818–1869)—and a Review of His Writings." *Journal of Canadian Studies* 23.3 (Autumn 1988): 5–38.

Charles Alexander Eastman
[Ohiyesa] (February 19, 1858–January 8, 1939)

Charles Eastman is, without a doubt, the best known of the early Native American authors. He produced nine monographs (an additional two are modifications of former texts) as well as a great number of articles that appeared in a wide range of major U.S. magazines. His works have been translated into French, German, Danish, and Russian; a few of his books have been reprinted several times, the most recent editions appearing in the 1990s. Aside from his notoriety as a writer, Eastman was also held up by the reformers of the late nineteenth century as a paragon of the "successful" Native American. His education was exceptionally thorough, and he held various important government positions in the course of his life. On the other hand, Eastman has occasionally been criticized as an unreliable source, whose writings contain many inaccuracies and comply with popular stereotypes.

Eastman was born near Redwood Falls in Minnesota, among the Wahpeton band of Santee Sioux. His mixed-blood mother, Mary Eastman, died shortly after his birth and his father, Jacob (Many Lightnings) Eastman was imprisoned for participating in the Minnesota Sioux uprising of 1862, thus leaving him in the care of his paternal grandmother and uncle. Following the uprising, the remaining Wahpeton fled to the area near present-day Manitoba. Young Eastman, or Ohiyesa (Winner), lived the first fifteen years of his life according to Santee customs, in relative isolation from Anglo-American society. This changed abruptly when his presumed-dead father, who had converted to Christianity while serving his term in prison, came to fetch his son to live with him in the Native American farming community of Flandreau, North Dakota. Here the young man was summarily enrolled in the local mission school and baptized under the name Charles Alexander Eastman.

In all, Eastman's educational advancement was to extend over a period of seventeen years: after he left the mission school in Flandreau, he attended Santee Normal Training School (1874–76), Beloit College (1876–79), Knox College (1879–81), Kimball Union Academy (1882–83), Dartmouth College (1883–87), and Boston University (1887–90). He graduated at age thirty-two, as one of the first licensed Native American physicians.

In the course of his life, however, Eastman had great difficulties making a living as a doctor. Following his graduation, he served as government physician at the Pine Ridge Agency until 1893, when he resigned due to personal conflicts with the reservation agent. Here he witnessed the events leading up to the tragedy at Wounded Knee, and met his future spouse, Elaine Goodale, who was then government supervisor of education for the Sioux.

For the next year, Eastman tried, without much success, to set up private practice in St. Paul. From 1894 to 1898 he assumed the position of field secretary for the Young Men's Christian Association, organizing some forty Native American associations. Toward the end of his affiliation with the YMCA, he became involved as representative of the Santee in their appeal to Washington to restore treaty annuities that had been cut off after the uprising of 1862. The fees he expected for his services but never received in full became the source of a long-lasting dispute between him, the tribe, and government representatives (Wilson 1983).

After a brief interim at Pratt's Carlisle Indian School (1899–1900), Eastman was hired as government physician for the Crow Creek Reservation in South Dakota. Again, strained relations with the agent led him to resign in 1903. With the aid of Hamlin Garland he was made head of a program to establish Christian names for the Sioux, ostensibly to protect their property rights (1903–08). In 1910, he traveled among the Ojibwa of northern Minnesota to procure artifacts for the University of Pennsylvania Museum. Following this short but obviously moving reencounter with more traditional Native American lifestyles, Eastman joined the naturalist movement that emerged between 1900 and 1920 and began what was to be a lasting association with the Boy Scouts of America.

At about this time (1910), Eastman was fast becoming a public figure in Native American affairs. He was invited regularly to attend the reformist conferences at Lake Mohonk and, in 1911, was elected to represent Native Americans at the First Universal Races Congress held in London. He was also one of the founding members of the Society of American Indians, though his participation in this organization was only sporadic and ceased altogether in 1919 because of disagreements on the issue of peyote (he was against its use).

From 1923 to 1925, Eastman held his last government position, as U.S. Indian Inspector. In this capacity he served as a member of the Committee of One Hundred Advisory Council, which was formed to discuss the Bursum Bill and Native American policy and laid the groundwork for the 1928 Meriam Report. In 1928, he went to England on a lecture tour sponsored by the Brooks-Bryce Foundation. The Indian Council Fire in Chicago honored him in 1933 with its first award for distinguished achievements. In 1939, he died of a heart attack in Detroit, at the age of eighty (Copeland 1978; Miller 1978; Stensland 1977; Wilson 1975 and 1983).

Charles Eastman began to write rather late in his life, encouraged and supported by his wife. One scholar (Miller 1978) feels that Elaine Goodale Eastman may have been her husband's ghostwriter. The fact that she already had a minor reputation as a poet and that he failed to publish much after their separation in 1921 seems to indicate that she played a more important role in his literary endeavors than her official co-authorship of only one monograph would lead one to assume.

Eastman's writings cover a wide range of Native American topics, but can be roughly arranged under the following headings: autobiographical accounts, fictive or traditionally based short stories, and interpretations of Native American ways of life and history. Though based primarily on his knowledge of the Sioux, his works tend to present a generalized view of Native Americans. They reflect in part his "transitional" role, to borrow one of his own terms, as an individual uprooted from Sioux traditions at an early age and then projected suddenly into modern American society as a test case for late nineteenth century reformist ideals. What Eastman consequently describes is often a somewhat idealized, nostalgic childhood memory, made to correspond to values adopted in the course of his later Christian upbringing. His works may thus be more valuable as an insight into his personality than a source of ethnographic data.

Eastman's first book, *Indian Boyhood* (1902), is a compilation of autobiographical sketches that had been serialized previously by *St. Nicholas*, a popular magazine for juveniles. Two of these, "Hakadah's First Offering" and "First Impressions of Civilization," were reprinted in *Current Literature* (1903) and *Harper's* (1904), respectively. Together, the sketches recount episodes from Eastman's childhood, ending with his introduction to Anglo-American society. *Indian Boyhood* sets the pattern for much of his later writing, presenting the Native American as a "child of nature" and role model for American youth. The harsher realities of Sioux life are occasionally filtered out for the benefit of Anglo readers, e.g., omitting the inevitable consumption of a sacrificed dog in "Hakadah's First Offering."

Between 1904 and 1909, Eastman published three collections of short stories. The first, *Red Hunters and the Animal People* (1904), is made up of twelve stories based upon traditional animal tales for children. The protagonists of most of these stories are animals whose cunning and valor in the daily struggle to survive make them role models for young hunters. A few of Eastman's most successful pieces are included here, such as "The

Gray Chieftain," which was first published in *Harper's* (1904) and was later selected by William Dean Howells and H. M. Alden for their anthology *Under the Sunset* (1906).

In *Old Indian Days* (1907), Eastman complements seven Plains warrior stories with eight stories about Native American women. His stated motive for including the latter was to dispell the widespread notion that Native American women were mere "beasts of burden." These stories resemble stories written by his contemporary Gertrude Bonnin in that the female protagonists here are just as heroic as their male counterparts and, consequently, seem to have slipped from one stereotypical role into another. The kinds of stories gathered in the two books mentioned above found ready publication with the rise of national magazines and the popularization of the short story by "local color" writers during the second half of the nineteenth century, which was carried over into the present century by regionalist and realist authors. Many appeared as well in *Harper's Sunset, Metropolitan, Ladies Home Journal, Outlook*, and other well-known publications. Eastman himself was acquainted with and supported by two leading members of the realist school of writers, William Dean Howells and Hamlin Garland.

With his wife, Eastman also prepared a collection of Sioux folktales, *Wigwam Evenings* (1909; later published as *Smoky Day's Wigwam Evenings*), which contain elements of the European fable tradition (Copeland 1978; Stensland 1977).

Eastman first touched upon the subject of Native American religion in an address, "Sioux Mythology," given at the World Columbian Exposition in 1893, and published in *Popular Science* the following year. He turned to it again after his visit to the Ojibwa living in the Great Lakes area in 1910. This "return to the woods," as he entitled the corresponding chapter in his second autobiography (Eastman 1916), occurred at a time in which disappointment with his own career and disillusionment with American society were precipitating a personal crisis. The brief confrontation with more traditionalist Native Americans must have accented his own alienation, symbolized at the end of said chapter by a giant turtle who makes him feel like an intruder in its domain. Although he continued to write books and articles for juveniles, he now turned increasingly toward a mature reading public. His *The Soul of the Indian* (1911) is thus the first of his truly "adult" monographs. Like some earlier Native American writers with a Christian education (e.g., William Apes), negative personal experiences with "civilization" led Eastman to conclude that traditional Native Americans actually lived out the principles formulated in Christian teachings. On the basis of his own understanding of Sioux religion, he creates a kind of universal Native American cosmology interwoven with Christian elements. Nevertheless, *The Soul of the Indian* represents the first attempt by a Native American author to interpret the essence of Native American religious thought and compare it favorably to Christianity. Curiously enough, another Sioux writer, Vine Deloria, Jr., was to take up the subject again some sixty years later.

At the turn of this century, Eastman also participated in a "back to nature" movement in the United States which led to the establishment of the National Park System, among other things. He was especially supportive of the Boy Scouts of America and the Camp Fire Girls organizations. With them in mind, he published a great number of articles on Native American crafts and woodlore, as well as a monograph dedicated to them: *Indian Scout Talks* (1914; reprinted as *Indian Scout Craft and Lore*, 1974). Here again, he found an appreciative forum for his presentation of the Native American as a model of virtue for youth, based upon his close contact to nature.

Eastman's political views are expressed in a number of articles he wrote for the Society of American Indians journal, *American Indian Magazine*, between 1916 and 1919 and a monograph published in 1915, *The Indian Today; The Past and Future of the First American*. As a product of the allotment era, he naturally shared most of the recommendations finally embodied in the Dawes Act of 1887, which he referred to as the "Emancipation Act of the Indian" (58). But he further advocated the gradual replacement of the Bureau of Indian Affairs with a special commission in which 50 percent of the members were to be Native Americans, and the establishment of an Indian Court of Claims. His enthusiasm, however, waned after the passage of the Burke Act, which he regarded as a step backward and decried as having been framed for the benefit of grafters (Eastman 1916:164).

In 1916, Eastman published his most important work, *From the Deep Woods to Civilization; Chapters in the Autobiography of an Indian*. It continues the narrative of his life from the point at which *Indian Boyhood* left off, delineating his educational experiences and ensuing career. It is both the most personal and critical book that Eastman ever wrote. Unlike his earlier autobiography, it is addressed to a mature reader, chronologically arranged, and replete with concrete dates. As his wife points out in her foreword to later editions, much of the story needs to be read between the lines. While the book ends in an emotional affirmation of his identification with America, it also discloses the traumatic events (Wounded Knee, a visit to slum areas in the East, confrontations with politicians during the Santee issue and the Burke Act) which led to his disillusionment with "civilization." Nor can it disguise his frustration at having been prevented from achieving that measure of success predicted by the reformers.

In his last monograph, *Indian Heroes and Great Chieftains* (1918), Eastman creates a Native American gallery of "founding fathers." It has been criticized (Hyde 1937) for containing historical inaccuracies; however, it has also been suggested (Stensland 1977) that it should not be viewed strictly as a historical text, but rather as a product of folklore, which often transforms historical figures into folk heroes as it is transmitted orally through generations during difficult times. In this sense, this collection of biographies, gathered at least in part through interviews with elders, is no more inaccurate than the popular accounts about the founders of the American nation.

As has been stated previously, Eastman ceased to write after his separation from Elaine Goodale (with the exception of a couple of articles that appeared in 1922). The remaining years in the life of a man who had personified the Native American success story of the allotment era were beset with financial difficulties. He supplemented the meager income from royalties with public appearances in Plains costume.

Bernd C. Peyer
Johann Wolfgang Goethe University

BIBLIOGRAPHY

Primary Sources

Eastman, Charles. "Sioux Mythology." *Popular Science* 46 (November 1894): 88–91.

———. *Indian Boyhood*. New York: McClure, Phillips & Co., 1902. Rpt. New York: Dover, 1971.

———. "Hakadah's First Offering." *Current Literature* 34 (January 1903): 29–32.

———. *Red Hunters and the Animal People*. New York: Harper and Brothers, 1904. Rpt. New York: AMS, 1976.

———. "First Impressions of Civilization." *Harper's Monthly Magazine* 108 (1904): 587–92.

———. "The Gray Chieftain." *Harper's Monthly Magazine* 108 (1904): 882–87.

———. *Old Indian Days*. New York: McClure Co., 1907. Rpt. Rapid City, SD: Fenwyn, 1970.

———. *Wigwam Evenings; Sioux Folk Tales Retold by Charles A. Eastman (Ohiyesa) and Elaine Goodale Eastman*. Boston: Little, Brown and Company, 1909.

———. *The Soul of the Indian; An Interpretation*. Boston: Houghton Mifflin Company, 1911. Rpt. Lincoln: U of Nebraska P, 1980.

———. *Indian Scout Talks; A Guide for Boy Scouts and Campfire Girls*. Boston: Little, Brown and Co., 1914. Rpt. as *Indian Scout Craft and Lore*. New York: Dover, 1974.

———. *The Indian Today; The Past and Future of the First American*. Garden City, NY: Doubleday, Page & Co., 1915. Rpt. New York: AMS, 1975.

———. *From the Deep Woods to Civilization; Chapters in the Autobiography of an Indian*. Boston: Little, Brown and Co., 1916. Rpt. Lincoln: U of Nebraska P, 1977.

———. "The Sioux Yesterday and Today." *American Indian Magazine* 5 (October–December 1917): 233–39.

———. *Indian Heroes and Great Chieftains*. Boston: Little, Brown and Co., 1918.

———. "The Indian's Plea for Freedom." *American Indian Magazine* 6 (Winter 1919): 162–65.

———. "Justice for the Sioux." *American Indian Magazine* 7 (Spring 1919): 79–81.

Secondary Sources

Copeland, Marion W. *Charles Alexander Eastman (Ohiyesa)*. Boise State U Western Writers Series. Caldwell, ID: Caxton, 1978.

Hyde, George E. *Red Cloud's Folk: A History of the Oglala Sioux*. Norman: U of Oklahoma Press, 1937.

Miller, David R. "Charles Alexander Eastman, the 'Winner': From Deep Woods to Civilization." *American Indian Intellectuals*. Ed. Margot Liberty. *Proceedings of the American Ethnological Society* (1978): 60–73.

Stensland, Anna L. "Charles Alexander Eastman, M.D., Santee Sioux." *American Indian Quarterly* 3.3 1977: 199–208.

Wilson, Raymond. "The Writings of Ohiyesa—Charles Alexander Eastman, M.D., Santee Sioux." *South Dakota History* 6 (1975–76): 55–73.

———. *Ohiyesa: Charles Eastman, Santee Sioux*. Urbana: U of Illinois P, 1983.

E. Pauline Johnson
[Tekahionwake or "Double Wampum"]
(March 10, 1861–March 17, 1913)

Renowned in Canada, Great Britain, and the United States for her power-ful oral interpretations of her own work, Johnson was one of the first Indian women to publish books of poetry and short stories. She is also among the earliest Indian writers to deal with the theme of the mixed-blood. Johnson also achieved acclaim as a reinterpreter of legends of the Northwest Coast Indians.

Born in 1861 on the Six Nations Reserve in the Grand River Valley near Brantford, Ontario, Emily Pauline Johnson was the daughter of George Henry Martin Johnson, a Mohawk chief, and Emily Susanna Howells, an English-born cousin of the American writer William Dean Howells. After their marriage, George Johnson built his bride an impressive house called Chiefswood, which became a gathering place for Indian and white visitors. Johnson and her siblings were educated primarily at home by their mother, who stimulated her children's love of literature by reading them the works of the English Romantics. Also strong influences were her grandfather, Smoke Johnson, a speaker in the Iroquois councils, and her father. Not all of Johnson's life was idyllic. Her father was severely beaten three times and shot in retribution for his attempts to eradicate the illegal alcohol and timber traffic on the reserve. George never recovered from these injuries and died in 1884. Financial difficulties caused the family to abandon Chiefswood and its gracious lifestyle.

From 1892, Pauline supported herself primarily as an interpreter of her own works, performing the Indian portion dressed in a fringed buck-skin dress of her own design and the remainder dressed in an evening gown. In 1894, Johnson appeared in London, where she arranged for the publication in 1895 of her first volume of poetry, *The White Wampum*. Its appearance increased the public's interest in Johnson as a performer. From

1897 until the end of her career, she toured with J. Walter McRaye, who became her partner and later her manager. In 1898, she became engaged to Charles Robert Lumley Drayton, who broke off the engagement in 1899. She probably became romantically involved with her unscrupulous manager, Charles Wurz, in 1900–1901. She alludes to a consummated-but-tragic love in three unpublished poems, "Morrow Land," "Heidelburgh," and "Song." Her grief over these relationships is reflected in her frequent treatment of the betrayal of Indian women by white men.

In 1903, Johnson published *Canadian Born*, which disappointed her critics because it included many poems written years earlier and lacked the fresh voice of her earlier volume. From 1907 to 1912, Johnson contributed stories and articles frequently to *Mother's Magazine* and *Boy's World*, both printed by the Cook Publishing Company, near Chicago. Through *Mother's Magazine*, which in 1910 had a circulation of 600,000, Johnson reached her largest audience in the United States. Her small income from the sale of her works enabled Johnson to retire from performing in 1908 and make her permanent home in Vancouver. She began her collaboration with Joe Capilano, the Squamish chief, refashioning the Chinook stories he told her and those she collected from others. These were published in 1911 as *Legends of Vancouver*. Dying of cancer, Johnson collected her poems in *Flint and Feather* (1912), which includes those published in the two previous volumes and additional work. The Women's Press Club of Vancouver attempted to aid Johnson financially by arranging for the publication of two collections of her work, which appeared after her death in 1913: *The Shagganappi*, stories written for *Boy's World*, and *The Moccasin Maker*, which included several of her stories about Indian and non-Indian women and her essay, "A Pagan in St. Paul's." Her ashes were buried in her beloved Stanley Park and in 1922, the Women's Canadian Club, assisted by the Daughters of the Empire, erected a monument to her. For several years, the Six Nations Reserve has sought funds to restore the family home at Chiefswood.

In her lifetime, Johnson was primarily known as a poet. Critics particularly praised her powerful treatment of Indian themes, her beautiful descriptions of nature, and the influence of Romanticism on her work. In his review of *The White Wampum* (1895), Hector Charlesworth called her the most popular figure in Canadian literature and "in many respects the most prominent one" (1895:478). Norman Shrive emphasizes in "What Happened to Pauline?" that she was one of the Canadian poets chosen for immortality by the "literary boosters" of the 1920s (1962:37).

Almost half the poems in *The White Wampum* utilize Indian themes, as do several of the poems in *Canadian Born*. Many of these characterize Indian women. In *White Wampum*, "Ojistoh" describes how a fierce Mohawk woman convinces her Huron captor that she loves him better than her husband, whom he killed, and then kills the captor. "Cattle Thief" describes how the daughter of a Cree slain by whites for stealing cattle defies their intention to cut up her father and fiercely rebukes them for the wrongs done her people by whites. In "Cry from an Indian Wife," a brave woman bids her warrior husband good-bye and urges him not to revolt against the Union Jack, despite what Indians have suffered at the hands of whites. One of Johnson's most touching poems about Indian women is "Corn Husker" from *Canadian Born*, which describes an old woman. Some of the Indian poems, such as "Dawendine" (*Canadian Born*) and "The Ballad of the Yaada" (*Flint and Feather*) deal with legends of lovers. Others, particularly in *The White Wampum*, deal with the harsh side of Indian life. Her oft-recited "As Red Men Die" depicts a fierce Mohawk captive who is willing to die but never to bend to his captors while "Wolverine," a narrative poem told by a white trapper, describes how whites killed a kind Indian, Wolverine, when he tried to return goods that whites had left behind. Johnson also wrote a great deal of nature poetry, and her lyrics were praised by critics for their simplicity and delicacy. Her most famous poems are "Shadowland" and "Song My Paddle Sings," which describes the power of the West Wind on the river. Generations of Canadian children have memorized these poems from *The White Wampum*. Johnson particularly liked to create tranquil scenes in nature. She often used melodramatic episodes and romanticized diction in her poetry, reflecting her youthful absorption of Scott, Byron, and Longfellow and her fondness for the versification of Tennyson and Swinburne.

Because of its treatment of the role of women on the frontier, Johnson's *The Moccasin Maker* is more important to the development of American Indian literature than is her poetry. Like nineteenth-century English and American women writers, Johnson champions the Victorian values of domesticity: men and women find their greatest happiness in the home and the network of human attachments it represents. For these writers, the home and the world become one. However, many of Johnson's heroines are alone—whether as widows, or as wives temporarily or permanently separated from their husbands. Even when husband and children are present, Johnson sometimes stresses the isolation a wife can feel if she follows her husband into the wilderness or when a quarrel separates family members. Several of her plots are based on true stories she heard, and she includes a fictional account of her parents' courtship and marriage. Mother love is a powerful theme in her characterization of Indian and non-Indian women. Another is the traumatic consequences of white contact for Indian life, which is frequently dramatized by the tragedies Indian women experience when they fall in love with white men. Her most memorable story of such a tragedy is "A Red Girl's Reasoning," which describes how a mixed-blood woman leaves her husband forever because he holds her parents' Indian marriage in contempt. Johnson often performed this story on stage.

Perhaps Johnson's best work is her *Legends of Vancouver* (1912). Here Johnson reveals an acute sense of the importance of setting, the interaction between storyteller and audience, and the act of storytelling. She opens each story with a description of a specific scene that figures in the legend. Johnson achieves a casual, conversational tone by telling how she learned the tale and by using dialogue between herself and Chief Capilano or other storytellers to introduce the legend. She is particularly adept at capturing her relationship with Capilano. In "The Sewash Rock," for example, Johnson denies that she knows a story in order to encourage Capilano to tell it. She also occasionally compares and contrasts the legends and customs of the Northwest Coast and Mohawk Indians, as she does in "Deep Waters." Although most of the stories deal with the Indians from the Vancouver area, she does include an account of the occasion when Arthur, the Duke of Connaught and grandson of Queen Victoria, was made a Mohawk Chief at the Six Nations Reserve. Her collection was among the most successful literary reinterpretations of oral literature of the period and was one of the early attempts to record the mythology of the Indians of the northern Pacific Coast.

The Shagganappi is a collection of boys' adventure stories, in which the Indians, ranging from the Northeast to the Northwest Coast, are characterized as always loyal, protective, and courageous in their relations with whites. The title story (whose title means "buckskin cayouse" in Cree) describes the triumph of a young mixed-blood named Fire Flint over the prejudice among the boys at his school. Although some later critics dismissed her work for its sentimentality and forced diction, Johnson remains an important figure in the evolution of American Indian women's literature.

A. LaVonne Brown Ruoff
University of Illinois—Chicago

BIBLIOGRAPHY

Primary Sources

Johnson, E. Pauline. *The White Wampum*. London: John Lake, The Bodley Head, 1895.
———. *Canadian Born*. Toronto: Morang, 1903.
———. *Legends of Vancouver*. Vancouver: Sunset, 1912. Rpt. Vancouver: McClelland, 1961.
———. *Flint and Feather*. Toronto: Musson, 1912. Rpt. Markam, Ontario: Paper Jacks, 1973.
———. *The Moccasin Maker*. 1913. Ed. with intro. by A. LaVonne Brown Ruoff. Tucson: U of Arizona P, 1987.
———. *The Shagganappi*. Vancouver: Briggs, 1913.

Secondary Sources

Charlesworth, Hector. "Miss Pauline Johnson's Poems." *The Canadian Magazine* 5 (May–October 1895): 478–80.

Foster, Mrs. W. Garland (Anne). *The Mohawk Princess, Being Some Account of the Life of Teka-hion-wake (E. Pauline Johnson)*. Vancouver: Lion's Gate, 1931.

Keller, Betty. *Pauline: A Biography of Pauline Johnson*. Vancouver: Douglas & McIntyre, 1981.

McRaye, Walter. *Town Hall To-Night*. Toronto: Ryerson, 1929.

——. *Pauline Johnson and Her Friends*. Toronto: Ryerson, 1947.

Shrive, Norman. "What Happened to Pauline?" *Canadian Literature* 13 (1962): 25–38.

John Joseph Mathews
(November 16, 1894–June 11, 1979)

Five books representing biography, fiction, history, and nonfiction comprise the bulk of John Joseph Mathews's published writing. Literary historians cite his *Sundown* (1934) as among the earliest novels written by an Indian, although there is general agreement that it is overshadowed by the more polished *The Surrounded* of D'Arcy McNickle, published two years later. More widely known in its time than his novel was *Wah'Kon-Tah* (1932), a Book-of-the-Month Club selection. Some of Mathews's most memorable prose is found in *Talking to the Moon* (1945), where his mixture of folklore, naturalistic description, and personal rumination has elicited comparison to Thoreau's reflections on his Walden experience (Ruoff 1983:164). His final book, *The Osages: Children of the Middle Waters* (1961), is regarded as one of the most "literary" tribal histories and an outstanding early example of the ethnohistorical mode.

Mathews was born of mixed white and Indian heritage. His father, a quarter-blood Osage with French ancestry, moved with the tribe from its Kansas reserve in 1874 to a final reservation located in northeastern Indian Territory. The family house, constructed of stone and boasting two stories, was perched on Agency Hill overlooking the burgeoning frontier town of Pawhuska, capital of the Osage Nation until allotment in 1906, and afterward the seat of government for Osage County, Oklahoma. The father made a comfortable life for his white wife and mixed-blood children with the earnings from a trading post and later the town's first bank.

After graduating from high school in 1914, Mathews enrolled at the University of Oklahoma, earning a degree in geology in 1920. Nearly three years of that period were spent in uniform. Enlisted in the cavalry, the young mixed-blood was transferred to the aviation section of the Signal Corps, and eventually became a flight instructor with the American

Expeditionary Forces in Europe. He rejected a Rhodes Scholarship offered him after graduation, but attended Oxford University in England anyway. Mathews probably turned down the scholarship because the discovery and development of petroleum resources beneath the Osage reservation provided him and his tribespeople with funds sufficient for all reasonable and, if need be, unreasonable wants.

In 1923, Mathews received his B.A. Oxon reading natural science, and then spent the next few years roaming Europe and North Africa. His pursuits included study in international relations; a stint as correspondent for the *Philadelphia Ledger*, covering the activities of the League of Nations; and extended hunting trips in Africa. He returned to Oklahoma in 1929 and built a secluded cabin on his allotted land in the forested hills near Pawhuska where he lived and wrote until his failing health forced him to relocate to town, where he continued to write until his death. During the 1930s, he was elected to the tribal council and played a major role in the struggles of the Osages to deal with drastic drops in their oil revenues and resulting hard times.

Mathews's writing career might have been limited to contributions to an alumni magazine, for which he wrote nine adventure sketches, had not friends intervened. In 1878, Quaker Laban J. Miles was appointed agent to the Osages. After thirteen years of service he retired, remaining in Pawhuska until his death in 1931. Mathews had been named beneficiary of the former agent's journals and papers. Learning of the bequest, Joseph Brandt, founder and editor of the University of Oklahoma Press, urged Mathews to use his legacy to write about the early reservation days.

Mathews maintained a spartan existence, leaving his typewriter only for brief respites spent hunting or listening to Indian music. The narrative was completed within months and appeared as the third volume of the Civilization of the American Indian series inaugurated by Brandt. The editor submitted the proofs to the Book-of-the-Month Club, which made *Wah'Kon-Tah: The Osage and the White Man's Road* its first university press selection.

The book sold well and received laudatory reviews in which Mathews's lack of romanticism in describing the Osages was especially praised. One reviewer compared *Wah'Kon-Tah* stylistically with Willa Cather's *Death Comes to the Archbishop* (1927). Mathews himself professed mild astonishment at his success and made no plans for a second project, preoccupied as he was with tribal politics. In 1934, however, he accepted an unsolicited offer of a new literary assignment. When interviewed in the 1970s Mathews recalled being very reluctant to attempt a novel, but having yielded to pressure, simply sat down and finished it as rapidly as possible, never looking at the published version (Wilson 1981:276–77). Not exactly a labor of love, *Sundown* has received a good deal of attention because of its subject matter, Indians and assimilation, and its Native American author-ship.

There is much that is autobiographical in the novel. The protagonist, Challenge (Chal) Windser, is a mixed-blood Osage growing up in Okla-homa from the time of allotment in 1906 through the oil boom of the 1920s. His father, a prototypical "progressive" mixed-blood, sends Chal to a public school, where the youngster excels in football and is recruited to play at the state university. Chal joins a fraternity there and stays in school although he is never fully at ease, partly for fear his full-blood friends on campus will shame him before the whites. He leaves school to join the air corps where he enjoys the anonymity of the uniform and the adventure of flying. The last portion of the novel focuses on Chal's inability to develop meaning and direction in his life after the war, wavering between the hedonism and decadence of oil-rich Indians and the hardheaded capitalism of the white men.

Carol Hunter, a mixed-blood Osage scholar, emphasizes the bitterness of Mathews's vision of the forced acculturation of his generation of Indi-ans, exacerbated by the great frenzy of the oil boom years (Hunter 1982:334–35). Interestingly, in contrast to Chal's failure to cope with culture change and his mixed-blood heritage, Mathews's life was a refutation of the help-lessness portrayed in the novel. Also autobiographical, but more successful in form and content, was *Talking to the Moon* (1945). When Mathews returned from Europe, he hoped to adjust himself to the rhythms of na-ture, keeping very limited contact with groups of mankind. For ten years he lived in a stone house resembling a hunting lodge. Situated eight miles from Pawhuska, astride a prominent ridge of the hilly, forested region of the eastern half of Osage County, the dwelling was meant to be a perma-nent and solitary retreat.

Filled with beautifully crafted passages celebrating the ecology of the ridge, *Talking to the Moon* avoids sentimentalism by gentle irony and a self-deprecatory wit characteristic of much Indian humor. Mathews scoffs at his own presumption of becoming part of the wild's balanced ways, upset-ting none of the natural order, giving up hunting to observe nature. Within a year, he realized that his very position was unnatural—feeding himself from cans and thus avoiding actual participation in the ridge's economic struggle for life. Before long, he introduced chickens and pheasants to his environment and brought other men to his home where they ate the game he shot, drank beer, and talked. Mathews's appreciation of nature never caused him to succumb to any facile exposition about Indians as "natural ecologists"; the Osages had been hunters from necessity, but he remained one by choice, exhilarated by the competition that he admitted was hard to understand but was certainly a part of life.

Mathews's *Life and Death of an Oilman: The Career of E. W. Marland* (1951) is probably the least read of his works. Reviewers found the biography of Mathews's close friend, an oil entrepreneur and governor of Oklahoma in the 1930s, to be a mature work, well researched and surprisingly objective. As in all his writing, Mathews's prose gained strength from his familiarity with the subject. Many passages effectively combined geologic and geographical accuracy with anthropomorphic metaphors to produce descriptions more common to fiction than biography. A literary agent wrote to Mathews about the possibility of a movie based on the book, but the negotiation never panned out (Wilson 1981:286–87).

The Osage writer's last book, *The Osages* (1961), attempted nothing less than the telling of his tribe's history from its beginnings. Although he did a credible job in researching available documents and using his tribal connection for extensive oral accounts, Mathews was quite aware that there would be gaps in his narrative; these he intended filling with instinct and imagination. Any historian reading that self-described methodology could have predicted an uncertain future for *The Osages* with scholarly reviewers. They found his book more art than history, epic rather than monographic.

Nonetheless, *The Osages* succeeds as ethnohistory. Mathews wrote from the perspective of the Indian, adopting a multidisciplinary research plan that relied heavily on oral sources and drew much from Mathews's knowledge of the Osage language. Custom and culture loom as large as battles and treaties, and all are presented nonlinearly. Ironically, because of this and its length, over 800 closely printed pages, many Osages find the book disappointingly daunting.

Mathews's correspondence reveals that he wrote a second novel entitled *Within Your Dream*, which was never submitted to a publisher. In 1974, the aging writer did show editors a massive autobiographical manuscript with the working title of *Twenty Thousand Mornings!* Readers expressed misgivings about its length, which would require two volumes to accommodate, but Mathews rejected suggestions to shorten it and was still polishing the writing at the time of his death five years later. In this as-yet-unpublished work, as in all his writing, Mathews was less interested in satisfying publishers than in satisfying himself.

Terry P. Wilson
University of California—Berkeley

Bibliography

Primary Sources

Mathews, John Joseph. *Wah'Kon-Tah: The Osage and the White Man's Road*. Norman: U of Oklahoma P, 1932.
———. *Sundown*. New York: Longmans, Green, 1934.
———. *Talking to the Moon*. Chicago: U of Chicago P, 1945.

————. *Life and Death of an Oilman: The Career of E. W. Marland*. Norman: U of Oklahoma P, 1951.

————. *The Osages: Children of the Middle Waters*. Norman: U of Oklahoma P, 1961.

Secondary Sources

Hunter, Carol. "The Protagonist as a Mixed Blood in John Joseph Mathews' *Sundown*." *The American Indian Quarterly* 6 (1982): 319–37.

Ruoff, A. LaVonne Brown. "Old Traditions and New Forms." *Studies in American Indian Literature: Critical Essays and Course Designs*. Ed. Paula Gunn Allen. New York: MLA, 1983.

Wilson, Terry P. "Osage Oxonian: The Heritage of John Joseph Mathews." *Chronicles of Oklahoma* 59 (1981): 264–93.

(William) *D'Arcy McNickle*
(January 18, 1904–October 18, 1977)

As Oliver La Farge pointed out in a 1936 review of D'Arcy McNickle's first novel, *The Surrounded*, McNickle was one of the earliest American Indian writers to publish a novel of historical as well as literary importance. Not only was his literary craftsmanship, honed by a year at Oxford University in England, as good as that of Hemingway, Fitzgerald, and other contemporary non-Indian writers, he also managed to take his subject—the situation of the American Indian on his reservation—beyond the established historical and literary stereotypes and preconceptions. McNickle's fictions advocate neither the romanticized American Indian of the popular frontier romances nor the unconditional assimilation predicated by writers of American history and by American Indian writers like John Milton Oskison and John Joseph Mathews. His fictional characters make clear that the American Indian had to find his own way in the drastically changed world of the twentieth century in order to maintain his spiritual values. And, finally, McNickle's *The Surrounded* foreshadowed N. Scott Momaday's Pulitzer Prize–winning novel *House Made of Dawn* (1968) by more than thirty years and, therefore, must be considered the first fiction of the Native American Renaissance.

(William) D'Arcy McNickle was born on January 18, 1904, as the son of an Irish American farmer and a half-blood French Cree mother at St. Ignatius, Montana. Even though the family seems to have lived on the Flathead Reservation, his mother, Philomene, and McNickle and his two older sisters were not adopted into the Salish Kootenai Confederated Tribes until 1905. McNickle's tenuous roots within the Flathead community, whose tribal unity and traditional social structures had been weakened by the forced relocation in 1872 and the allotment of reservation lands in 1910, were further weakened by his parents' divorce in 1914. His bitter experiences of growing up as a mixed-blood find expression in his novels, especially the early manuscript versions of *The Surrounded*, and caused him, as a young man, to reject his Indian heritage completely.

McNickle's formal education was extensive. He attended boarding school at Chemawa, Oregon, public high school in Montana and, finally, the University of Montana, which he left in his last year to go to England. In 1925, McNickle sold his allotment on the Flathead Reservation and used the money to study at Oxford, England, where he acquired his sure command of the subtleties of English.

McNickle's New York City years, 1927 (approximately) to 1935, were during the height of the Depression. His failure to make his way as a professional writer and his growing awareness of the abuses the American Indian had suffered led to a rethinking of his tribal heritage. Even before the financial failure of *The Surrounded* in 1936, financial pressures led McNickle to accept an appointment at the Bureau of Indian Affairs under the Commissioner of Indian Affairs, John Collier. After his resignation from the Bureau, McNickle worked for the American Indian Development from 1952 to 1966; that year he accepted an appointment to establish the Anthropology Department at the University of Saskatchewan, Regina Campus. He retired in 1971 at age sixty-seven to Albuquerque, New Mexico. His last, major professional involvement was with the Center for the History of the American Indian at the Newberry Library in Chicago, where he remained as director until his death in 1977. The Center houses the D'Arcy McNickle Collection.

McNickle's novel *The Surrounded* (1936) was followed by his nonfiction books, which explore the same historical and contemporary Indian-white relationship as his novels: *They Came Here First* (1949); *Indians and Other Americans* (1959), a collaboration with Harold E. Fey; and *Native American Tribalism* (1962). McNickle's second novel, *Wind from An Enemy Sky* (1978), was not published until the year after his death, but during his lifetime he did add a juvenile novel, *Runner in the Sun* (1954), with a pre-Columbian setting, and a biography of Oliver La Farge, *Indian Man* (1971), to his growing list of publications. The topics of his astonishing number of articles range from short biographies of Indian chiefs at the time of the Puritan settlement to the Peyote Cult; unfortunately, McNickle's only comment on fictions by and about American Indians is a short discussion of Oliver La Farge's fiction in *Indian Man*.

McNickle, in an attempt to find his own literary form and writing style, experimented with the common literary themes of the 1920s and 1930s, which had proved such productive decades in American literature. These experiments were particularly evident in his short fiction dealing with city life and the early manuscript version of *The Surrounded*, written in the late 1920s and early 1930s. The reader encounters the destructive materialism explored in F. Scott Fitzgerald's *The Great Gatsby* (1925), the exaggerated concern with the individual as shown in John Dos Passos's *Manhattan Transfer* (1925), and the shallowness of life reduced to money and the futile search for a new identity in Europe that, for example, Henry James's character undertakes in *The American* (1877). These stories are well written but are not as powerful as the Montana stories, which explore the individual's relationship to the land and the community. Drawing on his own experiences, McNickle paints a strong and convincing picture of the farmer's struggle to survive; the images are so starkly realistic that they call to mind Hamlin Garland's earlier stories of the Middle Border in *Main-Travelled Roads* (1891).

The short stories set on Indian reservations were probably written after McNickle started his major revisions of the earlier manuscript versions of *The Surrounded* in 1934. A progression in his treatment of the Indian-white theme can be noted that reflects McNickle's personal development during the New York City years; the complete rejection of his Indian heritage slowly gave way to a careful reexamination of his tribal roots. In the early manuscript version of his novel, McNickle re-created the image of the American Indian prevalent in American literature as far back as William Bradford's account of the Pilgrims' settlement in New England: the American Indian as locked in a primitive and savage state forever without hope of attaining civilization. McNickle's Indians in the manuscript version, described through the eyes of the acculturated half-blood protagonist, Archilde, and, at times, through the eyes of his respected Spanish father, Max, are lazy, diseased, and doomed to disappear under the pressures of civilized America. Max even goes so far as to say that they are children of the devil and, therefore, unfit for one of the fundamentals of American civilization, Christianity. Indians and half-bloods, like the protagonist Archilde, must prove themselves worthy of civilization; the high regard in which the Montana society holds the half-blood Archilde at the end of the novel is evidence of his complete rejection of his Indian heritage. It is a bleak affirmation of the popular belief that without complete and unquestioning acculturation of the American Indians, all tribes would be doomed to physical extinction. This view of the American Indian does not deviate from the one McNickle encountered in books by such respected American historians as Leo Hubermann *(We, the People)* and James Truslow Adams *(The Epic of America)*.

McNickle's diaries and correspondence of the early 1930s indicate, however, that McNickle, due to his personal development during the difficult years of the Great Depression, was beginning to examine more critically the assumptions of American historians and writers. His idealized view of American democracy changed to a sometimes bitter recognition of the physical and spiritual destruction it had caused among the American Indian tribes with its arrogant refusal to recognize value in an "uncivilized" society. McNickle's new understanding of history, which was in fact a complete reversal of the one held in the manuscript version of *The Surrounded*, is also, a little more tentatively perhaps, reflected in the short stories set on Indian reservations. The stories show that there is value in Indian communities, a sense of place and respect for the individual as a necessary part of the whole. It is this homogeneity that defeats the Superintendent of the Mountain Indians in "Hard Riding." That story also denies the popular belief that the mental ability, the overall racial intelligence, is lower in the American Indian than in the white American. The spokesman of the Mountain Indians assumes the role of trickster to defeat their Superintendent with words rather than with weapons. The victory of the Indians is one of Native intelligence over white stereotypes. The Indian short stories also indicate that Native American communities can adjust to a meaningful life within American civilization if given the time to find their own way. McNickle explores in "En roulant ma boule, roulant . . ." and "Hard Riding" what assimilation would mean for an Indian community: spiritual death. The materialism and individualism governing the American people will destroy tribal unity; American Indians will adhere to the letter of a law rather than the spirit of it.

McNickle never reduced the conflict between whites and Indian/half-bloods on the reservations to the simplicities of most popular fiction, especially not to the simplified version of the conflict that the frontier romances show. His protagonists are taken from both worlds; e.g., Superintendent Brinder in "Hard Riding" is an individual as well as the official representative of the federal government, and Dieudonné in "En roulant ma boule, roulant . . ." is closely linked with the traditional tribal patriarch. Even the white characters are painted with some sympathy; the Superintendent in "Train Time" may lack the sensitivity to understand the all-important bond between the grandparents and the boy, or he may not find the right words to prepare anxious children for their train journey to boarding school, but he does feel affection for the boy.

Out of the manuscript version and the short fictions developed an even more complete and complex picture of the white-Indian relationship in the published version of *The Surrounded*. Perhaps as early as 1934, when McNickle was completing the final revisions of *The Surrounded*, he wrote to John Collier that literature could not be separated from history. In 1971, he explained that idea in more depth; tribal histories, he indicated, must include various elements of oral literature, e.g., stories and legends, and not merely set down facts like Western history. It is not surprising, then, that *The Surrounded* offers a variety of different views of the Indian-white relationship, ranging from the official view of the federal government to the legendary figure of Big Paul.

The most important white spokesman in regard to the Indian-white relationship is the protagonist's father, Max. His development from a realistic but hostile recorder of Indian-white relationships to someone who accepts individual responsibility for the physical and spiritual destruction of the entire Flathead tribe, and his interaction with other white characters who hold various and even opposing views of their relationship with the Flatheads, create a comprehensive picture of the difficulties Archilde faces in joining the white community. Parker, the Superintendent of the Reservation, is an uneasy advocate of the official policy of unconditional acculturation. Moser, the merchant, shows himself to be interested only in the financial exploitation of Indians and whites alike. Father Grepilloux, the old missionary, has withdrawn from the terrible reality of reservation life to a historical period that had held out to whites and Indians the promise of a Jacksonian agricultural paradise. McNickle's juxtaposition of Louis's death with Father Grepilloux's funeral seems to usher in a new phase in the relationship between the white inhabitants of the Flathead Valley and its aboriginal inhabitants. It will be a much less peaceful coexistence; the whites will reject all responsibility for what has happened. In the end, even the Superintendent is not prepared to support his wards; his rejection of Archilde is the rejection of the tribe, of the traditional older generations and the lawless younger one alike.

This rich texture of different views of the Indian-white relationship is repeated for the traditional members of the Flathead tribe. Catherine, Max's full-blood wife, experiences a development similar to Max's. She too rediscovers her individual responsibility to the tribe and, by renouncing Christianity, takes once more the role of the tribal matriarch in a traditional community. But her renunciation of Christianity also means that she renounces the federal laws that have destroyed her family. Acculturation has failed for the Flatheads, and the older people withdraw into the spiritual world of their ancestors, waiting for the physical destruction that is sure to follow. They are indeed surrounded.

The half-blood protagonist's journey of self-discovery takes him more and more to the traditional Indian community of his mother, Catherine. It is a reversal of his beliefs in the first chapter where he considers himself acculturated and has nothing but amused tolerance for the Indian ways. Harshly realistic scenes of the reservation life, e.g., his encounter with the old Indian woman carrying guts for a meal on her child's wagon, combine powerfully with the whites' easy rejection of all responsibility for conditions on the reservation. At the end of the novel, Archilde might be arrested for a murder he has not committed, but he has regained his spiritual balance. He is a Flathead and, like them, he is surrounded.

The complex web of views on the Indian-white relationship in *The Surrounded* is supported by the rich texture of the novel. McNickle used juxtaposed broken narratives as structural elements, Flathead legends and myths, and personal reminiscences that are oral history. These different approaches to the Indian-white relationship give the reader a foundation on which to judge Archilde's final decision for spiritual rather than physical freedom. It also created the illusion of objectivity for the white American reading public of the 1930s who only recently had begun to accord American Indian tribes the right to self-determination as part of the New Deal. If the writer was a historian, as McNickle said to John Collier, then McNickle rewrote Flathead history in his novel *The Surrounded.* The protagonist's return to his tribal roots and the rich, supportive texture of the novel set *The Surrounded* apart from the fictions of earlier American Indian writers like Simon Pokagon and John Joseph Mathews.

In his second, posthumously published novel, *Wind from an Enemy Sky* (1978), McNickle examines the Indian-white relationship once more. Despite the more than forty years that elapsed between the writing of the two novels, the Indian-white relationship seemed unchanged to McNickle. If anything, the hope for Archilde held out at the end of *The Surrounded* has been replaced by pessimism. *Wind from an Enemy Sky* is set on the reservation of a fictional tribe, the Little Elk people. The chief of the Little Elk people, Bull, and Superintendent Rafferty fight for the return of the tribe's sacred medicine bundle, Feather Boy, to reestablish tribal unity. The short spiritual revival of the tribe's heritage is destroyed by the news that Feather Boy has been eaten by rats in Pell's museum basement. Bull, deprived of all hope for a meaningful acculturation, kills Rafferty, thereby removing all physical protection from his people, and also from Pell, thereby avenging Feather Boy.

The most prominent white character of the novel, Superintendent Rafferty, experiences some significant development. Rafferty has a sincere desire to help the Little Elk people; he sees their poverty and has respect for them and their way of life, but his administration is hampered by the fossilized church and the Bureau of Indian Affairs. Despite his lack of knowledge of either Indian culture or federal administration at the beginning of the novel, he manages to see a spiritual quality in the Indian community that he finds lacking in his own. His cultural sensitivity is closely linked with the landscape of the Little Elk reservation. A certain hostility toward the landscape that Rafferty feels at the beginning of *Wind from an Enemy Sky* is slowly replaced by an understanding of its rugged beauty and the demands it makes on people. More and more aware of his individual responsibility for the desperate situation of the Little Elk community, and burdened at the same time by his official responsibility for these "wards" of the government, Rafferty experiences a growing alienation from white values. He finds himself attracted to Bull and the Boy rather than to the rich, knowledgeable Adam Pell, who supposedly preserves Indian traditions in his museum but manages to destroy the spiritual center of the Little Elk people through carelessness. At the end of *Wind from an Enemy Sky*, Rafferty is caught between two worlds; because of Feather Boy's destruction, he will never be able to participate in the spiritual community of the tribe, but Rafferty's alienation from the white world makes refuge there impossible too. Death at Bull's hands is the only meaningful solution for him.

The church in the novel is the rigidly fixed one of the younger Jesuit priest in *The Surrounded*; it is certainly not the church of the old missionary Father Grepilloux who had realized that in order to create a meaningful belief system for the Flatheads, the church must include those elements of Native beliefs that did not violate the church's. American Indians, according to the old priest in *Wind from an Enemy Sky*, are inferior beings. They will undoubtedly become extinct, which to his mind is a reasonable solution of the Indian-white conflict. The church is no longer the mediator it was in former times and, therefore, has aligned itself with the official governmental policies demanding unconditional acculturation.

Bull, helplessly watching the whites harness the all-important water with their dam, feels that the physical and spiritual destruction of the tribe is imminent; despite his growing trust in the Superintendent that foreboding never quite disappears. His reconciliation with the brother, whom whites consider the model of an acculturated Indian, reinforces Bull's traditionalist views. Unconditional acculturation may bring food instead of hunger, but it also adds spiritual deprivation to an already physically precarious situation. In the end, Bull assumes his reponsibility for the community and avenges the loss of Feather Boy. *Wind from an Enemy Sky* is a didactic piece of writing; McNickle had a point to make about Indian administration and the careless destruction of the spiritual heritage of American Indian tribes, as his choice of a fictional tribe indicates. In the end, the Little Elk people have become a symbol for all other tribes under federal administration. Their experiences are prototypical. The novel is informative, contains some interesting characters, and shows fine literary craftsmanship, but it lacks the power of *The Surrounded*. It also lacks the personal involvement McNickle had shown in his earlier novel.

Birgit Hans
University of North Dakota

BIBLIOGRAPHY

Primary Sources

McNickle, D'Arcy. *The Surrounded*. 1936. Albuquerque: U of New Mexico P, 1978.

———. "Train Time." *Indians at Work* 3 (March 15, 1936): 45–7.

———. *They Came Here First: The Epic of the American Indian*. New York: J. P. Lippincott, 1949.

———. *Runner in the Sun*. New York: Winston, 1954.

———. *Indian Man: A Life of Oliver La Farge*. Bloomington: Indiana UP, 1971.

———. *Native American Tribalism: Indian Survivals and Renewals*. 1962. Rpt. New York: Oxford UP, 1973.

———. *Wind from an Enemy Sky*. New York: Harper & Row, 1978.

———. *The Hawk and Other Stories*. Ed. Birgit Hans. Tucson: U of Arizona P, 1992.

————, and Harold E. Fey. *Indians and Other Americans: Two Ways of Life Meet.* 1959. Rpt. New York: Harper & Row, 1970.

Original papers from the D'Arcy McNickle Collection at the Newberry Library in Chicago. These materials—letters, diaries, short fictions, and manuscript versions of both novels—are uncatalogued; more precise locations, therefore, cannot be given.

Secondary Sources

Adams, James Truslow. *The Epic of America.* Boston: Little, Brown, and Company, 1931.

Hubermann, Leo. *We, the People.* 1932. Rpt. New York: Harper & Brothers Publishers, 1947.

La Farge, Oliver. "Half-Breed Hero." Review of *The Surrounded* by D'Arcy McNickle. *The Saturday Review*, March 14, 1936.

Mourning Dove [Humishuma, b. Christine Quintasket; m. Christal McLeod, Christine Galler] (April 1882 [?]–August 8, 1936)

Mourning Dove was the first Native American novelist to organically incorporate aspects of the daily life, the oral traditions, and the religious perspectives of an Indian people into a novel, *Cogewea, the Half-Blood* (1927). With *Coyote Stories* (1933), she also was one of the first Indian writers to collect and publish Indian legends, thereby preserving much of their oral integrity. With the recent publication of *Mourning Dove: A Salishan Autobiography* (1990), a collection of her final unpublished papers, Mourning Dove also will come to be recognized as an important contemporary voice on the severe disruption of Indian life at the turn of the last century. Nonetheless, such achievements have not been appropriately recognized because of the extensive editing, even co-writing, of her books by L. V. McWhorter, Dean Guie, and now Jay Miller. The primary critical problem remains how to distinguish Mourning Dove's work from that of her editors in order to accurately assess her place in the literary canon.

Christine Quintasket, or Humishuma (Mourning Dove), was born in a canoe while her mother was crossing the Kootenai River near Bonner's Ferry, Idaho. This event took place between April 1882 and 1888 (Mourning Dove always refers to 1888, the Tribal Enrollment Services records indicate 1887, and allotment records indicate 1882, 1886, and 1887). Her mother, Lucy Stukin [Stuikin], was Schwelpi, or Colville, and Lake, from the Arrow Lakes Tribes of Canada. Her father, Joseph Quintasket, was descended from the Nicola band of the Thompson River Indians of British Columbia on his mother's side. Mourning Dove's tribal enrollment was Lake on the Colville Reservation, but she always referred to herself as an Okanogan. She did write of an Irishman named Haines, or Haynes, who worked for the Hudson Bay Company, as her grandfather. Yet allotment records indicate that a man named Haines may have been her biological father. Whatever the bloodline, Joseph's family was her family.

Her birth happened but a little more than a decade after the Battle of the Little Big Horn in which Custer and his troops were annihilated. Mourning Dove lived at a time when some of those who had fought in white-Indian conflicts were still alive, and when current federal assimilation policies denied Indians the right to speak their own languages or to practice their religious beliefs and tribal ceremonies. It was a time when the allotment system was exploited to force Indians to sell valuable tribal lands, and it was also a period of ongoing sexual exploitation. Mourning Dove grew up in such a world, and it was that world which serves as the backdrop for her novel and her final manuscripts, and which inspired her to preserve the Okanogan legends she feared might pass away with the dying of the older generation.

Those of an Indian heritage who had written before her, such as Zitkala Sa, had the advantages of a Euroamerican education. As a child, Mourning Dove did attend, with interruptions, the Goodwin Mission School and the Fort Spokane School. As a young adult, she pursued an education by serving as a matron at the Fort Shaw School west of Great Falls, Montana, and then, several years later, attended a business college in Calgary, Canada. Still, her formal education probably did not exceed the equivalent of eight years of schooling. She married twice; in both cases, life was hard financially and psychologically. She had to cope with spousal alcoholism and, at times, physical abuse. Many years she worked as a migrant worker or a camp cook. She also ran a boardinghouse for a short time. Moreover, she fulfilled all the demands of a member of a large extended family; although she had no children of her own, she often helped to parent children who lived with her or with others.

That was one part of her very demanding life. Another part was her desire to write. She met L. V. McWhorter in 1914, when she was in her late twenties or early thirties and he was fifty-four. She had completed the first draft of *Cogewea* two years earlier, in 1912, an effort inspired by witnessing the last buffalo round-up on the Flathead Reservation in Montana. She also had begun to collect "the old stories." In the winter of 1915–16, she stayed with McWhorter's family and they completed the first publishable version of the novel. Two publishers did consider this second draft, and had the cost of paper and other printing supplies been less during World War I, *Cogewea* might have been published as early as 1917 or 1918. But the volume was not published then, and in 1922, a frustrated McWhorter edited the work to the point of co-writing it. He misguidedly believed that by giving the novel more ethnographic substance and political context, the social significance of the novel would be self-evident. Therefore, he added long sections which addressed the plight of the Indians, exposed the corruption of the Bureau of Indian Affairs officials, and condemned Christian hypocrisy. These additions were not shared with Mourning Dove. When the manuscript was finally printed in 1927, she commented that she hardly recognized the text as her own. The book did very poorly. Mourning Dove and McWhorter could not even sell out the first edition. Nonetheless, her devotion to McWhorter for his faith in her, and his tireless efforts to see her novel published, led her to work with him and Dean Guie to publish twenty-seven of the thirty-eight Okanogan tales she had collected between 1912 and 1921. *Coyote Stories* was published in 1933. It achieved instant success, was nationally reviewed, and was in its second printing by 1934. The works she wrote between 1928 and 1933 on the life of the Okanogans were posthumously published in 1976 and 1990 and generated substantial interest.

Late in her life, Mourning Dove achieved a recognition that meant much to her. She was the first Indian to be made an honorary member of the Eastern Washington Historical Society (1927) and, later, a life member of the Washington State Historical Society. In 1935, she was elected to the Council of the Colville Tribes, a significant honor. On August 8, 1936, she suffered a massive brain hemorrhage and died. She is buried in Omak, Washington.

The critical comments on her work are quite instructive. *Coyote Stories* was universally praised in initial book reviews. Although this work is currently out of print, it is a delightful and informative collection of Okanogan tales which received national visibility. A review in the *Lexington Kentucky Leader* (December 17, 1933) by A. B. Guthrie compliments Mourning Dove for being an effective storyteller with "a fine simplicity of expression." He also compliments McWhorter for his unusually accurate and informative notes. A reviewer in the *Daily Oklahoman* (January 14, 1934) ponders why such collections are not available from the tribes within its boundaries, as *Coyote Stories* represents "a spiritual heritage which can never be replaced." Another review, in the *Oregonian* (December 24, 1933), asserts that the edition is more valuable than many volumes of "ethnological theorizing" in reconstructing the vivid life of Indians in the Pacific Northwest. Reviews in the *Boston Globe* (November 27, 1933) and the *Washington* (December 16, 1933) are equally enthusiastic.

With *Coyote Stories*, Mourning Dove and L. V. McWhorter accomplished what they had set out to do in 1914: they preserved an essential part of Indian culture, and they made that culture imaginatively comprehensible to the dominant Euroamerican population. These are extraordinary achievements given the times and the constraints upon them as self-taught writer and historian. The Dove/McWhorter/Guie collaboration can be examined in depth because the 1921 drafts that Mourning Dove sent to McWhorter, McWhorter's 1922 editing of those drafts, and the 1929–31 collaborative work with Guie are housed in the archives at Holland Library, Washington State University, Pullman.

It is to *Cogewea, the Half-Blood: A Depiction of the Great Montana Cattle Range*, however, that contemporary critics turn, and their assessment is ambivalent at best. Charles Larson's critique of the work in Appendix 1 of his *American Indian Fiction* (1978) sets the stage for its problematic reception. For Larson, it is not possible to distinguish Mourning Dove's story from McWhorter's writing, and the narration is so severely disjointed that the work is not salvageable. The ethnographic comments disrupt, the stilted language is unbelievable, and the moral center of the novel, Stemteema, is anti-white. Even Paula Gunn Allen (in *The Sacred Hoop*, 1986), who values the text for bringing the anguish of the half-breed to the fore, and for incorporating myth, tribal history, and ritual into the story, sees the work as maimed because of McWhorter's intrusions, and because Mourning Dove tried to satisfy both white and tribal literary requirements and failed. There is clear disappointment that Mourning Dove should have modeled her story on "the melodramatic dime-novel western." These criticisms are echoed by Andrew Wiget in the earlier *Native American Literature* (1985), where introductory comments highlight the confused narrative voice, the overblown language, the emotional tirades, and the lack of development in the characters.

Cogewea is a very disjointed novel, difficult to read because both rich and banal literary movements are juxtaposed. It is clearly the work of two writers with different literary aims and gifts. The critic with the most insight into the work to date is Alice Poindexter Fisher, who wrote a dissertation on Zitkala Sa and Mourning Dove (1979), and who is responsible for editing the 1981 reprint of the novel. She emphasizes that while there are serious problems, the work is an important historical artifact because it combines elements of the oral tradition of the Okanogans with an accurate record of the contemporary life that both Mourning Dove and McWhorter knew. She sees the work as a pioneering effort essential to the emergence of an American Indian literary tradition. Mary Dearborn (*Pocahontas's Daughters*, 1986) supports that view. She argues that outsiders to the dominant culture need "midwives" from the dominant culture, who through prefaces, appendices, glossaries, and annotations "translate" the foreignness of the text, making it safe and apprehensible for those in power. Authorship is compromised in this process, but it appears to be an essential first step to becoming a heard voice in the dominant literature.

It is natural for readers to want a unified text and to point out the flaws or try to explain what prevents that unity. But to comprehend this work, a different reading is required. When Mourning Dove completed the first draft of *Cogewea* in 1912, she wanted to communicate Indian experiences and modes of knowing and sharing. She wrote a western romance because those were undoubtedly the novels she and those about her read. But she also saw in them the warped and denigrating images of Indians, which even her heroine complains about. Mourning Dove chose, instead, to directly address the crises of mixed-bloods and the tribal fears of genocide. She also portrayed the poignancy of a rapidly passing way of life through the distinct choices of the three sisters. Even more important, she filled the novel with family narratives (discrete story units within the text itself), evolving cultural legends, and references to long-standing cultural myths. Moreover, in Stemteema, Mourning Dove created a quintessential Indian elder who is wise in self-knowledge, accurate in her perceptions about others, and true to traditional ways. Stemteema's stories are authentic oral narratives and those, and all the passages that reveal a storyteller's art, are Mourning Dove's.

McWhorter, on the other hand, was an amateur historian, one fascinated by Indian culture and perceptive about the integrity and authority of an oral tradition long before such narratives had scholarly credibility. He was also a profoundly ethical man, and he was morally outraged at the blatant exploitation and denigration of Indian peoples and their cultures. He became a confrontational advocate for Indian grievances, large and small. He was isolated and harassed because of that commitment, and his sections of *Cogewea* reflect his personal defensiveness and anger, particularly at Christian hypocrisy and corrupt government officials. As an ethnographer, he also was responsible for the explanatory notes both within the text and as footnotes, which are intended to preserve a knowledge of Indian ways. He believed that Native American peoples would not survive the twentieth century, and chapter headings as well as the shorter and longer inserts that presume that passing are his inclusions.

If the dual authorship can be understood, *Cogewea* becomes an important literary work in the rich diversity of its oral narratives, and an important sociological work in its representation of the pressures on Native peoples, and those who supported them, at a time of extreme cultural suppression. In differentiating the two voices, it also becomes clear that Mourning Dove is a literary grandmother of the Native American Renaissance.

She is also a courageous woman who chose to examine her own times. The publication of *Mourning Dove: A Salishan Autobiography* makes that clear. It is not an autobiography in a Western sense, but rather is an examination, through memories, reflections, and tribal history, of life on the Colville Reservation from around 1885–1900, a period of growing pressures to assimilate combined with the severe disruption of a culture. Her memories begin with camp migrations and end with a homesteaders' run. As so few voices recount that rending period for Native peoples, her last work will be an important one. Yet tragically, even in 1990, an editor can still reorganize material, write over a voice by correcting it grammatically, and deny a writer the legitimacy of her own experiences. There has yet to be a book published which adequately assesses Mourning Dove's literary achievements and her place in the Native American canon.

Alanna K. Brown
Montana State University

BIBLIOGRAPHY

Primary Sources

Mourning Dove. *Cogewea, the Half-Blood.* Boston: Four Seas Co. 1927. Rpt. Lincoln: U of Nebraska P, 1981.

———. *Coyote Stories.* Ed. Heister Dean Guie. Caldwell, ID: Caxton Printers, Ltd., 1933. Rpt. Lincoln: U of Nebraska P, 1990.

———. *Tales of the Okanogans.* Ed. Donald Hines. Fairfax, WA: Ye Galleon, 1976.

———. *Mourning Dove: A Salishan Autobiography.* Ed. Jay Miller. Lincoln: U of Nebraska P, 1990.

Secondary Sources

Allen, Paula Gunn. *The Sacred Hoop: Recovering the Feminine in American Indian Traditions.* Boston: Beacon Press, 1986.

Brown, Alanna K. "Mourning Dove, an Indian Novelist." *Plainswoman* 11.5 (1988): 3–4.

———. "Mourning Dove's Voice in *Cogewea.*" *The Wicazo Sa Review* 4.2 (1988): 2–15.

———. "Profile: Mourning Dove (Humishuma) 1888–1936." *Legacy: A Journal of Nineteenth-Century American Women Writers* 6.1 (1989): 51–58.

———. "Mourning Dove's Canadian Recovery Years, 1917–1919." *Canadian Literature* 124–25 (1990): 113–22.

Dearborn, Mary. *Pocahontas's Daughters: Gender and Ethnicity in American Culture.* Oxford: Oxford UP, 1986.

Fisher, Alice Poindexter. "The Transformation of Tradition: Study of Zitkala-Sa (Bonnin) and Mourning Dove, Two Transitional Indian Writers." Diss. City U of NY, 1979.

———. "The Transformation of Tradition: A Study of Zitkala and Mourning Dove, Two Transitional American Indian Writers." *Critical Essays on Native American Literature.* Ed. Andrew Wiget. Boston: G. K. Hall and Co., 1985. 202–11.

Larson, Charles R. *American Indian Fiction.* Albuquerque: U of New Mexico P, 1978.

Miller, Jay. "Mourning Dove: The Author as Cultural Mediator." *On Being and Becoming Indian: Biographical Studies of North American Frontiers.* Ed. James A. Clifton. Chicago: Dorsey, 1989. 160–82.

Wiget, Andrew. *Native American Literature.* Twayne's United States Authors Series. Boston: Twayne, 1985.

Samson Occom *(1723–July 14, 1792)*

Samson Occom (or Occum) was the first Native American to publish in English and to achieve some recognition as a writer. Though his works do not stand out much from those of other eighteenth-century clerics—a body of literature tending to emphasize the practical rather than the poetic—there are sections that give insight into his unique experiences as a Native American in the service of the church. On the whole, his marginal fame is undoubtedly due more to his peculiar situation, the anomaly (then) of being a Native American preaching in English, than to his talents as a writer. His primary importance is thus of a historical nature as the "father" of Native American literature.

Occom was born on an unrecorded day in 1723 into a remnant community of Mohegan near New London, Connecticut. His grandfather, Tomockham (alias Ashneon), is thought to have migrated to this area early in the seventeenth century. One of his sons, Joshua Ockham (Aucum or Mawcum), married a descendant of the renowned sachem Uncas, whose name has been recorded as "Widow Sarah Occom." She was among the first Mohegans to be converted in the wake of the Great Awakening (1734–42) and consequently provided the initial impetus to her son's career as a missionary.

His own interest in Christianity surfaced when he was sixteen years old, and two years later, in 1741, he was converted after having had a revelation at a religious camp meeting. He then began to teach himself how to read biblical texts in English. At this time he also assumed a position of responsibility as one of twelve appointed councilors of the Mohegan community.

Through his mother's arrangements, Occom was accepted in 1743 at Eleazar Wheelock's private school for young men, preparing to enroll in college. During his four years there, he obtained a rudimentary education in English and theology, as well as elementary Greek and Latin. His progress as a student motivated Wheelock to train Native Americans as missionaries, founding his famous Indian Charity School for that purpose. Occom's aspirations to attend college, however, were thwarted by poor health and failing eyesight.

The "Pious Mohegan," as Occom was popularly called, devoted the rest of his life to spreading the gospel among Native Americans throughout the Northeast. After leaving Wheelock's school, he taught in New London for two years and then transferred to Long Island, where he missionized the Montauk for eleven years. The Association of Windham County recognized his efforts and licensed him to preach; he was finally ordained by the Long Island Presbytery. The highlight of his career came in 1766, when he accompanied Rev. Whitaker on a fund-raising tour to England and Scotland. Here he delivered some 300 sermons and was well received by numerous important personages. His popularity netted about £11,000 in donations, which ultimately enabled Wheelock to found Dartmouth College. Upon his return, Occom remained among the Mohegan until 1786, undertaking several missionizing journeys to tribes in New England and New York. That year he removed to Brothertown, a Christian Native American community in New York which he had helped to found. He spent the last years of his life at New Stockbridge, another Christian community in the vicinity of Brothertown, where he died in 1792 of natural causes at the age of sixty-nine.

While Occom remained a faithful Christian throughout his life, his relationship with his superiors was often very strained. In 1764, while residing among the Mohegan, he became involved in a dispute over land between this group and the state of Connecticut (the Mason Controversy), joining up with the party that demanded restitution for expropriated territories. This political involvement met with the disapproval of his sponsoring organization, which threatened to cut off his funds and revoke his license. Under such pressure, he finally withdrew from the issue, consenting to write a public confession of having neglected his duties as a missionary (original letter in the archives of the Dartmouth College Library, 1765). Relations between him and Wheelock also began to deteriorate after his return from England in 1768; Occom accused Wheelock of not having properly taken care of his family during his absence and, above all, of misusing the funds he had collected abroad for the training of Native American missionaries at Dartmouth. In fact, Wheelock had changed his plans at this time and the ultimate development of Dartmouth as an institution for Anglo-American students seems to legitimize Occom's concern (Blodgett 1935; Brain 1910; Love 1899; Peyer 1982; Sprague 1859).

Occom began to write sporadically shortly after having enrolled in Wheelock's school. His work consists of a fragmentary diary, a short study of the Montauk, a brief autobiography, a few dozen letters, manuscripts of sermons, a published sermon and a book of hymns (most of the unpublished material is found in the archives of the Dartmouth College Library; some is in the collections of the Connecticut Historical Society).

The diary covers a period from December 6, 1743, to March 6, 1790, with many gaps in between. Unfortunately, it is almost entirely composed of superficial accounts of missionizing activities. In keeping with the practical orientation of missionary journals of the times, it maintains a careful record of his clerical activities (sermons preached, prayer meetings, conversions, etc.) and is devoid of personal contemplation or secular topics. The few passages relating historically relevant events in his life, such as his journey to England or the migration of Mohegan families to Oneida territory in New York, are reduced to a mere listing of events and dates (Blodgett 1935).

In 1761, Occom wrote a letter to Rev. John Devotion in which he described the marriage, naming, religious, curing, and burial customs of the Montauk on Long Island. With the exception of the final paragraph, which refers to these customs as "heathenish idolatry and superstition," his observations are surprisingly objective and well detailed. This valuable ethnographic document was published posthumously in 1809, in the *Collections of the Massachusetts Historical Society.*

Just prior to his tour to England, on November 28, 1765, Occom wrote a one-page sketch of his educational background. His stated purpose for doing so was to disprove certain rumors that had been circulating about him at this time, namely that he was not Mohegan and had just recently been converted as a special exhibit for England. In the spring of 1768, he wrote a lengthier, ten-page account of his life, describing further his conversion experience and consequent missionary activities. This piece, however, was never published independently; Love (1899) and Blodgett (1935) reprinted it much later in their biographies. In the latter part of his autobiography, Occom voices his disappointment at the way his efforts were recompensed by his superiors, criticizing them for having exploited his services as a missionary and paying him quite a bit less than his white counterparts. Of all his writings, this piece gives the clearest impression of what Occom could have produced if his position had permitted him more leeway: the language, which has been left unedited, is atypically vigorous and infused with elements of sardonic humor (original and typescript transcription in Dartmouth College Library).

Occom's major work, upon which his status as the first Native American author in the United States is actually based, is *A Sermon Preached at the Execution of Moses Paul, an Indian . . .* (1772). It is the written and expanded version of a widely acclaimed sermon he had preached September 4, 1772, at the public hanging of a Native American seaman who had been convicted of murder following a drunken brawl. After some initial hesitation on his part, Occom finally succumbed to public demand and allowed it to be published on October 31 of that same year. The edition sold out within two weeks; a second was printed by the same press November 13, followed by yet another on December 4. In all, the sermon went through at least nineteen editions, including a Welsh translation that appeared thirty-five years after his demise (Love 1899). The text itself, thirty-one pages in length, is a typical exhortation on sin and redemption, embellished with numerous quotations from the Scriptures. Its popularity, as Occom himself points out in the introduction, is due primarily to the fact that it came "from an uncommon quarter." In a rather subservient manner—also typical of such writings and not without coyness on his part—he apologizes for having decided to publish it and hopes that its plain language will render it of service to "children . . . poor Negroes . . . and [his] poor kindred." Its main subject is temperance, a problem that was to be addressed by future generations of Native American authors, into the twentieth century.

Two years later, in 1774, Occom published *A Choice Collection of Hymns and Spiritual Songs*. Not nearly as successful as his sermon, it nevertheless went through three printings. Occom's biographers agree that a few of the hymns in the collection were of his own creation, including one, "Awaked by Sinai's Awful Sound," which was apparently quite popular at the time.

Further insight into Occom's personal life and views can be gleaned from his private correspondence, which has been reprinted in part by Love (1899), Blodgett (1935), and Richardson (1933); see also McCallum (1932). The leitmotif in many of his letters is his financial dependency on missionary organizations and the severe economic hardships he was confronted with as the father of six children. He had to turn to various secular vocations as well as farming, hunting, and fishing in order to feed his family. Occom interprets his difficulties as a result of racial discrimination. In other letters, as well as unpublished manuscripts of addresses, there are brief references to Occom's political views: e.g., he counselled Native American neutrality during the Revolutionary War, favored the maintenance of a land base, and advocated the formation of centralized tribal governments.

Finally, Occom's efforts as a teacher were instrumental in the development of at least two Native American writers of the late eighteenth century: the Mahican Hendrick Aupaumut (1757?–1830), author of a travelogue and an ethnographic sketch of the Mahican, and the Mohegan Joseph Johnson (1752–1776?), who wrote several letters published in New England newspapers.

Bernd C. Peyer
Johann Wolfgang Goethe University

BIBLIOGRAPHY

Primary Sources

Occom, Samson. "A Short Narrative of My Life." Unpublished manuscript. 1768. Archives of the Dartmouth College Library.

———. *A Sermon Preached at the Execution of Moses Paul, An Indian Who Was Executed at New Haven on the 2nd of September 1772 for the Murder of Mr. Moses Cook, late of Waterbury, on the 7th of December 1771/ Preached at the Desire of said Paul by Samson Occom, minister of the gospel and missionary to the Indians, New Haven 1772*. New Haven: Press of Thomas and Samuel Green, 1772.

———. *A Choice Collection of Hymns and Spiritual Songs*. New London, CT: Press of Thomas and Samuel Green, 1774.

———. "An Account of the Montauk Indians, on Long Island." *Collections of the Massachusetts Historical Society* 10 (1809): 105–10.

Secondary Sources

Blodgett, Harold. *Samson Occom*. Dartmouth College Manuscript Series 3. Hanover, NH: Dartmouth College Publications, 1935.

Brain, Belle M. "Samson Occom, the Famous Indian Preacher of New England." *The Missionary Review of the World* 33 (1910): 913–19.

Love, William DeLoss. *Samson Occom and the Christian Indians of New England*. Boston: The Pilgrim Press, 1899.

McCallum, James D. *The Letters of Eleazar Wheelock's Indians*. Dartmouth College Manuscript Series 1. Hanover NH: Dartmouth College Publications, 1932.

Peyer, Bernd. "Samson Occom: Mohegan Missionary and Writer of the 18th Century." *American Indian Quarterly* 6. 3–4 (1982): 208–17.

Richardson, Leon B. *An Indian Preacher in England*. Dartmouth College Manuscript Series 2. Hanover, NH: Dartmouth College Publications, 1933.

Sprague, W. B. "Samson Occom." *Annals of the American Pulpit* 3 (1859): 192–95.

John Milton Oskison
(September 21, 1874–February 25, 1947)

John Milton Oskison and his writings are not currently familiar to very many readers, and he has not so far received much critical attention— unfortunate lapses because Oskison was unusual among Native Americans both as a man and as a writer. He was a cattleman and a scholar, a world traveler and a soldier, at home with the rich and powerful but equally comfortable in log cabins. He published newspaper and magazine articles, essays, editorials, short stories, and novels; he collected Indian tales for publication, and he began an autobiography. He served as an editor at *Collier's* and the *New York Evening Post* at their height.

He was born near Tahlequah, Indian Territory, to John Oskison, an unschooled English immigrant who, even at the end of his life, could barely write his own name, and to Rachel Connor Crittenden, who was one-quarter Cherokee. Interestingly, John Milton Oskison is himself listed on the census rolls as one-quarter degree of blood. Oskison spent his boyhood and youth in Indian Territory, working on his father's cattle ranch. His father was a harsh taskmaster, and there was a three-year period when Oskison and his brothers did not attend school at all, instead helping their father establish a profitable cattle business. He mourned the loss of that schooling, but the scenes, events, and images of running cattle in all condi- tions and seasons became the material for his short stories and novels. He did graduate in the first graduating class of Willie Halsell College in 1894 at the age of nineteen. He then entered Stanford University, where one of his friends was Herbert Hoover. He received a Bachelor of Arts degree in 1898 and then spent a year doing graduate work in English at Harvard. In 1899, with his story "Only the Master Shall Praise," he won a writing contest sponsored by *Century Magazine*. He continued to write short sto- ries even after he became an editor and editorial writer for the *New York*

Evening Post in 1903. In late 1906, he resigned from the *Post* to become an associate editor and then finance editor of *Collier's Weekly*, where he remained until 1912. By the time World War I began, almost every major popular magazine had published his writing. Throughout this time he was also writing articles for Native American magazines and newspapers. During World War I he enlisted in the army and eventually was sent to France as a first lieutenant in the American Expeditionary Force, about whose relief efforts he also wrote. After the war and his return to the United States, he devoted most of his time to writing novels about the peoples and places of Oklahoma. He preferred to live in New York City and Paris rather than Oklahoma, although he came home often for anecdotes and inspiration. He made seven trips altogether to Europe, as well as trips to Hawaii, Bermuda, and Palestine. At the time of his death, he was working on another novel and his autobiography. Some of his most interesting writing occurs in his unpublished autobiography, in which he is haunted by memories and impressions of his father, an orphaned and abused man who ran away to the gold fields at seventeen by stowing away in a California-bound wagon, and who lived a life more nomadic than settled ever after. Photographs of John Milton Oskison show a handsome, urbane man and seem to belie his own assertion that he inherited the restless, nervous, short-tempered soul of his father; but wander he did, ranging the globe in his travels and displaying great eclecticism and diversity in his writings.

His short works can be divided roughly into three categories. From 1897 to 1917, he wrote letters and articles about "Indian problem" issues, mostly for Indian Territory newspapers and Indian school journals but also finding a national audience with "Remaining Causes of Indian Discontent" in the *North American Review*, "Making an Individual of the Indian" in *Everybody's Magazine*, and "Arizona and Forty Thousand Indians" in *Southern Workman*. In these articles he made no secret of his own Indian blood. He also belonged to the Society of American Indians, and in 1911 his name appears, as a member of the "Temporary Executive Committee," on the letterhead of the American Indian Association, which also declares that active memberships apply to "Persons of Indian Blood Only." American Indian authors, Oskison included, writing during these years are often credited by critics with (or accused by them of) being assimilationists who proposed the idea that the "Indian problem" would disappear according to the natural laws of "social evolution." A naive reading of Oskison's articles on Indian topics would seem to justify aligning him with assimilationism, but a closer look at his rhetorical technique raises strong doubts. He often contrasts issues without making value judgments: the traditional elders vs. the acculturated young men, the old lifestyle vs. the new, getting an education vs. the freedom of the reservation, sympathetic Anglos willing to intermarry vs. insensitive separatists, childlike Natives needing help vs. the adroit jurisprudential skill of tribal courts. It is not at all clear which side he is on. In the texts of otherwise insouciant, apparently "assimilationist" articles, he often uses harsh phrases such as "destroy the Indian identity," "soiled relics" after white contact, "inglorious passing," "imprisonment," "stilling the voices" of wise Indians. The harshness of these occasional phrases undercuts any naive acceptance of assimilation. When he writes that the "new man" is "Indian only in blood" or that the red man is gaining a sense of personal responsibility or that young girls are learning to appreciate the household implements of the white culture, we do not know whether he personally applauds these directions or bemoans them. His stance and tone in these articles are consistently neutral. At crucial points in his arguments in these Indian articles, he often retreats behind quotations from others such as President Theodore Roosevelt, Indian agents, and commissioners, using their words which advocate assimilation, but which clearly are not Oskison's words and so are not necessarily his thoughts.

Also fascinating for their hidden metaphors and underlying structure are his short stories, which he was publishing between 1900 and 1925. Their subject matter was always the rugged frontier life of the Oklahoma Territory and the foibles of its saints and sinners, heroes and desperadoes. Here the hero or the quietly courageous stalwart or the savior of the white rancher is invariably an until-then-overlooked Indian or half-breed. Another interesting feature of these stories is how often they follow the coyote-tale format. His protagonists are wry and compassionate tricksters with their own agendas—often creators, often destroyers, often adulterers, and often butts of the joke or the mislaid plan. They are marginal characters, slipping in and out of their society's awareness—one foot in Anglo society, one in Indian—belonging to the land but often anachronisms in their own times.

Oskison loved to write about cattle rustling, train robberies, bronc busting, graft and greed, patient women, wise old Indians, sturdy farmers, and forgiving judges. Most of the events he wrote about had actually happened (many he had witnessed himself), far-fetched as they may sometimes seem; and most of his characters were based on real people, ingenuous though his presentation may be. And though an occasional reviewer has said he oversentimentalized events and often wrote without a judicious selection of detail, perhaps it is more accurate to say that he did not have the heart to understate his descriptions of nor his excitement over those fulminating Oklahoma days. Oskison continues this style of writing in his novels, which are also set in the Oklahoma Territory. *Wild Harvest* (1925) tells the story of Nan Forest, a young woman who comes to Indian Territory with her father to make a life. She absorbs into her blood the prairie magic. She loves the struggle, the black soil, and the wind-tossed grass. Her neighbors are full-blood and mixed-blood Indians and white settlers who are learning to get along in the face of the inevitable forced proximity. The Indians at this time are struggling to enforce quarantines against incoming Texas cattle, and Nan and her friends get involved in that effort. In this novel, Oskison mirrors but criticizes at the same time the structure and techniques of the sentimental western. While Nan is the central character, she must learn to adapt to the atmosphere of the Territory, which is the atmosphere of the Indians who endure.

Many of these same characters appear in *Black Jack Davy* (1926), Oskison's next novel. They help the nineteen-year-old Davy and his elderly adopted parents establish a farm in the Territory, which they have rented from Ned Warrior, a full-blood Cherokee. Since a corrupt and greedy neighboring rancher wishes to run the new family as well as the Warrior family off the land, a series of violent encounters soon occurs. Davy's adopted father is eventually killed, but the long conflict has established new, almost extended family relationships among all concerned. While this novel also depends on some of the conventions of the popular western, there are enough deviations from that style to guarantee interest. *Black Jack Davy* was dramatized by Richard Mansfield Dickinson and won second prize in the national Drama League competition in New York City.

Oskison's most graceful novel is *Brothers Three* (1935). Francis Odell comes to Indian Territory with a part-Cherokee wife and infant son. Odell and his wife establish successful ranching and mercantile endeavors thanks largely to the wife's dedication to the land. The novel describes the misguided investments the family makes after the death of the father and their struggle to regain their footing after the stock market crash of 1929. This is a strongly autobiographical novel with the fictional sons Timmy and Roger roughly corresponding to Oskison's brothers Richard and Bert and the character Mister to himself. This was also the longest novel written by an American Indian author up to that time. It is a generational epic of a family on the land and what happens to them financially and psychologically as they adjust and readjust their relationship to that land. It contains his best-sustained writing. He had hit his stride as an author. He also wrote fictionalized biographies—*A Texas Titan* (1929) about Sam Houston and *Tecumseh and His Times* (1938)—whose Indian settings and careful details seem to be meant to satisfy his own personal interests and longings. He was contributing articles on topics of national interest to popular mainstream American magazines. He wrote of money—how to earn it, how to save it, how not to be swindled out of it. He wrote of ingenuity and creativity, lauding inventors, scientists, industrialists, and politicians. He wrote of modern military might; World War II was imminent and he was impressed by its machinery. He also contributed an occasional letter or article for the armchair adventurers among his readers about his trips to Yosemite or to Europe or on deer hunting and hiking among the ruins in the American Southwest.

John Milton Oskison's personal complexity is evident. He wrote about national and international powers and their modes of production, but he was also compelled by the romance and history of the old days in the Oklahoma Territory, especially the roles and heritages of its Indian populations, whose whispers stirred his own blood.

Gretchen Ronnow
Wayne State College

BIBLIOGRAPHY

Oskison, John Milton. *Wild Harvest*. New York: Appleton, 1925.

———. *Black Jack Davy*. New York: Appleton, 1926.

———. *A Texas Titan*. New York: Doubleday, 1929.

———. *Brothers Three*. New York: Macmillan, 1935.

———. *Tecumseh and His Times*. New York: G. P. Putnam, 1938.

———. "Autobiography." Unpublished manuscript. 1947. Western History Collection, U of Oklahoma Library, Norman.

S*imon Pokagon* *(1830–January 1899)*

Simon Pokagon was the youngest son of Chief Leopold, who was chief of the Pokagon band for over forty years. Although the band was primarily located near South Bend, Indiana, its original territory encompassed present-day Chicago. During the late 1830s, they settled near Dowagiac, Michigan. In 1844, Pokagon enrolled at Notre Dame, probably at the university's manual labor school, where he spent three years. Pokagon subsequently studied for two years at Twinsburg Institute, near Cleveland, Ohio, which prepared students for college (Dickason 1971:136–39). Although Pokagon's admirers frequently called him the best-educated Indian in America, he did not attend college, as was often asserted.

Pokagon surfaced as a public figure in 1864, when he went to Washington as a member of the Potawatomi delegation that persuaded the Secretary of the Interior to pay back annuities. Never a principal chief, Pokagon did serve for several years as chair of the band's Business Committee. He aroused considerable anger among his band because in 1881 he sold for cash, without the consent of the band, discounted notes that were supposedly guaranteed by anticipated settlements of Potawatomi claims, and because in 1894 he established a rival, unauthorized Business Committee to pursue his own settlement claims. In 1895, the Potawatomi rejected his claims, petitioning the Commissioner to refuse him any special status or funds. Still energetic in the pursuit of his own cause, Pokagon in 1897, purportedly acting on behalf of the whole band but without their knowledge or consent, sold by quitclaim the band's whole interest in the Chicago lakefront (Clifton, *The Pokagons*, 86–87, 97, 103–4, 112–13). During these years, Pokagon's campaign to gain public support for his claims, his many speeches to whites as a spokesman for Indian causes, and his appearance as part of the 1893 Columbian Exposition in Chicago gained him considerable popularity among whites. Greatly lionized by the press during this period, Pokagon was inaccurately credited by a Chicago reporter for obtaining the 1896 settlement of Potawatomi claims (Clifton, *The Pokagons*, 107).

Although Pokagon has been credited with writing *O-gî-mäw-kwe Mit-i-gwä-kî* (*Queen of the Woods*), the first American Indian novel devoted to Indian life, his authorship is currently questioned. *Queen of the Woods*, which may have been ghostwritten by Mrs. Cyrus H. Engle, was published after Pokagon's death by Engle. Its Victorian diction differs considerably from the broken English Pokagon used in his letters. This highly sentimental romance contrasts the idyllic forest life led by the Potawatomi with the destructive forces introduced by the white man. Engle indicates in the preface that "nearly all the persons mentioned in the narrative bear their real names, and were personally known to many yet living" (i). Pokagon, who is the narrator, uses his wife's name, Lonidaw, for the female protagonist and includes some details of their backgrounds. The melodramatic deaths of the character Lonidaw and her daughter are fictional. In *Queen of the Woods*, Pokagon returns to living in the woods after attending school. There he meets and eventually marries Lonidaw, a kind of woodland nymph who is accompanied by a snow-white deer (sacred in Potawatomi mythology). The evils of the world destroy this life when their pre-adolescent son, sent away to school, becomes an alcoholic and when their daughter drowns after drunken whites in a boat run down her canoe. Lonidaw, who makes Pokagon promise to fight drunkenness, dies of a broken heart. After Lonidaw's death, the narrative disintegrates into an anti-alcoholism tract. A unique aspect of the romance is Pokagon's emphasis on the Potawatomi language. He incorporates Potawatomi words into the narrative, translating them parenthetically, and includes an essay on the Algonquin language. Engle published three of Pokagon's birchbark booklets: *Red Man's Greeting*, originally entitled *Red Man's Rebuke* (n.d.) and sold at the 1893 Exposition; *The Pottawatamie Book of Genesis—Legends of the Creation of Man* (1901); and *Algonquin Legends of South Haven* (n.d.). In addition, Pokagon published several essays on Potawatomi culture and history.

A. LaVonne Brown Ruoff
University of Illinois—Chicago

Bibliography

Primary Sources

Pokagon, Simon. *Algonquin Legends of South Haven*. Hartford, MI: C. H. Engle, n.d. Birchbark booklet.

———. *Red Man's Greeting*. Hartford, MI: C. H. Engle, ca. 1893. Birchbark booklet originally entitled *Red Man's Rebuke*.

———. "An Indian's Observations on the Mating of Geese." *Arena* 16 (July 1896): 245–48.

———. "The Massacre of Fort Dearborn at Chicago." *Harper's Monthly* 98 (March 1898): 649–56.

———. "Indian Superstitions and Legends." *Forum* 25 (July 1898): 618–29.

———. *O-gî-mäw-kwe Mit-i-gwä-kî: Queen of the Woods.* Hartford, MI: C. H. Engle, 1899. Rpt. Berrien Springs, MI: Hardscrabble Books, 1972.

———. "The Future of the Red Man." *Forum* 23 (August 1899): 698–708.

———. *The Pottawatamie Book of Genesis—Legends of the Creation of Man.* Hartford, MI: C. H. Engle, 1901. Birchbark booklet.

———. "The Pottawatomies in the War of 1812." *Arena* 26 (July 1901): 48–55.

Secondary Sources

Buechner, Cecelia Bain. *The Pokagons. Indiana Historical Society Publication* 10.5 (1933): 279–340. Rpt. Berrien Springs, MI: Hardscrabble, 1976.

Clifton, James. *The Pokagons, 1683–1983.* Latham, MD: UP of America, 1984.

———. "Simon Pokagon's Sandbar: Potawatomi Claims to Chicago's Lakefront." *Michigan History* 71.5 (1987): 12–17.

Dickason, David H. "Chief Simon Pokagon: 'The Indian Longfellow.'" *Indiana Magazine of History* 57 (1971): 127–40.

Engle, Cyrus H. "Biographical Sketch of Chief Simon Pokagon's Life." In *Queen of the Woods.* 5–33.

Alexander Lawrence Posey
[Chinnubbie Harjo] (August 3, 1873–May 27, 1908)

Alexander Lawrence Posey was the first American Indian to receive significant national notice as a lyric poet and humorist. Yet he has received little critical attention: no biography, authoritative editions of his works, or significant critical studies exist. Though his works are in many ways conventional, he defies the stereotype of the assimilated Indian. He had well-defined ideas concerning the Indian writer and the obstacles between him and the American reading public, but his hesitancy to confront those obstacles may have denied him a prominent place in literary history, despite the volume and quality of his works.

Born in the Creek Nation of a Chickasaw-Creek mother and a white father, who had been reared among the Creeks, Posey did not speak English until age fourteen, when his father insisted that he acquire a formal, American-style education. After attending the Creek national school at Eufaula and spending three years at Bacone Indian University, where he developed his literary tastes and began to write, he became superintendent of Creek schools at Okmulgee, Eufaula, and Wetumka; superintendent of public instruction; owner and editor of the *Indian Journal* at Eufaula; and a field worker for the Dawes Commission. He bought the *Indian Journal* a second time shortly before his death.

His occupations kept Posey close to the Creeks. From childhood he was familiar with their traditional history and lore, and as an adult he was close friends with older Creeks who were also knowledgeable in Creek history and lore. As a journalist, Posey interviewed elderly Creeks, and as a field worker for the Dawes Commission he sought out and talked with the most conservative members of Creek society. He had easy access to the older and most conservative Creeks because he spoke Creek fluently, his knowledge of Creek culture included traditional forms of etiquette and social protocol, he maintained a great respect for the old people as repositories of knowledge, and his town and clan membership demanded respect in return. A member of the powerful Wind clan, from which the Creeks traditionally chose leaders, Posey was from Tuskegee, one of the white or peace towns, which held the balance of political power among the Creeks from the Civil War onward. As a writer, he drew extensively upon his deep knowledge of the Creeks and the landscapes they occupied in his home district in the Creek Nation.

From 1890 to 1900, Posey directed his literary efforts to poetry. He produced about 125 poems, nearly a hundred of which were collected by his widow, Minnie, in a posthumous volume in 1910. The quality varies from doggerel to exquisite poetic expression. Though many of his poems appealed to contemporary readers, in only a handful of the lyrics does he sustain a level of poetic quality that appeals to the modern reader, perhaps because of his poetic models. Though familiar with the poetry of Emily Dickinson and Walt Whitman, whom he considered the most creative American poets, Posey followed more familiar models, including major and minor poets of the British Romantic and Victorian traditions and the popular poets of nineteenth-century America. While imitative in form, Posey's poetry often demonstrates a freshness of subject, including Creek national figures, life ways of the Creeks, and the local natural scene. A close observer and lover of nature from childhood, Posey rendered the flora, fauna, and landscape of the Tulledega region with enthusiasm, clarity, and sincerity, but at times his rendering is romanticized almost to triteness.

Perhaps his own reticence allowed him to be satisfied with imitative verse and prevented his striking out more boldly in his poems. Always reluctant to talk about his writing, he sought only a local audience. Part of that reluctance resulted from a belief that Indian writers had special difficulties in composing English poetry. While they thought naturally in the figurative concepts of their native languages, they found it difficult, if not impossible, to render those thoughts in English. To him, this barrier explained why no Indian had been successful as a poet in English. While most of Posey's works appeared in local publications, he received some national notice in 1900. Publishers outside the Indian Territory sought his work, but he refused to contribute, saying that he wrote for a western audience and feared that eastern readers would not appreciate his work. About 1900, he gave up poetry and after that wrote very little and nothing of quality.

During his period of intense poetic production, Posey also produced a number of prose pieces. While at Bacone, he had written a series of narratives of Creek traditional lore, four of them about Chinnubbie Harjo, the mischievous, sometimes cruel wit of Creek traditional history, whose name Posey adopted as a pen name for his poetry. After he left Bacone, he produced a series of narratives about his childhood, about which he planned, but failed, to write a book. Fiction had little appeal for him, and he especially disliked the serialized fiction of his day, which he believed was written simply to sell. For prose models, he turned to Irving, Emerson, Thoreau (whose *Walden* was his favorite work), biographers, and late nineteenth-century nature writers.

Posey's greatest literary success was his political humor in the famed Fus Fixico letters. In early 1902, as the new owner of the Eufaula *Indian Journal*, he refused to write editorials. However, the political dynamics of the day required that he adopt an editorial voice with which to address such issues as the Creek allotment, conservative Creek resistance to it, the movement toward Oklahoma statehood, local political races, the workings of the local and federal bureaucracy, the actions of ambitious office seekers, and graft and fraud in allotments, town lots, leases, and national resources. He chose the voice of Fus Fixico, or "bird without heart," who wrote letters to the editor in the English dialect spoken by the full-blooded Creeks. Fus Fixico was an alleged member of the conservative Snake faction of Creeks, who were then resisting the allotment process. He reported the monologues that Hotgun, a Snake medicine man, delivered to his listeners. Dissolution of the tribal land title had forced the Snakes to the fringes of society in the movement toward statehood. Thus Fus Fixico, Hotgun, and the others were political outsiders who watched with amusement and, at times, incredulity the actions of federal and local politicians and bureaucrats. In Fus Fixico, then, Posey had found a credible character for his dialect voice, whose detached observations and commentary provided the basis for humor.

From 1902 until 1908, he produced about sixty letters, which brought wider acclaim than his poetry had. They were instantly popular, and in 1903, Posey was besieged by requests for the letters from newspapers throughout the country. As he had done with his poetry, he refused, asserting again that he wrote for a western audience and that others would probably not appreciate his humor.

Posey was intensely conscious of himself as an Indian writer. His most accomplished works reflect a deep knowledge of the Creeks and their land. He was familiar with, and encouraged, the literary efforts of his fellow Creeks, Cherokees, and other Indian writers of the territory. He knew the works of writers such as Simon Pokagon, Zitkala Sa, and Charles A. Eastman, and recognized the obstacles of language and audience that Indian writers faced. Ironically, regarding the latter, by refusing to seek a wider audience than Indian Territory readers, he denied himself the limelight and with it, perhaps, a higher place in the history of American Indian literature than he now occupies.

Daniel F. Littlefield, Jr.
University of Arkansas—Little Rock

BIBLIOGRAPHY

Posey, Alexander Lawrence. *Alex Posey, the Creek Indian Poet*. Collected by Mrs. Minnie H. Posey. Topeka: Crovet Co., 1910.

———. *The Fus Fixico Letters*. Eds. Daniel F. Littlefield, Jr. and Carol A. Petty Hunter. Lincoln: U of Nebraska P, 1993.

———. *Journal of Creek Enrolment Party 1905*. Oklahoma City: Oklahoma Historical Society, 1968.

———. *Poems of Alex Lawrence Posey, Creek Indian Bard*. Rev. by Okmulgee Cultural Foundation and the Five Civilized Tribes Heritage. Muskogee, OK: Joffman Printing Co., 1969.

Posey, Minnie H., comp. *The Poems of Alexander Lawrence Posey*. Topeka: Crane, 1910.

John Rollin Ridge *[Yellow Bird, or Chees-quat-a-law-ny] (March 19, 1827–October 5, 1867)*

John Rollin Ridge, poet, essayist, fiction writer, and newspaperman, was born into an important Cherokee family in the most turbulent period in his people's history. His major works consist of some fifty-one poems, most of which have been gathered into a posthumous volume; a fictional romance based on historical events in the Gold Rush days, *The Life and Adventures of Joaquin Murieta, the Celebrated California Bandit*; essays on the American Indian published in California periodicals; and hundreds of editorials and newspaper articles on a variety of subjects. He was an eloquent spokesman for a national policy of treating the American Indian honestly and fairly, and a defender of assimilationist programs. Ridge is considered one of the major Cherokee writers of the nineteenth century.

Ridge was born in the eastern Cherokee Nation to John Ridge, a prominent Cherokee, and Sarah Bird Northrup, a white woman. His well-schooled parents ensured that Rollin and his siblings received a good education. The Ridges believed that adopting the values and practices of the white society was the only way that the Cherokees could survive. As a result, they used modern farming and business practices to amass considerable wealth in the Cherokee Nation. Rollin's father and grandfather led the Cherokee resistance to removal from their traditional lands to the West. Around 1832, however, the Ridges became convinced that the only course open to the Cherokees was to make the best bargain they could and to immigrate to the West. Accordingly, John and Major Ridge and others signed the Treaty of New Echota, which provided for ceding the Cherokee lands in Georgia and the removal of the people to a territory in present-day northeastern Oklahoma. The treaty led to the forced migration of thousands of Cherokees that became known as the Trail of Tears. When the Cherokees reached their new lands in 1839, John and Major Ridge were assassinated for signing the removal treaty. The killing of John Ridge took place in front of his family, including twelve-year-old Rollin.

The impact of the scene was never to leave Ridge and was to affect many of his subsequent actions. Fearful that more violence was forthcoming, Sarah Ridge moved her family to Fayetteville, Arkansas. Rollin received a good education there and later at Great Barrington Academy in Massachusetts, after which he studied law in Fayetteville. In 1847, he married and settled down on the family farm in the Cherokee Nation, where, in an altercation over a horse, he killed another Cherokee and then fled to Missouri. Convinced that he could not get a fair trial in the Cherokee Nation, he decided to join the wagon trains headed for the gold fields of California.

In California, Ridge soon found his niche as a writer. He had written and published poetry and political articles while in Arkansas. In California, he capitalized on local events and wrote *Joaquin Murieta* under the name "Yellow Bird," a translation of his Cherokee name. Later, he became the first editor of the *Sacramento Bee* and went on to edit or publish a series of California newspapers. He also published poetry and essays in many of the popular San Francisco literary magazines. Ridge was involved in politics in California and was one of the leaders in the state Democratic Party. As such, he vehemently opposed abolitionism and the policies of Abraham Lincoln. After a trip to Washington as a member of the southern Cherokee delegation in 1866, Ridge returned to California, where he died at age forty.

All of his mature life, Ridge considered himself a poet. Following the conventional romantic line of his era, he saw poets as special beings who have the ability to make their mystical perceptions visible to common people. The poet's role, for Ridge, is to use his special power to translate his own experiences, transcendental and otherwise, for his reader. The poet is to re-create, as far as is possible, his own special insights into the universe surrounding all of us. In view of this basic assumption, it is not surprising that much of John Rollin Ridge's poetry contains poetic conventions common in the works of English and American Romantic poets of the early nineteenth century, poets that Ridge most certainly must have read. Themes and structures in his work are often imitative of earlier writers, especially in those pieces that may be called nature poems, which attempt to re-create the poet's personal experiences with the natural environment. The experiences, like those of the more famous Romantic poets of the period, often have mystical or transcendental qualities. In addition, the power of the imagination is nearly always the driving force that makes the experience possible. One such poem, "Mount Shasta," is probably the most famous of his poetic works; it was widely reprinted in California newspapers and magazines.

Some of Ridge's poems are clearly autobiographical and intensely personal. An examination of these works—most of which were written in periods of extreme stress—leads to some conclusions about how he saw himself and his personal situation. He clearly regarded himself as a Byronic figure, an exile who, despite his great talent, was prevented by fate from carrying out the one heroic Great Act that would prove his true worth to the world. A tragic figure, he saw himself as an intense, passionate man who hated and loved deeply, like most heroes of literature and myth. He admitted that his passions led sometimes to reckless behavior, but that the darker side of his temperament could be calmed most times by a soothing female voice. His autobiographical poems reveal an exaggerated sense of self-importance and a few demonstrate a large capacity for self-pity. Closely related to these works are his love poems, which are, for the most part, conventional in that they use traditional language, imagery, conceits and exaggeration, and structure. Some are clearly written to his wife, while the objects of some others are uncertain. For all their conventionality, the love lyrics reinforce the conception of Ridge as a passionate, emotional man.

Ridge wrote four poetic works in California which can be termed "philosophical" poems as they comprise some of his major statements on the history of civilization and the impact of history on contemporary societies. These poems, two called simply "Poem," "The Atlantic Cable," and "California," are expressions of Ridge's basic philosophical beliefs. Ridge, like many thinkers in the nineteenth century, believed that the process of civilization is an evolutionary one. Societies, races, and nations are caught up in the inevitable march of progress and are constantly evolving toward higher and higher levels. Implicit in this belief is the idea that the various contemporary societies and races have reached different plateaus on the evolutionary scale because of environmental and other factors. Among the many implications of such a system is the premise that the "advanced" nations are morally obligated to spread their ideas and methodologies to the "benighted" peoples of the world. A corollary of this idea is that the less advanced people accept these offerings wholeheartedly and learn to live like their more civilized counterparts. The message for American Indians is obvious.

Ridge published *The Life and Adventures of Joaquin Murieta, the Celebrated California Bandit* in 1854. The book was widely read and reviewed and, eventually, highly plagiarized. Pirated versions appeared as books, were serialized in periodicals, and were translated into foreign languages. Adaptations appeared in verse, and at least one film based on Ridge's story was produced. While many of the versions were produced in the nineteenth century, others have appeared more recently, including a 1967 drama by Pablo Neruda. More important than the literary imitations, however, is the fact that prominent historians of nineteenth-century California adopted Ridge's tale as an essentially true account of the events surrounding the affair. Ridge himself purports the story to be a true one important to the early history of the state. While it is clear that *Joaquin* is not pure history, it isn't pure fiction either. It is more like today's television "docudramas" or the currently fashionable news novels, productions based loosely on facts or history, liberally sprinkled with embellishments and added emphasis designed to titillate the audience. Ridge gathered his basic facts from newspaper stories of the day. The major episodes in Ridge's book had been reported, reprinted, and rehashed, with or without some of the gory details, in the local press. While Ridge embellished the basic story, the meat for his literary stew had been provided for him. There is no doubt that the romance was meant to be sensational. That Ridge wanted a best-seller, the equivalent of a box-office smash, is clear; he expected to make money from his book, if not from the first edition, then from a subsequent one. Money was his prime motivation, while his quest for literary fame was a close second.

Ridge's writings on the Indians that appeared in California magazines, and in his and other newspapers, are for the most part derivative and offer little in the way of original insight. The main thrust of many of his Indian pieces was that Indians must assimilate into white society as quickly as possible. Ridge urged that U.S. government Indian policy work toward this end. He also asserted the need for the protection of Native Americans against physical and economic harm. His writings on Cherokee affairs, however, were based on personal experience and observation and were heavily political. He published early diatribes against the majority, or Ross, faction in Arkansas and continued his attacks in California.

James W. Parins
University of Arkansas—Little Rock

BIBLIOGRAPHY

Primary Sources

Ridge, John Rollin. *Poems*. San Francisco: Henry Payot & Co., 1868.

Yellow Bird. *The Life and Adventures of Joaquin Murieta, the Celebrated California Bandit.* 1854. Rpt. Ed. Joseph Henry Jackson. Norman: U of Oklahoma P, 1955.

Secondary Sources

Dale, Edward Everett. "John Rollin Ridge." *Chronicles of Oklahoma* 4 (December 1928): 312–21.

Farmer, David, and Rennard Strickland. *A Trumpet of Our Own: Yellow Bird's Essays on the North American Indians.* San Francisco: The Book Club of California, 1981.

Foreman, Carolyn Thomas. "Edward W. Bushyhead and John Rollin Ridge." *Chronicles of Oklahoma* 15 (September 1936): 295–311.

Parins, James W. *John Rollin Ridge: His Life and Words.* Lincoln: U of Nebraska P, 1991.

Ranck, M. A. "John Rollin Ridge in California." *Chronicles of Oklahoma* 10 (December 1932): 560–69.

Walker, Franklin. "Yellow Bird." *Westways* 30 (November 1938): 47–52.

(Rolla) *Lynn Riggs* (August 31, 1899– June 30, 1954)

Our foremost Native American playwright is Lynn Riggs, who also remains one of the greatest writers of folk drama. Author of thirty plays and many poems, Riggs attained fame, ironically, from a production on which he did *not* work: Rodgers and Hammerstein's *Oklahoma!*, which was based on Riggs's *Green Grow the Lilacs*.

He was born Rolla Lynn Riggs on August 31, 1899, in the Verdigris Valley three miles south of Claremore, in the Indian Territory, then one of the most isolated areas in North America. His father, William Grant Riggs, was a cowboy-turned-banker and his mother, Rosa Gillis Riggs, was one-eighth Cherokee. Because of this ancestry, Riggs later received a government land allotment near Claremore, Oklahoma.

As a boy, Riggs was sensitive and gentle, an avid reader of dime novels which influenced his later plots toward melodrama, and he was extremely musical, which motivated him to learn all the old Cherokee chants.

He was never very close to his three brothers, but was extremely close to his sister, Mattie, four years older than he. His mother died when he was a year old, and his father remarried. Unhappy with his domineering stepmother, Riggs, while still a child, went to live with his aunt, Mrs. Mary Riggs Brice, who ran a boardinghouse in Claremore. Stepmothers are often depicted harshly in Riggs's plays, but Mary becomes the lovable aunt in *Green Grow the Lilacs* and several other plays.

He graduated from the Eastern University Preparatory School in Claremore in 1917, then worked at odd jobs for two years in New York City, where he became an avid playgoer. In 1920, he enrolled as a speech major at the University of Oklahoma, where he edited the campus literary magazine. His first national publication was a poem in *Smart Set* magazine in 1922, and in August 1923, his work appeared in *Poetry* magazine. His first play, *Cuckoo*, was staged on campus in 1922. Set in the rural hills of his boyhood and filled with some of Riggs's favorite ballads, the short farce began his lifelong blend of folk comedy and music.

During his senior year, he had a nervous breakdown and pneumonia; leaving without a degree, he followed medical advice by moving to New Mexico where he worked outdoors at poet Witter Bynner's chicken ranch. Thus began his love affair with Santa Fe, where he later built his own adobe house at 770 Acequia Madre Street, then as now in the heart of the art colony. Ida Rauh Eastman, of the original Provincetown Players, encouraged him to write more plays, and by 1925 he had completed three. One, *Knives from Syria*, was staged successfully by the Santa Fe Players in 1925 and became his first published play in 1927. The one-act shows a genial middle-aged woman without a man, a romantic young woman, a hired man, a peddler both mysterious and comic, and a group of young men bent upon playing tricks in the dark. *Knives* anticipates the cast of characters of *Green Grow the Lilacs*.

Encouraged, he moved back to New York and wrote a dozen plays in the next five years. *Sump'n Like Wings* was optioned for Broadway, but not produced there. In 1927, his poetic tragedy, *Big Lake*, was staged at the American Laboratory Theatre and gained favorable notices. Critic Barrett Clark recommended him for a Guggenheim Fellowship, and Riggs became the first Oklahoman to receive this award. Clark, in his book *Study of the American Drama*, called Eugene O'Neill, Paul Green, and Lynn Riggs the equal of any of the European dramatists—high praise for Riggs, who had not yet reached Broadway.

Riggs then began a long association with Jasper Deeter's semi-professional Hedgerow Theatre outside Philadelphia, with such plays as *Rancor*, *The Lonesome West*, *The Cherokee Night*, *Son of Perdition*, *Roadside*, and *A Lantern to See By*. The latter is a powerful tragedy in the old Indian Territory.

The Guggenheim Fellowship allowed Riggs to travel in Europe in 1928, the same year he had eight poems in *Poetry* magazine. He returned to the United States in 1930, and moved to Hollywood, where he became a screenwriter for Pathé Pictures. In 1930, he also began writing *The Cherokee Night*, saw *A Lantern to See By* produced professionally in Detroit, enjoyed his first Broadway production with *Roadside*, published his first book of poetry, *The Iron Dish*, and saw *Green Grow the Lilacs* go into rehearsal by the Theatre Guild. Fame and fortune appeared imminent. But *Roadside*, the most exuberant of all his comedies, closed after only eleven performances. *Roadside*, set in 1905, is in the frontier humor tradition. Hannah, from Verdigris Switch, leaves her timid husband for the braggart-warrior Texas. The play makes important statements about the need for human freedom and dignity.

Green Grow the Lilacs opened on Broadway on January 26, 1931. Franchot Tone, later a Hollywood leading man, played Curly, with Lee Strasberg as the peddler. *Lilacs* had sixty-six performances and could have run much longer, but it had been scheduled for a nine-week national tour. Inflexible scheduling thus deprived Riggs of a hit. The most interesting aspect of *Lilacs* is its ballad-like quality. The script contains many of the Rodgers and Hammerstein songs in embryo, several of the lyrics taken almost verbatim from the dialogue.

Riggs's favorite play, *The Cherokee Night*, opened at Hedgerow on June 18, 1932. Although no one on Broadway would touch it, this play may well be his greatest artistic achievement. *Cherokee* is virtually a series of seven one-act plays which depict the disintegration of the western branch of the Cherokee tribe. The story takes place between 1895 and 1931, though not chronologically, and we see several characters at different stages of their lives. By far the most poetic of Riggs's plays, it says that for an Indian to deny his Indianness is to diminish himself as a human being. Riggs was decades ahead of his time in his ethnic sensitivity.

With Broadway not receptive to further productions, Riggs devoted a large part of the 1930s to writing films-by-committee in Hollywood. The folk dramatist was wasted in a series of clichéd westerns, romances, and Sherlock Holmes movies.

In 1935, he received a query from George Gershwin about collaborating on a folk musical, but nothing came of this, and Gershwin died in 1937. Had Gershwin lived, and had they collaborated, Riggs's Broadway career might have been vastly different. Riggs did, however, write *Russet Mantle*, a social comedy set in Santa Fe, which achieved his longest Broadway run: 117 performances in 1936.

On January 20, 1941, after five fruitless years of trying to reach Broadway again, Riggs finally returned with his tragedy of brother-sister incest, *The Cream in the Well*, which closed after twenty-four performances and savage damnation from the critics. Writing about incest was *not* to be permitted. Riggs created his own doomed House of Atreus on the shores of Big Lake, near Verdigris Switch, but the critics refused, as they always had previously, to pay any attention to the strong undercurrent of sexuality in Riggs's plays; they saw him only as a writer of congenial down-on-the-farm comedies. His Broadway career was virtually finished.

Drafted into the army of the United States in 1942, he was promoted three times to T/3, and remained on duty at Wright Field, Ohio, when *Oklahoma!* opened on March 31, 1943, to make musical history with its 2,202 performances. Many grew rich from that production, but Riggs received a weekly royalty of only $250. In April 1943, Riggs applied for and was granted a discharge to work for the Office of War Information.

He wrote several more plays, but the only one to reach Broadway was a revival of *Roadside* under the title *Borned in Texas*, in 1950. It closed after ten performances. At this time the State of Oklahoma inducted him into its Hall of Fame, and the University of Oklahoma gave him a citation for his achievements. Close-mouthed about his feelings, Riggs did not return to Oklahoma for either award. In those final years, Riggs wintered in New York City and summered on Shelter Island, and shared his quarters with a series of young male artists. He was toying with the idea of moving back to Santa Fe when he died on June 30, 1954. His death went almost unnoticed in the New York press, which had never been particularly kind to him. To this day he remains more praised than produced, never having been fully admitted to Broadway's inner circle. Broadway was the loser.

Thomas A. Erhard
New Mexico State University

BIBLIOGRAPHY

Primary Sources

Riggs, Rolla Lynn. *Knives from Syria*. New York: Samuel French, 1927. One-act comedy. Produced in Santa Fe, 1925.

———. *Big Lake*. New York: Samuel French, 1927. Full-length tragedy. Produced by American Laboratory Theatre, 1927.

———. *Reckless*. New York: Samuel French, 1928. One-act comedy. This is Scene One of the later *Roadside*.

———. *Sump'n Like Wings*. New York: Samuel French, 1928. Full-length drama. Produced by Detroit Playhouse, 1931.

———. *A Lantern to See By*. New York: Samuel French, 1928. Full-length tragedy. Produced by Detroit Playhouse, 1930.

———. *The Iron Dish*. New York: Samuel French, 1930. (Poems)

———. *Roadside*. New York: Samuel French, 1936. Full-length comedy. Produced on Broadway, 1930, and anthologized by Harper & Row, 1953.

———. *Green Grow the Lilacs*. New York: Samuel French, 1936. Full-length comedy-drama. Produced on Broadway, 1931, and anthologized by Crown Publishers, 1961.

———. *The Cherokee Night*. New York: Samuel French, 1936. Full-length tragedy. Produced at Hedgerow Theatre, 1932; produced by Federal Theatre off-Broadway, 1936.

———. *Russet Mantle*. New York: Samuel French, 1936. Full-length comedy. Produced on Broadway, 1936.

———. *The Cream in the Well*. New York: Samuel French, 1947. Full-length tragedy. Produced on Broadway, 1941.

———. *A World Elsewhere*. New York: Samuel French, 1947. Full-length tragedy. Produced on Broadway, 1941.

———. *The Dark Encounter*. New York: Samuel French, 1947. Full-length drama.

———. *The Year of Pilar*. New York: Samuel French, 1947. Full-length tragedy.

———. *Hang Onto Love*. New York: Samuel French, 1948. Retitling of the unproduced *Domino Parlor*.

———. *The Hunger I Got*. New York: Samuel French, 1949. One-act drama.

———. *Toward the Western Sky*. Cleveland: Western Reserve, 1951. Musical pageant-drama, written with Nathan Kroll. Produced at Western Reserve University, 1951.

Secondary Sources

Aughtry, Charles E. "Lynn Riggs, Dramatist: A Critical Biography." Diss. Brown University, 1959.

Clark, Barrett. *Study of the American Drama*. New York: Appleton, 1928.

Erhard, Thomas A. *Lynn Riggs, Southwest Playwright*. Austin: Steck-Vaughn Company, 1970.

Jane Johnston Schoolcraft
[Obahbahmwawagezhegoqua]
(1800–May 22, 1841)

Jane Johnston Schoolcraft, whose name in Ojibwa means literally "the Sound Which the Stars Make Rushing Through the Sky," was one of the first American Indian women to publish poetry and interpretations of Ojibwa myths.

She was the daughter of John Johnston, a Scottish-Irish immigrant, and Oshaguacodaywaygwa (Woman of the Green Prairie), whom he re-named Susan after their marriage. Susan's father was Chief Waubojeeg (White Fisher), an influential local headman. After their marriage, Johnston, a successful fur trader, settled at Sault Ste. Marie, a small settlement next to an Ojibwa village on the St. Mary's River on the southern shore of Lake Superior in what is now Michigan. In addition to teaching all eight children the Ojibwa language, culture, and myths, Susan educated them as well in the exploits of their grandfather and of their great grandfather, Ma Mongazida. Because there were no schools at Sault Ste. Marie, Johnston tutored the children in literature, history, and classics and developed a large library for their use. Later, their formal education was completed in Canadian private schools. As her father's favorite daughter, Jane often accompanied him on trips to Detroit, Montreal, and Quebec. In 1809, Johnston took Jane to Ireland, where she attended school for approximately four months while staying with a great-aunt. By 1810, father and daughter had returned home.

When Henry Schoolcraft arrived at Sault Ste. Marie in 1822 to serve as Indian agent for the Upper Great Lakes, he accepted Johnston's invitation to live with the trader's family. His close friendship with Johnston was strengthened when Henry and Jane married in 1823. Following their wedding, the couple continued to live with the Johnstons. Their first child, William Henry, was born in 1824. When a second was stillborn in 1825,

Jane almost died from sickness and grief. Before she could recover, she and Henry were devastated when William Henry suddenly died in 1826. She bore two more children: Jane Susan Anne (Janee) in 1826 and John Johnston in 1829. Shortly after Janee's birth, the family moved into Elmwood, a large, elegant Agency house which became a center for social life at Sault Ste. Marie. In the 1830s, the Schoolcrafts often spent the winters in Detroit, so that the children could go to school.

During that decade, the couple gradually became estranged. In a letter written in November 1830, Henry, who attributed William's death to idolizing the boy over God, announced that henceforth the family would follow Christ and urged his wife to cleave to him rather than her family. He reminded her that she had been brought up in a remote place "without a regular education" and "the salutary influence of society to form your mind, without a mother, in many things to direct & with an over kind father who saw everything in the fairest light . . ." (quoted in Bremer, 1987:111). Because of a series of illnesses and her loneliness during her husband's long business trips, Schoolcraft became very despondent. In 1838, the couple traveled to New York in hopes of improving her health. That same year, Henry sent the children to private schools in the East, a separation that was almost unbearable for Schoolcraft. In 1841, Henry resigned his position as agent and the family settled in New York City. When Henry decided to visit England that year, Schoolcraft stayed behind. She died shortly after his arrival there.

Schoolcraft's delicacy of manner, polish, and tasteful appearance were praised by visitors like Thomas L. McKenny, later Commissioner of Indian Affairs, and Anne Brownell Jameson, the Irish writer. Schoolcraft's youthful literary efforts were encouraged by her father, who also wrote poetry. She and Henry exchanged poems during their courtship. During the winter of 1826–27, Henry established a reading society at Sault St. Marie, which published *The Literary Voyager or Muzzeniegun*, a literary magazine that included poems and essays (mainly on Indian culture). The fifteen issues that appeared from December 1826 to April 1827 were eagerly read not only at Sault Ste. Marie but also in Detroit. Under the pseudonyms of "Rose" and "Leelinau," Schoolcraft contributed several poems and interpretations of Ojibwa stories. Her poems reflect a love of nature, gentle piety, and her reading of the English poets, especially those of the pre-Romantic and Romantic periods. Her "Lines Written to a Friend Asleep," which urges the friend to wake up to observe the beauty of nature, evokes Wordsworth's "Expostulation and Reply." "To Sisters on a Walk in the Garden, After a Shower" is a descriptive-reflective poem which uses a description of the delicate beauty of the garden after the rain to exemplify the lesson that pain and care, like showers, are supplanted by the bright calm of faith. Three other poems published in *The Literary Voyager* focus on the themes of stoic faith, grief, and suffering and undoubtedly express

Schoolcraft's despair over the death of young William in 1826: "Resignation"; "Lines Written Under Severe Pain and Sickness"; and "Lines Written Under Affliction," whose emphasis on the pleasure and ease that dark shades bring evokes Milton's "Il Penseroso." Far more forceful is "Invocation to My Maternal Grandfather on Hearing His Descent from Chippewa Ancestors," in which an angry Schoolcraft defends Waubojeeg from false stories about his "valorous youth." She also contributed her interpretations of three traditional Ojibwa stories: "The Origin of Robin: An Oral Allegory," "Moowis: The Indian Coquette," and "The Forsaken Brother." Schoolcraft uses a clear, direct voice and demonstrates an engaging storytelling style. She also contributed to the journal a translation of a narrative by her mother: "The Character of Aboriginal Historical Tradition."

Until her death, Schoolcraft collaborated with Henry on his Ojibwa research. She served as his interpreter and translated stories and ethnographic information her mother and other relatives gave to Henry. As he himself acknowledged, their contributions were invaluable to his work. Though he published twenty volumes and hundreds of articles describing his explorations and Indian culture, Henry is best known today for his six-volume *Historical and Statistical Information Respecting the History, Condition, and Prospects of the Indian Tribes of the United States* (1851–57) and his two-volume *Algic Researches* (1839).

A. LaVonne Brown Ruoff
University of Illinois—Chicago

BIBLIOGRAPHY

Primary Sources

The Literary Voyager or Muzzeniegun. Ed. Henry Rowe Schoolcraft. Ed. with an Introduction and Notes by Philip P. Mason. Westport, CT: Greenwood, 1974.

Secondary Sources

Bremer, Richard G. *Indian Agent, Wilderness Scholar*. Mt. Pleasant: Clark History Library, Central Michigan University, 1987.

Jameson, Anna Brownell. *Winter Studies and Summer Rambles in Canada*. 3 vols. London: Saunders and Otley, 1838.

Mason, Philip. "Introduction." *The Literary Voyager or Muzzeniegun*. xxi–xxvi.

McKenny, Thomas L. *Sketches of a Tour to the Lakes and Character and Customs of the Chippeway Indians. . . .* Baltimore, MD: Fielding Lucas, Jr., 1827.

Sarah Winnemucca *[M. Hopkins; Thocmetony] (1844–October 17, 1891)*

Author of *Life Among the Piutes: Their Wrongs and Claims* (1883), Sarah Winnemucca is the first Indian woman to publish a personal and tribal history. She was born in 1844 near the sink of the Humboldt River in Nevada and was raised as a traditional Paiute. Her grandfather was Truckee, whom she inaccurately claimed was the chief of all the Paiutes, and her father was Old Winnemucca, who succeeded Truckee as chief. She and her family followed Truckee's policy of peaceful co-existence with whites.

When Winnemucca was around ten, she accompanied her mother and Truckee to California. There she learned Spanish and began to pick up English while working for several white families. Her knowledge of English increased after 1857, when she and her sister Elma became companions to the daughter of Major William Ormsby in Carson Valley. Her beloved grandfather, who had been a strong influence, died in 1869. In accordance with his wishes, Winnemucca and Elma briefly attended a school at the Convent of Notre Dame in San Jose, run by the Sisters of Charity. Winnemucca variously gave the dates of her attendance as 1858 to 1860 and as 1861; the girls left because of whites' objections to their presence. Winnemucca continued her education on her own while working as a domestic in and around Virginia City.

Her involvement in Indian affairs began in 1866, when the Paiutes asked her and her brother Natchez (or Naches) to go to Fort McDermit to try to stop white raids on the tribe. At the request of the army, Winnemucca and Natchez persuaded their father, Old Winnemucca, and his band to settle on a reservation. Winnemucca worked intermittently as an interpreter for the military at Fort McDermit and Camp Harney and as an interpreter and teacher's aide at Malheur, Oregon. During the 1878 Bannock War, Winnemucca served as an interpreter for General Oliver Otis Howard's command and as a liaison between the army and the Paiutes, who had joined the Bannocks. She also later became an interpreter and teacher at the Yakima Reservation, where Paiute prisoners were detained. Throughout this period, Winnemucca strongly criticized the mistreatment of her people by Indian agents and missionaries, especially William Rinehart and the Rev. James Wilbur.

In 1879, after hostilities had ceased, Winnemucca gave a series of highly successful lectures in San Francisco and Nevada, castigating the agents for conditions at Malheur and Yakima. That same year, she, Natchez, Old Winnemucca, and Captain Jim traveled to Washington to plead their cause to government officials. Secretary of the Interior Carl Schurz authorized the release of Leggins's band at Yakima and agreed that Paiutes could return to the Malheur reservation. Unfortunately, Schurz authorized neither provisions nor escort for the move.

In 1883 and 1884, Winnemucca gave over 300 lectures in the East, attacking corrupt agents, unfeeling missionaries, and bad government policies. While in Boston, she became close friends with Elizabeth Palmer Peabody, a pioneer in kindergarten education, and her sister, Mary Tyler Mann, widow of Horace. Through their influence, Winnemucca spoke in the homes of Emerson, Whittier, and several congressmen. Among these was Senator Henry Dawes, sponsor of the 1887 General Allotment Act, which allotted Indian lands in severalty. Winnemucca and her family strongly supported this policy.

During her eastern tour, Winnemucca wrote her *Life Among the Piutes*, which was sold at her lectures. Largely at the instigation of Rinehart, government officials viciously attacked Winnemucca's ethics and morals. Despite Winnemucca's attempts to gain the Paiutes allotments on the Malheur lands, Congress failed to approve the grants. With money from Peabody and income from lectures and her book, a discouraged Winnemucca returned to Nevada to establish a school for Paiute children in 1884. That year she undertook another lecture tour in Nevada and California. After the school closed in 1887, Winnemucca settled with her sister at Henry's Lake Idaho, where she died in 1891.

Winnemucca led a difficult and controversial life. Her many marriages bought her neither security nor support and fueled attacks on her character. In 1871, she married First Lieutenant Edward C. Bartlett, an alcoholic wastrel who quickly ran though her money. After she left Bartlett, she apparently married in the Indian custom a Native American called Jones. Two years after her divorce from Bartlett in 1876, she married Joseph Setwaller; the date of this divorce is unclear. In 1882, Winnemucca married Lieutenant Lewis H. Hopkins, a dandy who ran up large gambling debts and who in 1887 defrauded Natchez and Winnemucca's friends of profits from a wheat harvest. He died that year from tuberculosis. Although Winnemucca mentions Bartlett and Hopkins in *Life Among the Piutes*, she does not allude to Jones and Setwaller.

Life Among the Piutes covers the period from Winnemucca's birth in 1844 to 1883, from the first contacts with whites through the Paiutes many conflicts with whites, resettlements, and negotiations to receive justice from the federal government. The book is one of the most colorful and personal tribal histories of the nineteenth century. Because of the attacks on her character, Winnemucca is careful to authenticate her narrative. Her editor, Mary Tyler Mann, emphatically states in the "Editor's Preface" that her own role was simply to copy "the original manuscript in correct orthography and punctuation" (ii). Winnemucca appends many documents from whites attesting to her high moral character and to her services as interpreter and intermediary for the government.

The central theme of her personal and ethnohistory is Indian-white relations. Part I consists of a single chapter on the background of her family and on the impact of white migration on Paiute life after 1844. Part II is a chapter on the domestic and social moralities of the Paiutes, and Part III contains six chapters on the conflicts between the Paiutes and whites from 1860 to 1863 as the Indians struggled to retain their native land, were moved from one reservation to another, and attempted to gain allotments on the Malheur Agency in Oregon.

Life Among the Piutes is far more personalized than are earlier Indian autobiographies. Winnemucca gives detailed accounts of her psychological reactions as a child. Especially powerful are her descriptions of her terror of whites, who she thought looked like owls, and her account of how her parents buried five-year-old Winnemucca and her sister up to their heads in order to hide them from nearby whites, who they feared would kill and eat the children. Winnemucca, however, gives little information about her personal life as an adolescent and adult.

Nevertheless, she does reveal more of her adult personality than do earlier Indian autobiographers. Casting herself in the role of a word warrior, she recounts episodes that emphasize her courage and stamina as she risked being killed or raped while she rode back and forth between the Paiutes and the army during the Bannock War of 1878. She also dramatizes her confrontations with corrupt Indian agents and indifferent government officials.

Winnemucca also describes Paiute beliefs and customs, especially those pertaining to family life and government. Especially significant is her emphasis on the roles played by women in Paiute culture. In the section devoted to Paiute-white relations from around 1860 to 1883, Winnemucca strongly criticizes the agency system. Also important is Winnemucca's use of dramatic re-creation of scenes and dialogue, which Margot Liberty attributes to the quotative style of Northern Paiute narratives (Fowler 1978:40).

Her only other work is the article "The Pah-Utes" (1882), which is a general introduction to the tribe's customs, language, and traditions.

A. LaVonne Brown Ruoff
University of Illinois—Chicago

BIBLIOGRAPHY

Primary Sources

Winnemucca [Hopkins], Sarah. *Life Among the Piutes: Their Wrongs and Claims.* Ed. Mrs. Horace Mann. 1883 Rpt. Bishop: Chalfant Press, 1969.

———. "The Pah-Utes." *The Californian* 6 (1882): 252–56.

Secondary Sources

Canfield, Gae Whitney. *Sarah Winnemucca of the Northern Paiutes.* Norman: U of Oklahoma P, 1983.

Fowler, Catharine S. "Sarah Winnemucca." *American Indian Intellectuals.* Ed. Margot Liberty. 1976 *Proceedings of the American Ethnological Society.* St. Paul: West, 1978. 33–42.

Ruoff, A. Lavonne Brown. "Nineteenth Century Autobiographers." *Redefining American Literary History.* Ed. A. LaVonne Brown Ruoff and Jerry W. Ward. New York: MLA, 1990. 251–69.

Sands, Kathleen Mullen. "Indian Women's Personal Narrative: Voices Past and Present." *American Women's Autobiography.* Ed. Margot Culley. Madison: U. of Wisconsin P, in press.

Stewart, Patricia. "Sarah Winnemucca." *Nevada Historical Quarterly* 14 (1971): 23–38.

Zitkala Sa *[Gertrude Simmons Bonnin]*
(February 22, 1876–January 26, 1938)

Zitkala Sa was a pioneer among Native American writers; elements of contemporary Native American literature can be found in her limited body of work. Her writing reflects her emotionalism about her traditional society and the cultural confusion of her own life, and it demonstrates her anger at the injustices dealt to the Native American. The tone of her work is sentimental, didactic, and inflammatory. Although she wrote as an American Indian and a female at a time when few similar voices were being heard, she did not flinch, nor did she moderate her voice.

Zitkala Sa, born Gertrude Simmons on February 22, 1876, at the Yankton Reservation in South Dakota, was raised as a traditional Sioux by her mother in the absence of her white father. At the age of eight, she begged to be allowed to go East to school in order to visit the "red apple country" portrayed so enticingly by visiting missionaries. Her traumatic experiences at White's Manual Labor Institute, a Quaker missionary school in Indiana, were later recounted in a magazine article, as were her recollections of her early traditional upbringing. After returning home from school three years later, she was quite unhappy and unable to adjust to her former life with her mother. Four years later, against her mother's wishes, she returned to Indiana to pursue her education, culminating with two years at Earlham College (1895–97). She was isolated and lonely at college; an incident that exemplified her sojourn was a statewide oratorical contest during which she burned with fury and humiliation as a banner with "squaw" written on it appeared in the audience. After winning second place in the competition, she accepted her award with feelings of bitter triumph.

After completing college, she went to Carlisle Indian Training School to teach briefly in 1898–99, but her disillusionment with the Indian boarding school system was not lessened by her new position on the other side of the desk. She began writing autobiographical articles and short stories for magazines with some success, which led to her return to the reservation to collect stories for her first book, *Old Indian Legends* (1901). While working as an issue clerk at the Standing Rock Reservation during this time, she met and married Raymond T. Bonnin, a Sioux employee of the Indian Service, in 1902. For the next fourteen years, the Bonnins lived and worked on the Uintah and Ouray Reservation in Utah, and her writing ceased. In 1916, Zitkala Sa was elected Secretary-Treasurer of the Society of American Indians (SAI), a pan-Indian assimilationist reform group, and edited its journal, the *American Indian Magazine*, from 1918–19; this gave her a forum once again for her writing. She and her husband moved to Washington, D.C., where she continued her unflagging work on behalf of her people, lobbying heavily for Indian legislation, speaking on behalf of Indian rights, and enlisting outside interest in Indian reform efforts. After the disintegration of the SAI in 1920, Zitkala Sa founded her own political organization in 1926, the National Council of American Indians, and served as its president until she died in Washington on January 26, 1938.

Zitkala Sa's three autobiographical pieces, "Impressions of an Indian Childhood," "The School Days of an Indian Girl," and "An Indian Teacher Among Indians," were originally published by the *Atlantic Monthly* during 1900, then reprinted in her book *American Indian Stories* in 1921. Fisher (1979:34) makes the point that these works were significant at the time because they may have been the first autobiographical literature to appear which was not written with the assistance of an interpreter, editor, or ethnographer. Bataille and Sands (1984:13) note that early self-written autobiographies were a form of literature typically produced by politically active women for whom the communication of a personal life story was only secondary. The articles are also unique when compared to the later Siouxan autobiographies of Charles Eastman and Luther Standing Bear, which tend to be more apologetic with regard to traditional upbringing and do not reveal the authors' feelings about the world at large. Though her language can be sentimental, Zitkala Sa uses her writing both as an outlet for personal expression and as a political weapon, which more closely aligns her with contemporary Native American writers (Stout 1984).

Zitkala Sa's first book contract with Ginn resulted in the publication of *Old Indian Legends* in 1901. For this book, she left her teaching position at Carlisle Indian Training School to return to the reservation to collect the stories she remembered being told in her childhood. Like her contemporaries, Charles Eastman, Marie McLaughlin, Luther Standing Bear, and Ella Deloria, she was driven by the need both to preserve the stories of her traditional past, a world which she saw fast slipping away, and to communicate information about her people to the Western world. Zitkala Sa was the first among her contemporaries to have a series of Sioux legends published. The fourteen legends, consisting primarily of Iktomi trickster tales and some tales of culture heroes, are *ohunkankans*, tales told at night primarily for entertainment, as distinct from another genre of tales, which are more mythic and sacred. In this volume, Zitkala Sa has reinterpreted the traditional stories for children of all cultures, as she indicates in her preface.

Fisher compares one of Zitkala Sa's stories with a more literal translation from the Lakota found in Ella Deloria's *Dakota Texts* in order to show the transformation from oral to literary narrative. That she reinterpreted the story in order to transmute the oral narrative aesthetic to the literary one, and to adapt it to an audience containing non-Sioux, is not inconsistent with an oral tradition in which various versions of a tale, imbued with the storyteller's style and suited to the audience of the event, are found. Her book is also a precursor to the works of contemporary Native American authors, signaling the legitimacy of joining a personal voice to traditional themes.

Zitkala Sa's second book, *American Indian Stories*, was published in 1921 by Hayworth. It reprinted the three autobiographical articles first published in the *Atlantic Monthly* as well as four stories and essays previously published in the general periodical literature in 1901–2. Three new stories and essays were included.

Although her literary output slowed after her marriage to Bonnin in 1902, her creative energies were never at rest, as she became increasingly involved in Native American reform efforts. The 1921 publication reflects the more combative, political turn in her life as compared with her earlier book of Indian legends.

Over half the book consists of the autobiographical essays, which express the confusion and isolation of those who were products of the boarding school system. "The Great Spirit" is a reprint of her article "Why I Am a Pagan," originally published in the *Atlantic Monthly* in 1902 and containing her repudiation of Christianity. "The Soft-Hearted Sioux" (originally published in the March 1901 *Harper's Monthly Magazine*) is a short story telling how Christian boarding school training has wholly unsuited a man for his traditional Indian life, with dramatic and devastating consequences.

Zitkala Sa continued to lecture and work for Indian reform as secretary-treasurer of the Society of American Indians. Her position as temporary editor of its journal, the *American Indian Magazine*, gave her a vehicle for her writing once again. During this period, she had fourteen pieces, primarily articles and editorial columns, published in that journal. Always outspoken, her articles reflected her views, which earned her supporters and detractors from both Indian and white ranks. She would never return to fiction as a literary form.

One later piece of work came as a result of her participation as a member of the General Federation of Women's Clubs as one of a trio of investigators sent to Oklahoma in 1923 whose published report, entitled

Oklahoma's Poor Rich Indians: An Orgy of Graft and Exploitation of the Five Civilized Tribes—Legalized Robbery (1924) was instrumental in the appointment of a federal commission of investigation (Dockstader 1977). This document shows Zitkala Sa at her most strident, at the peak of her political development.

Recognizably proficient as a writer of English, possessed of an active imagination, and coming from a background steeped in oral tradition while living a reality imbued with the politics of being an Indian in a white-dominated society, Zitkala Sa lived during the transitional years so often described in contemporary Native American literature. Yet her literary output, sublimated to the more pressing political work which faced her, contains only the embryo of a tradition which has come to maturity in the writings of contemporary Native American authors.

Mary A. Stout
Tucson Public Library

BIBLIOGRAPHY

Primary Sources

Zitkala Sa. "Impressions of an Indian Childhood." *Atlantic Monthly* (January 1900): 37–47.

———. "The School Days of an Indian Girl." *Atlantic Monthly* (February 1900): 185–94.

———. "An Indian Teacher Among Indians." *Atlantic Monthly* (March 1900): 381–86.

———. *Old Indian Legends*. Boston: Ginn, 1901. Rpt. Foreword by Agnes M. Picotte. Lincoln: U of Nebraska P, 1985.

———. "The Soft-Hearted Sioux." *Harper's Monthly Magazine* (March 1901): 505–8.

———. "The Trial Path." *Harper's Monthly Magazine* (October 1901): 741–44.

———. "A Warrior's Daughter." *Everybody's Magazine* (April 1902): 346–52.

———. "Why I Am a Pagan." *Atlantic Monthly* (December 1902): 801–3.

———. "The Indian's Awakening." *American Indian Magazine* (January–March 1916): 57–9.

———. "A Year's Experience in Community Service Work Among the Ute Tribe of Indians." *American Indian Magazine* (October–December 1916): 307–10.

———. "The Red Man's America." *American Indian Magazine* (January–March 1917): 64.

———. "Chipeta, Widow of Chief Ouray: With a Word About a Deal in Blankets." *American Indian Magazine* (July–September 1917): 168–70.

———. "A Sioux Woman's Love for Her Grandchild." *American Indian Magazine* (October–December 1917): 230–31.

———. "Editorial Comment." *American Indian Magazine* (July–September 1918): 113–14.

———. "Indian Gifts to Civilized Man." *American Indian Magazine* (July–September 1918): 115–16.

———. "Address by Mrs. Gertrude Bonnin." *American Indian Magazine* (Fall 1919): 153–57.

———. "Editorial Comment." *American Indian Magazine* (Winter 1919): 161–62.

———. "America, Home of the Red Man." *American Indian Magazine* (Winter 1919): 165–67.

———. "The Coronation of Chief Powhatan Retold." *American Indian Magazine* (Winter 1919): 179–80.

———. "Letter to the Chiefs and Headmen of the Tribes." *American Indian Magazine* (Winter 1919): 196–97.

———. "Editorial Comment." *American Indian Magazine* (Spring 1919): 5–9.

———. "Editorial Comment." *American Indian Magazine* (Summer 1919): 61–63.

———. *American Indian Stories.* Washington: Hayworth, 1921. Rpt. Foreword by Dexter Fisher. Lincoln: U of Nebraska P, 1985.

———, Charles H. Fabens, and Matthew K. Sniffen. *Oklahoma's Poor Rich Indians: An Orgy of Graft and Exploitation of the Five Civilized Tribes—Legalized Robbery.* Philadelphia: Office of the Indian Rights Association, 1924.

Secondary Sources

Bataille, Gretchen M., and Kathleen Mullen Sands. *American Indian Women: Telling Their Lives.* Lincoln: U of Nebraska P, 1984.

Dockstader, Frederick J. *Great North American Indians.* New York: Van Nostrand Reinhold, 1977.

Fisher, Alice Poindexter. "The Transportation of Tradition: A Study of Zitkala Sa and Mourning Dove, Two Transitional American Indian Writers." Diss. City University of New York, 1979.

Gridley, Marion E. "Gertrude Simmons Bonnin: A Modern Progressive." *American Indian Women.* New York: Hawthorn Books, 1974.

Stout, Mary. "Zitkala Sa: The Literature of Politics." *Coyote Was Here: Essays on Contemporary Native American Literary and Political Motivation.* Århus, Denmark: SEKLOS, 1984.

Young, Mary E. "Bonnin, Gertrude Simmons." *Notable American Women—1607–1950—A Biographical Dictionary.* Cambridge, MA: Belknap Press of Harvard UP, 1971.

A Native American Renaissance: 1967 to the Present

Contemporary Native American Writing: An Overview

Roots of a Renaissance

What has been called the "Native American Renaissance" in writing is generally dated from the end of the 1960s with the publication of N. Scott Momaday's *House Made of Dawn* (1968) and its subsequent Pulitzer Prize. Considering the importance and the effects of Momaday's success, there is certainly some justification for choosing Momaday's novel as the beginning of the modern period in American Indian writing. However, it might also be argued that the real beginnings of that so-called Renaissance are much earlier. Further, it might better be called a continuum than a renaissance since the issues have remained much the same for Indians and Indian writers not just over the last two decades, but for the last two centuries. The publication of Momaday's novel and its critical recognition only served to bring the concerns of the Native American into sharper focus and to open wider the curtain of that stage where the work of Indian writers could be seen.

Just what was going on in Native American writing in the years after World War II, the period which gave birth to both the McCarthy era and the Beats, as well as the policy of Termination? As far as poetry goes, it seems that until the early 1970s, there was precious little. True, a few of the current generation of Native American writers, such as Maurice Kenny, whose first book of poems, *Dead Letters Sent*, was published in 1958 by Troubadour Press, were appearing in print well before Momaday. However, their works and even those earlier writers themselves were usually not, at that time, recognizably "Indian." Kenny was himself peripherally involved with the Beat Generation, though he did not become a Beat poet. Though Carroll Arnett had poems in *Poetry* and *Saturday Review* in 1967, there was little evidence prior to the 1970s that he would later prove to be a significant Native American voice. One of the few recognizably Native American books of poetry published before the '70s was Gerald Vizenor's *Summer in the Spring: Lyric Poems of the Ojibway*, published in 1965 by Nodin Press in a limited hardcover edition. In terms of fiction, the only truly visible figure was D'Arcy McNickle, a writer who was (and still is) underrated, though relatively well published in his day. Like most other "visible" Native American writers prior to Momaday, McNickle was sometimes seen more as "spokesman" than literary figure. It was not until 1971 that a book of McNickle's, his biography of Oliver La Farge, was nominated for a National Book Award, and his third novel, *Wind from an Enemy Sky*, was published only posthumously in 1978. Navajo writer Emerson Blackhorse Mitchell's autobiography *Miracle Hill* was published in 1967 by the University of Oklahoma Press. Now out of print, Mitchell's story was part of a long line of Native American autobiographies, stretching back well before the twentieth century. However, those works and Mitchell's were generally regarded as something other than "literary." A sociological curiosity, they were worthy of consideration in an anthropology course, but not as an important part of American literature. (That problem still exists today. Although works by a few writers such as Louise Erdrich, Leslie Silko, and Michael Dorris may be found on the poetry and fiction shelves of American bookstores, most works by Native American writers can be found only in the Social Sciences sections—even when those works are books of poetry. Hopi/Miwok poet Wendy Rose has innumerable stories to tell about the times she has found her books only on the Anthropology shelf.) In the 1950s and 1960s, an Indian writer was a voice crying unheard in the civilized wilderness of American letters.

There is no question that Momaday's powerful novel and its recognition as a serious work of literature were extremely influential in changing the atmosphere in which the Native American writer could exist. Suddenly, with *House Made of Dawn*'s Pulitzer, it was possible that a Native American writer could be accepted by the literary establishment. Moreover, Native American writers could begin to see that they were not alone. For the first time, the possibility of Native American writing as something other than an isolated and isolating experience began to be a reality. Momaday's highly visible success and the ways in which that success influenced publishers to open their doors to other Native writers—in particular through the publication of American Indian anthologies—would be significant factors in the formation of a community of new Native American writers.

So many of the writers after him have presented similar scenes of Native American life that it may seem that Momaday is even more influential than in fact he is. For example, the main character of his first novel is a person whose life is out of balance because of the conflict between "traditional ways" and the "modern world." Healing the divisions without and within by a return to a spiritual path lit by the continuance of tradition (though that tradition may also show itself in new forms) is the road which Momaday's Abel must take to survive. It is a path which later Native protagonists in novels by Leslie Silko, James Welch, Paula Gunn Allen, and Janet Campbell Hale (to name just a few examples) either take and thereby find redemption or miss and thereby face destruction. A critic lacking knowledge of earlier Native writers or oral tradition might conclude that all of these writers are copying Momaday. But many of those scenes and images had appeared before. Many of the images and situations in the novel are virtual archetypes, in part due to the debt the novel owes to the oral traditions of the Southwest. (Momaday, to his credit, has always been straightforward in acknowledging his debt to those oral traditions.) Certainly *House Made of Dawn*'s now familiar theme of the Indian who has been away from his or her people (at school, at war, in prison) and returning to his or her own people as a semi-outsider is central to Leslie Silko's *Ceremony*, published in 1977. But it is also the central conflict in D'Arcy McNickle's 1936 novel of Indian life, *The Surrounded* (and in non-Indian writer Frank Waters's 1942 classic novel *The Man Who Killed the Deer*). It is not so much that Momaday did something new as it is that he did so many old things so well. Moreover, those things—those images, themes, and conflicts—were, are, and will continue to be central to Native American writers and Native American life.

The success which comes with a Pulitzer Prize could not have come to a more appropriate writer, in terms of helping open the door for a then unrecognized generation of new Native writers. Momaday refused adamantly to play the part of sole ethnic "spokesman for all of his people," a trap in which more than one recent African American writer has been caught. By not presenting himself as the only legitimate voice of Native American writing, Momaday left room for other writers. Because of what he said in that first novel, what he accomplished in terms of mainstream recognition, and how he responded to that recognition, Momaday was a true pathfinder. His role has been acknowledged by many other Indian writers. In a 1983 interview published in *Survival This Way*, Paula Gunn Allen credits *House Made of Dawn* in the strongest possible way, saying, "I wouldn't be writing now if Momaday hadn't done that book. I would have died" (Bruchac 1987:11).

Momaday's *The Way to Rainy Mountain* was published in 1969. Through its threefold exploration of his own Kiowa roots—presenting tales from the Kiowa oral traditions, a comment by Momaday on each tale, and then a related personal or family story of his own—Momaday became one of the first of the new generation of Native American writers to present work directly from the folk traditions in a literary context. Such use of the folk traditions and retellings of traditional tales would continue throughout the next two decades by numerous other Indian writers. One example is Dakota writer Elizabeth Cook-Lynn's *Then Badger Said This* in 1977. Leslie Silko's collection of stories and narrative poems is entitled *Storyteller*. Storytelling and the various uses of storytelling traditions are vitally important and will, I am certain, continue to be so for Native American writers. In more ways than one, in fact, Momaday's career to date may be seen as both a model and a reflection of some of the most vital aspects of contemporary Native American literature.

Of course, other things which would prove important for Native American writing were going on in America in the late 1960s besides the publication and recognition of one Indian author's book. It was also in 1969 that the first Native American "media event" took place with the well-publicized takeover of Alcatraz Island by the "Indians of All Tribes," who declared the island and its infamous abandoned prison to be Indian Land. Such events had happened before. One need only turn to non-Indian writer Edmund Wilson's 1959 volume *Apologies to the Iroquois* for an example. In that nonfiction study of the lot of the Iroquois people in the 1950s, Wilson tells the story of the more-or-less ignored "occupation" of some land on Schoharie Creek near Amsterdam, New York, by a small group of Mohawks led by Standing Arrow. However, it was not until Alcatraz that the full weight of international television would be brought to bear on "militant" Indian concerns. And Alcatraz would prove to be only the first of a series of such demonstrations of Native American presence, strength, and declared sovereignty which would continue through the '70s and '80s and into the present. The takeover of Alcatraz by the "Indians of All Tribes" was also led by a Mohawk, a steelworker named Richard Oakes. Native Americans from all over the continent came to Alcatraz. Lakotas, Hopis, Senecas, Cherokees, and Chippewas were only a few of the tribal nations represented by the hundreds of Indians who visited or resided on that short-lived "Indian Land" over the next nineteen months until June 11, 1971, when the "Indians of All Tribes" were removed by federal marshalls, ending the occupation. Among those visiting or living on the island during the takeover were a number of Native American writers. Probably the two best known were Peter Blue Cloud (another Mohawk) and Wendy Rose, an urban Indian poet of mixed (Hopi/Miwok) Native descent from the Bay area.

One of the earliest of the Native American anthologies, Brother Benet Tvedten's *An American Indian Anthology*, published in 1971 by Blue Cloud Quarterly Press, contained Peter Blue Cloud's poem "Alcatraz Visions." Peter Blue Cloud's editing of *Alcatraz Is Not an Island*, published by Wingbow Press of Berkeley in 1972, was probably Blue Cloud's most important work as a poet and editor to that point. The Alcatraz anthology contained essays by the "Indians of All Tribes" dealing with the takeover and with related Indian rights issues in California, an "Alcatraz Diary" written by Blue Cloud, and poems by Lydia Yellowbird, Raymond Lego,

Jerry Hill, and Blue Cloud himself. The book strongly expressed the tone that the next two decades of Native American political resistance would take. It gave voice and form to a pan-Indian militancy which would combine calls to honor the treaties with a celebration of traditional culture. It was a militancy quite unlike that of black America. Native American "Red Power" was a militancy with a decidedly spiritual and environmental base. That tone would be heard to a greater or lesser degree in virtually all of the voices of the generation of Indian writers which began to emerge in the early '70s. The Indian "takeovers" at the BIA in Washington and at Wounded Knee in 1973, the activism of the American Indian Movement's Dennis Banks and Russell Means, and the continuing struggle through the 1980s around the imprisonment of AIM activist Leonard Peltier can be found reflected in the poems and prose of contemporary Native Americans. It can also be found in the genre of Native American writing, which is overlooked by virtually all the modern anthologies—the lyrics of contemporary Native American songs written in the folk or country modes. (To my knowledge, the only literary publication which has given a forum to the lyrics of Native American writers is *Blue Cloud Quarterly*, which devoted an issue in the early '70s to Buffy Sainte-Marie.) The songs of Floyd Westerman, Buffy Sainte-Marie, Jim Pepper, Willy Dunn, David Campbell, Buddy Red Bow, A. Paul Ortega, and a number of others resonate with an awareness of the issues facing Native Americans today. The lyrics of many of their songs are, I feel, powerful poetry in their own right.

Although it can certainly be said that much of mainstream American writing has been and continues to be apolitical and that "political writing" has been branded as "mere propaganda" by many American critics, it can just as truly be said that much Native American writing seems to embrace the political as an integral ingredient. The roots of this political awareness in contemporary Indian writing have certainly been strengthened by the last three decades of political activities of Native American activists such as the take-overs and the fish-ins, the Longest Walk, and other demonstrations of Native unity and purpose. However, those political roots are, historically, very deep. The idea of governments being "of the people" comes as much from Native American traditions as it does from Europe, and Native American ideas of "women's rights" were far in advance of Europe. Many oral traditions of Native America—such as the Iroquois story of the founding of the Great League of Peace—are deeply political. Words are powerful things, and language—as the Cherokees with their Sacred Formulas well knew—can both create and kill. American Indian writers maintain that traditional respect for the power of the word and the "political" role of the artist. They seem to be unanimous in describing their work as something much different from "art for art's sake." In the collection of autobiographical essays *I Tell You Now*, Dakota poet Elizabeth Cook-Lynn describes her writing as "an act of defiance born of the need to survive." It is a question of both personal survival and the survival of cultures, and that strong relationship between a great many Native American writers and Native "political causes" will certainly continue and probably become even stronger over the next decade.

Native American Literary Freedom and the Press

The Native American press has a long history and has played an important role in American Indian life in the second half of the twentieth century. In a thought-provoking essay published in *Wicazo Sa Review* (Fall 1987), Renape writer Jack Forbes went so far as to state that the true way to define Native American literature is to say that it is literature produced *by* Indians *for* Indians and that such work is not to be found in the books and journals produced by the mainstream. Instead, Forbes insists, it is to be found in the "Indian-published periodicals." Such presses as Maurice Kenny's Strawberry Press and the many Native American newspapers to be found in North America are, to Forbes, the primary source of "real" Native American writing. Moreover, since the main focus of Native American newspapers is nonfiction, Forbes feels that nonfiction is the heart and the true spirit of American Indian literary endeavor. Whether or not one accepts that premise, it is hard to think of another publication that has published more contemporary American Indian poets than has the highly political Indian newspaper *Akwesasne Notes*. A list of the Indian writers who have appeared on the poetry pages of *Notes*, as it is affectionately called, would read like an anthology of modern Native American poetry. For two decades, both the known poets who wish to speak to an Indian audience and those appearing in print for the first time have found *Akwesasne Notes* hospitable. First published, interestingly enough, in 1969, *Notes* emanates from "The Mohawk Nation near Rooseveltown, N.Y." Today, *Akwesasne Notes* remains an important outlet for Native American writing. It is a prominent example of the ways the Native American press has been and will continue to be very significant for American Indian writers, placing their work in the context of the most current and controversial events in the Indian world, and often providing young Native writers with their first forum. The Native press remains, I feel, one of the two primary proving grounds for new Indian writing. The other important proving ground is the "small press."

Although major publishers have brought out books by contemporary Native Americans over the past two decades, in virtually all cases, the space on their lists for work by more than one or two token Native writers has not been made available. Harper & Row started an ambitious program of publishing Native American writers after the success of Hyemeyohsts Storm's controversial *Seven Arrows*, the first Native American "coffee table book." A number of books by Native American writers were published over the years between Storm's book in 1972 and Ray Young Bear's *Winter of the Salamander* in 1980. Simon Ortiz, James Welch, Vine Deloria, Jr., and someone named Nas'naga were among the Native American writers published. In the front of Young Bear's book, it is stated, "This book is the tenth in Harper & Row's Native American Publishing Program. All profits from this program are used to support projects designed to aid the Native American People." For a time, Duane Niatum worked for Harper & Row as editor of that series. However, with the resignation of a single person at Harper & Row, the commitment to the series died suddenly. With the exception of *Seven Arrows*, none of these books were kept in print by Harper & Row. Further, I have yet to hear of any specific project that "aids the Native American People" which received funds from that project. It was only at the small presses (and certain university presses), publishing companies with limited resources which often could produce only a few books a year in limited press runs, that real sustained commitment to Native American writing would be found in the decades of the 1970s and 1980s.

The real beginning of small press involvement in Native American literature can probably be dated to 1969 and the publication of a special issue of *South Dakota Review* entitled "The American Indian Speaks." John Milton, the magazine's editor, was a non-Indian. Like Brother Benet Tvedten, the founder and editor of *Blue Cloud Quarterly* (which was certainly one of the most important presses for Native American writers in the '70s and '80s), Milton recognized the promise of contemporary Native American writing and consistently published the work of Indian writers when other publications ignored them. Reissued that same year as a book, *The American Indian Speaks* was the first real anthology of contemporary Native American writing. Such important authors as James Welch, Janet Campbell Hale, Bea Medicine, and Simon Ortiz were among the more than forty writers and artists included.

The last twenty years have seen the publication of dozens of anthologies of Native American contemporary writing. The majority of them have been from small presses. Some have been in the form of special issues of magazines (as in the 1979 "Native American Issue" of *Shantih*, or the 1989 "Oklahoma Indian Markings" issue of *Nimrod*), while others have been full-fledged books, sometimes from major publishers. The anthologies have been of great significance to Native American poets in particular, though several anthologies of short fiction have also appeared and are of real note. Some of the anthologies which have been of major importance include Benet Tvedten's 1971 *An American Indian Anthology* (with sixteen writers); Dick Lourie's *Come to Power* (eleven writers) in 1974 from The Crossing Press; Duane Niatum's beautifully produced and strongly edited *Carriers of the Dream Wheel* (fifteen Native American poets and one Polynesian) in 1975 from Harper & Row; the Canadian Native writers anthology *Many Voices* (thirty-four Native American poets) in 1977, edited by Day and Bowering, from J. J. Douglas; my own *Songs from This Earth on Turtle's Back* (fifty-two American Indian poets) in 1983 from the Greenfield Review Press; *The Clouds Threw This Light* (seventy-seven poets), edited by Phil Foss and published by the Institute of American Indian Arts in 1983; and Niatum's second anthology from Harper & Row, *Harper's Anthology of 20th Century Native American Poetry* (thirty-seven writers, including poets from Canada and the United States) in 1988.

One major anthology which deserves special mention is Geary Hobson's *The Remembered Earth*. First published in 1979 by Hobson's own Red Earth Press and later reissued by the University of New Mexico Press, it remains—even after more than a decade—the best single introduction to the range of poetry, fiction, and nonfiction work by contemporary American Indian writers. Of particular note in the area of short fiction is Simon Ortiz's anthology of short stories by Native American writers, *Earth Power Coming*, which was published by Navajo Community College Press in 1983. Navajo Community College Press is a leader in the field of Native presses publishing Native work, but it has been unable to follow up with further projects in contemporary Native American literature because of a lack of money, even though its current director, Pawnee/Otoe writer Anna Lee Walters, has had numerous projects in mind. Two other very important anthologies are Rayna Green's 1984 anthology of Native American women's fiction and poetry, *That's What She Said*, from Indiana University Press, and Mohawk writer Beth Brant's *A Gathering of Spirit*, a collection of poetry and stories by North American Indian women which was originally published as a special issue of *Sinister Wisdom* magazine in 1984 and was reissued as a book shortly thereafter, and then republished by Firebrand Books in 1988. There is absolutely no question that some of the strongest voices in contemporary American Indian writing are the voices of women, and those two anthologies offer clear evidence of this. When considering the importance of anthologies of Indian writing, mention should also be made of the numerous collections of "Indian" writing translated by non-Indians, such as Jerome Rothenberg's *Shaking the Pumpkin*, published in 1972 by Anchor. While some of the translations of "traditional poetry of the Indian North Americas" in that book are good, too much of the material is mistranslated or misunderstood. Moreover, such anthologies may foster the idea that Indians are a part of the past by focusing on the "retranslation" by non-Indian writers (usually poets who at the time of their "retranslating" had never even met an Indian) of work collected in the late nineteenth and early twentieth centuries by ethnologists. Such anthologies have sometimes reinforced stereotypes and made it even more difficult for contemporary writers to be accepted, especially when their work has not seemed to fit the mold set by such collections.

An early anthology of Native American poetry which appeared in 1972 was Terry Allen's *The Whispering Wind*, published by Doubleday. The good thing about the collection was that it was visible evidence of the work in creative writing being done at the Institute of American Indian Arts (IAIA), a special school which offers study in everything from creative writing to sculpture, drama, and painting to Native Americans, who are usually of college age. The IAIA was founded in 1962, and a large number of Native American writers have either studied or taught there. The unfortunate thing about *The Whispering Wind* was that much of the poetry in it was not very good, and the fourteen writers (some of whom, such as Janet Campbell Hale, have since produced some very mature, powerful work) were rushed into print before they were ready. Terry Allen also edited a series of anthologies of poetry and prose by students in Native American high schools through the Creative Writing Project of the BIA; the first collection appeared in 1969 as *Arrow I*. With the exception of Joseph Concha, none of the eighty-six writers who appeared in the four *Arrow* anthologies between 1969 and 1972 appear ever to have published again.

The community of writers which has been made visible by the anthologies of the last twenty years includes not only younger Native Americans, but also some authors who are considerably older. Louis Littlecoon Oliver, a Creek Indian writer from Tahlequah, Oklahoma, saw his first publication (aside from letters to the editor in local papers) only in the early 1980s, when he was in his late seventies. Still writing at the age of eighty-five, with four published books of poetry and prose now to his credit, Oliver stated in an unpublished interview in 1983 that if it had not been for the visit to Tahlequah of Joy Harjo a few years earlier and her interest in his writing, he would have "crawled into his hole like an old groundhog and just disappeared." Oliver first became aware of Harjo's work through seeing it in a Native American anthology. In a similar fashion, Mary Tallmountain was encouraged and helped to find outlets for her poems by Paula Gunn Allen, who is a generation younger. Both Tallmountain and Oliver have been heavily influenced by the work of younger Native American poets, especially in terms of form. Until he encountered younger Indian writers in the 1980s, Oliver's conception of poetry was, as he put it, "old-fashioned." Within a few years, though, he had made the transition from rhymed poems with Victorian diction to both open forms and work drawing strongly on Creek oral traditions, including one entire chapbook in a bilingual format with poems in Creek and English.

It might be noted at this point that except for Pauline Johnson (1861–1913) and Frank Prewett (1893–1962), both of whom were Canadian Iroquois and both of whom were immersed from early childhood in English literature, few American Indian poets were published until the 1970s. Although autobiographies have a long tradition and there were a number of recognized Native American fiction writers before Momaday (who still describes himself as a poet first, a fiction writer second), Native American poets could be counted on the fingers of one hand. Until the 1970s, virtually the only "Native American poems" to be found in print were translations (usually by non-Indians) of American Indian chants and songs. Why was this so, and why are there so many Native American poets in print now? I asked this question of Cheyenne writer Lance Henson and his response was a simple one. "This is the first literate generation of Indian writers. In my own case, I'm the first Cheyenne to get a degree in Creative Writing." Whereas before there were a few isolated, even "acculturated" writers of Indian heritage here and there, for the first time in the 1970s and 1980s it became evident to the literary public and, more important, to Native Americans themselves, that (to paraphrase a poem of Simon Ortiz's) "Indian writers are everywhere." For the first time, there was the real possibility of *community*. That sense of community would be a turning point for older and younger poets alike. It would come at a time when the growth of Native presses and sympathetic small (and sometimes larger) press editors would provide more than occasional token outlets for the publication of this new work. *Opportunity and community*, not creative ability or inspiration, were the key words for the new Native American poets, who began to become visible in the '70s and '80s. At that point in American literary history, a larger number of Native writers than ever before were both prepared to write and provided with outlets for their work. That new climate of opportunity would even, in the 1980s, make it possible to bring back into print work by Native Americans of past decades or discover and publish for the first time works which did not find publishers at the time of their completion. The most obvious example of that at present is Ella Carr Deloria's novel *Waterlily*, which was completed in 1944 but published only in 1988—more than four decades later! In Canada, where the development of a community of Native writers has somewhat lagged behind the events in the United States, it appears that there is tremendous potential and talent. Although the border between the United States and Canada is not recognized by many Native nations (such as the Mohawks, who have yearly "border crossings" to assert their Native rights), Canadian-born Native writers such as Peter Blue Cloud found publication much easier in the United States and many do not realize that Blue Cloud might be claimed as a "Canadian." The opportunities found by Copway and Prewett and Johnson were not readily available to other Canadian Native writers until very recently, it seems. The appearance of Theytus Press in British Columbia and the publication of such exciting new "Canadian" Indian authors as Jeanette Armstrong and David Daniel Moses lead me to expect a great deal from north of the U.S. border in the next decade.

The successes of Pauline Johnson and George Copway remind us that there have been other times when Native American writing was given public attention. As Geary Hobson pointed out astutely in a 1976 essay in *New America*, there have been a number of periods in which "'interest' in Indians was prominent," followed by periods of disinterest, when the fad passed. Hobson identifies those times of interest as 1880 to 1910, the late 1920s and the 1930s, the period from 1947 to 1955, and the period beginning in 1969. He refers, therefore, to contemporary Native American writing as a "renascence" rather than a renaissance, a rising again into vigor rather than a rebirth. It is an important and insightful observation. Though there have been breaks in public interest, there have been no real breaks in the flow of energy from certain of the Native American oral traditions, for example, to the rhythms and concerns of many of the Native American poets of today.

If the current rise of Native American writing is only the most recent of a number of waves, are we to expect a similar receding from the shore, as happened in the late 1930s or around 1910? It is my own feeling that this current wave is one which is going to sink in, rather than ebb away. The growing strength of the Native press and the sheer, ever-increasing number of American Indian writers now in print have created a presence that is probably self-sustaining. In 1983, *Songs from This Earth on Turtle's Back* included fifty-two writers from more than thirty different tribes. Only seven years later, *New Voices from the Longhouse*, an anthology made up only of Iroquois writers, included only six writers who had been in the earlier volume. From fifty-two from many tribes to thirty from the Iroquois alone is quite a leap. I fully expect to see more regional and tribal-based collections in the years to come.

Another example of the probable staying power of the new generation of Native American writers can be found in the academic world. Courses in Native American writing are to be found in many colleges and even secondary schools, and for better or worse, the growing body of critical writings about contemporary Native Americans has made modern American Indian writing a legitimate field of academic endeavor. There is even a *European Review of Native American Studies*, published in English in Austria. One particularly promising sign is the emergence of competent Native American critics who are beginning to shed light on contemporary American Indian writing in ways which the non-Indian critics have sometimes failed to do. These new Indian critics include Paula Gunn Allen, whose landmark study of recovering the feminine in American Indian Studies, *The Sacred Hoop*, was published by Beacon in 1986, Geary Hobson whose as-yet-unpublished study of American Indian writing promises to be a significant work, and such other Indian critics as Elizabeth Cook-Lynn, Jack Forbes, and Ward Churchill.

Definitions

At this point, it may be worthwhile to make a few observations about just what Native American writing is, and what position it occupies in American literature. A good comparison might be made between the relationship of Native American writing to American literature and the relationship of African writing to British literature. In both cases, the writing is usually in the language of the colonizer. In both cases, cultural conflict is a major issue, and, ironically, the expression of traditional values in the language of the oppressor has been one of the results of introducing a European written language into predominantly oral cultures. As is the case with African literature, Native American oral traditions and traditional values have breathed new energy into the adopted language. Similarly, the current generation of colonized writers is as fluent in the adopted tongue as are the best writers whose roots are solely in European traditions. With American Indian contemporary writing, as with African literature written in English (where we now have a Nigerian winner of the Nobel Prize for Literature, Wole Soyinka), we have passed the point where that body of literary work can be seen only as a literary curiosity or a mere adjunct to the colonizer's literature. It is, indeed, part of the body of world literature written in English, but it is—just as much as American literature is no longer a colonial appendage of British tradition—also a literature which stands on its own and can be seen to have its own traditions and directions. Rather than trying to fit Native American literature in as a minor part of the American literary mainstream, it may be more appropriate to see Native American writing as a river in its own right. Or perhaps we might see it in terms of the image given us by the Iroquois in the famous two-row wampum belt which spelled out, more than two centuries ago, the relationship the Iroquois saw between themselves and the whites. The two rows on the belt represent two canoes going down the river. One is the white canoe, the other the Indian. They go in the same direction and may even be traveling at the same speed. However, they are separate boats and it is very hard to travel far or stay in balance when you have one foot in each boat.

Native American literature today is also not just being written in English. There is an American Indian literature in Spanish though it is little known to most English speakers, but it is as strongly connected to American Indian literature composed in English as African writing in French or Portuguese is linked to African writing in English. Moreover, there is a small but growing body of Native American writing going on in various original Native American languages. (I say "original" because I consider that such European languages as English, French, and Spanish when used by Native American communities raised to fluency in them are now "Native American languages.") There are well-organized efforts being made in many American Indian communities to strengthen or restore the place of such original Native languages as Seneca in New York State or Passamaquoddy in Maine, often through bilingual programs in the schools. Native-language radio stations exist in many parts of North America now, from the lands of the Dene in Canada to the Mohawk along the St. Lawrence River.

It is logical to expect more work—especially poetry and storytelling—written in original Native American languages. Perhaps it will appear in bilingual format, as has been done in the important Sun Tracks series from the University of Arizona, which in 1980 published *The South Corner of Time*, an anthology which focused on four southwestern Native American nations (Navajo, Hopi, Papago/Tohona O'odham, and Yaqui) and presented stories and poems in their Native languages with English on facing pages.

Such bilingual presentation solves the problem of limited audience faced by the Native writer who might know her or his language well enough to write in it but who is faced by the dilemma of having no more than a few dozen or a few thousand readers able to read that tongue. The options of bilingualism may be as exciting for the Native American writer fluent in an original American Indian language as they are to a Chicano or Puerto Rican poet able to switch between Spanish and English. This leads to a question now being asked by many. Who is Indian? If someone is only "part" Indian, can we still call him or her a Native American writer? It is an interesting question to be asked within a culture where anyone who has the smallest trace of African ancestry is often simply called "black." While it is no longer acceptable to talk of "Quadroons" when speaking about black writers, the terms "mixed-blood," "full-blood," and "half breed" are common currency in public thinking about American Indians. American racism takes some strange turns, and there seems to be a strong bias, even now, toward discounting certain writers by saying they are not Indian enough genetically to be called Indian writers.

This is ironic for a number of reasons. For one, there have been at least five centuries of "mixing" with people of European (and African) descent in the Americas. (If one accepts the well-documented theories of Viking colonies from the year 1000, that mixing perhaps goes even farther back.) For another, the terms "mixed-blood" and "full-blood" are seldom accurate descriptions. Donald Berthong, a scholar who has worked since 1952 assessing Cheyenne oral traditions in Oklahoma, concluded in the summer 1989 issue of *Meeting Ground* that the full/mixed-blood distinction "does not mean a lot. It has nothing to do with genetics, but rather situational rhetoric. A family will be identified as full or mixed blood by other families depending on the vested interests and the degree of tribal unity or factionalism involved" (3).

Most of the contemporary generation of Native American writers have some white ancestry. In some cases, the white blood is proportionately equal to or greater than the Native. Using blood quantum to discredit a Native writer's work or identity, however, is (pardon the expression) a red herring. I am not speaking of those writers who claim Indian blood with little proof or are simply fakers using "Indian ancestry" as a marketing gimmick. In his landmark anthology *The Remembered Earth*, Hobson cited several means to define someone as "Indian." The definition he found most essential was "the Indian tribe's or community's judgment." Being seen as an Indian in the eyes of your own Native American people (and being able to state, with certainty, just who those people are) is, I feel, an excellent way to establish oneself as a Native American writer. It is also probably the best way for Native American writers to recognize themselves.

Asserting that certain writers are not Indian because they are of mixed blood is yet another step toward the total displacement and final dispossession of Native Americans. It ignores the fact that American Indian cultures have shown and continue to show an incredible ability to survive, change, and yet remain distinctly "Indian." Like the Jews, American Indians have been stereotyped, labeled, despised, placed in concentration camps, and numbered. To that, however, has been added the additional insult of being told—after all of this oppression and dispossession—that you are not who you say you are. As long as Native Americans exist, they lay a claim on America's conscience. Contemporary Native American poets, fiction writers, essayists, and dramatists have been among the most vocal and the most effective in making the social and political realities of the Indian condition visible to Native peoples and the general public. The pan-tribalism which has long been sought by visionary Indians (from Metacomet and Tecumtha to Leonard Peltier and Vine Deloria, Jr.) characterizes much of contemporary Native American writing. It has grown stronger over the past two decades and will continue to grow in strength in the decades to come. At the same time, through the words of Native writers, the specific tribal realities of the many nations of Native America will come into clearer and clearer focus.

At present, many, perhaps most, of the contemporary Native American writers either come from "urban Indian" or nontribal community backgrounds or live outside of tribal communities. This is understandable when one realizes that the opportunities for both higher education and physical longevity have been much greater outside the tribal setting, whether reservation, reserve, or "nonrecognized" community. The jobs which can support a writer are usually only to be found in such settings as colleges or urban areas. It is, quite simply, a question of opportunity and access. But the possibilities of broadening that access have been greatly increased over the past two decades. True community-based education—Freedom Schools, for example—under Indian control and the potential availability of affordable technologies such as desktop publishing make for very interesting new scenarios. One of the new bright lights on the Indian literary horizon at the time of this writing is Theytus Press and the En'owkin Center with its International School of Writing. A community-based Native American press and writing school run by Native people in British Columbia, it has the potential to serve as a model for other similar endeavors and to help develop a whole new generation of American Indian writers, including more writers who come from and remain within tribal communities. More Indian schools and colleges and Indian publishers will mean more opportunity for Native writers. Support for such endeavors ought to be a major priority for anyone with a stake in Indian writing today. Such schools may also solve one of the biggest problems faced by Native American playwrights. It is relatively easy to write a play, but a play can come to life only when it is brought to the stage. The growth of Native American drama has been slowed by the difficulty of forming and supporting Native American theater groups, as well as finding places to do the actual plays. A number of promising theater projects in the 1980s—such as Oneida playwright Bruce King's company, which was based at the Turtle Museum in Niagara Falls—have vanished when financial support for the groups faded. Perhaps the En'owkin Center or similar Native American entities will provide lasting homes for the development of the new Native American theater.

It is interesting to note just how new the contemporary era of Native American writing really is. In more ways than one, it is still an open book. At this writing, not one of the important Native American writers whose work first came to light in this period has ceased writing. Most appear to have some of their best work still ahead of them. Because of this, any statements about the directions of particular writers or of Native writing as a whole can only be tentative. Further, it is vital to acknowledge that contemporary Native American writers—for all they have in common—are an uncommonly diverse group of individuals. With that in mind, it is amazing how much agreement and good feeling between writers does exist in the Native American writing community. It is not that all Native American writers like each other. (I still remember with some humor the remark made by a white writer after witnessing the Native American writing panel at the American Writers' Congress in the late 1970s. "My God!" that person said, "all you Indian writers LIKE EACH OTHER!") However, we are more like each other than we are like any other group of writers anywhere in the world today. Certain threads of experience and respect, sorrow and celebration, love and confusion, link the members of the current generation of Indian writers. One of the major problems faced by many transplanted American writers today—the feeling of isolation in a rootless culture built upon immigration and constant displacement—is a problem for the Native American writer only when he or she (like Momaday's Abel) forgets just how deeply rooted Native American experience still is. While mainstream America swings from trend to trend, the Native American view of "America" and of life as a whole has remained very different from the view held by the so-called majority culture. In a very real sense, despite five centuries of attack, the spirit of Native America—as we see it expressed in contemporary American Indian writing—has not changed.

Despite the fact that rates of poverty, suicide, and alcoholism still remain highest for Native populations among all the peoples of the United States and Canada, the essential strengths of Native American cultures remain. Those strengths include the ability to see themselves and non-Indian culture with clarity and honesty. Few non-Indian writers have succeeded in drawing realistic, fully realized Native American characters without creating further examples of the stereotyped "Noble Savage" or "Bloodthirsty Redskins" encountered in Fenimore Cooper. Yet the white characters encountered in such Native American novels as James Welch's *The Death of Jim Loney* or Louise Erdrich's *Love Medicine* are certainly not cardboard cutouts. Native American cultures have always stressed the importance of close observation of the natural world, which includes the human beings within that world. The kind of narcissistic turning inward characteristic of non-Native poetry is not a Native American direction. Seeing the world around one, with all of its complexity, is the Native way, and that seeing always includes the possibility of reproducing it in art, whether poem or song, story or dance. I have only to close my eyes to see the picture of a white tourist at a Hopi feast day being followed by a Hopi clown. The clown's every action was a reflection of that increasingly uncomfortable tourist. The tourist had come there to see the colorful Natives, not to be confronted by a mirror. That unwillingness to look into the painfully honest mirror which Native American writers hold up to America can be seen in some of the negative critical response—or lack of response—on the part of certain critics and all too many publishers to contemporary American Indian writing. The ratio of published to as-yet-unpublished, yet highly publishable Native American writing remains much too low in poetry, drama, and fiction.

However, if the outlets for their work increase, today's Native American writers may be in the strongest positions of any writers in North America today. Not only are they able now to draw upon the wealth of world literature, which is more available in North America than, perhaps, anywhere else in the world, but they also are able to refer to and draw from a variety of oral traditions. Not only are they able to take advantage of the freedoms of speech guaranteed by Canada and the United States, but they are also able to use that freedom to offer to the world not only good literature but also meaningful ways in which to praise and preserve that world. The physical and spiritual returns to those healing values of love of earth and respect for tradition, which prove the salvation of Momaday's

Abel, Silko's Tayo, Allen's Ephanie, and a host of others in American Indian writing, are paths which more human beings than Indians would do well to follow. I have no doubt that there will be many more Native American writers acting as guides and pathfinders along those ways.

Joseph Bruchac
The Greenfield Review

BIBLIOGRAPHY

Allen, Paula Gunn. *The Sacred Hoop*. Boston: Beacon, 1986.

Allen, Terry, ed. *Arrow I*. Creative Writing Project of the Bureau of Indian Affairs, United States Department of the Interior. Pacific Grove Press, 1969.

———. *The Whispering Wind*. New York: Doubleday, 1972.

Berthong, Donald. *Meeting Ground*. (Summer 1989): 3. Chicago: D'Arcy McNickle Center, Newberry Library.

Blue Cloud, Peter. *Alcatraz Is Not an Island*. Berkeley: Wingbow Press, 1972.

Brant, Beth, ed. "A Gathering of Spirit." *Sinsiter Wisdom* (July 1983).

Bruchac, Joseph, ed. *Songs from This Earth on Turtle's Back*. Greenfield Center, NY: The Greenfield Review Press, 1983.

———. *Survival This Way*. Tucson: U of Arizona P, 1987.

———. *New Voices from the Longhouse*. Greenfield Center, NY: Greenfield Review Press, 1990.

Cook-Lynn, Elizabeth. *Then Badger Said This*. Fairfield, WA: Ye Galleon Press, 1983.

Day, David, and Marilyn Bowering, eds. *Many Voices*. North Vancouver, BC: J. J. Douglas, 1977.

Deloria, Ella Carr. *Waterlily*. Lincoln: U of Nebraska P, 1988.

Erdrich, Louise. *Love Medicine*. New York: Holt, Rinehart and Winston, 1984.

Evers, Larry, ed. *The South Corner of Time*. Tucson: U of Arizona P, 1980.

Forbes, Jack. "Colonialism and Native American Literature: Analysis." *Wicazo Sa Review* (Fall 1987): 17–24.

Foss, Phil, ed. *The Clouds Threw This Light*. Santa Fe: Institute of American Indian Arts Press, 1983.

Green, Rayna, ed. *That's What She Said*. Bloomington: Indiana UP, 1984.

Hobson, Geary. "Round Dance: Native American Writing at the University of New Mexico." *New America* 2.3 (Summer–Fall 1976): 4–8.

———. *The Remembered Earth*. Albuquerque: Red Earth Press, 1979.

Kenny, Maurice. *Dead Letter Sent*. New York: Troubadour Press, 1958.

Krupat, Arnold, and Brian Swann, eds. *I Tell You Now*. Lincoln: U of Nebraska P, 1987.

Lourie, Dick, ed. *Come to Power*. Ithaca: Crossing Press, 1974.

McNickle, D'Arcy. *The Surrounded*. New York: Dodd, Mead, 1936.

———. *Indian Man*. Bloomington: Indiana UP, 1971.

———. *Wind from an Enemy Sky*. New York: Harper & Row, 1978.

Milton, John, ed. "The American Indian Speaks." *South Dakota Review* 7.2 (Summer 1969).

Mitchell, Emerson Blackhorse. *Miracle Hill*. Norman: U of Oklahoma P, 1967.

Momaday, N. Scott. *House Made of Dawn*. New York: Harper & Row, 1968.

———. *The Way to Rainy Mountain*. Albuquerque: U of New Mexico P, 1969.

Niatum, Duane, ed. *Carriers of the Dream Wheel*. New York: Harper & Row, 1975.

———. *Harper's Anthology of 20th Century Native American Poetry*. New York: Harper & Row, 1988.

Ortiz, Simon, ed. *Earth Power Coming*. Tsaile: Navajo Community College Press, 1983.

Ringold, Francine, ed. "Oklahoma Indian Markings." *Nimrod* 32.2 (Spring 1989): 6.

Rothenberg, Jerome, ed. *Shaking the Pumpkin*. New York: Anchor, 1972.

Silko, Leslie. *Ceremony*. New York: Viking, 1977.

Storm, Hyemeyohsts. *Seven Arrows*. New York: Harper & Row, 1972.

Tvedten, Benet, ed. *An American Indian Anthology*. Marvin, SD: Blue Cloud Quarterly Press, 1971.

Vizenor, Gerald. *Summer in the Spring: Lyric Poems of the Ojibway*. Minneapolis: Nodin Press, 1965.

Waters, Frank. *The Man Who Killed the Deer*. Chicago: Swallow Press, 1942.

Welch, James. *Winter in the Blood*. New York: Harper & Row, 1974.

———. *The Death of Jim Loney*. New York: Harper & Row, 1979.

Wilson, Edmund. *Apologies to the Iroquois*. New York: Farrar, Straus and Cudahy, 1960.

Young Bear, Ray. *Winter of the Salamander*. New York: Harper & Row, 1980.

Critical Approaches to Native American Literature

Let me suggest that there are three requirements for the development of any critical approaches to Native American literature: first, there must be a recognition of the fact that there is such a thing as Native American literature; second, there must be an understanding of the languages in which and the means by which that literature is presented; and, third, there must be a knowledge of the culture whose concerns that literature expresses and addresses. All three of these requirements would appear to be self-evident, although, in fact, the third has recently been called into question from two apparently different, although ultimately similar perspectives. But let us examine each of these items in turn.

1. Inasmuch as the indigenous people of the present-day United States did not rely upon alphabetic writing as a means of information storage and transmission, their unlettered condition seemed, in the eyes of the European invaders, to bar them from possession of any *littera*-ture, defined as the culture of letters (*littera*, letter). It was only from the European pre-Romantic period (1760 or so) forward that the meaning of *literature* shifted so that not the form of the presentation (writing) but the content of the presentation (imaginative and affective material) became the determining factor in the Western understanding of literature. By the time Bishop Percy's collection of Scottish ballads appeared to impress such as Wordsworth with the expressive powers of the "ordinary speech of ordinary men" (Preface to *The Lyrical Ballads*), it was no longer a contradiction in terms to speak of an *oral literature*. We may date the beginnings of the Euroamerican recognition of the existence of Indian literatures from this period and take what is probably the first translation of an Indian song into English by Lt. Henry Timberlake as the earliest critical approach to Native American literature.[1] This is to say that, however uncritical it may

look to us, Timberlake's translation illustrates that approach which attempts to render Indian literature comprehensible to the Euroamerican by presenting it in a form Euroamericans can easily recognize as indeed literary. Such an approach persists to the present day, though translators of Indian songs or stories do not employ, of course, the Drydenesque heroic couplets of Timberlake, but whatever contemporary manner may strike their readers as "literary."

So much, however sketchy, for Euroamerican recognition of the existence of a Native American literature, and an indication of one "primitive" sort of approach to that literature. What of Native American recognition of a Native American literature, and so the possibility of a Native American critical approach? In the West, the literary category is marked by the dominance of a *conjuncture of pedagogical and pleasurable functions*, as in Sir Philip Sidney's sense of poetry as preeminently capable of teaching and delighting.[2] Sidney's point was to emphasize literature's unique ability to join discursive functions that the West more usually took as separate, even opposed. In this very particular sense, Native American cultures have ceased to see virtually all discourse as "literary."

To illustrate by a somewhat crude analogy, let me point to the fact that in a traditional culture, a wooden club used for killing salmon might first have to be elaborately carved before it can work properly. In similar fashion, all, or a very good deal, of traditional Indian discourse, however specific its practical function (to cure, to assure proper rainfall, etc.), tends also to be "well-carved"—highly elaborated in its rhetorical and figural strategies—and so to appear "literary" to Westerners. But although Native people themselves certainly recognize functional differences among types of discourse, distinguishing between rain-assuring songs, for example, and—say—the "dream songs" (q.v.) of the Pima or Mojave, songs which are specifically *not* for curing or for assuring the fall of rain, still they do not abstract these differences into definitions of distinct discursive categories. Indians distinguish discourse *generically* (dreamsongs and rain songs, myth narratives, ceremonial rhetoric, etc.), but not *categorically* (literature, history, philosophy, science, fiction, nonfiction, etc.). Thus there is no Indian "literature" as such for Indians. The only operative indigenous "critical approach" is to verbal performance generally, and it is concerned with *comparisons of the effectiveness of variants*: some singers or tellers or speakers do this better, others do that; some go on too long, others not long enough, while some always seem to get it just right; some are always scary, some always funny; etc. The development of any further indigenous approach to Native American literatures would require some indigenous definitions of the category of literature. These can most probably be worked out, for it seems likely that they are implicit in varieties of Native American discourse. But this work remains to be done.

2. It is not clear just how much of the Cherokee language Lt. Henry Timberlake did or did not understand. A likely guess is that a Cherokee or mixed-blood person with some command of English "interpreted" for Timberlake. Much Indian literature has been "translated" in this way, with results whose accuracy may well be guessed. Although Indian languages were studied in the seventeenth-century (so that the Bible might be translated into those languages), and no less than George Washington and Thomas Jefferson (among others) collected Indian wordlists for learned societies in the eighteenth century, detailed comprehension of Native tongues reached a first plateau of relative sophistication only after the middle of the nineteenth century. While the labors of civil servants like Henry Schoolcraft among the Chippewa, or clerics like Bishop Riggs in the Dakotas, or early anthropologists like Washington Matthews and Frank Hamilton Cushing in the Southwest deserve the fullest recognition, one must date a more "scientific" study of Indian languages (as of much else) from the intervention of Franz Boas in the 1890s and after. Although a detailed account of this matter is beyond the scope of the present essay, it may not be amiss to note, as Dell Hymes has recently reminded,

> that the study of Native American languages has yet to take its materials seriously enough, and make them its first concern. The bibliographies of the languages grow, but there is hardly to be found anywhere a comprehensive, cogent presentation of what is known about a language, so that what is known can be used by anthropologists, folklorists, even just other linguists. . . . (1987:17–18)

and, of course, I would add, by students of Native American literature.

It seems reasonable to claim that any critical approach to any literature whatever is most immediately dependent upon any understanding of the linguistic code—the language—in which that literature appears or, short of that, at least upon access to a range of translations trustworthy for their linguistic comprehension. From this perspective, it would seem that critical approaches to traditional Native American literatures are still in a relatively early stage of development. This, of course, does not apply to written literature in English by Native Americans, although at least one contemporary Native American critic, Jack Forbes, has raised the question whether this latter is properly called "Indian" literature at all.[3]

Traditional Indian literatures were presented not only in languages entirely unfamiliar to Euroamericans, but in a mode which was largely unfamiliar to them as well, the mode of individual dramatic performance. Although the Puritan invaders of America were the contemporaries of Shakespeare, they were also the contemporaries of the King James version of the Bible, and preferred the latter in its apparently authoritative textual fixity (the unchanging word of God) to the potentially heretical openness of the former (the fickle words of men)—for all that the plays were first written to be spoken, the biblical texts passed on by word of mouth before being written down. Hence the problem not only of comprehending the language but also the dynamics of performance of traditional Indian literatures.

In point of historical fact, there seems to be extremely little in the way of the appreciation of performative dynamics before the twentieth century. Henry Schoolcraft, William Gilmore Simms, even Daniel Brinton and Jeremiah Curtin have little or nothing to say about these matters in the mid- and latter nineteenth century.[4] Only toward the end of the century, with the work perhaps foremost of Alice Fletcher, and then of Natalie Curtis Burlin, could one begin to recognize that Indian "songs" were indeed sung, and that chants were chanted.[5] The dynamics of storytelling would have to wait even longer, entering the accounts of Boas and his students only peripherally or incidentally. Indeed, critical translation-approaches to Native American literature oriented toward the production of, in Dennis Tedlock's phrase, a "performable text" (1983:6), privileging the performative dynamics of actual tellings, were not much in evidence before the 1960s with the seminal work of Tedlock himself and his occasional colleague, the poet Jerome Rothenberg. Both Tedlock and Rothenberg attempted to devise typographic presentations of Indian literature for the page that would at least suggest some of the dynamics (pauses, volume, pitch, audience response) of actual performance events. Dell Hymes's work has been essential in working out principles for line division in narratives that formerly had been presented in highly "unliterary" prose blocks. Given the obvious constraints upon any written approach to oral performance, it has been suggested recently by Andrew Wiget that traditional Indian literatures are perhaps best studied in filmed or videotaped format. Wiget has provided an example of performance analysis which may be taken as exemplary of one avenue of approach oriented to this aspect of our subject.[6] Of course, translations oriented toward an emphasis on performative dynamics inevitably tend to slight, or at least do less well by, the linguistic structure of the literature they translate—just as translations oriented toward emphasizing the linguistic structure (e.g., of the sort Hymes has pioneered in producing) somewhat slight that literature's dynamics. It may well be that no full solution to this problem is possible. For all that, current work by ethnomusicologists—Leanne Hinton, David McAllester, George List, and others—and by linguists and anthropologists—Donald Bahr, William Bright, David Gusa, Dell Hymes, M. Dale Kinkade, Anthony Mattina, Joel Sherzer, Dennis Tedlock, and others—is clearly expanding the range of possibilities for approaches to Native American literature based upon a close attention to its linguistic codes and also to its performance strategies.

3. In an essay called "Shakespeare in the Bush," the anthropologist Laura Bohannon recounts her attempt to offer a plot summary of *Hamlet* to the Tiv people of West Africa when, Bohannon having often asked them

to tell her their stories, they asked her to tell them one of hers. At every point in Bohannon's summary, the Tiv interrupted to assure her that she must be getting the story wrong—for no son would act as Hamlet did toward his mother, no young person behave that way to an elder, no spirit perform as she said Hamlet's father's ghost did, and so on. However "timeless" and "universal" we might think Shakespeare to be, *Hamlet* as he wrote it made little sense to the Tiv.

In just the same way, we may well recognize that Native American stories that include instances of mother-in-law avoidance may make the wrong kind of sense to Westerners, as mother-in-law jokes may confuse or disturb many Indian audiences: all narratives that involve kinship relations are sure to be somewhat baffling if one does not know how a given culture expects kin to behave to one another. Frequent patternings of fours and fives in Plains and Northwest Coast stories will seem odd to people whose own pattern numbers are three or seven. Those used to looking others in the eye, vigorously shaking their hand, and inquiring casually of their health will not readily understand why such behavior causes laughter or consternation among the Hopi and other Indian people. To develop a critical approach to the songs and stories that deal with such matters—and all songs and stories, all literature everywhere, deals with such matters—one needs, it would seem, a knowledge of that people's cultural assumptions. While no one disputes this in an absolute way, nonetheless, two sorts of objections have arisen recently. The one comes from the perspective of what I would call aesthetic universalism, which asserts that for all the differences of human customs, human art is still basically the same everywhere. Thus in his "An Introduction to the Art of Traditional American Indian Narration," Karl Kroeber writes that

> even an inexperienced reader can rewardingly apply to traditional Indian narratives the kind of critical attitude he brings to other literatures. When one does this, the primary discovery one makes is that *diversity* of interpretation is possible because the narrative truly is a work of art. (8)

"A majority of Indian stories," Kroeber continues,

> . . . appeal to enough common features in human nature to allow us at least entrance to their pleasures—if only we can relax sufficiently to enjoy them. (9)

Jarold Ramsey approvingly quotes the Nez Perce storyteller and translator Archie Phinney to the effect that

> Any substantial appreciation of these [Nez Perce] tales must come . . . from vivid feelings within oneself, feeling as a moving current [of?] all the figures and the relationships that belong to the whole myth-body. (in Kroeber:xxi).

Ramsey rhetorically asks, "doesn't Phinney's formula ring true for us, too, literature being what it is, and our imaginations of life being what they are?" (xxi). The difficulty, of course, is that just what literature "is," as I have noted, not to say what "our imaginations of life" in different languages and modes of presentation "are," may not be so clear or universal as Ramsey assumes. Even Kroeber's ideally "relaxed" reader, for all that she may spot "common features in human nature" in Indian literatures and permit herself the very greatest "*diversity* of interpretation," may find her readings either trivial or simply mistaken. A reading of Indian literature that discovers in it, for example, the observations that people age and die, or that spring brings renewal to nature, produces the likeness of Indian literature to all other literatures by ignoring the particular and possibly unique manner in which such observations are presented. And such a reading may simply be misinterpreting specific cultural details, reading them in a manner that would be quite appropriate to Western culture but which is not at all appropriate to Native American cultures. "Diversity" of interpretation is certainly possible for any rich literature, but it is not the case that anything goes; egregiously mistaken interpretations are the most usual consequence of an "inexperienced" reader applying "the kind of critical attitude he brings to other literatures" to the literatures of a very different culture.

The second type of objection to an insistence on the importance of ethnographic information in the understanding of Native American literature is more recent, and derives from what may broadly be called the context of "postmodernism." Gerald Vizenor, the Anishinabe (Chippewa) poet, novelist, and critic, is the foremost proponent of the anti-social-scientific, postmodernist approach to Native American literature. Vizenor's sense, in common with postmodernist anthropologists like Stephen Tyler, is that social scientific "knowledge" is predominantly knowledge of its own rules, codes, and concepts for making sense of culture, not of culture itself. Human linguistic behavior—"literature"—like human behavior generally, for Vizenor is best exemplified by the figure of the trickster, whose shape-changing, limit-transgressing antics provide the best guide—it is inherent in the nature of the trickster *not* to provide a model—to who and what we are, and, as well, to how we ought to read. It might be noted here that this, too, is a version of aesthetic universalism, one that insists on the absolute individual difference of all acts and all texts from one another—on the irreducible uniqueness of phenomena—rather than on the ultimate sameness of phenomena, at least of those phenomena we take as art or "literature." Inasmuch as it has been easier thus far to call for a postmodernist critique of Native American literature than actually to produce one (this is the case as well, as several commentators have noted, with the call for a postmodernist ethnography), we will have to await further developments before offering a fuller assessment.

I have proposed thus far that all approaches to Native American literatures require a recognition of something that might properly be called
Native American literature; that they require a comprehension of the language and the presentational strategies of that literature; and that they
require some knowledge of the cultural concerns that literature expresses
and addresses. Approaches to Native American literature may thus be
distinguished in terms of their relative emphases on one or another of
these requirements. Henry Timberlake in the 1760s and Mary Austin in
the late 1910s and 1920s of this century, for example, emphasized the
literariness of Native performances in presenting them as conformable to,
on the one hand, heroic couplets, and, on the other, imagist free verse.

Oriented toward the performative dynamics and the linguistic structure of Native American literature, Dennis Tedlock produces "oral texts,"
texts at least potentially performable, while Hymes produces written texts
with a strong feel for the verbal patterning of narrative. Although his
approach differs radically from that of Hymes, Anthony Mattina has also
worked from an orientation to the language of the text, attempting to get
the "feel" of Indian narrative by presenting it in a language at once strange
and familiar to Western readers, the "Red English" that many "nowaday
Indians" (Lincoln 1983) speak.

Focus on Native American literature in relation to its cultural ground
has also produced a variety of approaches. A great number of readings of
traditional and modern texts exist which carefully attempt to use their
knowledge of the specificities of the cultural matrix to achieve useful and
meaningful interpretations. Critics less concerned with such specificities
have produced broad, thematic, almost archetypal readings (in the case of
Kroeber, Ramsey, and others) of Indian literature, while the postmodernist
determination of Gerald Vizenor to loosen the bounds of cultural "knowledge," permitting language the fullest freeplay, attempts to produce readings whose nature it is still too soon to specify. It is also the case that some
of the newer approaches to Native American literatures, e.g., the feminist
work of Paula Gunn Allen, also privileges the domain of cultural address
and expression—here, the question of women and gender difference, as
this appears in Indian literature. A Marxian approach does not strictly exist
as yet, although Arnold Krupat's work has occasionally adopted Marxian
terms in its commitment to a form of cultural materialist study. Such an
approach also is concerned with the cultural work of literature in a given
social formation.

For all of this, it needs to be said that a great many, perhaps the
majority of Euroamerican commentators on Native American literature
have not been very clear about or conscious of the particular *approach* they
actually were taking. In the twentieth century, outside the ranks of professional linguists and anthropologists, "literary" criticism of Native American literature has been marked by rather casual unself-consciousness and

eclecticism. I do not mean to suggest that one must myopically pursue a single approach; I do mean to suggest that it is useful for a critic to know what she is doing. Allen's unmistakably feminist approach, Vizenor's postmodernist approach, along with the recent appearance of explicitly Lacanian and Bakhtinian approaches, will, if they do nothing else, urge commentators to greater self-awareness and sophistication. The major contemporary anthologies of critical essays on Native American literature—Abraham Chapman's *Literature of the American Indians* (1975), Karl Kroeber's *Traditional American Indian Literatures* (1981), Brian Swann's *Smoothing the Ground* (1983), Andrew Wiget's *Critical Essays on Native American Literature* (1985), and Swann and Krupat's *Recovering the Word* (1987)— have all been quite intentionally eclectic in their selections, permitting the widest range of approaches to appear. Doubtless there is room for new collections of this sort. But it may also be that the study of Indian literatures has developed to the point where more specialized volumes are now both necessary and possible. The field currently seems open and exciting.

Arnold Krupat
Sarah Lawrence College

NOTES

1. Here are a few lines from Timberlake's "Translation of the WAR-SONG. *Caw waw noo dee*, & c.":

   > Where'er the earth's enlightened by the sun
   > Moon shines by night, grass grows, or waters run,
   > Be't known that we are going, like men, afar,
   > In hostile fields to wage destructive war;
   > Like men we go, to meet our country's foes,
   > Who, woman-like, shall fly our dreaded blows. (81)

2. See Sidney's "Defence of Poetry."
3. See Jack Forbes, "Colonialism and Native American Literature: Analysis."
4. See, for example, Schoolcraft's *Algic Researches*, from which Longfellow took his Hiawatha material, and also the essays by Brinton, Curtin, and Simms reprinted in Abraham Chapman's collection.
5. See Fletcher's essay in Chapman, as well as her *Indian Story and Song from North America*. Burlin's major contribution is *The Indians' Book*.
6. See Andrew Wiget, "Telling the Tale: A Performance Analysis of a Hopi Coyote Story."

BIBLIOGRAPHY

Austin, Mary. Introduction. *The Path on the Rainbow: An Anthology of Songs and Chants from the Indians of North America*. Ed. George W. Cronyn. New York, 1918.
———. *The American Rhythm: Studies and Reexpressions of Amerindian Songs*. 1923. Rpt. Boston, 1930.

Burlin, Nathalie Curtis, ed. *The Indians' Book: An Offering by the American Indians of Indian Lore, Musical and Narrative, to Form a Record of the Songs and Legends of Their Race.* 1907. Rpt. New York: Dover, 1968.

Chapman, Abraham, ed. *Literature of the American Indians: Views and Interpretations.* New York: New American Library, 1975.

Fletcher, Alice. *Indian Story and Song from North America.* 1907.

Forbes, Jack. "Colonialism and Native American Literature: Analysis." *Wicazo Sa Review* 3 (1987): 17–23.

Hymes, Dell. *"In Vain I Tried to Tell You": Essays in Native American Ethnopoetics.* Philadelphia: U of Pennsylvania P, 1981.

———. "Tonkawa Poetics: John Rush Buffalo's Coyote and Eagle's Daughter." *Native American Discourse: Poetics and Rhetoric.* Ed. Joel Sherzer and Anthony Woodbury. Cambridge: Cambridge UP, 1987. 17–61.

Kroeber, Karl. "An Introduction to the Art of Traditional American Indian Narration." In Kroeber, 1–24.

———, ed. *Traditional American Indian Literatures: Texts and Interpretations.* Lincoln: U of Nebraska P, 1981.

Krupat, Arnold. *For Those Who Come After.* Berkeley: U of California P, 1985.

———. "Post-Structuralism and Oral Literature." In Swann and Krupat, 113–28.

Lincoln, Kenneth. *Native American Renaissance.* Berkeley: U of California P, 1983.

Mattina, Anthony, and M. de Sautel, trans. *The Golden Woman: The Colville Narrative of Peter Seymour.* Tucson: U of Arizona P, 1985.

Ramsey, Jarold. "From 'Mythic' to 'Fictive' in a Nez Perce Orpheus Myth." In Kroeber, 25–44.

———. *Reading the Fire: Essays in the Traditional Indian Literatures of the Far West.* Lincoln: U of Nebraska P, 1983.

Rothenberg, Jerome, ed. *Shaking the Pumpkin: Traditional Poetry of the Indian North Americas.* Garden City, NY: Doubleday, 1972.

Schoolcraft, Henry Rowe. *Algic Researches.* New York, 1839.

Sidney, Sir Philip. "A Defence of Poetry." 1595.

Swann, Brian, ed. *Smoothing the Ground: Essays on Native American Oral Literature.* Berkeley: U of California P, 1983.

———, and Arnold Krupat, eds. *Recovering the Word: Critical Essays on Native American Literature.* Berkeley: U of California P, 1987.

Tedlock, Dennis, trans. *Finding the Center: Narrative Poetry of the Zuni Indians.* 1972. Rpt. Lincoln: U of Nebraska P, 1978.

———. *The Spoken Word and the Work of Interpretation.* Philadelphia: U of Pennsylvania P, 1983.

Timberlake, Lt. Henry. *Memoirs: 1756–1765.* Johnson City, TN.

Tyler, Stephen. "Post-modern Ethnography: From Document of the Occult to Occult Document." *Writ-Culture: The Poetics and Politics of Ethnography.* Ed. James Clifford and George Marcus. Berkeley: U of California P, 1986.

Vizenor, Gerald. "A Postmodern Introduction." *Narrative Chance: Post-modern Discourse on Native American Literature.* Ed. Gerald Vizenor. Albuquerque: U of New Mexico P, 1989.

Wiget, Andrew. *Native American Literature.* Boston: Twayne, 1985.

———. "Telling the Tale: A Performance Analysis of a Hopi Coyote Story." In Swann and Krupat, 297–338.

———, ed. *Critical Essays on Native American Literature.* Boston: G.K. Hall, 1985.

Wordsworth, William. Preface. *Lyrical Ballads.* 1798.

European Responses to Native American Literatures

The Native inhabitants of North America have always held great fascination for the Europeans, forming a target of their curiosity and study ever since the discovery of America. Perception of the "New World" and the strange creatures that were to be found here—denying them the status of legitimate dwellers in that land—was for many centuries identified with discovery of the alien, the other, and, as such, was felt to threaten disruption of the established certainties of man and medieval society.

The flowering of European studies on American Indians has seen several different phases. From the Renaissance up to roughly the end of the eighteenth century, the Indian was conceived of either as the "Red Devil" or the "Noble Savage," thereby incarnating two opposite trends, or two cultural figments of the collective European imagination. In the nineteenth century, attention was focused above all on archaeology, ethnohistory, and ethnography, leading up to the dawn of the new century, when research into cultural anthropology was launched.

The influence of these particular trends is still felt today in contemporary studies on American Indians. One of the first consequences is that some of the most active American anthropologists, such as Adolph Bandelier (1840–1914), Robert H. Lowie (1833–1957), and Franz Boas (1858–1942), all of whom dedicated lifetime fieldwork to Indians, received their normal education in Europe, subsequently leaving for the United States in the massive flow of migration at the turn of the century.

The other consequence is that even today, interest in Native Americans is primarily of a historical-anthropological nature. Despite the rich literary output over the last decades by American writers of Indian origin, the various journals, newsletters, and conferences on topics relating to Native cultures show a proportion heavily weighted against exegetic studies on contemporary Native American literature, although, as will be seen, over the last few years interest has increased substantially and has led to the publication of excellent critical contributions and the setting up of publishing projects of interuniversities research.

On the organizational level, this interest made it possible to establish the American Indian Workshop in Amsterdam in 1980, as a branch of the European Association for American Studies. The publication of a *Newsletter*, edited by Christian F. Feest of the Museum of Anthropology in Vienna, offered the opportunity for cooperation between scholars in the various disciplines as well as annual meetings in many European capitals. The *Newsletter*, which since June 1981 has also included a bibliography of all items written by European scholars on North American Indians, merged in 1987 with the *European Review of Native American Studies* with two editorial offices, one in Vienna (Christian F. Feest) and the other in Budapest (Laszlo Borsanyi). Among feature articles and shorter notes dealing with Native American topics in the first three issues (1987–89), the contributions on Native American literature are limited to one short note and two essays.

In other European literary journals, studies on Native American authors begin to appear more regularly. Recently there has also been the publication of special issues devoted to Native American culture *(Revue Française d'Études Américaines* and *Storia Nord Americana*, for example). The first issue of a new journal, *Native American Literatures*, totally devoted to literary topics, has been published in Italy by the University of Pisa Research Group on Native Cultures.

In European universities, Native American literature as a field of literary specialization is becoming more firmly established. Courses and seminars are offered in many universities; in the past few years, a number of dissertations have been written on contemporary authors, a sizable group of students and scholars have been entering the field, and many English or American Studies departments already have a good library of journals, primary and secondary sources dealing with Indian cultures. Funds have been granted to carry out research on contemporary Native writers. Publishing activity includes collections of essays by European and American scholars, fiction and poetry translations, and series devoted to major works in translation, with meticulous notes, extensive bibliography, and solid introductory essays. Such a format should provide the general reading public with proper information on the individual author and his tribal background and also meet the requirements of sound scholarship accompanying the text. As far as readership is concerned, it seems in fact quite appropriate and beneficial to offer some basic information to convey a more realistic appreciation of the American Indian: the novelistic literature of the last century (by Karl May and Emilio Salgari, to name only two of the most prolific writers, not to speak of Anglo-American writers such as James Fenimore Cooper) has been extremely detrimental, establishing a romantic and exotic image, mixed up later on with the Hollywood Indian of the American frontier.

Although, as we have seen, anthropological and historical studies are by far the most cultivated among European Indianists, we must also admit that in the past few years an increasing number of scholars have devoted their research to contemporary Native American literature. The critical analysis focuses on established authors such as N. Scott Momaday, James Welch, and Leslie Marmon Silko, or less-known writers who have traveled extensively in Europe giving poetry readings. The approach tends to be multidisciplinary, although the strongest evidence from this point of view can be found only in Italy, where Elémire Zolla, professor of American literature at the University of Rome, played a pivotal role with his teaching and his many publications, including the pioneering work on Indian authors, *I letterati e lo sciamano* (1973). Such activity is obviously stimulated by the increasing output of Native American writers, both well-known novelists and poets as well as younger, talented authors such as Joy Harjo and Louise Erdrich.

But this interest is also stimulated by a growing concern regarding ethnicity, and by the interplay, currently at work, between mainstream literature and minority cultures. Much scholarship tends to point out multiculturalism in American society and outline the ethnic presence in American writing. Given these premises, current European scholarship is heading toward a redefinition of American identity as well as a reappraisal and a fresh look at American literature and the canon. The rich ethnic participation in American culture has indeed opened a new and unique perspective.

The "new Indian" as he is portrayed in contemporary Native American literature not only transcends stereotypes, but can well embody, from a European viewpoint, the struggle for cultural survival, the affirmation of renewal within traditional values, the reunion with the land and the reacquisition of one's sense of place, and the quest for a new identity in the standardizing contemporary society.

The "melting pot" concept is now reshaping itself into a "mosaic" concept, or "patchwork quilt" of ethnic groups, proud of their diversities and traditions. It reflects a multicultural society of which people both in Europe and in the United States are increasingly aware. The bibliography on European contributions to contemporary Native American literature indicates that Indian people have a prominent place in this society. As a group, they are among the most productive artists, witnessing once more the Native "investment" and "appropriation" of their homeland.

Laura Coltelli
University of Pisa

341

BIBLIOGRAPHY

Primary Sources

Abbey, Mark. "Saga of the Translator's Sons." *Times Literary Supplement* (November 11–17, 1988): 1255. (Includes a review of Brian Swann and Arnold Krupat, eds., *I Tell You Now*, among other books on Indians.)

Bruchac, Joseph. "New Voices from the Longhouse: Some Contemporary Iroquois Writers and Their Relationship to the Tradition of the Ho-de-no-sau-nee." *Coyote*. Ed. B. Schöler. Århus: Seklos, 1984. 147–60.

Churchill, Ward. "Generations of Resistance: American Indian Poetry and the Ghost Dance Spirit." *Coyote*. Ed. B. Schöler. Århus: Seklos, 1984. 40–56.

Niatum, Duane. "History in the Colors of Song: A Few Words on Contemporary Native American Fiction." *Coyote*. Ed. B. Schöler. Århus: Seklos, 1984. 25–34.

Ortiz, Simon J. "Always the Stories: A Brief History and Thoughts on My Writing." *Coyote*. Ed. B. Schöler. Århus: Seklos, 1984. 57–69.

Peyer, Bernd C. *The Elders Wrote: An Anthology of Early Prose by North American Indians 1768–1931*. Beiträge zur Kulturanthropologie. Berlin: Dietrich Reimer Verlag, 1982.

Rose, Wendy. "Just What's All This Fuss About Whiteshamanism Anyway?" *Coyote*. Ed. B. Schöler. Århus: Seklos, 1984. 124–33.

Walters, Anna Lee. "American Indian Thought and Identity in American Fiction." *Coyote*. Ed. B. Schöler. Århus: Seklos, 1984. 35–39.

Secondary Sources

Béranger, Elisabeth. "Anna Lee Walters Nos Donne de Bonnes des Pawnees dans *The Sun Is Not Merciful*." *Annales du CRAA* 13 (1988).

Biagiotti, Cinzia. "Orchestrazione di una Morte." Afterword to James Welch, *La morte di Jim Loney [The Death of Jim Loney]*, trans. and ed. C. Biagiotti. Collana Indianoamericana. Milan: La Salamandra, 1989. 193–224.

Cellard, Bernadette Rigal. "Aliénation et Initiation Mystique dans *Winter in the Blood* de James Welch." *Le Facteur Religieux en Amerique* 7 (1986): 133–59.

———. "La Langage des Lieux dans *The Death of Jim Loney*." *Annales du CRAA* (1987): 61–77.

———. "Femme et Araignée dans *The Woman Who Owned the Shadows* de Paula Gunn Allen." *Annales du CRAA* 13 (1988): 33–42.

———. "Noanabozho contre Chronos on les Ambiguités de l'Histoire Chez Vizenor." *Annales du CRAA* (forthcoming).

Clute, John. "Janus Faced Fables." *Times Literary Supplement*, October 28–November 3, 1988. 1211. (Review of Louise Erdrich's *Tracks*.)

Coltelli, Laura. "Lo Storytelling de Leslie Marmon Silko." Introduction to Leslie Marmon Silko, *Raccontare [Storyteller]*, trans. and ed. L. Coltelli. Collana Indianoamericana. Milan: La Salamandra, 1983. 11–47.

———. "Reenacting Myths and Stories: Tradition and Renewal in *Ceremony*." Ed. Laura Coltelli. *Native American Literatures*. Forum I. Pisa, 1989. 173–83.

———. *Winged Words: American Indian Writers Speak*. Lincoln: U of Nebraska P, 1990.

———. "Linguaggio, immaginazione e memoria." Afterword to N. Scott Momaday, *I nomi [The Names]*, trans. and ed. L. Coltelli. Collana Indianoamericana. Milan: La Salamandra (forthcoming).

———, guest ed. "Native American Literature 1968–1988. A Bibliographical Evaluation." Special Issue of *Storia Nord Americana* (1990).

D'Amico, Maria Vittoria. "*Wordarrows* di Gerald Vizenor: le antiche frecce di un nuovo indiano." Afterword to Gerald Vizenor, *Parolefrecce*. Collana Indianoamericana. Milan: La Salamandra (forthcoming).

Feest, Christian F. "Indians and Europe." Editor's Postscript in Christian Feest, ed., *Indians and Europe: An Interdisciplinary Collection of Essays*. Aachen: Ed. Herodot, 1987. 609–20.

Giordano, Fedora. "Translating the Sacred: The Poet and the Shaman." *North American Indian Studies*. Ed. Pieter Hovens. Göttingen: Ed. Herodot, 1981. 109–21.

———. "Jaime de Angulo: La parola e Il Potere." *L'esotismo nella Letteratura Americana*. Ed. Elémire Zolla. Rome: Lucarini, 1982. 3: 3–117.

———. "Jaime de Angulo: A European Among the Californian Indians." *In Their Own Words* 3 (1986): 117–34.

———. "North American Indians in Italian (1950–1981). A Bibliography of Books." *Indians and Europe*. Ed. Christian F. Feest. Aachen: Ed. Herodot, 1987. 491–503.

———. *Etnopoetica, Le avanguardie Americane e la Tradizione Orale Indiana*. Rome: Bulzoni, 1989.

Gradoli, Marina. *"The Surrounded* di D'Arcy McNickle: alle origini del Rinascimento Indiano Americano." Afterword to D'Arcy McNickle, *L'Accerchiamento*, trans. Giancarlo Baccelli, ed. Marina Gradoli. Collana Indianoamericana. Milan: La Salamandra (forthcoming).

Horelitz, Jean Hanff. "Rough-Country Magic." Review of Louise Erdrich's *The Beet Queen*. *Times Literary Supplement*, February 27, 1987. 206.

Hornisch, Inge. "Ursprünge indianischer Dichtung." *Magazine für Amerikanistik* 10.4 (1986): 58–64; illus.

———. "Vom Ursprung indianischer Dichtung und neuer indianischer Poesie." *Americana* 8.3 (1988): 23–30.

Hovens, Pieter. "Introduction: A Short History of European Contributions to North American Indian Studies." *North American Indian Studies*. Ed. Pieter Hovens. European Contributions. Göttingen: Ed. Herodot, 1981. 3–10.

Hunter, Carol. "An Interview with Wendy Rose." *Coyote*. Ed. B. Schöler. Århus: Seklos, 1984. 40–56.

Lincoln, Kenneth. "Common Walls: The Poetry of Simon Ortiz." *Coyote*. Ed. B. Schöler. Århus: Seklos, 1984. 79–94.

Ludovici, Paola. "Un Cavallo Bianco, una Mucca e un Ginocchio Ferito." Afterword to James Welch, *Inverno nel Sangue [Winter in the Blood]*, trans. G. Mariani and P. Ludovici; ed. P. Ludovici. Savelli, 1978. 151–57.

———. "La Cerimonia dell'Oblio." Introduction to Leslie Marmon Silko, *Cerimonia [Ceremony]*, trans. and ed. P. Ludovici. Rome: Ed. Riuniti, 1981. 7–12.

———. "Narrativa Indiana Contemporanea." *Novecento Americano*. Ed. Elémire Zolla. Rome: Ed. Lucarini, 1981. 663–93.

Lumer, Helga. "Die Produktivitär indianischer Mythen bei dem Chippewa-Autor Gerald Vizenor." *Zeitschrift für Anglistik und Amerikanistik*. 34.1 (1986): 60–64.

Lutz, Hartmut. *Indianer und Native Americans. Zur sozial- und literaturhistorischen Vermittlung eines Stereotyps*. Hildesheim: Georg Olms, 1985.

Manske, Eva. "Nachwort." Afterword to N. Scott Momaday, *Haus aus Dämmeruna [House Made of Dawn]*. Leipzig: Philipp Reclam jun., 1988. 202–21.

Mariani, Giorgio. "Art Made of Dawn: An Introduction to Contemporary Native American Poetry." In P. Hovens, ed., *North American Indian Studies* 2 (1984): 174–89.

Meli, Franco. "Dove stai andando?" Introduction to N. Scott Momaday, *Casa fatta di alba [House Made of Dawn]*, trans. L. Willis and F. Meli; ed. F. Meli. Milan: Guanda, 1979. 7–20.

———. "Charles A. Eastman: Parabola of Integration." In P. Hovens, ed., *North American Indian Studies* 2 (1984): 162–73.

Murray, David. *Modern Indians.* South Shields, England: BAAS Pamphlets. In *American Studies* (1982).

Peyer, Bernd C. "A Bibliography of Native American Prose Prior to the 20th Century." *Wassaja/The Indian Historian* 13.3: 3–25.

———. "Reconsidering Native American Fiction." *Amerikastudien/American Studies* 24.2 (1979): 64–274.

———. "Autobiographical Works Written by Native Americans." *Amerikastudien/American Studies* 6.3/4 (1981): 386–402.

———. "The Importance of Native American Authors." *American Indian Culture and Research Journal* 5.3 (1981): 1–12.

———. *The Elders Wrote: An Anthology of Early Prose by North American Indians 1768–1931.* Beiträge zur Kulturanthropologie. Berlin: Dietrich Reimer Verlag, 1982.

———. "Die englisch-sprachige Literatur der Indianer Nordamerikas." *Native Americans.* Ed. D. Herms and H. Lutz. Berlin, 1985. 95–107.

Prampolini, Gaetano. "Per *House Made of Dawn.*" (December 1980): 30–46.

———. "Molti viaggi in uno *The Way to Rainy Mountain* e l'opera di N. Scott Momaday." Afterword to N. Scott Momaday, *Il Viaggio a Rainy Mountain*, trans. and ed. G. Prampolini. Collana Indianoamericana. Milan: La Salamandra, 1989. 111–66.

Ruppert, James. "The Poetic Language of Ray Young Bear." In *Coyote.* Ed. B. Schöler. Århus: Seklos, 1984. 24–133.

Schöler, Bo, ed. "Images and Counter-Images: Ohiyesa, Standing Bear and American Literature." *American Indian Culture and Research Journal* 5.2: 37–62.

———. "Indianerbilleder. Familieportraet eller skraemmebillede." *Stofskifte* 6.9 (1983): 79–100.

———. "Trickster and Storyteller. The Sacred Memories and True Tales of Gerald Vizenor." *Coyote.* Ed. B. Schöler. Århus: Seklos, 1984. 34–146.

———. "Mythic Realism in Native American Literature." *American Studies in Scandinavia* 17.2 (1985).

———. Postscript (in Danish). In *Windornen: Abenakiindianernes fortaeuinger om Gluskabi.* [The Wind Eagle: Abenaki Stories About Gluskabi]. (Stories as told by Joseph Bruchac, trans. and retold by B. Schöler, illus. by Kahiones.) Århus. CDR Forlag (1985).

———. "To Live and to Notice It: An Introduction to Native American Studies in Denmark." *Engelsk Meddelelser* 32 (Special issue). 110 pp. Copenhagen, 1985.

———. ". . . I Would Save the Cat. An Interview with Ralph Salisbury." *American Studies in Scandinavia* 17.1 (1985): 27–34.

———. "Interpretive Communities and the Representation of Contemporary Native American Life in Literature." *European Review of Native American Studies* 1.2 (1987): 7–30.

Schubnell, Matthias. "Frozen Suns and Angry Bears: An Interpretation of Leslie Marmon Silko's 'Storyteller.'" *European Review of Native American Studies* 1.2 (1987): 21–25.

Steenhoven, G. Van. "Gedachten over Gedichten. I" [Thoughts on Poems—I]. *De Kiva plain* 23.4 (1986): 60–63. (Thoughts based on Bruchac's *Songs from This Earth on Turtle's Back.*)

———. "Gedachten over Gedichten. 2" [Thoughts on Poems—2]. *De Kiva* 25.5 (1986): 86–90. (On the Grandmother motif in Bruchac's *Songs from This Earth on Turtle's Back.*)

Stout, Mary. "Zitkala-Sa: The Literature of Politics." *Coyote.* Ed. B. Schöler. Århus: Seklos, 1984. 70–78.

Taylor, Linda. "On and Off Reservation. Review of Louise Erdrich's *Love Medicine.*" *Times Literary Supplement*, February 25, 1985, 196.

Vangen, Kate Shanley. "The Devil's Domain: Leslie Silko's *Storyteller.*" *Coyote.* Ed. B. Schöler. Århus: Seklos, 1984. 116–23.

Vaschenko, Alexander. *Indieitsev Severnoi Ameriki mifologiia* [North American Indian Mythology]. *Mify narodov mira* [Myths of the Peoples in the World]. *Moskva Sovietskaia Entisiklopediia,* 2 vols. (1980): 1–512.

———. "Indieiskaia territoriia v literaturie SShA" [Indian Territory in the Literature of the U.S.A.]. *Problemy stanovlieniia amerikanoskoi literatury* [The Problems of the Formation of American Literatures]. Moskow: Ed. Nauka, 1981.

———. "Istochnikovedchieskiie problemy eposa indieitsev SShA" [Some Textual Problems of the North American Indian Epics]; *Folklor: Poetika i traditsii* [Folklore: Poetics and Tradition]. Moskow: Ed. Nauka, 1982. (Walam Olum and the Great League epic cycle.)

———. "Mir, sotvorenyi slovom" [The World, a Creation of the Word]. *Ia sviazan dobrom s zemlici [I Stand in Good Relation to the Earth].* Ed. A. Vaschenko. Moscow: Raduga, 1983. 5–15. (Introduction to a reader of contemporary Native American literature, including translations by the editor of works of N. Scott Momaday, Duane Niatum, James Welch, Gerald Vizenor, Simon Ortiz, Leslie Silko, Ray Young Bear, Hyemeyohsts Storm, Thomas Sanchez, and Vine Deloria, Jr.)

———. "Problemy stnicheskikh literatur" [On the Problem of "Ethnic Literatures"]. *Literatura SShA 70–Kh godov XXv* [U.S. Literature in the 1970s]. Moscow: Ed. Nauka, 1983.

———. "Sovremennyi indieitskii pistatel SShA" [Contemporary Indian Writing in the U.S.A.]. *Istoricheskie Sudby.* Ed. V. Tishkov. Moscow, 1985. 349–57.

———. "Some Russian Responses to North American Indian Cultures." *Indians and Europe: An Interdisciplinary Collection of Essays.* Ed. Christian F. Feest. Aachen: Ed. Herodot, 1987. 307–20.

———. *Serdtsye v ritme s prirodoi [In Nature's Heartbeat: Literature by Native Americans and Native Siberians].* 2 vols. Moscow: Laitim, 1992.

Walters, Anna Lee. "American Indian Thought and Identity in American Fiction." *Coyote.* Ed. B. Schöler. Århus: Seklos, 1984. 35–39.

Zolla, Elemire. "Antropologia Poetica Mary Austin, Jane Belo, Maya Dei." *Novecento Americano* 3. Ed. E. Zolla. Rome: Lucarini, 1981. 711–23.

———. "The Teaching of Carlos Castaneda." *North American Indian Studies.* Ed. Pieter Hovens. Göttingen: Ed. Herodot, 1981. 247–53.

———. *I letterati e lo sciamano.* Milan: Bompiani, 1986; New York: Harcourt, 1973. Venice: Marsilio, 1989 (rev. and updated ed.).

Teaching Indian Literature

An essay on "Teaching Indian Literature" should cover practically everything that an essay entitled "Teaching Literature" would, since Native American literature embraces all the major forms of expression typically, or even untypically, called Literature: performed oral literature, song, chant, and narrative, ceremonial or not; various forms of nonfictional prose, including histories, essays, and autobiography; fiction; poetry; and drama. To complicate matters, all these forms of literary expression have been communicated in both English and tribal languages, and some of the oral literatures have the historical depth of thousands of years. Despite these almost overwhelming diversities, there are several common challenges that teachers face when presenting Indian literature. I will focus on four: How much, if any, background material should be introduced? How crucial are questions of translation and transformation? What ethical responsibilities accompany the teaching of Indian literature? How can Native American texts be effectively and responsibly introduced into literary survey courses?

The background issue grows out of two interrelated assumptions: (1) American Indian literature is *unfamiliar* to most students; hence, they need cultural, historical, and biographical contexts to help them to understand the texts, and (2) Indian literature is *different* from most types of literature previously encountered by students. To avoid misreadings, which at worst could lead to old or new forms of racism, teachers should offer contexts that define the differences. These assumptions have been developed into convincing arguments voiced by leading scholars in the field (e.g., Dorris 1979; Evers 1975; Ramsey 1979). Nevertheless, as both Ballinger and Beidler have cautioned, too much emphasis on background and too little on the text can turn exciting artistic creations into dull artifacts. One approach to this dilemma is to first allow the students to enjoy the assignment and to

347

raise questions. In response to these questions, instructors should find opportunities to discuss the *functions* of the text in relevant tribal and nontribal contexts and the *Native American aesthetics* or combinations of Native and Euroamerican aesthetics that inform the text and help shape audience response.

The importance of knowing the original functions of a Native American text is obvious when that text is a tribal story, song, or ceremony. For example, students might initially be confused by the length, the frequency of repetition, and the references to unfamiliar deities in the Navajo Nightway, a nine-day curing ceremony. Much of their confusion can be minimized if the teacher explains that the functions of the ceremony extend beyond the healing of a particular individual or individuals to an attempt to restore harmony in the universe; that the healing calls for reenacting the exploits of Navajo Holy Beings who, when suffering afflictions similar to the patient's, solved their problems; and that the Navajo view of healing aims at the maintenance or reestablishment of *h'ozh'o*, a concept combining beauty, harmony, balance, and order (see Witherspoon in Evers's *South Corner*). Students can also "see" the functions by watching excerpts from a performance of the Nightway in the BBC movie *Navajo* (1972) or by watching Andrew Natonabah sing and explain one Nightway song in the "By This Song I Walk" videotape from the *Words and Place* series (Evers 1981).

When studying various forms of autobiography, students can benefit from an awareness of the assumptions about functions that shaped the texts. To illustrate, questions about the lack of descriptions of childhood in coup tales from oral Plains cultures or about the dominant position of childhood visions in an as-told-to autobiography like *Black Elk Speaks* (1931) could be handled by providing definitions of the types of masculine, public identities the coup tales were supposed to create and with descriptions of crucial functions of visionary experiences for an Oglala Sioux *wicasha wakan* (holy man). (See Brumble in Roemer's *Approaches*; and Castro 1983:84–85.)

Even a student's reading of a novel can be enhanced by an awareness of authorial statements about function. Louise Erdrich claims that she is driven by a question of survival: Why, after centuries of genocide, has she been one of the Indians "picked" to survive? Obviously, she can never answer the question, but that question drives her with a sense of commitment to tell and retell her people's stories (*Interview*). Her statements imply a concept of the function of literature that can help students to understand Erdrich's fiction, as well as many of the works of N. Scott Momaday, Leslie Silko, James Welch, Gerald Vizenor, Michael Dorris, and other contemporary Native American novelists and poets.

As students work more closely with specific elements of a text, it may be necessary to share with them different, though not unrelated, types of background context: the aesthetic concepts and literary conventions informing the literature. Students conditioned by the aesthetic criteria of formalism can certainly find delight in many works of poetry, fiction, and nonfiction written by Indians. They may not, however, know what "to make out of" traditional oral literatures. Background about specific conventions will help to answer questions about, for instance, introductory and closing formulas (e.g., Tedlock 1972:xxvii–xxviii), repetition (e.g., Evers and Molina 1988:36), and characterization, notably the unpredictable alterations between heroic and idiotic acts of trickster figures. Even more significant is an understanding that in many forms of sacred ceremonialism, conservation, not innovation, is celebrated. The traditional Navajos, for example, assume that the universe is a dangerous place susceptible to unpredictable eruptions of imbalance. Ceremonies counter these dire possibilities and realities with the re-creation, in powerful words, of a familiar, orderly, and beautiful universe that reaffirms the Navajo way and compels reality to become harmonious. Understanding this traditional aesthetic can not only help students to comprehend ceremonial literature, it can also help them to comprehend the references to ceremonialism in modern works of poetry and fiction. The implications of the tensions surrounding Betonie's experiments with Navajo ceremonialism in Silko's *Ceremony* (1977) become, for example, more accessible to students acquainted with traditional Navajo aesthetics.

How instructors deal with translation/transformation issues is just as important as how they respond to questions about background contexts. When teaching traditional tribal literatures, instructors should, whenever possible, use bilingual texts that exhibit sensitivity to linguistic, performance, and cultural contexts—for instance, translations such as Tedlock's Zuni stories (1972), translations in the Evers et al. anthology *The South Corner of Time* (1980), or the performances of songs and stories in the video series *Words and Place* (Evers 1981).

Instructors who teach nonfiction, especially as-told-to autobiographies, and even works composed in English still should be concerned about how non-Indian editors and contemporary Indian authors "translate" tribal materials for non-Indian audiences. A rearrangement of interviews into a chronological order and several key additions and deletions enabled John G. Neihardt to preserve the spirit of Black Elk's message while communicating it to a general reading audience (see Castro 1983:79–97). In *The Way to Rainy Mountain* (1969), N. Scott Momaday does not include mention of the Kiowa trickster figure Saynday in his collection of tribal and family stories, but he does add a historical commentary and a personal memory to each story. The omission makes the book more unified. Saynday would introduce moods potentially disruptive to the prevailing lyric and meditative tones of the book. The additions render the Kiowa stories more accessible to non-Kiowas in both intellectual and emotional ways. Neihardt and Momaday are only two examples of important non-Indian and Indian editors, essayists, novelists, and poets who have struggled to create "valid" Indian literature communicable to non-Indian audiences. Teachers should make their students aware of these struggles, especially the successful literary acts of transformation.

The ethics of teaching Indian literature constitute one of the instructors' most difficult areas of struggle. In this brief essay, I certainly cannot do justice to such a complex topic, but at least I can draw attention to two crucial issues. First, when teachers present sacred ceremonial literature or origin narratives, they should treat them with a respect appropriate to the discussion of the liturgical literatures and creation accounts of Christianity, Judaism, Hinduism, Buddhism, and other great world religions. An instructor who has made conscientious attempts to introduce functional and aesthetic backgrounds and has obtained a sophisticated translation or video performance will probably achieve this sensitivity. Second, when teaching any type of Native American literature, instructors should be careful not to reinforce old or create new stereotypes. After reading such novels as Momaday's *House Made of Dawn* (1968) or Silko's *Ceremony* (1977), Erdrich's *Love Medicine* (1984), James Welch's *Winter in the Blood* (1974) or *Jim Loney* (1979), careless readers might conclude that the drunken Indian stereotype was true. Such readers might also read the Hollywood Plains warrior stereotype into *Black Elk Speaks* (1932) or Welch's *Fools Crow* (1986). It is the responsibility of the teacher to help these students to read carefully enough to see how the best Indian authors undercut old stereotypes (see Bo Schöler's essay "Young and Restless"). Instructors should also avoid creating new stereotypes, notably the counterimage of the stoic savage, the image of the singing Indian—the notion that within the heart of every real Indian lies a ceremonial chant, an epic tale, a lyric poem, a novel, or a stinging satirical essay. Enthusiastic English teachers may be especially tempted to propagate this stereotype. Of course, the best way to minimize the possibility of teaching stereotypes or of mishandling sacred literatures is to invite Native American scholars, creative writers, or religious or political leaders to speak to the students.

So far, I have emphasized the challenges and responsibilities of exposing students to important background contexts (without reducing the works to artifacts), of raising awareness about translation and transformation, and of guarding against mishandling sacred texts and perpetuating and creating stereotypes. These emphases may make the teaching of Native American literature seem particularly difficult, even burdensome, particularly for instructors new to the field. I would like to counter that impression by concluding on two positive notes.

Since the early 1970s, numerous articles and several books have appeared directed at encouraging the teaching of Indian literature. Especially useful for teachers are A. LaVonne Brown Ruoff's concise twenty-one-page overview "American Indian Literatures" (1986), which is followed by her excellent *American Indian Literatures: An Introduction and Selected Bibliography* (1990). Other resources include Paula Gunn Allen's extensive collection of essays and course descriptions, *Studies in American Indian Literature* (1983); Andrew Wiget's *Native American Literature* (1985); Kenneth M. Roemer's *Approaches to Teaching Momaday's "The Way to Rainy Mountain"* (1988), which includes background material and essays by instructors who have found Momaday's book to be especially appropriate for writing curricula and a variety of surveys and specialized courses; and the special issue of *Studies in American Indian Literatures* devoted to teaching (1991). Paul Lauter's *Reconstructing American Literature* (1983) also contains course descriptions that include Indian literature, important elements of which were included in the new *Heath Anthology of American Literature.*

Kenneth M. Roemer
University of Texas—Arlington

BIBLIOGRAPHY

Allen, Paula Gunn, ed. *Studies in American Indian Literature: Critical Essay and Course Designs*. New York: MLA, 1983.

The American Experience. Englewood Cliffs: Prentice Hall, 1989.

American Literature: A Prentice Hall Anthology. Vol. 2. Ed. Emory Elliott et al. Englewood Cliffs: Prentice Hall, 1991.

Ballinger, Franchot. "A Matter of Emphasis: Teaching the 'Literature' in Native American Literature Courses." *American Indian Culture and Research Journal* 8.2 (1984): 1–12.

Baym, Nina. "The Heuristic Powers of Indian Literatures: What Native Authorship Does to Mainstream Texts." *Studies in American Indian Literatures*. 2nd Series. 3.2 (1991): 8–21.

———, et al. *The Norton Anthology of American Literature*. 3rd ed. New York: Norton, 1989.

Beidler, Peter G. Review of *Studies in American Indian Literature*, ed. Paula Gunn Allen. *American Indian Quarterly* 9 (1985): 468–71.

Castro, Michael. *Interpreting the Indian: Twentieth-Century Poets and the Native American*. Albuquerque: U of New Mexico P, 1983.

Dorris, Michael. "Native American Literature in Ethnohistorical Context." *College English* 41 (1979): 1147–62.

Erdrich, Louise. *Love Medicine*. New York: Holt, 1984.

———. *Louise Erdrich: Interview with Kay Bonetti*. Audiotape. American Audio Prose Library, No. 6022, 1985.

Evers, Larry. "Native American Oral Literatures in the College English Classroom: An Omaha Example." *College English* 36 (1975): 649–62.

———. *Words and Place: Native Literature from the American Southwest*. New York: Clearwater, 1981. 8 videocassettes.

———, and Felipe S. Molina. "Coyote Songs." *Dispatch* 6.2 (1988): 34–41.

Evers, Larry, et al., eds. *The South Corner of Time: Hopi, Navajo, Papago, and Yaqui Tribal Literature*. Tucson: U of Arizona P, 1980.

Lauter, Paul, ed. *Reconstructing American Literature: Courses, Syllabi, Issues*. Old Westbury, NY: Feminist Press, 1983.

————, et al., eds. *The Heath Anthology of American Literature*. Lexington, MA: Heath, 1990.

McQuade, Donald, et al., eds. *The Harper American Literature*. New York: Harper & Row, 1987.

Momaday, N. Scott. *House Made of Dawn*. New York: Harper & Row, 1968.

————. *The Way to Rainy Mountain*. Albuquerque: U of New Mexico P, 1969.

Navajo: The Fight for Survival. BBC/Time-Life Film, 1972. 16mm.

Neihardt, John G., ed. *Black Elk Speaks. . . .* New York: Morrow, 1932.

Ramsey, Jarold. "The Teacher of Modern American Indian Writing as Ethnographer and Critic." *College English* 41 (1979): 163–69.

Roemer, Kenneth M. *Approaches to Teaching Momaday's "The Way to Rainy Mountain."* New York: MLA, 1988.

Ruoff, A. LaVonne. "American Indian Literatures: Introduction and Bibliography." *American Studies International* 24.2 (1986): 2–52.

————. *American Indian Literatures: An Introduction and Selected Bibliography*. New York: MLA, 1990.

Schöler, Bo. "Young and Restless: The Treatment of a Statistical Phenomenon in Contemporary Native American Fiction." *Native American Literatures*. Ed. Laura Coltelli. Pisa: Servizio, 1989.

Silko, Leslie Marmon. *Ceremony*. New York: Viking, 1977.

Studies in American Indian Literatures. Ser. 2. 3.2 (1991). Special Issue.

Tedlock, Dennis. *Finding the Center: Narrative Poetry of the Zuni Indians*. New York: Dial, 1972.

Welch, James. *Winter in the Blood*. New York: Harper, 1974.

————. *The Death of Jim Loney*. New York: Harper, 1979.

————. *Fools Crow*. New York: Viking, 1986.

Wiget, Andrew. *Native American Literature*. Boston: Twayne, 1985.

Native Literature of Canada

When we discuss Canadian literature and Native people, we generally talk about the use that Canadian writers have made of Native people and Native culture, and we spend most of our critical energy drawing lines from writers such as Duncan Campbell Scott, Isabella Valancy Crawford, and E. J. Pratt to more contemporary literary figures such as Howard O'Hagan, Robert Kroetsch, Sharon Pollock, W. O. Mitchell, W. P. Kinsella, and Rudy Wiebe. We do so because the literary Indian is a rather visible feature of Canadian literature. Indeed, the list of Canadian authors who have *not* made use of the Native is almost easier to compile than the list of those who have.

Canadian Native literature (literature produced by aboriginal people in Canada), on the other hand, does not enjoy the same sort of visibility, and instead of drawing connecting lines between authors (and their works), we tend to draw lines that divide. The most obvious division we make is separating oral literature from written literature. We have the body of oral literature that was collected by a small army of anthropologists, missionaries, ethnographers, folklorists, linguists, and the like, and we have the body of written literature that ranges from autobiographies, sermons, histories, diaries, and journals to the more contemporary offerings of poetry, prose, and drama, and while we understand that Native storytellers and Native writers have produced both, we treat the oral and the written as two separate literary traditions. As well, we suggest by this division that the oral and the written are mutually self-exclusive, the oral (pure and authentic) predating the arrival of the European but dying out sometime in the nineteenth century and the written (corrupt and specious) appearing in the twentieth century primarily as a consequence of providing the contemporary descendants of proper Indians with an education. All of this overlooks the continuing presence of traditional Native communities of contemporary Native people and the symbiotic relationship that exists between the spoken and the written word, a relationship that recognizes oral literature as a continuing, developing, changing tradition, and written literature as its modern complement and companion. In the contemporary world, our main access to literature is through books or plays or movies, and unless we are a part of those more traditional communities, we see little of the oral. What we see is the written, lying, as it does on the surface, a tip, suggesting, as it should, a much larger body just below.

Our concern here is with the tip, that portion of what we call Native literature that is written (and, in particular, that portion written in English). We can begin our discussion with George Copway (Ojibway; 1818–1869), who in 1847 published his autobiography, *The Life, History, and Travels of Kah-ge-ga-gah-bowh, a Young Indian Chief of the Ojebwa Nation, a Convert to the Christian Faith, and a Missionary to His People for Twelve Years; With a Sketch of the Present State of the Ojebwa Nation, in Regard to Christianity and Their Future Prospects. Also an Appeal; With All the Names of the Chiefs Now Living, Who Have Been Christianized, and the Missionaries Now Laboring Among Them. Written by Himself,* a title which tends to give away the plot of the book. Copway's autobiography is generally considered to be the first book in English by a Canadian Native. The life story of an Indian, even a young one (Copway was twenty-nine when he wrote his autobiography), proved to be a very popular item, and by the end of 1848, the book had gone through seven printings. Copway was more than equal to the task that fame thrust upon him, and for years he was one of the most visible Indians in North America. He corresponded with Washington Irving, William Cullen Bryant, and James Fenimore Cooper, and within two years of the publication of his autobiography, he was visiting with such luminaries as Francis Parkman and Henry Wadsworth Longfellow.

In addition to *The Life, History, and Travels of Kah-ge-ga-gah-bowh,* Copway also wrote *The Traditional History and Characteristic Sketches of the Ojibway Nation* (1850), generally conceded to be the first tribal history in English by a North American Indian; *The Ojibway Conquest: A Tale of the Northeast* (1850), a poem about the last major battle between the Ojibway and the Sioux, attributed to him, though he may not have written it; and *Running Sketches of Men and Places in England, France, Germany, Belgium and Scotland* (1851), a narrative of Copway's extensive international travels.

Contemporary with Copway were other Native writers such as Peter Jones (Ojibway; 1802–1856), Peter Jacobs (Ojibway; 1807–1890), Henry Budd (Cree; 1810–1875), George Henry (Ojibway; b. 1810), Francis Assikinack (Odawa; 1824–1863), Peter Dooyenate Clark (Wyandot), Louis Jackson (Mohawk; b. 1843), John Brant Sero (Mohawk; b. 1867), Oronhyatekha (Dr. Peter Martin, Mohawk; 1841–1907), and Lydia Campbell (Inuit; b. 1818). Peter Jones was a leading Methodist preacher of the times and a friend to George Copway (he performed the wedding ceremony of Copway and Copway's wife, Elizabeth Howell). Jones's autobiography, *Life and Journals of Kah-He-Wa-Quo-Na-By, Wesleyan Minister* (1860), his *History of the Ojibway Indians with Special Reference to Their Conversion to Christianity* (1861), and his *A Collection of Ojibway and English Hymns* (1877) were not published until after his death. Lydia Campbell's *Sketches of Labrador Life* (1894) described Inuit life at the turn of the century and was the first autobiography we know of by an Inuit.

Early work by Native writers was, in the main, limited to autobiography, histories, diaries, and journals. While Copway, Jones, and Campbell have enjoyed a modicum of contemporary interest (Copway's autobiography was reprinted in 1970, while his *Traditional History and Characteristic Sketches of the Ojibway Nation* was reprinted in 1972; Jones was the subject of a 1987 biography by Donald Smith; and Campbell's *Sketches* was reprinted by Them Days in 1980), most of the other Native writers of this period have remained unknown. Peter Jacobs and Henry Budd published their journals and diaries, which dealt primarily with their missionary work. Jacobs's *Journal of the Reverend Peter Jacobs, Indian Wesleyan Missionary from Rice Lake to the Hudson's Bay Territory, and Returning. Commencing May 1852. With a brief account of his life and a short history of the Wesleyan Mission in that country* (1855) was a first-person account of Jacobs's trip from Toronto to York Factory (along with a rather nasty attack on Indian religion and values), while Budd's *The Diary of The Reverend Henry Budd 1870–1875* was an account of Budd's life, particularly his years as an Anglican missionary in Rupert's Land.

Peter Dooyenate Clark, Louis Jackson, and Oronhyatekha all wrote histories. Clark's *Origin and Traditional History of the Wyandotts, and Sketches of Other Indian Tribes of North America* (1870) dealt, in large part, with historical characters and events. Louis Jackson's *Our Caughawagas in Egypt: A Narrative of What Was Seen and Accomplished by the Contingent of North American Voyageurs Who Led the British Boat Expedition for the Relief of Khartoum up the Cataracts of the Nile* (1885) described the 1884–85 Nile expedition to the Sudan, part of whose complement consisted of eighty-six Indians, fifty-two from Caughnawaga. While Clark and Jackson wrote histories that dealt with Indians, Oronhyatekha went slightly further afield and wrote the *History of the Independent Order of Foresters*, an organization of which he was the Supreme Chief Ranger from 1881 to 1907.

Other Native writers such as George Henry, Francis Assikinack, and John Brant Sero produced a variety of pamphlets and articles. George Henry, who was in charge of a troupe of Ojibway dancers, wrote two pamphlets on their travels in Europe and the impressions that the troupe formed of Europeans in the various countries they visited. His *Remarks Concerning the Ojibway Indians, by One of Themselves, Called Maungwudaus, Who Has Been Travelling in England, France, Belgium, Ireland, and Scotland*

(1847) and *An Account of the Chippewa Indians, Who Have Been Travelling among the Whites in the United States, England, Ireland, Scotland, France and Belgium* (1848) were among the first written reactions to whites by Native people. Francis Assikinack wrote several articles for the *Canadian Journal* in 1868: "Legends and Traditions of the Odahwah Indians," "The Odahwah Indian Language," and "Social and Warlike Customs of the Odahwah Indians." Between 1899 and 1911, John Brant Sero authored a series of articles—"Some Descendants of Joseph Brant," "A Memorial for Brant," "The Six Nations Indians in the Province of Ontario, Canada," "Dekanawideh: The Law-Giver of the Caniengahakas," "Indian Rights Association After Government Scalp," "View of a Mohawk Indian," and "O-no-dah"—for publications such as *Ontario Historical Papers and Records, Wilshire's Magazine,* the *Journal of American Folklore,* and the *Globe and Mail.* A man of varied interests and tastes, he translated "God Save the King" into Mohawk, and while he was in Folkestone, England, in 1903, he entered and placed third in a male beauty contest.

Another interesting and certainly more famous writer of the period, though not with the eclectic range of Assikinack or Sero, was Louis Riel (Metis; 1844–1885). Riel is generally known for his political and military activism on behalf of the Metis in Manitoba, but he was also a poet whose *Poésies religieuses et politiques* was published in 1886. Riel's collected writings, which consist, to a great extent, of letters, have been published in a five-volume set (1985). The third volume of the set, edited by Glen Campbell, contains all of Riel's known poetry.

Many of the early examples of Native writing were published by missionary societies, while the works of these and other Native writers also appeared in short-lived journals such as *Petabun* (1861–62), the *Algoma Missionary News and Shingwauk Journal* (1877–84), *Na-Na-Kwa* (1898–1903), *The Canadian Indian* (1890–91), and a journal called *The Indian,* which evidently was the first journal in Canada edited by an Indian for Indians. It was the work of Peter Edmund Jones, the son of Peter Jones, and ran for twenty-four issues (1885–86).

Although we began this discussion of early Native writers with George Copway and ended it (more or less) with Louis Riel, that is not exactly accurate. While Copway is considered to be the first Canadian Indian to have published a book in English, John Richardson (Ottawa; 1796–1852) predates Copway by at least fifteen years. Richardson was born in Upper Canada in 1796 and during his lifetime wrote poetry, newspaper articles, travel accounts, and a series of sometimes lurid, sometimes sentimental, almost always gothic novels which included *Wacousta; or, The Prophecy* (1832), *The Canadian Brothers; or, The Prophecy Fulfilled* (1840), *The Monk Knight of St. John: A Tale of the Crusades* (1850), *Hardscrabble; or, The Fall of Chicago* (1851), and *Wau-Nan-Gee; or, The Massacre at Chicago* (1852), among others; the most famous of which was *Wacousta.*

Richardson was part Indian, Ottawa on his mother's side. While he did not go out of his way to make this information known, it was a fact of which his contemporaries were aware. Ironically, though many of his novels deal with Indians, the Indians in Richardson's works are generally cast as standard gothic villains poised to wreak Jacobean mayhem on sentimentally drawn whites. Of these early Native writers, Richardson is probably the most familiar to students of early Canadian literature. A number of his works have been reprinted and are used in classrooms, while selected pieces are traditionally included as part of standard anthologies.

Richardson is normally not included in a discussion of Native writers, probably because he was a mixed-blood, arguably because he did not write anything that we might want to call "Native," and certainly because he did not display his Indianness in the ways that a writer such as E. Pauline Johnson chose to display her work and her life.

While John Richardson might properly begin a discussion of the early period of Native literature in Canada, E. Pauline Johnson (Mohawk; 1861–1913) most certainly represents its proper end. In terms of reputation, Johnson is one of Canada's best-known Native writers. Her two volumes of poetry, *The White Wampum* (1895) and *Canadian Born* (1903); a collection of Indian legends and stories, *Legends of Vancouver* (1911); and her two collections of short stories, *The Shagganappi* (1913) and *The Moccasin Maker* (1913) (both collections published posthumously), all dealt with Native people and her own Indian heritage. She was eminently successful as a reader and a lecturer, traveling across Canada, the United States, and Europe, and, more than any other single person of her time, brought public attention to Native people and to Native culture through the powerful descriptions in her poetry and prose of Native life and the natural world.

Yet for all Johnson's popularity and for the geographical distance she covered on the lecture circuit, she seems to have had little effect on other Native writers of her time. Indeed, after Johnson, there appears to be a gap of some fifty-odd years in which we do not see Natives writing. This is, most probably, an optical illusion. Native people such as Khalserten Sepass (Chilliwack; 1840–1945), Edward Ahenakew (Cree; 1885–1961), Deskaheh (Cayuga; 1873–1925) (whose efforts to secure recognition of Nationhood for Six Nations through the League of Nations took him to Geneva in 1923 as a statesman and a speaker), and Dan Kennedy (Assiniboine; 1877–1973) were making speeches, producing articles, writing poetry and stories during this period. Also, examples of Native autobiography such as Anauta's (Inuit) *Land of the Good Shadows: The Life Story of Anauta, an Eskimo Woman* (1940) and Charles James Nowell's (Kwakiutl; b. 1870) *Smoke from Their Fires: The Life of a Kwakiutl Chief* (1940) continued to find audiences. But as yet, we have not discovered any novels, collections of short stories, volumes of poetry, plays, and the rest. It could be that there is little to find, that most of the writing that Natives did appeared in periodicals, newspapers, and local journals while any major pieces that might have been produced have been lost or misplaced. More likely, however, we simply have not been able to find and identify these works as yet.

Whatever the reasons, Native writers and their work do not become visible again until the 1960s. In the United States, N. Scott Momaday's (Kiowa/Cherokee; 1934–) *House Made of Dawn* (1968) won the Pulitzer Prize, and the following year, Vine Deloria, Jr.'s (Sioux; 1934–) book *Custer Died for Your Sins*, a collection of ironic and humorous essays, received considerable critical and popular acclaim. In Canada, the advent of contemporary Native literature can be marked, in part, by the upsurge of Canadian nationalism that began in the early 1960s in anticipation of the 1967 centennial celebration—a celebration that fostered a renewed pride in being a Canadian and which also focused peripheral attention on Natives—and by the release of a political document, the *1969 White Paper, or, More Properly the Statement of the Government of Canada on Indian Policy*. The *White Paper* was essentially a termination document that called for the federal government to abrogate its legal obligations to Indians through the simple expedient of unilaterally terminating the government's relationship with treaty and status Indians.

The literary reaction to the *1969 White Paper* took at least three forms, the first of which—cultural narratives, memoirs, tribal histories, autobiographies—had little to do with the *White Paper* itself. However, the interest in Indians that nationalism and the *White Paper* created helped to foster an atmosphere in which cultural narratives such as Norval Morriseau's (Ojibway; 1933–) *Legends of My People, the Great Ojibway* (1965), Nuligak's (Inuit; 1895–1966) *I, Nuligak* (1966), and George Clutesi's (Nootka; 1905–1988) *Son of Raven, Son of Deer* (1967) flourished. The same year that the *White Paper* was released, Gray's Publishing released Clutesi's second book, *Potlatch*; Yale University Press published James Sewid's (Kwakiutl; b. 1913) *Guests Never Leave Hungry*; and the National Museum of Canada (Anthropological Series) published Zebedee Nungak and Eugene Arima's *Eskimo Stories*. These were followed by a steady stream of other such books which included John Tetso's (Slavey; 1921?–1964) *Trapping Is My Life* (1964; rpt. 1970), Tom Boulanger's (Cree; b. 1901) *An Indian Remembers: My Life as a Trapper in Northern Manitoba* (1971), Pitseolak (Ashoona)'s (Inuit; 1907?–1983) *Pitseolak: Pictures Out of My Life* (1971), Marty Dunn's (Micmac; 1941–) biography of Duke Redbird, *Red on White* (1971), Henry Pennier's (Metis; 1904–) *Chiefly Indian: The Warm and Witty Story of a British Columbia Halfbreed Logger* (1972), Dan Kennedy's *Recollections of an Assiniboine Chief* (1972), James Redsky's (Ojibway; 1926–) *Great Leader of the Ojibway: Mis-Quona-Queb* (1972), Maria Campbell's (Metis; 1940–) *Halfbreed* (1973), Wilfred Pelletier (Odawa) and Ted Poole's *No Foreign Land: The Biography of a North American Indian* (1973), Jane Willis's (Cree; 1940–) *Geniesh: An*

Indian Girlhood (1973), Alma Greene's (Mohawk) *Tales of the Mohawk* (1975) and *Forbidden Voice: Reflections of a Mohawk Indian* (1971), Peter Pitseolak's (Inuit; 1902–1973) *People from Our Side* (1975) and *Peter Pitseolak's Escape from Death* (1977), Armand Togoona's (Inuit; 1926–) *Shadows* (1975), Peter Erasmus's (Cree; 1833–1931) *Buffalo Days and Nights* (1976), Anthony Apakark Thrasher's (Inuit; 1937–) *Thrasher, Skid Row Eskimo* (1976), Alice French's (Inuit; 1930–) *My Name Is Masak* (1976), Chief John Snow's (Stoney; 1933–) *These Mountains Are Our Sacred Places* (1977), Minnie Aodla Freeman's (Inuit; 1936–) *Life Among the Qallunaat* (1978), Kuskapatchee's (Cree) *Swampy Cree Legends* (1978), Mike Mountain Horse's (Blood; 1888–1964) *My People the Bloods* (1979), Joseph Dion's (Cree; 1888–1960) *My Tribe the Cree* (1979), Norman Eekoomiak's (Inuit; 1948–) *An Arctic Childhood* (1980), Beverly Hungry Wolf's (Blood; 1950–) *The Ways of My Grandmothers* (1980) and a second book written with her husband, *Shadows of the Buffalo: A Family Odyssey Among the Indians* (1983), Basil Johnston's (Ojibway; 1929–) *Tales the Elders Told* (1981) and his *Ojibway Ceremonies* (1982), Kermot Moore's (Nishnabi; 1926–) *Kipawa: Portrayal of a People* (1982), Jean Goodwill (Cree) and Norma Sluman's *John Tootoosis* (1982), Lilly Harris et al., *Enough Is Enough: Aboriginal Women Speak Out* (1987), Alexander Wolfe's (Soto; 1927–) *Earth Elder Stories* (1988; a collection of oral stories in much the same vein as Johnston's *Tales the Elders Told*), Lee Maracle's (Salish/Cree/Metis; 1950–) collection of essays, stories, and poetry, *I Am Woman* (1988), and her biography of a young Indian, *Bobbi Lee: Indian Rebel* (1990), As is the case with *Potlatch* and *Guests Never Leave Hungry*, these works combine autobiography, biography, ethnography, sociology, literature, and history, creating a cultural mosaic of Indian life and thought.

A second form, one directly related to the *White Paper*, consisted of a series of reactions to what Natives rightly perceived as an attack by the government on treaties and the special status tribes that had over the years bought with land cessions and related agreements. The most immediate reaction to the *White Paper* was the Anglican Church of Canada's Bulletin 201, which contained the responses of prominent Native people to the proposed policy and Harold Cardinal's (Cree; 1945–) *The Unjust Society* (1971), the first of a series of books critical of the government's suggestion that termination would prove to be a benefit for Natives by making them equal citizens in Canadian society. Cardinal's argument was countered by William Wuttunee's (Cree) *Ruffled Feathers: Indians in Canadian Society* (1971), which argued in favor of the government's plan. But Wuttunee's book was the exception to the general opposition to the *White Paper*. George Manuel's (Shuswap; 1921–) *The Fourth World: An Indian Reality and Social Change* (1973), Howard Adams's (Metis; 1926–) *Prison of Grass: Canada from the Native Point of View* (1975), Harold Cardinal's second book, *The Rebirth of Canada's Indians* (1977), and Duke Redbird's (Metis,

1939–) *We Are Metis* (1980) continued a decade of criticism of the federal government and its terminationist leanings.

The third form that reaction to the *White Paper* took is what is traditionally thought of as literature. One could argue that the *White Paper* had little to do with the increase in poetry, prose, and drama, but the increase in these genres immediately after its release suggests that the document and its aftermath was a stimulus in much the same way that the publication of *House Made of Dawn* and its winning the Pulitzer Prize appears to have stimulated Native writing in the United States.

Prior to 1969, much of Native literature was confined to local publications—newspapers, journals, and so on—and very little of it reached a provincial market, let alone a national market. It is therefore not surprising that contemporary Native literature initially appeared in anthologies. One of the first of these anthologies was Kent Gooderham's *I Am an Indian* (1969), a collection of short essays, stories, myths, and poems. Many of the stories were anthologized from earlier ethnographic collections, while much of the newer material was somewhat romantic and appears to have been chosen for its effect, though the excerpts from Edith Josie's (Loucheaux; 1925–) columns in the *Whitehorse Star* that describe life in the Indian village of Old Crow on the Porcupine River in the Yukon were engaging for both their style and voice (Josie's columns had been collected and published in 1963 in *Old Crow News: The Best of Edith Josie* and in 1966 in *Here Are the News*). A second anthology was published in 1970. Edited by Waubageshig (Harvey McCue) (Ojibway; 1944–), *The Only Good Indian: Essays by Canadian Indians* contained essays on a variety of social and political topics as well as several poems by Duke Redbird and an essay by Chief Dan George. This was followed by a series of anthologies on Inuit songs and stories: James Houston's *Songs of the Dream People: Chants and Images from the Indians and Eskimos of North America* (1972), Tom Lowenstein's *Eskimo Poems from Canada and Greenland* (1973), and Charles Hoffman's *Drum Dance: Legends, Ceremonies, Dances and Songs of the Eskimo* (1974). Walter Lowenfels's *From the Belly of the Shark: A New Anthology of Native Americans* (1973) contained both Indian and Inuit materials, while another general anthology, *Native Peoples in Canadian Literature* (1975), edited by William and Christine Mowat, contained much the same type of material as had *The Only Good Indian*. These initial anthologies were followed by David Day and Marilyn Bowering's *Many Voices* (1977), an anthology of poetry by Canadian Natives (though the work of several non-Native poets, most notably Cam Hubert [Anne Cameron] was also included). Robin Gedalof's *Paper Stays Put: A Collection of Inuit Writing* (1980) emphasized contemporary literature and was one of the first anthologies to do so, while John Robert Colombo's *Poems of the Inuit* (1981) and his two-volume *Songs of the Indian* (1983) made use of older ethnographic collections such as Knud Rasmussen's ten-volume report *The Fifth Thule Expedition: The*

Danish Ethnographical Expedition to Arctic North America, 1921–24, while at the same time adding to our knowledge of Inuit poets such as Aua and Orpingalik. Two companion anthologies were published in 1983 and 1988. Penny Petrone's *First People, First Voices* (1983) and *Northern Voices: Inuit Writing in English* (1988) were extensive and eclectic noncritical chronologies of writing by Indian/Inuit people beginning with early speeches and running to contemporary literature. Both are extremely valuable for their range and quantity of historical material.

The first anthologies to deal strictly with contemporary literature by Native writers—in this case, short prose—were Maria Campbell's *Achimoona* (1985), which featured the work of eight Native writers, and a special issue of *Canadian Fiction Magazine* (No. 60, 1987) edited by Thomas King (Cherokee; 1943–), which collected eighteen stories by fourteen Native writers. Four other anthologies are Heather Hodgson's (Cree; 1957–) *Seventh Generation: An Anthology of Native Poetry and Prose* (1989), Agnes Grant's *Our Bit of Truth: An Anthology of Canadian Native Literature* (1989); an anthology of Native women's writing (essays, poetry, prose, and autobiography) edited by Jeanne Perreault and Sylvia Vance (in press); and a second collection of short fiction by Native writers edited by Thomas King (in press). Other more general anthologies, such as *The Last Map Is the Heart: Western Canadian Fiction*, have begun to feature Native writers.

There have been only a limited number of volumes of poetry published by Native writers in Canada. Certainly, E. Pauline Johnson—in terms of number of books—remains Canada's major Native poet. More contemporary poets are beginning to appear, however, and their work is starting to receive attention. Sarain Stump's (Shoshone; 1945–1975) book of poems and drawings *There Is My People Sleeping* was published in 1970. The next year saw the publication of a chapbook called *Sweetgrass* (1971) which contained the poetry of three Metis writers, Orville Keon (1929–), Wayne Keon (1949–), and Ronald Keon (1953–). One year later, Daylight Press published Skyros Bruce's (Salish) *Kalala Poems* (1972) and Griffen House published Shelia Erickson's (Cree) *NOTICE: This Is an Indian Reserve* (1972) (edited by Kent Gooderham), a collection of photographs and poetry. Howard Norman's excellent collection of Swampy Cree narrative poems, *The Wishing Bone Cycle*, was released in 1976, while in 1977, Highway Books published three chapbooks, two by Ben Able (Okanagan; 1938–) *Okanagan Indian* (poetry and prose) and *Wisdom of Indian Poetry*, while the third, *Native Sons*, was a collection of Native poetry and drawings by Native inmates at the Guelph Penitentiary. In the same year, Chimo Press released George Kenny's (Ojibway; 1952–) collection of poetry and short prose *Indians Don't Cry*. Kenny's collection was followed by Rita Joe's (Micmac; 1931–) *Poems of Rita Joe* (1978), Daniel David Moses's *Delicate Bodies* (1980), Duke Redbird's *Loveshine and Red Wine* (1981), Rita Joe's second volume of poetry, *Song of Eskasoni* (1988) and Joan Crate's (Cree; 1953–) *Pale as Real Ladies: The Pauline Johnson Poems* (1989).

This rather limited collection of chapbooks, however, does not represent the number of Native poets in Canada. Contemporary poets such as Beth Cuthand (Cree; 1949–), Jeannette Armstrong (Okanagan; 1948–), Michael Paul Martin (Cree; 1948–), Shirley Bruised Head (Blood; 1951), Frank Connibear (Salish), J. B. Joe (Nootka; 1948–), Anneharte (Saulteaux; 1942–), Gina Simon (Odawa/Ojibway; 1960–), Joane Cardinal Schubert (Peigan; 1942), Simon Frog (Ojibway; 1943–), Lorraine Rekmans (Metis; 1963–), Edna H. King (Ojibway), and Lenore Keeshig-Tobias (Ojibway; 1950–) have all published in various journals, and several of these writers are currently working on book-length manuscripts.

Contemporary fiction, like contemporary poetry, began to appear with regularity in the 1970s. Markoosie's (Inuit; 1941–) short novel, *Harpoon of the Hunter* (1970), which was originally serialized in *Inutitut* and later published in book form by McGill-Queen's University Press, can be used to mark the beginning of contemporary fiction, though there may be earlier novels of which we are not aware. *Harpoon of the Hunter* was followed seven years later by Orville and Wayne Keon's *Thunderbirds of the Ottawa* (1977) and Lynn Sallot and Tom Peltier's (1936–) *Bearwalk* (1977). Basil Johnston's collection of humorous short stories about reserve life, *Moose Meat and Wild Rice*, was published in 1978. Howard Norman's collection of Swampy Cree stories *Where the Chill Came From* was published in 1982, and in 1983, Pemmican Press released Beatrice Culleton's (Metis; 1929–) *In Search of April Raintree*, a novel that dealt with the foster-home system and the difficulties Indians had in trying to make a place for themselves in a white world. In 1984, Douglas and McIntyre published Bill Reid's (Haida; 1920–) *Raven Steals the Light*, a collection of Raven stories. The following year, Theytus Press brought out Jeannette Armstrong's novel *Slash* (1985). *Slash* is part history lesson, part novel, in that it follows the fictional travels of a young Indian man as he participates in most of the major political events of the late 1960s and early 1970s (the Trail of Broken Treaties, Wounded Knee). Ruby Slipperjack's (Ojibway; 1952–) first novel, *Honour the Sun*, was published in 1987. *Honour the Sun* began to move away from focusing on a single alienated Native character (a mark of earlier novels in both the United States and Canada) and dealt instead with the idea of community and communal concerns. This focus was shared by Basil Johnston's second book, *Indian School Days* (1988). Advertised as an autobiography, the book is in reality a fine episodic novel that looks at the Native and non-Native community that forms at a Jesuit boarding school. The same year saw Yvonne M. Klein's translation of the first and second volumes of Jovette Marchessault's (Montagnais; 1938–) autobiographical trilogy: *Like a Child of the Earth*, which won the Prix France-Quebec in 1976, and *Mother of the Grass*. Generally known as a dramatist—her short story "Night Cows" was adapted for the stage and received critical praise—Marchessault is also an artist and a prose writer whose *Lesbian Triptych* (1985) (also translated by Klein) is a major piece of feminist writing. The decade is rounded out by Harry Robinson's (Okanangan; 1901–) *Write It on Your Heart* (1989), a seminal collection of stories that represents a transitional form of prose standing between traditional oral stories and contemporary written stories; Jordon Wheeler's (Cree; 1964) *Brothers in Arms* (1989), a collection of three novellas; and Thomas King's episodic novel *Medicine River* (1990).

Native drama in Canada is at present the most vibrant of the contemporary genres, having been sparked, in no small degree, by the wide critical acclaim accorded Tomson Highway's (Cree; 1951) play *The Rez Sisters* (1988). While the play was certainly not the first by a Canadian Native, it is arguably one of the best. It won the Dora Mavor Moore Award for the best new play of 1988, was runner-up for the Floyd S. Chalmers Award, and was short-listed for the prestigious Governor General's award in drama. The play centers on a group of Native women on a reserve and weaves both traditional and contemporary materials together to create a resilient community that draws strength from both the past and the present. Highway has also written *Aria*, a one-woman play that portrays individual women from Hera to a contemporary Indian woman on the street; *Juke Box Lady*, about alcohol and drug abuse; *The Sage, the Dancer, and the Fool*, which chronicles a day in the life of a Native in a city; and *Dry Lips Oughta Move to Kapuskasing*, a play that Elaine Bomberry of the Native Earth Production Company—the company that has produced most of Highway's plays—calls "the flip side" of *The Rez Sisters*, dealing as it does with a group of Native men (*Dry Lips* and *The Rez Sisters* are two parts of a projected seven-part collage of plays about Natives). While Highway is the most visible figure in Native drama, he is only one of a growing number of Native playwrights.

One of the first contemporary plays by a Native writer to be produced was Minnie Aodla Freeman's *Survival in the South*, which was produced for the Dominion Drama Festival in 1971. It was followed by George Kenny's *October Stranger*, which opened at the Todmorden Mills Theatre in Toronto on July 27, 1977, and Jim Morris's (Cree) *Ayash*, which was performed in February 1981 at Sioux Lookout. Maria Campbell's *The Book of Jessica* was first performed at the 25th Street Theatre in Saskatoon in 1983 and published as a book by Coach House in 1989. Shirley Cheecho (Cree; 1952–) has been involved with the writing and production of at least three plays: *Nanabush of the 80s* by Kennetch Charlette (Cree; 1958–), Shirley Cheecho, and Alanis King (Ojibway/Odawa; 1965–); *Nothing Personal*; and *Shadow People* (Shirley Cheecho). On the West Coast, Sadie Worn Staff (Chiricahua Apache) has written and produced a number of plays for the Spirit Song Native Indian Theatre Company in Vancouver, which include *The Tribes of*

Dawn (1987), *Winter Moon Magic* (1987), and *Shadow Warrior* (1988). Other plays and playwrights include Duke Redbird's *Wasawkachak*, Daniel David Moses's *Coyote City* and *Deep Shit City*, John McLeod's (Ojibway; 1949–) *Diary of a Crazy Boy*, Drew Taylor's (Ojibway; 1962–) *Up the Road* (Taylor has also written four television scripts that have been produced, three for *The Beachcombers* and one for *Street Legal*), Floyd Favel's (Cree) *The Learning*, Ben Cardinal's (Cree; 1958–) *Bones*, Billy Merasty's (Cree; 1960–) *Waskeechoos' Family*, Nancy Paul Woods's (Ojibway; 1945) *I Hate White Girls*, and Monique Mojica's (Cuna/Rappanho) *Princess Pocohontas and the Blue Spots*. In 1986, Fifth House published *The Land Called Morning*, a book of plays that dealt with Native themes. One of them, Valerie Dudoward's (Tshishia) "Teach Me the Ways of the Sacred Circle" (produced by Spirit Song Native Indian Theatre Company in 1986), was written by a Native. The other two, Lone Borgerson's *Gabrielle*, and John Selkirk's *The Land Called Morning*, were written by non-Natives in collaboration with Native students.

The health of contemporary Native poetry, prose, and drama is due, in part, to the journals, magazines, and newspapers that specialize in Native material, such as *Inutitut, Towow, Taqrauk, The Magazine to Reestablish the Trickster, Isumasi*, and *Whetstone* (every fourth issue of which is a Native issue), and the occasional special journal issue such as *Poetry Toronto* (March 1987) and *Canadian Fiction Magazine* (No. 60, 1987), devoted to Native literature. Native-run publishing companies and small presses interested in Native material include Theytus Press, Pemmican, Fifth House, Write-On Press, and Them Days. Theater companies which workshop and produce Native plays include Native Earth Performing Arts in Toronto, De-ba-jih-mu-jig Theatre Group on Manitoulin Island, Spirit Song Native Indian Theatre Company in Vancouver, and Saskatoon Native Theatre in Saskatoon.

Native literature is also assisted by the critical works that are beginning to be produced which examine the uses that white writers have made of Native culture and Native people, and works which deal with Native literature itself. Such books include Leslie Monkman's *A Native Heritage: Images of the Indian in English-Canadian Literature* (1981), Robin McGrath's *Canadian Inuit Literature* (1984), and *The Native in Literature* (1987), a collection of critical essays edited by Thomas King, Cheryl Calver, and Helen Hoy (see also Penny Petrone's essay on "Indian Legends and Tales" and "Indian Literature," and Robin Gedalof McGrath's essay on "Inuit Literature," in *The Oxford Companion to Canadian Literature*, edited by William Toye), and by programs such as the En'owkin International School of Writing, a Native-run writing program for Native people in Penticton, British Columbia, and the Native Theatre School in Heathcoate, Ontario, which trains Native people in acting, playwriting, and stagecraft.

Thomas King
University of Minnesota

BIBLIOGRAPHY

Able, Ben. *Okanagan Indian*. Cobalt, Ontario: Highway Books, 1977.

———. *Wisdom of Indian Poetry*. Cobalt, Ontario: Highway Books, 1977.

Adams, Howard. *Prison of Grass: Canada from the Native Point of View*. 1975. Rpt. Saskatoon: Fifth House, 1989.

Ahenakew, Edward. "An Opinion of the Frog Lake Massacre." *Alberta Historical Review* 8.3 (1960): 9–15.

———. "The Story of the Ahenakews." Ed. Ruth M. Buck. *Saskatchewan History* 17.1 (1964): 12–23.

Anauta. *Land of the Good Shadows: The Life Story of Anauta, an Eskimo Woman*. With Heluiz Chandler. Washburne, NY: John Day, 1940.

Armstrong, Jeannette. *Slash*. Penticton, British Columbia: Theytus, 1985.

Assikinack, Francis. "Legends and Traditions of the Odahwah Indians." *The Canadian Journal* 14 (March 1858): 115–25.

———. "Social and Warlike Customs of the Odahwah Indians." *The Canadian Journal* 16 (July 1858): 297–309.

———. "The Odahwah Indian Language." *The Canadian Journal* 18 (November 1858): 481–85.

Augusta [Mary Augusta Tappage]. *The Days of Augusta*. Ed. Jean E. Speare. Vancouver: J. J. Douglas, 1973.

Batisse, Ken George, et al. *Native Sons*. Cobalt, Ontario: Highway Book Shop, 1977.

Boulanger, Tom. *An Indian Remembers: My Life as a Trapper in Northern Manitoba*. Winnipeg: Peguis, 1971.

Bruce, Skyros. *Kalala Poems*. Vancouver: Daylight Press, 1972.

Budd, Henry. *The Diary of the Reverend Henry Budd 1870–1875*. Ed. Katherine Pettipas. Winnipeg: Manitoba Record Society, 1974. n.p., n.d.

Burr, Mike, ed. *Found Poems of the Metis*, n.p., n.d.

Campbell, Lydia. *Sketches of Labrador Life*. 1894. Rpt. Goose Bay, Labrador: Them Days, 1980.

Campbell, Maria, ed. *Halfbreed*. Toronto: McClelland and Stewart, 1973.

———. *Achimoona*. Saskatoon: Fifth House, 1985.

———. *The Book of Jessica*. Toronto: Coach House, 1989.

Cardinal, Harold. *The Unjust Society: The Tragedy of Canada's Indians*. Edmonton: Hurtig, 1969.

———. *The Rebirth of Canada's Indians*. Edmonton: Hurtig, 1977.

Clark, Peter Dooyenate. *Origin and Traditional History of the Wyandotts, and Sketches of Other Indian Tribes of North America*. Toronto: Hunter, Rose, 1870.

Clutesi, George C. *Son of Raven, Son of Deer*. Sidney, British Columbia: Gray's, 1967.

———. *Potlatch*. Sidney, British Columbia: Gray's, 1969.

Colombo, John Robert. *Poems of the Inuit*. Ottawa: Oberon, 1981.

———. *Songs of the Indian*. 2 vols. Ottawa: Oberon, 1983.

Copway, George. *The Life, History and Travels of Kah-ge-ga-gah-bowh*. 1847. Rpt.

———. *The Ojibway Conquest: A Tale of the Northeast*. New York: G. P. Putnam, 1850.

———. *The Traditional History and Characteristic Sketches of the Ojibway Nation*. 1850. Rpt. Toronto: Coles, 1972.

———. *Running Sketches of Men and Places in England, France, Germany, Belgium, and Scotland*. New York: J. C. Riker, 1851.

Cowan, Susan, ed. *We Don't Live in Snow Houses Now*. Ottawa: Canadian Arctic Producers, 1976.

Crate, Joan. *Breathing Water*. Edmonton: NeWest, 1989.

———. *Pale as Real Ladies: The Pauline Johnson Poems*. Ilderton, Ontario: Brick, 1989.

Culleton, Beatrice. *In Search of April Raintree*. Winnipeg: Pemmican, 1983.

————. *Spirit of the White Bison*. Winnipeg: Pemmican, 1985.

Day, David, and Marilyn Bowering, eds. *Many Voices*. Vancouver: J. J. Douglas, 1977.

Deloria, Vine, Jr. *Custer Died for Your Sins*. Toronto: Macmillan, 1969.

Dion, Joseph. *My Tribe the Cree*. Calgary: Glenbow Museum, 1979.

Dudoward, Valerie. "Teach Me the Ways of the Sacred Circle." *The Land Called Morning*. Saskatoon: Fifth House, 1986.

Dunn, Marty. *Red on White*. Toronto: New Press, 1971.

Eekoomiak, Norman. *An Arctic Childhood*. Oakville, Ontario: Chimo, 1980.

Erasmus, Peter. *Buffalo Days and Nights*. As told to Henry Thompson. Calgary: Glenbow-Alberta Institute, 1976.

Erickson, Shelia. *NOTICE: This Is an Indian Reserve*. Ed. Kent Gooderham. Toronto: Griffin, 1972.

Freeman, Minnie Aodla. *Life Among the Qallunaat*. Edmonton: Hurtig, 1978.

French, Alice. *My Name Is Masak*. Winnipeg: Peguis, 1976.

Gedalof, Robin (see also Robin McGrath). *Paper Stays Put: A Collection of Inuit Writing*. Edmonton: Hurtig, 1980.

George, Chief Dan. *My Spirit Soars*. With Helmut Hirnschall. Surrey, British Columbia: Hancock House, 1982.

Gooderham, Kent, ed. *I Am an Indian*. Toronto: J. M. Dent and Sons, 1969.

Goodwill, Jean, and Norma Sluman. *John Tootoosis*. 1982. Rpt. Winnipeg: Pemmican, 1984.

Grant, Agnes. *Our Bit of Truth: An Anthology of Canadian Native Literature*. Winnipeg: Pemmican, 1989.

Greene, Alma. *Forbidden Voice: Reflections of a Mohawk Indian*. Toronto: Hamlyn, 1971.

————. *Tales of the Mohawk*. Toronto: J. M. Dent, 1975.

Harris, Lilly, et al. *Enough Is Enough: Aboriginal Women Speak Out*. As told to Janet Silman. Toronto: The Women's Press, 1987.

Henry, George [Maungwudaus]. *Remarks Concerning the Ojibway Indians by One of Themselves, Called Maungwudaus, Who Has Been Travelling in England, France, Belgium, Ireland, and Scotland*. London: G. A. Wilson, 1847.

————. *An Account of the Chippewa Indians, Who Have Been Travelling among the Whites in the United States, England, Ireland, Scotland, France and Belgium*. Boston: By the Author, 1848.

Highway, Tomson. *The Rez Sisters*. Saskatoon: Fifth House, 1988.

————. *Dry Lips Oughta Move to Kapuskasing*. Saskatoon: Fifth House, 1989.

Hodgson, Heather, ed. *Seventh Generation: An Anthology of Native Poetry and Prose*. Penticton, British Columbia: Theytus, 1989.

Hoffman, Charles. *Drum Dance: Legends, Ceremonies, Dances and Songs of the Eskimo*. Agincourt, Ontario, Canada: Gage, 1974.

Houston, James. *Songs of the Dream People: Chants and Images from the Indians and Eskimos of North America*. Don Mills, Ontario: Longman, 1972.

Hungry Wolf, Beverly. *The Ways of My Grandmothers*. New York: William Morrow, 1980.

————, and Adolf Hungry Wolf. *Shadows of the Buffalo: A Family Odyssey Among the Indians*. New York: William Morrow, 1983.

Jackson, Louis. *Our Caughawagas in Egypt*. Montreal: W. Drysdale, 1885.

Jacobs, Peter. *Journal of the Reverend Peter Jacobs, Indian Wesleyan Missionary*. New York: Carlton and Phillips, 1855.

————. *A Collection of Ojibway Hymns*. Sarnia, Ontario: n.p., 1886.

Joe, Rita. *Poems of Rita Joe*. Halifax: Abanaki, 1978.

————. *Song of Eskasoni*. Charlottetown, Prince Edward Island: Ragweed, 1988.

Johnson, E. Pauline. *The White Wampum*. Toronto: Copp Clark, 1895.

————. *Canadian Born*. Toronto: Morang, 1903.

————. *Legends of Vancouver*. 1911. Rpt. Toronto: McClelland and Stewart, 1961.

————. *Flint and Feather*. 1912. Rpt. Markham, Ontario: Paperjacks, 1973.

————. *The Moccasin Maker*. 1913. Rpt. Tucson: U of Arizona P, 1987.

————. *The Shagganappi*. Vancouver: Briggs, 1913.

Johnston, Basil. *Moose Meat and Wild Rice*. Toronto: McClelland and Stewart, 1978.

————. *Tales the Elders Told*. Toronto: Royal Ontario Museum, 1981.

————. *Ojibway Ceremonies*. Toronto: McClelland and Stewart, 1982.

————. *Indian School Days*. Toronto: Key Porter, 1988.

Jones, Peter. *Life and Journals of Kah-He-Wa-Quo-Na-By, Wesleyan Minister*. Toronto: Anson Green, 1860.

————. *History of the Ojibway Indians with Special Reference to Their Conversion to Christianity*. 1861. Rpt. Toronto: Canadiana House, 1973.

————. *A Collection of Ojibway and English Hymns*. Toronto: Methodist Church Society, 1877.

Josie, Edith. *Old Crow News: The Best of Edith Josie*. Whitehorse, Yukon Territory: Whitehorse Star, 1963.

————. *Here Are the News*. Toronto: Clarke, Irwin, 1966.

Kennedy, Dan. *Recollections of an Assiniboine Chief*. Ed. James R. Stevens. Toronto: McClelland and Stewart, 1972.

Kenny, George. *Indians Don't Cry*. Toronto: Chimo, 1977.

————. *October Stranger*. With Denis Lacroix. Toronto: Chimo, 1978.

Keon, Orville, and Wayne Keon. *Thunderbirds of the Ottawa*. Cobalt, Ontario: Highway Book Shop, 1977.

Keon, Orville, Wayne Keon, and Ronald Keon. *Sweetgrass*. Eliot Lake, Ontario: W.O.K. Books, 1971.

King, Thomas. *Medicine River*. Toronto: Penguin, 1990.

————, ed. *Canadian Fiction Magazine* 60 (1987).

————, Cheryl Calver, and Helen Hoy, eds. *The Native in Literature: Canadian and Comparative Perspectives*. Toronto: ECW, 1987.

Kuskapatchee. *Swampy Cree Legends*. Ed. Charles Clay. Bewdley, Ontario: Pine Ridge, 1978.

Lowenfels, Walter. *From the Belly of the Shark: A New Anthology of Native Americans*. New York: Vintage Books, 1973.

Lowenstein, Tom. *Eskimo Poems from Canada and Greenland*. Pittsburgh: U of Pittsburgh P, 1973.

Manuel, George. *The Fourth World: An Indian Reality and Social Change*. Don Mills, Ontario: Collier-Macmillan, 1973.

Maracle, Lee. *I Am Woman*. North Vancouver: Write-On, 1988.

————. *Bobbi Lee: Indian Rebel*. Toronto: The Women's Press, 1990.

Marchessault, Jovette. *Lesbian Triptych*. Trans. Yvonne M. Klein. Vancouver: Talonbooks, 1985.

————. *Like a Child of the Earth*. Trans. Yvonne M. Klein. Vancouver: Talonbooks, 1989.

————. *Mother of the Grass*. Trans. Yvonne M. Klein. Vancouver: Talonbooks, 1989.

Markoosie. *Harpoon of the Hunter*. Kingston and Montreal: McGill-Queen's UP, 1970.

————. *Wings of Mercy*. Dorval, Quebec: Kativik School Board, 1984.

Metayer, Maurice, ed. *Tales from the Igloo*. Edmonton: Hurtig, 1972.

McGrath, Robin. *Canadian Inuit Literature: The Development of a Tradition*. Mercury Series No. 94. Ottawa: National Museum of Man, 1984.

Momaday, N. Scott. *House Made of Dawn*. New York: Harper & Row, 1968.

Monkman, Leslie. *A Native Heritage: Images of the Indian in English-Canadian Literature*. Toronto: U of Toronto P, 1981.

Moore, Kermot. *Kipawa: Portrayal of a People*. Cobalt, Ontario: Highway Book Shop, 1982.

Morriseau, Norval. *Legends of My People, the Great Ojibway*. Ed. Selwyn Dewdney. Toronto: Ryerson, 1965.

Moses, Daniel David. *Delicate Bodies*. Vancouver: Blewointment P, 1980.

Mountain Horse, Mike. *My People the Bloods*. Calgary: Glenbow Museum, 1979.

Mowat, William, and Christine Mowat. *Native People in Canadian Literature*. Toronto: Macmillan, 1975.

"Native Issue." *Whetstone* (Spring 1985).

"Native Issue." *Whetstone* (Spring 1987).

"Native Issue." *Whetstone* (Fall 1988).

"Native Writers in Toronto." *Poetry Toronto* 135 (March 1987).

Norman, Howard, ed. *The Wishing Bone Cycle: Narrative Poems from the Swampy Cree Indians*. New York: Stonehill, 1976.

———, ed. *Where the Chill Came From*. San Francisco: North Point, 1982.

Nowell, Charles James. *Smoke from Their Fires: The Life of a Kwakiutl Chief*. Ed. Chellan Stearns Ford. 1940. Rpt. Hamden, CT: Archon, 1968.

Nuligak. *I, Nuligak*. Trans. Maurice Metayer. Toronto: Peter Martin, 1966.

Nungak, Zebedee, and Eugene Arima. *Eskimo Stories*. Ottawa: The National Museums of Canada Anthropological Series No. 90. Bulletin No. 235, 1969.

Oronhyatekha [Dr. Peter Martin]. *History of the Independent Order of Foresters*. Toronto: Hunter, Rose, 1894.

Pelletier, Wilfred, and Ted Poole. *No Foreign Land: The Biography of a North American Indian*. Toronto: McClelland and Stewart, 1973.

Pennier, Henry. *Chiefly Indian: The Warm and Witty Story of a British Columbia Halfbreed Logger*. Ed. Herbert L. McDonald. Vancouver: Graydonald Graphics, 1972.

Petrone, Penny. *First People, First Voices*. Toronto: U of Toronto P, 1983.

———. *Northern Voices: Inuit Writing in English*. Toronto: U of Toronto P, 1988.

Pitseolak [Ashoona]. *Pitseolak: Pictures Out of My Life*. Ed. Dorothy Eber. Montreal: Design Collaborative Books, 1971.

Pitseolak, Peter. *People from Our Side*. Ed. Dorothy Eber. Edmonton: Hurtig, 1975.

———. *Peter Pitseolak's Escape from Death*. Ed. Dorothy Eber. Toronto: McClelland and Stewart, 1977.

Rasmussen, Knud. *The Fifth Thule Expedition: The Danish Ethnographical Expedition to Arctic North America, 1921–24*. 10 vols. 1932. Rpt. New York: AMS, 1976.

Redbird, Duke. *We Are Metis: A Metis View of the Development of a Native Canadian People*. Willowdale, Ontario: Ontario Metis and Non-Status Indian Association, 1980.

———. *Loveshine and Red Wine*. Serpent River Indian Reserve, Cutler, Ontario: Woodland Studios, 1981.

Redsky, James. *Great Leader of the Ojibway: Mis-Quona-Queb*. Toronto: McClelland and Stewart, 1972.

Reid, Bill. *Out of the Silence*. New York: Harper & Row, 1972.

———. *Raven Steals the Light*. Vancouver: Douglas and McIntyre, 1984.

Richardson, John. *Tecumseh; or, the Warrior of the West: A Poem of Four Cantos*. London: James Moyer, 1828.

———. *Wacousta; or, The Prophecy*. 1832. Toronto: McClelland and Stewart, 1967.

———. *The Canadian Brothers; or, The Prophecy Fulfilled*. 1840. Rpt. Toronto: U of Toronto P, 1976.

———. *The Monk Knight of St. John: A Tale of the Crusades*. New York: n.p., 1850.

———. *Hardscrabble; or, The Fall of Chicago*. New York: Dewitt and Davenport, 1851.

———. *Wau-Nan-Gee; or, The Massacre at Chicago*. New York: H. Long and Brother, 1852.

Riel, Louis. *The Collected Writings of Louis Riel.* 5 vols. Gen. ed. George F. G. Stanley. Edmonton: U of Alberta P, 1985.

———. *Poésies religieuses et politiques.* Montreal: n.p., 1886.

Robinson, Harry. *Write It on Your Heart.* Penticton and Vancouver: Theytus and Talonbooks, 1989.

Sallot, Lynn, and Tom Peltier. *Bearwalk.* Toronto: Musson, 1977.

Sark, John Joe. *Micmac Legends of Prince Edward Island.* Charlottetown, Prince Edward Island: Lennox Island Band Council and Ragweed Press, 1988.

Sepass, Khalserten. *The Songs of Y-Ail-Mihth.* Vancouver: Indian Time, 1955.

Sero, John Brant. "Some Descendents of Joseph Brant." *Ontario Historical Papers and Records* 1 (1899): 113–17.

———. "Dekanawideh: The Law-Giver of the Caniegahakas." *Man* (1901): 166–70.

———. "Indian Rights Association After Government Scalp." *Wilshire's Magazine* (October 1903): 70–75.

———. "View of a Mohawk Indian." *Journal of American Folklore* 18 (1905): 160–62.

———. "O-no-dah." *Journal of American Folklore* 24 (1911): 251.

———. "A Memorial for Brant." *Shocked and Appalled: A Century of Letters to the Globe and Mail.* Ed. Jack Kapica. Toronto: Lester and Orpen Denneys, 1985.

Sewid, James. *Guests Never Leave Hungry: The Autobiography of James Sewid, a Kwakiutl Indian.* Ed. James P. Spradley. 1969. Rpt. Montreal: Queen's UP, 1972.

Slipperjack, Ruby. *Honour the Sun.* Winnipeg: Pemmican, 1987.

Smith, Donald. *Sacred Feathers: The Reverend Peter Jones (Kahkewaquonaby) and the Mississauga Indians.* Lincoln: U of Nebraska P, 1987.

Snow, Chief John. *These Mountains Are Our Sacred Places.* Toronto: Samuel-Stevens, 1977.

Stump, Sarain. *There Is My People Sleeping: The Ethnic Poem-Drawings of a Sarain Stump.* Sidney, British Columbia: Gray's, 1970.

Tagoona, Armand. *Shadows.* Toronto: Oberon, 1975.

Tetso, John. *Trapping Is My Life.* 1964. Rpt. Toronto: Peter Martin, 1970.

Thrasher, Anthony Apakark. *Thrasher, Skid Row Eskimo.* In collaboration with Gerard Deagle and Alan Mettrick. Toronto: Griffin, 1976.

Toye, William, ed. *The Oxford Companion to Canadian Literature.* Toronto: Oxford UP, 1983.

Waubageshig [Harvey McCue]. *The Only Good Indian: Essays by Canadian Indians.* Toronto: New Press, 1970.

Wheeler, Jordan. *Brothers in Arms.* Winnipeg: Pemmican, 1989.

Willis, Jane. *Geniesh: An Indian Girlhood.* Toronto: New Press, 1973.

Wolfe, Alexander. *Earth Elder Stories.* Saskatoon: Fifth House, 1988.

Wuttunee, William. *Ruffled Feathers: Indians in Canadian Society.* Calgary: Bell, 1971.

New Native American Fiction

If a date can be ascribed to the advent of new Native American fiction, it would be February 14, 1936, for on that day D'Arcy McNickle (Metis; 1904–1977) saw the publication of his first novel. For years, editors had praised, and rejected, his drafts, thus forcing the young man through agonizing revisions as he sought to make his work true to the tribal themes he wished to convey, but also marketable. In the former regard, *The Surrounded* was a marvelous success; in the latter, it was a dismal failure. Critics praised it, but the book did not sell. When it was released again, in 1977, *The Surrounded* found the audience for which it was suited. In the intervening forty years, the reading public had changed; it was ready for a novel that did not espouse either of two extremes: the Noble Savage or the Indian on the brink of extinction. As the recent popularity of McNickle's works attests, he was forty years ahead of his time, for the resolutions he found to the dilemma of publication and veracity are echoed today.

The Surrounded clearly prefigures the works of other contemporary Indian writers. Like them, McNickle wrote to articulate a Native American point of view, a Native identity, so he was ever mindful of the need to remain true to a tribal worldview: in *The Surrounded*, the cultural attitudes and beliefs that mark the Salish as a distinct, homogenous people. He achieved this accuracy, but also the publication of his novel, by setting the novel in the specific landscape of the Salish (the land of his youth) and by incorporating tribal narratives into his book in two ways. He "told" several stories, at length, by reproducing a storytelling event, but he also used tribal narrative devices and verbal motifs. A four-part framework and repetition are used throughout to dramatize the stories of Catherine, Archilde, and the Salish as they face the apparent demise of their heritage and their culture. Rather than perpetuate the popular image of the "Indian going

371

bad," he shows his characters rising to the occasion by reaffirming, through communal action, traditional tribal values and lifeways in modern times. Thus was born a hybrid fiction, derivative of spoken and written literatures, that emerged from the desire to celebrate tribal identity, and to promote tribal autonomy. As Simon Ortiz (Acoma Pueblo; 1941–) notes in the introduction to his edited anthology of short fiction, *Earth Power Coming* (1983), the title of which comes from another McNickle novel, the survival of Native cultures has always rested in the stories and the voices that give them life. Since 1936, the voices are in print as well as in sound.

However, individual authors vary considerably in the emphasis that each places on the traditional and tribal, and even a brief, but representative, survey illustrates the diversity that lies between the retelling of the old stories and the creation of new. Although they derive from quite disparate cultures and personal backgrounds, the authors share equally the concern for identity and perpetuity found in McNickle's life and works.

The fiction of Peter Blue Cloud (Mohawk; 1927–) exemplifies how the old stories provide the impetus for modern, written storytelling. In "Coyote Meets Raven" (in Ortiz's anthology), he reconstructs these two tribal tricksters in all their self-centered detail. In the story, the two vie for the upper hand, to see whose powers are stronger, so at first the contest suggests a tribal rivalry as well, between those who tell Coyote stories and those who tell Raven. However, as the contest reaches its climax, a third character—or voice—enters the drama; the creative force, here called Thunderbird, intervenes, putting a stop to the conflict and chastising the two for their egotistical rivalry. The message is clear and unequivocal. Each culture has its heroes and its powers, and each is a force to contend with in its own landscape. If they allow a desire for individuality to dictate their actions, however, tribal people lose their power and can no longer move freely to direct their own futures. As always, the storyteller provides a pointed moral and food for thought. Like that of his colleagues, Blue Cloud's work has more behind it than the individual ego of one writer; it has the voice of a people.

This is not to suggest that Native fiction avoids a sense of loss, of change that may not be for the better. It can be found in almost every piece, but it is, more often than not, qualified by either an implicit or explicit statement of continuity. This, too, is strongly representative of the connections between the verbal and written traditions: in the former, stories supply the crucial bridge between the past and the present, thus allowing people to interpret present events and react to them with the knowledge contained within the narratives.

Joseph Bruchac (Abenaki; 1942–) seems well aware of the sustaining connection between the old and new stories. In his *Survival This Way: Interviews with American Indian Poets* (1987), he notes the widespread propensity to reaffirm the traditional. This tendency can be found in his own writings as well. In "The White Moose," an old Cree hunter, Jean Maurice, makes a pact to kill a white bull moose and send its hide to a museum in Quebec City (*The White Moose*, 1988). In modern times, it seems no longer possible to adhere to old mores, such as a proper respect for such an extraordinary, exemplary animal. Although he is patient enough to allow the moose time to promulgate its kind, and although he performs the hunt in its proper way, he hunts the moose for profit, for money, and the results are disastrous. The white hide brings misfortune to whoever touches it, until it is finally turned dark by a mysterious fire in the museum. It also affects Jean Maurice, who loses all his possessions. However, he recognizes the cause of his adversity. He gives the museum money to the church, and vows never to hunt for museums again. His ways changed, he is allowed once more to take pride in and confidence from his reciprocal relationship with his world and its endless cycles of life.

Bruchac's story speaks to the point. Although their world has changed since the incursion of the Europeans, Native Americans still have the means to exert power over their own destinies. Some of the knowledge garnered over the long habitation of this continent remains and is available for those who understand it. Much has changed, but much remains for those who listen and learn, and stories are still being created to emphasize the point.

This message is found elsewhere. In "The Sin of Niguudzagha" (in Ortiz) by Mary Tall Mountain (Koyukon; 1918–), the lifeways of the old Niguudzagha's people have been affected by the "dominant culture," and its priests. He recognizes that much of the old knowledge will be lost; however, he persists in performing the rituals and obligations to the old ways. He is a man of power, one who has spirit helpers and a very personal, intimate relationship with his landscape and the forces that inhabit it. Tall Mountain shows how he acquired this power, and how he uses it for the benefit of his people. Although a modern, fictional creation, Niguudzagha is strongly reminiscent of characters from older tribal narratives. His life is exemplary, the dramatization of the *potential* that exists in the world for those who recognize it, respect it, and use it wisely for the survival of humankind.

In the works of Anna Lee Walters (Pawnee-Otoe; 1946–), one also finds bleak aspects of modern existence subtly balanced by the enduring relationship between a people and a place. In "Going Home," Sun and Nita seem doomed to divorce after twenty years of marriage, but on her way home to her own people, she gives a ride to one of the old women of Sun's tribe who suggests a perspective that goes beyond the limited and personal.

The place Nita has inhabited for twenty years and the people with whom she has shared it are now her home, for they have shaped her identity, and this relationship with the larger community of people and place is something immensely more enduring and valuable than the personal and transitory. She turns around, and dissolution turns to affirmation.

She is killed by Sun in a car accident while returning home, but even in this tragedy there is a brief moment of insight and confirmation. As Sun sits immobilized by the pain of Nita's loss, he begins to sing his pain, and the landscape seems to respond; birds come to perch on the fence near him, the sun rises, and the song clarifies his place in the world and his course of action. He takes a gun from his truck. Walters paints dark images of modern life for her characters—marital problems, drunkenness, traffic fatalities, suicide—but she also softens these images with very poignant, suggestive detail. Life has always been difficult, but there have always been mitigating influences: family, community, and a sensitive and responsible identification with one's landscape.

These two closely related imperatives are very clearly stated in the title piece to Walters's collection of short fiction, *The Sun Is Not Merciful*. Its main characters, Lydia and Bertha, have lived on the same small piece of land their whole lives; all their memories, actions, and stories are tied directly to this place where their ancestors are buried. However, the government wants the land for a hydroelectric project, and despite their refusal to sell, the inevitable happens. Interestingly, when the land is lost, Lydia also loses a part of herself: a leg. Loss of land is thus equated with the loss of physical self. But Walters qualifies even this. While Lydia and Bertha fish the new reservoir, they remember their father, referred to simply as Old Man—a name suggestive of characters from tribal verbal arts. He taught them how to fish, and how to cope with the debilitating heat of an unrelenting sun. In short, he taught them how to survive, and they learned their lessons well. Although the land they have lived on for seventy years has undergone drastic change, they have accommodated that change and made the best of it to endure. As Old Man told them again and again, they come from a long line of fisherpeople who have always been drawn to water. (Perhaps, in this case, the water was drawn to them.) They also have the stories of the past and faith in their own abilities, and that unrelenting faith wears down the opposition: the young game warden who would give them citations for practicing their ancient lifeway. Even in modern times and against seemingly insurmountable forces, Native cultures survive and exert their powers.

However, once the Native writer moves the setting of his or her story away from the specificity of a tribal landscape, the power is not as clearly defined. In Luci Tapahonso's (Navajo; 1953–) "The Snakeman" (in *The Remembered Earth*, ed. Hobson, 1979) one finds very few hints about the identities of the young girls who live in a dormitory in the city. Their fears, anxieties, and characters seem universal, until the mystery of one girl's nightly disappearance is explained: she goes to meet with her dead mother.

As in older narratives, this is possible even in an urban, prison-like setting, and, ironically, the dark meetings provide the only affirmation in the girl's otherwise bleak existence.

This is true likewise for Donna and Sullie in Linda Hogan's (Chickasaw; 1947–) "New Shoes" (in Ortiz). Urban existence is not satisfying, despite its apparent attractions. Isolated from family and community, Sullie must watch her daughter drift into the confusing, threatening life of the city, powerless to help her become a woman with direction and deliberation. The only hope that Donna may exert control over her own fate comes from the unspoken, familial tie that can be seen in reflection, but not directly.

The brevity of short fiction often requires that the familial, communal, and traditional remain implied, and largely underdeveloped. In the novel, however, these things find elaboration. In *A Yellow Raft on Blue Water* (1987) by Michael Dorris (Modoc; 1945–), one is presented with the personal narratives of three generations. Working backward through time to unravel the mysteries of family history, Dorris portrays the complex search for identity in modern times, and one aspect of his style underscores the difficulty.

His book is woven through with references to popular media, in particular television and video. These influential aspects of modern existence are unavoidable in the lives of his characters, and they subtly play into their perceptions of self and place. However, despite these recent "prime movers," the characters are still much like those found in McNickle's novel fifty years earlier. Rayona, Christine, and Ida, like Archilde, Catherine and Modeste, face problems that derive from mistakes of the past. They must confront the past to rectify the present, and thereby reaffirm—despite the influences of Euroamerican society—the basis of tribal identity: communal ties.

Dorris's novel opens with Rayona's visit to her mother in the hospital. Christine has just braided her daughter's hair. The book ends with a distant scene in the past in which Christine has given Ida a hairdo. Ida converts the style in the cold dark of pre-dawn, braiding the three strands into one: an apt symbol for the concluding of the narrative, and the lives of the three main characters. Much as the Salish are woven together at the end of *The Surrounded*, Dorris's characters are inextricably tied to one another. It is a common refrain in contemporary Native American literature: the touch of one generation upon another, and the continuity it suggests.

New Native fiction depicts Indian survivors, no matter where they may be found. From the ranch setting of Elizabeth Cook-Lynn's (Crow Creek Sioux; 1930–) "Dragon Mountain" in Vietnam, and from reservations and cities around the country, people and lifeways are shown enduring. This is true even for characters of mixed ancestry, most numerous in fiction since McNickle's protagonist in *The Surrounded*. Even characters who have never lived in the traditional landscape of their ancestors are not locked out. As in older verbal narratives, recent works emphasize commitment to community, reciprocity with a landscape, and the power of self-determination that they provide.

John Lloyd Purdy
Central Oregon Community College

BIBLIOGRAPHY

Armstrong, Jeannette. *Slash*. Pentication, BC: Theytus Books, 1988.

Bruchac, Joseph. *Survival This Way: Interviews with American Indian Poets*. Tucson: U of Arizona P, 1987.

———. *The White Moose: Stories by Joseph Bruchac*. Marvin, SD: Blue Cloud Quarterly, 1988.

Dorris, Michael. *A Yellow Raft on Blue Water*. New York: Henry Holt & Co., 1987.

Hobson, Geary, ed. *The Remembered Earth: An Anthology of Contemporary Native American Literature*. Albuquerque: U of New Mexico P, 1979.

McNickle, D'Arcy. *The Surrounded*. New York: Dodd, Mead, 1936.

Ortiz, Simon J., ed. *Earth Power Coming: Short Fiction in Native American Literature*. Tsaile, AZ: Navajo Community College P, 1983.

Walters, Anna Lee. *The Sun Is Not Merciful*. New York: Firebrand Books, 1985.

The New Native
American Theater

Intermittently over the past twenty years, there have been bursts of creative energy and enthusiasm aimed at the development of an American Indian theater. There have been so many problems, however, that some of the few brave souls who struggled for that goal have given up, exhausted by frustration and a failure of nerve.

Companies have come and gone: Red Earth Performing Arts in Seattle, A-Tu-Mai in Southern Ute, Native Americans in the Arts in New York City, American Indian Theatre Company of Oklahoma in Tulsa, and Navajoland Outdoor Theatre at Navajo. It is sad to recall those honorable casualties, but it is also heartening to reflect that their efforts were not in vain, if viewed as steps toward an ideal, which still beckons and entrances the survivors.

The movement toward an Indian theater had its roots in the social and political upheavals of the late 1960s and early 1970s. In hindsight, it is easy to see that much of the effort to improve life for ethnic and other minorities was misdirected and unproductive; many wrong things were done, even for the right reasons, and some reformers—including some pioneers of Indian theater—tried to move too far and too fast. The result was often a shoddy simulacrum of progress, based on immature talent, arrogant optimism, and too little experience. On the other hand, it was a wonderful time of awakening for many who had never before appreciated their own or their group's uniqueness or felt an urge to assert it. Native Americans, whom President Richard Nixon, in a statement of his Indian policy in June 1970, described as "the most deprived, the most isolated" of American minorities, launched a drive for self-determination among the 326 tribes. This drive was made possible by improved education, a freeing-up of funds to enhance the quality of life for minorities, and the emergence of a pan-

Indian consciousness. For too long, Indian groups had tended to keep to themselves, with little exchange of ideas or desire for cooperation, but pan-Indianism was kicking up dust not only in politics but in the arts also. The desire for more communication among themselves, and a willingness to open up dialogue with non-Indians, stimulated, among other things, the development of a number of Indian theater groups throughout the country, mostly in large cities. Almost all of them depended on funding for survival, and all of them closed as the money dried up.

In the tribal past, communication had been person-to-person, group-to-group, through storytelling, dance, and ceremony in a familial setting. These were the primary means of instruction. Winter was for tales, summer for dances, early fall for feasting. Life wheeled around the regularly ordained ceremonies. But these classic modalities began to disappear with the suppression of Indian religions, enforced separation of family members, the drift from the land to the cities, and a falling-off in the speaking of Native languages. The dominant white culture seemed poised to swamp everything in its path. Much, indeed, was gone forever, and realists knew that it could not be artificially re-created. Many non-Indians seemed ready to give Native American culture an honorable burial under museum glass, but despite dirges over the "vanishing American," that same American was not only failing to vanish but had actually begun to adapt to change and to evolve new modalities, a sure sign that the species was not ready for extinction. By the late 1960s it was apparent that everything traditional need not and should not be discarded, and that new and original forms could also emerge from tradition.

Many Indians now realized that show dancing and historical pageants designed for the entertainment of non-Indians need not be the only concept of Native American theatricality. These things have their place, no doubt, but they appeal mainly to uninformed audiences. Now came, in addition to traditional tales dramatized on the stage, a series of realistic Indian plays written by Indians, addressing Indian issues, and intended for a primarily Indian audience. As a legacy from the past, this theater also encompassed music and dancing, and some of its pioneers felt that Indians who did not understand or participate in traditional ceremonies might find in this medium a new respect for ritual and form. It would be an acceptable outgrowth of the religious heritage of the race and would strengthen the badly weakened sense of tribe, but it could also help Indians to define their own identities, by encouraging self-esteem, and by accurately reflecting modern life. It could also counter hostile, uninformed, and insensitive attitudes of the film and television industries toward Indians, as well as misguided attempts by political zealots, who, without much caring about Indian people themselves, might use Indian issues as another means of flagellating the conscience of white America. Provided that they could control it, the stage seemed to offer Indians yet another means of self-realization through the presentation of truth and nature.

False images of the "redskin"—comic, noble, child of nature, savage, bloodthirsty, monosyllabic, grunting, poetically inclined, poker-faced, and so on—had formed in Europe and the English colonies in America long before the latter declared their independence. In America, they quickly surfaced in drama; and from the late eighteenth century until the early decades of the twentieth, there were many plays on the American stage about Indian life or in which Indian characters appeared. The authors were all non-Indians, and their Indian characters were little more than dramatic machinery for boisterous masquerade, melancholy rumination, or fashionable depiction of the Noble Savage. Novelists and poets like Cooper, Longfellow, Helen Hunt Jackson, and Hawthorne perpetuated the stereotypes that had already appeared in drama, while eastern yellow journalism and the "penny dreadfuls" about frontier life emphasized the image of the bloodthirsty, crazed aborigine. These stereotypes were staple fare in films at least until the 1960s. More responsible works like John Barth's *Sot-Weed Factor* (1960), Arthur Kopit's play *Indians* (1969), Ken Kesey's play and film *One Flew Over the Cuckoo's Nest* (1962 and 1976), and Thomas Berger's novel and film *Little Big Man* (1964 and 1971) struck some wrong notes, first because their authors were not Indians and lacked the authentic voice, and second because they were not so much interested in depicting real Indians as in using Indians as pathetic supernumeraries to rub the face of white America in its own guilt. The Noble Savage of Rousseau had returned as the counterculture hero commenting on the evils of the modern rat-race. Unfortunately, many progressive thinkers took these works and sometimes even completely bogus ones like the *Billy Jack* films as significant statements.

Meanwhile, where were the Indian authors who might have righted the balance? There were some good novels by Indians, such as James Paytiamo's *Flaming Arrow's People* (1936), John Joseph Mathews's *Sundown* (1934), John Oskison's *Brothers Three* (1935), and D'Arcy McNickle's *The Surrounded* (1936). There was even an arresting, curious drama about the life of Cherokee Indians in eastern Oklahoma, Rolla Lynn Riggs's *The Cherokee Night* (1932), which failed in its pre-Broadway tryout, being considered too remote and structurally unconventional. Other works by Indian authors include the memoirs of Black Elk, the works of Charles Eastman, James Welch's *Winter in the Blood* (1974), and N. Scott Momaday's *House Made of Dawn* (1968) and *The Way to Rainy Mountain* (1969). All of these examine the Indian's alienation and search for personal identity, but they have probably been more widely read and discussed by non-Indians than by Indians themselves. Even the works of Vine Deloria, Jr., though useful in calling attention to wrongs done to Indian people, were basically polemics addressed to whites. Neither the novel nor the polemic has proved effective as a means to inspire and stir up dialogue among Indians them-selves. This leaves the theater to accomplish the task.

What ideals might a Native American dramatist strive for? First, he or she—for convenience the pronoun "he" will be used from this point on—should have full ethnic identity. He must know who he is and who the people are for whom he is writing. He must have experienced the multifac-eted life of an Indian, preferably at the grass roots, and have known the frustrations, sorrows, joys, and satisfactions that ordinary Indian people know; he cannot afford to have led a sheltered life, especially in a non-Indian setting. He must know instinctively and from experience what pro-tocols must be observed, what customs respected, what limits observed, and what sacred cows may fittingly be scourged or taunted. On the other hand, he cannot shun contact with the non-Indian world. He must read good newspapers and magazines, and good books of all kinds. He has a duty to make himself as educated as possible; there is nothing incompat-ible between writing ethnic drama and reading Shakespeare or H. Rider Haggard. It will help, too, if he develops a business sense and public-relations skills, the more so if he directs a company, because otherwise his group will founder, and his plays will never reach the public. He must know every facet of the theater, study the techniques of writing plays, and be generally prepared to adapt, patch, make, and mend at a moment's notice. Finally, he must be able to conceive and develop a storyline, write dialogue untainted by artificial stiffness and anachronistic poeticisms (a vice that afflicts much of what passes for the authentic Indian voice), and, in short, have some genuine talent. At this stage, what Indian theater needs most are playwrights willing to go the distance. There is also a need for more actors, directors, designers, technical personnel, administrators, and producers, but without good plays there will be no theater. The trick cannot be done by feathers and drums alone, and there are no shortcuts.

One of our bright hopes at this time is William Yellow Robe, an Assiniboine Sioux from Montana, who has created some jolting one-act plays, *Sneaky*, *Wink Dah*, and *The Closing of Another Circle*, among others. Such a rising talent might well be fostered by a major university, much as August Wilson has been supported by Lloyd Richards at Yale. Similarly, many tribes have the resources to maintain a tribal dramatist, or to provide the financial backing for well-conceived theatrical projects. This would have a healthy social effect and could prove a source of financial profit. So far, there has been too little response and no backing from those who stand to gain the most, the tribes themselves.

Some of the problems which have occurred in various Indian compa-nies need to be frankly addressed. There has sometimes been a lack of team spirit at critical junctures. Indians have always been a bit indepen-dent, but no enterprise can survive persistent lateness or absence from rehearsals, drinking at inappropriate times, or insubordination. It is often difficult for young Indians to adapt to the many disciplines of the theater, but adapt they must. A second problem is a tendency to psychological dependence on grant money. Failure to plan for financial self-sufficiency has caused the demise of several promising groups.

On the credit side, many new Indian talents in all aspects of the theater have been uncovered in the past twenty years, and not all of them will be lured away by the film and television industries. The first phase of the New Native American Theater is over, and the next has already begun.

Hanay L. Geiogamah
University of California—Los Angeles

Indians in Anglo-American Literature, 1492 to 1990

At the heart of any literary exploration of the American experience stands the image of the Native American. As he plays the role of Other to the American Self, he holds a mirror to an ever-emerging sense of identity. In his landmark study of Euroamerican images of Native Americans, *The White Man's Indian*, Robert Berkhofer writes, "to understand the White image of the Indian is to understand White societies and intellectual premises over time more than the diversity of Native Americans" (1979:xvi). No single statement can be more fundamental to a study of the Indian in American literature, for the merging of various distinct peoples under the generalized term "Indian" was central first to European, and later to American thought and art, and was a vital concept in the dialectics of self-definition, political development, and literary independence. What follows is a survey of the literary uses of the Indian over centuries which attempts to synthesize the diverse intellectual and moral currents of Anglo-American thought.

Early exploration accounts of Native Americans varied wildly. Some described a people living in an earthly paradise with an abundance of food, little need for clothing, a gracious attitude toward visitors; other accounts created a darker image of degenerate wildness rife with wanton murder and cannibalism. Columbus himself seems to have projected both images of the peoples he met. Throughout Europe, the discovery of the new continent and the people who inhabited it played a key role in major philosophical discussions, and the structure of those theoretical discussions required that all Native Americans be generalized by one term, "Indian." The explorers' experiences of the various tribal groups were seized by eager moral and philosophical speculators and marshalled to prove almost any point. Two philosophers as divergent as Locke and Hobbes were convinced that the moral condition of the "Indian" proved their varying theories on the relation of the individual to society and on the nature of civilization.

However, early explorers and colonists judged the Indian by European standards of civilization and Christianity, and even the staunchest supporters of the Indian's natural goodness found that the Indian must be led to adopt the European world. The image of the Indian in American literature, expressed clearly in early contact literature, is constructed from three basic elements: an ambivalent attitude toward the "Indian" moral character, the conviction that civilization and progress were inevitable and right, and the belief that the spiritual depravity of "Indian" superstition required a Christian tonic. However these attitudes were appropriated to promote social criticism, they remained active presuppositions.

In his classic work *Savagism and Civilization*, Roy Harvey Pearce chronicles how the colonists eventually convinced themselves that while there might be savage virtues, natural virtues, there were no noble savages in North America. No place could be perceived for the wild Indian in civilization's destiny. Pearce concludes:

> For the Indian was the remnant of a savage past away from which civilized men had struggled to grow. To study him was to study the past. To kill him was to kill the past. History would thus be the key to the moral worth of cultures; the history of American civilization would thus be conceived of as three-dimensional, progressing from past to present, from east to west, from lower to higher. (1965:49)

However, underneath this conviction in the inevitable superiority of European civilization, the lure of the savage wilderness still remained. The Indian was thought to reveal how man behaved when removed from oppressive social restraints on human behavior. This image of freedom was both promising and threatening. Of all the colonial settlers, it was the Puritans who reacted the most strongly and articulately to this implicit and immediate challenge to their worldview.

Richard Slotkin, in *Regeneration Through Violence*, explores how the Puritans conceptualized their journey into the savage wilderness in terms of their personal conflict between conscience and sin. The projection of their fears and repressed desires onto the Indians made the cleansing of sin from themselves possible only with the extermination of the Indian. The underlying tension stemming from Puritan acculturation to the New World, the process of adjusting their mores and worldview to the requirements of life in an alien environment, encouraged all colonists and especially the Puritans to define themselves through negation. The more they attacked the Indian, the more they affirmed their European values and heritage. The vast popularity of war narratives such as *The History of King Philip's War* by Increase Mather (1687), religious instruction by religious leaders such as Cotton Mather, and captivity narratives such as *A Narrative of the Captivity and Restoration of Mrs. Mary Rowlandson* (1682) served to teach readers that while natural virtues might appear desirable, the reality of the Indian proved these supposed virtues to be a devilish illusion. The colonists' only hope to survive and build a new world lay in defeating forces which would erode their promised social and spiritual well-being. Though other well-known accounts of seventeenth-century colonial life and thought such as John Smith's *A General Historie of Virginia* (1624), William Bradford's *A History of Plymouth Plantation* (1646), and *A Relation of Maryland* (1635) may not present the Indian in the role of a hell-worshiping devil in a drama for the souls of Christian colonizers, Indians were seen as intractable savages unwilling to advance from their primitive surroundings, capable at a moment of perpetrating the most horrible atrocities for obscure reasons. The Noble Savage of European philosophy had little credence on the cutting edge of expansion and colonization.

In the eighteenth century, the writings of Thomas Jefferson, William Byrd, and other American disciples of the Enlightenment discussed the philosophical possibilities of educating the Indian to the ideas of Christian progress. As the Indians and border warfare receded deeper into the American wilderness, some writers and thinkers were convinced that reasonable appeals could induce the Indian to give up his culture and way of life. They struggled to explain why this had not happened previously and used their conviction to justify continued appropriation of the land for the common good of Indian and colonist alike. While the Indian no longer had to be exterminated, there was no question but that he must progress, and that progress would be the final proof of a relationship they saw developing between the land and the new American political experiment through which freedom and civilization would evolve into the highest form of human society.

The philosophical debate over the fate of the Indian and the nature of the colonists' acculturation to the new continent continued in the parlors of the affluent and educated. However, the popular imagination was still more completely fired by captivity narratives and tales of border warfare. What was popularly seen as the irrational violence of the savage Indian seemed to point up the senselessness of debate, and emphasized the frontiersman's ethic of action. To the frontiersman, the Indian presented a path to self-definition, even if it was a negative one, and he personified the wildness of the American continent. This popular trend finds its most literate expression in Charles Brockden Brown's gothic classic *Edgar Huntly* (1799), where the Indian's role is one of perpetrator of atrocities.

In the later eighteenth and early nineteenth centuries, the Indian began to appear in poetry. Works by Joel Barlow, Timothy Dwight, and Hugh Henry Brackenridge sought to create a scheme of American experience which presented the Indian in an essentially Romantic light. The

Indian was seen as no longer personifying natural reason and virtues; now he was a man of emotion and sensibility. He was more an artifact of the past than a contributor to the present. Through their vision of history and of the glorious future of America, these writers sought to mediate between the savage and the civilized, the settler and the Indian, and to elucidate the contributions of each toward the unique experience of America. The settler brought order and cultivation, the Indian love of nature and passion. The two were destined to merge, but, of course, on civilized Christian ground.

At the same time that serious literature was beginning to occupy itself with the philosophical considerations of the Indian, popular literature expanded the booming category of travel literature on the West. Filled with exotic tales of Indians and frontiersmen, these books kept alive an image of the wild, savage Indian which frightened and yet titillated many readers. The sense of wild freedom and adventure associated with daring chiefs and rugged self-made men lured many would-be settlers from the populous Eastern seaboard, while reminding others that the newly formed United States was an inland nation as well as a maritime one.

One of the most popular and accomplished of the writers of this period was Philip Freneau (1752–1832). Freneau's Indians were noblemen of nature, but they were aware of themselves as members of a dying race. His poems were typical of a literary sentiment that was more concerned with the Indian of the past or of a present competition that was soon to pass. His poems emphasize the naturalness of the Indian's attitude about life and death, his essential goodness, and his wisdom. Freneau paints the Indian with a sense of the wild sublime in fundamental conflict with the civilized life of social conventions. Civilization is ultimately seen as a hindrance to the immediate and direct experience of nature and of life. The Indian plays much the same role as a critic of society as did the Romantic artist himself.

Between the War of 1812 and the Civil War, the Indian held a central place in American literature and art, a position he has yet to regain. As the influence of European Romanticism made itself felt in the United States, the Indian emerged as vital to the new sensibility because through him the Romantic writer could explore the indigenous traditions, folk customs, and glorious national past that was so central to much Romantic writing. Perhaps the most popular image of the Indian was created by John Augustus Stone in his play *Metamora, or the Last of the Wampanoags* (1829). While drama focusing on American Indians was popular throughout the nineteenth century, it was most influential during the first half, and no other play came close to the blockbuster status of *Metamora*, a melodramatic tragedy centered around a heroic, patriotic warrior with idealized moral features struggling against deceitful colonists.

As subject, the Indian was used by early nineteenth-century writers to evoke a variety of emotions. The writer had only to utilize the already existing ambivalent feelings about the Indian and the American wilderness to achieve his Romantic goals. Key to any image of the Indian was the premise that Indians were members of a rapidly dying race. Whether good or bad, they were inevitably being eliminated by the callous advances of a civilization that was also eliminating a sublime landscape in favor of more mundane concerns. Both the heroic chief who was trying to stop the encroachment of the settlers and the last member of a dead tribe were poetic subjects who could evoke pity, wonder, and tragedy.

This Romantic sensibility of writers fused with an equally strong sentiment to declare American literary independence. Though the United States had political freedom, many writers still felt subject to European artistic dictates. In an attempt to establish their own literature, American writers sought truly American subjects such as the American Indian and the American wilderness. Since the Indian was believed to be dying out, critics maintained that it was the writer's duty to capture the true spirit of the original inhabitants. Only Americans could write faithfully of American history and experience, and by doing so, a truly independent American literature would be created.

Historical narrative poems reveal one main thread of American Romanticism beginning around 1790 and continuing into the 1850s. These poems often centered on Indians, sometimes great chiefs, or heroic frontiersmen who were closely associated with Indians. While espousing historical fact and accurate portrayal, these narratives evoked what reviewers called the sublime, the wonderful, the picturesque, and the pathetic. Civilization and social norms could be implicitly criticized, while the uniqueness of the American past was celebrated. One of the earliest of these was Mrs. Sarah Wentworth Morton's *Ouabi; or, The Virtues of Nature* (1790), but the tradition continued with *Yamoyden, A Tale of the Wars of King Philip* (1820) by James Eastburn and Robert Sands, *Frontenac* (1849) by Alfred Street, and many others. Images of the Indian were common also in the work of a group of writers known as "The Knickerbocker School." Centered around the prestigious *Knickerbocker Magazine*, these writers produced poetry, sketches, and novels which presented historical Indians in predominantly Romantic postures. Fitz Greene Halleck published *Red Jacket* (1828), and Charles Fenno Hoffman wrote *A Winter in the West* (1835) and "A Vigil of Faith" (1842). In *Koningsmarke, The Long Finne* (1823), James Kirke Paulding satirically presented both positive and negative images of the Indian. These Romantic stoics were capable of violence when wronged or when plows disturbed the bones of their ancestors, but they also remembered kindnesses and offered hospitality to strangers.

The best-known "Knickerbocker" was Washington Irving. After a number of essays, early in his career, which proposed the Noble Savage as a fit subject for Romantic fiction, Irving gave the Indian a major role in three of his works: *A Tour of the Prairies* (1835), *Astoria* (1836), and *The Adventures of Captain Bonneville* (1837). In these historical travel-oriented accounts, the savage, degenerate side of the Western Indians appears, though Irving is careful to show the depredations of uncivilized frontier settlers which provoke Indian response.

Perhaps the most famous Indian images of the early nineteenth century were produced by James Fenimore Cooper. In his *Leatherstocking Tales* as well as other novels and essays, Cooper popularized a Romantic image of the Indian. Drawing on the historical novels of Sir Walter Scott, Cooper sought to create epics of the American frontier, a world poised between savagism and civilization where the moral character of Indian and settler could be tested. Cooper's frontiersmen and Indians are motivated by emotion, but emotion modified by their natural social position, culture, and individual moral codes. Cooper was able to embed his narratives with both the popular and the poetic images of the Indian; he could be both a howling hell-hound and a natural nobleman. Cooper's interest was less in the Indian than in the paradoxical influence of the savage and the wilderness on the civilized man and the future of the American nation.

The popularity of the Indian as literary subject in the first half of the nineteenth century was widespread. No major writer could escape the subject. John Greenleaf Whittier, James Russell Lowell, and William Cullen Bryant all seriously explored the cultural implications of the Noble Savage in historical poems. Southern writers such as William Gilmore Simms in *Yamasee* (1835) and *The Wigwam and the Cabin* (1853), and Robert Montgomery Bird in *Nick of the Woods* (1835), were more concerned with puncturing the stereotype of the Noble Savage by using the more popular violent images of the Indian's degraded moral character. For them, though the result of ignorance and not vice, savagism still inevitably withered when confronted with the superiority of civilization, especially southern civilization.

In 1839, Henry Rowe Schoolcraft published *Algic Researches*. As the first collection of authentic Indian oral tales, Schoolcraft's work provided a new direction for writers. In the 1840s and 1850s, many poems emerged which drew heavily on mythological material from the supposedly uncivilized savages. In addition to being taken as a proof of the moral nature of the Indian mind, these oral tales tended to reinforce the Romantic idea of a golden age of the Indian before the advent of the European. The best known of these mythological poems was, of course, Henry Wadsworth Longfellow's successful *The Song of Hiawatha* (1855). Abstracting the Indian from a historical to mythological plane allowed Longfellow to present the most Noble of Savages without dealing with the backlash of border violence.

Other major writers of the American Renaissance were deeply concerned with the American Indian. While not completely Romantic in their appraisals of the Indian, they still appreciated the Indian's supposed natural integrity, his spiritual relation to the land, and his stoic acceptance of fate. And of course, the tragedy of his imminent passing was lost on none. Ralph Waldo Emerson expressed in his journals the wish to retain something of the natural life and practical knowledge of the Indian; Henry David Thoreau, in *The Maine Woods* (1864) and in his unpublished manuscript on Indians, promoted an image of the Indian as fundamental man, the man inside every civilized man, but without the artifice and with his natural characteristics still untamed. And Herman Melville's moralistic attacks on stereotypical thinking, American mythmaking, and all forms of self-delusion placed him in a position sympathetic to the Indian. In works such as *The Confidence Man*, Melville's examination of civilized values encompassed the frontier and the popular traditions of border violence. Walt Whitman used the Indian as a model for the sensuous apprehension of nature.

In contrast to these writers, the great Romantic historians of the period, Francis Parkman and George Bancroft, while using Romantic narrative techniques, consistently portrayed the Indian as a savage standing obstinately in the way of the inevitable progress of civilization and Christianity. The Indian would be eliminated by a superior civilization, and his fate was well deserved. After the Civil War, the Indian as subject became increasingly identified with sectional and regional literature. Local color writers employed the Indian as an indication of the unique social characteristics which made up their individual provinces. However, the Indian did not play a key role in any extended philosophical discussion of the nature of man, as he had in the first half of the nineteenth century. Writers such as Bret Harte tended to marginalize Indian characters when they appeared at all. However, Joaquin Miller and Helen Hunt Jackson perceived the disregard and deadly misunderstanding which characterized contemporary attitudes toward Native Americans and responded with books which presented Indians in idealized Romantic characterizations, respectively *My Life Among the Modoc* (1873) and *Ramona* (1884).

Writers associated with American literary realism seldom chose the Indian as a subject for serious consideration. When they did, it was usually to ridicule Romantic stereotypes, sometimes by brutal character attacks which some have charged amounted to literary racism. Samuel Clemens writing in *Roughing It* (1872) and *The Adventures of Tom Sawyer* (1876), and some of the short fiction of Stephen Crane, provide numerous examples.

While the Indian slipped from consideration in serious literature, popular culture and popular literature seemed full of fantastic re-creations of historical encounters. The dime novels published by Beadle and Adams exemplified the sensationalism which fed public taste with increasingly violent images of the Indian as thoughtless savage killer and destroyer of civilized institutions. Realist writers saw themselves as supplying a necessary antidote to Romanticism and sensationalism in all subjects, including the Indian.

With the emergence of regionalist writers, the Indian once again was seen as a topic for serious consideration by American writers. However, in the writing of Hamlin Garland, Jack London, Charles Lummis, John Neihardt, Willa Cather, Mary Austin, and others, the dynamics of Indian social and philosophical life began to be perceived. Building on the intellectual foundations of turn-of-the-century biology and anthropology, regionalist writers explored the culture of the Indian with a growing sense of cultural relativism. Books such as London's *The Son of the Wolf* (1900), Garland's *The Captain of Grey Horse Troop* (1902), Neihardt's *The Lonesome Trail* (1906), and Austin's *Isidro* (1904) developed Indian characters and cultures with an eye toward explaining Indian worldviews. These regionalist writers constituted the leading edge of the second wave of serious literary and artistic interest in the American Indian, a wave which lasted into the 1930s.

A variety of new sources opened for American writers which encouraged their interest in presenting more balanced images of Native Americans, and in considering the possibility that Indian culture and literature had something positive to say to twentieth-century America. With the increased availability of reliable ethnographic material and an attitude of cultural relativism flourishing in anthropology, many writers felt they could now speak with some authority and common sense when dealing with Indian topics. Also, the publishing world of magazines and books was encouraging the publication of firsthand accounts of contacts with Native Americans. Equally significant was the fact that some Native writers, such as Charles Eastman, Gertrude Bonnin, Pauline Johnson, Luther Standing Bear, Geronimo, and a few years later Black Elk, John Mathews, John Oskison, and D'Arcy McNickle, were being published. In all these materials, American writers found a renewal of a sense of community, spirituality, and land-orientation as well as a revitalized sense of the essential power of art and literature. While this may appear to represent a countertendency to the flow of modernism in America, in reality many American modernists saw "primitivism" and thus the world of the American Indian as a base on which to erect a new, reawakened vision of modern man's relationship to the cosmos. It became acceptable once again to say that the American Indian had something important to teach American society.

Many writers felt that the most immediate access into the American Indian world was through the wealth of ethnographic song/poetry which existed in the early twentieth century. After the interest of poets like Carl Sandburg, Alice Corbin Henderson, and others associated with *Poetry* magazine launched the publication of the first anthology of American Indian poetry, *The Path on the Rainbow* (1918), literary magazines and publishers seemed open to work that presented what seemed to be authentic positive images of Indians and Indian culture. Poets as diverse as Amy Lowell in *Ballads for Sale* (1927) and *Legends* (1921), Witter Bynner in *Indian Earth* (1929), and Lew Sarrett in *Box of God* (1922) won acclaim with their work. But dozens of other writers, such as Mary Austin, John Gould Fletcher, Hartley Burr Alexander, and John Neihardt, used Indian cultural material at one point or another to expand America's cultural horizons. Michael Castro summed up the sense of an era when, in writing about the Indian as symbol in the work of Vachel Lindsay, Hart Crane, and William Carlos Williams, he concluded, "The red man himself served as a symbol of both the American continent and a new American identity based on a harmonious relationship—a mystical participation—with the land. . . . To each, the Indian was a being at one with the land and so was a powerful symbol in the battle against alienation that was so painfully widespread in America of the 1920s" (1983:49).

Many similar attitudes toward the Indian were expressed in pre–World War II American fiction. Regional books and westerns such as Zane Grey's *The Vanishing American* (1925), Willa Cather's *Death Comes for the Archbishop* (1926), Edna Ferber's *Cimarron* (1929), and Kenneth Roberts's *Northwest Passage* (1937) began to explore Indian characters and cultures with the idea that the Indian should be presented with the complexity and psychological depth common to any other character, and the building of the new Indian even extended to mainstream American literature as well with the Pulitzer Prize–winner *Laughing Boy* (1929) by Oliver La Farge, and works by William Faulkner like *Go Down, Moses* (1942) and especially "The Bear." Many modern writers acknowledged that to understand the American experience and the American self, it was vital to attempt to understand the Indian. However, these were still non-Native patterns and images based on the interpretation of Native Americans by the non-Native world. It would be left to a later generation of Native writers to individualize the images of tribal peoples and to speak with authority about the internal cultural dynamics of the Native American experience.

After World War II, as the United States tried to return to normal life, writers produced few images of the Indian. As termination and relocation swept the reservations, the American public looked to a new prosperity built on the righteousness of a victorious way of life. While much American poetry was dominated by the tenets of New Criticism, some writers following the tradition of William Carlos Williams were pushing for "a new American poetry, a new relationship to place and nature, and new values and identity. Olson, Rothenberg, and Snyder each studied Indian cultures as a source of poetic renewal" (Castro 1983:102). Charles Olson as the prime force behind the Black Mountain School, Jerome Rothenberg at the center of the New York Deep Image movement, and Gary Snyder, prominent West Coast Beat poet, encouraged other writers who wished to create a new American consciousness which was mythic, more in harmony with the American landscape, and which could unify fragmented modern experience.

The interest and exploration of Indian literature and culture rose until it peaked in the Ethnopoetics movement of the late 1960s and early 1970s. Indicative of the level of interest was the Pulitzer Prize award Gary Snyder received for his book of poems and essays inspired by Indian cultures, *Turtle Island* (1974). Though Snyder first published a book of poems influenced by Native American thought in 1960 (*Myths and Texts*), it was not until the publication of *Technicians of the Sacred* (1969) and *Shaking the Pumpkin* (1972) edited by Jerome Rothenberg that the Ethnopoetics movement became influential. Rothenberg attempted to draw on "American Indian poetics as the basis for developing new, postmodern performance forms" (Castro 1983:117). The movement dissipated when its prime journal, *Alcheringa*, ceased publication in the mid-1970s, though linguistic anthropologists use the term "ethnopoetics" to refer to the poetic structures of oral literature. The decline may have been due in part to the rising number of Indian writers who were creating literature which more accurately expressed tribal perspectives and Native self-image as well as to some specific attacks by Native writers chiding the ethnopoet to explore his own cultural backgrounds. The image of the Indian that emerges throughout this period is that of the primitive equivalent of a sophisticated modern artist, who expresses the ideal of spiritual, ecological, and communal harmony so earnestly pursued by the 1960s counterculture.

Post–World War II fiction writers seemed much less interested in the Indian as source of inspiration. Some novels using Indian characters were published, mostly in the field of western American literature. Most notable were the works of Frank Walters, especially *The Man Who Killed the Deer* (1942), Mari Sandoz's *Cheyenne Autumn* (1953) and *The Horsecatcher* (1957), Conrad Richter's *The Light in the Forest* (1953), and Dan Cushman's *Stay Away Joe* (1953). While none of these books produced large sales, they began to show the Indian in a more sympathetic light, usually as a melancholy figure caught between two worlds. This approach did require that the authors explore Indian values and worldview, but the message to most readers was one of the tragic and inevitable loss of something pristine and beautiful. Ken Kesey's *One Flew over the Cuckoo's Nest* (1962) marks the movement of the image of the Indian from the fringes of western American literature to the center of the counterculture of the late 1960s and early 1970s. Once again, nobleness and freedom are united with social criticism to create a popular image. Hal Borland's *When Legends Die*, Thomas Berger's *Little Big Man* (1964), Margaret Craven's *I Heard the Owl Call My Name* (1967), Arthur Kopit's *Indians: A Play* (1969), and *Rabbit Boss* (1973) by Thomas Sanchez fleshed out the political and social implications of this image. But it was Dee Brown's *Bury My Heart at Wounded Knee* (1971) which fixed for a generation the image of the patriotic, humanitarian Indian chief reluctantly fighting to protect his land against the murdering and deceitful government military forces waging a relentless war. The contemporary parallels were perceived by many readers. Yet an even more alluring facet was to be added in the late 1960s, when the counterculture attempted to incorporate Indian values and philosophy into its perspective. The republication of *Black Elk Speaks* in 1961 initiated a widespread exploration of Indian religious and mystical thought that culminated in Carlos Castaneda's *The Teachings of Don Juan: A Yaqui Way of Knowledge* (1968) and its increasingly fantastic sequels. The Indian became everything contemporary America was not. He was the first ecologist, an original communalist, and a peace-loving democrat whose religion and philosophy expressed profound practical and mystical wisdom.

Though a version of this construct was presented in 1979 with the publication of *Hanta Yo* by Ruth Beebe Hill, the image had faded by the late 1970s under the onslaught of Native American writers. The degree of change can be measured by the uproar of criticism from tribal people and literary critics which accompanied *Hanta Yo*'s publication. Since the 1970s, Native American writers have seemed to claim the cultural and moral high ground for the production of literary images of Indian characters. With this emerging corps of writers, new themes and images relating to Native concerns are being created. For the 1980s, few lasting Anglo-American literary images have taken shape. Notable exceptions are the Canadian W. P. Kinsella's *The Moccasin Telegraph and Other Indian Tales* (1983), and the string of increasingly successful Tony Hillerman mystery novels starting with *The Blessing Way* (1970) and *Dance Hall of the Dead* (1973) and ending with *Coyote Waits* (1990).

What has flourished is a series of accounts with seers, shamans, medicine men, and medicine women aimed at a New Age readership ready to resurrect the more mystical and ecological aspects of the late 1960s image of the Indian. It is as difficult to consider them as literature as it is to take seriously their claims to authenticity and accuracy when contemporary Native American writers so clearly express Native American worldviews and culture. The tenacity of this present reincarnation of Romantic ideals gives testimony to the continuing need for American culture and letters to come to terms with difference and otherness as represented in Native American peoples.

James Ruppert
University of Alaska—Fairbanks

BIBLIOGRAPHY

Berkhofer, Robert F. *The White Man's Indian: Images of the American Indian from Columbus to the Present.* New York: Random House, 1979.

Castro, Michael. *Interpreting the Indian: Twentieth-Century Poets and the Native American.* Albuquerque: U of New Mexico P, 1983.

Fussell, Edwin. *Frontier: American Literature and the American West*. Princeton: Princeton UP, 1965.

Keiser, Albert. *The Indian in American Literature*. Oxford: Oxford UP, 1933. Rpt. New York: Octagon Books, 1970.

Pearce, Roy Harvey. *Savagism and Civilization: A Study of the Indian and the American Mind*. Baltimore: Johns Hopkins UP, 1953. Rev. ed., 1965.

Ruppert, James. "Discovering America: Mary Austin and Imagism." *Studies in American Indian Literature*. Ed. Paula Allen. New York: MLA, 1983.

Slotkin, Richard. *Regeneration Through Violence: The Mythology of the American Frontier 1600–1860*. Middletown: Wesleyan UP, 1973.

Smith, Henry Nash. *Virgin Land: The American West as Symbol and Myth*. Cambridge, MA: Harvard UP, 1950.

"Teaching the Indian in American Literature." *Studies in American Indian Literature*. Ed. Paula Allen. New York: MLA, 1983.

P*aula Gunn Allen* (*October 24, 1939–*)

Paula Allen is a noted writer, scholar, and teacher. Her writing displays a wide range of cross-cultural knowledge and perceptual skills. A highly polished poet and essayist, she has received wide notice for her work, significantly influencing many writers and scholars. She has published seven volumes of poetry, one novel, and a collection of critical essays and has contributed numerous poems and essays to magazines and anthologies. Finally, her work as editor and teacher is equally well known.

Paula Allen was born in Albuquerque, New Mexico, and raised in the small Hispanic land-grant village of Cubero on the edge of the Laguna Pueblo, of which she remains a member. She was born to a mother of Laguna Pueblo–Sioux ancestry and a father of Lebanese-American ancestry, and her childhood was a confluence of cultures and aesthetics. She grew up listening to half a dozen languages and musical traditions, yet Allen shows an unabashed bias for Laguna's traditions as well as its understandings and values. Both the land which delineates Laguna sacred cosmology and Pueblo cultural traditions have continued to form the bedrock of her understanding of the world and her place in it. Much of her creative and critical work originates in insights derived from her early experiences.

After education at Catholic schools in Albuquerque, at the Colorado Women's College, and at the University of New Mexico, she attended the University of Oregon, where she received a B.A. in English in 1966. Two years later, in 1968, she received an M.F.A. in Creative Writing from the same institution, and then taught for a year at De Anza Community College. She remained in California for several years before returning to Albuquerque. From 1971 to 1973, she taught at the University of New Mexico while taking courses toward her Ph.D. In the mid-1970s, she taught at San Diego State University, College of San Mateo, and the

California State University at San Francisco. Her first book of poetry, *The Blind Lion* (1974), was published by Thorp Springs Press. In 1975, she received her Ph.D. in American Studies from the University of New Mexico. She remained in Albuquerque working in a variety of professional positions, and in 1978–79 she taught at Fort Lewis College. In 1981, she moved to Los Angeles to accept a fellowship at UCLA. From 1982 to 1990, she taught at the University of California at Berkeley in the Native American Studies Department. In 1990, she accepted a position in the English Department at the University of California at Los Angeles. In the same year, she was awarded the Native American Literature prize, and her anthology *Spider Woman's Granddaughters* received the American Book Award. The late 1970s and early 1980s were productive years for her poetry. She published *Coyote's Daylight Trip* (1978), *A Cannon Between My Knees* (1981), *Star Child* (1981), and *Shadow Country* (1982). In 1977, she helped organize the first curriculum development seminar on Native American Studies sponsored by the Modern Language Association, which took place at Northern Arizona University. Later she compiled and edited the results of that seminar in a volume published by the MLA, entitled *Studies in American Indian Literature* (1983).

Allen has had significant recognition for her work. She received a National Endowment for the Arts fellowship for essay writing in 1977, a postdoctoral fellowship in American Indian Studies at UCLA in 1981, and in 1984 was awarded a postdoctoral research grant by the Ford Foundation–National Research Council to study oral traditional elements in Native American novels.

Her recent publications reveal the variety of her talents. She has published a novel, *The Woman Who Owned the Shadows* (1983); a book of poetry, *Wyrds* (1987); and a critical volume, *The Sacred Hoop: Recovering the Feminine in American Indian Traditions* (1986). She edited a collection of writings by Native American women entitled *Spider Woman's Granddaughters* (1989). *Skins and Bones*, a collection of her poems selected from 1979–87, was published in 1988. In 1991, she published *Grandmothers of the Light: A Medicine Woman's Sourcebook*, a collection of essays and traditional tales.

In both her creative and critical work, Allen forges conscious connections between her life and the life of the Laguna Pueblo. Laguna was founded by people from several different pueblos, and it has always included Navajos, Mexicans, and whites. Allen sees this confluence structuring her ancestry and her life. This diversity could be a source of fragmentation, but, for her, it is more importantly a source of strength. She sees the people at Laguna functioning as mediators, and her own life as a half-breed as reflecting centuries of Laguna experience. Both her critical and creative work rise out of the necessity of talking from at least two perspectives at once—an act that is both illuminating and alienating. For Allen, the mediator's role is more than just making peace between warring factions of experience; it is an act in which the epistemological framework of one group is used to define meaning and value in another system. Her creative acts of mediation are both personal and cross-cultural. Allen has said, "to me a poem is a recording of an event of the mind" ("I Climb the Mesas," 18). In her work, the event of the mind is always mediational.

In determining the nature of this "event of the mind," it is helpful to consider the Black Mountain poets Robert Creeley and Charles Olson, whom Allen acknowledged as influential. On the surface, her line length and breath unit reveal a similar sense of craft, but, more important, the movement of Allen's poetry is informed by Olson's demand for projective movement in the poem—one perception must lead immediately to a further perception. For Olson, as for Creeley, with whom Allen also studied, the act of observation is previous to the poem, so poetry is less concerned with description than with perception. Or as Lincoln (1983:215) describes the movement of Allen's poetry, "impression leads toward thought." However, the nature of Allen's perception is quite different from that of the Black Mountain poets. Her act of mind is one in which Native perception forges the interconnections between a structuring series of opposing foci—physical/spiritual, contemporary/traditional, woman/man, wilderness/civilization, grounded/disconnected, personal/mythic, and white/Indian; her field of composition is one of spirit, value, and continuance.

Many of her poems, such as those in her volume *Shadow Country*, are grounded in perceptions which reconcile the opposites in the contemporary Native American experience. Native perception and contemporary American reality meet in the text of the Native American poet, who must "develop metaphors that will not only reflect the dual perceptions of Indian/non-Indian but that will reconcile them. The ideal metaphor will harmonize the contradictions and balance them so that internal equilibrium can be achieved, so that each perspective is meaningful and, in their joining, psychic unity rather than fragmentation occurs" ("Answering the Deer," 42). Many of her poems contrast assimilation and colonization with spirit-infused and land-centered values to find a metaphoric balance between the despair created by loss and the hope inherent in continuance.

Allen's critical work reveals her analytical insight into literature and has engendered worldwide respect. One focus of her analysis is Native American oral tradition. Her often quoted article "The Sacred Hoop: A Contemporary Perspective" (in *Studies in American Indian Literature*) explores the basic assumptions behind traditional Native American literature. In "The Sacred Hoop," she discusses the expressive forms of traditional song and poetry. Moreover, she attempts to reveal the epistemological underpinnings of Native literary impulses as contrasted to the literary tradition of Western civilization.

A second focus of her critical and creative work is the clarification of the experience of Native American women, in both traditional and contemporary societies. Allen's feminism is an act of mythic and cross-cultural insight as well as a social position. Wiget (1985:118) has observed that Allen "celebrates Native women as the source of connections, the focus of relationships, the well of creativity." While Allen discusses woman's role in mythic terms, referring to the Laguna figure Spider Woman, maker of the world, she also presents women as healing agents. For Allen, creativity and curing (on many levels) are always intricately connected. Native women especially draw strength for themselves, their families, and their societies from their spiritual sources, their roles as sexual and cultural mediators, their connectedness with the earth and its creatures, and their historical consciousness. She concludes by saying that the poetry of Native women expresses these distinguishing characteristics; thus, their work is seen as essential for Native physical and spiritual survival. As the mythic figures of traditional tales make and renew the world, so contemporary Native women writers renew and re-create the vital connections and visions which allow for tribal continuance. The bedrock of these connections, of course, is their relation to spirit: "American Indian women who write have as our first and most significant characteristic a solid, impregnable and ineradicable orientation toward a spirit-informed view of the universe, which provides an internal structure to both our consciousness and our art" ("This Wilderness in My Blood," 95). For Allen, then, Native American world views are fundamentally mystic and spiritual.

In *The Sacred Hoop*, she adds to her previous positions the contention that Native American societies promoted an essentially "woman-centered world view." She offers what critic Elaine Jahner, in her review of that book, has called "alternate he-tories" (1986:102). Critic Elizabeth Hanson, while commenting on the limited supporting evidence provided for Allen's "gynocratic" view of tribal life, concludes: "Subjunctive at points, reflective of a chosen audience at others, Allen's criticism is ambitiously large-scale, enthusiastic, mythic, prolix and uneven in tone" (1990:18). Jahner, noting the scope of Allen's task, writes, "Because of her maturity and breadth of experience, Allen succeeds in giving us what no one else has, a highly intelligent yet personal critique of basic cultural assumptions from a Native American feminist perspective" (1986:104).

In both her creative and critical work, Allen strives to forge connections between the physical and the spirit, between peoples and various cultural structures, between the past and the present, between the individual and the forces of the cosmos. This connectedness to the spirit of all things, to the intelligent consciousness of all things, which Allen sees in contemporary American Indian literary work, is also the link to American Indian traditional poetry and tribal poetry around the world. For Paula

Allen, studies of traditional poetry and contemporary poetry are, necessarily, similar acts, spiritual acts.

James Ruppert
University of Alaska—Fairbanks

BIBLIOGRAPHY

Primary Sources

Allen, Paula Gunn. *The Blind Lion*. Berkeley: Thorp Springs Press, 1974.
———. *Coyote's Daylight Trip*. Albuquerque: La Confluencia, 1978.
———. *A Cannon Between My Knees*. New York: Strawberry Press, 1981.
———. *Star Child*. Marvin, ND: Blue Cloud Quarterly Press, 1981.
———. "Answering the Deer." *American Indian Culture and Research Journal* 6.3 (1982): 35–45.
———. *Shadow Country*. Los Angeles: American Indian Studies Center, 1982.
———. *The Woman Who Owned the Shadows*. Argyle, NY: Spinsters Ink, 1983.
———. "This Wilderness in My Blood: Spiritual Foundations of the Poetry of Five American Indian Women." *Coyote Was Here: Essays on Contemporary Native American Literary and Political Mobilization*. Ed. Bo Schöler. Aarhus, Denmark: Seklos, 1984.
———. *The Sacred Hoop: Recovering the Feminine in American Indian Traditions*. Boston: Beacon Press, 1986.
———. "The Autobiography of a Confluence." *I Tell You Now: Autobiographical Essays by Native American Writers*. Ed. Brian Swann and Arnold Krupat. Lincoln: U of Nebraska P, 1987.
———. "I Climb the Mesas in My Dreams: An Interview with Paula Allen." *Survival This Way: Interviews with Contemporary Native American Poets*. Ed. Joseph Bruchac. Tucson: U of Arizona P, 1987.
———. *Wyrds*. San Francisco: Taurean Horn, 1987.
———. *Skins and Bones: Poems 1979–87*. Albuquerque: West End Press, 1988.
———. *Spider Woman's Granddaughters: Traditional Tales and Contemporary Writing by Native American Women*. Boston: Beacon Press, 1989.
———. *Grandmothers of the Light: A Medicine Woman's Sourcebook*. Boston: Beacon Press, 1991.
———, ed. *Studies in American Indian Literature: Critical Essays and Course Designs*. New York: MLA, 1983.

Secondary Sources

ASAIL. Bibliography 5. *Studies in American Indian Literature Newsletter* 7.3 (1983): 55–80.
Hanson, Elizabeth. *Paula Gunn Allen*. Western Writers Series. Boise: Boise State UP, 1990.
Jahner, Elaine. "A Laddered, Rain-bearing Rug: Paula Allen's Poetry." *Women and Western American Literature*. Ed. Helen Winter Stauffer and Susan Rosowski. Troy: Whitston, 1982. 311–26.
———. "A Review of *The Sacred Hoop*." *Parabola* 11.4 (1986): 102+.
Lincoln, Kenneth. *Native American Renaissance*. Los Angeles: U of California P, 1983.
Ruppert, James. "Paula Gunn Allen and Joy Harjo: Closing the Distance Between Personal and Mythic Space." *American Indian Quarterly* 7.1 (1983): 27–40.
Wiget, Andrew. *Native American Literature*. Boston: Twayne, 1985.

399

Joseph Bruchac *(October 16, 1942–)*

Storyteller, poet, publisher, editor, Joseph Bruchac has devoted his considerable energies to bringing American Indian verbal and written art to the eyes and ears of a generation of readers, both in America and abroad. He has authored more than twenty volumes of his own work, and his poems and stories have appeared in more than 400 publications. He has also earned a considerable reputation as a storyteller, traveling around the country and performing both contemporary and traditional stories. Perhaps Bruchac is best known in the field as an editor and promoter of new talent. As editor and co-founder of the Greenfield Review Press, he has been the single most important force in the nation in publishing and promoting the work of emerging Native American writers. Bruchac is perhaps most widely known for his editing of two key volumes: *Songs from This Earth on Turtle's Back* (1983), a collection of the work of fifty-two poets, as well as the more recent collection of interviews with American Indian writers, *Survival This Way* (1987).

In an interview in 1988 in the *Glen Falls Review*, Bruchac stated that it was futile to try to talk in isolation about his various editing projects, his storytelling forays across the country, or even his own writing. "You have to talk about where I live, about my family, about the things around me" (4).

Born in Saratoga Springs, New York, of mixed ancestry—Slovak on one side and Abenaki and English on the other—Bruchac remembers the value both in his family and in his community of the art of storytelling. Though he has lived and traveled throughout the world, Bruchac now lives in the same town where he grew up in a house built by his grandfather. He began learning stories of the Adirondacks as a child from his grandfather, Jesse Bowman, who came from a long line of Adirondack woodsmen and was of Abenaki Indian ancestry. Later, Bruchac earned a degree in English with a minor in zoology from Cornell University and went on to earn his M.A. in writing from Syracuse University. In 1966, he and his wife, Carol, went off to teach in Ghana. The three years they spent there were a time when he wrote seriously and began to formulate his priorities. "Living in another country made us realize certain things about . . . who we were and what we wanted to do. And when you are an ex-patriot, you are not rooted in your own land" ("Informal Conversation," 7). A sense of one's roots and one's dynamic link to the community, two fundamental ingredients of Bruchac's vision, melded in Ghana with constant contact with the oral tradition. The African peoples the Bruchacs taught shared stories, and the couple saw the integrity of these stories in their lives.

It was during the years in Africa that the Bruchacs decided to return home to the house his grandfather had built, and from there to launch a substantial publishing effort—a journal that would feature the work of minority writers, writers whose substantial talent had not found a way into print. For years, *The Greenfield Review* placed those voices from the margin at its center. The *Review* was always original, fresh, and long. Bruchac would later express concern that each volume was a book, but that its readers saw it as a single volume, a "throwaway." It was this attitude that led Bruchac and his wife to restructure their publishing activities. *Greenfield Review* was phased out, and in its place was born a new publishing house, the Greenfield Review Press. The list of Native American writers whose first volume was brought out by Greenfield Press reads like a Who's Who in contemporary Native American literature: Janet Campbell Hale, Barney Bush, and Linda Hogan are just a few of the many writers whose publication careers began at Greenfield.

When one reads through Bruchac's numerous volumes of poetry and prose, one is struck by the presence of the natural world. Often geographically fixed, the poems and stories offer encounters with animals, rocks bearing maps of the land, neighbors, work horses, squirrels, frogs. Bruchac chooses not to select the lofty pose; his poems seem at first simple evocations of sights and sounds, often with a moment of perception or renewal at the end. Read more carefully, they are indeed transformative. For Bruchac, the act of seeing, of looking carefully, and *really* seeing, is the essence of both art and life. In "Compost" (*Near the Mountains*, 27) the narrator is caught in the act of turning the compost, and he observes that even as the spading fork slips into the earth, his "hands feel ready to spout / strong roots and grow green." The moment of man transcending his humanity and becoming more closely aligned to the natural circle, as well as the theme of being rooted, of a fierce and loyal attachment to place, to the land—these are paramount issues in Bruchac's work.

The theme of ethnicity is another concern throughout his career. Many of the poems and stories celebrate his own Abenaki connections, but many other poems have a less exclusive realm. Several pieces celebrate the Slovak half of the family, and there are poems about Africans, poems set in Navajo country around Ship Rock, and poems featuring Kokopilau, the Hopi's Humped Back Flute Player. Bruchac's evident interest in his own ethnicity has given him a more expansive appreciation of other cultures and traditions.

At moments in the writing, the feeling is spiritual, religious in a way that defies easy categorization. Bruchac's poetic voyages lead to moments of self-realization and transcendence that demand to be examined in spiritual ways. In "Prayer" (*Near the Mountains*, 20), we are offered an invocation stunning in its simplicity and its magnitude. The narrator asks only for "the blessing of the crayfish / the beatitude of the birds" as he strives to find his place in the universe and to fashion his songs.

Bruchac is a poet of names. He is a man who has looked closely, and studied the world around him. In his work, we learn the names of the birds, the trees, the flowers. Yet even this naming has a further dimension. At moments in the work it becomes an incantation, a recipe for spiritual connection not only with "nature" but also with ancestors, shadowy spirits who share the land with him.

Bruchac has not been content to stay at home and write his work. He has earned a substantial reputation as a traveling storyteller. His stories reflect the legends and lore of his own region as well as incorporate his travels around the world. Bruchac not only sees storytelling as a fine kind of entertainment, but sees as well how stories are a part of us all. They reassert our humanity while they remind us that we all have stories to tell. He has likened stories to breath itself—they are an integral part of us, and like breath, they join us to other things and are meant to be shared ("teller").

Bruchac's writing and storytelling have earned him a number of awards, including grants from the National Endowment for the Arts as well as a Rockefeller Foundation Award. Yet if his own writing has brought him international acclaim, one can only say his editing has placed him squarely at the heart of the field. As noted earlier, the journal *The Greenfield Review* was later followed by the steady stream of volumes and chapbooks that the Greenfield Press released, through which Bruchac introduced a procession of new writers into the eyes of the international literary community. He has also edited a number of anthologies to introduce the work of not only Native American writers, but Asian American writers, and even prison writers, as well. Throughout his career, Bruchac has insisted on enlarging the canon of American literature, of moving the margins into the spotlight. His acclaimed text *Songs from This Earth on Turtle's Back* (1983) introduced readers to a new generation of Native writers—almost all of whom have gone on to win major critical acclaim. This anthology was the first of its kind and would later encourage the larger publishing houses to "discover" contemporary American Indian poetry. More recently, his *Survival This Way* (1987) offers readers of Native American literature a series of probing and insightful interviews with the finest writers in the field today. Among those interviewed are James Welch, Mary Tall Mountain, and Duane Niatum.

Rereading Bruchac's stories, poems, and essays, one tends to find a quiet voice, one that is revealing yet gentle, spoken in steady tones and not shouted. Yet there is no more political writer than Bruchac. In fact, underlying everything he does, the stories and poems he writes, the stories he tells, the struggling writers that his press and anthologies have promoted, is a political credo that writing has power. In an interview in 1988 in *Newswatch*, he commented, "A writer has a role in society. . . . Poetry helps us see the world, and what is more important than seeing and hearing? . . . And even more it builds culture, it is the thing that distinguishes us as individuals, peoples, nations, tribes, clans. . . . It is vitally at the center of all things that are best in us" ("The Earth, My Inspiration"). At the center of Bruchac's vision is the belief that words can change the world. It would appear that he is right. Now, as curriculum committees across the country join ranks with publishers and scholars to find ways to incorporate marginal voices into the canon of Western thought, we find ourselves turning again and again to Bruchac's work.

Andrea Lerner
California State University—Chico

BIBLIOGRAPHY

Primary Sources

Bruchac, Joseph. *Indian Mountain and Other Poems*. Ithaca, NY: Ithaca House Press, 1971.

————. *The Buffalo in the Syracuse Zoo*. Greenfield Center, NY: Greenfield Press, 1972.

————. *Flow*. Austin: Cold Mountain Press, 1975.

————. *The Road to Black Mountain*. Berkeley, CA: Thorp Springs Press, 1976.

————. *Entering Onondaga*. Austin: Cold Mountain Press, 1978.

————. *There Are No Trees Inside the Prison*. Brunswick, ME: Blackberry Press, 1978.

————. *The Good Message of Handsome Lake*. Greensboro, NC: Unicorn Press, 1979.

————. *Breaking Silence: An Anthology of Asian American Poetry*. Greenfield Center, NY: Greenfield Press, 1983.

————. *Songs from This Earth on Turtle's Back*. Greenfield Center, NY: Greenfield Press, 1983.

————. *The Light from Another Country: A Collection of Poetry from Americans in Prison*. Greenfield Center, NY: Greenfield Press, 1984.

————. *Iroquois Stories: Heroes and Heroines, Monsters and Magic*. Illus. by Daniel Burgevin. CA: Crossing Press, 1985.

————. *The Wind Eagle and Other Abenaki Stories*. Illus. by Kahionhes. Bowman Books, 1985.

————. *North Country: An Anthology of Contemporary Writing from the Upper Hudson Valley and the Adirondacks*. Greenfield Center, NY: Greenfield Press, 1986.

————. *Tracking*. Ion Books, 1986.

————. *Walking with My Sons*. Lockland Press, 1986.

————. *Near the Mountains: New and Selected Poems*. White Pine Press, 1987.

————. *Survival This Way: Interviews with American Indian Poets*. Tucson: U of Arizona P, 1987.

————. *The Faithful Hunter: Abenaki Stories*. Illus. by Kahionhes. Bowman Books, 1988.

————. *The White Moose*. Drawings by Angie Eagle. Vol. 34, No. 2. Marvin, SD: Blue Cloud Quarterly, 1988.

————. *Langes Gedachtnis* [Long Memory]. Osnabruck, Germany: O.B.E.M.A. Editions, 1989.

————. *Return of the Sun: Native American Tales of the Northeast Woodlands*. Illus. by Gary Carpenter. Crossing Press, 1989.

————. *New Voices from the Long House: Contemporary Iroquois Writing*. Greenfield Center, NY: Greenfield Press, 1990.

————, and Michael Caduto. *Keepers of the Earth: Native American Stories and Activities for Children*. Illus. by Kahionhes and Carol Wood. Fulcrum Press, 1988.

————, and Michael Caduto. *All Our Relatives: Native American Animal Stories and Activities for Children*. Fulcrum Press, 1991.

————. *The Next World: An Anthology of Poetry in English from Africa, Asia, and the Caribbean*. Greenfield Center, NY: Greenfield Press.

————. *Stone Giants and Flying Heads*. Iroquois Folk Tales. Crossing Press.

————. *Turkey Brother*. Iroquois Folk Tales. Crossing Press.

Secondary Sources

"Teller of Tales." *Utica Dispatch-Observer*, February 6, 1986.

"The Earth, My Inspiration." *Newswatch*, September 12, 1988.

"An Informal Conversation with Joe Bruchac." *The Glen Falls Review* 6 (1988–89).

Elizabeth Cook-Lynn (1930–)

The northern plains have always been important to Elizabeth Cook-Lynn. Born in 1930 on the reservation at Fort Thompson, South Dakota, she attended schools on the Fort Thompson and Big Bend reservations, eventually receiving a B.A. in journalism from South Dakota State College in 1952 and an M.Ed. in education, psychology, and counseling from the University of South Dakota in 1971.

At an early age, she was fascinated with writing, soon becoming a voracious reader. She credits much of her interest in writing to the influence of her grandparents, who were among the first writers in the Sioux language, and she sees her work as an extension and continuation of a growing body of Sioux literary expression. She also acknowledges a certain dismay at her discovery as she was growing up of the impoverished characterizations of Sioux culture in Euroamerican writing. These early experiences led her to believe in writing as an act of defiance, as an act which ensures survival and defies oppression.

Subsequently, as a member of the Crow Creek Sioux, her heritage as a Dakotah woman set the foundations for her approaches to myth and history. Dakotah oral tradition, as she has experienced it, provides her with rich sources for an exploration of the nature of myth and its role in contemporary life, a subject she expresses in many poems and short stories. She acknowledges the singers and drummers as the real poets of the Dakotah, and she sees the contemporary poet as one who must "consecrate history and event, survival and joy and sorrow, the significance of ancestors and the unborn" ("You May Consider," 59). In this way, contemporary writing can sustain the legacy of ancestors. It can perceive the traditional Dakotah values and explore what they have to say to today's experience.

Her first book, *Then Badger Said This* (1977), is an illustrated multigenre exploration of the sources of Dakotah life and values in which Cook-Lynn juxtaposes poetry, myth, personal history, and cultural history. In the creation of this book, she acknowledges the influence of N. Scott Momaday, and specifically *The Way to Rainy Mountain* (1969), in an effort to do for the Dakotah what Momaday did for the Kiowa. The chapbook *Seek the House of Relatives* (1983) includes a number of poems which introduce kinship and inheritance in personal and cultural terms, as well as one short story which is included in a later collection. Both books explore historical events to reveal cultural values which structure cross-cultural interactions.

The Power of Horses and Other Stories (1990) brings together previously published short fiction with unpublished stories. The thirteen stories present portraits of contemporary and traditional Sioux people surviving and responding to the challenges of this century from World War I to Indian activism, but responding in a way which confirms Sioux values without glossing over individual weaknesses.

Her novel *From the River's Edge* (1991) treads consciously political ground as it explores the assimilationist effects of Sioux/white relations through a trial over cows stolen from the farm of a Dakotah man. John Tatekeya has not lived up to his own and his mentors' expectations in life. The novel probes the corrupting influence of Euroamerican colonialism, which leads to betrayal and near-destruction of communal integrity. As realization grows in the protagonist, he takes a few small steps back toward tribal honor and a renewed understanding of tradition.

Much of her thinking about contemporary Native American experience and literature can be found in the pages of the *Wicazo Sa Review*, an Indian Studies journal, which she founded in 1985 and continues to edit.

She taught for four years at the secondary level. From 1971 to 1989, she taught English and Native Studies at Eastern Washington University. She is Professor Emeritus at EWU and has been a Visiting Professor at the University of California–Davis. Currently she lives and writes in Rapid City, South Dakota. Of her work, she writes that it "arises from what I know and want to express concerning Dakotah beliefs and values and experiences and imagination" ("Survival," 51).

James Ruppert
University of Alaska—Fairbanks

BIBLIOGRAPHY

Cook-Lynn, Elizabeth. *Then Badger Said This.* 1977. Rpt. Fairfield, WA: Ye Galleon Press, 1983.
———. *Seek the House of Relatives.* Marvin, SD: The Blue Cloud Quarterly Press, 1983.
———. "Survival." *The Wicazo Sa Review: A Journal of Indian Studies* 1.1 (Spring 1985): 49–52.

————. "As a Dakotah Woman." Interview with Joseph Bruchac. *Survival This Way: Interviews with American Indian Poets*. Ed. Joseph Bruchac. Tucson: U of Arizona P, 1987. 57–71.

————. "You May Consider Speaking About Your Art." *I Tell You Now: Autobiographical Essays by Native American Writers*. Ed. Brian Swann and Arnold Krupat. Lincoln: U of Nebraska P, 1987. 55–63.

————. *The Power of Horses and Other Stories*. New York: Arcade Publishing, 1990.

————. *From the River's Edge*. New York: Arcade Publishing, 1991.

Roemer, Kenneth. "Review of *Then Badger Said This*." *ASAIL Newsletter* n.s. 2 (Winter 1978): 55–58.

Ruppert, James. "The Uses of Oral Tradition in Six Contemporary Native American Poets." *American Indian Culture and Research Journal* 4 (1980): 87–110.

Vine Deloria, Jr. (March 26, 1933–)

Vine Deloria, Jr., is the most significant voice in this generation regarding the presentation and analysis of contemporary Indian affairs, their history, present shape, and meaning. He has a command both of the English language and of information about the "legislation" pertaining to Indian affairs from Pope Alexander VI's *Inter Caetera* bull of 1493 (in which the good pope did "give, grant, and assign forever to you and your heirs and successors, kings of Castile and Leon, all singular the aforesaid countries and islands . . . hitherto discovered . . . and to be discovered. . . . together with all their dominions, cities, camps, places, and villages, and all rights, jurisdictions, and appurtenances of the same" [*God Is Red*, 274–75]), to the 1978 demise and renewal of the Indian Claims Commission and the controversies over varying interpretations of the American Indian Religious Freedom Act of 1976. No other voice, Indian or white, has as full a command of the overall data of Indian history and affairs, and no other voice has the moral force, the honesty, to admit mistakes and to redress them, or the edge to bite through the layers of soft tissue, through the stereotypes, myths, and outright lies, to the bone, to the bone marrow, of Indian affairs.

What is it, precisely, that Deloria tells us? In *Custer Died for Your Sins* he examines the prevailing myths about Indians which locate them in the past and render them invisible. He calls this work "an Indian Manifesto"; it is a call to consciousness and action by Indian people every bit as much as it is a challenge to the so-called dominant society. He shows us that the Indian wars continue, for example, with the U.S. violation of the Pickering Treaty as recently as the 1960s, building the infamous Kinzua Dam that flooded the Seneca Reservation, while at the same time squandering "one hundred billion dollars" in Vietnam to supposedly "keep its commitments." He proves that the whole popular understanding of treaties is backwards.

411

No Indian tribes were ever given land by the United States; the tribes gave the U.S. land in order to have their title to the remaining land confirmed. On the issue of tax exemption, he tells us that most tribes believe that "they paid taxes for all time when they gave up some two billion acres of land to the United States" (*Custer*, 4). This is the information, the message, coming out of his analysis of contemporary Indian affairs.

Vine Deloria, Jr., was born in Martin, South Dakota, on the border of the Pine Ridge Indian reservation, and is an enrolled member of the Standing Rock Sioux Tribe. He comes from a distinguished Sioux family: his great-grandfather, Saswe, was a medicine man of the Yanktons; his grandfather was a Yankton chief who converted to Christianity in the 1860s and spent the rest of his life as a missionary on the Standing Rock Reservation. His father spent thirty-seven years as an Episcopal missionary in South Dakota among the Sioux, ending his career as Archdeacon of the Missionary District of South Dakota. His aunt, Ella Deloria, was an anthropologist trained by Franz Boas, with distinguished books (*Speaking of Indians* and *Dakota Texts*) to her credit. Deloria himself served in the U.S. Marine Corps, and after graduation from college attended the Augustana Lutheran Seminary in Rock Island, Illinois, for four years, earning his B.D. degree in 1963. After seminary he worked for the United Scholarship Service in Denver, Colorado, to develop a program to get scholarships for Indian students in eastern preparatory schools. In 1964, he became Executive Director of the National Congress of American Indians (NCAI) in Washington, D.C. In September 1967, he entered law school at the University of Colorado, hoping that Indian legal programs could do for the tribes what the Legal Defense Fund had done for the black community. He has been a member of the Board of Inquiry on Hunger and Malnutrition in the U.S.A. (where in 1967 he discovered black children in the Mississippi delta eating red clay on alternate days in order to fill their bellies (*We Talk, You Listen*, 194) and a member of the National Office for the Rights of the Indigent. He appeared as an expert witness at the four Wounded Knee trials; founded the Institute for the Development of Indian Law in Washington, D.C.; served as a consultant on the movie *Soldier Blue*; and was professor of political science at the University of Arizona in Tucson until 1990, directing the graduate program in American Indian Policy Studies. He also serves on the board of the Indian Rights Association. At present, he teaches in the department of law, history, political science, and religious studies at the Center for Studies in Ethnicity and Race in America at the University of Colorado at Boulder. More than all his, however, through his writing Vine Deloria, Jr., has been the spokesperson for Indian people as they are today, their history, their condition, their concerns, their views of white society, their best prospects for the future.

Anyone first approaching Deloria's written work is impressed by the sheer amount of it (fourteen books, nine of them as sole author; six "special reports" for government agencies or private foundations; more than a dozen editorials or articles as contributing editor; fourteen introductions to books; and more than eighty-five articles in a wide spectrum of magazines and journals). In addition to the amazing volume of this written work, there is the scope of it. He has been trained as a theologian, lawyer, and political scientist, and has written on all aspects of contemporary American Indian affairs, from the meaning and history of the treaties to the religious dimension of Indian life.

His early work *Custer Died for Your Sins* (an extremely popular book from the late 1960s) revealed a surface attraction sustained by the depth of the work. That surface attraction is evident in the title itself, in the elements of Custer—Death—Sin, and in the aiming of these elements aggressively at the reader. Early on, we learn that the title originally was a bumper sticker, common in Indian country, that struck back with humor and bite at the sort of religious consciousness in America that still expressed itself by erecting "Christ Died for Your Sins" signs at key points on the landscape, while at the same time erecting mission churches and schools on the choicest pieces of reservation land stolen through the Allotment Act. (It is worth pointing out that as of January 1989, Navajos converting to certain evangelical Christian churches were still *required* to publicly destroy, by burning, any of the *jish*, or medicine bundles, still in their safekeeping.) This bumper sticker title clearly states, as does the whole of Deloria's corpus, that sin is a major aspect of the American experience, but the sinners are those who have stolen and desecrated the land, and General George himself is *the* symbol of the greed, arrogance, aggression, and deceit that guides/fuels this desecration. Deloria is wise enough to realize that orgies of guilt and confession over past sins too often have been substituted for a significant change in attitude toward and/or treatment of American Indians, allowing us to avoid the central question of history: "Why must man repeat his mistakes?" As he points out, accepting responsibility for current and future continuations of the patterns of oppression and abuse is much harder than wallowing in guilt.

One aspect of Deloria's work that is especially clarifying is his ability to make suggestions for change after criticizing the status quo. For instance, in *The Nations Within: The Past and Future of American Indian Sovereignty*, co-authored in 1984 with fellow attorney and political scientist Clifford Lytle, Deloria sets forth his most detailed recommendations. This volume is mostly a carefully described narrative of the Indian New Deal policies of John Collier, which culminated in the Indian Reorganization Act of 1934. Deloria and Lytle describe the whole process of reform, debate, and compromise out of which this bill ultimately emerged, the problems of its implementation, and the "barren" decades of 1945–65 when the drive to terminate Indian reservations and federal responsibilities to the tribes was at its height. This narrative serves as the backbone for addressing contemporary Indian affairs. In a final chapter, "The Future of Indian Nations," Deloria and Lytle recommend (1) a call for structural reform of tribal governments that is basic, but that still allows connection between the past and present; (2) lasting, deep cultural renewal that will address the question of Indian identity in the modern world; (3) economic stability for Indian communities that recognizes the Indianness of the reservation while being efficient in present-day economic terms; and (4) stabilization and mutual respect in relations between tribes and federal and state governments. That chapter, then, is composed of sections which detail the prospects for and obstacles to each of these recommendations. It is this steady commitment to the details of the actual conditions of and prospects for the renewal processes of Indian communities as they now exist that makes Deloria's work so valuable.

The depth of Deloria's commitment to the cause of Indian rights, to the issue of sovereignty for Indian nations, to the calling for truth and justice in this nation's dealings with Indian peoples is unquestionable. But Deloria's work seeks dimensions far beyond the surface realities of contemporary Indian affairs or the history of white-Indian encounters in North America. Deloria shows us the nature of the huge rift between the spiritual "owners" of the land, the Indians, and the political owners of the land, the whites—a rift which creates obvious turbulence throughout the political, moral, and psychic life of the nation. Deloria believes that until a reconciliation between the two is achieved, our society will be unstable and very dangerous. It is this vision of a reconciled society that gives his treatment of Indian affairs and history such depth and bite.

Deloria never allows us to forget that the heart and soul of all aboriginal society is the connection to the land. As he puts it, "the fundamental choice of this century is between history and nature," or between the ideas of progress and evolution and the sacredness of one's actual place in the universe. As Deloria sees it, a belief in history, in progress, allows us to act immorally toward anything or anyone that stands in its way. Morality, right action, ethical maturity, is a matter of rootedness, of deep knowledge of and connection to place, of the capacity for establishing such connection even when one's place must change, or one must change one's place. In lecturing on this preeminence of the land itself in aboriginal experience, Deloria once quoted Carl Jung to precisely locate the root of his own work:

> Certain Australian primitives [sic] assert that one cannot conquer foreign soil, because in it there dwell strange ancestor-spirits who reincarnate themselves in the new born. The foreign land assimilates its conquerors. (Jung 1928:49)

He went on to ponder the effects of the earth on human personality, how specific places might be formative to particular kinds of personalities. Such pondering appears to be the deep source for all his work on Indian affairs, and of his awareness of the dangers of rootlessness/ruthlessness in those societies cut off from both conscious and unconscious links to the soil. In stating this preeminence of the land itself in aboriginal experience, Deloria quotes Curley, a Crow chief, in 1912, refusing to give any more of his land to the federal government:

> The soil you see is not ordinary soil—it is the dust of the blood, the flesh and the bones of our ancestors. We fought and bled and died to keep other Indians from taking it, and we fought and bled and died helping the whites. You will have to dig down through the surface before you can find nature's earth, as the upper portion is Crow. The land as it is, is my blood and my dead; it is consecrated; and I do not want to give up any portion of it. (*God Is Red*, 166–67)

Roger Dunsmore
University of Montana

BIBLIOGRAPHY

Primary Sources

Deloria, Vine, Jr. *Custer Died for Your Sins*. New York: Macmillan, 1969.

———. "This Country Was Better Off When the Indians Were Running It." *New York Times Magazine*, March 8, 1970. Rpt. in Alvin Josephy, ed. *Red Power*. New York: McGraw-Hill, 1971.

———. *We Talk, You Listen*. New York: Macmillan, 1970.

———. *God Is Red*. New York: Grosset and Dunlap, 1973.

———. "The Question of the 1868 Sioux Treaty . . . A Crucial Element in the Wounded Knee Trials." *Akwasasne Notes* (Spring 1973).

———. "The Indian Movement out of a Wounded Past." *Ramparts Magazine* (March 1975).

———. "Why Indians Aren't Celebrating the Bicentennial." *Learning Magazine* (November 14, 1975).

———. "The Fascination of Heresy." *Katallagete—Be Reconciled* (Spring 1977).

———. "Colorado Requiem on the Ravages of Rootlessness." *Quote Magazine* (September 1978).

———. *The Metaphysics of Modern Existence*. San Francisco: Harper & Row, 1979.

———. "Education and Imperialism." *Integrateducation* 109–110 (1982).

———. "Circling the Same Old Rock." *Marxism and Native Americans*. Ed. Ward Churchill. Boston: South End Press, 1983.

———. "The Indian Student Amid American Inconsistencies." Unpublished.

———, ed. *Sender of Words: The Neihardt Centennial Essays*. Salt Lake City: Howe Brothers, 1984.

———, and Sandra Cadwalder, eds. *The Aggressions of Civilization*. Philadelphia: Temple UP, 1984.

———, with Clifford Lytle. *The Nations Within*. New York: Pantheon Books, 1984.

Evers, Larry. "A Conversation with Vine Deloria, Jr." *Sun Tracks* (1978).

Secondary Sources

Jung, Carl. "Mind and Earth." *Contributions to Analytic Psychology*. Trans. C. F. and H. G. Baynes. London: Routledge and Kegan Paul, 1928.

Michael (Anthony) Dorris
(January 30, 1945–)

Michael Dorris has become significant to the field of Native American literature through his anthropological writings concerning the well-being of contemporary Native American culture groups, Native American history, and social concerns, and for his contributions to contemporary fiction. He and his wife, Louise Erdrich, have become widely known for their collaborations on several works of fiction, which have been published under Dorris's name, Erdrich's name or both. They also co-author under the pen name Milou North.

Dorris was born in Dayton, Washington, on January 30, 1945. Dorris is a Modoc tribal member, whose Indian ancestry comes from his father. When he was two years old, his father, Jim Dorris, died; his mother, Mary Besy (Burkhardt) Dorris, did not remarry. Dorris has remarked that his family life was characterized by the strength of single women. His mother and grandmother, both widows, and an unmarried aunt provided important role models for his own life and for his fiction. As a young unmarried man, he felt he had the support and ability to start his own family. He adopted his first son, Adam, in 1971. He later adopted two more children, Sava and Madeline. In 1981, he married Louise Erdrich; they have three daughters: Persia, Pallas, and Aza. These relationships have variously influenced Dorris's writing. His oldest son, Adam, suffered from Fetal Alcohol Syndrome. The struggles of diagnosing and treating Adam's consequent learning disabilities are detailed in the nonfiction book *The Broken Cord* (1989). Collaboration with his wife has resulted in several critically acclaimed novels, and his experiences as a father have been translated into several articles for educational publications and popular parenting magazines.

The range of Dorris's works includes articles for scholarly journals, articles and short fiction for general interest magazines for both adult and young adult audiences, novels, and nonfiction. In 1975, he wrote the text for *Native Americans: 500 Years After*, a documentary study of American Indian life through black-and-white photographs by Joseph C. Farber. In 1976, Dorris began a series of articles on racism in the classroom for the Council on Interracial Books for Children. "Why I'm Not Thankful for Thanksgiving" (1978) and "I Is Not for Indian" (1982) were reprinted in *Books Without Bias* (1989), edited by Beverly Slapin and Doris Seale. Dorris also served as editor with Arlene B. Hirschfelder and Mary Gloyne Byler on an earlier book, *Guide to Research on North American Indians* (1983). This resource work includes extensive bibliographies for research in anthropology, ethnology, archaeology, history, and contemporary urban issues.

His journal articles include "Native American Literature in an Ethnohistorical Context" (*College English* 41 (1979:147-62) and "The Grass Still Grows, the Rivers Still Flow: Contemporary Native Americans" (*Daedalus*, 1981). The first of these articles argues against the kind of reductionist thinking that allows for the full range of expression included in Native American literature to be taught as if there were widespread commonalities between tribes. Dorris advocates teaching the literature of a culture group with the ethnohistory of that group, to create academic depth. In "The Grass Still Grows, the Rivers Still Flow," Dorris offers a historical overview of Native Americans which includes major governmental policies toward Indians, precedent-establishing legal cases, and some of the society-shaping literary works of the last two hundred years of the U.S. history.

In 1972, Dorris accepted a position as Instructor of Anthropology and Chairman of the Native American Studies Department at Dartmouth University. He advanced during the 1970s and 1980s to become Professor of Anthropology and Native American Studies.

In 1981, he married Louise Erdrich and began to expand his writing into the area of fiction. In 1987, his first novel, *A Yellow Raft on Blue Water*, was published under his name only. The collaboration between Dorris and Erdrich is close, but certain characters are reserved for publication under one name or the other, or occasionally under the pen name of Milou North. This close working relationship has become a matter of great interest to both the general reading public and to literary critics. In interviews, Dorris and Erdrich are frequently asked about their collaborative process, which includes an exchange of multiple drafts and readings. This process is repeated until they achieve consensus on every aspect before the piece is published. This process has led some to speculate on the political implications of dual authorship in a dominant culture that values the exceptional individual. In a 1987 interview with Hertha Wong, Dorris and Erdrich seemed to agree with the suggestion that their collaboration was another reason that *Love Medicine* is a Native American novel. However, they also place great emphasis on the fact that they work well together and trust each other's judgment (Wong 1987:202).

Also in 1987, a nonfiction contribution entitled "Indians on the Shelf" was published in Calvin Martin's *The American Indian and the Problem of History*. The eight-page article is Dorris's most succinct and controlled effort on a theme he frequently addresses: the distorted image of Native Americans as the result of mythologizing by Western European culture.

> In advertising [Indians] are inextricably linked with those products (corn oil, tobacco) the general public acknowledges as indigenous to the Americas. But flesh and blood Native Americans have rarely participated in or benefited from the creation of these imaginary Indians, whose recognition factor, as they say on Madison Avenue, outranks, on a world scale, that of Santa Claus, Mickey Mouse, and Coca-Cola combined. (99)

> A survey of literature dealing with Indians over the past two or three hundred years would seem to imply that Indians are motivated more often by mysticism than by ambition, are charged more by unfathomable visions than by intelligence or introspection, and in effect derive their understandings of the world more from an appeal to the irrational than to empiricism. Since the whys and wherefores of Native American society are not easily accessible to those culture-bound by Western traditional values, there is a tendency to assume that Indians are creatures either of instinct or whimsy. (101)

Dorris also writes for a variety of popular publications. *Seventeen Magazine* has published his short fiction, and *Parents Magazine* has published several pieces of nonfiction, usually as part of a regular column about fathers, as well as short fiction. *Mother Jones* published the short story "The Bench Mark" in 1990.

The Crown of Columbus, the first novel to be published under both Dorris's and Erdrich's names, appeared in the first part of 1991. The book met with mixed reviews because of the odd combination of characters: Vivian Twostar, a mixed-blood Associate Professor of Native American Studies, and Roger Williams, a poet. Both are instructors at Dartmouth and become involved in a convoluted search for a legendary crown Columbus left as a gift to an Indian chief in the New World. Kirkpatrick Sale, writing for *The Nation*, found the plot fatally flawed by a historical error, but at least one reviewer found the action entertaining enough to look forward to the possibility of a movie version. Remarking on the collaborative effort, Ann Rayson states in her article for *Studies in American Indian Literatures* (Winter 1991) that "Vivian Twostar defines her marginal status to imply that beneath the surface levity of this novel Erdrich and Dorris celebrate a new cohesion, the confluence of Indian-white heritages and male-female voices" (27).

Probably the strongest and most revealing of Dorris's solo works is his nonfiction work *The Broken Cord*. The widespread problems of alcohol abuse are detailed in the experiences of his Lakota son in a moving story that shatters the assumption that "a little alcohol can't hurt." The book illustrates the desperate need for all communities including reservations to provide education on the hazards of alcohol abuse and encourages treatment for alcohol and drug addiction. Dorris unashamedly reveals his hopes and heart-felt expectations that Adam will manage to overcome his handicaps. Adam's life is full of struggle, however, and then ends abruptly.

Dorris's novel *A Yellow Raft on Blue Water* preceded the publication of *The Broken Cord*, but it too demonstrates Dorris's concern for alcohol abuse among Native Americans. Of the three narrating characters in *A Yellow Raft*, Christine is a chronic abuser. Like the other novels of the Dorris and Erdrich collaboration, this one allows for several versions of the same story, overlapping or contradicting the stories of the other narrators. Christine is from a Native American family living in Montana, but leaves that rural area for Seattle, where she eventually marries a black man. Christine, her mother, and her racially mixed daughter, Rayona, each try to reconcile their needs for love and independence with the conflicting values of family, society, and racial biases. Dorris captures the voices of the adult women and creates believable complexity and personality. To my reading, Dorris's upbringing in a household of women must have served him favorably in the creation of these characters. Rayona is a less successful characterization and seems, especially in light of Dorris's son Adam, to be something of a miracle child, given her mother's drinking. Her intelligence and independence seem at times to be a little too remarkable for a teenaged girl, and are in sharp contrast to Dorris's experiences with the painfully slow process by which Adam learned and forgot basic lessons of self-maintenance. To my mind, Dorris could make a greater contribution to our understanding of life among Native Americans if his fiction was more consistently grounded in his personal experience. Given the strength of his historical articles and his ability to reach general reading audiences of several age groups, I am more inclined to hope for his autobiography than for another novel of prose fiction.

Dorris is prolific. In fact, he writes like a man with hard-nosed determination in life to educate every possible reader to the ill effects of subtle or unintentional racism. From his earliest writings on, Dorris displays an energetic passion for correcting the misguided or ignorant perceptions of Native Americans. The strength of both his convictions and his arguments are clearly expressed in his articles "Native American Literature in an Ethnohistorical Context" and in "Indians on the Shelf." He recognizes that many of the perceptual problems that persist concerning Native Americans are held by the "average" American and are bone-marrow deep in the American mythos. Dorris tries to complicate the simplistic ideas of what Native Americans were like, what they are like, and what they hope for. While perhaps not truly literary, there is a continued need for such contributions, and for his persistent voice, which unflinchingly draws our attention to the ways in which we too casually categorize and devalue people of color.

Barbara K. Robins
New Mexico State University

BIBLIOGRAPHY

Primary Sources

Dorris, Michael. "Why I'm Not Thankful for Thanksgiving." *Council on International Books for Children Bulletin* 9 (1978). Rpt. *Books Without Bias: Through Indian Eyes.* Ed. Beverly Slapin and Doris Seale. Berkeley: Oyate, 1989 (rev. ed.).

——. "Native American Literature in an Ethnohistorical Context." *College English* 41 (1979): 147-62.

——. "Native American Studies and Curriculum." Paper presented to the Second Annual Conference on Special Emerging Programs, 1979. Available as ERIC doc. ED190282.

——. "The Grass Still Grows, the Rivers Still Flow: Contemporary Native Americans." *Daedalus: Journal of the American Academy of Arts and Sciences* 110 (Spring 1981): 43–69.

——. "I Is Not for Indian." *American Indian Stereotypes in the World of Children.* Ed. Arlene B. Hirschfelder. Metuchen, NJ: Scarecrow Press, 1982. Rpt. *Books Without Bias: Through Indian Eyes.* Ed. Beverly Slapin and Doris Seale. Berkeley: Oyate, 1989 (rev. ed.).

——. "The Best of Pen Pals." *Seventeen* 46 (August 1987): 272.

——. "Hard Luck." *Seventeen* 46 (March 1987): 262–63+.

——. "Indians on the Shelf." *The American Indian and the Problem of History.* Ed. Calvin Martin. New York: Oxford UP, 1987: 98–105.

——. "The Queen of Christmas." *Seventeen* 46 (December 1987): 128–29.

——. "Why Mr. Ed Still Talks Good Horse Sense." *TV Guide* 36 (May 28–June 3, 1988): 34–36.

——. *A Yellow Raft on Blue Water.* New York: Warner, 1988.

——. *The Broken Cord.* New York: Harper & Row, 1989.

——. "Rites of Passage." *Parents* (June 1989): 246–48.

—— "The Bench Mark." *Mother Jones* (January 1990): 19–21, 47–48.

——. "A Desperate Crack Legacy." *Newsweek* 115 (June 25, 1990): 8.

——. "Fetal Alcohol Syndrome." *Parents* (November 1990): 238–45.

——. "The Minnie Mouse Kitchen." *Parents* (December 1990): 234–35.

——. "Ode to an Author Escort." *Publishers Weekly* 238 (June 7, 1991): 34.

——. "What Men Are Missing." *Vogue* 181 (September 1991): 511.

——, and Louise Erdrich. "Who Owns the Land? Chippewa Indian and the White Earth Indian Reservations." *The New York Times Magazine* 137 (September 4, 1988): 32, col. 1.

——, and Louise Erdrich. *The Crown of Columbus.* New York: HarperCollins, 1991.

——, and Joseph C. Farber, photographer. *Native Americans: 500 Years After.* New York: Crowell, 1975.

——, Arlene B. Hirschfelder, and Mary Gloyne Byler, eds. *Guide to Research on North American Indians.* Chicago: American Library Association, 1983.

North, Milou. "Change of Light." *Redbook* 158 (March 1982): 78–79.

Secondary Sources

Coltelli, Laura. "Louise Erdrich and Michael Dorris." *Winged Words: American Indian Writers Speak.* Lincoln: U of Nebraska P, 1990.

Mannes-Abbott, Guy. "Native Speech." *New Statesman Society* (July 26, 1991): 35.

Oldham, Gerda. "Review: *The Crown of Columbus*." *Antioch Review* (Spring 1991): 303.

Rayson, Ann. "Shifting Identity in the Work of Louise Erdrich and Michael Dorris." *Studies in American Indian Literatures* 3 (Winter 1991): 27–36.

Sale, Kirkpatrick. "Roll On, Columbus, Roll On." *The Nation* (October 21, 1991): 1, 486–90.

Wong, Hertha. "An Interview with Louise Erdrich and Michael Dorris." *North Dakota Quarterly* 55 (Winter 1987): 196–218.

(Karen) *Louise Erdrich*
(June 7, 1954–)

Louise Erdrich's rise to prominence in Native American literary circles is noteworthy for two reasons. First, it took place in a relatively brief span of time. Her first book, a collection of poetry entitled *Jacklight*, was published in 1984 and was swiftly followed, in four years, by a trilogy of powerful novels: *Love Medicine* (1984), *The Beet Queen* (1986), and *Tracks* (1988). Second, her work has been critically acclaimed and widely popular, so her writings continue to garner influential critical attention while also reaching a broad, multicultural audience. Consequently, she is successful financially as well as artistically as she explores the potential of written literature to express—and perhaps to perpetuate—tribal points of view. Few Indian writers have been so fortunate.

Erdrich is popular because she is a talented storyteller whose stories are engaging, compelling, and pertinent, and because her earliest work exhibited a skillful use of language in provocatively constructed narratives, she immediately drew the attention of editors and critics often interested only in established writers. Short stories that were to become *Love Medicine* appeared in *The Atlantic Monthly*, *Kenyon Review*, *The Best Short Stories of 1983*, and *O. Henry Prize Stories*, and the novel itself won the National Book Critics Circle Award for Fiction, the American Academy and Institute of Arts and Letters' Sue Kaufman Prize for fiction, and the *Los Angeles Times* Book Prize for best novel. Moreover, each of her books has received complimentary reviews from such bastions of mainstream sensibilities as *The New York Times Book Review*, as well as the attention of scholars and their journals: *Studies in American Indian Literatures* devoted an entire issue to her first two books.

Her popularity with critics is understandable. As one scholar noted very early on, Erdrich's *Love Medicine* is strongly reminiscent of William

Faulkner's *Go Down, Moses*. This comparison with the Nobel Prize winning writer is quite perceptive, for it suggests two of Erdrich's greatest strengths as a novelist and storyteller: her complete absorption in one specific landscape and the people who inhabit it—the North Dakota equivalent of Faulkner's Yoknapatawpha County—and her ability to "layer" points of view through a diversity of characters, a polyphony of voices speaking of this place and each other over a long period of time. Her works have depth through their elaborately developed characters—some heroic, some tragic, some both—whose lives play out beside family and clan histories, and the larger story of their implied community, which changes, yet stays much the same. In a word, her writings possess epic qualities.

Born in Little Falls, Minnesota, Erdrich grew up in Wahpeton, North Dakota. She entered Dartmouth College in 1972, where she began her writing career with the Cox Prize in fiction and also a prize for poetry from the American Academy of Poets. After receiving her bachelor's degree from Dartmouth, she returned home to teach in poetry programs in North Dakota, but returned to graduate school at Johns Hopkins University, where she received her Master of Arts degree in 1979. Her list of accomplishments since that time includes fellowships from the MacDowell Colony (1980), the Yaddo Colony (1981), and the National Endowment for the Arts (1982). Erdrich is a member of the Turtle Mountain Band of the Anishinabe (Chippewa) people, and her grandfather was once tribal chairman, but she is also of German-American descent. This is noteworthy because the interplay between Euroamerican and Native American voices can be found in all her early works; one of the four sections in *Jacklight* is devoted to the Euroamerican side of her family, and her second novel, *The Beet Queen*, is set away from the reservation and is comprised mainly of nontribal characters. Like many of her contemporaries, she incorporates the mixed-ancestry dilemma into her art, and although her works occasionally depict characters who lose themselves in the confusion surrounding their identity, they more often provide an array of characters who find resolution, fulfillment and affirmation in their Native blood. As she once told Joseph Bruchac (1987:77), she felt uncomfortable, at first, when her Chippewa voice began to assert itself, but her uneasiness subsided when she allowed it free rein. Interestingly, she also became an immensely successful writer at that point.

In the same interview, Erdrich reveals another aspect of her art. She states that a writer has no control over "subject and background," those elements that give her own writing its singular character, and if a writer recognizes this and if "he or she is true to what is happening, the story will take over" (77). This belief, coupled with the strength of her Chippewa voice, speaks to her power as a narrator. The stories she tells have a strongly autobiographical, cultural basis in her desire to reestablish identity by conveying a sense of place and history, and her ability to tell them is the result of at least three main influences. There are several storytellers in her family, so she grew up listening to stories about her kin and community; she has also received college training in writing fiction and poetry; and she is married to another Native American author, Michael Dorris, whose contributions to her work are noted in the dedications of each of her novels. Therefore, Erdrich draws heavily upon both verbal and written traditions of expression to achieve her purpose as an American author.

The poems in *Jacklight* are early indications of the directions in which her creative choices would take her. The book is divided into four sections, four thematic concerns for her to explore through her art the confusion inherent in her generation, the inescapable past with its history of change and loss, the character and relationships of the German-American side of her family, and, most telling, the myths from the verbal arts that help define the Anishinabe and their place, but that also enlighten the preceding sections. In brief, the book moves from dilemma to the implication of ancient resolutions, from the story of what is happening to a people now to those that tell of what happened to them in the past. In her first major work, she strikes upon themes shared by her contemporaries—D'Arcy McNickle, Leslie Silko, James Welch, to name just a few—and considers what they have likewise noted: that although Native American cultures have changed since the incursion of the European, many of them are still alive and vital and using tribal stories to help them address current events. Thus, the people survive, and Erdrich's emphasis on the endurance of her people places her at the very heart of current Native American literature, which, through its very existence, displays this survival while dramatizing its means.

The title poem of the book is both a prologue and a preparatory synopsis of what follows in Erdrich's canon. In "Jacklight," the nocturnal, illegal hunting of game suggests the history of Euroamerican-Indian relations. Like deer in the forest drawn toward an artificial, false light, the Anishinabe have been drawn toward assimilation and therefore death, personally and communally. However, in the final stanza Erdrich reverses the roles, rewriting what many have presumed to be the inevitable outcome of the confrontation between Native and colonist. Rather than emerge from their hiding places to be undone by those who seek to kill them, the narrators of the poem turn back into the woods, luring the hunters after them. The trap has not only been avoided; it has become the demise of those who use it to destroy. Their advantage is short-lived and transitory.

As the first section, "Runaways," suggests, the remaining poems are not always as hopeful, the emphasis on survival not so clearly stated. As in life, the potential for endurance is not always immediately apparent. The reality of the moment is not always pretty. Boarding schools, alcoholism, violence, and the pervasive misunderstandings that cause them are a part of contemporary experience, but Erdrich balances these ills with compassionate and caring relationships, "A Love Medicine." No matter how desperate some characters in *Jacklight* may seem, they all have access to the potential for renewal, for transformation, through the love of another human being, or through the curative power of a re-identification with a landscape conveyed through myth. Family—as well as the extended family or community—and their stories heal. In "Night Sky," a woman and her husband watch the ascent of Arcturus, and remember the old story of the woman who is transformed, acquiring the powers of a bear and traveling to the stars. The world is deep with the immensely evocative stories that ignite one's wonder, direct one's actions, and draw isolated individuals closer together.

That is why the stories are so important to Erdrich, and no doubt why she has foregone writing poetry for novels. Poetry is "a great surprise," the product of her subconscious, but fiction provides the added challenge of bending that urge into elaborate tellings and retellings of interrelated stories. In fact, several of the images first introduced in *Jacklight* reappear in her more recent work. "Family Reunion" and "A Love Medicine," to name only two, act as transitions between this book of poetry and her first novel, which explores, in greater detail, the issues raised in the poems.

Love Medicine brought Erdrich immediate acclaim. With its complex interplay of individual narratives, its unblinking examination of people's lives and choices, and its poetic use of language, it exemplifies Erdrich's talent for storytelling. As noted by Kathleen Sands, the novel deviates somewhat from other recent Native novels in its use of the secular tradition of gossip as a major narrative device. This is not to imply that Erdrich does not incorporate traditional tribal verbal arts into her work. Anishinabe literary motifs are found throughout: the westward road of the dead, the prevalence of water as a metaphor and allusion to tribal history, the image of fish and fishing, the respect and awe for people of power who possess obscure knowledge. Erdrich, however, supplements these ancient narrative elements with recent personal histories, and intertwines communal gossip with her characters' autobiographical revelations. The result is an expansive understanding of family/tribal, and perhaps universal, events filtered through several, sometimes contradictory, points of view.

The love triangle between Marie Kashpaw, her husband, Nector, and Lulu Lamartine is the heart of the novel. Their stories cover fifty years, from 1934 to 1984, and touch the lives of every other character in the book. Against their long lives, however, Erdrich places the relatively short existence of June Morrissey/Kashpaw, whose death in the opening chapter sparks the memoirs of the other characters as they try to explain the events leading to her loss, and their relationships to her. The result is a complex woven fabric in which no single character possesses the knowledge necessary to understand all the connections and therefore to accurately interpret all the events. That insight is reserved solely for the reader, who is the intimate, the confidant, of each character and who must continuously construct and reconstruct a satisfying point of view as personal narratives unfold, shedding new light. Erdrich's works are immensely engaging in this way, and therefore reflect qualities of traditional verbal arts in which audience involvement is equally active and mandatory.

Love Medicine examines the interlacing of the lives of several Anishinabe characters and families. *The Beet Queen*, on the other hand, incorporates only four Indian characters into its central stories of Mary and Karl Adair. At first this may be construed as a movement away from the tribal concerns that figure so prominently in her earlier works, but these narratives give depth to the expansive history of the specific landscape that Erdrich develops throughout her canon, and provide an important link between her first and third novels. *The Beet Queen* covers the years 1932–72 in the town of Argus, so it runs almost concurrently with the first, but tells, instead, what happens off the reservation to those who migrated to the northern plains long after the Chippewa, but who profoundly, perhaps disastrously, altered the face of the land for all people.

Wallace Pfef is such a character. He launches a campaign to change the economic base of the farmlands around Argus by introducing the sugar beet. He does so not out of a desire for the good of the community, or necessarily for his own ambition, but out of a series of events that links his first homosexual encounter and a late-night confrontation with a police officer. Thinking of his first lover when Officer Lovchik finds him parked alone on a dark lovers' lane, Pfef attempts to hide his confusion by babbling about a sugar beet display he saw at a convention in Minneapolis. Erdrich's irony is telling: such are the sources of inspiration that have changed forever the lives of individuals, and directed the future of a land.

Like her earlier works, *The Beet Queen* conveys Erdrich's clear image of people's sometimes wanting lives. Each character is somehow deficient; each lives a life of isolation. This leads to conflict, but also to the qualified affirmation so characteristic of Erdrich's art. Although Mary vies for the affection of Celestine's daughter, Dot, and although this results in hard feelings between longtime friends, the result is a closer relationship between all members of their family as long-standing involvement leads to the emergence of life-narratives, stories that allow for broader perspective and deeper understanding on the part of the people who possess them. As in *Love Medicine*, where Marie and Lulu become close friends in later years despite, or perhaps because of, their conflict, Celestine and Mary come to realize that their love and concern for Dot is all that is important, and that no matter how closely they wish to influence Dot's life, they are doomed to fail because she must respond to forces often beyond their ken and control. This free and unqualified transmission of love and compassion is the redemptive force in the novels; it is not always the means to security for individuals, but it does identify them as members of a specific group and provides them with hope, attachments, and a strong sense of self.

In *Tracks*, Erdrich takes her readers still further into the past of her landscape. Here, however, there are only two narrators, whose perspectives on events gradually grow more disparate, and of the two tellers, old Nanapush seems more believable, or realistic. He provides an expanded view of events, often employing comparisons with past happenings, clan or family histories, or his own obvious wit and insight and concern for his people. He gives readers a clear appraisal of what is actually transpiring. Pauline, however, grows steadily more introverted and her reliability as a storyteller suffers accordingly. This point is important, because Erdrich writes about a time (1912 to 1924) when sweeping changes took place for the Anishinabe, a time when events and actions dictated the way things are today. The last old-growth forests fell, changing the land forever, and families fought over how the tribe should react. Nanapush, therefore, becomes representative of the ways that such change may be confronted— sometimes with positive effect, sometimes without, but always with dignity—and Pauline becomes a nun, thus representing how new forces may supplant and subvert the old. Nanapush is laudable because he is concerned with others and because he wants to retain and nourish the good that his people have acquired over the long span of their existence as a people. Once again, Erdrich expresses concerns and attitudes shared by other tribal artists, and does so with such skill that her readers come to share her conviction.

In *Love Medicine*, Erdrich added a new dimension to contemporary American Indian written literature by incorporating gossip as a central device for her narrative. Such stories are important because, like all verbal traditions, they help to define identity and appropriate behavior by granting points of comparison between our own stories and those of others. As one narrator in *Tracks* notes, the story "comes up different every time, and has no ending, no beginning" (31). Each person must cultivate the ability to recognize current events, current "stories," for what they are, and thereby determine appropriate actions. As old Nanapush says of his family history, "There is a story to it the way there is a story to all, ever visible while it is happening" (34). *Tracks* is a storytelling session in which Erdrich makes the invisible apparent to her readers, and the lesson it provides compelling. In this way, her books fit not only into the relatively recent tradition of written fiction by Native Americans, but also into the ancient traditions of spoken literatures on this continent.

John Lloyd Purdy
Central Oregon Community College

BIBLIOGRAPHY

Primary Sources

Erdrich, Louise. *Jacklight*. New York: Henry Holt and Company, 1984.
———. *Love Medicine*. New York: Holt, Rinehart and Winston, 1984.
———. *The Beet Queen*. New York: Henry Holt and Company, 1986.
———. *Tracks*. New York: Henry Holt and Company, 1988.
———. *Baptism of Desire: Poems*. New York: Harper & Row, 1989.

Secondary Sources

Ainsworth, Linda. "Response to *Love Medicine*." *Studies in American Indian Literatures* 9.1 (Winter 1985): 24–29.
Bruchac, Joseph. *Survival This Way: Interviews with American Indian Poets*. Tucson: U of Arizona P, 1987.
George, Jan. "Interview with Louise Erdrich." *North Dakota Quarterly* 53.2 (Spring 1985): 240–46.
Kroeber, Karl, ed. "Louise Erdrich." In "Bibliographies of Fourteen Native American Poets." *Studies in American Indian Literatures* 9, Supplement (1985).
Sands, Kathleen M. "Response to *Love Medicine*." *Studies in American Indian Literatures* 9.1 (Winter 1985): 12–24.

Hanay Geiogamah (1945–)

We, the Native Americans, reclaim the land, known as America, in the name of all American Indians, by right of discovery. We wish to be fair and honorable with the Caucasian inhabitants of this land, who as a majority wrongfully claim it as theirs, and hereby pledge that we shall give to the majority inhabitants of this country a portion of their land for their own to be held in trust by American Indian people—for as long as the sun shall rise and the rivers flow down to the sea! We will further guide the majority inhabitants in the proper way of living. We will offer them our religion, our education, our way of life—in order to help them achieve our level of civilization, and thus raise them and all their white brothers from their savage and unhappy state.

This statement, proclaimed by the narrator in Hanay Geiogamah's *Foghorn*, contains very powerful words when read from the script. However, this cannot compare to the impact these words have on an audience that hears these words spoken during a live performance. Because a play is written to be performed, a play's true literary value can be measured only during a performance. Thus, a play's success begins with the playwright's abilities to envision all theatrical aspects of a play, to bring the printed word to life, so the meaning is seen, heard, and felt. As the most prominent Native American contemporary playwright, Hanay Geiogamah successfully conveys his theatrical visions through the printed word. In his *New Native American Drama*, a collection of three plays, Geiogamah displays his talents as a dramatist through the theatricality of his plays.

Born in Lawton, Oklahoma, in 1945, Hanay Geiogamah, a Kiowa-Delaware Indian, studied journalism at the University of Oklahoma. He has taught creative writing, Native American theater, and the role of the arts in contemporary Native American life at several colleges and universities. Geiogamah conceived the idea for an all-Indian acting troupe in 1970.

The motivation for assembling his troupe stemmed from Geiogamah's belief that "for decades American Indians have been portrayed in films and on television in a manner entirely derogatory to the cultural and mental well-being . . ." of Native American people (quoted in Phillips 1972). With the organization of the Native American Theatre Ensemble (NATE) in New York in 1972, Hanay Geiogamah set out to create a more realistic picture of the Native American.

Body Indian, written by Geiogamah and performed by NATE, opened October 25, 1972, at the La MaMa Experimental Theatre Club. The successful opening was highlighted by a glowing review from Clive Barnes, at the time the distinguished critic for the *New York Times*. According to Barnes, theater gives Native Americans the "opportunity to preserve a cultural heritage clearly in danger of erosion" and is an important vehicle to use as a "modern means of expression." Geiogamah's first and most highly acclaimed play, *Body Indian* has a plotline which is presented in a realistic chronological order. Within the five scenes of the play, *Body Indian* boldly addresses the contemporary problem of alcoholism among Native Americans, while stressing the social and moral obligations of the people themselves. The central figure of the play is Bobby, who at the end of each scene passes out from too much alcohol consumption and gets rolled by "friends" and relatives alike. These "friends" and relatives take their turns at Bobby and try to justify their actions. The horror of this abusive treatment of Bobby is intensified by Geiogamah's use of lighting and sound effects. After each time Bobby is rolled, the actors freeze their actions while the blasts of a train whistle are heard and the images of a railroad track are projected across the stage. The symbolic representation of the train serves as a reminder to Bobby of the accident which took his leg and left him disabled. However, from a broader spectrum, the theatrical effects—the tracks and the whistle of the train—can also symbolize the arrival of white settlers to "civilize" the Indian lands. The effects of the surrealistic lighting and sound juxtaposed against the realistic setting in *Body Indian* can come to fruition only during a performance of the play.

The most traditional of the three plays in Geiogamah's collection, *49* was first performed by NATE on January 10, 1975, at Oklahoma City University. Using a traditional Native American ceremonial ground as the setting, *49* takes place in a time period ranging from about 1885 to the present. The central figure in this play is Night Walker, an ageless, timeless ceremonial leader of his tribe. Night Walker represents the spirit of the people, floating between the past and the present, connecting the two time periods with one setting. In his unique way, Geiogamah blends the historical with the contemporary, the traditional with the modern, the spirit with the flesh, to produce a flowing, meaningful piece of dramatic literature. Unlike the script for *Body Indian*, which demands a full contemporary set, the script for *49* calls for a relatively sparse stage setting, minimal props, and actors to pantomime and create their own environment. Although a challenge to actors, the use of pantomime compels audience members to use their imaginations, thus heightening the ethereal qualities of Night Walker and the sacred ceremonial grounds. Another interesting aspect of *49* is that the only characters on stage are those belonging to the tribe, past and present. The tribal police who attempt to break up the ceremony are only heard through the sound system. This gives unity and strength to the people of the tribe which transcends the spoken/written word. Unlike *Body Indian*, whose lighting and sound effects interrupt the action of the play, lighting and sound effects in *49* are blended together with the setting to create the environment.

On October 18, 1973, Geiogamah's *Foghorn* opened at the Reichskabaret in Berlin. In contrast to both *Body Indian* and *49*, *Foghorn* is a series of fast-paced vignettes utilizing a variety of theatrical techniques. Yet beneath the surface of frivolity lies a hard-hitting message. Because of Geiogamah's wide use of the technical theater as well as his creative abilities as a writer, the absurdity of the stereotyping of Native Americans has a dramatic impact on audiences viewing the production.

In the spring of 1984, the Tiospaye Council at the University of South Dakota asked me to direct its production of *Foghorn*. Working with Geiogamah's script, I learned the importance of the theatricalities of *Foghorn*, for the technical aspects of the script as described in the production notes make the message of the play clear. In addition, the author's notes were extremely important in establishing a unified concept for the production. Geiogamah stresses that the stereotypical characters be "almost . . . pushed to the point of absurdity" and that the "satire" be "playful mockery rather than bitter denunciation." The seriousness of the play is more obvious if "the heavy hand is avoided" and a "light, almost frivolous" atmosphere is created (Geiogamah 1980:9). Characters are to avoid a preachy tone and to allow the laugh lines to occur naturally. Through the author's notes I was better able to envision the concepts Geiogamah was striving to present in the production of *Foghorn*.

Probably the most important theatrical aspect of *Foghorn* is the style in which the script itself is written. *Foghorn* has eleven scenes presenting a historical overview of Native Americans since the arrival of Columbus. These eleven scenes circle, beginning with the serious and moving on to the absurd, then to the ridiculous, to the hysterical, and back to the serious. This circle symbolizes the circle of the Indian nations, which is the strength of the people. This concept is enhanced by the traditional drum group which performs at various times throughout the play, representing the heartbeat of the people who are the circle. *Foghorn* opens with the performers depicting a forced journey, one similar to the Trail of Tears. This journey is interrupted by Columbus's "discovering" America, European settlers screaming derogatory comments at the travelers, and Congressmen plotting to move the Indians onto reservations. The journey continues, and scene 1 flows into scene 2.

Scene 2 is set on Alcatraz Island during the occupation on Thanksgiving Day 1969. The narrator steps forward in this scene to make the proclamation quoted at the beginning of this essay. This is followed by a traditional song performed by the drum group. With the final beat of the drum still echoing in the theater from the end of scene 2, scene 3 begins with an organ blasting out church music. The play progresses into the lighter, more satirical scenes. Scene 3 depicts a Catholic nun sent to bring "the one true religion" to the "pagans." Her Bible is the Yellow Pages of the phone book, and her cross is made of paper money. One hysterical scene follows another in the central section of the play. Bringing "education" to the "savages," the white teacher waves her tiny American flags as she attempts to teach English, "the most beautiful language in all the world," to the children of the tribe. The first word she wants them to learn is "hello" because, according to her, this is the one word they "must know to become civilized" (61).

Another scene depicts Pocahontas and her hand-maidens laughing at the color of the white man's skin and his lack of manliness. The truth is finally revealed in the scene between the Lone Ranger and Tonto. Tonto is the real hero of this infamous duo; the Lone Ranger has been taking undue credit for their good deeds all these years.

A series of scenes follows satirizing American politics. In one scene, the First Lady announces that more Indian land will be taken away for a national park, while another scene parodies the Watergate scandal and a possible tribal revolution. The humor and absurdity of the characters and situations are obvious if these scenes are kept at a light, quick pace. These scenes build up to the tenth scene, which can be the most riotous of all. With carnival music in the background, Indians with brightly colored headdresses, stick horses, rubber knives, and children's bows and arrows frolic on the stage in a scene which pokes fun of the old-style Wild West shows.

The tone suddenly changes as a single gunshot is heard, and the performers fall on the stage as if dead. Scene 10 merges into scene 11, and the audience suddenly find themselves at Wounded Knee, South Dakota, during the 1973 occupation. This theatrical manipulation of the audience serves to drive home the point that Native Americans are ". . . NOT GUILTY!" of the crimes committed against them. The theatrical use of humor and satire, coupled with a circular script and utilization of the traditional drum group, enhances the point that Native Americans are not responsible for the negative images perpetuated by stereotyping.

Whether he uses the theatrical techniques to blatantly point up symbolism as in *Body Indian*, or subtly blends lighting and sound to create an ethereal atmosphere as in *49*, or gaily decorates the stage with the color, lights, and sounds of a cabaret as in *Foghorn*, Geiogamah's power as a playwright lies in his ability to envision the stage production as a whole. He is then able to communicate this vision through his writing. Even though Geiogamah is able to share his ideas with the reader, his excellence as a dramatist can best be appreciated by directors and actors who work with his scripts and by audiences who view the final productions. This is the mark of a true dramatist—to be able to write a script for a meaningful and successful production.

Sue M. Johnson
University of South Dakota

BIBLIOGRAPHY

Barnes, Clive. "Stage: American Indian Repertory." *New York Times*, October 29, 1972, Sec. l, p. 69 col. 1–3.

Geiogamah, Hanay. *New Native American Drama*. Norman: U of Oklahoma P, 1980.

Phillips, McCandish. "Indian Theatre Group: Strong Beginning." *New York Times*, November 9, 1972, Sec. 1, p. 56 col. 1–4.

Joy Harjo *(May 9, 1951–)*

Joy Harjo's poetry attempts to resolve polarities to bring this world into balance. She emphasizes the concept of androgyny, an acceptance of the male and female within each person and all of nature, as essential to wholeness. As Harjo stated when interviewed by Joseph Bruchac:

> Native American experience has often been bitter. . . . I like to think that bitter experience can be used to move the world. We're human beings ultimately, and when it's all together, there won't be these categories . . . we will be accepted for what we are and not divided. (96)

Since the publication in 1979 of *What Moon Drove Me to This?* Harjo's poetry has received attention and acclaim from literary critics such as Paula Gunn Allen and Andrew Wiget, and her work has been included in all major anthologies of Native American poetry. In 1989, Bill Moyers featured Harjo and her work in his television series *Power of the Word*.

While Harjo's poetry has obviously evolved from her own experience, it consistently moves toward something much larger. As Wiget puts it, "at her best the energy generated by this journeying creates a powerful sense of identity that incorporates everything into the poetic self, so that finally she can speak for all the earth" (1989:117). And Paula Allen calls her "a poet whose work is concerned with metaphysical as well as social connections" (1986:166).

Born in Tulsa, Oklahoma, to Allen W. and Wynema Baker Foster, Harjo grew up in an urban environment and in a broken home and has referred to herself as a half-breed; she is Cherokee on her mother's side, Creek on her father's ("Three Generations," 29). She seems to have learned much of her Indian identity from her great aunt, Lois Harjo Ball (1906–1982), to whom she dedicated her book *She Had Some Horses* (1983). In a

"Bio-Poetics Sketch for *Greenfield Review*," Harjo recalls digging in the "dark rich earth" as a child, a formative experience in her development as a poet (8).

Like most published Native American poets, Harjo has an academic background, with a B.A. from the University of New Mexico (1976) and an M.F.A. from the University of Iowa (1978). Harjo has taught at the Institute of American Indian Arts, Arizona State University, the University of Colorado, and the University of Arizona. She has been a writer and consultant for the Native American Public Broadcasting Consortium, the National Indian Youth Council, and the National Endowment for the Arts. She wrote a script for Silver Cloud Video which was produced in 1985, and she is co-author of "The Beginning," a script for the Native American Broadcasting Consortium. She has edited *High Plains Literary Review*. In addition to writing, Harjo plays tenor saxophone and has performed with a big band in Denver. She has two children, Phil and Rainy.

Harjo began writing poetry in the mid-1970s, when she was a student at the University of New Mexico. Writers she has mentioned as influencing her work are Simon Ortiz, Leslie Silko, Flannery O'Connor, James Wright, Pablo Neruda, Meridel Le Sueur, and African and African-American writers (Bruchac, 98, 99, 101, 102). Country-western songs, Creek preachers, stomp dance songs, jazz, and blues have also influenced her poetry ("The Woman . . ." 39). Consistent with the traditional Native American respect for language, Harjo told Bruchac: "I realize writing can help change the world. I'm aware of the power of language which isn't meaningless words. . . . Sound is an extension of all, and sound is spirit, motion" (100).

Yet life in contemporary America, even among those aware of this power, tends to separate people from each other and from their own voices. Like the rest of American society, modern Indians communicate by telephone, a mode that cannot quite remove the distance they feel from each other. Several poems in Harjo's first three books describe unsuccessful efforts by people who love each other to communicate by phone. In "Are You Still There," it is difficult for the woman who called her man to say anything; she is lonely and his voice overwhelms her: "'i have missed you' he says / the rhythm circles the curve / of mesita cliffs / to meet me / but my voice is caught / shredded on a barbed wire fence / at the side of the road / and flutters soundless / in the wind" (*The Last Song*, n.p.). In "Half-Light," a woman is awakened by a call in the night from a man she cannot live with, but still loves: "now he wants me again, in durango, / and i still love the father of my daughter / even in the emptiness / we are mad for each other, / but it twists me the fear his voice makes" (*What Moon Drove Me to This?*, 63). And in "Your Phone Call at 8 AM," the voice of the woman's former lover is reduced to a "skeleton," wanting; the woman says, "anything, to cancel / what your heart ever saw in me that you didn't" (*She*

Had Some Horses, 57). Besides understanding the emotional distancing the man is trying to effect, the woman/poet is coming to an emotional independence from him, as indicated by the ending: "this poem isn't for you / but for me / after all" (57).

To become articulate, however, means more to Harjo than achieving confidence in one's own voice, though that is certainly a beginning. As a poet, Harjo views language as more than merely a means of humans communicating with each other. This is the opening of her poem, "For Alva Benson, and for Those Who Have Learned to Speak": "And the ground spoke when she was born. / Her mother heard it. In Navajo she answered / as she squatted down against the earth / to give birth" (*She Had Some Horses*, 18). This is the traditional image of the earth mother who remains grounded because she knows her source of life and her relationship to it. Women like Alva Benson who have "learned to speak for the ground" are images of strength and continuity in Harjo's poetry. However, Harjo does not romanticize the lives of Indian women; she casts a direct gaze on the fragmented family lives of many urban Indians and their consequent suffering.

In "Conversations Between Here and Home," Emma Lee's husband beats her up because he wants money "to drink on" (*What Moon Drove Me to This?*, 18). She is one of many; and the final stanza of the poem describes a group of women who will no longer put up with such brutality: "angry women are building / houses of stones / they are grinding the mortar / between straw-thin teeth / and broken families" (18). These images drive home the point that such a life is hard. It wears a woman down. While the strength of these women must be admired, there are personal, emotional, and physical costs involved in being single parents without men.

Drinking is a cause of family disintegration, but Harjo's poetry, like that of most Native American writers, shows both sides of drinking. It is associated with romance in a number of Harjo's poems, such as "There Was a Dance, Sweetheart": "She ran the bars with him, / before the motion of snow / caught her too, and he moved in. / It was a dance" (*What Moon Drove Me to This?*, 21). But more important to the romance than the drinking is the presence of nature, the dance, and the voice of the woman's lover, "come here come here" (22).

Harjo's poems explore some of the reasons Indians drink, as in "Night Out": "another shot, anything to celebrate this deadly / thing called living" (*She Had Some Horses*, 21). Many are trapped in a vicious cycle of alcoholism. The poem ends: "You are the circle of lost ones / our relatives. / You have paid the cover charge thousands of times over / with your lives / and now you are afraid / you can never get out" (21).

The trap of alcoholism historically used to snare Native Americans catches not only adults in the bars, but also American youth. And Harjo's "The Friday Before the Long Weekend" expresses an adult's frustration about this: "You come in here / drunk child / pour your beer / down the drain, /'apple juice,' / bullshit. / . . . / I can see the stagger / in your eyes / . . . / What can I teach you / what can I do?" (*She Had Some Horses*, 35).

Perhaps the only hope is that someday the drunk child or adult will come to an awareness such as that of the woman in "Alive," who learns to accept herself as a part of the creation (*She Had Some Horses*, 56). Throughout Harjo's poetry, nonhuman elements are brought into and related to the human body: "an ancient chant / that my mother knew / came out of a history / woven from wet tall grass / in her womb" (*The Last Song*, n.p.). In "To a Black-haired Daughter Sleeping," "she is taking in / her fetal water history / bone cliffs / of her chest rising" (*What Moon Drove Me to This?*, 4). And in "She Had Some Horses," there are many kinds of horses, representing various elements of the earth—"bodies of sand," "blue air of sky"— and all types and polarities of people "who got down on their knees for any saviour" or "who thought their high price had saved them" (*She Had Some Horses*, 63–64). Through blending human and nonhuman nature and conflicting feelings and attitudes, Harjo moves toward an acceptance of the whole human condition, acknowledging the constant duality of love and hate in every human relationship that is alive and real.

Many of Harjo's poems express a woman's frustration at not achieving connection with those she wants to be close to, as in "White Sands." The woman driving to Tulsa for her sister's wedding does not have a traditional American marriage; she never wore a white gown and does not fit her mother's image of what her daughter should be. But the woman's image of herself—"I will be dressed in / the clear blue sky"—gives her, as Paula Allen has stated, an "unbroken and radiant connection with something larger and more important than a single individual," her mother (1986:124).

The women in Harjo's poetry long for the security of mother and home that is often lost to Native American women living in cities: "When she was young she ate wild rice on scraped down / plates in warm wood rooms. It was in the farther / north and she was the baby then. / They rocked her" (*She Had Some Horses*, 22). In one of her most moving poems, "The Woman Hanging from the Thirteenth Floor Window," Harjo evokes this woman "hanging by her own fingers, her / own skin, her own thread of indecision / . . . / . . . crying for / the lost beauty of her own life" (*She Had Some Horses*, 23). Not just one crazy, suicidal woman in Chicago, she is a mother of three children and "several pieces between the two husbands / she has had," a sex object, broken by these men. She is symbolic: "all the women of the apartment / building who stand watching her, stand watching themselves" (23). Will she fall to her death, discarding the "4 a.m. lonelinesses that have folded / her up like death?" (23); or will her memories of beauty make her climb "back up to claim herself again?" (23). At the end of the poem, both options remain. The suicidal woman's consciousness was the aim; and Harjo achieved that in the poem.

Harjo explained the composition of this poem in an interview published in the first issue of *Wicazo Sa Review*. Her visit to the Chicago Indian Center planted the seed, but two years passed before she wrote it. Though she imagined the woman hanging, the image evoked in the poem seems so real that women have often come up to Harjo following a reading to tell her they are sure they know the woman in the poem or that they have read a newspaper article about her ("The Woman Hanging . . . ," 40).

There are similarities between the life of the woman hanging and that of Noni Daylight, a persona in a number of Harjo's poems. In "Kansas City," "Noni Daylight's / a dishrag wrung out over bones" (*She Had Some Horses*, 33)—what more precise image for a worn-out woman? And yet this woman accepts her life: "she chose to stay / in Kansas City, raise the children / she had by different men, / all colors. Because she knew / that each star rang with separate / colored hue, as bands of horses / and wild / like the spirit in her" (33). And so, because she has lived fully, she does not despair.

What Harjo's poetry finally achieves is something akin to the life of Daylight. Creativity, like living fully, requires the fearless expenditure of passionate energy. The contradiction will always exist that the ones you love most hurt you most, but what is life worth without "Ice Horses": "They are the horses who have held you / so close that you have become / a part of them, / an ice horse / galloping / into fire" (*She Had Some Horses*, 67). Noni Daylight may be just one Native American woman in contemporary America, but she lives in the middle part of the country and certainly represents many. While it has been her impulse to live, she has also had to confront fear, as expressed in Harjo's poem "Heartbeat": "It is not the moon, or the pistol in her lap / but a fierce anger / that will free her" (*She Had Some Horses*, 37). The implication of this poem is that Daylight must turn her anger outward into a force for social change. Wiget says that in Harjo's poetry, the "moon represents all that the sun does not, loneliness, failed relationships, the night world of her other self, the persona she calls Noni Daylight. . . . Yet it is not so simple." He goes on to explain that "the moon is often addressed in an almost sisterly manner and consoles her in her isolation" (1985:117).

Increasingly, Harjo's poetry has included references to the history of U.S. colonization. Of course, the misuse of nature is an inextricable part of this process, as in the poem "Backwards": "The moon came up white, and torn / at the edges. I dreamed when I was / four that I was standing on it. / A whiteman with a knife cut pieces / away / and threw the meat / to the dogs" (*She Had Some Horses*, 20). Like Wiget, Allen has noted the prominence of the moon as a symbol in Harjo's poetry. In *The Sacred Hoop*, she writes: "the poetry of . . . Harjo finds itself entwining ancient understandings of the moon, of relationship, of womanhood, and of journeying with city streets, rodeo grounds, highways, airports, Indian bars, and powwows.

From the meeting of the archaic and the contemporary the facts of her life become articulate . . ." (160).

Harjo's book *She Had Some Horses* is an exorcism of the kind of fear that can paralyze an individual or a whole culture. The chant "I Give You Back" powerfully confronts past and present from both perspectives, the cultural—"I give you back to the white soldiers / who burned my home, beheaded my children, / raped and sodomized my brothers and sisters. / I give you back to those who stole the / food from our plates when we were starving" (73)—and the individual—"I am not afraid to be hungry. / I am not afraid to be full. / I am not afraid to be hated. / I am not afraid to be loved. / to be loved, to be loved, fear" (73–74). Harjo's use of such repetition is consistent with her belief in the power of language. She has stated, "Repetition has always been used, ceremonially, in telling stories, in effective speaking, so that what is being said becomes a litany, and gives you a way to enter in to what is being said and a way to emerge whole but changed" ("The Woman Hanging . . . ," 39). This poem does not end with an attitude of merely rejecting fear, but rather with an affirmative statement about the courage necessary to live—"But come here, fear / I am alive and you are so afraid / of dying" (74).

Overcoming fear of the oppressor in whatever form is the essential thing that Harjo has been striving for as a poet. *In Mad Love and War*, published in 1990, is a cross-cultural view of humanity and inhumanity. From the blues lament "Strange Fruit" to "Resurrection," set in Nicaragua, the poetry in this powerful collection insists on telling the terrible truth about oppression, while at the same time celebrating the beauty of the natural world of being.

The poetry in this book, especially the poem "For Anna Mae Pictou Aquash," responds in a personal and spiritual way to the violation of those whose voices and lives have spoken for justice on this earth. Harjo remembers the ghost dancers who, like Aquash, were murdered at Pine Ridge, at the end of the poem: ". . . we have just begun to touch / the dazzling whirlwind of our anger, / we have just begun to perceive the amazed world the ghost dancers / entered / crazily, beautifully" (8).

Harjo's poetry has become increasingly visionary, not escapist. This is evident in "Transformations," which Harjo calls "a letter" addressed to someone who she says "would like to destroy me" (294). The poem continues, "Bone splintered in the eye of one you choose / to name your enemy won't make it better for you to see" (294). In *The Sacred Hoop*, Allen calls transformation "the oldest tribal ceremonial theme" and says that "it comes once again into use with the American Indian poetry of extinction and regeneration" (162).

The transformation Harjo seeks to effect is from hatred to love; but for this to occur, the other she is addressing must come to accept the feminine part of consciousness: "On the other side / of the place you live stands a dark woman. / She has been trying to talk to you for years. / . . . / She is beautiful. / This is your hatred back. She loves you" (59). A statement by Harjo is pertinent here: "I have a sense of how I keep going deeper and deeper. . . . there are worlds in which polarity isn't the law. You don't have good/evil, sun/moon, light/dark. . . . When I really feel that other place, this place seems insane" (quoted in Allen 1986:166).

In Mad Love and War won the Poetry Society of America's William Carlos Williams Award. *In Mad Love and War* extends Harjo's enduring interest in the permanent tangle of human relations. The book breaks new ground for Harjo, however, in presenting for the first time many "prose poems" in which Harjo is clearly seeking to capture the poetic nature of emotionally charged scenes and dream speech. The volume is evidence of Harjo's continuing commitment to personal growth and the evolution of her craft.

We can change the world only if we first have some vision of that other world. Only then can we shape a culture that we can more than survive in. This is the pulse of Harjo's poems—they seek a means for us to communicate within and express love for ourselves and others. Harjo's honest expression and assessment of contemporary American life makes her poetry a valuable tool toward the change of consciousness necessary for the holistic vision all of us so desperately need.

Norma C. Wilson
University of South Dakota

BIBLIOGRAPHY

Primary Sources

Harjo, Joy. *The Last Song*. Las Cruces, NM: *Puerto Del Sol* Chapbook No. 1, 1975.
———. *What Moon Drove Me to This?* New York: I. Reed Books, 1979.
———. "Bio-Poetics Sketch for Greenfield Review." *The Greenfield Review* 9.3–4 (1981): 8–9.
———. *She Had Some Horses*. New York: Thunder's Mouth Press, 1983.
———. "The Woman Hanging from the Thirteenth Floor Window." *Wicazo Sa Review* 1.1 (1985): 38–40.
———. "Transformations." *Harper's Anthology of 20th Century Native American Poetry*. Ed. Duane Niatum. San Francisco: Harper & Row, 1988. 294–95.
———. *In Mad Love and War*. Middletown, CT: Wesleyan UP, 1990.
———. "Three Generations of Native American Women's Birth Experience." *Ms.*, 2.1 (1991): 28–30.

Secondary Sources

Allen, Paula Gunn. *Studies in American Indian Literature*. New York: MLA, 1983.
———. *The Sacred Hoop*. Boston: Beacon Press, 1986.
Bruchac, Joseph. *Survival This Way: Interviews with American Indian Poets*. Tucson: U of Arizona P, 1987.
Wiget, Andrew. *Native American Literature*. Boston: Twayne Publishers, 1985.
———. "Nightriding with Noni Daylight: The Many Horse Songs of Joy Harjo." *Native American Literature*. Ed. Laura Coltelli. Pisa: SEU, 1989. 185–96.

Lance (David) Henson
(September 20, 1944–)

The frequency with which Lance Henson and his work have been sought by editors, publishers, anthologists, and sponsors of readings and workshops here and in Europe offers more than adequate testimony that Lance Henson is the foremost Cheyenne poet now writing. In the literary circles of Indian country and in the few journals that notice contemporary American Indian literature, his critical reputation is secure. His books quickly sell out. Virtually all his readers and listeners like and admire the man and his poems, and want more of both.

Born in Washington, D.C., and reared by his grandparents on their Cheyenne allotment near Calumet, Oklahoma, Henson is an honorably discharged Marine, a member of the Cheyenne Dog Soldier Warrior Society, the Black Belt Karate Association, and the Native American Church. Each of these affiliations bears upon his work. He holds a B.A. in English from Oklahoma College of Liberal Arts and an M.A. in creative writing from Tulsa University.

He is a poet of the earth, its creatures, and especially its seasons. Though he writes of all four seasons, it is winter that predominates. Indeed, winter and night or darkness or some blend of them informs most of his poems. He is attracted to the changing times of day, sunrise and sunset, moonrise and moonset, when visual experience grows or diminishes, rises or relaxes. This growth and diminution are seen and felt in the movement of the earth's creatures and their life sources—images of birds, animals, rain, and particularly the wind, which is a manifestation of spirit life and a constant in western Oklahoma, the poet's home. If a central theme were to be singled out, one around which related themes and images cluster, it would be that of smallness. In the tape-recorded reading cited in the bibliography, the poet remarked: "I like to try to cherish small things in the world—pebbles. . . ." The word *small* or its cognates appear very often. The poems themselves are physically small, the collections of them are small. And within that smallness is the concentration of spiritual energy, the intensity of spirit animate in pebbles, the wind, hawks and crows, bones and trees, dreams of past and present in the whirling circle of living within the mystery of this earth, the blessed gift we spend our lives trying to return in some measure to the old ones and the children, all of them.

The poet's recent reading tours in Europe coincided with the appearance of new poems showing wider, more pronounced social and political concerns. In "riding late into the ohio dark," he conjures grim pictures of people sleeping in cardboard boxes in urban alleys as counterparts to those in junk cars on the reservations; "something other than roses blooming" stares at the government's continuing theft of Indian land; "after the sunday oklahoman and times article" responds defiantly to the ongoing genocide of forced assimilation. A note of solidarity is sounded in "to a miskito poet" for those indigenous people of South America whose oppression parallels that of northern Native people; "for a fallen uncle" remembers warriors who have given their lives to and for their people. Saddest of all is this book's title poem, which lays a curse upon America for murdering its own children (*Another Song for America*, 26–31). These poems are too small for the clutter of standard capitalization or punctuation. Instead, line length, line breaks, and phrasal units direct the reader's eye and ear through the images and the rhythms. Though only a few are labelled *song* in their titles, nearly all the poems *are* songs: lyrics of personal celebration, prayer songs of exhortation and thankfulness and blessing. They are formalized rituals in which satire or banter would be inappropriate. The poet himself has a delightful, delighting, and subtle sense of humor, but it is seldom apparent in the poems. Nor should it be, given their ceremonial purpose. In the taped reading mentioned above, the poet comments: "To me a poem is a story—shortened." These stories are movingly sacramental, never solemnly dull.

This ceremonial quality is evident even in the travel poems found in *Another Song for America*, pieces such as "fresno to albuquerque," "lines written near osnabruck west germany," and "sketches from vienna," in which the sights and scenes are not merely recalled but are memorialized by gestures as simple as popping open a can of beer, exhaling frosted breath on a cold German morning, listening to a distant saxophone near the oldest church in Vienna. Again and always, the small things mean the most because they remind us—those who will listen—that small as our selves are, we still have a place and a purpose that can be sustained only through constant renewal of our lives and our spirit, a renewal that touches in recognition the value of everything in our lives from one day to the next.

Gogisgi Carroll Arnett
Mecosta, MI

BIBLIOGRAPHY

Henson, Lance. *Keeper of Arrows*. Johnstown, PA: Renaissance Press, 1972.

———. *Naming the Dark*. Norman, OK: Point Riders Press, 1976.

———. *Mistah*. New York: Strawberry Press, 1977.

———. Audiotape. Central Michigan University, November 29, 1979.

———. *Buffalo Marrow on Black*. Edmond, OK: Full Count Press, 1980.

———. *In a Dark Mist*. Merrick, NY: Cross-Cultural Communication, 1982.

———. *A Circling Remembrance*. Marvin, SD: Blue Cloud Quarterly, 1984.

———. *Selected Poems 1970–1983*. Greenfield Center, NY: Greenfield Review Press, 1985.

———. *Another Song for America*. Norman, OK: Point Riders Press, 1987.

Linda Henderson Hogan
(July 16, 1947–)

"As energy, language contains the potential to restore us to a unity with earth and the rest of the universe" ("Who Puts Together," 112). The poetry, fiction, and essays of Linda Hogan uncover realities that are not easy to name or comprehend; from the tiny atom to the atomic bomb, her vision is whole. Hogan's writing gained recognition with the publication of *Calling Myself Home* in 1978. Since then, Joseph Bruchac (whose Greenfield Review Press published that first book), Paula Gunn Allen, N. Scott Momaday, Andrew Wiget, Simon Ortiz, Duane Niatum, Marge Piercy, and others have shown their high regard for Hogan's writing in critical essays, in interviews, or by including her work in anthologies.

Born in Denver, Hogan lived part of her childhood in a housing project in Colorado Springs and in Germany. Because her family originates from Oklahoma, she maintains close ties there. Her father is Chickasaw; her mother is from an immigrant Nebraska family. Hogan has stated that there were no books in her home, but that stories told by her father and uncle were a literary resource that has enriched her writing (autobiographical statement, 78).

In her early twenties, Hogan moved to California where she worked as a nurse's aide and later began adult education classes. She later moved to Maryland, outside of Washington, D.C.; it was there that she began writing poetry (Bruchac 1987:121). She returned to college in 1975 and went on to complete an M.A. in English and creative writing at the University of Colorado. Hogan has been poet-in-residence for the Colorado and Oklahoma Arts Councils. She has taught at the University of Colorado, Colorado College, Colorado Women's College, and the University of Minnesota; and has presented lectures, readings, and workshops at many other universities, in Native American communities, and at conferences.

Among her many fellowships and awards are an American Book Award from the Before Columbus Foundation for *Seeing Through the Sun* (1985), a Yaddo Artists Colony Residency Fellowship, a D'Arcy McNickle Memorial Fellowship, a John Simon Guggenheim fellowship, a National Endowment for the Arts grant in fiction, and the Five Tribes Museum Playwriting Award.

Her poems, essays, and short stories have been published widely in such magazines as *Prairie Schooner, Denver Quarterly, The Greenfield Review, Ms.*, and *Parabola*.

She has two daughters, Sandra and Tanya, both adopted, and for the last ten years Linda Hogan has called Idledale, Colorado, her home.

Hogan's writing examines people's essential relationship to land, animals, and each other from a Chickasaw-feminist-humanist perspective that recognizes the precariousness and complexity of these relationships in the nuclear age. Her imagination and politics have been informed by Chickasaw tradition, by living close to the earth, and by the working- and poverty-class life of her childhood. Her poetry and prose have consistently evolved from a culturally specific to a universal consideration of human relationships and responsibilities to place and to each other. Her early poems in *Calling Myself Home* are made up of the spare imagery of the Oklahoma landscape and are more obviously rooted in Chickasaw tradition than her later work. The turtle, the most frequent animal in this book, is symbolic of Hogan herself and of the Chickasaw people who have carried their homes with them, each body a shelter, a shell, a home. In "turtles," the first poem, they are associated with women (Chickasaw women traditionally dance with turtle shells on their legs in healing ceremonies). The poem celebrates this relationship:

> Wake up, we are women.
> The shells are on our backs.
> We are amber, the small animals
>   are gold inside us. (3)

As in many other poems in *Calling Myself Home*, females are valued here as the source of new life. The mother-child, particularly the mother-daughter, relationship is central to later work such as in *Daughters, I Love You* (1981), a section of *Eclipse* (1983), the short story "New Shoes" (1983), and the novel *Mean Spirit* (1990). Hogan presents this relationship as tender yet painful for the mother who is unable to protect her daughter from suffering and who must finally be separate from the daughter she holds so dear. In *Daughters, I Love You*, the mother grieves that she cannot protect her daughters, their unborn, or the planet from being poisoned by radiation. In "New Shoes," Sullie, whose daughter, Donna, is growing up "Like a stranger" (10), finally understands that though Donna is becoming independent of her, she can be glad that her daughter is becoming a woman. Loving her, she says, "You sure look pretty" (20). *Mean Spirit* features the strong matriarch Belle Graycloud, a protective presence central to her Osage community.

In her essay "Let Us Hold Fierce," Paula Allen writes of Hogan's work: "Being an Indian enables her to resolve the conflict that presently divides the non-Indian feminist community; she does not have to choose between spirituality and political commitment, for each is the complement of the other. They are the two wings of one bird, and that bird is the interconnectedness of everything" (1986:169).

Hogan's poetry and fiction illuminate the injustice of poverty in the center of the United States and south of the border. From the ironic statement of "Blessing" in *Calling Myself Home*—"Blessed are the rich / for they eat meat every night. / They have already inherited the earth" (26)—through "Wall Songs" in *Seeing Through the Sun* and her novel *Mean Spirit* she casts new light on generally accepted platitudes and conventions. "Wall Songs" ends, "boundaries are all lies" (68). Her novel *Mean Spirit* wraps around a community and examines a new/old way of living.

Something should be said here about Hogan's contributions to literary criticism. Two essays in particular have brought original research and critical insights to light. In "The 19th Century Native American Poets," Hogan surveys the literary tradition that preceded contemporary Native American poets. Discussing the poetry of E. Pauline Johnson, Alexander Posey, John Rollin Ridge, and Gertrude Bonnin, Hogan points out "the conflicts forced upon Native Americans by federal government policies and by the educational system for Indian children in the late 19th century" (29). In "Who Puts Together," Hogan examines N. Scott Momaday's use of the "oral concept of language where words function as a poetic process of creation, transformation, and restoration" (103) in *House Made of Dawn*. Both the historical and the theoretical and linguistic analyses in these essays have bearing on Hogan's own life and writing.

What is so remarkable about Hogan's writing is her scope. She is not narrow or sectarian. Her work carries the message that all the various cultures on this earth must accept and love each other if we are to survive. In "Black Hills Survival Gathering" (1980), the drum beat of the Buddhist monks, like the beat of the Native American drum, is the same as the human heartbeat, which is the same as the heartbeat of the planet earth (*Eclipse*, 28–29). Like Leslie Silko, Hogan has a global vision of nature that necessitates confronting the nuclear threat to all. Like Silko, Hogan recognizes the power of language to heal or to destroy. In "The Women Speaking," women of Russia, India, and America "walk toward one another" to "bless this ground" (*Eclipse*, 30). But language also has the power to destroy, as we read in "Folksong":

> The men are in assembly
> They speak, yes or no
>   and change the living
>   to the dead. Such is the power of words. (*Seeing Through the Sun*, 8)

There is an intricate mystery about Hogan's writing, partially the effect of assorted images that fit together in the random ways that life fits together—not placed there neatly, but in a wonderful, unpredictable reality. The story "Amen," for example, could have expressed themes quite different from the statement it ends with. There is a parallel between Jack, the old, one-eyed man, and the large, old, one-eyed fish. And there is a parallel between the fish and the Chickasaw people that make Sullie, the girl in the story, have a certain reverence for it, that it survived so many years. She is reluctant to eat it. But eat it she must. For that is what the fish is for. "Amen," say the women, as Jack tells her to eat the "Indian fish" (282).

Norma C. Wilson
University of South Dakota

Bibliography

Primary Sources

Hogan, Linda. *Calling Myself Home*. Greenfield Center, NY: Greenfield Review Press, 1978.

——. Autobiographical statement in *Sun Tracks* 5 (1979): 78.

——. "The 19th Century Native American Poets." *Wassaja* 13 (1980): 24–29.

——. "Who Puts Together." *Denver Quarterly* 14.4 (Winter 1980): 103–10.

——. *Daughters, I Love You*. Denver: Research Center on Women, 1981.

——. "Amen." *Earth Power Coming*. Ed. Simon J. Ortiz. Tsaile, AZ: Navajo Community College Press, 1983. 276–87.

——. *Eclipse*. Los Angeles: U of California P, 1983.

——. "New Shoes." *Earth Power Coming*. Ed. Simon J. Ortiz. Tsaile, AZ: Navajo Community College Press, 1983. 3–20.

——. *Seeing Through the Sun*. Amherst: U of Massachusetts P, 1985.

——. *Savings*. Coffee House Press, 1987.

——. *Mean Spirit*. New York: Atheneum, 1990.

——. *The Book of Medicines*. Coffee House Press, 1993.

Secondary Sources

Allen, Paula Gunn. *The Sacred Hoop: Recovering the Feminine in American Indian Traditions*. Boston: Beacon Press, 1986.

Bruchac, Joseph. *Survival This Way: Interviews with American Indian Poets*. Tucson: U of Arizona P, 1987.

M*aurice* **Kenny** *(August 16, 1929–)*

Kenny is a penetrating and dynamic poet often associated with the Native American Renaissance. His writing and editorial work have influenced many Native and non-Native writers toward an appreciation of Native American values and political insights. While completing over fifteen volumes of poetry and prose, editing and contributing to anthologies, co-editing the magazine *Contact II*, publishing books for Strawberry Press and Contact II Press, teaching, and working on numerous other projects, he has maintained an intensely active public reading schedule through which he has promoted Native writers and Native publications all over the country. His work has been widely acclaimed and his influence widespread.

Born on August 16, 1929, of a mother of Seneca ancestry and a father of Mohawk ancestry, Kenny spent the first years of his life around Watertown, New York—"a small town nesting in the foothills of the Adirondacks on the shores of the Black River, which flows out of the mountains and into the great Lake Ontario" ("Writing at the Edge," in Swann 1987:46). Kenny's identification with nature was forged from days spent wandering the woodlands alone and from his father's love of the beauty and freedom of the woods and streams.

Kenny's early ramblings led him to Butler University, where he earned a B.A. in English literature in 1956 and nurtured his love of poetry. As his early sense of craft was molded by his teachers at Butler, so were his expectations for precision in writing. Soon after graduation, he moved to New York, beginning a long and fruitful association with that city. Though Kenny was in contact with many of the best-known writers of the late 1950s, his relationship with poet Louise Bogan proved to be the most significant and influential one for him. Her technical expertise and tragic spirit fired the young writer's imagination and helped direct his growing sense of voice and craft. Also influential was Willard Motley, author of *Knock on Any Door*. While working as his secretary, Kenny learned the discipline necessary to be a successful writer.

In 1962, Kenny left New York for extended journeys to Mexico and the Virgin Islands, which ended with a stint in Chicago writing obituaries for the *Chicago Sun*. When Kenny returned to New York in 1968, he was writing prolifically, though much of the fruit of this period was not published until the mid-1970s. In November 1976, after working together on *Dodeca*, Kenny and J. G. Gosciak began to co-edit a new magazine, the influential *Contact II*, dedicated to mapping the growing and emerging poetic world of contemporary America. During the same period, he established the Strawberry Press to publish the poetry and art of Native people. Kenny traveled extensively across the United States during the late 1970s and early 1980s, visiting a dazzling array of college campuses, arts organizations, bookstores, and broadcast programs. As he gave readings, he promoted publications and encouraged Native writers. Concurrently, he continued to intensify his ties to Iroquois country, placing special emphasis on his association with *Akwesasne Notes*.

In the 1980s, Kenny began to receive wide recognition for his accomplishments. In 1983, *Blackrobe* was nominated for a Pulitzer Prize, and in 1984 it was given the National Public Radio Award. Also in 1984, *The Mama Poems* won the American Book Award. He received North Country Community College's Hodson Award in 1987 for his contributions to community service, and he received a citation from St. Lawrence University for his contributions to letters.

In 1985, Kenny began teaching at North Country Community College. The move from Brooklyn placed him home once again in the upstate New York of his boyhood. Living in the city of Saranac Lake, he again faced the Adirondacks, feeling the ties of nature and culture, and enjoyed a sense of renewal and accomplishment—"All the elements important to my poems, to my life, surround me presently" ("Writing at the Edge," in Swann 1987:53). Though he continues to consider Saranac Lake as home, he has taught at a number of institutions such as the University of Oklahoma and the University of British Columbia.

For a number of years, Maurice Kenny has stated his philosophy: "I am committed to the earth and the past; to tradition and the future. I am committed to people and poetry." This commitment translates itself into many poems in which the narrative voice speaks from the point of view of the natural object. Kenny seeks to restructure the perception of his readers so as to bring them in tune with their most basic sensual experiences with the world, yet his poems provoke an intellectual appreciation of human history and culture. Kenny wants his readers to feel at home in this world. In his poetry, "home" is the place of harmony between nature, song, spirit, and the past. Kenny exposes the extent to which the Native American past can be read in that harmony; in contrast, the Euroamerican past seems dominated by dislocation and misperception.

Many of his poems pick up the rhythms of songs and dances of the Iroquois longhouse. These highly musical poems reveal a lyric vision which celebrates the intertwining of human and natural rhythms while expressing the pain and anguish which separation from home, the past, nature, and culture can create. These lyrical insights often find delineation in a Whitmanesque identification with the natural world, but a world in which the Native American perception of spirit negates ego in favor of celebrating the songs of the world around us. While one may see Williams's influence here ("No Ideas But in Things"), one can also see the influence of Native American cosmology. Thus Kenny's natural images are doubly powerful: the natural image evokes Native cultural and social connotations while Kenny as narrator becomes a spirit-infused voice for the experiences of things.

Early poetry such as the work in *Dead Letters Sent* (1958) reveals Kenny's long-standing concern with the intertwining of the rhythms of man and nature, and an awareness of the lyrical tradition of English poetry, but a Pound/Williams emphasis on the natural symbol's appropriateness, combined with the use of musical and natural speech rhythms, modifies any hint of academic presentation.

While Kenny continued to write and publish in the 1960s, it was not until 1976, with the publication of *I Am the Sun*, that his work found a wide audience. The poem, based on a Sioux ghost dance song, reveals a shifting emphasis in his work—toward oral tradition, toward performed poetry, toward persona, and toward cultural stances with political implications. Both *North: Poems of Home* (1977) and *Dancing Back Strong the Nation* (1979) expand the direction of *I Am the Sun* while focusing its emergent themes on familiar ground—the interaction of man and nature.

Perhaps the most powerful of his persona work is the masterpiece *Blackrobe* (1982). In this work Kenny combines poetry, drama, and history as he presents the voices of the main characters surrounding the life and death of a Jesuit missionary, Isaac Jogues, who was killed by the Mohawk he had come to convert. Through his use of a variety of voices, Kenny is able to present a dynamic Mohawk perspective on the killing of Jogues. The priest's arrogance, lack of cultural understanding, and inflexibility are explored in a way that not only clarifies an event from history, but also succeeds in drawing important contemporary political parallels. The dramatic power of the poetry in the volume overwhelms a reader. As an acknowledgment of Kenny's presentational abilities, a cassette version of Kenny reading *Blackrobe* has been released. Kenny has finished a similar volume dealing with a figure from Mohawk history, Molly Brant.

In *The Mama Poems* (1984), Kenny turned his attention to his own boyhood. Though highly autobiographical in nature, the poems effectively reach out to explore an individual's connection to the land and Mohawk culture. Kenny's personal pain and dislocation mirror the land's and the culture's struggles with change and loss. As always in Kenny's work, both memory and change work over the materials of life, subtly shifting the narrator's perception and understanding of his experience until he must forge the vital and life-sustaining connections with family, land, and culture through an act of will and self-definition. This book is such an act of will and definition of identity.

In *Is Summer This Bear* (1985), Kenny returns to an exploration of the natural world with an emphasis on the experiences of animals. His poems are songs by and about Bear, Hawk, Coyote, and other animals which suggest their mythic, cultural, and physical domains. This focus leads Kenny to poems which express the tension between Native perceptions and the contemporary American world, a world that Native people cannot ignore and which influences their perception of themselves and nature. Not far beneath the surface of both contemporary and nature poems is the struggle to retain and define both identity and tradition which informs the contemporary Native American experience.

Kenny's most recent publications include the anthology *Wounds Beneath the Flesh: 15 Native American Poets* (1983), *Humors and/or Not So Humorous* (1988), *Short and Long of It* (1990), *Last Mornings in Brooklyn* (1991), and *Tekonwatonti: Molly Brant, Poems of War* (1992). *Between Two Rivers* (1987) is an excellent selection of Kenny's poetry, revealing the diversity, intensity, and significance of his vision. As a testament to Kenny's singular accomplishment, the book spans thirty years of creative endeavor. It contains work from all the previously cited books as well as *Only As Far As Brooklyn* (1979), *Kneading the Blood* (1981), and *The Smell of Slaughter* (1982).

James Ruppert
University of Alaska—Fairbanks

BIBLIOGRAPHY

Primary Sources

Kenny, Maurice. *Dead Letters Sent*. New York: Troubador Press, 1958.

———. *I Am the Sun*. Akwesasne, NY: *Akwesasne Notes*, 1973. Rpt. New York: Dodeca, 1976, Buffalo: White Pine Press, 1979.

———. *North: Poems of Home*. Marvin, SD: Blue Cloud Quarterly Press, 1977.

———. *Dancing Back Strong the Nation*. Marvin, SD: Blue Cloud Quarterly Press, 1979.

———. *Only As Far As Brooklyn*. Boston: Good Gay Poets, 1979.

———. *Boston Tea Party*. San Francisco: Soup, 1981.

———. *Kneading the Blood*. New York: Strawberry Press, 1981.

———. *Blackrobe: Isaac Jogues*. Saranac Lake, NY: North Country Community College Press, 1982.

———. *The Smell of Slaughter*. Marvin, SD: Blue Cloud Quarterly Press, 1982.

———. *The Mama Poems*. Buffalo: White Pine Press, 1984.

———. "The Creative Process: Wild Strawberry." *Wicazo Sa Review* 1.1 (Spring 1985): 40–44.

———. *Is Summer This Bear*. Saranac Lake, NY: Chauncy Press, 1985.

———. *Rain and Other Fictions*. Marvin, SD: Blue Cloud Quarterly Press, 1985. Rpt. Buffalo: White Pine Press, 1990.

———. *Between Two Rivers: Selected Poems 1956–84*. Fredonia, NY: White Pine Press, 1987.

———. "Our Own Pasts: An Interview with Maurice Kenny." *Survival This Way: Interviews with American Indian Poets*. Ed. Joseph Bruchac. Tucson: U of Arizona P, 1987.

———. "Writing at the Edge: Words Toward a Life." *I Tell You Now: Autobiographical Essays by Native American Writers*. Ed. Brian Swann and Arnold Krupat. Lincoln: U of Nebraska P, 1987.

———. *Greyhounding This America*. Chico, CA: Heidelberg Graphics, 1988.

———. *Humors and/or Not So Humorous*. Buffalo: Swift Kick, 1988.

———. *Short and Long of It*. Little Rock: U of Arkansas Native Studies Program, 1990.

———. *Last Mornings in Brooklyn*. Norman: Renegade Press, 1991.

———. *Tekonwatonti: Molly Brant, Poems of War*. Buffalo: White Pine Press, 1992.

———, ed. *Wounds Beneath the Flesh*. Marvin, SD: Blue Cloud Quarterly Press, 1983. Rpt. Fredonia, NY: White Pine Press, 1987.

Secondary Sources

ASAIL Bibliography 4. *Studies in American Indian Literature Newsletter* 7.1 (1983): 1–13.

Bruchac, Joe. "New Voices from the Longhouse: Some Contemporary Iroquois Writers and Their Relationship to the Tradition of the Ho-de-no-sau-nee." *Coyote Was Here: Essays on Contemporary Native American Literary and Political Mobilization*. Ed. Bo Schöler. Åarhus, Denmark: Seklos, 1984.

———. "Our Own Pasts: An Interview with Maurice Kenny." *Survival This Way: Interviews with American Indian Poets*. Tucson: U of Arizona P, 1987.

Ruppert, James. "The Uses of Oral Tradition in Six Contemporary Native American Poets." *American Indian Culture and Research Journal* 4.4 (1980): 87–110.

Scott, Carolyn. "Baskets of Sweetgrass: Maurice Kenny's *Dancing Back Strong the Nation* and *I Am the Sun*." *Studies in American Indian Literature* 7.1 (Winter 1983): 8–13.

"Special Focus on Strawberry Press." *The Greenfield Review* 9.3–4 (1981): 194–214.

Wiget, Andrew. *Native American Literature*. Boston: Twayne, 1985.

Thomas King *(April 24, 1943–)*

Although he was born and educated in the United States, Thomas King has become one of the foremost writers of fiction about Canada's Native people. Born in Sacramento in 1943, King was raised in Roseville, California. He is the son of Kathryn K. King, whose ancestry is Greek and German, and Robert Hunt King, whose ancestry is Cherokee. From 1970 to 1981, King was married to Kristine Adams. Their son, Christian King, was born in 1971. He and his partner, Helen Hoy, currently reside in St. Paul with their two children, Benjamin Hoy (b. 1985) and Elizabeth King (b. 1988).

King graduated from high school in Roseville. At age twenty-one, he took a tramp steamer to Australia and New Zealand, where he worked as a photojournalist. After he returned to the United States, he worked at Boeing Aircraft as a tool designer. He subsequently entered California State University, Chico, where he earned his B.A. in English in 1970 and his M.A. in English in 1972. King received his Ph.D. in American Studies and English from the University of Utah in 1986. His dissertation was "Inventing the Indian: White Images, Native Oral Traditions, and Contemporary Native Writers."

Since 1989, King has been associate professor of American Studies and Native Studies at the University of Minnesota, where he is also chair of Native Studies; from 1979 to 1989, he was assistant professor of Native Studies at the University of Lethbridge, where he was also chair of Native Studies from 1985 to 1987. Other positions he has held include coordinator of the History of the Indians of the Americas Program, University of Utah (1977–79), associate dean for Student Services at California State

University, Humboldt (1973–77), and director of Native Studies at the University of Utah (1971–73).

King's first novel was *Medicine River* (1990), set in the fictional town from which it takes its title, located near the Blood Reserve in Alberta. Like the protagonists of many twentieth-century novels, Will, the protagonist, is a passive mixed-blood who tries to learn more about himself, his family, and the Indians and mixed-bloods of his hometown. Son of an Indian mother, Will becomes increasingly involved with the people of Medicine River. The catalyst in his decision to return home, and for his return home, is his friend Harlen Big Bear, who is full of enterprises that never quite come off, misguided advice for Will, and rambling stories. The novel received high praise for its accurate portraits of life in an off-reservation town and on the reserve.

Although *Green Grass, Running Water* (1993), King's second novel, retains the realistic portraits of *Medicine River*, it is far more ambitious and sophisticated in its narrative form. The plot focuses on a cast of characters who attempt to determine their relationships to one another and to their Indian relatives and homeland. The novel is a very clever trickster story, filled with humorous twists of fate that change the lives of the characters and with satires of the depictions of American Indians in movies and western adventure novels. King also shows how Indians overturn these. Letisha Morningstar, for example, got her Indian-sounding name from her white husband. She owns the highly successful Dead Dog restaurant, where she persuades gullible tourists that they are eating authentic Indian dog meat. In one hilarious scene, Alberta Frank, a university professor, attempts to teach Indian history to a recalcitrant class that includes such stalwarts as Henry Dawes and Elaine Goodale. Adding to the fun is Coyote's origin myth, which is interwoven throughout the novel and is a patchwork of creation stories from such disparate groups as the Iroquois, Blackfoot and Ojibwa, and Navajo. Also interspersed are the conversations between the members of a trickster chorus, composed of four old Indians who have escaped from a mental hospital (Hawkeye, Lone Ranger, Ishmael, and Robinson Crusoe).

Written for children, his *A Coyote Columbus Story* (1992) is a delightfully witty book that brings Columbus into Indian trickster stories. It was nominated for the 1992 Canadian Governor General's award. Though he is primarily a fiction writer, King has also published poetry in such journals as *Canadian Literature, Soundings, Whetstone*, and *Tonyon Review*.

King has edited two collections of fiction by Canadian Native peoples: *An Anthology of Short Fiction by Native Writers in Canada*, a special issue of *Canadian Fiction Magazine* (1988); and *All My Relations: An Anthology of Contemporary Canadian Native Fiction* (1990). In addition, he co-edited, with Cheryl Calver and Helen Hoy, *The Native in Literature* (1987), which grew out of the University of Lethbridge's "Conference on the Native in Literature: Canadian and Comparative Perspectives" (1985).

A. LaVonne Brown Ruoff
University of Illinois—Chicago

BIBLIOGRAPHY

King, Thomas. *Medicine River*. Toronto: Penguin, 1990. Fiction.

———. *A Coyote Columbus Story*. Toronto: Groundwood, 1992. Children's fiction.

———. *Green Grass, Running Water*. New York: Houghton, 1993; Toronto: HarperCollins, 1993. Fiction.

———. *Medicine River*. Toronto: Canadian Broadcasting Corporation, 1993. Film script.

———. *Medicine River*. Edmonton: Canadian Broadcasting Corporation, 1993. Radio drama.

———, ed. and intro. *An Anthology of Short Fiction by Native Writers in Canada*. Special Issue of *Canadian Fiction Magazine*. Toronto: *Canadian Fiction Magazine*, 1988.

———, ed. and intro. *All My Relations: An Anthology of Contemporary Canadian Native Fiction*. Toronto: McClelland, 1990.

———, Helen Hoy, and Cheryl Calver, eds. *The Native in Literature: Canadian and Comparative Perspectives*. Toronto: ECW, 1987.

N(avarre) Scott Momaday
(February 27, 1934–)

I

In 1969, when Kiowa author N. Scott Momaday won the Pulitzer Prize for his first novel, *House Made of Dawn* (1968), the world took note of the high quality of Native American writing and of the complexity of the Kiowa, Navajo, and Pueblo oral mythological traditions that terrace this contemporary fiction. Distinguished as one of the finest twentieth-century American novels, *House Made of Dawn* has been translated into Dutch, Italian, German, Swedish, Norwegian, and Polish, and Momaday's *The Way to Rainy Mountain* (1969) into French, German, Italian, and Japanese. Yet the full long-range impact of Momaday's literary contribution is hard to assess—not only because Momaday is still active as a writer, but also because other Indian writers, whose imaginations and opportunities unfolded as a result of his path-breaking efforts, are still dreaming of songs and stories to come.

Although known primarily for his impressive literary achievements—including *The Way to Rainy Mountain*—N. Scott Momaday has also been recognized for his considerable artistic skills. In the last decade, his paintings and drawings have increasingly appeared as cover art on his books—*The Ancient Child* (1989) and the recent Sun Tracks/University of Arizona Press reprint edition of *The Names* (1976)—and as dust jacket illustrations for books of criticism/interviews on his works, such as Kenneth Roemer's (ed.) *Approaches to Teaching Momaday's "The Way to Rainy Mountain"* (1988), Charles L. Woodard's *Ancestral Voice: Conversations with N. Scott Momaday* (1989), and Joseph Bruchac's *Survival This Way: Interviews with American Indian Poets* (1987). The imagery of Momaday's artwork centers around the same themes that crisscross his poetry, fiction, and expository writing. He has drawn tribal elders and ancestors, powerful symbolic shields, mad buffalo, and meditative sitting bears. These images vibrantly suggest a personal quest for identity among his Kiowa people, and his relationship to nature as articulated through art, ritual, and language.

Momaday is interested in multiple ways of telling a story; and the oral storytelling tradition, a verbal phenomenon generated by a polyphonic interaction of human voices over millennia, provides him with the primary symbols, structures, and themes which he deftly transposes into written literature. For Momaday, pictographs or painted rock images also tell stories that stretch into mythic time. In his second novel, *The Ancient Child*, when the protagonist Locke Setman examines his own paintings he finds them "dark abstractions, set in bright, whirling depths, mysterious, and profound as ancient rock paintings, beasts, and anthropomorphic forms proceeding from the far reaches of time" (213). These awesomely beautiful images express the confluence of Momaday's historical, literary, and artistic interests. For Momaday, an image of an Anasazi shield-bearer, for instance, may suggest a story in rock that has emerged from the distant past to speak meaningfully, however obliquely, to the modern world.

Given his love of visual images, it is not surprising, therefore, that Momaday is reluctant to be known only as a writer. The corpus of Momaday's work is significant because he insists on showing the life-giving qualities of the arts and the interrelationships of the arts to other components of tribal culture. Through his autobiography, fiction, poetry, painting, and drawing, Momaday reveals the essential wholeness and unity of experience that Indian communities recognize as a fundamental dimension of the order of the universe. When Momaday draws a "self-portrait" of author as Bear, he re-creates an image of a primordial animal spirit whose ferocity and healing powers are legendary among diverse North American Indian tribes. The bear characterizes Momaday's own precarious journey out of the open country of sweet grass and traditional Kiowa storytelling into the predominantly urban, "alien spheres" of American arts and letters.

Momaday's novels, *House Made of Dawn* and *The Ancient Child*, are kin to other novels by Native American writers that began to be published nearly one hundred years ago, when Simon Pokagon's *Queen of the Woods* (1899) appeared in the closing days of the nineteenth century. Works such as Mourning Dove's *Cogewea, the Half-Blood: A Depiction of the Great Montana Cattle Range* (1927), John Joseph Mathews's *Sundown* (1934), D'Arcy McNickle's *The Surrounded* (1936), and more recently James Welch's *Winter in the Blood* (1974), Leslie Marmon Silko's *Ceremony* (1977), Paula Gunn Allen's *The Woman Who Owned the Shadows* (1983), and Louise Erdrich's trilogy: *Love Medicine* (1984), *The Beet Queen* (1986), and *Tracks* (1988)— among others—have shared Momaday's abiding concern with the dilemma of a young Indian protagonist trying to maintain an unbroken link to the natural world and his/her community amid threats of conflict and violence from the dominant white culture.

Of these writers, Momaday was the first to significantly transform the novel into a narrative structure that is capable of generating healing energy through its embedded mythic patterns. The life-giving story, song, and prayer texts that center *House Made of Dawn* voice Navajo, Pueblo, and Kiowa beliefs about the continuously generated healing powers of the natural world. The Navajo story patterns in particular—which Momaday incorporates into *House Made of Dawn*—tell of "heroes" (from the Twins in the origin myth to the healing ceremonial Nightway) or a "heroine" (Elder Sister in the Mountainway chant) who are separated from family and home to venture out into a dangerous world. After suffering near-death experiences, they are ritually aided by the Holy People (deities) who bestow detailed ceremonial knowledge on them and restore them to a state of spiritual and physical health. Eventually the "heroes" are able to return home, remade in an image of *hozho*, of beauty, order, and harmony.

This basic Navajo hero pattern is well suited to form the basis of *House Made of Dawn*'s story line. Abel, the protagonist of the novel, experiences the grave difficulty of remaking his life in an image of holiness after he has been shattered by combat overseas during World War II and by confrontation with an evil, albino witchsnake figure upon returning home to Jemez Pueblo, New Mexico. Abel's life parallels the Navajo hero's journey into dangerous mythic space, and it is not until he has extensive contact with the transformative powers of Bear that he is capable of surviving with dignity. The significance of Bear as an embodiment of wilderness and healing energy is carried over into *The Ancient Child*, wherein the protagonist Set, is actually possessed by Bear and becomes the "reincarnation of the bear—the boy bear [Kiowa bearboy]" (Woodard 1989:15) who figures prominently in Kiowa legend. As the ethnomusicologist David McAllester notes, "native empowerment is the theme" of *The Ancient Child* (1990:114). And this empowerment largely occurs through the presence of Bear.

N. Scott Momaday saw that American Indian fiction could be "deepened" to tell culturally meaningful stories from Native points of view by using indigenous modes of expression. Recognizing the novel as inherently flexible enough to accommodate portions of old stories from oral tradition—what I call "storysherds"—Momaday let these mythic "fragments" bleed into the fictional matrix of the text, becoming its lifeblood. Thus, Momaday initiated and set up many of the literary patterns for other Indian writers.

Leslie Marmon Silko in *Ceremony* has created a distinctive, original tale of a young half-breed man's search for wholeness and spiritual balance when he returns home from the Philippine jungles to Laguna Pueblo as a dislocated war veteran. What we recognize as Momaday's influence and contribution to the Silko text is threefold. First, Silko follows Momaday in modeling her protagonist's life journey on ancient Pueblo and Navajo mythic hero patterns. Second, she does this, in part, by paralleling Tayo's contemporary story to the mythic stories of his people that tell of the origins of the world, and of the strained relationships that existed between the earth people and the creative deities (e.g., Corn Woman) after the time of emergence from the underworlds. Because of tension or disharmonies between elements of the created world, it is necessary for heroic action to redress the imbalance. Tayo, *Ceremony*'s protagonist, then engages in positive actions that correct the patterns of misbehavior around Laguna that have caused drought to grip the land. This theme of the healing of both person and place, which Silko develops so extensively in *Ceremony*, is dominant in southwestern Native American oral traditions, but was first elevated to significance in written literature by Momaday.

Most strikingly, in *Tracks*, Chippewa novelist Louise Erdrich has developed the theme of healing in the context of the medicine practices and sacred knowledge of her people in the northern lake country, shortly after the turn of the century. Not only is Erdrich intrigued, like Momaday, with bear power—witness her characters Fleur and Margaret, who possess it—but also she, like Silko and Momaday, creates a medicine person (Moses Pillager) upon whose skills the plot turns. These medicine powers are transmitted through the generations from Old Man Pillager to his grandson Lipsha Morrisey in *Love Medicine*.

Although it would have been possible for Silko and Erdrich to have developed the theme of healing in their narratives based solely on their knowledge of ritual and oral traditions in their home cultures, N. Scott Momaday's vision of embedding mythology and old healing stories in a contemporary novel provides a vital, compelling model for younger writers to build upon. Among the Southwest Indian writers who also voice many of Momaday's concerns with relationships of persons to their cultural/geographic homelands, Paula Gunn Allen, Laguna Pueblo author of numerous volumes of poetry, a novel, and *The Sacred Hoop: Recovering the Feminine in American Indian Traditions* (1986)—a collection of essays on Native women's spiritual traditions—has stated publicly that N. Scott Momaday was a formative influence on her work, and that, indeed, reading *House Made of Dawn* helped to save her life. Other writers whose themes and images on occasion echo Momaday's are Simon J. Ortiz (Acoma Pueblo), Wendy Rose (Hopi/Miwok), Luci Tapahonso (Navajo), Harold Littlebird (Laguna/Santo Domingo), and the Oklahoma poets Joy Harjo (Creek) and Linda Hogan (Chickasaw) who have lived many years in the Southwest. Simon Ortiz has written that he was "happy to discover" N. Scott Momaday's writing in the 1960s when he (Ortiz) was searching for "Native American literary works and authors" ("Always the Stories," 63). Just as Ortiz has written: "There are tracks / at river's edge, raccoon / coyote, deer, crow, / and now my own . . ."—so have Ortiz and Momaday gone into the back country for water and spiritual sustenance (Ortiz, "Bend in the River," *Going for the Rain*, 82). Several fine southwestern Native writers (such as Simon Ortiz) have amassed an impressive body of creative work that, while not directly derivative of Momaday's writing, has developed in tandem or parallel to it.

In the 1970s and 1980s, Momaday's work was widely anthologized. Every major anthology of American Indian literature offered a substantial selection of Momaday writings, and the landmark anthologies *Carriers of the Dream Wheel* (1975) and *The Remembered Earth* (1979) bear his phrases as titles. The recently published two-volume *Heath Anthology of American Literature* (1990) features lengthy excerpts from *The Way to Rainy Mountain* and situates N. Scott Momaday among dozens of other contemporary ethnic and "mainstream" writers.

In the 1980s, two important books appeared that focus on N. Scott Momaday's work. First, Matthias Schubnell, a German scholar, published *N. Scott Momaday: The Cultural and Literary Background* (1985). This largely historical study traces the evolution and development of Momaday's artistry predominantly in terms of his Euroamerican influences, and helped to catapult Momaday further into the national and international literary limelight. And in 1988, Kenneth M. Roemer's *Approaches to Teaching Momaday's The Way to Rainy Mountain* was published in the Modern Language Association's "Approaches to Teaching World Literature" series. This series features Momaday's work in the "context" of the literary achievements of other writers—such as Chaucer, Dante, Ibsen, Melville, Shakespeare, and Homer. Recently, my own investigation of Momaday's first novel has been published as *Landmarks of Healing: A Study of House Made of Dawn* (1990). This critical study examines mythic patterns from Navajo, Pueblo, and Kiowa oral traditions, especially sacred stories about twins and bears, that Momaday has transformed in order to place his characters and readers into a symbolic relationship with the healing and regenerative powers of the natural world.

Since *House Made of Dawn* and *The Way to Rainy Mountain* were published in the late 1960s, scores of critical articles have appeared on Momaday's work. Roemer's *Approaches to Teaching Momaday's The Way to Rainy Mountain* alone contains seventeen original essays on various aspects of Momaday's contribution to world literature and pedagogical techniques for articulating his relationship to tribal and "mainstream" literatures. Within months of the fall 1989 release of his second novel, *The Ancient Child*, critics began responding to the new work. And by 1990, especially after the recent publication of Charles Woodard's *Ancestral Voice: Conversations with N. Scott Momaday*, Momaday studies had accelerated to a point of intensity, not coincidentally during a period when our collective American consciousness has deepened and broadened to value the aesthetic beauty and plurality of our national literatures. At present, N. Scott Momaday enjoys a well-deserved reputation as a master storyteller and world-class literary artist.

II

Momaday was born at Lawton, Oklahoma, on February 27, 1934, to Natachee Scott Momaday, a mixed French and Cherokee woman, and Alfred Momaday, a full-blooded Kiowa man. In August, during the first summer of his life, Scott Momaday was given his Kiowa name by Pohd-lohk, an elder of the tribe. As Pohd-lohk held the baby in his arms near the bank of Rainy Mountain Creek, he proclaimed him Tsoai-talee, "Rock-tree Boy," linking his spirit with that of the place known as Devil's Tower on the ancient Kiowa migration route. The family took Scott on a long journey to Wyoming so he could contact that ancestral landmark repeatedly honored in Kiowa mythological traditions. Momaday's bond to Tsoai, the place for which he was named, forms the basis for his identity, and the Kiowa story of the bear/children incident that took place there becomes the central story that Momaday retells in all of his major works.

Between 1936 and 1943, Momaday lived with his parents on the Navajo reservation at Shiprock, Chinle, and Tuba City. This arid redrock landscape of Navajo *Dine bikeyah* ("homeland of the people") had a lasting impact on the child, who, in later years, would assiduously study the culture and return time after time for inspiration along the gullies, arroyos, and mesas. It seems that the vastness of this terrain must have appealed tremendously to the young boy from the plains of Oklahoma whose first landscape was a sea of mixed grasses. Navajo country is the setting for poems such as "Earth and I Gave You Turquoise" and "To a Child Running with Outstretched Arms in Canyon de Chelly" (*The Gourd Dancer*, 15–16, 49), and it is the sacred locale of Ben Benally's stories and songs in *House Made of Dawn* and the setting of the later scenes near Grey's Lukachukai home in *The Ancient Child*.

In 1946, when Momaday was twelve years old, his parents moved to Jemez Pueblo, New Mexico, where they took positions as teachers at the Jemez Day School for elementary students. Al Momaday, an artist, was the principal and his wife, a writer, specialized in teaching the youngest students. The Momadays remained teachers at the school for a good many years. During Momaday's adolescence at Jemez Pueblo, he was fortunate to witness many plaza dances and to travel north to the Valle Grande, an ancient volcanic caldera that would become one of the Jemez settings for *House Made of Dawn*. But Momaday could not receive all of his schooling locally. After Scott had attended junior high and high schools in Santa Fe, Albuquerque, and Bernalillo, he left the region temporarily in 1951 to finish high school at a military academy in Virginia.

Momaday returned to the Southwest to graduate with a B.A. in political science from the University of New Mexico in 1958. After college, Momaday taught school for a year on the Jicarilla Apache reservation in Dulce, New Mexico. This experience in an isolated northern New Mexico community served to deepen Momaday's ties to place and refine the depth and sensibilities of his literary vision. His familiarity with the 7,000-foot plateau country along the continental divide has provided inspiration for poems such as "Long Shadows at Dulce" (*The Gourd Dancer*, 50), and for the climactic scene at Stone Lake in the closing pages of *The Ancient Child*.

Desiring to return to his studies, Momaday began graduate school at Stanford University, quickly received an M.A., and completed his Ph.D. in English there in 1963 under the tutelage of the renowned poet Yvor Winters. By 1964, Momaday took his first university teaching job at the University of California at Santa Barbara where he taught in the English department with other distinguished faculty such as Hugh Kenner, Basil Bunting, Marvin Mudrick, and Kenneth Rexroth. In 1965, his dissertation was published by Oxford University Press as *The Complete Poems of Frederick Goddard Tuckerman*. Momaday demonstrates his command of scholarly apparatus in his introduction to the volume where he both criticizes this nineteenth-century American poet and praises him for his fine-tuned, careful observations of nature. In the summer of 1969, Momaday was honored with a gourd rattle and an eagle-feather fan when he was initiated into the Kiowa Gourd Dance Society.

By the fall of 1969, Momaday was teaching at the University of California, Berkeley, and in 1972 took a position as professor at Stanford University. In the spring of 1974, he taught at the Moscow State University as the first exchange professor in American literature in the Soviet Union. Momaday has also taught at the University of Regensburg in Germany. Since 1981, Momaday has been Regents Professor of English at the University of Arizona, and over the years he has received nine honorary doctorates. Apart from Momaday's own autobiographical statements, Matthias Schubnell's *N. Scott Momaday: The Cultural and Literary Background* (1985) provides the most concise, detailed information about the author.

III

During the years that Momaday was teaching in Santa Barbara, he was working on a novel that would be published as *House Made of Dawn* in 1968. A year later it would win the Pulitzer Prize for fiction. To date it is probably the best-known novel by an Indian author, yet for many readers it remains nearly inexplicable and mysterious at heart. The novel tells the story of a young Jemez Pueblo man, Abel, the protagonist, who leaves home to fight in World War II. When he returns to the Pueblo in the mid-

1940s, he is profoundly estranged from his culture, and is provoked into killing an albino Pueblo man who appears to Abel as a witchsnake rather than as a human being. After an affair with a white visitor to Jemez, Angela St. John, Abel is relocated to a Los Angeles prison where he spends some lost years. Upon Abel's leaving prison, his new friends Milly and Ben Benally, a Navajo, attempt to help him pull his life together. But Abel is harassed by the slick Kiowa preacher-peyote road man Tosamah, and is drawn into a fight with the wicked cop Martinez, who brutally beats him almost to death. Ben and Angela appear in a Los Angeles hospital room to sing and encourage Abel back from the edge of death. As Abel slowly mends, Ben sees him off on the Santa Fe train eastbound for Arizona and New Mexico. At the end of the novel, Abel returns home just in time to care for his dying Grandfather Francisco. As Francisco's spirit begins traveling to the other world, Abel runs on the snowy wagon road at dawn to reaffirm his ties with the land.

The structure of this novel is convoluted by Euroamerican standards, but makes perfect sense when one considers that Momaday is deliberately trying to break up the planes of our conventional narrative vision in order to show us a world informed by myth. By creating a circular, nonlinear narrative, replete with disjunctures and multiple storytelling voices, Momaday is trying to tell a complicated story—from several points of view and several tribal perspectives—in a way that is consistent with his understanding of the structures of oral tradition and the cyclic nature of time. Momaday was the first Indian writer to end his novel as it began—with the image of a man running at dawn. The circularity of this affirmative scene, which expresses the potentiality of life at its fullest, is complemented by the novel's four-part structure, which also conveys a sense of wholeness. Since ritual actions performed four times are considered complete, sacred, and efficacious, Abel's healing at the "end" of the novel is convincingly enacted. Silko's novel *Ceremony*, published nearly a decade after *House Made of Dawn*, likewise incorporates mythic structures and ritual patterns that provide us with new angles of vision and perceptions about the unity of experience. When Silko frames her novel with the word "Sunrise," she, like Momaday, symbolically indicates that blessings are continuously being bestowed on the characters and the land.

Although many of the events and issues in *House Made of Dawn* are cryptic—such as why Abel is sought out by both the albino and by Martinez—the surface events of the novel clearly show Abel to be a lost, alienated person with little family and seemingly few deep abiding ties to the land and community where he was raised. This socio-psychological dimension of the text is the one upon which most serious criticism of *House Made of Dawn* has been based. Actually, however, churning beneath the surface of the plot, the eruptive deep structure of the novel suggests that Abel is inarticulate not only because he is muted by contact with the dominant white world, but also because he is a contemporary remanifestation of one of two maimed Navajo culture hero brothers—the Stricken Twins—who have suffered for having an unknown father and for having wandered off outside the boundaries or limits of culturally defined space. Vidal, Abel's older brother, is the other "twin" boy. When Abel takes on some of Vidal's attributes after he dies, a "twin reunification" takes place and a sense of wholeness is reconstituted (Scarberry-Garcia 1990:32–33).

There is considerable critical disagreement about the role of the character Angela in the novel. Marion Willard Hylton, for example, views Angela as an instigator of misery while Harold S. McAllister sees her as a saint or angel of mercy for Abel. In my reading of Angela, although she is initially deceptive and cunning in her relationship with Abel, through her intuitive knowledge of bear power and her identification with the Navajo mythological figures Changing Bear Maiden and Bear Maiden, she comes to realize that her own former viciousness to Abel was inhumane. After this recognition, she becomes Abel's nurturer and one of his healers (Scarberry-Garcia 1990:62–66).

In the last scene in *House Made of Dawn*, when Abel runs at dawn, even though he is still injured, he is no longer spiritually ill, as he has been through most of the narrative. Some early critics of the novel, such as Charles Larson, saw the gesture as a death run (Larson 1978:92), but most critics follow Larry Evers, who in "Words and Place" (316–17) explains that language, such as Abel's singing of the "House Made of Dawn" prayer as he runs, acts to restore wholeness and inner harmony. Momaday has built upon mythic episodes recorded in various ethnographic texts (by Washington Matthews and Aileen O'Bryan, among others) in order to show that when images of the land are internalized in characters and human beings, through repetition in song, prayer, and story, now as always, spiritual transformation and physical healing may occur.

A year before *House Made of Dawn* was published, Momaday had one hundred copies of *The Journey of Tai-me* (1967) privately hand-printed in Santa Barbara. This slim volume became the prototype for a longer, more extended study of Kiowa oral traditions known as *The Way to Rainy Mountain* (1969). One of the attractions of *The Way to Rainy Mountain*, besides its brevity, is its unflinching clarity of vision. Of all of Momaday's works, it most forthrightly articulates the land ethic that has made him famous as a philosopher of environmental issues.

Graced by pen-and-ink illustrations by Al Momaday, *The Way to Rainy Mountain* is probably Scott Momaday's most popular book. From the first illustration of the bear rearing against the Devil's Tower to the final illustration of the falling stars over a Kiowa encampment, this book, which is a compilation of oral history and autobiography, speaks eloquently of human relationships to specific landscapes. Framed by the poems "Headwaters" and "Rainy Mountain Cemetery," the heart of the book beginning with the "Prologue" and the "Introduction" conveys a sense of who the Kiowa people are. In three distinct narrative segments, the story is told of a long journey of the Kiowas over a span of three hundred years and a thousand miles from the headquarters of the Yellowstone in present-day western Montana to the Southern Plains around Rainy Mountain, Oklahoma. Through three central sections—"The Setting Out," "The Going On," and "The Closing In"—the book charts the Kiowa migration beginning in the late 1600s, its culmination in a "golden age" between 1740 and 1830 when the horse culture flourished, and the rather rapid "decline" of the tribe beginning in 1833, the year the stars fell, until 1879 when the buffalo, the focus of Kiowa spiritual life, were essentially gone. "The Epilogue" dwells on the event of the falling stars' meteor shower as heralding the decline of the culture, but ends with the positive image of the hundred-year-old woman Ko-sahn, a living embodiment of tribal memory.

Momaday's quest for identity, a major theme that runs through all of his work, is expressed in *The Way to Rainy Mountain* in terms of another great theme—humanity's relationship to the natural world. Part of the last passage in section XXIV reads: "Once in his life a man ought to concentrate his mind upon the remembered earth, I believe. He ought to give himself up to a particular landscape in his experience, to look at it from as many angles as he can . . ." (83). This meditative writing, based on lived experience in a given place, anticipates many of the eco-writers such as Barry Lopez and Gretel Ehrlich who have tried through their own refined sensibilities to articulate a land ethic of reciprocity that is viable for contemporary Americans.

Momaday's trademark style of precisely describing the minutest details of animal life and the lay of the land, in "elevated" formal diction, has earned him the respect of a wide and diverse audience. Over the years Momaday has cultivated a distinctive narrative voice that is recognized orally for its deep resonances and visually, in print, for its "scope" and range as it describes the grandeur and colorations of landforms in the shimmering distance. Momaday's serious, often grave tone of voice lends an air of solemnity to his descriptions of such places as the Washita River and the Staked Plains.

In many respects, the story of Momaday's journey to retrace the paths of his ancestors is the story of the Kiowas' relations with animals. Most of Al Momaday's illustrations here are of animals and insects—horses, buffalo, bear, alligator, spider, and cricket. Other animals that figure prominently in *The Way to Rainy Mountain* are dogs, moles, grasshoppers, and various birds including red bird, bobwhite, and peyote bird. Storm horse and peyote bird are mythical creatures who figure in stories about creation and transformation. And the sacred Sun Dance doll, Tai-me, who manifests some of the most potent powers of the Kiowa cosmos, is part deer and part bird, her body a union of the powers of earth and sky. For Momaday, these animals and spiritual figures are, like his grandparents Aho and Mammedaty, repositories of knowledge worthy of close attention.

For students and critics of this book, Kenneth M. Roemer's (ed.) *Approaches to Teaching Momaday's The Way to Rainy Mountain* is indispensable. These helpful essays range over the territory of biographical and cultural background, to forms, structures, and themes of the book, to pedagogical contexts for using the book in composition and literature courses. In *The Way to Rainy Mountain*, Momaday's love of the land, expressed through his love of language, becomes one of the highest values of his life.

The 1970s were active literary years for Momaday. In 1970, he published his best-known essay, "The Man Made of Words," which makes the point that the imaginative use of language can be a survival tool. This is the case for the Arrowmaker who saved himself by using his wits and speaking judiciously. The piece is full of ethical and moral charges to responsibility, especially to take care of the land. Yet the essay equally charges its listener/readers to take great care with the language they use, for it is one of the most potent, though invisible, elements of existence.

In 1973, Momaday collaborated with photographer David Muench to publish a book on the changing seasonal landscape of Colorado, entitled *Colorado: Summer, Fall, Winter, Spring.* Momaday's lyrical text does for Colorado nearly what *House Made of Dawn* did for New Mexico and *The Way to Rainy Mountain* did for Oklahoma. Martha Scott Trimble's *N. Scott Momaday* (1973) appeared about this time as the ninth volume of the Boise State College Western Writers Series. This pamphlet provides an introduction to Momaday's early works and a selected bibliography of works by and about the author (Schubnell's book remains the most helpful bibliographic source on Momaday). The year 1974 saw the publication of *Angle of Geese*, Momaday's first chapbook of poetry. These metrically complex poems are filled with light and dark imagery, and contain flight/running motifs that are associated with reintegration, death, and eternity. *The Gourd Dancer*, which appeared in 1976, contains all of the poems in *Angle of Geese* and an additional two dozen poems. One of these poems, "Forms of the Earth at Abiquiu," movingly describes Momaday's "gift of a small, brown stone" to the artist Georgia O'Keeffe (60). During this same period, Momaday wrote weekly columns for *Viva*, the Santa Fe *New Mexican* newspaper's Sunday magazine. These columns, such as "The Night the Stars Fell," significantly illuminate Momaday's other, better-known material. But perhaps Momaday's most widely read essay of the 1970s is the eloquent "A First American Views His Land," which appeared in the Bicentennial issue of *National Geographic* (1976). Here, Momaday makes the point that Native Americans profoundly care about the land because for millennia the Indian has been "at home" on the continent.

The Names: A Memoir, which was published in 1976, is Momaday's extended prose narrative account of his personal genealogy, tribal heritage, and childhood experiences. Unlike *The Way to Rainy Mountain*, which is a collection of compact stories, almost vignettes, about his place in the history of the Kiowa people, *The Names* is a longer "documentary" piece about his place in the Kiowa lifestream. Most of Part Three is an unpunctuated, nearly breathless recollection of impressive events that occurred to him as a little boy, told from the point of view of a child. The colloquial language here is appropriate for descriptions of the world as seen by a young person who may have been uncommonly observant and sensitive, but who had not yet developed into the famous writer with an oracular voice.

Replete with black-and-white photographs of family members and of significant places where he spent his childhood, Momaday's book traces his immediate family's personal history back, four generations before him, to his great-great-grandparents on both sides. In typical Momaday fashion, for those for whom there is no photograph on the genealogical chart he sketches facial portraits, consistent with the way that he imagines them to have looked. Momaday may not have been directly influential on Leslie Marmon Silko, but her *Storyteller*, published in 1981, bears a resemblance to *The Names*. In its broadest outlines, *Storyteller* also is composed of photographs, and of stories from oral history about personal family tradition, but is expanded to include original poetry and fiction, as well as lengthy retellings of traditional Keres mythology. Silko's *Storyteller*, then, while loosely modeled on Momaday's concept of autobiography, is really more like a synthesized compilation of both *The Way to Rainy Mountain* and *The Names*—in a decidedly rearranged, Laguna woman's context—laced together by Silko's own narrative genius. Both Silko and Momaday hear and develop multiple storytelling voices as a way of opening up new possibilities for seeing who they are. Even though Schubnell (172–73) may suggest that echoes of Dinesen, Camus, Whitman, Faulkner, Proust, and Joyce may be found in *The Names*, one is at least as likely to hear Natachee, Mammedaty, and Pohdlohk speaking.

In some ways, as a number of critics have noted, Momaday seems to be telling the "same story," over and over again. *The Ancient Child* (1989) seems to bear this observation out. This most recent work is immediately familiar to a seasoned reader of Momaday. Early in the novel, half-Kiowa protagonist Locke Setman is described as a successful artist living in San Francisco. Yet he is deeply unsettled and easily disturbed. Barely aware of his Kiowa heritage, Locke is summoned "home" to Oklahoma by a telegram that announces his "grandmother" Kope'mah's impending death. The trip evokes memories of Locke's troubled, orphaned childhood and thrusts him into a state of illness that is mitigated only by his growing curiosity about his identity. At his grandmother's grave he feels out of place, and it is not until the young half-Kiowa, half-Navajo medicine woman Grey gives him a powerful medicine bundle that he begins to feel a bond with his ancestors and a hint of his personal bear power to come. This old Momaday theme of the healing powers of Bear, which appeared in four bear stories in *House Made of Dawn*, appears even more pervasively in *The Ancient Child*. By the end of Book One, Locke flashes back to his father's story of the sudden appearance of a small boy in a Piegan camp. Since the little boy in some senses is said to be inarticulate and to transform into a bear, the boy becomes an archetypal model for Locke, who needs to define his identity, learn to feel at home in the wilderness, and be healed.

The rest of the novel (Books Two through Four) is a working out of Locke's wrestling with his self-images, his women, his artistic direction, his past, his dreams, his illness (which culminates in a mad scene in which he exposes the medicine bundle without proper ritual control), and his growing bear power. His life conforms to the monomythic hero pattern, already discussed in regard to Abel in *House Made of Dawn*. As he begins to acknowledge the dual bear qualities of enemy and healer within him, he grows stronger and is more capable of love. By the time he has gone on a long journey through New Mexico, experienced the transformative slap of a bear paw on his throat, participated in a peyote ceremony, and witnessed a Navajo Yeibichai dance, he is ready for the epiphanal experience at Tsoai where his sense of smell grows acute as he becomes Bear.

The Ancient Child contains other elements—such as the appearance of the legendary characters Billy the Kid and Set-angya—that stretch the scope of the novel. Momaday is seriously playing with mythic materials in order to show that history reimagined becomes a cluster of stories that still resonates meaningfully into our contemporary time. Like his other work, *The Ancient Child* is heavily autobiographical and, although Momaday did not know Set-angya and Billy the Kid in the flesh, he knows them intimately in his mind's eye.

N. Scott Momaday has written in *The Names*: "I have seen Grendel's shadow on the walls of Canyon de Chelly . . ." (60). Momaday is imaginatively oriented toward that place where myths intersect, where the visual image becomes indistinguishable from the story that is being told. As readers of Momaday's collected works, we have come to expect exquisite descriptions of landscape, especially of landforms seen by a Plains man from a distance. The clean, exhilarating prose that distinguishes Momaday's writing may ennoble us because it allows us to take a fresh look at the world, at the time of creation, when everything is bursting with original, transformative energy. Momaday's recent shield project (*Sun . . .*, 1992 a and b), enlarges a familiar vision with more high-quality illustrations and a new gathering of stories about those old emblems of personal power—

shields—that in their own swirling and symmetrical designs become images of the cosmos conceived in beauty.

Susan Scarberry-Garcia
Fort Lewis College

Bibliography

Primary Sources

Momaday, N. Scott. *The Journey of Tai-me*. Santa Barbara: Privately Printed, 1967.

———. *House Made of Dawn*. New York: Harper & Row, 1968. Rpt. New York: Perennial Library, Harper & Row, 1989.

———. *The Way to Rainy Mountain*. Albuquerque: U of New Mexico P, 1969. Rpt. Albuquerque: U of New Mexico P, 1976.

———. "The Man Made of Words." *Indian Voices: The First Convocation of American Indian Scholars*. Ed. Rupert Costo. San Francisco: Indian Historian Press, 1970. 49–84. Rpt. in *Literature of the American Indians: Views and Interpretations*. Ed. Abraham Chapman. New York: New American Library, 1975. 96–110.

———. "The Night the Stars Fell." *Viva* 14 (1972).

———. *Angle of Geese and Other Poems*. Boston: David R. Godine, 1974.

———. "A First American Views His Land." *National Geographic* 150.1 (1976): 13–18.

———. *The Gourd Dancer*. New York: Harper & Row, 1976.

———. *The Names: A Memoir*. New York: Harper & Row, 1976. Rpt. Tucson: U of Arizona P, 1976.

———. *The Ancient Child*. New York: Doubleday, 1989.

———, and David Muench. *Colorado: Summer, Fall, Winter, Spring*. New York: Rand McNally, 1973.

Tuckerman, Frederick Goddard. *The Collected Poems of Frederick Goddard Tuckerman*. Ed. N. Scott Momaday. New York: Oxford UP, 1965.

Secondary Sources

Allen, Paula Gunn. *The Woman Who Owned the Shadows*. San Francisco: Spinsters Inc., 1983.

———. *The Sacred Hoop: Recovering the Feminine in American Indian Traditions*. Boston: Beacon Press, 1986.

Bruchac, Joseph. *Survival This Way: Interviews with American Indian Poets*. Tucson: Sun Tracks and the U of Arizona P, 1987.

Erdrich, Louise. *Love Medicine*. New York: Holt, Rinehart and Winston, 1984.

———. *The Beet Queen*. New York: Henry Holt and Co., 1986.

———. *Tracks*. New York: Henry Holt and Co., 1988.

Evers, Lawrence J. "Words and Place: A Reading of *House Made of Dawn*." *Western American Literature* 11 (1977): 297–320. Rpt. in *Critical Essays on Native American Literature*. Ed. Andrew Wiget. Boston: G. K. Hall, 1985. 211–30.

Hobson, Geary, ed. *The Remembered Earth: An Anthology of Contemporary Native American Literature*. Albuquerque: Red Earth Press, 1979. Rpt. Albuquerque: U of New Mexico P, 1981.

Hylton, Marion Willard. "On a Trail of Pollen: Momaday's *House Made of Dawn*." *Critique, Studies in Modern Fiction* 14.2 (1972): 60–69.

Larson, Charles. *American Indian Fiction*. Albuquerque: U of New Mexico P, 1978.

Lauter, Paul, et al., eds. *The Heath Anthology of American Literature*. Vol. 2. Lexington, MA: D. C. Heath and Co., 1990.

Mathews, John Joseph. *Sundown*. 1934. Rpt. Boston: Gregg, 1979.

Matthews, Washington. *The Night Chant: A Navaho Ceremony*. Memoirs of the American Museum of Natural History, Vol. 6. New York, 1902.

McAllester, David P. "Review of *The Ancient Child*." *Parabola: The Magazine of Myth and Tradition* 15.2 (1990): 110–14.

McAllister, Harold S. "Incarnate Grace and the Paths of Salvation in *House Made of Dawn*." *South Dakota Review* 12.4 (1974): 115–25.

McNickle, D'Arcy. *The Surrounded*. 1936. Rpt. Albuquerque: U of New Mexico P, 1978.

Mourning Dove. *Cogewea, the Half-Blood: A Depiction of the Great Montana Cattle Range*. Boston: Four Seas, 1927. Rpt. Lincoln: U of Nebraska P, 1981.

Niatum, Duane, ed. *Carriers of the Dream Wheel: Contemporary Native American Poetry*. New York: Harper & Row, 1975.

O'Bryan, Aileen. *The Dine': Origin Myths of the Navaho Indians*. Bureau of American Ethnology Bulletin 163. Washington, DC: GPO, 1956.

Ortiz, Simon J. *Going for the Rain*. New York: Harper & Row, 1976.

———. "Always the Stories: A Brief History and Thoughts on My Writing." *Coyote Was Here: Essays on Contemporary Native American Literary and Political Mobilization*. Ed. Bo Schöler. Åarhus, Denmark: Seklos, 1984. 57–69.

Pokagon, Chief Simon. *Queen of the Woods*. Hartford, MI: C. H. Engle, 1899. Rpt. Berriaen Springs, MI: Hardscrabble Books, 1972.

Roemer, Kenneth M., ed. *Approaches to Teaching Momaday's "The Way to Rainy Mountain."* New York: MLA, 1988.

Scarberry-Garcia, Susan. *Landmarks of Healing: A Study of "House Made of Dawn."* Albuquerque: U of New Mexico P, 1990.

Schubnell, Matthias. *N. Scott Momaday: The Cultural and Literary Background*. Norman: U of Oklahoma P, 1985.

Silko, Leslie. *Ceremony*. New York: Viking Press, 1977. Rpt. New York: Penguin Books, 1986.

———. *Storyteller*. New York: Seaver Books, 1981.

Trimble, Martha Scott. *N. Scott Momaday*. Boise State College Western Writers Series, No. 9. Boise, ID, 1973.

Welch, James. *Winter in the Blood*. New York: Harper & Row, 1974. Rpt. New York: Penguin Books, 1986.

Woodard, Charles L. *Ancestral Voice: Conversations with N. Scott Momaday*. Lincoln: U of Nebraska P, 1989.

Duane (McGinniss) Niatum
(February 13, 1938–)

The author of four books of poetry and a number of chapbooks, Klallam writer Duane Niatum is one of the most widely published Native American poets. Born in Seattle and a longtime resident of that city, Niatum is undoubtedly the best-known American Indian poet of the Northwest. He has also written short fiction and numerous critical essays. Niatum's position as editor for Harper & Row's Native American Authors Series in 1973–74 also led to his becoming widely recognized as an editor of Native American poetry. His anthologies, *Carriers of the Dream Wheel* (1975) and the *Harper's Twentieth Century Native American Poetry* (1988), are considered the major texts for courses in American Indian literature. An artful poet, a probing and intelligent critic, and a skilled editor, Duane Niatum is a leading figure in American Indian literature.

Duane Niatum was born in Seattle in 1938 under the name Duane McGinniss. He cites his parents' divorce when he was five as an important turning point in his life, for it was at this point that the boy and his Klallam grandfather became very close. Serving as a "surrogate father," the older man taught the boy not only values that would shape his life, but introduced him to Klallam traditions which Niatum would tap increasingly in his writing. In 1971, he changed his name to Niatum, his maternal great grandfather's Indian name. After serving in the Navy, Niatum earned a B.A. at the University of Washington, where he was influenced by Theodore Roethke, Nelson Bentley, and Elizabeth Bishop. He earned his M.A. in the writing program at Johns Hopkins University. He has taught in a number of writing programs and has given readings throughout the world. Niatum is currently living in Ann Arbor, Michigan, where he is completing his Ph.D. in Northwest Coast American Indian art.

In Niatum's first collection of poetry, *After the Death of an Elder Klallam* (1970), many themes are visible that would continue to be dominant in his later work. The sources of his poems emerged from his exploration of his Klallam roots, his insistence on grounding his poems in precise geographical settings, and his interest in spirituality. Throughout that decade, with the publication of *Taos Pueblo* (1973), *Ascending Red Cedar Moon* (1973), and *Digging Out the Roots* (1977), Niatum refined his style while his vision became increasingly wedded to his Klallam heritage. In 1981, Niatum published a chapbook entitled *Pieces*; that same year, the University of Washington Press put out a larger collection, *Songs for the Harvester of Dreams* (1981). In 1987, Blue Cloud Quarterly Press published another chapbook, *Stories of the Moons*. A prolific writer and a dedicated craftsman who continuously revises his poems, Niatum is currently preparing the manuscript of *New and Selected Poems*.

In an essay entitled "History in the Colors of Song: A Few Words on Contemporary Native American Poetry," Niatum discusses what he perceives to be some common elements in contemporary Native American poetry. Although he is discussing the work of his peers, the article applies directly to his own work. For Niatum, central to an appreciation of Native American poetry is a sense of the writer's identity in relation to all things, both animate and inanimate. A second point in his article is the importance of the author's relationship to place. In contemporary Native American poetry, Niatum feels the presence of the "soul chanting for kinship." In Niatum's own poetry, that kinship comes alive to his readers not only in the names and the dedications that are sprinkled throughout the poems, but also in connections with spiritual entities. Not only does the forest of his native Washington figure prominently in his work, but Niatum makes the place come alive to us by populating it with the animals, the trees, and the ghosts of his people. Niatum's poetry is the poetry of naming. The table of contents in *Songs for the Harvester of Dreams* is a roll call of the animals of the forest. Titles include "The Bear," "Wolf," "Grasshopper," "Loon," "Kingfisher," "Eagle," "Spider," and "The Heron at Low Tide." Many of these poems begin with the presence of the animal, often named only in the title, then proceed through a brief description of physical, behavioral, or spiritual characteristics of the animals, and usually end with some identification of the poet with the animals. Sometimes the animals function as a guide or bridge to the spirit world where we are introduced to the figures of Cedar Man or First People or Trickster.

In a recent interview with Joseph Bruchac, Niatum responded to the challenges of being an ethnic writer in the United States. He likened the pose to that of "a tightrope walker between the two cultures who is never really a part of either" (Bruchac 1987:204). The tension of such a pose between worlds is reflected in Niatum's writing virtually throughout his career. The poems are replete with dualities. Sometimes they are expressed in the relations between Indians and non-Indians, between traditional and modern lifestyles, or between life in the city and life in the country. Many of Niatum's poems are anchored firmly to Klallam settings or traditions, yet others are contemporary and explore issues of love, art, relationships, and so on. Some detail the shifting of the seasons, while others navigate carefully in a world where spirits walk and speak with the living. Yet in all of these polarities, the dominant theme is finding ways to forge relations. Dualities for Niatum strain toward connection. Rather than finding solutions through rejecting one or the other world, Niatum's poetry becomes an occasion for the poet and his readers to forge connections. Perhaps the metaphor of the tightrope may be viewed less as a symbol of exclusion and more as a symbol that forms a slender thread to tie two poles together. It is the poet, then, in the guise of the agile and graceful acrobat, who allows us all to walk that bridge between those worlds. Such power of reconciliation lies in the use of the imagination. His poems become ways of bringing opposites together, and of reinforcing the old to give continuity and vitality to the new.

With the publication of *Carriers of the Dream Wheel* (1975), Niatum established his reputation as an editor. Containing the work of sixteen young writers, and published by a major press, the anthology brought a new generation of American Indian poets to a wide audience. Beautifully illustrated by poet Wendy Rose, the book features the work of a number of college-educated and scholarly young writers. In 1988, Niatum published an updated version, *Harper's Twentieth Century Native American Poetry*. The contributors are geographically diverse and offer a stunning array of the finest poetry that is being written today by American Indian authors. These books have sold widely and well; they serve as texts in college classrooms and yet have wide, popular appeal.

Niatum's critical reputation rests on a large number of articles, book reviews, and essays published throughout his career. Perhaps his most widely discussed essay, "On Stereotypes," argues against the limited view of writers of Indian origin to be defined, taught, and presented as "Native American artists." Niatum here raises his voice against such practices, arguing for these artists to be seen "as individuals rather than as Indians, as human beings and not as assemblages of tribal traits" (1987:561). This view has been echoed repeatedly by Native American writers including James Welch and N. Scott Momaday. For Niatum, such "stereotyping" forbids the reader from approaching the work free of preconceived notions. In later years, however, Niatum's feelings on the issue have softened, as he has perceived the tension that seems inevitable in the position of being an artist and a "Native American" artist.

For twenty-five years, Duane Niatum has been active in the American Indian literary community. His books have been translated into a number of languages, and his work has been widely anthologized. Throughout these years, his pace has never slackened; he has consistently produced writing of the highest caliber. Aside from a steady stream of new poems finding their way into publication, Niatum is an avid craftsman who is constantly reshaping and revising his older poems. His craftsmanship and his interest in fostering Native American writers to publication have singled him out as a talented, respected, and generous figure in the American literary community.

Andrea Lerner
California State University—Chico

BIBLIOGRAPHY

Primary Sources

Niatum, Duane. *After the Death of an Elder Klallam*. Phoenix, AZ: Baleen Press, 1970.
———. *Ascending Red Cedar Moon*. New York: Harper & Row, 1973.
———. *A Cycle for the Woman in the Field*. A Chapbook. Laughing Man Press, 1973.
———. *Digging Out the Roots*. New York: Harper & Row, 1977.
———. *Turning to the Rhythms of Her Song*. A Chapbook. Seattle, WA: The Jawbone Press, 1977.
———. *To Bridge the Dream*. A Story Chapbook. Laguna, NM: AP Ltd., 1978.
———. *Pieces*. New York: Strawberry Press, 1981.
———. *Songs for the Harvester of Dreams*. Seattle: U of Washington P, 1981.
———. *Raven and the Fear of Growing White*. Amsterdam, Holland: Bridges Press, 1983.
———. "History in the Colors of Song: A Few Words on Contemporary Native American Poetry." *Coyote Was Here*. Ed. Bo Schöler. Århus, Denmark: Seklos, 1984.
———. "On Stereotypes." *Recovering the Word*. Ed. Brian Swann and Arnold Krupat. Berkeley: U of California P, 1987.
———. *Stories of the Moons*. Marvin, SD: Blue Cloud Quarterly Press, 1987.
———, ed. *Carriers of the Dream Wheel*. New York: Harper & Row, 1975.
———, ed. *Harper's Twentieth Century Native American Poetry*. New York: Harper & Row, 1988.

Secondary Sources

Bruchac, Joseph, ed. "Closing the Circle: An Interview with Duane Niatum." *Survival This Way*. Tucson, AZ: Sun Tracks & U of Arizona P, 1987. 193–210.
Ramsey, Jarold. "Word Magic." Rev. of John Bierhorst, ed., *Four Masterworks of American Indian Literature*; Michael Borich, *The Black Hawk Songs*; and Duane Niatum, *Ascending Red Cedar Moon*. In *Parnassus* 4.1 (1975): 165–75.

S*imon J. Ortiz* (May 27, 1941–)

Though his work has received scant attention from the mainstream critical establishment, Simon Ortiz is generally recognized by critics and scholars of American Indian literature as one of the most talented and accomplished writers of the "Native American Renaissance" of the 1960s and 1970s. While productive as an essayist and short story writer, his reputation is usually associated with his poetry. Joseph Bruchac asserts that Ortiz may be the Native poet best known to other American Indians (1987:211); both Paula Gunn Allen (1986:132) and Kenneth Lincoln (1983:189–200) offer his work as a model of the traditional American Indian voice holding its own in the contemporary world. His role as a leading figure in the struggle to preserve and continue traditional forms and themes is acknowledged, for instance, in the title of Joseph Bruchac's anthology of interviews with American Indian poets, *Survival This Way*—a line borrowed from one of Ortiz's poems. The voice of the Acoma traditionalist which informs his early work expands in his later work to encompass concerns usually identified with the pan-Indian nationalism of the 1970s and 1980s; even in these works, however, the voice of militant protest, the quality of anger and defiance heard in the work of Jimmy Durham or Carol Sanchez, is subsumed and subordinated to the gentler rhythms of assurance and continuity characteristic both of his early work and of traditional Pueblo oral narrative and song.

Born in Albuquerque, Simon Ortiz was raised in the Acoma village of McCarty's (called Deetziyamah in the Acoma language and in several of his works) in an Acoma-speaking family. The shaping power of these early years upon his own creative vision and self-concept as a writer is evident in much of his work, as Ortiz himself both acknowledges and celebrates in his essays "Always the Stories" and "The Language We Know." In 1948, he began attending the BIA day school in McCarty's. Beginning with the seventh grade, he attended the St. Catherine's and the Albuquerque Indian Boarding schools, and later attended Fort Lewis College (1962–63), the University of New Mexico (1966–68), and the University of Iowa (1968–69). To support his writing career, Ortiz spent much of the following decade on the move, teaching at San Diego State (1974), the Institute of American Indian Arts (1974), Navajo Community College (1975–77), the College of Marin (1976–79), the University of New Mexico, and Sinte Gleska College. Recurring images of bus depots, airports, and subway stations in his poetry of this period record a demanding schedule of lecture tours and speaking engagements.

Ortiz's commitment to preserving and expanding the literary tradition into which he was born—the oral tradition of Acoma—accounts for many of the themes and techniques characterizing his work. Ortiz regards himself less as a "poet" than a "storyteller"; however, the repertoire of the traditional Pueblo storyteller includes not only oral narrative materials which, given their oral texture, adapt easily to short story or essay form (e.g., anecdotal historical material), but also songs, chants, winter stories, and the more sacred oral narratives associated with origin stories and their attendant ceremonies. Such materials when recited aloud have a distinctly "poetic" texture.

Ortiz's role as a storyteller in the traditional Acoma sense is made explicit in the structure of his early collections of poetry, *Going for the Rain* (1976) and *A Good Journey* (1977). Read separately, many of the ninety poems that make up *Going for the Rain* seem lyric fragments, voicing a spectrum of human emotions ranging from exuberance ("A Pretty Woman") to despair ("The Wisconsin Horse") and a range of occasions from an overheard barroom anecdote ("A Barroom Fragment") to an intimate interior monologue ("Earth Woman"). Read within the context suggested by the prologue to the volume, however, the individual poems become steps of an integrated four-stage journey, the overall motion of which recapitulates the sacred motion of the *shiwana* or Cloud People of Acoma ceremonial tradition, whose function is to ensure continued life for the land and the people by ensuring the periodic return of rain. By metaphorically entering into identity with the motion of the life of Acu (the place where life happens), the persona of these poems ensures his own return, or re-emergence, into the life of Acumeh hano (the Acoma people), which is at the same time a "return to himself." Thus contextualized, moments of both joy and despair experienced during the journey (which in this text takes the persona to such far-flung places as Florida, San Diego, Wisconsin, New York City, and [closer to home] Gallup, Hesperus, and Albuquerque) become appreciable as gifts or blessings, brought home to the people in prayer. This journey in all directions further reestablishes Acu—the point of origin as well as the destination of what otherwise appear to be pointless wanderings—as the geographical as well as spiritual center of the storytelling persona's identity, a pattern which incidentally confirms the traditional American Indian concept of the healing power of human identity with sacred place.

Ortiz's small chapbook *A Poem Is a Journey* (1981) is patterned along the same lines as *Going for the Rain*; here, the persona follows the trail of Tsaile Creek from Tsaile Lake to where it disappears into the earth of the Lukuchukai Mountains, a journey that reveals in passing the land's own need for some analog of a *shiwana* priest to bring the water back from "underneath, moving silently," into human consciousness and voice. In the final movement of this work, the persona, finding himself on the California coast, completes the journey of the poem by entering into motion with the clouds forming there, a motion that carries the combined life forces thus created eastwards, in the persona's regenerative vision, toward a reunification with the "thunder on Kaweshtima" and a vision of "moving grass at Aacqu."

This reemergence aspect of the journey motif also informs several of the sixty poems comprising *A Good Journey*, Ortiz's most accessible volume. In "Heyaashi Guutah," the *shiwana* spirit still moves across the land on its southwest-to-northeast axis, linking the mesas southwest of Acoma to Kaweshtima (Mt. Taylor), and in poems like "Notes for My Child" (part of which appeared in *Going for the Rain* as "To Insure Survival"), human life still takes its distinctive colors and texture from the land of its origin. In the overall structure of *A Good Journey*, however, the center of the persona's identity is less a place on the land and more immediately the oral tradition that "lives" there, and the journey is about keeping that tradition (and, of course, the cultural values it encodes) in motion. The title of the volume derives from an interview statement (included in the volume's prefatory materials) in which Ortiz asserts that his creative vision is addressed to the continuum of generations of which he is a part—his children at one end, his grandparents on the other—and that the "good journey" is the movement from previous generations down through his own to the newest ones: the preservation through retelling of the stories of "how they were born, how they came to this certain place, how they continued." The titles of the five sections of this volume, beginning with "Telling" and ending with "I Tell You Now," contextualize the enclosed poems as oral events rather than merely objects, and in many of the individual works in the collection, techniques such as multiple voicing, direct address, embedded quotation, and internal glossing further enhance the impression of oral performance while at the same time bringing the voices of elders into contact with the voices (or sometimes simply the audience) of children. The frequency with which Coyote, the popular and in some ways populist trickster/transformer figure of Acoma oral tradition, appears in this volume (five of the nine pieces in "Telling," the opening section, are coyote stories) provides Ortiz not only with some delightful storytelling opportunities but also, as Patricia Clark Smith has pointed out, implicates Ortiz's storytelling persona in the search for new strategies of survival at both the personal and communal levels ("Coyote Ortiz," 1983). This concern also informs overtly the poems of the volume's fourth section, "Will Come Forth in Tongues and Fury," as well as much of Ortiz's later published work.

The theme of survival at the communal level is the major focus of the (lamentably neglected) works collected in *Fight Back: For the Sake of the People, for the Sake of the Land* (1980). Published in journal form jointly by the Institute for Native American Development and the University of New Mexico's Native American Studies program as a tricentennial commemoration of the Pueblo Revolt of 1680, most of the nineteen poems and the lengthy mixed-format piece comprising this volume are stories of "now-day Indians" and their co-workers (Cajuns, Okies, Blacks, Mexicans) struggling against government and corporate exploitation—exploitation of the land in the form of the Kerr-McGee uranium mining and refining operations at Ambrosia Lake in Acoma country and those of Anaconda at the Jackpile site in neighboring Laguna country, and exploitation of the people in the form of economic and political control over the lives of the people, workers and nonworkers, living in or near these places. Despite the preface to the volume by Roxanne Dunbar, which proposes an ideologically Marxist reading of both Pueblo history and Ortiz's work in this volume, the strong recurring theme in these works—the way Ortiz proposes to ensure survival—is that the people have survived and continue to survive both as individuals and, more importantly, as a collective entity by identifying themselves with "the creative forces of life" ("Mid-America Prayer," the first poem of the collection). Heroism, or "fightback," in these works takes the form of maintaining and promulgating the old ways, of preserving life in the oral traditional way, as, for instance, in what happens in "Ray's Story" when the story of how Lacey (an Indian from Muskogee) died in the mines becomes "Ray's Story," preserved in Ray's voice and further kept alive in Ortiz's written version of it. The role of storytelling in the preservation of the land and the people is the point of one of the finest poems in this collection, "That's the Place Indians Talk About." Here, the story of the spiritual significance of the Ambrosia Lake area, regarded in Acoma oral tradition as the emerging place of the Acoma people, enters into identity with the story of Coso Hot Springs, a sacred place of the Shoshonean people. In this poem, the voice of an elder Paiute man, telling the story of how his people still draw strength from this place despite the fence around it built by the China Lake Naval Station, combines with the voice of Ortiz's persona to confirm the ongoing "moving power of the voice" as a creative force of life in which are identified the moving powers of both "the earth" and "the People."

Perhaps the clearest stylistic indication of Ortiz's overall purpose in this collection (a purpose informing later works as well) is the mixed format of "No More Sacrifices," which takes up nearly half the volume. Formally, it presents itself as a prose essay interspersed with stanzas of a journey poem. Generically, it reads as an autobiography, contextualized within a cultural history of the Southwest (focused on the history of the Acoma area) and responsive internally to the embedded journey poem, which uses the traditional quest-for-water motif to make the point that changes in the life of the land oblige in the lives of the people who identify with it. Within the poem, the "sacrifice" takes the form of a sacred spring which is losing its energy; within the essay, Ortiz points out *inter alia* the extravagant wastes of water involved in "Mericano" railroad and mining operations in the area, operations also involving the kinds of human sacrifices to "progress" recorded in the stories comprising the rest of the volume—most notably episodes of physical relocation, spiritual dislocation, and surrenders of land. To upset the fragile balance of life on the land is to upset the life of the people as well. But what is equally apparent in the structure and texture of this piece, as in the volume as a whole, is that the roots of Ortiz's story lie not in the political ideology of the times but rather in his heritage of received oral tradition, recalled and celebrated as a source of continuing life here as it is in his earlier work. Even so, there is a certain strained tone to the works in *Fight Back*, as though the healing power of oral tradition were barely a match for the sheer quantity of pain encoded in the lives of the characters Ortiz tells of and thereby makes a part of his own story.

This strain constitutes the dominant impression of *From Sand Creek* (1981). Like "No More Sacrifices," *From Sand Creek* is a dual-format work composed of forty-two poetic sketches, each accompanied by a short (frequently one-sentence) prose meditation on the facing page. As a whole, the work is set in the Fort Lyons, Colorado, Veterans Administration Hospital, where Ortiz himself underwent treatment in 1974–75. The storytelling persona of these works seems less informed by the regenerative (healing) power of Acu in Acoma oral tradition than by the memories, the cultural heritage, of this non-Acoma place, Fort Lyons, understood not only as the site of the contemporary VA Hospital but also as the headquarters of the U.S. troops who, along with the Colorado Volunteers under the command of the Reverend Colonel John Chivington, massacred about a fifth of the Cheyenne and Arapaho people camped along Sand Creek under a U.S. flag in the winter of 1864. Despite the images of regeneration and renewal with which the volume opens and closes, the tone of these works is almost unremittingly bleak. Andrew Wiget sees in these poems the operations of "a compassionate vision that would transform grief and guilt into hope" (1986:46); and Ortiz's own willingness and ability to enter not only into identity with the spirits of Native victims of

Sand Creek (and Korea, and Vietnam) but also, astonishingly, into sympathetic identity with the diseased and dangerous spirits of all the parties to that massacre, Chivington included, certainly evidences the poet's compassion. Still, Ortiz's storytelling power in *From Sand Creek* seems strained beyond its ability to heal, this far away from its Acoma wellsprings and given the amount of pain and disease that his persona enters into identity with in this collection.

The power of the creative vision informing much of Ortiz's poetry is somewhat attenuated in his prose fiction. In all, twenty-four of his short stories have been published in three volumes. Four of them appear in Kenneth Rosen's 1974 anthology, *The Man to Send Rainclouds*; another four comprise Ortiz's *Howbah Indians* (1978); and *Fightin': New and Collected Stories* (1983) contains nineteen short stories, three of which appear also in earlier collections ("Kaiser and the War" in *The Man to Send Rainclouds*, "Men on the Moon" in *Howbah Indians*, and "To Change in a Good Way" in *Fight Back*, presented there in poetic format). As Wiget has observed, Ortiz's short stories (like many of the works collected in *Fight Back*) "deal principally with the nature and consequences of cross-cultural encounters" (1986:24), encounters ranging in anecdotal gravity from an old Acoma grandfather's exposure to, and eventually successful struggle to come to terms with, twentieth-century technology in the form of a television ("Men on the Moon") to a younger Acoma man's ambush and slaying of a New Mexico state policeman ("The Killing of the State Cop," in *The Man to Send Rainclouds*). Typically, though, the potential violence of these encounters is gentled not only within the plot structure but also by the point of view—the storytelling persona—Ortiz creates in order to convey the events of each story: as in much of his poetry at its best, it is the narrative voice which commands our attention and gives life to the story it tells. Such devices as the telling of stories within stories, multiple voicing, and direct quotation occur frequently in these stories, foregrounding the oral texture of the printed text. As significant as many of these stories may be as storytellings, however, they still read as more "prosaic" and to that extent less vital than Ortiz's poetry at its best, perhaps because of the monotonic appearance they have in prose form (compare, for instance, "To Change in a Good Way" in *Fight Back* with the prose version in *Fightin'*). Even so, Ortiz's short stories bespeak the same values that characterize the persona of his poetry and give cause for celebration: he is a spokesman for, and his work has the power to evoke in us, "respect, compassion, and the promise of hope" (Wiget 1986:50).

Robert M. Nelson
University of Richmond

BIBLIOGRAPHY

Primary Sources

Ortiz, Simon J. *Naked in the Wind*. Chapbook. Pembroke, NC: Quetzal-Vihio, 1971.

———. *The Man to Send Rainclouds: Contemporary Stories by American Indians*. Ed. Kenneth Rosen. New York: Viking Press, 1974.

———. *Going for the Rain*. New York: Harper & Row, 1976.

———. *A Good Journey*. Berkeley: Turtle Island, 1977. Rpt. Tucson: Sun Tracks and U of Arizona P, 1984.

———. *Howbah Indians*. Tucson: Blue Moon, 1978.

———. *Fight Back: For the Sake of the People, for the Sake of the Land*. Albuquerque: Institute for Native American Development, U of New Mexico, 1980.

———. *From Sand Creek*. New York: Thunder's Mouth, 1981.

———. *A Poem Is a Journey*. Bourbonnais, IL: Pteranodon, 1981.

———. "Towards a National Indian Literature: Cultural Authenticity in Nationalism." *MELUS* 8.2 (Summer 1981): 7–12.

———, ed. *Earth Power Coming: Short Fiction in Native American Literature*. Tsaile, AZ: Navajo Community College P, 1983.

———. *Fightin': New and Collected Stories*. New York: Thunder's Mouth, 1983.

———. "Always the Stories: A Brief History and Thoughts on My Writing." *Coyote Was Here*. Ed. Bo Schöler. Århus, Denmark: Seklos, 1984. 57–69.

———. "The Language We Know." *I Tell You Now: Autobiographical Essays of Native American Writers*. Ed. Brian Swann and Arnold Krupat. Lincoln: U of Nebraska P, 1987. 185–94.

———. "The Story Never Ends." *Survival This Way: Interviews with American Indian Poets*. Ed. Joseph Bruchac. Tucson: Sun Tracks and U of Arizona P, 1987. 211–29.

Secondary Sources

Allen, Paula Gunn. *The Sacred Hoop*. Boston: Beacon Press, 1986.

Gingerich, Willard. "'The Old Voices of Acoma': Simon Ortiz's Mythic Indigenism." *Southwest Review* 64.1 (Winter 1979): 18–30.

Lincoln, Kenneth. "Common Walls: The Poetry of Simon Ortiz." Rpt. in *Native American Renaissance*. Berkeley: U of California P, 1983. 183–200.

Smith, Patricia Clark. "Coyote Ortiz: '*Canis Latrans Latrans*' in the Poetry of Simon Ortiz." *Studies in American Indian Literature: Critical Essays and Course Designs*. Ed. Paula Gunn Allen. New York: MLA, 1983. 192–210.

Wiget, Andrew. *Simon Ortiz*. Western Writers Series No. 74. Boise: Boise State U, 1986.

Carter Revard *[Nompehwathe]*
(March 25, 1931–)

While he has not received the critical attention that some younger Native American writers have received, Carter Revard has published extensively: he has produced collections of his poems, published individual poems and fiction in literary journals, and is represented in a dozen anthologies. He has also published essays and made numerous presentations on Native American topics at professional meetings and elsewhere (all of this in addition to his scholarship as a specialist in medieval literature). Frequently, these publications and presentations have been by request, an indication of the respect with which he is regarded. Some of his literary publications are not Native American in either theme or style, but it is his Native American work that is his most successful.

Born in Pawhuska, Oklahoma, Revard is part Osage on his father's side. He grew up in the area of Pawhuska and Buck Creek Valley on the Osage reservation with his twin sister and among the half-Osage children of his stepfather, the full-blooded Addison Jump, as well as among Ponca relatives. In September 1952, his Grandmother Jump, along with Osage elders, sponsored a naming ceremony for him at which he received his Indian name, Nompehwathe (Make Afraid or Fear Inspiring, a reference to a Thunder Being). Revard's frequent allusions to the ceremony and to the mythology surrounding it testify to the profound significance the event had for him as an act fixing him within the Osage tradition. He discusses the relationship between Osage naming practices, the naming ceremony, and the Osage origin myth in "History, Myth, and Identity Among the Osages and Other Peoples" (1980) and in "Traditional Osage Naming Ceremonies: Entering the Circle of Being" (1987). Revard earned degrees from the University of Tulsa, Oxford University (as a Rhodes Scholar), and Yale University. Since 1961, he has taught at Washington University, St. Louis.

Revard's earliest collections of poetry were *My Right Hand Don't Leave Me No More* (1970) and *Nonymosity* (1980). *Ponca War Dancers* (1980) is his most significant collection to date in that it draws upon earlier work and develops themes frequently central to his Native American work as a whole. Divided into three sections, this largely autobiographical collection has poems on growing up ("Getting Across"), honoring relatives ("Home Movies"), and, in the last section ("Ponca War Dancers"), poems about his Ponca relatives and drawing upon his Osage heritage. In the first two sections, there is little that strikes one as overtly "Indian." Still, one could argue that embedded in some of the poems are themes familiar in contemporary Native American poetry: the power and understanding to be learned from communion with the natural world (characterized by close observation of and a familiar footing in the natural), the transforming powers of song and ceremonial consciousness, and the sustaining power of the extended family. In the rhythms achieved by his line breaks, there may also be suggestions of the Osage voice speaking in English. In fact, Revard credits the first poem in the book, "Coyote," with giving him the speech sounds of the people of Osage County, Oklahoma, including the Indian voices ("Something That Stays Alive"). In the "Ponca War Dancers" section of the book, both transformation of various sorts and the family themes found elsewhere in Revard's work are particularly emphatic.

In general, Native American traditions see no contradiction between myth and "history," as Ameropean (Revard's term) traditions do. Evidence of this lies in the ease with which Native American oral traditions have mythologized (a form of transformation through language) current events and present "realities," for example, in contemporary Trickster stories. Revard's work, too, mythologizes: he has stated that he wants to transform contemporary science and traditional stories into myth ("Walking Among the Stars"). Hence, in a short story, a Native American physicist harnesses the energy of black holes to transport himself into sacred mythic time which coexists with "historical" time ("How the FBI Man Nearly Found God"). In two poems, Revard weaves mythic and contemporary technological facts with Las Vegas, a place prominent in certain aspects of Ameropean myth. In "People from the Stars" (*Ponca War Dancers*), he tells how the Wazhazhe (the Osages) came into this world from the stars and how the beings of this world—golden eagle, cedar tree, Nompehwathe, and others—agreed that the Wazhazhe could use their bodies in this world. The Wazhazhe may return to the star world whenever they wish, unlike the Europeans' ancestor Satan who was kicked out of Heaven permanently. In the meanwhile, the people use their oil royalties from the Europeans to fly about in airplanes between the real star world and the artificial star worlds created by the invaders, places like Las Vegas where the Osages can be entertained by the white world while talking of Indian matters. A later poem, "Close Encounters," whose science fiction title alludes to another contemporary Ameropean mythology, develops similar themes but with Las Vegas even more an image of artificiality as its lights contrast vacantly with the stars and other natural lights.

In yet other poems, Revard creates an interpenetration of modern science and Osage tradition to suggest the transforming powers in his own life. In "How the Songs Came Down" (*Ponca War Dancers*), he depicts people as black holes while, among other themes, illustrating the oral tradition in the person of his Aunt Jewell, who sang a Ponca song to give the young Carter and the other children courage. "Dancing with Dinosaurs" (*Ponca War Dancers*) begins with details drawn from other modern sciences: descriptions of birds' reptilian ancestors as dinosaurs modulate into images of modern birds migrating or singing. These images in turn lead to the ceremony in which Revard was named Nompehwathe, a winged being. Reptiles evolving into birds in the struggle for survival, birds migrating and singing for survival, sacred Thunder Beings: all meld into the singing and dancing of the naming ceremony by which young Osages are transformed for their survival with the Osages in their mythic world.

In his autobiographical essay, "Walking Among the Stars" (a title which implies his own sense of being in the Osage world), Revard compares himself to a mockingbird who has many songs; yet, he says, these songs are not his alone but are his people's. In *Ponca War Dancers*, his Osage relatives provide the mythic ground of his self-image and his writing; his Ponca relatives contribute to a more political sense of "Indianness." While Revard has said that the collection *Nonymosity* probably contains his most political poems, the title poem of *Ponca War Dancers* demonstrates a somewhat more militant Indian consciousness. This poem is first of all an honoring of his Uncle Gus McDonald, a great Ponca dancer, who, although circumscribed by the white world, nevertheless sustained his spiritual freedom—achieved in a vision—in the circle of dancers. It is also a tribute to his cousin Carter Camp and others, contemporary warriors at Wounded Knee and elsewhere. In this poem, Revard is self-deprecating when comparing himself to Camp. Indeed, Revard does not strike one as a very militant person. Still, there is in some of his writing a strong social consciousness, frequently expressed in satire. While not all of his satires are thematically Native American, the most successful are. "Discovery of the New World" (*Ponca War Dancers*) uses a science fiction premise to satirize the ideological rationalizations by which Europeans justified the conquest and destruction of Western Hemisphere tribal civilizations. Similarly, a mixed poetry and prose composition, "Report to the Nations: Claiming Europe" (1983), is a report to the Osage elders on the narrator's successes and failures as he travels Europe claiming lands for the Osage Nation. Frequently, he questions the feasibility of civilizing the Europeans just as the

Europeans did in their accounts of conquering the peoples of the American continents. Revard hopes to expand such short prose pieces into a novel; consequently, this aspect of his writing may find a more emphatic voice than it has had in the past.

Franchot Ballinger
University of Cincinnati

BIBLIOGRAPHY

Revard, Carter. *My Right Hand Don't Leave Me No More*. St. Louis: Eedin Press, 1970.

——. "History, Myth, and Identity Among the Osages and Other Peoples." *Denver Quarterly* 14.4 (1980): 84–97.

——. *Nonymosity*. Richfield, VT: Samisdat, 1980.

——. *Ponca War Dancers*. Norman, OK: Point Riders Press, 1980.

——. "Report to the Nation: Claiming Europe." *Earth Power Coming: Short Fiction in Native American Literature*. Ed. Simon Ortiz. Tsaile, AZ: Navajo Community College Press, 1983. 166–81.

——. "How the FBI Man Nearly Found God." *The Greenfield Review* 11.3–4 (1984): 46–60.

——. "Something That Stays Alive: An Interview with Carter Revard." *Survival This Way: Interviews with American Indian Poets*. Tucson: Sun Tracks and the U of Arizona P, 1987. 231–48.

——. "Traditional Osage Naming Ceremonies: Entering the Circle of Being." *Recovering the Word: Essays on Native American Literature*. Ed. Brian Swann and Arnold Krupat. Berkeley: U of California P, 1987. 444–66.

——. "Walking Among the Stars." *I Tell You Now: Autobiographical Essays by Native American Writers*. Ed. Brian Swann and Arnold Krupat. Lincoln: U of Nebraska P, 1987. 65–84.

——. "Close Encounters." *River Styx* 25 (1988): 38–40.

Wendy Rose *(May 7, 1948–)*

Wendy Rose speaks for women—rejected, used, sold, or worse—in a society that values the dollar above everything, even above the capacity for regeneration. Her writing, an uncompromising indictment of callous capitalism, is unsettling and powerful.

Rose first gained attention in the mid-1970s when her poems and watercolor illustrations appeared in Duane Niatum's *Carriers of the Dream Wheel*. Rose's drawings continue to extend the meaning of her poetry, adding an intuitive dimension to her words.

Born in Oakland, California, Rose was raised by her mother. In an interview, she referred to herself as "physically separated from one-half of my family and rejected by the half that brought me up" (Bruchac 1987:254). Raised a Roman Catholic, she is Hopi-Miwok on her father's side. During the 1970s she was involved in academia, eventually earning a Ph.D. in anthropology and teaching in the American Indian Studies Program at the University of California at Berkeley and at California State University in Fresno. Later she served as Coordinator of American Indian Studies at Fresno City College. Increasingly, her insights as an anthropologist have extended and enriched her poetry.

Rose has published nine volumes of poetry, and her poems have been included in more than fifty anthologies. She has also served as general editor of *American Indian Quarterly*. Currently she is compiling a bibliography of Native American writings from 1700 to the present.

The search for identity, central to Rose's work, has extended from her own personal search to a fierce indictment against a segment of society that reduces everything, even human beings, to commodities. As Andrew Wiget has pointed out, "Of all native poets now writing, none, with the possible exception of Momaday, has more consistently reasserted the creation of personal identity through art" (1985:103).

Rose began writing under the name "Chiron Khanshendel," which she gave herself. The assertion of her Hopi identity is at the heart of her first book, *Hopi Roadrunner Dancing* (1973). One of the poems, "Newborn Woman, May 7, 1948," is about having been born unwanted. The refrain "i could not help it" is repeated throughout this poem about her birth. But the poem ends in self-affirmation:

> Dreams of my mother i shattered, i arrived. . . . i indian
> i desert, i newborn woman. (9)

Essential to Rose in this search was making contact with her father. In a tender poem, "Oh Father," she wrote of the closeness she felt to him: "fingertips melting into each other, / spirits merging" . . . "all I have to do is look into your eyes." The poem ends: "i'm sorry i guess / but i have to know: / oh father, who am I?" (11)

Rose and her husband, Arthur Murata, traveled to Arizona to visit her father in August 1977. She wrote of this visit in *Builder Kachina: A Home-Going Cycle* (1979). More grounded in and celebratory of place than her other books, *Builder Kachina* is about going back to find herself. This journey was essential to Rose as an artist and as a person: "Must I explain why / the songs are stiff and shy? / . . . / California moves my pen / but Hotevilla dashes through my blood / like a great / and crazy dragonfly" (n.p.).

From her father she learned that building roots is a process: "Carefully / the way we plant the corn / in single places, each place / a hole just one finger around. / We'll build your roots / that way. . . . / What we can't find / we'll build but / slowly, / slowly." *Builder Kachina* chronicles the gentle, careful personal effort of a woman, whose community is "urban Indian" and "*pan* tribal" (Bruchac 1987:254), to understand the Hopi side of her identity. In contrast with the voice of *Builder Kachina*, that of *Academic Squaw* (1977), which forms part of her later book, *Lost Copper*, is angry, ironic, and pan-Indian. The poems in *Academic Squaw* are a direct result of her study of anthropology. They condemn the pricing of Native American cultures. Museums even buy and sell bones, a practice that Rose condemns, for, she believes, "bones are alive. They're not dead remnants but rather they're alive" (Bruchac 1987:262). "Three Thousand Dollar Death Song" is an outcry against the pricing of bones. Another poem in the book denounces the pricing of the remnants of the 1890 Wounded Knee massacre. In this poem, a woman victim at Wounded Knee speaks powerfully of her suffering. Even though she could not stop the massacre, the poem ends hopefully because "Now / the ghost dances / impervious / to bullets." In *Academic Squaw*, Rose treats these Native Americans of the past, not as anthropological specimens, but as people whose lives and struggles are to be respected; she gives them voice and allows them to speak their pain.

Rose's poetry constantly moves back and forth between historical and contemporary contexts and between her own experiences and those of many other people. As a chronicler of the larger American historical and social sphere, Rose is foremost among Native American poets. Her book *What Happened When the Hopi Hit New York* (1982) illustrates her broad vision. The poems form a journal of a trip across the United States, beginning in California, going on to the Hopi Reservation, to Alaska, Iowa City, New Orleans, Chicago, Connecticut, Vermont, New Hampshire, and finally to Brooklyn. The book ends with her flight back to California. Poems about each of these places describe the life of the people in them; they are perceptive, and often funny. In "Punk Party Brooklyn 1978," she writes of the shallow relationships between some people: "Like any party / they photograph each other but / forget to develop / the film." Rose's poetry has steadily improved, and her book *The Halfbreed Chronicles* (1985) is her best. These are not pretty poems. They shock us in documenting the brutal ways that people have continued to exploit one another in what purports to be a civilized Euroamerican culture. Combining her Native American sensibility and her knowledge as an anthropologist with the use of personae, a technique she used in *Academic Squaw* and which she may have derived from nineteenth-century British poetry, Rose gives voice to Truganniny, Yuriko, and Julia, among others. These women, tortured in many ways, dramatize a few of the many horrors of our time.

Truganniny, the last Tasmanian, utters her death wish: "put me where / they will not / find me" ("Truganniny," 57). The note that introduces this poem informs us that Truganniny, like her husband who died before her, was "stuffed, mounted and put on display for over eighty years."

Yuriko, "born severely retarded," says of her mother, a victim of the bombing of Hiroshima: "Radiation / came like a man / and licked her thighs; / I was a tiny fish / boneless within / and I felt nothing" ("Yuriko," 64). Julia Pastrana, a Mexican Indian woman, was a mid-nineteenth-century singer and dancer in the circus, billed as "The Ugliest Woman in the World." After her death, her husband had her and their infant son stuffed and mounted and put on display. Their bodies were exhibited as recently as 1975 in Europe and the United States. In the poem, "Julia," the title character, still wanting to believe that he loves her, appeals to her husband:

> Tell me it was just a dream
> my husband, a clever trick
> made by some tin-faced village god
> or ghost coyote, to frighten me
> with his claim that our marriage is made
> of malice and money. (69)

Indigenous people, women, children—these are among the people to whom Rose gives voice. The poems in *The Halfbreed Chronicles*, like all of Rose's work, are often poignant, but more important, they arouse a rage in our social conscience, not to permit anything like this to happen again.

Norma C. Wilson
University of South Dakota

BIBLIOGRAPHY

Primary Sources

Rose, Wendy. *Hopi Roadrunner Dancing*. Greenfield Center, NY: The Greenfield Review, 1973.

———. *Academic Squaw*. Marvin, SD: Blue Cloud Quarterly, 1977.

———. *Builder Kachina: A Home-Going Cycle*. Marvin, SD: Blue Cloud Quarterly, 1979.

———. *Lost Copper*. Banning, CA: Malki Museum Press, 1980.

———. *What Happened When the Hopi Hit New York*. New York: Contact II Publications, 1982.

———. *The Halfbreed Chronicles and Other Poems*. Los Angeles: West End Press, 1985.

Secondary Sources

Bruchac, Joseph. *Survival This Way: Interviews with American Indian Poets*. Tucson: Sun Tracks and U of Arizona P, 1987.

Wiget, Andrew. *Native American Literature*. Boston: Twayne, 1985.

Leslie Marmon Silko
(March 1, 1948–)

Publication of Leslie Silko's writing in the 1970s coincided with the international awakening of interest in American Indian literatures as sources for culturally specific insights and perspectives that are increasingly endangered in a technologically dominated world. Silko presented the world with narratives that make a specific dramatic impact while simultaneously enlarging our understanding of narrative as a cultural force absorbing and redirecting the developmental dynamics in the daily lives of people negotiating change of all kinds. She dedicated her book *Storyteller* to "the storytellers as far back as memory goes and to the telling which continues and through which they all live and we with them."

Leslie Silko, born in 1948, is a member of the Laguna Pueblo tribe. She grew up at Laguna, attending high school in Albuquerque and then entering the University of New Mexico. After graduation, she decided to study law but changed to English. She taught at several colleges and universities before settling in Tucson, Arizona, where she is currently working on her next novel and other projects.

The publication of *Ceremony* in 1977 brought Silko's writing to general public attention. Critics lauded the precisely crafted quality of the novel but generally sidestepped the implications of the fact that it is distinguished as a novel by its innovative structural and stylistic adaptations to accommodate the dynamics of oral literature. Many attentive readers found themselves in accord with the poet James Wright's expressed sense that Silko's work brings "us all into the presence of something truly remarkable." Like Wright, even enthusiastic readers and critics found it difficult to specify the adjective "remarkable." Wright himself continued his tribute to Silko by trying to characterize his reactions to *Ceremony*: "In some strange way it seems inadequate to call it a great book, though it is surely that, or a perfect work of art, though it is one. I could call *Ceremony* one of the four or five best books I have ever read about America and I would be speaking the truth. But even this doesn't say just what I mean. I think I am trying to say that my very life means more to me than it would have meant if you hadn't written *Ceremony*. But this sounds inadequate also" (Wright, in *The Delicacy and Strength of Lace*, 3).

The inadequacy that Wright and others felt so acutely was more than the usual experience of humility in the presence of art. It included an awareness that language and its narrative realizations were working in ways that required an unusual slight shift away from responses conditioned by previous experiences of literature; and while cultural differences were clearly implicated in this shifting, they could not entirely account for them. Since Silko's work first reached general public notice, critics and teachers of American Indian literatures have continued the attempt to articulate some of what remains elusive about Silko's art. A steady small stream of critical writing traces the development of an informed community of readers that is slowly growing beyond the defined perspectives of American Indian literatures. Silko's place in American letters is enhanced by the fact that her short stories and poems can now be found in several anthologies of general American writing.

While the experience of art always exceeds the language of critics, the quality of Silko's art allows for much richer and more exactly comprehensive interpretive specification than has yet been given it. Part of the difficulty in specifying dimensions of Silko's style derives from the underdeveloped general academic understanding of cultural restraints within the epistemological presuppositions that guide so much literary criticism. Unrefined critical assumptions have been most unquestioningly blatant in the criticism of oral narrative. Concentration on plot structures has so overshadowed attention to style and its capacity to accommodate different epistemological modes that cultural outsiders have appropriated American Indian materials while denying the vitality of a given community's adaptations of their own traditions. This stance focused Silko's anger and occasioned one of her rare critical essays, entitled "An Old-Time Indian Attack," written in the late 1970s. Her infrequent critical writings often include more or less direct expressions of similar frustrations over writing about Native American peoples which unself-consciously imposes an outsider's judgment on an insider's experience. As they perpetuate the limitations of their own confusions about how culture curtails assumptions of universal processes, literary critics fall into what Silko has called "one way knowing." In several published interviews, she has identified herself as fundamentally, experimentally, and very consciously "two-way," relational in every sense of the word. Each configuration of relationships in her writing allows for a different interpretive perspective. Some configurations, though, are more basic than others.

Perhaps the most important relationship in Silko's writing is that existing between individual expression and cultural narrative. Or, to put it in terms that Silko herself uses, the crucial relationship is the one between listener and storyteller. This quickly calls to mind another interaction existing on an entirely different analytic level, that between oral storytelling and the modern novel. For Silko the two are intimately interactive in ways that had little or no precedent in world literature outside of N. Scott Momaday's work. Silko's particular concentration on the relationship between listener and storyteller as a fundamental nexus of choice and imaginative growth, always endangered from without by lies and from within by psychic abjection, brings readers to an unusually intense awareness of origins and artistic foundations. She herself expressed the essence of the relationship simply and directly in one of her letters to James Wright, noting analogies in the immediate emotional intensity that the visual arts evoke in sensitive viewers. "Even on the post-card I can appreciate the vitality in Vermeer's paintings and how alive they remain by bringing something seldom touched in ourselves alive too—life-giving process, as with the listeners who make it possible for the storyteller to go on" (41–42).

All of Silko's writing is an extended, imagistically realized commentary on how listening and storytelling can be life-giving processes. They are the essential dynamics of a way of knowing, an epistemological process that allows us to glimpse images and narratives as generative factors within the developmental trajectory of a person's psycho-linguistic growth. The crucial implications of the previous statement for constitutive interactions between individual subjectivity, cultural presuppositions, and their narrative realizations are dramatized in Silko's work. One stanza from the initial poetic sequence in *Ceremony* has achieved epigrammatic force as a banner line for Silko's writing and—by extension—for the entire field of Native American literature. "You don't have anything / if you don't have the stories."

Silko's sense of story encompasses the entire dynamic of culturally specific symbolic interaction with brief narratives serving as dramatic distillations of the larger symbolic and semiological processes. Distinct narratives are responses to situations—symbolic dosages, prescribed for the event of the moment. Stories in the broad sense in which Silko uses the term, so broad that gossip is an integral part of the story process, create the bond between subject and society. The verb "create" carries extraordinary weight in reference to Silko's work because for her that bond is always fragile. She concentrates on moments when it is threatened and renewed. Her sense of story is not so broad, though, that it universalizes the process at any but the most abstract levels. Specific cultures teach their own ways of relating to stories. This culturally defined interpretive dimension, always dependent on a living, interpreting community, is a boundary-determining factor that Silko incorporates into her plots, her style, and even the structure of her works. The pervasiveness of this boundary means that it defies simple characterizations of its functions. Her short stories allow us to glimpse the main features of the dynamic process of Silko's sense of story, a process which becomes considerably more complicated in the novel *Ceremony*.

"Storyteller" is a tale about traditional knowing and acting that incorporates the most basic elements of Silko's art, the motifs found in all the other stories and even in many of the poems. The central character, a young Yupik woman, claims to have killed a white man in order to avenge the murder of her parents. The State Troopers tell her that all the circumstances of the case point to the impossibility of her having murdered the man. Yet she insists she did. The story tells us how and why. It lets us glimpse the coming together of knowledge and desire in and through storytelling; and it pulls readers into the murderous compulsions of desire run amuck. The girl's parents were murdered by those who take whatever they want with no regard for person or community, so she turns that unconstrained desire against the man who killed her parents by sexually directing it toward herself and then leading the man bent on rape to his death. But "Storyteller" dramatizes positive desire too and links it to narrative dynamics. Desire springs from the prelinguistic anteriority of instinct seeking objects of need. Reflected and refracted through symbolic articulation, it becomes a force for community and continuity, always reaching toward the future. This fundamental human condition of need animates the plot of "Storyteller" so directly that the actual plot seems only a thin but impenetrable membrane separating us from the inner workings of desire. Yet the verbal materiality of that membrane incorporates the distance of cultures as well as the inevitable distance imposed by any structured realization of prelinguistic need.

Two elements of this short story recur throughout Silko's work and constitute thematic constellations. One is an emphasis on telling a story in exact detail, avoiding shortcuts or lies. Silko gives this theme a stylistic touch that verges on the uncanny. Characters must live the story so that their actions obey a retroactive anteriority. The teleological becomes immediate motivation—an opaque yet urgent guide to choices. Critical language can state the outlines of temporality implicit in this sacred worldview, but only immediate experience of Silko's style can turn it into narrative tension and make the "warnings" work artistically. That tension is fed by Silko's references to getting the smallest details of the stories right and by her own skill in achieving the exactness in writing that her dying character strives for in his tales. In "Storyteller," a dying old man passionately recounts the story of a bear that he must chase to the death, his death. "The old man would not change the story even when he knew the end was approaching. Lies could not stop what was coming. He thrashed around on the bed, pulling the blankets loose, knocking the bundles of dried fish and meat on the floor" (32).

Getting the details right requires an alertness that is the result of disciplined training achieved through listening to stories. This introduces the second thematic element implicit in all of Silko's work—the emphasis on feeling. For Silko, feeling takes on unique ramifications that are far from its general mass-media connotations. In Silko's writing, feeling is disciplined desire. (If that appears a contradiction to many for whom desire, by definition, is beyond discipline, then the contradiction permeates Silko's work and may yet prove to be the most culturally substantive dynamic in her writing.) In "Storyteller," the young woman experiences the old man's passion through sex; but more than that, she listens to him transfer it to the exacting language of his story and she learns how to stay alert, feeling her way through observation and story into what still lies in the future. "She could feel the silence the story left, and she wanted to have the old woman go on. . . . These preparations were unfamiliar, but gradually she recognized them as she did her own footprints in the snow" (25, 27).

By learning to understand feeling in relation to exact observation of all the conditions surrounding it, the young woman lures the white man to his death, feeding his sexual passions and then making him chase her across the ice of the Bering Sea in spots where she knows it is weak. "They asked her again, what happened to the man from the Northern Commercial store. 'He lied to them. He told them it was safe to drink. But I will not lie.' She stood up and put on the gray wolfskin parka. 'I killed him,' she said, 'but I don't lie'" (31).

For Silko, the relationship between storyteller and listener is a maternal one, no matter what the biological sex of the participants may be. Themes of maternity are realized within a rich constellation of images and plot transformations. An underlying cultural consideration must be the fact that Laguna Pueblo is a matriarchal culture. The Pueblo existing within its symbolically invested landscape is a mother who has been mistreated and misunderstood by colonizers. This socio-historical context colors our awareness of Silko's passionate maternal figures, whom blonde social workers quickly label as unfit mothers in total disregard for the enormous nurturing capability these characters possess. The story "Lullaby" reveals the essential lineaments of the maternal themes in Silko's writing to date. This story was selected as one of the best short stories of 1975. (See Martha Foley, *Best Short Stories of the Year.*)

Silko's signature opening move, the use of nature descriptions to refer to psychological and cosmic temporality, sets the tone of "Lullaby" in immediate sharp contrast to the title. "The sun had gone down but the snow in the wind gave off its own light." Ayah, the mother in this story, is old, "her life had become memories," and her warmth in winter comes from a wool Army blanket that had once belonged to a son killed in military action. But if her blanket is literally a faded, raveled connection to a lost son, memory connects it to an entire maternal tradition of weaving things of beauty. The swift, sure, direct connections that Silko makes between the blanket as object and its remembered connections is a superb example of her ability to achieve the connotative mimesis that is characteristic of her art. "Ayah pulled the old Army blanket over her head like a shawl. Jimmie's blanket—the one he had sent to her. That was a long time ago and the green wool was faded, and it was unraveling on the edges. She did not want to think about Jimmie. So she thought about the weaving and the way her mother had done it" (43).

After precise evocation of the details of weaving, Silko moves from memory to immediate physical sensations which then become the transition to another memory. This use of physical sensation to make the body a living, feeling, responsive embodiment of memorized story is basic to Silko's style. "She felt peaceful remembering. She didn't feel cold any more. Jimmie's blanket seemed warmer than it had ever been. And she could remember the morning he was born" (44).

If the blanket can bestow warmth though its maternal associations, the inexorable progression of these same associations reverses everything. The reversal of birth is not death. It is severed nurturing. It is the lullaby cut off before need is over. It is the maternal gesture used as a betrayal of the maternal. First there is the disappearance of Jimmie. "It wasn't like Jimmie died. He just never came back, and one day a dark blue sedan with white writing on its doors pulled up in front of the boxcar shack where the rancher let the Indians live."

Then comes the event that chokes off the lullaby. Ayah cannot read white writing. She loses her children because of it. Believing that by signing her name, she can save her children, she actually gives them up to the care of social workers. All that had once evoked maternal care now causes recoil, a twist inward to unbearable pain. (Silko's text sets up and uses the polyvalence of the word "bear.") "She did not sleep for a long time after they took her children. She stayed on the hill where they had fled the first time, and she slept rolled up in the blanket Jimmie had sent her. She carried the pain in her belly and it was fed by everything she saw . . . the pain filled her stomach and there was no room for food or for her lungs to fill with air. The air and the food would have been theirs" (47). But if her belly full of pain stems from being unable to read white writing, Ayah does know how to read human need and she can respond with courageous clarity. After the loss of her children, she hates her husband "because he had taught her to sign her name. Because it was like the old ones always told her about learning their language or any of their ways: it endangered you" (47). Years later, though, when her husband is sick, his shivering becomes a sign of a need that she understands profoundly. She knows that "only her body could keep him warm" (47) and she returns to nurturing maternity. As the story progresses, we learn that only her body can bear him to his own peaceful death. She knows all the signs of land, sky, and heart, and she "reads" the right time to arrange his death. Then she sings him to this transitional sleep with words of loving parenting and together-ness. "She tucked the blanket around him, remembering how it was when Ella had been with her; and she felt the rush so big inside her heart for the babies. And she sang the only song she knew to sing for babies" (51). That exquisitely tender reading of the story's ending, though, co-exists with another; and much of the story's significance derives from the disparity between alternative readings. The other account of the ending that the tale requires us to see is that which shows a wife murdering her sick husband by getting him drunk and then watching and singing while he freezes in the cold. Even if readers ascribe to the tender and positive ending so carefully established by the style of the story, they have to remember that the law would lean toward the other interpretation. Silko explicitly situates her writing amid conflicting interpretations that depend to a large degree but never entirely on cultural perspectives. "Tony's Story" is another story that expands this aspect of Silko's work.

Silko's writing achieves moments when images are flush with the en-ergy of origins. Birth and death are bound together with an intensity few writers achieve. "I knelt above you / that morning / I counted the rattles / the last whistles / in your throat. / I put my mouth on yours / . . . I saw how you would go / spilling out / between ivory ribs / seeping under the tall gate / where earth sucked you in / like rainwater" ("A Hunting Story").

Her stories dramatize how desire, need, and sexuality are all variations of the same psychic dynamics feeding the wellsprings of life, conscious-ness, and culture. Silko brings readers close to the moments when sexual-ity and storytelling participate in the same gestures of becoming. She does it with startling directness and a simplicity that makes James Wright's choice of a Vermeer postcard so appropriate a response to Silko's own artistic genius. Sexual intimacy that is not just connection to another hu-man being but is also a transgressive and augmentative relationship to an organically developing tradition is dramatized in the short story "Yellow Woman."

A married woman and man, strangers who meet by the river, under-stand their sexual attraction in terms of the old legends about the abduc-tion of Yellow Woman. In Silko's story, the compulsive precariousness of overwhelming sexual attraction becomes precisely analogous to the risks of seeking meaning outside the already given constraints of the symbolic system. But if such meaning is still outside the communally encompassed tradition, it is so, not by virtue of any essential antagonism but simply because it is a new development that may or may not become part of the tradition. The tentativeness of this development provokes a tension which Silko persistently evokes, touching as it does on the birthing passage from individual experience to cultural resource. "But I only said that you were him and that I was Yellow Woman—I'm not really her—I have my own name and I come from the pueblo on the other side of the mesa" (55). The questioning about whether or not they are really following the signs of tradition or only the siren songs of their private and socially inappropriate desires leads to speculation about origins of the traditional legends. "I was wondering if Yellow Woman had known who she was—if she knew that she would become part of the stories. Maybe she'd had another name that her husband's relatives called her so that only the ka'tsina from the north and the storytellers would know her as Yellow Woman. But I didn't go on; I felt him all around me, pushing me down into the white river sand. . . . All I could know was the way he felt, warm, damp, his body beside me. This is the way it happens in the stories, I was thinking, with no thought beyond the moment she meets the ka'tsina spirit and they go" (55–56).

If the characters question, the overall development of the story resolves the questioning affirmatively so that we finally understand the narrative as an evocation in story form of the dynamics of legend formation. Readers are immersed in the experiential immediacies underlying legend formation which charts the path from instinctual desire to impetuous risk to new meaning that can, in its turn, be passed on through added legends that link old and new and initiate further seeking, subsequent returns to originary experiences. The images of individuals seeking each other in desire and hope, tracing each other's footsteps along the sands of a river where individuals have traced similar quests, are directly realized from the very first words of the story. "My thigh clung to his with dampness, and I watched the sun rising up through the tamaracks and willows. . . . I felt hungry and followed the river south the way we had come the afternoon before, following our footprints that were already blurred by lizard tracks and bug trails . . . I walked north with the river again, and the white sand broke loose in footprints over footprints" (54).

In 1981, Silko published a collection of stories and poems called *Storyteller*. Previously published short stories and poems become part of a new whole as they are interwoven with autobiographical commentaries revealing formative influences in Silko's personal and artistic development. Revelation here is never exhaustive or even exact. It shimmers as suggestion that is enhanced by the fact that so much of the personal reminiscence is presented in verse form, giving the added meaning and ambiguity of poetic rhythms. Every item takes on added significance from what surrounds it. The settings for the stories, poems, and reminiscences include photographs which function less as illustrations than as incentives to another kind of contemplation. While working on the book, Silko wrote to James Wright: "I am interested now in the memory and imagination of mine which come out of these photographs—maybe I am more affected by what I see than I had heretofore realized. Strange to think that you heard something—that you heard someone describe a place or a scene when, in fact you saw a picture of it saw it with your own eyes. Now that I look at all this, it seems so obvious—this is what makes a poet a poet and not a painter or photographer" (65).

Storyteller belongs with that small collection of books in world litera-ture that are structurally adapted explicitly in order to illustrate the devel-opmental interrelationships between individuals and a living tradition. This book, to date, has received minimal attention from critics, perhaps because of general inattentiveness to the psycho-linguistic ramifications of living oral traditions. This oversight seems to have blinded critics to the signifi-cance of the style of *Storyteller* which is so bound up with the dynamics of oral transmission and their educative process. Traditional learning, prop-erly guided, is timed to correspond with major and minor transitional events in a person's developmental trajectory, and the autobiographical sections of *Storyteller* let us glimpse the workings of such learning as al-most no other work of literature does. Traditional transmission of narra-tive is intimately relational in a way that no relationship other than the maternal approaches. *Storyteller* celebrates that intimacy.

Poems are a crucial part of *Storyteller* and correspond to the way poems work to structure the novel *Ceremony*. A sure sense of rhythm governs them. Rhythm harnesses the emotions implicit in basic human gestures realized within a context where similar gestures can evoke a connotative history. Frequently Silko explicitly links intimately described gesture to tradition with brief references to stories. Other poems are predominantly narrative with a clear, controlled dramatic line presented in terms of its emotional efflorescence. Synesthesia is often used to present the connota-tive force of environment in relation to action. In *Storyteller* and in *Cer-emony*, the poems function to set past and present in emotional relation-ship to each other so that the affective structuring and channeling that the stories achieved in the past can achieve their interpretive role in the present.

In the novel *Ceremony* all the themes, images, and characteristic moves found in Silko's other writing take on added meaning as they are compli-cated by the way issues of culture change and contact intrude upon their development. These issues affect more than just content. They pose a more fundamental tension that informs narrative and poetic rhythms as they are modulated by structure and orchestrated through the micro-ele-ments of style. *Ceremony* is so precisely crafted a novel that analogies to the plastic or musical arts come to mind with an appropriate critical ease. Any given thematic strand can be traced from beginning to end in its connec-tions to all others, and the fundamental strands can be followed back into the short stories and poems. Emphasis on crafted precision, though, should not preclude the way the novel shatters contemplative securities. The novel is much more than a celebration of recovered mythic meaning; it dramatizes the excruciating precariousness of such recovery while simultaneously valorizing it.

The character Tayo is a man attuned to the ways of knowing taught through the old stories. From his uncle Josiah and from the woman who first taught him the power of sexual knowing, he has learned to feel the story in life. But unlike the characters in the short stories for whom such feeling leads directly to action, Tayo is trapped in situations where the logic of action contradicts feeling. A World War II veteran supposedly suffering from shell shock, Tayo is really a victim of feeling (as Silko uses the word) severed from action, and like Ayah in "Lullaby" his capacity to feel his way into appropriate action is turned painfully inward. "He shivered because all the facts, all the reasons made no difference any more; he could hear Rocky's words, and he could follow the logic of what Rocky said, but he could not feel anything except a swelling in his belly, a great swollen grief that was pushing into his throat" (8–9). Tayo's way of feeling the stories leaves him a shivering wreck of a man because the interpretive dynamics so basic to Silko's sense of storytelling are out of balance not only for Tayo but for the entire culture. Therein lies the peculiarly modern force of the novel. A healer tells Tayo, "'There are some things we can't cure like we used to,' he said, 'not since the white people came'. . . He pulled the blue wool cap over his ears. 'I'm afraid of what will happen to all of us if you and the others don't get well,' he said" (38).

Tayo's response indicates Silko's way of switching reference away from simple social concerns and into more comprehensive matters of mind, spirit and story. "The old man only made him certain of something he had feared all along, something in the old stories. It took only one person to tear away the delicate strands of the web, spilling the rays of sun into the sand, and the fragile world would be injured" (38).

Tayo needs communal interpretation of what is happening to him. Only such externalized understanding can grant him the truth of what he feels and give him a way to turn that feeling to action. For Silko, the move outward to community is always the moment of ideological stress. An oppressive history has complicated that move and Silko's writing reveals the impact of that oppression. But the subject's need for communal reference is more fundamental than political history, which she consistently presents as a passing, superficial although dangerous phenomenon. Any subjectivity which separates itself emotionally and referentially from living community is, for Silko, even more deadly than isolated political acts, and in Silko's writing such separation is linked to witchcraft.

Artistic reference binds but it also bridges the way from individual emotion to communal possibility. It is relational. The most fundamental artistic references are ceremonial. Without ceremonial participation the people lose their communal references. "The sensitivity remained; the ability to feel what the others were feeling in the belly and chest; words were not necessary, but the messages the people felt were confused now" (68).

With the novel *Ceremony* Silko addresses the formation of an interpretive community appropriate to the twentieth century. She presents the right teachers, men and women who are "different." One such person is a Mexican dancer and she tells Tayo. "'They are afraid, Tayo. They feel something happening, they can see something happening around them and it scares them. Indians, Mexicans or whites—most people are afraid of change. They think that if their children have the same color of skin, the same color of eyes, that nothing is changing.' She laughed softly, 'They are fools. They blame us, the ones who look different. That way they don't have to think about what has happened inside themselves'" (100).

Silko's envisioned new interpretive community, while profoundly traditional, incorporates global understandings in order to keep the traditional story processes alive. It explicitly requires multicultural knowing (and not just "knowledge," which implies already posited structurations). "'This is the only way,' she told him. 'It cannot be done alone. We must have power from everywhere. Even the power we can get from the whites'" (150).

The feelings which are the instinct for the story-in-formation are stylistically essential to the development of *Ceremony*. All the transitions between old and new, mythic and prophetic, sacred and secular, local and global, disease and health, solitude and community, require characters to feel their way into the right course of action. "He did not expect to find Josiah's cattle near Herefords, because the spotted cattle were so rangy and wild; but without Betonie he wouldn't have hoped to find the cattle at all. . . . So he had gone, not expecting to find anything more than the winter constellation in the north sky overhead; but suddenly Betonie's vision was a story he could feel happening—from the stars and the woman, the mountain and the cattle would come" (186).

The enduring characters in *Ceremony*, like the cattle they raise for a livelihood, have indelible homing instincts; and they are tough, able to survive what would kill others. These are the people strong enough to "feel" the story. They create transitions that take characters and readers into the future and presage the future of Silko's own writing as well as the learning that the world in general seeks as it struggles toward a more knowing multiculturalism.

Silko's fascination with story has also led to experimentation with film. "Film," says Silko, "is a way of seeing very like the oral tradition. It operates on a highly refined, simultaneous, personal level. It makes one aware of the visual signals in the language and helps me realize a way of seeing, of organizing as a whole instead of through fragments of experience. Film gives the feeling that we get going for a walk, experiencing many things at once in a simple, elemental way" (Jahner 1981:385).

Presenting the simple and elemental with enough technical know-how and skill that the aura of retained enigmas continues to surround the simple is Silko's talent. The enigmatic quality of all Silko's writing continues to beckon as audiences and readers move into interpretations that reveal and conceal simultaneously.

Elaine A. Jahner
Dartmouth College

BIBLIOGRAPHY

Primary Sources

Silko, Leslie Marmon. *Laguna Woman*. Greenfield Center, NY: Greenfield Review Press, 1974.

———. *Ceremony*. New York: Viking, 1977.

———. *Storyteller*. New York: Seaver Books, 1981.

———. *Almanac of the Dead*. New York: Simon and Schuster, 1991.

———, and James Wright. *The Delicacy and Strength of Lace: Letters between Leslie Marmon Silko and James Wright*. Ed. Anne Wright. St. Paul, MN: Greywolf, 1986.

Secondary Sources

Allen, Paula Gunn. "The Psychological Landscape of *Ceremony*." *American Indian Quarterly* 5 (1979): 7–12.

———. "The Feminine Landscape of Leslie Marmon Silko's *Ceremony*." *Studies in American Indian Literature: Critical Essays and Course Designs*. New York: MLA, 1983.

Anderson, Laurie. "Colorful Revenge in Silko's *Storyteller*." *Notes on Contemporary Literature* 15.4 (September 1985): 11–12.

Barnes, Kim. "A Leslie Marmon Silko Interview." *Journal of Ethnic Studies* 13.4 (Winter 1986): 83–105.

Bell, Robert C. "Circular Design in *Ceremony*." *American Indian Quarterly* 5 (1979): 47–62.

Biedler, Peter G. "Animals and Theme in *Ceremony*." *American Indian Quarterly* 5 (1979): 15–18.

Blicksilver, E. "Traditionalism vs. Modernity: Leslie Silko on American Indian Women." *Southwest Review* 64 (1979): 142–60.

Brown, Patricia Clare. "The Spider Web: A Time Structure in Leslie Silko's *Ceremony*." *DAI* 47.5 (November 1986): 1726A.

Coltelli, Laura. "Reenacting Myths and Stories: Tradition and Renewal in *Ceremony*." *Native American Literatures*. Pisa, Italy: SEU, 1989.

Crow, Stephen Monroe. "The Works of Leslie Marmon Silko and Teaching Contemporary Native American Literature." *DAI* 47.10 (April 1987): 3757A.

Danielson, Linda L. "*Storyteller*: Grandmother's Spider's Web." *Journal of the Southwest* 30.3 (Autumn 1988): 325–55.

Evers, Larry. "A Response: Going Along with the Story." *American Indian Quarterly* 5 (1979): 71–75.

———. "The Killing of a New Mexican State Trooper: Ways of Telling a Historical Event." *Wicazo Sa Review* 1.1 (Spring 1985): 17–25.

Garcia, Reyes. "Sense of Place in *Ceremony*." *MELUS* 10.4 (Winter 1983): 37–48.

Hirsch, Bernard. "'The Telling Which Continues: Oral Tradition and the Written Word in Leslie Marmon Silko's *Storyteller*.'" *American Indian Quarterly* 12.1 (Winter 1988): 1–26.

Hoilman, Dennis. "A World Made of Stories: An Interpretation of Leslie Marmon Silko's *Ceremony.*" *South Dakota Review* 17.3 (1979): 54–66.

Jahner, Elaine. "An Act of Attention: Event Structure in *Ceremony.*" *American Indian Quarterly* 5 (1979): 37–46.

———. "The Novel and Oral Tradition: An Interview with Leslie Marmon Silko." *Book Forum* 5.3 (1981): 383–88.

Lucero, Ambrose. "For the People: Leslie Silko's *Sting Fellow.*" *MV* 5.12 (Spring 1981): 110.

McBride, Mary. "Shelter of Refuge: The Art of Mimesis in Leslie Marmon Silko's 'Lullaby.'" *Wicazo Sa Review* 3.2 (Fall 1987): 15–17.

Mitchell, Carol. "*Ceremony* as Ritual." *American Indian Quarterly* 5 (1979): 27–35.

Nelson, Robert M. "Place and Vision: The Function of Landscape in *Ceremony.*" *Journal of the Southwest* 30.3 (Autumn 1988): 281–316.

Purdy, John. "The Transformation: Tayo's Genealogy in *Ceremony.*" *Studies in American Indian Literature* 10.3 (Summer 1986): 121–33.

Ruoff, A. LaVonne. "Ritual and Renewal: Keres Traditions in the Short Fiction of Leslie Silko." *MELUS* 5.3 (1978): 2–17.

Ruppert, James. "Story Telling: The Fiction of Leslie Silko." *Journal of Ethnic Studies* 9.1 (1987): 53–58.

———. "The Readers Lessons in *Ceremony.*" *ARQ* 44.1 (Spring 1988): 78–85.

St. Andrews, B. A. "Healing the Witching: Medicine in Silko's *Ceremony.*" *ARQ* 44.1 (Spring 1988): 86–94.

Sands, Kathleen M., ed. "A Special Symposium Issue on Leslie M. Silko's *Ceremony.*" *American Indian Quarterly* 5 (1979): Preface 1–5.

Sands, Kathleen M., Paula Gunn Allen, Peter G. Biedler, Susan J. Scarberry, Carol Mitchell, Elaine Jahner, and Robert C. Bell. "A Discussion of *Ceremony.*" *American Indian Quarterly* 5 (1979): 63–70.

Scarberry, Susan J. "Memory as Medicine: The Power of Recollection in *Ceremony.*" *American Indian Quarterly* 5 (1979): 19–26.

Seyersted, Per. *Leslie Marmon Silko.* Western Writers Series 45. Boise: Boise State U, 1980.

———. "Two Interviews with Leslie Marmon Silko." *American Studies in Scandinavia* 13 (1981): 17–33.

Swan, Edith. "Healing via the Sunrise Cycle in Silko's *Ceremony.*" *American Indian Quarterly* 12.4 (Fall 1988): 313–28.

———. "Laguna Symbolic Geography and Silko's *Ceremony.*" *American Indian Quarterly* 12.3 (Summer 1988): 229–49.

Vangen, Kate Shanley. "The Devil's Domain: Leslie Silko's *Storyteller.*" *Coyote Was Here: Essays on Contemporary Native American Literary and Political Mobilization.* Ed. Bo Schöler. Århus, Denmark: Seklos, 1984. 116–23.

Hyemeyohsts (Chuck) Storm
(May 23, 1935–)

Hyemeyohsts Storm is the author of *Seven Arrows* (1972) and *Song of Heyoehkah* (1981), the first of which inaugurated the Harper & Row Native American Publishing Program and also stirred a controversy which raised fundamental issues regarding historical and ethnographic accuracy in Native American fiction and the rights of Native American authors to represent and interpret tribal religion without tribal authorization.

Storm was born in Lame Deer, Montana, the son of Arthur Charles (a carpenter) and Pearl (Eastman) Storm. He attended Eastern Montana College in Billings and has four children. He has also written a play, *The Beaded Path*, a book of short stories entitled *Reliability Mirrors*, and in 1979 had a work in progress, *The Magii Ship*, under the pseudonym Golden Silver. These are unpublished (*Contemporary Authors*, 1979). According to his publishers, he is a Northern Cheyenne, and was raised on the Cheyenne and Crow reservations. Although he is a speaker of Crow and Cheyenne, his Native American roots were initially doubted by his detractors (Costo 1972; Moore 1973), but they are now accepted.

What can be added, from personal acquaintance, is that before beginning *Seven Arrows* in 1969, Storm was also a cowhand, logger, and hunting guide, though he is hard to pin down on biographical details. By turns serious and playful, innocent and wise, didactic and fanciful, he fears labels that would establish and fix him in preexistent hierarchies. He prefers to be a sort of wandering seeker and healer, envisioning the great prehistoric teachers of the American plains in the same way: men and women whose "camps" were seldom fixed for more than a few months and whose deeds were reported only by word of mouth, hand signs, and "shields." In these ways, he seems to try to continue to live as a member of an oral culture. It is probable, too, that his distress with the facts preserved in print (and thus the hierarchies and authorities of cultures relying on them) is related to his own partial blindness. During the years that he wrote *Seven Arrows* and *Song of Heyoehkah* he had cataracts on both eyes and could barely read. He could not read the histories and ethnographies his detractors checked him against, and for his own knowledge and interpretations of Cheyenne stories he relied on memories of earlier readings of George Bird Grinnell and of oral versions he had heard. His writing was done on a typewriter, and for editing he had friends and his second wife, Sandy, read his drafts aloud to him. Because he could not read much classical or contemporary fiction, his style frequently seemed based on the pulp westerns that he had read before the cataracts developed.

Seven Arrows is, however, a unique book. Combining historical fiction and a religious vision, it describes a number of people of the Cheyenne and other tribes living and growing up and dying during the warfare of the late nineteenth century. The connecting theme or purpose is their desire to bring about a Sundance, or "Renewal," as Storm calls it, which would unite them against the whites and help them to preserve their traditional, peaceful customs. The most important of these customs, to Storm, are the Vision Quest, the Peace Shields, and the Medicine Wheel. The first enabled youths to find out who they were. The men's shields (or women's belts) then expressed who they were. And the Medicine Wheel, whether as circle of stones, circle of lodges, Sundance lodge, or a circle of people, represented the forces of the world acting together in harmony and equality. Along this path to the Sundance, which occurs but is not described in the book, various teachers tell traditional stories, interpreting them for their listeners. In this way, the tales become parables or "teachings," as Storm called them, with universal meanings most readers had never seen in previous collections of Indian tales.

Newspaper and magazine reviewers called *Seven Arrows* a brilliant, instructive book, praising it also for the well-chosen photographs of Indians, landscapes, and animals that not only illustrated but illuminated the tales. They also liked the brightly colored plates of "Shield Paintings" by Raren Harris, although some pointed out that the colors were more psychedelic than Plains Indians.

Controversy began with Rupert Costo's "'Seven Arrows' Desecrates Cheyenne." Costo had shown the book to Cheyennes at Lame Deer in June 1972, and they were shocked. Storm's version of Cheyenne religion was called "a blasphemous travesty." The paintings were deemed garish and monstrous. Storm had "outraged and insulted the Cheyenne, their tribal traditions, beliefs, and religion." John H. Moore, an anthropologist who had worked with the Cheyenne, listed further inaccuracies in Storm's description of Cheyenne religion. Storm's presentation of the medicine wheels and shields, he went on, magnified what to the Cheyenne were "minor elements."

On the other hand, Vine Deloria, Jr., wrote that *Seven Arrows* "begins a new and very important development in Indian literature." Storm had written a book of wide popular appeal that was physically beautiful, politically powerful, and unified by an intensely Indian consciousness and sense of time and space. To fault it for theological inaccuracies or historical anachronisms was to misunderstand totally what it was. "*Seven Arrows* is a religious statement, not a statement about religion, if the difference can be understood" (Deloria 1972).

Later critics, however, primarily challenged Storm's right to speak as a Cheyenne and for the Cheyenne in a manner unauthorized by the Cheyenne people. As William C. Sturtevant wrote (1973), the issues in evaluating Indian literature are larger than the "authors' claims of Indian identity." ". . . It does no favor to the 'real' Sioux or Apache or Cherokee to believe every writer who identifies himself as such." He also found Storm's teachings "pompous and rather patronizing . . . in the style of old-fashioned children's fairy tales about animals" (Sturtevant 1973:37–38). Little Joe Coyote expressed the views of Cheyenne religious leaders in a letter to Harper & Row: "Perhaps the most disturbing aspect of Mr. Chuck Storm's book *Seven Arrows* is the fact that some of the beliefs which he presents in his book as having been derived from our spiritual ways are completely unfounded and extremely repugnant to the sensitivities of our people who are knowledgeable and qualified to speak about such things, not merely as the product of imagination, but as the result of actual lived experience" (quoted in Chapman 1974).

Doug Latimer, Storm's editor at Harper & Row, later met with Cheyenne elders, apologized for misleading implications in the book's advertising, and reportedly paid the tribe "thousands of dollars" in what some Cheyenne called "reparations" (Jaeger 1980), but Storm himself has not publicly answered his critics. The irony, to some writers, is that the book presents a version of Cheyenne cosmology that is truly universal and encompassing, especially because of its emphasis on the Medicine Wheel and Peace Shields, and yet the Cheyenne traditionalists do not wish to be included in its compass (Smith 1983; DeFlyer).

Song of Heyoehkah is also a religious book, but it has been less controversial. Estchimah, meaning Sleep or Dreamer, is an Indian orphan girl living both in time (the Plains wars) and in eternity, and seeking to become a shamaness. During the same historical period, a small party of white goldminers, Evan, Calvin, and their girlfriend Pearlie, are rescued from starvation by three Indians. Pearlie marries an Indian but is eventually killed in a massacre, and Evan rejects the Indian way and goes crazy in his lust for gold. But under the alternately harsh, puzzling, and tricky instruction of Crazy Dog, a Cheyenne contrary or sacred clown, Calvin slowly rejects the white world (his Calvinism) and becomes an enlightened man of peace.

515

The book's principal fault is that it is slow-moving and dull. The characters have little individuality and are just instruments for preaching or being preached to, in a series of "teachings" that never seems to end. Everything is so transparently symbolic—animals, rivers, mountains, moons, twins, mirrors—that it is somehow never real. As Raymond J. DeMallie concluded, it reaches for satori but "produces only ennui."

Storm's humor does occasionally show through, however, as does a sense of rage and frustration that are not unsympathetic, despite being inconsistent with his mask of omniscient tranquility. There is a rebellious rage against established "laws" and "hierarchies"—and equal rage at the encrusted customs which men and women impose upon themselves, making them feel humble and inferior. "Law Born In Ignorance laws," "the old Feel Sorry For Yourself law," and "the old I Will Beat Myself law" are some of the laws with which Crazy Dog confutes his pupil Dancing Tree (the old Calvin). His gift to Dancing Tree, after this, is not another allegorical tale but, dug out of his "medicine bag," a whalebone corset. "The woman who wore it no doubt thought that it made her pretty. No one forced her to . . . at least, no *person* did so. It was her own law of ignorance. . . . You, my son, wear similar devices that hold you in."

Readers of Lynn Andrews's *Medicine Woman* have found Storm honored there as one of her teachers. He has also had a successful operation for his cataracts. Apart from this, little is known of his current life and work. Both willingly and accidentally, however, he has been an important writer and teacher and surely will be so again.

Robert F. Sayre
University of Iowa

BIBLIOGRAPHY

Primary Sources

Storm, Hyemeyohsts. *Seven Arrows*. New York: Harper & Row, 1972.
———. *Song of Heyoehkah*. New York: Harper & Row, 1981.

Secondary Sources

Chapman, Abe. *Literature of the American Indian*. New York: Meridien, 1974.
———. *Contemporary Authors*. Vols. 81–84. Detroit: Gale Research, 1979. 546.
Costo, Rupert. "'Seven Arrows' Desecrates Cheyenne." *Indian Historian* 5 (Summer 1972): 41–42.
DeFlyer, Joe. "On Seven Arrows." Unpublished paper, U of Nebraska.
Deloria, Vine, Jr. "The Cheyenne Experience." *Natural History* 81 (November 1972): 96–100.
———. "Interview. . . ." *Suntracks* 4 (1978): 84–85.
DeMallie, Raymond J. "Song of Heyoehkah." *Parabola* 6 (Fall 1981): 100–102.
Jaeger, Lowell. "*Seven Arrows*: Seven Years After." *Studies in American Indian Literatures Newsletter* n.s. 4 (Spring 1980): 16–19.
Moore, John H. "*Seven Arrows*." *American Anthropologist* 75 (1973): 1040–42.

Smith, William F., Jr. "A Modern Masterpiece: *Seven Arrows*." *Midwest Quarterly* 24 (1983): 229–47.
Sturtevant, W. C. "Domestic Noble Savages." *New York Times Book Review*, March 18, 1973. 36–38.

Gerald Vizenor (October 22, 1934–)

Gerald Vizenor has emerged as one of the leading Native American writers of our time. He has published three novels, three collections of short fiction and essays (the categories tend to merge in Vizenor), and ten books of poetry. His 1987 novel *Griever: An American Monkey King in China* won the Fiction Collective/Illinois State University Prize for 1986. Vizenor is a mixed-blood Chippewa or, as the Chippewa prefer to call themselves, Anishinaabe. His family is originally from the White Earth Reservation in northern Minnesota. Clement Beaulieu, a paternal ancestor whose name Vizenor often uses as a *nom de guerre*, was a half-blood who served as lieutenant colonel in the Minnesota State Militia. Clement's son-in-law Theodore Beaulieu was founder and editor of the reservation newspaper, *The Progress*. Vizenor has recently reissued in *Summer in the Spring* (1981) the Nanaboozho stories that Theodore Beaulieu ran in *The Progress* in 1886.

Vizenor's father, Clement, a house painter and paperhanger by trade, left the reservation to live in Minneapolis, where Gerald was born. When Gerald was two, Clement was murdered, probably by a black man. The police apprehended the chief suspect but did not feel the case was worth pursuing, believing that any Indian must be a vagrant, and so they let the suspect go. "We never spent much time on winos and derelicts in those days," the arresting officer told Vizenor twenty years later ("I Know What You Mean, Erdupps MacChurbbs," 1976); "who knows, one Indian vagrant kills another." Vizenor's uncle and his stepfather also died violent deaths.

Given a childhood filled with violence and desertion—his mother often left him for long periods with his grandmother on the reservation—it is not surprising that the world of Vizenor's fiction is full of bizarre and bloody events. The tone of his work is never marred with despair, however; Vizenor has learned to battle absurdity and injustice with the élan of Nanaboozho, the Anishinaabe trickster whose exploits he learned from his grandmother during his stints on the reservation.

At fifteen, Vizenor lied about his age to get into the National Guard, and as soon as he was able, enlisted in the Army and went to Japan. In Japan, he began to write haiku. The short poems, which traditionally are rooted in images from nature, have certain resemblances to traditional Chippewa songs, particularly as they appear in print in the collections of Frances Densmore and others. Another connection with tribal poetry, as Vizenor explains in *Matsushima*, "is a visual dream attribution in haiku which is similar to the sense of natural human connections to the earth found in tribal music and dream songs."

The cryptic and graphic nature of the haiku has had strong appeal for Vizenor, who has issued five collections of haiku over the years: *Two Wings of the Butterfly* (1962), *Raising the Moon Vines* (1964), *Seventeen Chirps* (1964), *Slight Abrasions* (1966), and *Matsushima* (1984).

When Vizenor returned from the Army he attended New York University for two years, then transferred to the University of Minnesota, where he earned a B.A. and did several years of graduate work. Subsequently he worked for the Minnesota Department of Corrections, the Minneapolis *Tribune*, and the Chippewa Tribe, before becoming a professor, first at Lake Forest University, then at Bemidji State College, the University of Minnesota, the University of California at Berkeley, and finally the University of California at Santa Cruz.

Vizenor published a few short pieces of fiction and nonfiction in the early 1970s, but his big breakthrough as a writer came in 1978 with the publication of *Wordarrows*, a collection of short pieces, and in 1979 with *Darkness in Saint Louis Bearheart*, a novel. These books, a unique blend of truth and fantasy which Vizenor calls "mythic verism," established him as an extremely talented storyteller and stylist with a very original way of looking at things and describing them.

Wordarrows, subtitled *Indians and Whites in the New Fur Trade*, is about the interactions and misadventures of Indians and whites in urban forests of the Twin Cities. It describes institutions like the Bureau of Indian Affairs and the American Indian Employment and Guidance Center, but principally it is a series of character sketches about local Indians and mixed-bloods and their problems with alcoholism, unemployment, and survival in the white world in general. Two of the most vividly drawn characters, Lilith Mae Farrier, the woman who had boxers (dogs, not athletes) as lovers, and Matchi Makwa, the urban shaman with his cloud of flies, appear in *Bearheart* as well.

Lilith Mae and Makwa, who seem exaggerated to the point of farce, are good examples of the way Vizenor works, taking something from life, extracting and intensifying its essence, and presenting it in a way that makes us see it differently. Vizenor begins the introduction to *Wordarrows* with a quotation from Morroe Berger (*Real and Imagined Worlds*, 1972) about fulfilling the "reader's desire for a combination of the recognizable and the unusual."

Matchi Makwa is certainly "recognizably unusual" to those familiar with the intersections of the white and Indian worlds. Vizenor describes Makwa as a "conference savage" or "nomadic committee bear," an Indian sufficiently attuned to white governmental and academic ways that he can live on foundation funds and government grants, hopping from one conference to another, loving up "idealistic and romantic white women," giving them body lice in return for their sensitive understanding. Makwa smells so bad that his friends won't sit with him and attracts so many flies that "some friends argued that several determined generations of reservation flies followed him from one conference to another."

A bit farfetched, perhaps, as is Lilith Mae's coupling with her boxer dogs. But in describing mythic verism ("Trickster Discourse," 1989) Vizenor argues that it involves a "narrative realism that is more than mimesis or a measure of what is believed to be natural in the world . . . [it] is a concordance, the discourse we choose to hear and believe in a work."

In other words, the author may move into what bourgeois whites identify as fantasy—Indians are somewhat less arbitrary in separating reality from fantasy, or waking from dreaming—in order to convey a more vivid sense of a deeper reality, or to change the metaphor, a reality with another dimension. But although the author departs from what M. M. Bahktin (*The Dialogic Imagination*, 1981) calls "quotidian reality," he renders the world he depicts in very precise detail, using the techniques of realism adopted from the modern novel. What Vizenor calls mythic verism, Bakhtin calls in Rabelais "fantastic realism," in which "grotesque fantasy is combined with the precision of anatomical and physiological analysis."

Darkness in Saint Louis Bearheart is noteworthy as Vizenor's first trickster novel. If there is one thing that Vizenor is known for in America today, it is his depiction of the trickster. He has written three trickster novels—*Bearheart, Griever: An American Monkey King in China* (1987), and *The Trickster of Liberty* (1988)—produced a trickster film, *Harold of Orange* (1983), and written (in *Narrative Chance*, 1989) and lectured (School of American Research, Santa Fe, 1986) on the trickster as a linguistic phenomenon.

The trickster, one of the most widespread of literary and mythic archetypes, is universal among American Indian tribes, and before Vizenor, N. Scott Momaday and James Welch created characters who have elements of the Trickster in their makeup, or act like tricksters at one time or another. But Vizenor carries this process further; *Bearheart* is a novel that employs a trickster narrator and focuses on characters that are explicitly based on the tribal trickster archetype.

The narrator, Saint Louis Bearheart, a minor functionary in the BIA, has written a novel, *Cedarfair Circus: Grave Reports from the Cultural World Wars*, the story of what happens when America runs out of gas: the government moves onto the reservations and steals the Indians' trees to use as fuel. Proude Cedarfair, an Anishinaabe from the Red Cedar Reservation in Minnesota, sees that the Indians are no match for the evil white tree killers, so he leads a small band of tribal refugees on a cross-country odyssey in which they fall in and out of the clutches of the Evil Gambler, the fast food fascists, and a populist paramilitary organization which has taken over New Mexico.

Proude is the trickster in the role of savior. The other facet of the trickster, the irresponsible, violent, oversexed scoundrel, is Benito Saint Saint Plumero, aka "Bigfoot," a "mixed-blood clown and new contrarion," as he puts it. Splitting the trickster figure is not new: Prometheus, the "forethinking" tricker who steals fire from the gods, and Epimetheus, the "afterthinking" trickee who welcomes Pandora and her box, represent the two faces of trickster in Greek mythology.

Proude, the trickster/savior, becomes so serious in his leadership role that he neglects his wife, Rosina, sexually. Bigfoot, the trickster/scoundrel who accepts no responsibility, is killed while having sex with Rosina. The novel ends with Proude's magic flight into the fourth world, leaving Rosina forlornly looking at the tracks vision bears had left in the snow.

Bearheart is marked by its bizarre violence: characters are strangled, castrated, poisoned, immolated, and torn limb from limb. The tone is one of black humor, appropriate to a trickster tale, which traditionally was comic. In many ways Bearheart fits the description of what Gerald Graff ("The Myth of the Postmodernist Breakthrough," 1973) and others have called the "postmodern novel": it refuses to take art seriously, attacks cultural pretensions, stretches language to its limits, departs from traditional realism, and employs ritual and visionary experience.

Vizenor's most interesting trickster, Griever de Hocus, appears in his next novel, *Griever: An American Monkey King in China*. Griever, like Proude Cedarfair, is a compassionate mixed-blood trickster from the Rez in Minnesota. In *Monkey King* we find him teaching English at Zhou Enlai University in Tianjin.

Tricksters are natural rebels against authority, and Griever, who is very skeptical of the legitimacy and accomplishments of the Revolution, uses his trickery to attempt to liberate man and beast in China. As a liberator he is not very successful. He frees a nightingale from its cage, but the bird flies back. He buys chickens in a market to free them from being killed by a brutal butcher, but they don't fly away. In his most daring trick he attempts to free some condemned prisoners by driving off with the truck that is to carry them to their execution, but some of the prisoners won't leave the truckbed, and the rest are shot as they try to escape.

But Griever is more—or less—than a liberator. As a trickster he constantly tries to gratify his appetites, particularly for sex, and many of his tricks aim to annoy the Chinese rather than liberate anyone. For example, he substitutes "The Stars and Stripes Forever" for the patriotic Chinese songs that play in his compound every morning, and he crashes the opening of Maxim's in Peking, disrupting the dinner of the Chinese dignitaries and foreign guests.

Griever is not only conscious of the trickster tradition of his Anishinaabeg heritage, the exploits of Nanaboozho; because he is in China, he conceives himself also as Monkey, the mythical Chinese trickster, hero of folk epic and opera. In the classic account of his adventures, *Journey to the West*, Monkey, who styles himself the "Great Sage, Equal of Heaven," flouts the authority of the Jade Emperor, gets drunk at the Queen of Heaven's banquet, and even urinates on Buddha's hand. Buddha imprisons Monkey under a mountain, but finally releases him so that he can help bring religious teachings back from India. On his sacred quest Monkey is joined by Sandy and Pigsy, former marshals of the hosts of heaven who have been punished by being transformed into monsters.

In Vizenor's novel, when Griever is photographed for his identification documents, he paints his face to resemble Monkey as he was depicted in operas like *Havoc of Heaven*. In his struggles with the Chinese authorities, Griever is joined by modern avatars of Sandy and Pigsy.

Griever pays a high price for defying authority; the woman he loves is murdered because she is carrying his child. Griever escapes in his ultralight airplane, accompanied by his pet rooster and a blonde Chinese woman.

Although "novel" seems to be the most appropriate term to use for Vizenor's next book, *The Trickster of Liberty*, in terms of genre the book falls somewhere between *Wordarrows*, a set of sketches, and *Griever*, a cohesive narrative. What unity *Trickster of Liberty* has derives from the fact that the sketches all concern characters who originally came from the same reservation.

Griever has a cameo role in *Liberty*, appearing very briefly. We do learn about his origins and his probable fate. His father, a mountebank traveling with a caravan called the Universal Hocus Crown, seduced his mother, an Anishinaabe, on a trip through White Earth Reservation. And apparently Griever has escaped successfully to Macao in his ultralight.

The tales and sketches that make up *The Trickster of Liberty* concern the grandchildren of Luster Browne, Baron of the Township of Patronia on White Earth Reservation by order of Teddy Roosevelt. Tune Browne founds the New School of Socioacupuncture at Berkeley. Tulip Browne, a private eye, solves the case of the stolen computer in the Native American Mixedblood Studies Department at Berkeley. Father Mother Browne renounces the priesthood to run a tavern and sermon center on the Rez, and Slyboots Browne manufactures microlight airplanes at White Earth.

In the prologue to *Trickster of Liberty*, "Tricksters and Transvaluations," Vizenor presents his ideas about trickster as a linguistic phenomenon. Vizenor is reacting against the theories of social scientists (a group for whom he often expresses contempt) who assert that trickster represents something, that he is a reflection of an idea or model of some sort. Vizenor argues that trickster is a function of language, "a wild venture in communal discourse." Vizenor calls trickster a "comic holotrope," insisting that he is not a "real person or 'being' in the ontological sense," but a "comic nature in a language gone."

Vizenor makes a valid point not only about trickster, but about all literary characters, mythic or otherwise, who are, after all, illusions fleshed out largely by the reader's imagination from a number of linguistic clues the storyteller provides. Nonetheless, for all his special pleading on this score, Griever de Hocus, Tune and Tulip Browne, et al. are vivid characters who as signifiers, linguistic entities, may be inmates in the prisonhouse of language, but nonetheless give as distinct an impression of being "real" as do the characters of Dickens, Faulkner, or Hemingway.

Vizenor has always been a writer of great exuberance, which manifests itself not only in bizarre and hilarious events and situations—the Scapehouse of Weirds and Sensitives and Bioavaricious Word Hospital of *Bearheart*, the chicken liberation and Maxim's scene of *Griever*—but even more in the imaginative war he has waged on language, which has intensified with each new work, reaching its peak in *Trickster of Liberty*. Vizenor often uses the trope of catachresis, bending or straining the words or images: e.g., "geometric blood," "cultural striptease," or sentences like "The Trickster . . . saluted the museum overseers, mounted the seasons down to the wild sea, overturned weathered barriers and minimal names in a comic parade." This use of catachresis shows language at its most self-reflexive, forcing the reader to pay attention to the medium as well as the message, and making him/her alter ways of looking at things. This is one of Vizenor's most effective ways of achieving defamiliarization, and exposing and exploding cultural pretensions.

Alan R. Velie
University of Oklahoma

Bibliography

Primary Sources

Vizenor, Gerald. *Two Wings of the Butterfly: Haiku Poems in English*. St. Cloud, MN: Privately Printed, 1962.

———. *Raising the Moon Vines: Original Haiku in English*. Minneapolis: Callimachus, 1964.

————. *Seventeen Chirps: Haiku in English*. Minneapolis: Nodin, 1964.

————. *Slight Abrasions: A Dialogue in Haiku*. With Jerome Downes. Minneapolis: Nodin, 1966.

————. "I Know What You Mean, Erdupps MacChurbbs." *Growing Up in Minnesota: Ten Writers Remember Their Childhoods*. Ed. Chester Anderson. Minneapolis: U of Minnesota P, 1976. 79–111.

————. *Wordarrows: Indians and Whites in the New Fur Trade*. Minneapolis: U of Minnesota P, 1978.

————. *Darkness in Saint Louis Bearheart*. St. Paul, MN: Truck, 1979.

————. *Summer in the Spring: Ojibwe Lyric Poems and Tribal Stories*. Minneapolis: Nodin, 1981.

————. *Harold of Orange*. Film and unpublished screenplay. St. Paul: Film in the Cities, 1984.

————. *Matsushima: Pine Islands*. Minneapolis: Nodin, 1984.

————. *Griever: An American Monkey King in China*. New York: Fiction Collective; Normal: Illinois State UP, 1987.

————. *The Trickster of Liberty: Tribal Heirs to a Wild Baronage at Patronia*. Minneapolis: U of Minnesota P, 1988.

————. *Narrative Chance*. Albuquerque: U of New Mexico P, 1989.

————. "Trickster Discourse: Holotropes and Language Games." *Narrative Chance*. Ed. Gerald Vizenor. Albuquerque: U of New Mexico P, 1989. 187–212.

Secondary Sources

Bakhtin, M. M. *The Dialogic Imagination*. Austin: U of Texas P, 1981.

Berger, Morroe. *Real and Imagined Worlds*. Cambridge, MA: Harvard UP, 1972.

Graff, Gerald. "The Myth of the Postmodernist Breakthrough." *TriQuarterly* 26 (1973): 383–417.

Wu Ch'eng-En. *Monkey: Folk Novel of China*. Trans. Arthur Waley. New York: Grove, 1943.

*A*nna Lee Walters *(1946–)*

Anna Lee Walters's first memories center around words, an intimate and mystical experience of the oral traditions of two tribal cultures. She sees these oral influences as central to her writing and her identity. Voices from these cultures carry the ancient visions, stories, and experiences which are at the core of Pawnee and Otoe identity even today. Through the oral tradition, past and future generations are connected. This concept holds a key position in Walters's fiction: "My stories and other writings are a counterpart, therefore, to the voice of oral tradition *and* to all literature with which I have come into contact since I first drew breath. I write for tribal people more than any other group" (*Talking Indian*, 100).

Anna Lee Walters was born in Pawnee, Oklahoma, in 1946 of a Pawnee mother and an Otoe-Missouria father. She has had a varied and productive career, working as a library technician at the Institute of American Indian Arts in Santa Fe from 1968 to 1974. During that time she attended the College of Santa Fe. After working as a technical writer for the Dineh Corporation, she contributed to curriculum development at Navajo Community College (N.C.C.) from 1976 to 1984. Since then she has functioned as Director of Public Information and Relations, and as Director of the Navajo Community College Press. Throughout her career, she has served as publisher and editor of a number of textbooks published by N.C.C. and other institutions. She has also taught English, creative writing, and history at N.C.C.

Walters holds a B.A. and an M.F.A. in Creative Writing from Goddard College, and her fiction and essays have been included in many anthologies and journals. Her book *The Sacred* (1977), co-authored with Peggy Beck, was a pioneering work in the study of Native American thought and world view. In it, the authors discussed a number of cultural events common to many tribal groups in North America so as to reveal philosophical and religious principles. These were juxtaposed to specific studies which explored integrated cultural expressions of traditional sacred values and worldviews.

Her collection of short stories, *The Sun Is Not Merciful* (1985), won the American Book Award in 1986. This collection of eight stories contains vivid portraits of people carved out of Walters's Oklahoma past. In these stories of struggle with the delegitimizing influence of contemporary life, Walters's characters draw on cultural values and oral tradition to redefine identity and establish continuity. They struggle to retain the beauty and integrity of their lives while they balance personal and communal needs and demands.

In *Ghost Singer*, Walters draws on her experiences working in the National Anthropological Archives at the Smithsonian Institution. The story follows the mysterious deaths of museum officials who work with Native human remains. When Natives and non-Natives see the spirits of the people whose remains have been archived, a Navajo medicine man and an Ioway healer from Oklahoma make their way to Washington to help their relatives. While presenting something of the spiritual world in Native thought, Walters emphasizes the beauty and mystery of the human spirit as well as the role of belief in perceiving those intangible qualities.

The Spirit of Native America (1989) reveals the breadth of her commitment to the discussion of Native American cultural expression. Drawing on the insight gained through her studies with Charles Loloma, Allan Houser, and Fritz Scholder, and on her far-reaching explorations of the Native American world view, she seeks to reveal some of the principles underlying American Indian art.

Her most recent book, *Talking Indian: Reflections on Survival and Writing* (1992), fuses autobiography, fiction, tribal history, reflections on Native American thought, and family photographs, some dating back to 1898. Walters examines her understanding of her tribal ancestry and animates the members of her family who contributed to her sense of identity. As she writes of her growth and maturity, she expands her personal experience to encompass that of contemporary Native peoples. Her goal is not only to discuss her life as a writer, but also to outline the foundations of cultural continuity and the strengths which engender Native survival.

As a writer, Walters seeks to describe a part of human experience that mainstream American literature does not normally include, but more important, she sees herself as carrying the timeless dream and vision of tribal people into contemporary society. Her fiction concentrates on values and choice, and on the negotiation of tribal identity in a contemporary setting. These themes rise out of her background, her family, and her personal journey: "All these experiences had everything to do with becoming a writer, and my identity as a tribal person and a woman shapes and inspires the words I've since written" (*Talking Indian*, 98).

James Ruppert
University of Alaska—Fairbanks

BIBLIOGRAPHY

Beck, Peggy, and Anna Lee Walters. *The Sacred: Ways of Knowledge, Sources of Life*. Tsaile: Navajo Community College Press, 1977.

Ryan, Matthew. "Interview with Anna Lee Walters." *Wildfire* 4 (Summer 1989): 16–21.

Walters, Anna Lee. "Odyssey of Indian Time." *Book Forum* 5 (1981): 396–99.

———. *The Otoe-Missouria Tribe, Centennial Memoirs. 1882–1982*. Red Rock, OK: Otoe-Missouria Tribe, 1982.

———. "American Indian Thought and Identity in American Fiction." *Coyote Was Here: Essays on Contemporary Native American Literary and Political Mobilization*. Ed. Bo Schöler. Århus, Denmark: Seklos, 1984. 35–39.

———. *The Sun Is Not Merciful*. Ithaca, NY: Firebrand Books, 1985.

———. *Ghost Singer*. Flagstaff: Northland Publishing, 1988.

———. *The Spirit of Native America: Beauty and Mysticism in American Indian Art*. San Francisco: Chronicle Books, 1989.

———. *Talking Indian: Reflections on Survival and Writing*. Ithaca, NY: Firebrand Books, 1992.

James Welch *(November 18, 1940–)*

Despite the invitation and welcome Indian writers received into mainstream 1970s American literary culture, those writers were frequently "caught in a tyranny of expectations." As Elaine Jahner notes, non-Indians often expected Indian writers to assume the role of either "mystic exemplars of an archaic sensibility" or "colorful rebels and tragically powerless victims of technology" (Jahner 1981:343). On the other hand, Indian political leaders often expected Indian writers to represent their struggles—past, present, and future—in the same stereotypical ways non-Indians hoped to see Indians portrayed, to serve the purposes of various causes. The role "visible" Indians played then and, indeed, play now often amounts to "representation" of all Indian peoples and causes. Perhaps more than any other Indian writer of that time, James Welch (Blackfeet/Gros Ventre) has resisted both prescriptions for Indian writing. Instead, in his works, Welch presents cultural losses and individual struggles for cultural survival in satirical and ironic ways, thwarting the possibilities for nostalgic catharsis. Yet Welch's realism, his refusal to paint a rosy picture of contemporary Indian life, paradoxically embodies a politic all its own, a politic based on the way things were then, and still are, for many Indian people.

The personae of his poems and the protagonists of his first two novels are not particularly extraordinary individuals; rather, they are "ordinary" people who struggle however they can, using whatever means they have at their disposal to recover a sense of honor and a feeling of purpose. Whatever dignity and wisdom they achieve or preserve may not seem great in contrast to the grand character that individuals of past epochs achieved, but in the context of contemporary struggles, surviving alone sometimes seems heroic. Welch's third novel, *Fools Crow*, extends the themes of failed dreams, honor versus shame, and resistance to cultural and literal disappearance. He turns back the clock one hundred years, to the time when the real troubles began and when the honor/shame social contract which enabled dignity in defeat was intact. As his career has expanded into new genres and broadened in historical scope and depth, including his latest, nonfictional work in *The Last Best Place* (an anthology of Montana writers), Welch has earned an important and honored place among contemporary American as well as Indian writers.

James Welch was born in 1940 in Browning, Montana, "a town of two thousand in northwestern Montana that serves as the headwaters and trade center for the Blackfeet Reservation" (Velie 1982:67). He attended school on the Blackfeet and Ft. Belknap reservations—the former being the home of his father, the latter being the home of his mother in northeastern Montana. In 1958, he graduated from high school in Minneapolis, where his family had moved so that his father could find work as a welder. Welch attended the University of Minnesota and Northern Montana State University at Havre, and eventually earned a B.A. from the University of Montana. In between enrollments in college, he worked as a firefighter, as an Upward Bound counselor, and at various odd jobs. After completing his B.A., he was enrolled briefly in the M.F.A. program at the University of Montana, but left to pursue writing full time. Welch has taught, however, at the University of Washington and at Cornell. He has served on the Parole Board of the Montana Prisons System for the past ten years, and on the Board of Directors of the Newberry Library D'Arcy McNickle Center for the History of the American Indian for almost as long. He currently resides in Missoula.

Through the encouragement of two teachers at the University of Montana, John Herrmann and Richard Hugo, Welch began thinking seriously of writing as a career. Herrmann made him realize, he states, that "writing . . . was something that a person could really do—an average person." Hugo reinforced the idea that "if you could use language well enough, you can really create something that would be art. . . . [A]fter three years I made a commitment to myself that this is what I wanted to do for the rest of my life" (Bevis 1982:183).

Welch began writing poems in the late 1960s, and published his first volume of poetry, *Riding the Earthboy 40*, in 1971 through World Publishing Company. The edition was not distributed and soon went out of print; it was reissued in augmented form in 1975, as the sixth book in Harper & Row's Native American Publishing Program. For the most part, the poems grew from his experiences in the small towns along U.S. Highway 2, the surrounding countryside, and the ranch where his father was leasing a forty-acre tract of land from the Earthboy family. The poems tell stories of what it means to live in that barren, cold part of the country, what it means to be Indian—living on U.S.D.A. commodities, drinking in bars, hunting a land where few wild game survive, talking of the "old ways"—and what it means to face a future with limited possibilities for prospering. The poems in *Riding* speak from inside Indian Country.

Throughout the collection, Welch subtly moves from grief and despair through anger and bitterness toward guarded hope; in the end, the cycle turns back toward grief, despair, and a sort of lame defiance. *Riding* is divided into four sections: "Knives," "The Renegade Wants Words," "Day After Chasing Porcupines," and "The Day the Children Took Over." Images of death dominate the first section; in "Verifying the Dead," the narrator speaks of finding a dead man—"It's him all right / I heard old Nine Pipe say." The poem ends with "a woman blue as night" singing "of a country like this far off" (4). In "Blue Like Death," the road becomes a metaphor for a life of drinking—"You see, the problem is / no more for the road" (9); death becomes the occasion through which to instruct the living. Young Indian men who walk along the railroad track tempt death—"Fools by chance, we traveled / cavalier toward death"; the train represents a threatening force that "will know us by the noise we chose— / black train rattle, steel on steel" (21). Throughout the poems, images of fish, birds, bones, and winter pull the theme of death together with elegiac quietness.

"The Renegade Wants Words" moves into historical portrayal and, understandably, the tone shifts toward anger and bitterness. A "slouching dwarf with rainwater eyes" comes from Washington with treaties that promise "life will go on as usual . . . everyone— / man, woman and child— would be inoculated / against a world in which we had no part, / a world of money, promise and disease" (35). The other poems in the section illustrate how false and self-serving such promises actually were. "Renegade Indians" continue their war of resistance; Indian men drink themselves to death in bars; and one man wonders how he can change his appearance and his ways to make himself acceptable to "those who matter" (34). Though full of a sense of anger, despair, and futility, satirically and ironically presented, these poems contain an underpinning of grief and compassion.

The philosophical tone of the next two sections leads toward guarded hope. As the titles "There Is a Right Way" and "The Versatile Historian" suggest, Welch presents images of Indian ways of adapting and surviving— not the assimilation policymakers envision, however. The title poem of the last section depicts children running outside in winter to build a snowman, "to create life, in their own image" (57). The irony of their building something traditionally Euroamerican—a snowman—contrasts with their youthful energies and willingness to dream. The circle within the collection comes around again and again to a desolate present; the ritual Welch seems to be enacting is akin to "vision-seeking" in the Indian religious sense—envisioning one's place in relation to natural and human realities.

The fact that the scenes Welch depicts reveal contrasts between despair and longing, acquiescence and struggle, mythological grandeur and cultural disintegration, brought favorable responses. William Stafford began his review of *Riding* with an echo from Herman Melville, "Call me Welch," and ended with "Call me Welch if you like. Or call me Horseman. Call me Speakthunder" (1976:107–8). That Welch's poetic voice evokes a comparison with Herman Melville's Ishmael is no accident; like Ishmael, Welch defiantly announces himself—the illegitimate "Native" son. His "bastard's tale" is told to a mainly Euroamerican audience that has for centuries been so busy naming, taming, defining, and studying "the Indian" that they have imagined there are no real Indians left.

Welch began his first novel, *Winter in the Blood*, in 1971 because he wanted to expand on the context in his poems. It was published in 1974 as the third book in the Harper & Row Native American Publishing Program. Before its publication, Welch described the book as being about a man close to his own age, "who is haunted by abstract furies." He goes on to describe him as "a do-nothing lowlife" who "will discover that he is human if insignificant" (Milton 1971:54). Given the apparent degradation of the nameless character, one might not think that a novel about a "do-nothing lowlife" discovering that "he is human if insignificant" would cause a stir, but Welch's novel was very well received. One critic proclaimed that the novel "assures James Welch's literary reputation," and indeed it has (Biedler 1974:202). Not only is it finely crafted, but it appears, in fact, to be cleverly and defensively designed against "a tyranny of expectations." The result is that "the Indian" one encounters in it is unlike any other in Indian or non-Indian literature.

The humor in the novel may be its most accessible aspect. Even at that, the surrealistic scenes that we might take to be funny may not be funny to the protagonist at all—we cannot be sure. The plot is also fairly accessible; it involves a restless young man moving between town and the ranch where he lives with his stepfather, mother, and grandmother. Throughout, he reflects on the past events in his life and longs for some kind of meaningful relationship, despite his claims of being "distant" from everyone. Although it is straightforward enough, the narrator's story resembles neither the first-person narrations of Indian autobiography nor fiction.

Welch states, in fact, that when he began writing, he did not "know any Indian writers, other than . . . Momaday, Ortiz, and McGinnis" (Milton 1971:53). Although Indians have been recording their personal and tribal histories in the English language virtually since the beginning of the nation, and writing poetry and fiction for nearly a century, most of the works have until recently been buried in research libraries (Ruoff 1983). In other words, when Welch began writing, it would have been difficult for him to read works by earlier Indian writers. Speaking about non-Indian writers who portray Indians, Welch says, "they are either sentimental or outraged over the condition of the Indian." About Indian writers, he says, "Only an Indian knows who he is . . . he will naturally write about what he knows. And hopefully he will have the toughness and fairness to present his material in a way that is not manufactured by conventional stance" (Milton 1971:54). "Tough" and "fair" are terms that certainly describe Welch's work, but his stance eludes easy description or categorization, particularly in *Winter in the Blood.*

Throughout Welch's work, we find a ritual of exorcism—a tough way of writing about the grievous aspects of contemporary Indian life, a fair way of writing that is grounded upon an unshakable trust in the positive worth of Indian beliefs. The narrator of *Winter* lives amid great tragedy, but he finds a positive way to live with the "distance" he feels from other people. By connecting with nature and finding a living male relative, he dispels some of his grief over the deaths of his father and brother, renews his optimism and his belief that he can win the love of the woman he desires, can turn his life around. At the end of the novel, however, we are still left wondering what "turning one's life around" might mean to him. The novel's closure denies its readers the catharsis of an unrealistic hopefulness.

The Death of Jim Loney, published in 1979, has attracted none of the attention of its predecessor. Its protagonist, Jim Loney, struggles to determine events in his past life, much as the narrator in *Winter* does, but struggles in vain. Although he discovers a few details about the woman who cared for him when his white father deserted him and his sister, Kate, nothing seems to add up to a purpose in living. He also learns how his Gros Ventre mother gradually succumbed to drink and the attentions of men, but nothing in that helps him to find a direction for himself. He, too, drinks to effect a "controlled oblivion" (59); he cannot, however, ignore the haunting recurrence of two metaphysical signs—a dark bird which appears to him when he's drinking and a Bible verse which keeps popping into his head. He is killed in the end by an Indian policeman, but he creates the circumstances that make his death inevitable.

Although Loney is presented as a sensitive, intelligent "halfbreed" who once possessed great talent as a basketball player and a student, his life in the time period of the novel (approximately two months) appears to add up to nothing in particular. In Jim Loney, Welch has again created an Indian who does not become a stereotype.

Judeo-Christian myth, the Myth of the West, and a rather mysteriously mythic Gros Ventre force overpower Loney in significant ways. White America does in one sense win, but in another sense Loney's death exceeds Western typologies, since the story is somewhat allegorical in its depiction of "the Indian's" place in those typologies. When Welch situates Loney amid the clichés of the Wild West as they are being lived out in the 1970s, he depicts another lowlife person like the narrator in *Winter in the Blood,* only this man contemplates the question: What is the opportunity afforded man by life itself? Insofar as Loney tries, however subconsciously, to answer that question, he transcends the labels "halfbreed" and "Indian," though he cannot transcend history—his own personal history and the history of Gros Ventre people. His task, like the author's, is to create a new place for himself, a place that will allow him authenticity of being and, ideally, recognition for who he is.

Where an author goes after writing a book like *The Death of Jim Loney* is a tricky matter. Welch decided to write a historical novel, *Fools Crow* (1986), depicting the events that have over the last century caused men like Jim Loney to feel a deep-seated defeat they could not quite identify and with which they could not cope. By giving an Indian context to the historical moment when the Blackfeet (Pikuni) suffered their most dramatic defeat, the Massacre on the Marias in January 1870, Welch both looks back and looks ahead. He generates a Pikuni story which contrasts the fullness of the people's fictionally re-created lives with the cultural devastation they began to suffer at the hands of the Euroamerican policymakers, soldiers, and traders in the mid-nineteenth century. Through the protagonist Fools Crow's struggle to develop into manhood and win a place for himself among the Lone Eaters, we witness the power of the individual Pikuni's dreams, offered for communal interpretation and meant to provide guidance for the group in war, hunting, ceremonial life, and interpersonal relations, a power which enlivens the plot with mystery. Through Fools Crow's powerful dreams, nestled in a visionary blend of mythic and historic time, we see how it is that Pikunis have survived near genocide and can determine their own future.

Taken as a whole, Welch's works comprise a literary enterprise akin to archaeological excavation—a reconstruction, re-creation, and revision of a people's honor lost. The pieces, fit together, represent honor regained, shame dispelled, and dreams revitalized.

Kathryn S. Vangen
University of Washington

BIBLIOGRAPHY

Primary Sources

Welch, James. *Winter in the Blood*. New York: Harper & Row, 1974.
———. *Riding the Earthboy 40*. New York: World Publishing Company, 1971. Rpt. New York: Harper & Row, 1975.
———. *The Death of Jim Loney*. New York: Harper & Row, 1979.
———. *Fools Crow*. New York: Viking Penguin, 1986.
———. *The Indian Lawyer*. New York: W. W. Norton, 1990.

Secondary Sources

Bevis, Bill. "Dialogue with James Welch." *Northwest Review* 3.1 (1982): 163–85.
Biedler, Peter G. "Book Review." *American Indian Quarterly* 1.3 (Autumn 1974): 202.
Jahner, Elaine, ed. "Introduction." *Book Forum* 5.3 (1981): 343–56.
Kittredge, William, and Smith. *The Last Best Place: An Anthology*. Seattle: U of Washington P, 1988.

Milton, John R. *South Dakota Review* 9.2 (Summer 1971): v–viii; 53–54.

Ruoff, A. LaVonne Brown. "Old Traditions and New Forms." *Studies in American Indian Literature: Critical Essays and Course Designs*. Ed. Paula Gunn Allen. New York: MLA, 1983. 147–68.

Stafford, William. "Book Review." *Journal of Ethnic Studies* 4.3 (Fall 1976).

Velie, Alan R. *Four American Indian Literary Masters*. Norman: U of Oklahoma P, 1982.

Roberta Hill Whiteman
(February 12, 1947–)

The title image of Roberta Hill Whiteman's book, *Star Quilt*, is a perfect metaphor for her poetry. Within its carefully crafted form, each poem is richly evocative. Through synesthetic and impressionistic language in lines like these from "Winter Burn," she fills her poetry with spiritual implications: "When birds break open the sky, a smell of snow / blossoms on the wind. You sleep, wrapped up / in blue dim light, like a distant leaf of sage" (*Star Quilt*, 31). When interviewed by Joseph Bruchac, Whiteman said: "I guess in some way . . . my writing has been, to try . . . to just look at life, to appreciate life, its mystery, how mysterious it is" (Bruchac 1987:328). There is an attitude of acceptance in the Native Americans who live in Whiteman's poems—no matter how they have conducted their lives, they have within them a sense of wonder at the magnificent experience of life they are part of.

Since the publication of her poems in *Carriers of the Dream Wheel* (1975), Whiteman's poetry has appeared in most anthologies of American Indian poetry and in literary journals and anthologies such as *The American Poetry Review*, *The Nation*, and *The Third Woman*. Poet Carolyn Fourche stated in the foreword to *Star Quilt* (1984): "One finds in this work a map of the journey each of us must complete . . . as children and exiles of the Americas. So there is a spiritual guidance here, uncommon in contemporary letters" (ix).

A member of the Oneida tribe of Wisconsin, Whiteman grew up near Green Bay and Oneida, Wisconsin. She remembers her grandmother as an influence on her love of poetry: "I remember . . . sitting in her lap and listening to her tell stories. . . . She left us . . . some of the very few books that we had and they were poetry, Wordsworth and Shakespeare. . . . as a child that was my favorite pastime, sitting underneath the dining room table and trying to wade through the books" (Bruchac 1987:327).

Whiteman's mother died when she was young, which, Whiteman has said, "led me to a real awareness of life" (327). Her father was a teacher and a musician, and Whiteman has credited him with her love of language and rhythm (327). However, even though she had written in journals from childhood, her father encouraged her to study science in college. As an undergraduate at the University of Wisconsin, she majored in creative writing and psychology, then went on to study creative writing with Richard Hugo at the University of Montana. She completed her M.F.A. in 1973.

Whiteman has presented readings of her poetry throughout the country, and she has been a Poet-in-the-Schools in Minnesota, Arizona, Wyoming, South Dakota, Oklahoma, Montana, and Wisconsin. She has taught on the Oneida Reservation in Wisconsin and on the Rosebud Reservation in South Dakota, and at the University of Wisconsin–Eau Claire.

In 1980, she married Ernest Whiteman, an Arapaho artist who illustrated her book *Star Quilt*. He and their children, Jacob, Heather and Melissa, appear in her poetry.

Whiteman credits the writing of the poem "Star Quilt," which opens her book, with helping her to conceive of the act of writing poetry as a process with a purpose: "It can be thought of as making something—like a quilt. . . . it can be used for something. . . . the quilt made . . . for a fast or a guest helps that person" (Bruchac 1987:326). In choosing the star quilt as symbol, Whiteman selected a useful form of folk art made by contemporary Native American women, thus linking herself to a tradition of women artists. And what she asks the quilt to do in this poem is what she seems to want her poems to do: "anoint us with grass and twilight air, / so we may embrace, two bitter roots / pushing back into the dust" (1). She seeks to write poems that will nurture us in a hard and bitter time. This poem, like all those in the collection, is carefully crafted within a pattern. It is made up of seven clusters of three lines; some are end stopped, others enjambed. There is frequent alliteration. And the outer shape is filled with images of light:

> These are notes to lightning in my bedroom. A star forged from linen thread and patches. Purple, yellow, red like diamond suckers, children of the star gleam on sweaty nights. The quilt unfolds against sheets, moving, warm clouds of Chinook. It covers my cuts, my red birch clusters under pine. (1)

Juxtaposed with abundant images from nature are others from ordinary domestic life, characteristic of Whiteman's poetry.

Star Quilt is arranged in four sections of seasonal poems, moving from fall ("Sometimes in Other Autumns") to winter (". . . Fighting Back the

Cold with Tongues") to spring ("Love, the Final Healer"), to summer ("Music for Two Guitars").

In the autumn section, one of the strongest poems is "Leap in the Dark." Quoting from this poem, Paula Gunn Allen has remarked that Whiteman's poetry exemplifies the theme of reconciliation and that she is one of the poets who have negotiated "the perilous path between life and death, between bonding and dissolution, between tribal consciousness and modern alienation" by means of the "transformational metaphor" (Allen 1986:161–62). This is certainly true of much of Whiteman's poetry. While she begins another poem in this section, "In the Longhouse, Oneida Museum," with the line "House of five fires, you never raised me," and moves on to describe her house of youth as "a shell of sobs," the poem ends in an affirmation of her connection to traditional Oneida life:

> House of five fires, they take you for a tomb,
> but I know better. When desolation comes,
> I'll hide your ridgepole in my spine
> and melt into crow call, reminding my children
> that spiders near your door
> joined all the reddening blades of grass
> without oil, hasp or uranium. (16, 17)

In the second section of *Star Quilt*, "Reaching Yellow River" is almost entirely a monologue, from the perspective of Mato Heholgeca's grandson, in whose memory the poem was written. The poem, imagining the last binge before the death of an alcoholic, is witty and poignant, and the words ring true: "For six days / I raced Jack Daniels. / He cheated, told jokes. / Some weren't even funny. / That's how come he won" (26). Finally, at the end, the young Lakota man is united with nature: "Foxtails beat / the grimace from my brow / until I took off my pain / like a pair of old boots. / I became a hollow horn filled / with rain, reflecting everything" (27–28). Another poem in this section, "Beginning the Year at Rosebud, S.D.," describes life on the reservation in images unrelenting in their truth: "Raw bones bend from an amber flood of gravel, / used clothing, whiskey. We walked, and a dead dog / seemed to leap from an iced shore, barks swelling her belly" (30). There is another, life-affirming side to life on the reservation: "A withered grandmother's face trickles wisdom / of buffalo wallows and graveyards marked with clumps of sage" (30). But that is the past, and the poem ends in sadness: "I know of a lodestone in the prairie, / where children are unconsoled by wishes, / where tears salt bread" (30).

The spring section appropriately centers on love. One of the poems, "An Old Man's Round for the Geese," is written in four-line ballad stanzas, with alternating end rhyme. The old man looks up at the migrating geese, relating them to the impulse of his life: "I know why the wild goose flies, / the blood in its veins is burning. / I know why the wild goose flies, / filled with incredible yearning" (46). Though he may have followed the urge to travel, he can't fly like the geese, nor has he been able to mate like them. The poem ends: "I wasn't as lucky as the geese / that meet to love a lifetime. / I wasn't as lucky as the geese / Bring me more wine, more wine" (46).

Other poems in the spring section are addressed to or are about Whiteman's family. In "For Heather, Entering Kindergarten," the mother fears that in school her daughter will learn to discard her Indian heritage: "I'm afraid / she'll learn the true length of forlorn, / the quotient of the Quick / who claim that snowflakes never speak, / that myths are simply lies" (54). In "Minor Invasions," Whiteman remembers the monotonous and miserable life of her mother as a housewife fighting dust: "Dust knows the value of lost days, / days when do, do, do wrenches / from us the screech of boxcars" (57). In "Love, the Final Healer," a mother tries to teach her son to accept his life: "Scared and hot, you fussed for hours / in the light of a motel, / . . . / We're caught in some old story. / I'm the woman winter loved / and you, the son of winter, ask / where did he go and why. / This poem gets cut to just one sentence: / You grow old enough and I get wise" (59). The poem ends in an affirmation of love: "After every turn of innocence and loss, / . . . . / when we give what's true and deep, / . . . / love, the final healer, makes certain / that we grow. A bug, a bird, a phrase from some old story or a friend will find us. / Then we'll remember winter as a cleansing. . . ." (59).

The summer section title poem, "Music for Two Guitars," is dedicated to Whiteman's husband, Ernie. The metaphor she chooses for the two of them is a musical instrument: "You have robbed my hesitation and distrust. / You have taken my fears and wrapped them in fires. / Full of possibilities, I cannot name what rings me. / Bell or empty bowl? Guitars on the verge of song" (63). Whiteman conceives of herself as an instrument through which poetry is written. When interviewed by Bruchac, she remembered something Lance Henson said about where thoughts come from: "'When you're walking on the earth, they come up through your feet'" (Bruchac 1987:334). This led Whiteman to think of Oneida women dancing in the traditional way: "When you dance . . . you massage the earth. And I like to think of that connection, that the earth is telling us things" (334). The theme of this summer section, and an important concept in Whiteman's poems, is that it is essential in life and in art to allow oneself to be influenced by nature, rather than to attempt to control it. In "Woman Seed Player," dedicated to Yanktonai Sioux artist Oscar Howe, Whiteman writes, "She doesn't force the day / to fit her expectations. / Now she pulls me through" (74).

Another of Whiteman's expressions of this theme is "Conversation Overheard on Tamalpais Road." The dialogue is between two women, Barnarda, crippled in a wheelchair, and her sister. When her sister asks, "Aren't you bitter?" Barnarda's answer reveals a wisdom and spirituality that allow her to transcend her physical state. Though the former flamenco dancer can no longer dance "in the stomp sting of stepping / to the music of guitars" (125), she now has come to the understanding "that we are most alive when letting go," and Barnarda says, "I dance on, gladdened / by a purling world. Can your guarded eyes / believe this reach of wind, this transparent sea?" There is a quiet dignity in this voice and in that of Roberta Hill Whiteman, a firm footing that acknowledges the source of human life and its great spiritual possibilities. These she affirms and celebrates.

Norma C. Wilson
University of South Dakota

BIBLIOGRAPHY

Primary Sources

Hill, Roberta. "Conversation Overheard on Tamalpais Road." *The Third Woman*. Ed. Dexter Fisher. Boston: Houghton Mifflin, 1980. 124–25.
Whiteman, Roberta Hill. *Star Quilt*. Minneapolis: Holy Cow! Press, 1984.

Secondary Sources

Allen, Paula Gunn. *The Sacred Hoop*. Boston: Beacon Press, 1986.
Bruchac, Joseph. *Survival This Way*. Tucson: U of Arizona P, 1987.

Ray (Anthony) Young Bear
(November 12, 1950–)

In an early "Introduction" to Young Bear's poetry, the late Richard Hugo observed with enthusiasm and no small amount of admiration,

> Ray A. Young Bear is magic. He writes as if he lived 10,000 years ago in a tribe whose dialect happens to be modern English. That timelessness is well taken. I can imagine a poet reading Young Bear and having a nagging feeling that he too could write this way once but got educated and sophisticated and lost his natural gift for direct imaginative response. (Hugo 1973:2)

Hugo made this insightful observation in 1973, when Young Bear was twenty-three years of age, a young man and a young poet with a reputation as an American Indian poet, or, indeed, as an American poet, still to be secured. Hugo, of course, knew poetry and he knew his poets. Now, some twenty years into what was then Young Bear's future, he is recognized by fellow poets and critics alike as a poet whose magic continues to startle readers into a kind of breath-catching amazement. The world which was all before Young Bear as an aspiring poet in the early 1970s has unfolded so that now any mention of contemporary Native American poetry simply must take account of Young Bear—his name, his past and present work, his achievements, and his prospects for further inspiration and growth.

Much of his inspiration—his achievement and his promise, his magic—still resides in the atavism, the "primitivism" which Hugo identified, for whatever Young Bear's present and future, they are largely defined by his heritage as a Mesquakie, as a "woodland singer" whose purpose and pleasure is to confirm the beliefs and the voicings of his ancestors. Perhaps like no other contemporary poet, Young Bear's Native voice sings out loud and vibrant. Ironically, this is what is now placing him more and more, and will eventually establish him, within the mainstream of modern American poetry and the oral traditions upon which its distinctively "American idiom," as William Carlos Williams termed it, is based.

Young Bear was born on November 12, 1950, in Marshalltown, Iowa, some few miles west of Tama, Iowa, and the Mesquakie Tribal Settlement which is his family home. The Mesquakie Settlement has existed since 1852 when the Mesquakies purchased eighty acres of land which had originally been settled by the Sauk (Sac) and Mesquakie (mistaken as a tribe by a clan name, Fox, by early French explorers) prior to the Black Hawk War in 1832. Throughout the 1800s, the Sauk (mainly in what is now Illinois) and Mesquakie (in Iowa), along with the Potawatomi, the Winnebago, and the Sioux were forced to cede their lands to the federal government (Lamar 1977:574). After the 1852 repurchase of lands which became the Mesquakie Tribal Settlement, more acquisitions increased settlement land to the present holdings of nearly 3,000 acres.

Coming from a Sauk (Sac) and Mesquakie (Fox) heritage of "Red Earth People" who long hunted and trapped the valleys of Iowa's rivers and were led in their resistance to external settlement by chiefs such as Black Hawk, Young Bear has a proud Woodland ancestry. His maternal grandmother, Ada Kapayou Old Bear, especially influenced his early poetic sensibility. His wife, Stella L. Young Bear, has consistently encouraged his efforts as a poet and Mesquakie singer, and it is to her that Young Bear dedicates his second book of poetry, *The Invisible Musician* (1989), continuing the spirit of gratitude reflected in his dedication of *Winter of the Salamander* (his first book of poetry, 1980) "to those who helped me."

Young Bear first began writing poetry in 1966 and in the 1970s enrolled, as opportunities arose, at colleges and universities in California (Claremont College) and in Iowa (Grinnell, the University of Iowa, Iowa State, Northern Iowa). He has carried the education obtained in these institutions and his knowledge of the old Mesquakie ways with him in readings across the country and in workshops with young poets, through various arts councils, in South Dakota, Iowa, and the West. Recently he has held visiting faculty positions at Eastern Washington University (1987) and the University of Iowa (1988).

With Stella L. Young Bear he co-founded, in 1983, the Woodland Song and Dance Troupe of Arts Midwest, a performing arts program which includes several states. Combined with dancers, Young Bear's group has also performed traditional Mesquakie music in both this country and the Netherlands.

Any attempt to fully understand Young Bear's poems in a completely logical, totally coherent way is futile. Rather, one must approach Young Bear's poems, both individually and collectively, as attempts to simply "be Mesquakie" and reaffirm his ancestral heritage—on both the conscious and unconscious level, the real and the surreal. Young Bear's primary motive is to recognize and transmit, to nourish and retain, his Native voice, his ancestral tribal language. As a result of this, his persona is "keeper of importance," a Mesquakie singer, an "invisible musician"—invisible in that his voice, distinctive and idiosyncratic as it may seem to most readers (even "sophisticated" readers of modern, stream-of-consciousness, stop-time, bent-time, reflexive techniques), is the collective voice of his grandfathers and grandmothers, especially Ada K. Old Bear. To paraphrase one of his poems, his persona simply (yet wondrously, magically) wants to be there— in the past of memory and dream, in a kind of blood consciousness— standing beside his grandfathers, just being himself (Young Bear, *Winter of the Salamander*, 118).

The magic of Young Bear's poetry, as Hugo alluded to it, is that he is able to transport himself, along with his reader, into a world which is convincingly, actually "there," as authentic as singing and listening can make it through the illusions not just of art and literature, of "poesy" in the Keatsian sense, but of certain "primal" feelings and subliminal awareness. Few have really associated Young Bear with the traditions of romance as Hawthorne thought of it or of "Magic Realism" as conceived by certain Latin American writers. But Magic Realism it is, once inside Young Bear's poems. For like the poems of Pablo Neruda (a poet with whom Young Bear identifies) and other Latinos, the poems in *Winter of the Salamander* and *The Invisible Musician* and in the scores of little magazines he has published in over his twenty-odd-year career, mix and mingle the real and the marvelous—that which *is* with that which *isn't*. Such is the stuff of the poetic imagination to be sure. But in Young Bear it comes with such an aboriginal presence and resonance as to evoke goosebumps of recognition, the rising of some vague but vivid shadow of a magnitude.

In *Winter of the Salamander* he served up, in eighty-odd poems from the Woodlands of his home, his memory, and his dreams, the darkly beautiful longings of regeneration, the abilities of the salamander, as animal/fish and as fetish, to renew itself, systematically, seasonally. As such, this volume confirmed his talents and gave them new impetus which carries over into *The Invisible Musician*. Young Bear's "vision and voice" is paradoxically despairing and angry, hopeful and life-loving, in both works, evidencing a kind of staying power, an endurance that promises to take him far into other genres, into fiction and nonfiction that will, no doubt, be brimming with the seering images, the hauntingly profound enigmas which characterize his essentially poetic nature.

In *The Invisible Musician*, Young Bear offers more explanation, by way of notes especially, of the riddles and bafflements of his strongly autobiographical and deeply personal allusiveness. Even so, poems like "The Personification of a Name," "The Language of Weather," and "Mesquakie Love Song," to name a few, remain ultimately inaccessible to the reader. In part this is because Young Bear's English is so authentically oral, so much so that when Mesquakie words appear, as they often do, the bilingualism is obscured by the essence of sound, the beauty of sound—the saying and the hearing. This is not to say, as some have suggested, that Young Bear's poems just do not make sense, do not work. They mean. They work. They mean and work magically. And the magic is moving and elemental. Young Bear's poetry moves the reader, quite simply, as close as one can come to being there with the elders, being Mesquakie, being Native American.

Robert F. Gish
California State Polytechnic University—
San Luis Obispo

BIBLIOGRAPHY

Primary Sources

Young Bear, Ray A. *Winter of the Salamander*. New York: Harper & Row, 1980.
———. *The Woodland Singers: Traditional Mesquakie Songs*. Cassette tape. Phoenix: Canyon Records Productions, 1987.
———. *The Invisible Musician*. Minnesota: Holy Cow! Press, 1989.

Secondary Sources

Gish, Robert F. "Memory and Dream in the Poetry of Ray A. Young Bear." *Minority Voices* 2.1 (1978): 21–29.
———. "Mesquakie Singer: Listening to Ray A. Young Bear." *A Journal of Contemporary Literature* 4.22 (1979): 24–28.
———. "On First Reading Young Bear's *Winter of the Salamander*." *Studies in American Indian Literature* 6.3 (1982): 10–15; Special issue on Young Bear with articles by Gretchen Bataille and James Ruppert.
Hugo, Richard. Introduction. *American Poetry Review* (November–December 1973): 22.
Lamar, Howard, ed. *The Reader's Encyclopedia of the American West*. New York: Harper & Row, 1977.

Index

Index

Index

Koningsmarke, The Long Finne, 387
Kopit, Arthur, 379, 392
Korean War. *See* War
Koyukon, 27, 28, 29
Krauss, Michael, 28
Kristeva, Julia, 101
Kroeber, Alfred L., 48, 50, 70, 120
Kroeber, Karl, 196, 333, 334, 335
Kroeber, Theodora, 48
Kroetsch, Robert, 353
Krupat, Arnold, 5, 175, 178, 182, 183, 183n, 335, 336
Ksa. *See* Iktomi (Ikto) the Trickster
Kuskapatchee, 359
Kutchin, 27, 28
Kutenai people, 34
Kwakiutl people, 34, 37; cosmology, 133; *Kwakiutl Tales*, 34; *Smoke from Their Fires: The Life of a Kwakiutl Chief*, 357; writers, 358

L

La Farge, Oliver, 251, 252, 391; *Indian Man: A Biography of Oliver La Farge*, 151
La Flesche, Francis, 95, 150, 151
La Flesche, Susette, 152
La MaMa Experimental Theatre Club, 432
Lacanian approaches to Native American literature, 336
Ladies Home Journal (periodical), 234
Laguna people, 55, 499–510; Coyote character, 102; Laguna Pueblo, 396, 465, 466; "Toe'osh: A Laguna Coyote Story— for Simon Ortiz" (comic poem), 201
Laird, Carobeth, 48, 50
Lakota people: and Alcatraz Island takeover, 314; autobiographies, 178; culture, 71, 213, 214; culture giver, 70; fiction, 213; healing ceremonies, 213; histories, 213; myths, 70, 213; religion, 212, 213, 214; sacred symbols, 213; White Buffalo Calf Pipe Woman, 70; Wooden Cup (prophet), 215
Lame Deer, 178
Land, 434; claims, Indian, 431; Concentration of Tribally Owned (table), 160; confiscation, 146–147, 159, 164, 446, 546; Distribution of Indian, 1880 (table), 158; Distribution of Indian, 1934 (table), 159; Indian connection to the, 391, 414– 415; inheritance, *see* Heirship
Land Called Morning, The (play), 364

Land of the Good Shadows: The Life Story of Anauta, an Eskimo Woman (autobiography), 357
Landmarks of Healing: A Study of The House Made of Dawn, 467
Language, 260, 331; Confusion of Tongues (biblical) 135–136; families in the Southwest, 54; Mesquakie, 547–548; "The Odahwah Indian Language" (article), 356; Ojibway, 228; origin of, 68; power of, 438, 442, 449, 451; as a survival tool, 473; white man, 115–116
"Language of Weather, The" (poem), 547
"Language We Know, The" (essay), 483
Lankford, George E., 85
Lantern to See By, A (play), 290
Larson, Charles, 262, 470
Last Best Place, The (anthology), 532
Last Map Is the Heart: Western Canadian Fiction, The (anthology), 361
Last Mornings in Brooklyn, 456
Latimer, Doug, 515
Laughing Boy (novel)
Lauter, Paul, 351
Law: "Dakawawideh: Law-Giver of the Caniengahakas" (article), 356; Ever- binding, 95; Great, 78; *Indian Nullifica- tion of the Unconstitutional Laws of Massachusetts, Relative to the Marshpee Tribe: Or, the Pretended Riot Explained* (monograph), 208; Institute for the Development of Indian Law, 412; *Legends, Traditions, and Laws of the Iroquois*, 147; Massachusetts miscegena- tion, 146. See also Federal Indian policy
Lawson, John, 91
Lazy Lawrence Murders, The (detective novel), 152
Le Sueur, Meridel, 438
League of Nations, 246, 357
League of the Iroquois. *See* Iroqouis/ Iroquoians
League of the Six Nations. *See* Iroqouis/ Iroquoians
"Leap in the Dark" (poem), 541
Learning, The (play), 364
Leasing Act, 161–162, 164–165
Leatherstocking Tales, 388
Lee, Jason, 135
Leechman, Douglas, 28
Leelinau. *See* Schoolcraft, Jane Johnston
"Leetle Bateese" poems. *See* Drummond, W.H.

Index

N

NaDene linguistic phylum, 27

Names: A Memoir, The (autobiography), 182, 464, 474, 475

Naming: ceremony, 491; renaming, 149; songs, 120

Nanaboozho (Chippewa Trickster), 519, 520, 523

Nanabush of the 80s (play), 363

Na-Na-Kwa (periodical), 356

Nanapush, 92

Nanih Waiya. *See* Mounds

Nanticokes, in Wallamolum epic, 93

Narragansett people, 73; autobiographies, 179

Narratives/Narration: Apache (Western) Narrative Genres (figure), 56; chanting of, 59; constraining structures, 12; continuing a, 76; educational, 179; epic, 91–96; epic, religion in, 92; ethnopoetic analysis of, 48; fabulistic, 91; grammatical patterns in oral, 48; interaction with nature, 55; "An Introduction to the Art of Traditional American Indian Narration," 333; Iroquois Great League, 95–96; kinship, 333; length of, 74; *Narrative Chance*, 102; *Narrative of the Captivity and Restoration of Mrs. Mary Rowlandson, A*, 385; *Narratives*, 35; Paiute, 301; printed, 41; religious, in the Southwest, 85–86; restrictions on, 55; tale as a major type of, 49; topology of cross-cultural, 11; types of, 19–20, 74, 76. *See also* Epic narratives, Historical narratives

Narrators, gifts for, 74

Nas'naga, 316

Natchez people: oral literature of, 85; succession of governors, 91

NATE. *See* Native American Theatre Ensemble

Nation (periodical), 419, 539

National Anthropological Archives, 528

National Congress of American Indians, 153, 412

National Council of American Indians, 304

National Endowment for the Arts, 424, 438

National Geographic (periodical), 473

National Indian Youth Council, 438

National Office for the Rights of the Indigent, 412

National Park System, 235

Nations Within: The Past and Future of American Indian Sovereignty, The, 413

Native American. *See also* American Indian, Indian

Native American Authors Series, 479

Native American Broadcasting Consortium, 438

Native American Church, 445

Native American culture. *See* Culture

Native American literature. *See* Literature

Native American oral literature. *See* Oral literature

Native American Public Broadcasting Consortium, 438

Native American Publishing Program. *See* Harper & Row Native American Publishing Program

Native American Studies, 321, 408, 418, 419, 459, 460, 495; *European Review of Native American Studies*, 321, 340; Native American Studies program, University of New Mexico, 486

Native American Theatre Ensemble, 431–432

Native American writing. *See* Writing

Native Americans in the Arts (theater company), 377

Native Earth Performing Arts, 364

Native Earth Production Company, 363

Native Heritage: Images of the Indian in English-Canadian Literature, A, 364

Native in Literature, The (critical essays), 364, 460–461

Native Language Center, University of Alaska

Native Peoples in Canadian Literature (anthology), 360

Native Sons, 361

Native Theatre School, 364

Nativists, 226

Natonabah, Andrew, 348

Natural resources, use of, 161, 169, 486

Nature. *See* Cosmology

Naukanski Siberian Yupik. *See* Yupik people

Navajo people, 53, 54; assessment of Euroamericans, 128; Athapaskan cycle, 58; Bear Maiden character, 470; ceremonials, 59, 349; country, 468; creation myths, 132, 349; deities, 348; fascination with traveling, 115; medicine men, 14; metaphysics, 10; myths, 133,

Index

Index

Index